PERSONAL LAW

ERIC L. RICHARDS

INDIANA UNIVERSITY

 **West Educational Publishing Company**

An International Thomson Publishing Company I(T)P®

Cincinnati • Albany • Boston • Detroit • Johannesburg • London • Madrid • Melbourne • Mexico City
New York • Pacific Grove • San Francisco • Scottsdale • Singapore • Tokyo • Toronto

Publisher/Team Director: Jack W. Calhoun
Sr. Acquisitions Editor: Rob Dewey
Acquisitions Editor: Scott D. Person
Developmental Editor: Susanna Smart
Production Editor: Sharon L. Smith
Production House: The Left Coast Group, Inc.
Manufacturing Coordinator: Georgina Calderon
Cover Design: Joe Pagliaro, Cincinnati
Cover Photo: PhotoDisc © 1997
Internal Designer: Jennifer Lynne Martin
Cover & Internal Icons: Jean Tuttle/Stockart.com © 1998
                          Jennifer Lynne Martin
Marketing Manager: Michael Worls

Copyright © 1999
By West Educational Publishing Company / I(T)P®
An International Thomson Publishing Company

ISBN: 0-538-87032-X (Text with *Quicken Business Law Partner*® *3* CD-ROM)
ISBN: 0-324-00313-7 (Text Only)

1 2 3 4 5 6 BR 3 2 1 0 9 8
Printed in the United States of America

I(T)P®

International Thomson Publishing
West Educational Publishing is an ITP Company.
The ITP trademark is used under license.

CONTENTS

During my many years of university teaching, I have not forgotten my experiences as a student. Like many students now, I was disenchanted with the course work and instruction, which often seemed boring and largely disconnected from my personal life. I naturally blamed my professors—who did not seem to understand me—and my textbooks—which were not relevant to the important things in my life. I found it difficult to wade through assigned readings or to stay focused during class sessions, and in large measure, I merely went through the motions of learning—memorizing a few key words or phrases—without comprehending the real value of the ideas read and discussed.

These experiences have largely shaped my teaching philosophy, which makes certain critical assumptions about teaching and learning. First, texts and lectures are but one part of the educational process. For example, while words can describe a swimming pool, real understanding begins after one takes a swim. Second, the things that often pass as knowledge—the facts and figures—are by themselves meaningless. They only gain real and lasting value when placed within the context of our own experiences and objectives. Such a connection to the self is often necessary to comprehend a topic. Thus, as educators, we must assist students in the process of discovering the relevance of their course materials to themselves. When this occurs, students will make the leap and immerse themselves in their education. That is when real teaching and learning begin.

Personal Law was written to help students understand many of the personal law issues of practical importance to their lives. It is premised on the notion that critical thinking depends on students enthusiastically approaching each lesson. This book provides legal concepts and cases that will generate immediate interest and enthusiasm. From these materials, students will be able to formulate analytical models that are readily transferable to any number of situations in their present and future lives.

A properly written text will become an integral part of the teaching and learning experiences shared by faculty and students for many years to come. Great care has been taken to write this text in a friendly and interesting style. In addition, the materials in this book have been tested in my classroom and the results have been extremely favorable. The cases and topics have triggered lively discussions among students both in and out of the classroom. Through these interpersonal connections, my students are sustaining the enthusiasm and intellectual curiosity essential for sophisticated learning. As a teaching resource, these materials have made my teaching mission much easier and more fulfilling.

Features in This Text

The text employs several pedagogical devices that assist students in the critical analysis of complex legal concepts.

- Each chapter is introduced by a *Chapter Opening Vignette* designed to catch the reader's interest. The actual legal resolution of these openers is then discussed in relevant sections of the chapter.
- Interspersed throughout each chapter are brief *Ethical Issues* sections designed to encourage active consideration and debate of the pertinent legal rules.
- Flowcharts, figures, and sample documents visually illustrate the chapters and reinforce key legal concepts.
- Six to ten current, high-interest *Cases* demonstrating the application of important legal rules can be found in each chapter. The cases are briefed to more simply present the pertinent legal rules and their practical application. However, the facts and decisions are edited from the language of the court to provide students with a useful tool for refining their analytical skills.
- Numerous *Problem Cases,* with the actual legal outcomes and with citations provided in the instructor's manual, are included at the end of each chapter.
- Important in this age of technology, *Internet Addresses* are included where appropriate in the margins and at the ends of many cases. These direct students to related material on the Internet, and give them a taste of the Internet as a research tool.
- Additionally, a few *800-Numbers* are also included, so that students can be aware that a variety of public services and other resources exist in most states.

Supplements

For Students

Quicken Business Law Partner® 3

The *Quicken Business Law Partner® 3* CD-ROM is included in the back of the text as a special complementary supplement for the course. This valuable product contains numerous sample documents, including forms and letters, that are useful for personal business as well as in the workplace.

You Be the Judge Software

This easy-to-use program presents students with new cases and directs them to resolve the relevant issues.

For Instructors

West is committed to providing you, our educational partners, with the finest educational resources available. Because we prepare our instructor resources with a variety of teaching environments in mind, it is likely that you will need only a portion of these for your course. Before you request an item, we ask that you please read thoroughly the description of each resource. If you still need more information about resources, we urge you to contact your local ITP/West sales representative or visit our Web site at *www.westbuslaw.com.* Many teaching and learning resources can be downloaded directly from this site.

Instructor's Manual with Test Bank

The instructor's manual contains solutions and citations to cases, and answers to Questions and Problem Cases. In addition, a test bank with multiple choice, true/false, and essay questions is found at the end of the instructor's manual.

West's Business Law Supplements

Ten Complementary Hours of *WestLaw*

West's computerized legal research gives instructors and students access to U.S. Code, federal regulations, and numerous special libraries. With *WestLaw,* you also have access to Dow Jones News/Retrieval, a comprehensive source of business and financial information.

Court TV Trial Stories

In courtrooms across America, dramatic stories of people in conflict unfold every day. Since 1991, Court TV has covered hundreds of these cases, each one a balance of right and wrong, fact and fiction, truth and lies. Court TV's *Trial Story* series features highly relevant cases condensed into one-hour programs. Each *Trial Story* captures the whole story of a trial, including news footage, courtroom testimony, and interviews with defendants, plaintiffs, witnesses, lawyers, jurors, and judges. Each *Trial Story* video engages students while presenting important legal concepts.

CNN Legal Issues Video Update

You can update your coverage of legal issues, as well as spark lively classroom discussion and deeper understanding, by using the *CNN Legal Issues* Video Update. This video update is produced by Turner Learning, using the resources of CNN, the world's first 24-hour, all-news network.

Business Law and Legal Environment Video Library

The Video Library includes seven different types of professionally produced legal videos: *Drama of the Law* and *Drama of the Law II, The Making of a Case, Law and Literature, Ethics in America,* American Bar Association and other mock trial videos, *Equal Justice Series,* and *West's Business Profiles.*

Supreme Court Audiocassette Library

These audio tapes feature 10 unedited arguments made before the Supreme Court.

Acknowledgments

I would like to thank Debbie McKinney and Jan Lundy at Indiana University. Their tireless, and often unrewarded, efforts have greatly assisted me in this project. I also wish to acknowledge the assistance of the undergraduate students at Indiana University who have worked with the early drafts of the book. Likewise, I wish to thank the following reviewers. Their ideas and insights have helped shape the final product.

RALPH BAKER
Ball State University

ROBERT H. BERGER
University of Washington

JAMES H. COX
Jefferson Community College

JAMES C. FOSTER
Oregon State University

RODNEY GRUNES
Centenary College of Louisiana

PAULINE M. HARRINGTON
Bridgewater State College

PENNY HERICKHOFF
Mankato State University

DEBORAH A. HOWARD
University of Evansville

JULIA S. INGERSOLL
Pierce College

GAIL KREBS
Commonwealth College

KAY Y. RUTE
Washburn University

DEAN J. SPADER
University of South Dakota

DAREL F. SWENSON
North Hennepin Community College

Thanks to Rob Dewey of West Educational Publishing for his faith in me, and to Sharon Smith, also of West Educational Publishing, for her support throughout this project. Gary Morris is to be commended for his editing of the original manuscript. Let me also thank The Left Coast Group for their cheerful and professional handling of the production process. Finally, I extend special thanks to Susanna Smart at West Educational Publishing. Her hard work and patience were key to the completion of the book.

ERIC L. RICHARDS
Indiana University at Bloomington

THE AMERICAN LEGAL SYSTEM

LAW AND THE LEGAL SYSTEM

After noticing that Kathy Harnett's new baby was not eating well and was small for his age, doctors tested him for drugs. When the test results proved positive, Harnett admitted that she smoked crack cocaine less than 13 hours before giving birth to her son. She was charged with the crime of *"delivery of a controlled substance to a minor"* by "delivering" the crack to her baby via the umbilical cord.

Has Harnett delivered a controlled substance to a minor?
Was this law intended to govern situations like this?
Does it matter if it was?
What is the role of law in our society?

Consider these questions as you read this introductory chapter.

Introduction

What is law? What roles does it play in our lives? These are important questions to consider as you read this first chapter. People view law in many different ways. Some think of police officers, while others imagine rules governing day-to-day behavior. Each perception is partially correct. To truly comprehend American law and the U.S. legal system, one must understand the nature of our society. For law is a reflection of the people and values it simultaneously controls and serves. Never lose sight of the dynamic nature of our legal system. It draws from the past, reflects the present, and paves the way for the future.

Chapter Overview

This chapter explores the fundamental role of law in our society and introduces several important classifications encompassed within the concept of law. This is followed by a brief examination of the constitutional framework that is a hallmark of the U.S. legal system. Attention is then turned to the basic sources of law in this country. The chapter closes with an examination of the analytical structure judges and lawyers employ when they consider legal disputes.

Law and the American Legal System

Law is much more than a set of rules. It also encompasses a process and structure for creating, enforcing, and interpreting those rules. This section looks at the idea of rules, the reasons for having rules, and the structure that manages them.

Legal Rules

At its most basic level, law can be seen as rules that limit people's freedom of action. These rules may be called "laws," "statutes," or "ordinances"; the label doesn't really matter. The important thing is that they all require people to conform their behavior to some particular standard. This concept of law may be viewed as a **set of principles** that

1. have **general application** to society,
2. were developed by a **legitimate authority** within society, and
3. threaten **sanctions** against those who fail to comply with the principles.

Functions of Law

The reasons for having legal rules are many and varied. However, there are four basic functions upon which most people can agree. (See Figure 1–1 on page 4.) They are:

1. keeping the peace,
2. maintaining order,
3. facilitating planning, and
4. promoting social justice.

In the case that opened this chapter, the rule prohibiting the delivery of controlled substances establishes certain standards of conduct in an attempt to **maintain order** and, perhaps, **keep the peace.** Later chapters examine areas like criminal law, tort law, and property law that also promote these two functions.

Figure 1–1: Functions of Law

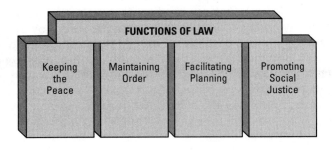

Chapters discussing contract law, employment law, and insurance law provide many examples of rules intended to **facilitate planning.** And the chapters discussing individual rights and employment law illustrate the role of law in **promoting social justice.** However, you should realize while you read the book that each area of the law generally fulfills more than a single function.

Types of Rules

Legal rules can be categorized in many ways. Four basic classifications are discussed here: procedural law, substantive law, criminal law, and civil law.

Procedural Law

Some rules are designed to control the manner in which rights and duties are determined. This is called **procedural law.** Such rules determine which tribunal may hear a dispute (jurisdiction), who may bring a suit (standing), how a hearing is to be conducted, and how a final decision is to be enforced.

There are several procedural requirements imposed by law on legislatures that help make people aware of a statute's existence. For example, all bills that are introduced are published so citizens as well as legislators can know about them. A bill is assigned to a committee, which may hold a public hearing on it. If reported out of the committee, the bill is discussed on the floor of the house that originated it. Amendments are likely both in committee and on the floor. The same process is then followed in the other house. If signed by the chief executive, the bill becomes law. It is then published in its final form.

The Constitution prohibits **ex post facto laws.** This means a new statute applies only to actions taken after it becomes effective. Since one cannot adjust one's conduct to a statute not yet passed, this requirement is essential to justice.

The *Administrative Procedure Act* requires federal rule-making agencies to publish notices of intent to issue regulations and the text of final regulations in the *Federal Register.* It also requires agencies to hold hearings or consider comments from interested parties about the proposed rules. The new rules then are printed in the *Code of Federal Regulations* (CFR), where all administrative rules are published. (Chapter 2 discusses procedural safeguards in greater detail.)

Substantive Law

Much of law establishes the rights and duties that members of society possess. These rights and duties generally are known as **substantive law.** Thus, rules that tell people they cannot discriminate or must pay taxes create duties. And rules protecting speech or privacy grant people rights that must be honored by the government and, sometimes, by private individuals.

Confusion arises when substantive law imposes duties on people that conflict with their legal rights. This dilemma is illustrated later in the chapter in a case involving an attempt by Pennsylvania to limit women's right to an abortion. And, in the case that follows, the court wrestles with a conflict between students' rights and the university's attempt to keep the peace, maintain order, and promote social justice.

Iota Xi Chapter v. George Mason University

993 F.2D 386 (4TH CIR. 1993)

FACTS   Sigma Chi Fraternity held an annual event planned and conducted both as entertainment and as a source of funds to be donated to charity. An "ugly woman contest" was one of the events staged in the cafeteria of the student union of George Mason University. As part of the contest, 18 fraternity members were assigned to one of six sorority teams cooperating in the events. The involved fraternity members appeared in the contest dressed as caricatures of different types of women, including one member dressed as an offensive caricature of a black woman. The fraternity, which later apologized to the university officials for the presentation, conceded the contest was sophomoric and offensive. Following the contest, 247 students signed a petition condemning the racist and sexist implications of the event. A university vice president stated that the message conveyed by the skit—that racial and sexual themes should be treated lightly—was completely antithetical to the school's mission of promoting diversity and providing an educational environment free from racism and sexism. A dean asserted that the university does not and cannot condone this type of on-campus behavior that perpetuates derogatory racial and sexual stereotypes, tends to isolate minority students, and creates a hostile and distracting learning environment. Such behavior is incompatible with and destructive to the university's mission of promoting diversity, and sends a message that the school is not serious about hurtful and offensive behavior on campus. The university imposed sanctions against the fraternity, including a requirement that Sigma Chi plan and implement an educational program addressing cultural differences, diversity, and the concerns of women.

ISSUE   Do the sanctions violate the students' First Amendment rights?

DECISION   Yes. First Amendment principles governing live entertainment are relatively clear; short of obscenity it generally is protected. Even crude street skits come within the First Amendment's reach. It would seem, therefore, the fraternity skit, even as low-grade entertainment, was inherently expressive and thus entitled to First Amendment protection. As evidenced by the statements of the university officials, the university sanctioned the fraternity because the message conveyed by the contest ran counter to the views the university sought to communicate to its students

continued

and the community. The First Amendment will not permit the university to punish those who scoff at its goals of racial integration and racial neutrality, while permitting, even encouraging, conduct that would further the viewpoint expressed in the university's goals. The university, however, urges us to weigh Sigma Chi's conduct against the substantial interests inherent in educational endeavors. George Mason certainly has a substantial interest in maintaining an educational environment free of discrimination and racism, and in providing gender-neutral education. On the other hand, a public university has many constitutionally permissible means to protect female and minority students. The First Amendment forbids the government from restricting expression because of its message or ideas. Accordingly, the university must accomplish its goals in some fashion other than silencing speech on the basis of its viewpoint.

Ethical Issue

The court upheld the fraternity's right to conduct the "ugly woman contest." How would you feel if the fraternity decided to put on this skit as a regular event?

Criminal Law

http://
www.law.cornell.edu/
topics/criminal.html
provides a brief
overview of criminal
law, with links to
related sites, includ-
ing federal agencies.

If people breach duties to society at large, as determined by statutes and other forms of legal rules, they violate **criminal law**. When criminal transgressions (like theft, kidnapping, or murder) occur, society (through prosecutors or district attorneys) brings judicial action against the violator. These may result in sanctions such as fines, imprisonment, or a death penalty being assessed against the criminal.

In the case that opened this chapter, the statute prohibiting the delivery of a controlled substance to a minor is an example of a criminal law. If Harnett has violated this rule, she may be punished under the criminal law system. (Criminal law and procedure are discussed in Chapter 6.)

Civil Law

http://
www.law.cornell.
edu/topics/civil_
procedure.html pro-
vides an overview of
civil procedure, with
links to related fed-
eral and state sites.

Sometimes duties are imposed on people by the **civil law** system. For instance, John may agree to rent an apartment from Michelle. If he violates the terms of the lease, he could be sued for monetary damages in a civil suit. However, since he has not violated any statutes, he has not committed a crime and, therefore, is not subject to criminal punishment.

Civil law duties often arise from contracts (discussed in Chapters 8–10). They also may spring from tort law (Chapter 7), which imposes an obligation to exercise care for others. Suits for violations of civil duties must be brought by the injured person. Further, civil law remedies generally are confined to monetary damages designed to compensate the victim for the injuries she has suffered. However, in cases of outrageous or intentionally harmful conduct, the defendant may be required to pay punitive damages as well.

Sometimes the same behavior violates both criminal and civil law. For instance, a drunk driver who strikes a pedestrian with his car has both violated criminal statutes prohibiting driving under the influence of alcohol, and breached a civil duty to exercise reasonable care while driving a motor vehicle. As a result of his conduct, the driver might be prosecuted for the crime in one trial and sued for damages by his victim in another.

The Legal System

Later chapters provide more insight into what is meant by the U.S. **legal system.** Chapter 2 looks at the role of the courts. Chapter 3 examines the legal profession and functions that lawyers perform in the day-to-day execution of laws. However, there are other actors involved in the legal system. For instance, legislative bodies make rules that govern our behavior. And administrative agencies (described in Chapter 4) often perform similar functions. Likewise, the various police forces are actively involved in the enforcement of criminal laws (discussed in Chapter 6). Finally, the U.S. Constitution (examined in Chapters 4 and 5) lies at the foundation of the legal system.

Law and the Constitution ▄▄▄▄

To fully understand our legal system, you must be familiar with its constitutional foundation. The U.S. Constitution is the highest source of law in the country. It defines and organizes the governmental bodies that make, enforce, and adjudicate legal rules. The Constitution is the source of governmental power as well as a safeguard of the rights of individuals against arbitrary exercise of that power. Further, it creates a system of checks and balances, including a federalist structure, that preserve its democratic foundations.

http://
*www.law.cornell.
edu:80/constitution/
constitution.overview.
html* contains links
to the articles of the
U.S. Constitution.

Checks and Balances

When drafting the U.S. Constitution, the Founding Fathers feared a return of the monarchy and autocratic practices that triggered the Revolutionary War. Accordingly, they devised a system of **checks and balances** within the national government. The three branches of government—legislative, executive, and judicial—were created with equal and complementary powers to prevent any one branch from dominating the others.

Thus, statutes cannot be enacted into law unless the president and both houses of Congress approve them. While the president possesses a veto power, it can be overridden by a two-thirds majority of each house. And Congress cannot enforce a statute; that function is left to the initiative of the executive branch. However, the executive must go to the judiciary to punish those who violate statutes. And the judiciary possesses the power to interpret statutes and other sources of law. Accordingly, in the previous case, only the court had the authority to decide if George Mason University violated the students' First Amendment rights.

Federalism

After the Revolutionary War, the original 13 colonies first became a loose confederation of sovereign states. However, they quickly realized the advantages of creating a stronger national government to protect themselves from outside forces and from each other. Still, each new state feared that it might be dominated by a central government that was too strong.

The solution to this dilemma was to create a system of **federalism,** which is another manifestation of the concept of checks and balances. While there is a national legal system, each state also has its own system. Although the Constitution's *supremacy clause* declares that legitimate national power overrides conflicting state powers, the national authority is limited to the powers specifically granted by the Constitution.

Congressional Power

As noted above, congressional authority to legislate is limited by the U.S. Constitution. Unless some provision in the Constitution gives Congress the power to address a particular issue, any law Congress creates that does so is unconstitutional. Most national laws are derived from Congress's authority to regulate interstate and foreign commerce. Over the years the courts have interpreted the *commerce clause* quite broadly and, as a result, the national government's power has grown. (Congressional power is examined in Chapter 4.)

Constitutional Restraint

The Constitution's **Bill of Rights** (the first 10 amendments) restrains the power of the state and national governments to arbitrarily interfere with people's rights. While judicial interpretations of the existence and magnitude of these rights have varied over time, courts have always recognized a need to balance governmental power against individual rights. (Chapter 5 explores the individual rights protected by the judiciary today.)

Sources of Law

Within the federalist system, state and national laws originate from a variety of sources. (See Figure 1–2 on page 10.) The primary sources of law are

1. constitutions,
2. legislation,
3. treaties,
4. administrative rules and decisions,
5. executive orders,
6. judicial decisions, and
7. private law.

Constitutions

The highest source of law in the United States is the U.S. Constitution. All other sources of public law (both national and state) must be consistent with the Constitution or they will be overturned by the courts. Each state also has a constitution, many of them much more detailed than their national counterpart. While state constitutions are subordinate to the national Constitution, they are the highest source of state law. Note in the *Coalition for Economic Equity* case, appearing later in this chapter, how the court balances a state constitution against the U.S. Constitution.

Legislation

Laws, in the form of **statutes**, are enacted by both the national and the state legislatures. As noted earlier, however, state laws may not conflict with legitimate national statutes. Statutes may be enacted for a variety of reasons. For instance, all criminal law is statutory law. There also are uniform statutes governing the sales laws of most of the states.

Legislation may also be passed by the lawmaking bodies of various governmental units within each state, such as cities and counties. Such legislation, often called **ordinances**, may cover a variety of topics ranging from zoning regulations to prohibitions against various types of discrimination. City and county ordinances may not conflict with national or state laws.

Treaties

The Constitution also recognizes treaties as an important source of law within the United States. To have legal effect, however, these pacts must be signed by the president and ratified by two-thirds of the U.S. Senate. Treaties may be overridden by subsequent national legislation.

Administrative Rules and Decisions

The complexities of modern life have triggered the growth of administrative agencies. Both Congress and the state governments have established numerous agencies to regulate particular industries and activities. The rules and decisions of properly constituted administrative agencies are another source of national and state law. (Administrative agencies are more closely examined in Chapter 4.)

Executive Orders

Congress may delegate rule-making authority to the president. Similarly, a state legislature may give such power to the state governor. As long as these executives remain within the guidelines established by the legislatures, their executive orders have the force of law.

Judicial Decisions

Most people do not realize that courts also make law. They do so in three ways:

1. through interpretation they give meaning and effect to the other sources of law;
2. through common law they find law when no other source offers a solution to a legal dispute; and
3. through judicial review they determine the constitutionality of acts of the legislative and executive branches.

We will now look at the common law and then at the process of judicial review. The notion of judicial lawmaking through statutory interpretation is examined later in the chapter as part of a more comprehensive discussion of legal reasoning.

Figure 1–2:   Sources of Law

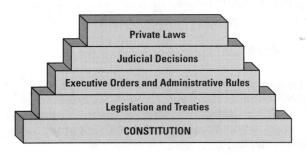

Common Law

http://
*www.commonlaw.
com* is a site with
links to common law
historical excerpts
and other relevant
sites.

Court-created law is called **common law.** It arises when courts are called upon to resolve disputes for which there is no statute or other source of law establishing a rule. The idea of a common law (or *decisional law*) springs from our early English heritage. After the Normans defeated England in 1066, William the Conqueror and his successors attempted to unite the country by dispatching royal judges to hold court in each of the cities. This practice replaced the varying customs and rules of each locality with a uniform, or *common,* system of laws.

The law evolved as more and more disputes were heard by the judges. Uniformity was furthered by the practice of following *precedents.* This meant that whenever the facts of a dispute were similar to those of an earlier case, the judge generally would follow the earlier decision. (This doctrine, known as *stare decisis,* is discussed later in the chapter.) When the American colonies won their freedom from England, they adopted the large body of English common law.

The notion of **equity** is another source of common law. The early English legal system provided a *court of chancery,* which provided equitable remedies not available to the common-law courts. Equity was more flexible than early common law. Rather than adhering blindly to past precedents, the court of chancery sought fundamental fairness. While most states have dispensed with a separate court of chancery, their courts are free to seek equitable solutions when strict adherence to established law would bring about a grave injustice. (Equity is discussed further in Chapter 8.)

Judicial Review

Courts also make law through their authority to interpret the meaning of the other sources of law (constitutions, statutes, etc.). Under the power of **judicial review** a judge may render a legal rule unenforceable by declaring it in conflict with a constitution. Similarly, higher courts may decide that lower court decisions are invalid.

In the following case, the court balances a state constitutional provision against the U.S. Constitution. Note the manner in which the court tries to avoid unnecessarily finding a conflict between these two important sources of law.

Coalition for Economic Equity v. Wilson
110 F.3D 1431 (9TH CIR. 1997)

FACTS   California voters adopted an initiative that amended their state constitution. The amendment provides: *"The state shall not discriminate against, or grant preferential treatment to, any individual or group on the basis of race, sex, color, ethnicity, or national origin in the operation of public employment, public education, or public contracting."* This amendment was challenged as imposing an unequal political structure that denies women and minorities a right to seek preferential treatment from the state and local governments. This was claimed to violate the Fourteenth Amendment to the U.S. Constitution, which prohibits race and gender discrimination.

ISSUE   Does the state constitutional provision violate the U.S. Constitution?

DECISION   No. The U.S. Supreme Court recently reminded federal judges that we should not even undertake a review of the constitutionality of state law without first asking: "Is this conflict really necessary?" Warnings against premature adjudication of constitutional questions bear heightened attention when a federal court is asked to invalidate a State's law, for the federal tribunal risks friction generating error when it endeavors to construe a novel state Act not yet reviewed by the State's highest court. However, we are satisfied that "yes, this conflict really is necessary." Under the U.S. Constitution any governmental action that classifies individuals by race or gender is presumptively unconstitutional and subject to the most exacting judicial scrutiny. However, this amendment to the California constitution prohibits the state from classifying individuals by race or gender. A law that prohibits the state from classifying individuals by race or gender does not violate the U.S. Constitution.

http://www.law.vill.edu/Fed-Ct/fedcourt.html

Private Law

All of the sources of law discussed above are derived from public institutions (legislatures, administrative agencies, courts, etc.). However, private persons also may create legally binding obligations on one another through their power to contract. When people enter into contractual agreements, the courts generally enforce their terms. But **private law** is subordinate to the other sources of law. As such, contracts are unenforceable when they conflict with the other sources of law or public policy. (Contracts and their enforceability are discussed in Chapters 8 and 9.)

Legal Reasoning

Much of law school is spent learning how to "think like a lawyer." Many non-lawyers view this thought process with suspicion, as if it were somehow a distortion of reality. However, **legal reasoning** is a useful tool for understanding and persuading. It combines basic analytical thinking with a recognition of the special features of the U.S. legal system. Legal reasoning is a type of critical thinking that proves useful in both legal and nonlegal situations.

This final section introduces three components of legal reasoning. It begins with a look at how judges and lawyers interpret the words in statutes and other legal rules. This is followed by an examination of the doctrine of *stare decisis* that underlies our common law system. The chapter closes with a brief exploration of how our legal philosophy affects the form and content of our decisions.

Legal Interpretation

Courts determine law through a process of **legal interpretation.** Many words are ambiguous by nature. Further, most statutes are written in very broad and general language. Thus, the court's power to interpret is an important one. It is especially important when a case involves a situation the legislature did not foresee when it passed the law. Through such interpretation judges can broaden or narrow the reach of a law. In interpreting legal rules, courts generally

1. look to the plain meaning of the language,
2. examine the legislative history of the rule,
3. consider the purpose to be achieved by the rule, and
4. try to accommodate public policy.

Where a statute has been interpreted by a government agency, the courts traditionally defer to that interpretation if it seems reasonable.

Plain Meaning

Generally, the first step in interpreting a statute or other source of law is to look at the **plain meaning** of the words. A judge would not say the legislature meant to establish a 65-mile-per-hour speed limit when the statute says 55. Some courts refuse to go beyond this step. They claim that they should apply a rule according to its literal language and not concern themselves with anything else. To do otherwise, in their minds, would result in imposing their will on the legislature.

Remember the case at the beginning of this chapter where Kathy Harnett was accused of delivering a controlled substance to a minor? The court needs to interpret two words: "delivery" and "minor." First, did Harnett "deliver" the crack cocaine to her child when she ingested it while pregnant? Second, was the child a "minor" while it was in her womb? The prosecutor could argue around the second issue by claiming the child received cocaine through the umbilical cord after he was expelled from the birth canal but before the cord was severed. However, it is not clear if the plain meaning of the word "delivery" applies to the facts of this particular case. This might compel the court to use other methods of legal interpretation.

Legislative History

Most courts refer to a statute's **legislative history** when the language is unclear. This involves an examination of investigative committee reports, legislative hearings, and press announcements. They also may look at discrepancies between how a bill was first introduced and how it finally was enacted for guidance on how to interpret its meaning.

Refer again to the court's problem in deciding if Kathy Harnett violated the "delivery" statute when she ingested crack cocaine while pregnant. Suppose an examination of this law's legislative history revealed that the legislature considered and rejected a specific statutory provision authorizing criminal penalties against mothers for giving birth to drug-addicted children. This probably would convince a judge that this particular law did not cover her behavior.

Purpose

Part of the court's investigation into a law's legislative history is to determine the **purpose** of the rule. This is because judges generally do not wish to interpret a law in a manner that conflicts with the objectives of the original lawmakers. Therefore, when the court looks into the legislative history of the law prohibiting the delivery of a controlled substance to a minor, it hopes to discover the objectives of the legislature when it enacted that particular measure. If it is clear that the legislature was responding to the problems posed by pregnant drug users, Harnett's behavior probably falls within the reach of the law.

Public Policy

Judges also may look to general concepts of **public policy** when interpreting legal rules. For instance, criminal prosecution of mothers like Kathy Harnett might undermine a public policy of keeping families intact. By incarcerating Harnett, the state could destroy the family. Of course, another court might believe that a public policy of prohibiting drug use compels a broad interpretation of all anti-drug statutes. In this particular case, the court may well decide that public policy dictates that ambiguous language in criminal statutes should be construed in a manner that favors the accused.

As you can see, there is no firm and fast definition of what constitutes public policy. It is precisely because of this ambiguity that some courts refrain from using public policy analysis when interpreting laws.

Bailey v. United States

116 S.Ct. 501 (U.S. Sup. Ct. 1995)

FACTS   A federal statute imposes a five-year minimum prison sentence upon a person who *"during and in relation to any crime of violence or drug trafficking crime . . . uses or carries a firearm."* After police officers stopped Roland Bailey for a routine traffic violation, they saw 27 bags of cocaine in the passenger compartment of his car. A search of his trunk revealed a large amount of cash and a bag containing a loaded 9mm pistol. Undercover police officers made several controlled buys of narcotics from Candisha Robinson. When the police arrested her and made a lawful search of her apartment, they found in a locked trunk a marked $20 bill from one of their controlled buys and an unloaded, holstered .22-caliber derringer. Both Bailey and Robinson were convicted of "using" a firearm in relation to their drug trafficking crimes and, as a result, received automatic five-year prison sentences. The trial courts used an "accessibility and proximity" test that held that a firearm is "used" whenever one puts or keeps a gun where it can be accessed if and when it is needed to facilitate a drug crime.

ISSUE   Should the convictions for "use" of a firearm be upheld?

DECISION   No. We start, as we must, with the language of the statute. The word "use" in the statute must be given its "ordinary or natural" meaning. The dictionary
continued

definitions of "use" imply that the prosecution must show an active employment of the firearm by a defendant before the statute is violated. However, we consider not only the bare meaning of the word but also its placement and purpose in the statutory scheme. The meaning of statutory language, plain or not, depends on context. We cannot believe that Congress intended the words "use" and "carry" to be redundant. We assume that Congress used two terms because it intended each term to have a particular, nonsuperfluous meaning. A broad reading of "use" undermines virtually any function for the word "carry." A more limited, active interpretation of "use" preserves a meaningful role for "carries" as an alternative basis for a criminal charge. Under the interpretation we adopt today, a firearm can be used without being carried. This reading receives further support from the context of the statute. Another section of this statute provides for the forfeiture of any firearm that is "used" or "intended to be used" in the commission of a crime. However, the provision before us attaches liability only in cases of actual use, not intended use. The difference between these two provisions demonstrates that, had Congress meant to broaden application of the statute beyond actual "use," it could have and would have so specified as it did in the forfeiture section.

http://www.law.vill.edu/Fed-Ct/fedcourt.html
http://supct.law.cornell.edu/supct/

Stare Decisis

Law must be predictable so people can plan their affairs. On the other hand, in a society where technological and social change is rapid, law must adapt to changing conditions. This is especially true where basic values are shifting. A fundamental dilemma faced by any legal system is the need to promote certainty and stability while simultaneously accommodating flexibility and change. Without providing some method for permitting **orderly change**, a legal system is unlikely to stand the test of time.

Stare decisis is the feature of decisional law that is most important in permitting orderly change. (The Latin phrase "stare decisis" means "let the decision stand.") This doctrine says that a court, in making a decision, should follow the rulings of prior cases that have similar facts (*precedents*). Three steps are involved in applying *stare decisis*:

1. finding an earlier case or cases with similar facts,
2. deriving a rule of law, and
3. applying that rule to the case at hand.

Predictability

Stare decisis lends predictability to decisional law by relying on prior decisions. This promotes a degree of consistency among judicial decisions. Of course, there are some limits to this certainty. State court decisions are binding only within the same state. Hence, the common law differs from state to state. A court in California may follow a precedent established by a court in Arizona, but it is not bound to do so. In the following case, consider the Supreme Court's deference to prior decisional law.

Planned Parenthood of
Southeastern Pennsylvania v. Casey
505 U.S. 833 (U.S. Sup. Ct. 1992)

FACTS   Pennsylvania enacted a statute limiting the right of women to have an abortion. Citing *Roe v. Wade* (a landmark case recognizing women's constitutional right to abortions), five abortion clinics challenged the constitutionality of the state statute. The executive branch of the United States asked the Court to overrule *Roe* and uphold the provisions in the Pennsylvania statute.

ISSUE   Should the court overrule *Roe v. Wade*'s recognition of a constitutional right to have an abortion?

DECISION   No. We acknowledge our decisions after *Roe v. Wade* cast doubt upon the meaning and reach of the holding. State and federal courts, as well as legislatures throughout the Union, must have guidance as they seek to address this subject in conformance with the Constitution. Given these premises, we find it imperative to review once more the principles defining the rights of the woman and the legitimate authority of the state respecting the termination of pregnancies by abortion procedures. *Roe*'s essential holding recognizes the right of the woman to have an abortion before viability of the fetus and to obtain it without undue interference from the state. The obligation to follow precedents begins with necessity; no judicial system could do society's work if it eyed each issue afresh in every case that raised it. Therefore, we should not overrule a prior decision without first inquiring whether: its central rule has been found unworkable; its limitation on state power could be removed without serious inequity to those who have relied upon it; the law's growth in the intervening years has left the prior decision's central rule discounted by society; and its premise have so far changed in the intervening years as to render its central holding somehow irrelevant or unjustifiable in dealing with the issue it addressed. Although *Roe* has engendered opposition, it has in no sense proven unworkable. Further, for two decades of economic and social developments, people have organized intimate relationships and made choices in reliance on the availability of abortion in the event that contraception should fail. No evolution of legal principle has left *Roe*'s doctrinal footings weaker than they were when it was decided in 1973. There clearly has been no erosion of its central determination. Finally, while time has overtaken some of *Roe*'s factual assumptions about the time when viability occurs, these go only to the scheme of time limits on the realization of competing interests. They have no bearing on the validity of *Roe*'s central holding that viability marks the earliest point at which the State's interest in fetal life is constitutionally adequate to justify a legislative ban on nontherapeutic abortions. The sum of this precedential inquiry shows *Roe*'s underpinnings unweakened in any way affecting its central holding. Thus, our duty in the present case is clear. In 1973, we confronted the already-divisive issue of governmental power to limit personal choice to undergo abortion. Whether or not a new social consensus is developing on that issue, its divisiveness is no less today than in 1973, and pressure to overrule the decision, like pressure to retain it, has grown only more intense. A decision to overrule *Roe*'s essential holding under the existing circumstances would come at the cost of both profound and unnecessary damage to the Court's legitimacy, and to the Nation's commitment to the rule of law. It is therefore imperative to adhere to the essence of *Roe*'s original decision.

http://supct.law.cornell.edu/supct/

Adaptability

Stare decisis does not render law rigid and unchanging. To understand how flexibility in the common law is possible, one must understand more about the operation of *stare decisis.*

First, a court has considerable freedom in picking precedent cases. Seldom are all of the facts in a case exactly the same as in an earlier case. Therefore, the judge or lawyer can choose, within limits, which facts to emphasize and which to disregard in seeking precedent cases. Certainly a lawyer for the plaintiff (the party bringing the lawsuit) will choose as precedent those cases in which the decision favors the plaintiff's position. He seeks to persuade the judge that they are the precedents that should be followed. The defendant likewise argues for precedents favorable to her position.

There also is flexibility at the second step; the lawyer or judge can state the rule to be applied from the precedent cases broadly or narrowly. A difference of a few words in the way the rule is phrased may either include or exclude the case in dispute. The third step—application—follows the first two almost automatically. If the analysis appears acceptable in the first step and the description of the rule seems reasonable in the second step, the third step is convincing.

Furthermore, the highest appeals court in a jurisdiction can **overrule** a precedent case. This does not occur frequently; more often a court will **distinguish** the case before it from the precedent by finding differences in facts between the current case and the precedent cases. The constitutional prohibition of *ex post facto* laws does not apply to common or decisional law. Therefore, precedent determined to be in error or out-of-date may be overruled without prior notice, and the new rule may be applied to the current case. Finally, a legislature may override *stare decisis* and change a common law rule by enacting a statute. The rule established by the statute applies thereafter.

Although the *Casey* decision upheld *Roe*'s recognition of the woman's right to an abortion, it simultaneously gave states broader latitude in restricting abortions. It did this, in spite of its strong pitch for *stare decisis,* by rejecting part of *Roe*'s fundamental holding. Consider the following portion of the *Casey* decision in light of our discussion of how *stare decisis* permits predictability as well as change.

Planned Parenthood of
Southeastern Pennsylvania v. Casey
505 U.S. 833 (U.S. Sup. Ct. 1992)

FACTS Pennsylvania's abortion statute required women seeking abortions to be counseled by a physician and offered literature listing alternatives. After counseling, women would then have to wait 24 hours before having the procedure performed. Women under the age of 18 needed written permission from a parent, and married women were required to sign a statement verifying that they had notified their husbands of their intent to have an abortion. *Roe v. Wade* had established a trimester framework to govern abortion regulations. Under this elaborate but rigid construct, almost no regulation at all was permitted during the first trimester of pregnancy;

regulations designed to protect the woman's health, but not to further the State's interest in potential life, were permitted during the second trimester; and during the third trimester, when the fetus is viable, prohibitions were permitted provided the life or health of the mother was not at stake.

ISSUE   Does *Roe v. Wade* render the Pennsylvania statute unconstitutional?

DECISION   No. All of the provisions in the abortion control regulation (except the spousal notification requirement) are constitutional. We reject *Roe*'s trimester framework as a rigid prohibition on all previability regulation aimed at the protection of fetal life. The trimester framework suffers from these basic flaws: in its formulation it misconceives the nature of the pregnant woman's interest; and in practice it undervalues the State's interest in potential life. Before viability, *Roe* treats all governmental attempts to influence a woman's decision on behalf of the potential life within her as unwarranted. This treatment is incompatible with the recognition that there is a substantial state interest in potential life throughout pregnancy. The very notion that the State has a substantial interest in potential life leads to the conclusion that not all regulations must be deemed unwarranted. Some guiding principles should emerge. What is at stake is the woman's right to make the ultimate decision, not a right to be insulated from all others in doing so. Regulations which do no more than create a structural mechanism by which the State, or the parent or guardian of a minor, may express profound respect for the life of the unborn are permitted, if they are not a substantial obstacle to the woman's exercise of the right to choose. Pennsylvania's requirement that a woman be informed of the availability of information relating to fetal development and the assistance available should she decide to carry the pregnancy to full term is a reasonable measure to insure an informed choice, one which might cause the woman to choose childbirth over abortion. This requirement cannot be considered a substantial obstacle to obtaining an abortion. Similarly, the 24-hour waiting period is not unconstitutional. The idea that important decisions will be more informed and deliberate if they follow some period of reflection does not strike us as unreasonable, particularly where the statute directs that important information become part of the background of the decision. A state is permitted to enact persuasive measures which favor childbirth over abortion, even if those measures do not further a health interest. However, the statute's spousal notification requirement is unconstitutional. The vast majority of women notify their male partners of their decision to obtain an abortion. In many cases in which married women do not notify their husbands, the pregnancy is the result of an extramarital affair. Where the husband is the father, the primary reason women do not notify their husbands is that the husband and wife are experiencing marital difficulties, often accompanied by incidents of violence. Thus, the spousal notification requirement is likely to prevent a significant number of women from obtaining an abortion. It does not merely make abortions a little more difficult or expensive to obtain; for many women, it will impose a substantial obstacle. A husband has a deep and proper concern and interest in his wife's pregnancy and the growth and development of the fetus she is carrying. Before birth, however, it is an inescapable biological fact that the state regulation with respect to the child a woman is carrying will have a far greater impact on the mother's liberty than on the father's. The parental consent provision is constitutional. As long as there is an adequate judicial bypass procedure, a State may require a minor seeking an abortion to obtain the consent of a parent or guardian. Finally, the recordkeeping and reporting requirements are permissible since they are reasonably directed to the preservation of maternal health and properly respect a patient's confidentiality and privacy. At most they might increase the cost of some abortions by a slight amount.

Legal Jurisprudence

http://
www.law.cornell.
edu/topics/topic2.
htm is a Cornell
University site where
you can choose a
topic under number
17 on Legal Theory
(jurisprudence).

Law is much more than a set of rules. It is a dynamic, living institution that reflects the ideas and events of the day. Yet an often overlooked aspect of law is the legal philosophy of judges and jurors. Their individual values and philosophies can greatly shape the decisions they render. The chapter closes with a brief discussion of the four schools of **jurisprudence** (legal philosophy) that are predominant today: legal positivism, natural law, sociological jurisprudence, and legal realism.

Legal Positivism

Legal positivists are unlikely to consider public policy and their own sense of morality when interpreting the law. They see law as the command of legitimate political institutions and, as such, believe it must be enforced to the letter. Legal positivist judges confine their analysis to the plain meaning of the words in order to strictly follow the will of the lawmakers. While **legal positivism** often creates harsh results by refusing to recognize equitable exceptions, it provides a great sense of predictability to the enforcement of legal rules.

Ethical Issue

Legal positivists strictly apply the law even when it brings about harsh results. Is this fair? Is it wrong for a judge to bend the rules to bring about more compassionate results?

Natural Law

Natural law thinkers recognize a higher set of rules that override the legitimacy of laws promulgated by political institutions. They disagree with the idea that law and morality are separate. Thus, natural law judges consider their own sense of morality and may refuse to enforce statutes they believe are unjust. A major criticism of natural law jurisprudence is that it does not provide the level of predictability attained by legal positivism because each judge's sense of morality may differ.

Sociological Jurisprudence

Legal sociologists have a vision for where society is going or should be going and make decisions that promote this social agenda. When interpreting statutes they look beyond the plain meaning of the words and fully consider the legislative purpose as well as the prevailing public policies. Unlike legal positivists, legal sociologists stress the need for law to change and keep pace with the evolution of society. Under **sociological jurisprudence** each case and legal decision is viewed as a piece of a much bigger, and more important, puzzle.

Legal Realism

Legal realism focuses on *law in action* rather than on the theoretical rules themselves. It stresses that law must be considered in light of its day-to-day application. Legal realists suggest that decision makers often mask the true basis for their decision behind the rhetoric of the law. They believe that decisions often are more attributable to the biases and moods of decision makers than they are to the formal legal rules that are supposed to determine the outcome. In one sense, legal realism suggests that decision makers don't always tell the truth when explaining the reason for a particular decision.

QUESTIONS AND PROBLEM CASES

1. What is the difference between statutory law and common law?

2. What are the primary functions of law?

3. How does criminal law differ from civil law?

4. *Roe v. Wade* has been considered the landmark case in which the Supreme Court recognized a woman's right to obtain an abortion. However, in *Planned Parenthood v. Casey* the Supreme Court again examined a state restriction on abortion rights—a statute requiring parental notice, spousal notice, and a 24-hour waiting period. Carefully explain how the *Casey* decision illustrates the legal notion of *stare decisis*. In particular, explain how it simultaneously promoted *predictability* and *adaptability*.

5. A city passed an ordinance limiting the days on which people could drive vehicles. People whose last name began with A through L could only drive on Monday, Wednesday, and Friday. All others could drive only on Tuesday, Thursday, and Saturday. Nobody could drive on Sunday. The ordinance was passed in order to decrease traffic congestion, save gasoline, and cut down on pollution. Terry Bates was charged with violating the ordinance when a policeman caught him riding his bicycle on a Tuesday. He now must persuade Judge Stern that he has not violated the law. However, he knows that Judge Stern recently convicted her eight-year-old daughter of violating another city ordinance that prohibited the driving of vehicles on the sidewalk when she rode her bicycle on the sidewalk. How can Terry convince the judge that he is innocent? Explain.

6. The U.S. Constitution sets forth qualifications for membership in the House of Representatives and the Senate. Despite this fact, an amendment was made to the Arkansas State Constitution placing term limits on candidates for the House or Senate. Specifically, the names of candidates to represent Arkansas in the House were prohibited from appearing on the ballot if the candidate already had served three terms. Senate candidates could serve no more than two terms. Under the U.S. Constitution, Congress has no power to alter the qualifications. And the states possessed no such power prior to ratification of the Constitution. Is the state's term limit provision unconstitutional?

7. One wheel on an automobile manufactured by Buick Motor Company was defectively made. Buick would have discovered the defective condition if it had made a reasonable inspection of the wheel. Buick sold the car to an automobile dealer who in turn sold it to MacPherson. MacPherson was injured when the wheel collapsed. MacPherson sued Buick for negligent failure to inspect the wheel. Buick's main defense was that it had not dealt directly with MacPherson and thus owed him no duty. The general rule governing such suits at the time of this action was that a buyer could not sue a manufacturer for negligence unless there was a contract between the buyer and the manufacturer. However, there had been a previous case, *Thomas v. Winchester*, where a manufacturer falsely labeled a poison that was sold to a druggist, who in turn sold it to a customer. The customer was able to recover damages against the manufacturer. Further, in *Devlin v. Smith*, a contractor was held liable when he improperly built a scaffold for a painter and the painter's employees were injured when it collapsed. Based on this information, explain how the court could permit MacPherson to recover from Buick.

8. In December 1988, Jennifer Johnson, while pregnant with a daughter, suffered a crack

cocaine overdose. She told paramedics she had taken cocaine earlier that evening and was concerned about the effects of the drug on her unborn child. She was hospitalized again on January 23, 1989, when she was in labor. Jennifer told an obstetrician she had used rock cocaine that morning while she was in labor. After giving birth to the child, she told an investigator for the Department of Health she had smoked pot and crack cocaine three to four times every other day throughout the duration of her pregnancy. Jennifer was convicted of violating a state law that provided: *"It is unlawful . . . to deliver any controlled substance to a person under the age of 18 years."* The state's theory of the case was that Jennifer "delivered" cocaine to her child via blood flowing through the child's umbilical cord in the 60-to-90-second period after the baby was expelled from her birth canal but before the cord was severed. She appealed her conviction. Should Jennifer's conviction be upheld on appeal?

9. Jan Swearingen purchased a Vietnamese pot-belly pig from a breeder after hearing that the pigs make good pets. She keeps the pig, Sassy, in her home and backyard and walks it with a leash. Sassy weighs between 125 and 150 pounds. She eats mini pig chow and dog food, drinks from a water dish, and uses a litterbox. After receiving complaints that a pig was being kept in a city residence, the city zoning administrator visited Swearingen's home and determined that Sassy did reside on the property. The city concluded the pig's presence violated the zoning code, which prohibits the keeping of "livestock" in a residential district. The term "livestock" is defined in the code as: *"Domestic animals kept for farm purposes, especially those marketable animals, and raising or breeding of domestic animals, such as cattle, horses, sheep, goats, and ponies, etc."* Swearingen testified she is not raising Sassy for slaughter, breeding, market, or farm purposes. Should the court order Sassy's removal from the city residence?

10. Kaiser Hospital implemented an affirmative action program that gave special consideration to black applicants for its job training program. Weber, a rejected white applicant, would have qualified for the program if the racial preference had not existed. Weber argued that Kaiser's affirmative action program violated federal laws prohibiting discrimination on the basis of race. In deciding in favor of Kaiser, the court stated that: *"A thing may be within the letter of a statute and yet not within the statute because it is not within its spirit."* In the context of your readings in this chapter, carefully explain what the court is saying.

CHAPTER 2

THE COURTS AND DISPUTE RESOLUTION

Rich Hill placed a telephone order for a computer and paid by giving the seller, Gateway 2000, his credit card number. The computer arrived in a box containing the computer and a list of terms said to govern the contract unless Hill returned the computer within 30 days. One of the terms required that all disputes be arbitrated. When Hill later tried to sue Gateway 2000 over shortcomings in the computer, the company argued the dispute must be submitted to an arbitrator.

Hill v. Gateway 2000, 105 F.3d 1147 (7th Cir. 1997).

What is arbitration? How does it differ from litigation?
When will a court require that a legal dispute be resolved
by arbitration?
Should the court enforce this arbitration clause?

Introduction

Each day television and the newspapers bombard us with evidence that we are living in a litigious society. It seems that most important issues eventually end up in court. Despite this stampede to the courtroom, most people know little about the actual workings of the courts beyond what they have seen on television or in the movies. This chapter attempts to provide a more focused view of this country's judicial system and the processes for resolving legal disputes.

Chapter Overview

The chapter opens with an overview of the structural aspects of the American judicial system. It compares and contrasts the various courts serving both the federal and the state governments. The next section looks at litigation and the fundamental prerequisites that must be met before a court may entertain a lawsuit. Attention is then turned to the actual procedures governing the filing, trying, and enforcement of a legal claim. This includes a brief glimpse at how to appeal an adverse judgment. This is followed by a review of several alternatives to litigation. The chapter closes with a section exploring strategies for reducing the risk of legal problems.

The Judicial System

It is somewhat of a misstatement to describe the American judicial system in the singular. In reality, the court system exists at two levels: the federal and the state. Because each state has its own set of courts, there are 51 court systems (one for the federal government and one for each state).

Federal Courts

http://
www.uscourts.gov provides access to information about the federal court system.

Legal disputes can be heard by the federal courts in either of two ways. First, cases involving a **federal question** may be brought before a federal court. A federal question arises when a federal law has been violated or there has been a violation of rights protected by the U.S. Constitution. Bankruptcy, patent, and copyright issues also raise a federal question.

Second, the federal courts also may hear **diversity** cases. These arise when the parties to a legal dispute are citizens of different states or countries. When this occurs and the amount at issue in the case is $50,000 or more, the plaintiff may file the case in federal court. If the plaintiff files in a state court instead, the defendant may petition to have the matter removed to a federal court.

Civil lawsuits brought in a state court are **removable** to a federal district court when the federal court has jurisdiction. However, the matter is not removable if one or more of the defendants is a citizen of the state where the action was originally brought unless the case involves a federal question. Suppose a Michigan plaintiff sued an Indiana defendant in an Indiana state court for $100,000 in damages resulting from a traffic accident. The Indiana defendant could not have the case removed to a federal district court. But if the lawsuit had originally been filed in Michigan, it could be moved.

Figure 2–1:   The Federal Courts

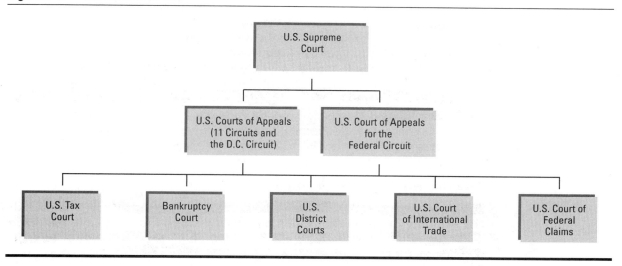

Although the U.S. Constitution only requires the existence of a national Supreme Court, it authorizes Congress to create subordinate federal courts. However, to protect against undue political pressure, all federal judicial appointees may be removed only for cause through an impeachment process. There are three tiers of courts in the federal system: district courts, courts of appeals, and the Supreme Court. (See Figure 2–1.)

Federal District Courts

Every state has at least one federal **district court** and most states have at least two. The district courts hear both criminal and civil matters and are the *trial courts* in the federal system. They perform both fact-finding and law-finding functions. The federal district courts are the only federal courts that use juries, although the defendant may waive this right and demand a *bench trial* where the judge decides the matter without the assistance of a jury.

There are several specialized courts at the district court level within the federal judicial system. For instance, the Tax Court hears appeals from decisions of the Internal Revenue Service, and the U.S. Claims Court is authorized to resolve contract claims against the federal government. When disputes arise over the customs duties assessed by the U.S. Customs Service, they are brought before the Court of International Trade. Finally, bankruptcy cases are heard by a Bankruptcy Court within each of the federal districts.

Federal Courts of Appeals

Appeals from a federal district court generally are heard by a **court of appeals.** There are 13 of these appellate courts. The states are divided into 11 circuits. A 12th circuit court hears appeals from the District of Columbia. There are many appeals from that region because the federal regulatory agencies are located there. The 13th appellate court is the U.S. Court of Appeals for the Federal Circuit, which reviews appeals of the decisions made by the various specialized courts at the district court level. (See Figure 2–2.)

With the exception of the U.S. Court of Appeals for the Federal Circuit, the courts of appeals review the decisions of the district courts that fall within their geographic region (circuit). Unlike the district courts, they generally do not perform a fact-finding function. Instead, they determine whether the lower courts have properly interpreted and applied the law. Each of the district courts within a particular circuit is expected to follow the decision of its court of appeals.

Because they are not fact-finders, courts of appeals do not hear testimony and do not have juries. Only the lawyers for each side make an appearance before the court. Most reviews at the circuit court level are heard by a panel of three judges. However, some matters are heard *en banc*. This means they are decided by all of the judges in the circuit.

The United States Supreme Court

The highest appellate court is the United States **Supreme Court.** It is the final judicial authority on the interpretation of federal statutes and the U.S. Constitution. All lower courts are expected to abide by its rulings. As an appellate court, the Supreme Court confines its review to questions of law and only the parties' attorneys appear at its hearings. Appeals to the Supreme Court generally come from the courts of appeals or the state supreme courts. However, it may act as a trial court for controversies between two or more states or cases brought against foreign ambassadors or ministers to the United States.

Figure 2–2:   The 13 Federal Judicial Circuits

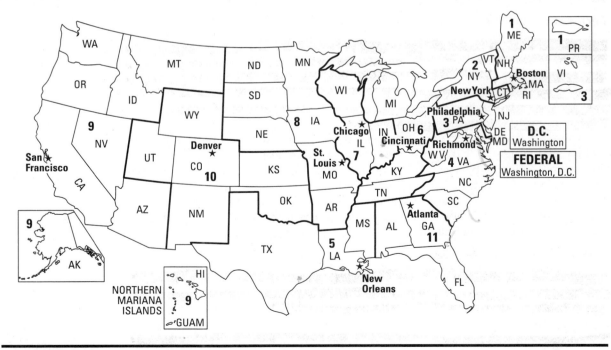

This is from *West's Federal Reporter* 3rd Series.

Most of the disputes that come before the Supreme Court fall within its **certiorari** jurisdiction. When the Supreme Court issues a *writ of certiorari*, it has indicated that it is willing to review a lower-court decision. *Certiorari* generally is not granted unless there are conflicting decisions among the various courts of appeals, or the highest court in a state has decided a matter involving a right guaranteed by the U.S. Constitution or federal law. However, the granting of *certiorari* is entirely within the discretion of the Supreme Court and it hears only a small percentage of appeals to it. When the Supreme Court denies *certiorari* (refuses to hear an appeal), the decision of the lower court stands.

State Courts

Although not all states use the same names for their courts, they basically share the same structure as the federal judiciary. They generally have one tier of trial courts and two tiers of appellate courts. However, some states have only one appellate level. Most states also have various types of inferior courts that hear less complicated or important cases.

http:// lawlib.wuacc.edu/ washlaw/uslaw//state law.html is a site with links to each state. Select a state and look up information on courts.

Trial Courts

Trial courts, like the federal district courts, determine questions of both fact and law. If there is a jury trial, the jury determines the facts and the judge instructs the jurors as to the proper rule of law. The jurors then apply the law to the fact to render a decision. In a bench trial, the judge determines the facts, the law, and the decision.

State trial courts generally serve specific geographic territories within a state. However, many states categorize their trial courts by functions. For instance, some trial courts hear only criminal matters while others hear civil claims. There also may be probate courts (to handle the estates of the deceased), family courts (to hear divorce and child custody matters), and juvenile courts.

State Appellate Courts

Most states have two levels of appellate courts. There are intermediate courts, like the federal circuit courts, as well as a single appellate body, like the U.S. Supreme Court, that serves as the final judicial authority. Generally, the intermediate courts are called courts of appeals and the highest court is the state supreme court. However, a few states call their highest court the court of appeals, and New York calls its trial courts the supreme courts. Finally, a few states have only one appellate court. As with the federal system, the state appellate courts do not hear witnesses or decide facts. They review the trial court proceedings to make certain the trial court has not made any legal mistakes.

Small Claims Courts

Most consumer complaints involve disputes over relatively small amounts of money ($1,000 or less). Even when an attorney can be found to handle such cases, much of the recovery is spent paying the lawyer's fees. The states formed **small claims courts** to address this problem. They provide an inexpensive forum where small civil suits may be resolved informally without the need for an attorney. Generally, for a filing fee as low as $30, a person may file a contractual claim against another person or business for amounts up to several thousand dollars. (The actual amounts vary by state.)

Small claims proceedings typically dispense with the formal rules of evidence that govern traditional trials. Each party is permitted to tell his or her side of the story in plain language. The judge may ask questions and, without the use of a jury, renders a decision, usually immediately at the conclusion of the trial. The rules regarding when or if a party may be represented by an attorney vary among the states. Small claims courts seldom are *courts of record.* This means they do not keep a record of the actual proceedings. Because there is no transcript of the original testimony, any appeal requires a *trial de novo* in a regular trial court. A *trial de novo* means the parties must completely retry the case as if they never had the original proceeding.

Litigation

Disputes often arise during daily life; however, in most instances people are able to adjust their expectations and arrive at a peaceful solution. In those instances where a voluntary settlement cannot be reached, more drastic measures may be contemplated. One such course of action, **litigation,** occurs when the disputants petition the courts to settle their differences.

Litigation generally should be the option of last resort rather than a favored dispute-resolution strategy. For one thing, the costs (both in time and money) associated with maintaining a lawsuit can be quite high. Further, lawsuits frequently place irreparable strains on personal and business relationships, destroying the likelihood of future cooperation. This section examines the fundamental prerequisites that must be met before courts may consider a lawsuit.

Standing

Before a court may hear a lawsuit, the plaintiff must have **standing** to bring the claim. Standing has three basic elements. First, the plaintiff must have suffered an *injury in fact.* This is an interference with one of the plaintiff's legally protected rights. Courts do not entertain a lawsuit if the plaintiff's claims are merely hypothetical. There must be actual or imminent harm to the plaintiff. Second, there must be a *causal connection* between the plaintiff's injury and the conduct of the defendant. Third, it must be clear that the *injury will be redressed* by a favorable decision from the court.

The standing doctrine is designed to guarantee that courts hear only real cases or controversies. Plaintiffs must have legitimate grievances that can be protected by the court. And they must assert their own claims, not those of third parties.

Jurisdiction

A court must have authority over the issues involved in the conflict (subject matter jurisdiction) and over the parties being sued (personal jurisdiction) before it may properly hear a dispute. This section briefly examines each of these issues.

Subject Matter Jurisdiction

All courts operate under some set of procedural rules that determine the type of cases or issues with which they may deal. This is known as **subject matter jurisdiction.** For instance, we have seen that the federal district courts may only hear cases involving federal questions or diversity jurisdiction. If a court lacks subject matter jurisdiction, it cannot hear the dispute, and the plaintiff must refile in an appropriate court. This initial mistake can result in the loss of valuable time and money.

Personal Jurisdiction

A court also is precluded from adjudicating a legal dispute unless it has **personal jurisdiction** over the defendant. This generally is not a problem when the defendant resides in the state where the court is located. However, the situation is more uncertain when the plaintiff files a lawsuit against a nonresident. In those instances, the court does not have personal jurisdiction unless it can be shown that the nonresident defendant has certain **minimum contacts** with the state where the suit is brought.

The minimum-contacts requirement generally is met if the defendant intentionally conducts business in the state or was served process (notified of the suit) while physically present in the state. Consider the following case and the court's determination that it had personal jurisdiction.

CompuServe v. Patterson

89 F.3D 1257 (6TH CIR. 1996)

FACTS   CompuServe is a computer information service headquartered in Ohio. It contracts with individual subscribers to provide access to computing information services via the Internet. It also operates as an electronic conduit to provide its subscribers computer software products, which may originate from CompuServe itself or from other parties. Software generated and distributed in this manner is often referred to as "shareware." Shareware makes money only through the voluntary compliance of the "end user," who pays the voluntary fee directly to CompuServe. The company then takes a 15 percent fee before forwarding the balance to the shareware's creator. Richard Patterson, a resident of Texas, placed items of "shareware" on the CompuServe system for others to use and purchase. When he became a "shareware" provider, Patterson entered into a Shareware Registration Agreement with CompuServe. The agreement expressly provided that it was entered into in Ohio and was to be governed and construed in accordance with Ohio law. Patterson's assent to the agreement was first manifest at his own computer in Texas, then transmitted to the CompuServe computer system in Ohio. A dispute later arose over Patterson's software product. CompuServe filed a lawsuit against him in the federal district court for the Southern District of Ohio. Patterson moved to dismiss on the ground that the court lacked personal jurisdiction because he had never visited Ohio.

ISSUE   Does the district court have personal jurisdiction over Patterson?

DECISION   Yes. Patterson's contacts with Ohio, which have been almost entirely electronic in nature, are sufficient to support the district court's exercise of personal jurisdiction over him. Breakthroughs in the communications and transportation industries have led to a relaxation of the limits on court's jurisdiction because all but the most remote forums are easily accessible. The Internet represents perhaps the latest and greatest manifestation of these globe-shrinking trends. It enables anyone

continued

with the right equipment and knowledge to operate an international business cheaply, and from a desktop. To determine whether personal jurisdiction exists over a defendant, federal courts apply the law of the forum state. Ohio law allows the state to exercise personal jurisdiction over nonresidents on claims arising from the non-resident's transacting any business in Ohio. This jurisdictional requirement must comport with federal constitutional law which requires that Patterson have had sufficient contacts with Ohio that the exercise of jurisdiction is fair. The court employs three criteria to make this determination. First, the defendant must purposefully avail himself of the privilege of acting in the forum state. Second, the lawsuit must arise from his activities there. Third, the acts of defendant or consequences he causes must have a substantial enough connection with the forum to make the exercise of jurisdiction over the defendant reasonable. There can be no doubt that Patterson purposefully transacted business in Ohio. Moreover, this was a relationship intended to be ongoing in nature. Because Patterson entered into a contract with CompuServe, an Ohio company, and injected his software into the stream of commerce, he has ample contacts with the state. Further, CompuServe's claims arise out of Patterson's activities in Ohio. Finally, this exercise of jurisdiction is reasonable in light of the state's strong interest in resolving a dispute involving an Ohio company and Patterson's voluntary participation in the company's Shareware Registration Agreement.

http://www.law.emory.edu/6circuit/

Venue

Frequently more than one court has jurisdiction over the parties and the subject matter of their dispute. It is then necessary to determine which court is the proper place for the lawsuit to be brought. This concept is known as **venue.** When contracts cross state borders, venue often is proper in both the seller's and the buyer's state. If the contract is formed in a third state and is performed in a fourth, it is conceivable that courts in at least four states have proper venue. When this happens, if the amount in controversy is $50,000 or more, the case also may be filed in a federal district court under its diversity jurisdiction.

Forum Non Conveniens

Sometimes a court meets jurisdictional and venue requirements, but the trial would be more convenient and just if it were conducted in another forum. Under these circumstances a judge is permitted to dismiss the case under the doctrine of **forum non conveniens.** In deciding whether to use this doctrine, courts utilize a three-step process.

Step One   The court looks to see if there are any **alternative forums** with subject matter jurisdiction over the dispute and personal jurisdiction over the defendant. If there are none, the court won't dismiss the suit. In some instances a court won't dismiss on *forum non conveniens* grounds unless the defendant first agrees to submit to the jurisdiction of another forum acceptable to the plaintiff.

Step Two   In this part of the inquiry, the court weighs various **private factors** in order to evaluate the relative advantages and obstacles to a fair trial. Included among the private interests are: (a) the ease of access to evidence; (b) the costs of summoning witnesses; (c) the need to actually view any premises; and (d) the enforceability of the court's judgment.

Step Three   In deciding if the lawsuit should be removed to another forum, the court considers certain **public factors.** These include: (a) the amount of congestion the court is experiencing; (b) the desire to avoid burdening jurors with issues that have little relevance to the community; (c) the importance of having the trial in a community with a strong interest in the outcome; and (d) the desire to have the case decided in a forum that is familiar with the law governing the dispute.

Courts seldom disturb the plaintiff's choice of forum unless the balance tilts strongly in favor of the defendant. Further, the scales are weighted even more heavily in the plaintiff's favor if she is a resident of the state where the case originally was filed.

Hansen v. Owens-Corning Fiberglas

59 Cal. Rptr. 2d 229 (Cal. App. 1 Dist. 1996)

FACTS   John Hansen filed suit in California against Owens-Corning Fiberglas Corporation, alleging personal injury from his own exposure to asbestos. He claimed this exposure occurred while he was working as a laborer for Boeing in Seattle, Washington, from 1939 to 1940; as a boilermaker's helper in Montana from 1940 to 1942; while serving in the military in South Carolina, Illinois, and Louisiana from 1942 to 1945; as plumber's helper in Montana from 1946 to 1949; and as the owner of his own sheet metal company in Montana from 1949 to 1996. He further alleged that, as a result of his exposure to asbestos, he had been diagnosed with mesothelioma, a cancer often caused by asbestos exposure. Owens-Corning moved to dismiss the California lawsuit on the ground of *forum non conveniens.*

ISSUE   Should the lawsuit be dismissed because of *forum non conveniens?*

DECISION   Yes. Most of the interactions between the parties and other relevant contacts occurred in Montana rather than California. Hansen lived in Montana continually since 1945 and never lived in California. Most of the asbestos exposure is alleged to have occurred in Montana, while none is alleged to have occurred in California. Most of the potential witnesses are from Montana. Nearly all medical treatment for Hansen was given in Montana, and all of the treating doctors still reside there. Also, most of his former coworkers are residents of Montana. Owens-Corning does business nationwide and is subject to jurisdiction in both states. It is reasonable to conclude that Montana provides a suitable alternative forum. Further, the private factors—ease of access of proof, the cost of securing witnesses, and the availability of compulsory process over witnesses—weigh in favor of Montana. Finally, the public factors also weigh in favor of Montana. California courts are overburdened with asbestos litigation and have little or no interest in litigation involving injuries incurred outside of California. Although a plaintiff's choice of forum is entitled to great weight, in this case the balance is strongly in favor of Montana.

http://www.findlaw.com/

Ethical Issue

Plaintiffs frequently file their lawsuits in the court that provides them the greatest tactical advantage. Is it ethical to intentionally file a suit in a court that is inconvenient for the defendant?

Conflict of Laws

If a contract between the disputing parties does not specify which body of law governs any dispute, it is determined by the rules of the forum where the lawsuit is filed. The process by which a court chooses the appropriate law is known as **conflict of laws.** There are well-established conflict-of-laws rules. For instance, for sales of goods under the Uniform Commercial Code, courts have a great deal of discretion since they are to apply the law that bears an appropriate relation to the contract. The common law has two predominant approaches. Under the simpler approach, if the dispute is over the actual formation of the agreement, the applicable law is that of the place where the contract is made. When the conflict concerns the actual performance of the contract, the governing law generally is that of the place where performance was to have occurred.

Another widely used approach applies the law of the jurisdiction with the *most significant contacts.* For contracts, this involves an examination of: (1) the place of contracting; (2) the place of negotiation; (3) the place of performance; (4) the location of the subject matter of the contract; and (5) the domicile, place of incorporation, and place of business of the parties.

For tort claims, the majority of U.S. courts discover the jurisdiction with the most significant contacts by examining four factors: (1) the domicile, place of incorporation, and place of business of the parties; (2) the place where the tortious conduct occurred; (3) the place where the relationship of the parties is centered; and (4) the place where the injury occurred.

Judicial Procedures

http://
www.law.cornell.edu/
rules/frcp/overview.
htm provides an
index of topics on
the federal rules of
civil procedure,
many of which are
covered in the
following pages.

The federal government and the states have developed elaborate procedures governing the litigation process. These rules are designed to guarantee that trials are fundamentally fair. The basic procedural rules are examined in this section. It also identifies some of the important differences between civil procedure and criminal procedure. (A fuller discussion of criminal law and procedure appears in Chapter 6.)

Pleadings

The litigation process begins at the **pleadings** stage. This is the formal communication between the disputing parties in which they notify each other and the court of their legal claims. Failure to properly plead a case may result in that party losing without the benefit of a trial.

The Complaint

A civil case begins when the plaintiff files a **complaint** (sometimes called a petition) with the court (see Figure 2–3). This document sets out the basis of the claim against the defendant. It details the plaintiff's interpretation of the relevant facts

Figure 2–3: The Complaint

IN THE UNITED STATES DISTRICT COURT FOR
THE WESTERN DISTRICT OF _____

Civil Action, File No. _____

_____

_____ _____ Avenue

_____ , _____
                        PLAINTIFF ⎤
        v.   ⎥
_____ Corporation   ⎥
100 W. Main Street   ⎬ COMPLAINT
_____   ⎥
                                  ⎥
_____ , _____   ⎥
                        DEFENDANT ⎦

Plaintiff for his claim for relief against defendant states:

1.   Plaintiff is a citizen of the State of _____ and defendant is a corporation incorporated under the laws of the State of _____ having its principal place of business in a State other than the State of _____ . The matter in controversy exceeds, exclusive of interest and costs, the sum of ten thousand dollars.

2.   On the 20th day of July, 19_____, at or near the intersection of _____ Boulevard and _____ Drive, in _____, _____, _____ so recklessly, negligently, and carelessly operated an automobile belonging to the defendant as to cause said automobile to come into collision with the automobile owned and being operated by the plaintiff.

3.   At the time of the collision mentioned in paragraph 2 above, _____ was operating the automobile owned by the defendant with its permission and on its business.

4.   As a direct and proximate result of the collision and _____'s negligence described in paragraph 2 above, the plaintiff suffered severe, painful and permanent injuries to his head, neck, and back, including the brain, nerves, muscles, and ligaments thereof; he sustained a concussion of the brain and was unconscious for a period of time after the accident; he has suffered and will continue to suffer great and excruciating pain, distress and anguish of both mind and body; and his earning power has been and now is permanently impaired; all to his damage in the sum of $15,000.

5.   As a further direct and proximate result of the aforesaid collision and _____'s negligence, plaintiff has incurred and will in the future be compelled to incur expenses for medical care, physicians' services, nursing, braces, and medicines in at least the amount of $700.

6.   As a further direct and proximate result of the aforesaid collision and the negligence of _____ as heretofore alleged, the motor vehicle owned by the plaintiff was damaged so that the difference in its market value immediately before and immediately after said accident was $203.18.

Wherefore plaintiff demands judgment against defendant in the sum of thirty thousand dollars and costs and for all other relief to which he may appear to be entitled.

_____
Attorney for Plaintiff

_____
Address.

Source: *West's Federal Practice Manual,* Revised 2nd ed.

and legal issues as well as the remedy she is seeking. Evidence may not be presented at trial unless it is related to the statement made in the complaint. (In a criminal case, the judicial process begins with the prosecutor filing an *information* or a grand jury handing down an *indictment*.)

Service of Process

Upon receiving the complaint, the clerk of the court prepares a **summons**, which notifies the defendant of the claims and orders him to appear (see Figure 2–4). The actual presentation of the summons to the defendant is known as **service of process**. A defendant generally is not subject to the personal jurisdiction of a court unless he received service of process. This formal notification provides the defendant with the summons and complaint, which gives him legally sufficient notice of the lawsuit filed against him. The usual method of serving process is personal delivery of the notice, followed by the filing of written proof of that service. This normally is carried out by a county sheriff or a professional *process server* employed by the plaintiff's attorney.

An alternate and less expensive method of "personal delivery" is to have the Postal Service deliver the process to the defendant through registered or certified mail with a return receipt requested. When process is mailed in this fashion, the return receipt signed by the defendant and a copy of the process that was mailed is filed. This provides the court with a great deal of certainty that the requisite notice was given. Consider the following case examining the constitutionality of a state statute authorizing service of process by first-class mail.

Miserandino v. Resort Properties

691 A.2d 208 (Ct. App. Md. 1997)

FACTS   Gerard Miserandino, a resident of Maryland, borrowed money from a Virginia lender to purchase land in Virginia. Later, when a dispute arose over repayment of the loan, Resort Properties filed a claim for $4,211.82 against Miserandino in Virginia. A Virginia statute authorizes plaintiffs to serve process on nonresident defendants by first-class mail. Pursuant to this statute, Resort Properties mailed a first-class letter to Miserandino notifying him of the legal claim against him. When Miserandino did not appear at the Virginia hearing, the court entered a judgment against him. Miserandino now argues that the judgment should be set aside because he was not properly served with process.

ISSUE   Was the service of process constitutionally sufficient?

DECISION   No. The importance of giving adequate notice cannot be overstated. Miserandino does not contend that the procedure required under Virginia law was not followed in this case. That the notice was sent, however, does not answer the question of whether the means employed for transmittal of the notice was constitutionally sufficient. Personal delivery by a sheriff or process server, followed by filing written proof of that service, provides a high degree of probability that the defendant has received adequate notice. And mailing the notice return receipt requested by registered or certified mail provides a less expensive alternative. We find no special or unique circumstances to justify relaxation of the ordinary and available methods of service that offer a considerably higher degree of probability of actual notice than does delivery by first-class mail. Miserandino's nonresidency is not of such significance or compelling interest to justify shifting the balance to the point where notice by first-class mail alone is sufficient. We fail to see why traditional methods of personal service on residents become so much more difficult or costly when applied to nonresidents. In particular, service by mail requiring a signed return receipt would be no more difficult or expensive in the case of a nonresident than that of a resident. The Virginia statute is constitutionally inadequate because notice by first-class mail alone is not reasonably calculated to reach those who could easily be informed by the traditional means.

Figure 2–4: The Summons

STATE OF INDIANA   IN THE _____ CIRCUIT
COUNTY OF _____   SS: COURT
                               CAUSE NO. _____

_____
             Plaintiff,
       v.
_____
           Defendant.

TO DEFENDANT: *[Name]*
                  [Address]

You are hereby notified that you have been sued by the person named as plaintiff in the court indicated above.

The nature of the suit against you is stated in the complaint which is attached to this summons. It also states the relief sought or the demand made against you by the plaintiff.

An answer or other appropriate response in writing to the complaint must be filed either by you or your attorney within twenty (20) days, commencing the day after you receive this summons (or twenty-three (23) days if this summons was received by mail), or a judgment by default may be rendered against you for relief demanded by plaintiff.

If you have a claim for relief against the plaintiff arising from the same transaction or occurrence, you must assert it in your written answer or response.

Dated: _____

                            [Signed] _____ *[Seal]*
                                       Clerk

The following manner of service of summons is hereby designated.

_____   Registered or certified mail.
_____   Service on individual (Personal or copy) at above address.
_____   Service at place of employment, to wit:
_____   Service on agent. (Specify)
_____   Other service. (Specify) _____

                               [Signed] _____

                                 Attorney for Plaintiff
                                 [*Address*]
                                 [*Telephone Number*]

Source: *West's Indiana Practice* Vol. 9 2nd ed., by Stephen E. Arthur.

The Answer

After receiving the summons and complaint, the defendant makes an appearance by filing an **answer** to the complaint with the court and forwarding a copy to the plaintiff (see Figure 2–5). This document responds to the complaint paragraph by paragraph. If the complaint does not state a claim protected by law, the defendant may file a **motion to dismiss.** For instance, suppose state law requires that tort claims be filed within two years of the injury arising. If the plaintiff waits three years to file a tort complaint, the court will dismiss the claim.

If a defendant does not make an appearance by filing an answer, the plaintiff may petition the court for a **default judgment.** When this occurs, the plaintiff wins everything requested in her complaint. The basic purpose of a default judgment is to protect the parties from undue delay in the judicial proceedings. However, courts prefer to have cases decided on the merits and, as a result, may be persuaded to vacate the default judgment and conduct a trial if the defaulting party establishes that: (1) the default was not willful; (2) he has a meritorious defense; and (3) the nondefaulting party will not suffer undue prejudice.

American Alliance Insurance v. Eagle Insurance
92 F.3d 57 (2nd Cir. 1996)

FACTS   On February 14th, a fire damaged a commercial garage owned by Michael Feidelson, who was insured by American Alliance Insurance. Shimoe Brake & Wheel, which leased the building, was insured by Eagle Insurance. However, because Shimoe had not paid all of its insurance premium, Eagle claimed that it had canceled the policy on the previous January 14th. After paying Feidelson, American sued Shimoe for the amount of the fire damage. Eagle was notified of the action and declined to defend Shimoe on the ground that it had canceled its policy with Shimoe. Because Shimoe never answered the complaint, a default judgment was entered against it. American then commenced an action against Eagle, seeking to collect from Eagle the default judgment entered against Shimoe. The summons and complaint were sent to Eagle's Uniondale office. However, Eagle's in-house counsel accidentally placed the pleadings in the wrong file and failed to answer them. When Eagle did not attend a pretrial conference, the court issued a default judgment against the company. After the court froze Eagle's bank account, the company requested that the default judgment be vacated.

ISSUE   Should the default judgment be vacated?

DECISION   Yes. Eagle's failure to answer the complaint was due to a filing mistake that went unnoticed for two months. Such conduct, though grossly negligent, was not willful, deliberate, or evidence of bad faith, though it weighs somewhat against granting relief. Eagle has presented a meritorious defense—the claim that it does not insure Shimoe because the policy was canceled due to nonpayment of the premium before the fire occurred. Further, it does not appear that American would be prejudiced by hearing at this date. In light of the strong preference for resolving disputes on the merits, the default judgment should be vacated.

http://www.tourolaw.edu/2ndcircuit/

Figure 2–5:   The Answer

IN THE UNITED STATES DISTRICT COURT FOR
THE WESTERN DISTRICT OF _____

Civil Action, File No. _____

_____

_____ _____ Avenue

_____ , _____   PLAINTIFF ⎤
                                                     ⎟
                    v.   ⎟
_____ Corporation   ⎬   ANSWER
100 W. Main Street   ANSWER   ⎟
_____   ⎟
                                                     ⎟
_____ , _____   DEFENDANT ⎦

Defendant for its answer to plaintiff's complaint states:

First Defense

1.   Defendant admits the allegations contained in paragraphs 1 and 3 of plaintiff's complaint; admits that a collision between automobiles driven by the plaintiff and _____ occurred as alleged in paragraph 2 of plaintiff's complaint, but denies each and every other allegation contained in said paragraph; and alleges that it is without knowledge or information sufficient to form a belief as to the truth of the allegations contained in paragraphs 4, 5, and 6 of plaintiff's complaint.

Second Defense

2.   At the time and place and on the occasion mentioned in paragraph 2 of plaintiff's complaint, the plaintiff was himself negligent, his negligence caused or so helped or contributed to cause and bring about the accident and alleged injuries and damages of which he complains, that but for such negligence on his part, said accident would not and could not have occurred and his alleged injuries and damages, if any, would not and could not have been sustained.

Wherefore defendant demands judgment that the plaintiff's complaint be dismissed, that it recover its costs in this action, and that it be granted any and all other relief to which it may appear to be entitled.

_____
Attorney for Defendant

_____
Address

Source: West's *Federal Practice Manual,* Revised 2nd ed.

Discovery

During the next stage of a judicial proceeding, the parties gather the information necessary to resolve the dispute. This process is known as **discovery.** It involves the use of depositions, interrogatories, and requests for documents. Failure of any party to fully cooperate in the discovery process may result in fines. If the plaintiff does not comply, her claim could be dismissed.

Depositions

Perhaps the most common method of discovery is the **deposition.** It involves a witness's oral testimony under oath prior to trial. Depositions normally take place in an attorney's office with a court reporter recording the lawyer's questions and the witness's answers. One purpose of a deposition is for the attorneys to discover the facts and issues of a case prior to trial. Depositions also are useful in making certain that a witness's story does not change over time.

Interrogatories

An attorney may submit detailed lists of written questions, called **interrogatories.** Even though they are answered in writing and under oath, interrogatories are cheaper to administer than depositions since a court reporter is not needed. Because the parties write out their responses to interrogatories, they also may provide clearer answers. However, unlike in a deposition, the questioning attorney is not present and able to observe a party's demeanor when the interrogatories are answered. The answers may also be less candid since the answering party may consult with her attorney and carefully draft a response.

Requests for Documents

Each side may formally request that the other produce documents, photographs, or other evidence relevant to the trial. It may also petition the court to issue a **subpoena** ordering potential witnesses to appear at the trial. The discovery process is less liberal in criminal trials because a criminal defendant cannot be forced to incriminate himself. Therefore, the prosecutor can be forced to produce documents, while the criminal defendant need not cooperate.

Parties normally may obtain discovery of any documents or evidence that is (1) not privileged and (2) relevant to the subject matter of the lawsuit. Consider the following case, which examines the privilege issue.

Mason v. Stock

869 F.Supp. 828 (D. Kan. 1994)

FACTS While driving through the city of Haysville, Paul Mason was stopped by Haysville police officer Timothy Stock and accused of driving under the influence of alcohol. Mason claims he was roughed up, detained, and taken to the hospital for several hours. His blood alcohol content was found to be 0.00. Mason sued both Stock and the city, claiming excessive use of force and false arrest. He alleged that the city permitted, encouraged, and ratified a pattern of unjustified and unreasonable excessive uses of force and false arrests by police officers, particularly against persons accused of driving under the influence of alcohol. As a part of the discovery process, Mason requested production of the police personnel files and internal affairs files. He claimed to be entitled to them because they would reveal the existence of similar complaints against the city and its police force. The city objected to the request on the ground that the information sought was privileged.

ISSUE   Should the city be required to produce the files?

DECISION   Yes. Haysville police officers have constitutionally based privacy interests in the personal matters contained within their police files. However, privileges are to be narrowly construed. Further, the privacy interests of police officers should be especially limited in view of the role played by the police officer as a public servant who must be accountable to public review. With this in mind, only one type of item in the personnel files is so highly personal and sensitive in nature that it should be safeguarded as privileged: the psychological evaluations of each of the police officers. All other items concern more official, duty-connected types of information, such as payroll and vacation/absence records, official oaths, letters of appreciation, and periodic performance evaluations. These clearly are not privileged. The city claimed that the internal affairs files must be privileged because disclosure of such information would chill the willingness of officers to candidly criticize fellow officers during internal investigations. This argument is rejected. It is unlikely that citizens and police officers will absolutely refuse to cooperate in investigations because of a few isolated instances of disclosure.

Pretrial Conference

Some judges take an active role in attempting to narrow issues and encourage the parties to settle their dispute. The **pretrial conference** allows the judge to meet privately with both attorneys and honestly assess the nature of the claims. They determine which factual issues are not in conflict. By encouraging the attorneys to *stipulate* (agree) to key facts, the trial can be shortened by avoiding the need to present witnesses on issues over which there is no real disagreement.

Summary Judgment

When the pleadings (and the parties' stipulations) indicate there are no factual issues over which the parties are in disagreement, there is no need for a trial. Because the only issues in dispute are questions of law, and the judge determines legal questions, a **summary judgment** may be appropriate. With a summary judgment, the judge decides the case based on the information in the pleadings and facts uncovered during the discovery process.

The Trial

When hearing a civil case, a federal district court must honor the parties' request for a jury trial if the amount at issue exceeds $20. Most states also guarantee a right to a jury in civil cases. For criminal prosecutions, at either the state or federal level, the accused has a right to speedy and public trial, by an impartial jury of the state and district where the crime was committed. However, this jury-trial right in criminal cases is reserved for prosecutions of serious offenses. There is no right to a jury in a trial for a petty offense. An offense carrying a maximum prison term of six months or less is presumed to be petty.

Lewis v. United States
116 S.Ct. 2163 (U.S. Sup. Ct. 1996)

FACTS   Ray Lewis was a mail handler for the United States Postal Service. One day, postal inspectors saw him open several pieces of mail and pocket the contents. The next day, the inspectors routed "test" mail, containing marked currency, through Lewis's station. After seeing him open the mail and remove the currency, the inspectors arrested him. He was charged with two counts of obstructing the mail. Each count carried a maximum authorized prison sentence of six months. Lewis requested a jury trial, but the district court judge granted the government's motion for a bench trial. Lewis complained that since he was being prosecuted in a single proceeding for two petty offenses where the combined authorized prison term exceeded six months, he was entitled to a jury trial.

ISSUE   Is Lewis entitled to a jury trial?

DECISION   No. The Constitution reserves the jury-trial right to defendants accused of serious, rather than petty, crimes. A criminal offense carrying a maximum prison term of six months or less is presumed petty. Here, the maximum authorized penalty for obstruction of mail is six months' imprisonment—a penalty that presumptively places the offense in the petty category. However, we face the question that Lewis is nevertheless entitled to a jury trial, because he was tried in a single proceeding for two counts of the petty offense and therefore could have been sentenced to twelve months in prison. By setting the maximum authorized prison term at six months, the legislature categorized the offense of obstructing the mail as petty. The fact that Lewis was charged with two counts of a petty offense does not revise the legislative judgment as to the gravity of that particular offense, nor does it transform the petty offense into a serious one, to which the jury-trial right would apply. The Constitution's guarantee of the right to a jury trial extends only to serious offenses, and Lewis was not charged with a serious offense.

http://www.law.vill.edu/Fed-Ct/fedcourt.html
http://www.supct.law.cornell.edu/supct/

Conducting the Trial

A civil case begins with the plaintiff's attorney making an *opening statement* outlining her case. The defendant's attorney has the option of following with his own opening statement. The plaintiff's attorney then calls her witnesses and presents the evidence supporting her claim. The defendant's attorney may *cross-examine* each witness and challenge the admissibility of evidence.

At the conclusion of the plaintiff's case, the defendant's attorney frequently requests a **directed verdict,** which results in the trial ending in favor of the defendant. A directed verdict is granted only when the plaintiff fails to present evidence sufficient to support her legal claim. If the request for a directed verdict is denied, the defendant's witnesses and evidence are introduced. At the conclusion of the defendant's case, the plaintiff's attorney usually requests a directed verdict.

The Verdict

After both sides have presented their witnesses and evidence, they summarize their positions. In a jury trial, the judge then instructs the jury as to the legal rules governing the dispute. In a civil trial, the plaintiff has the burden of proving her case by a *preponderance of the evidence*. The burden is even higher for the prosecutor in a criminal trial; he must prove the defendant's guilt *beyond a reasonable doubt*.

The decision by the jury or the judge (in a bench trial) is called the **verdict**. In civil cases, it generally only requires a three-fourths majority to render a verdict. However, criminal cases usually require unanimity. After the jury reports its verdict in a civil trial, the judge may overrule their decision by granting the losing party a **judgment n.o.v.** (*judgment non obstante veredicto*, or notwithstanding the verdict). However, he may not overrule a "not guilty" verdict in a criminal trial. The judge also may grant a motion for a new trial if she believes there has been a serious legal error.

Ethical Issue

Judges generally don't win any popularity contests when they overrule a jury's verdict. How do you feel about a judge issuing a judgment n.o.v. to override the unanimous verdict of a jury?

Enforcing Judgments

At the conclusion of a lawsuit, the court instructs the losing party, the **judgment debtor,** to pay damages or otherwise abide by its decision. While many parties voluntarily obey the court, others do not readily comply. The winning party, the **judgment creditor,** may need to return to court to obtain a **writ of execution.** This directs the sheriff to seize listed assets of the judgment debtor to satisfy the judgment. If the judgment debtor and her assets are located outside of that jurisdiction, the judgment creditor must seek enforcement from a court in that state. The *full faith and credit clause* of the U.S. Constitution requires that each state fully recognize and enforce the judgments of the courts of the other 49 states.

Appealing Judgments

If a disputing party believes the evidence did not support a verdict or the court made an error of law, he may appeal. Appellate courts, as noted above, do not hear witnesses or gather evidence. Instead, they read the lower-court transcripts, read briefs prepared by the attorneys, and listen to the attorneys' oral arguments. Appellate court decisions are based on majority rule. If the appellate court agrees with the lower-court's verdict, it **affirms** the decision. If it believes the lower court erred, it **reverses** the decision. If the case needs to be reheard because of an improper interpretation of law, the case is **reversed and remanded** for the lower court to retry.

Alternative Dispute Resolution

http://
*www.law.cornell.
edu/topics/adr.html*
provides information
and links on the topic
of ADR.

Many people and businesses look for alternatives to the judicial system when civil disputes arise. There are four major advantages associated with the basic methods of **alternative dispute resolution (ADR).** First, ADR generally is faster than litigation. Most court dockets are overcrowded, causing civil disputes to languish for many years. Second, ADR procedures tend to be flexible and can be tailored to the particular needs of the disputing parties. Third, through ADR the parties may submit their dispute to an expert who fully understands the complexities of their case. Judges and juries often are ill-equipped to deal with complex disputes. Finally, unlike a judicial proceeding, the parties may agree to maintain confidentiality. This final section discusses four ADR mechanisms: (1) negotiation, (2) mediation, (3) mini-trial, and (4) arbitration.

Negotiation

Unlike litigation, where a judge presides over the conflict, with **negotiation** the parties themselves decide how to resolve the matter. Of course, this won't succeed unless both sides make a good-faith effort to arrive at a solution. After reaching an agreement, the parties generally draw up a binding contract spelling out their new obligations.

Mediation

With **mediation,** the disputants call in a neutral third party to help them reach a compromise. Although mediators may be given authority to compel a solution, generally their role is to persuade the parties to accept a common position. As with negotiation, after resolving a dispute through mediation, the parties are likely to draft a contract incorporating their new agreement.

Mini-Trial

A **mini-trial** is similar to litigation in that lawyers from each side formally present their legal and factual arguments to each other. There may be a discovery process where they exchange relevant information. Like mediation, mini-trials generally are officiated by a neutral third party who issues a nonbinding decision at the culmination of the lawyers' presentations. As with negotiation and mediation, however, it is up to the parties themselves to voluntarily reach a settlement agreement.

Mini-trials seem best suited for disputes involving complex facts. They permit the parties to avoid complicated legal issues and instead focus on the practical business aspects of their dispute.

Arbitration

The generally preferred method of resolving business disputes is through **arbitration.** This involves the settlement of legal controversies by a nonjudicial third party. Frequently, the arbitrator issues a binding decision, although nonbinding arbitration also is fairly common. As with the three previous ADR mechanisms, the parties must voluntarily agree to arbitrate. They have the power, through their agreement, to select the arbitrator as well as the rules that govern the arbitration process.

Private parties have a great deal of discretion over the arbitration forum and the substantive rules that govern their dispute resolution process. Generally, they make these choices during the contract negotiation stage (before any disputes arise) and incorporate them into their final agreement. However, the decision to arbitrate may be made after a dispute arises.

Enforcing the Arbitration Agreement

The *Federal Arbitration Act* requires that private agreements to arbitrate be enforced according to their terms. Thus, the parties to a contract may (1) require that any disputes be arbitrated, (2) select the arbitrator, and (3) determine the rules governing the arbitration process. Because decisions to arbitrate are contractual in nature, a court may invalidate an arbitration agreement if it was secured by fraud, duress, or unconscionability. (These contract defenses are discussed in Chapter 9.)

For instance, in the case that opened this chapter, Hill argued that the arbitration agreement was unenforceable because the arbitration clause was buried in the list of terms. However, the court rejected this argument since nothing in the *Federal Arbitration Act* requires that an arbitration clause be prominent. It held that people who accept a contract take the risk that unread terms may later prove unwelcome.

Doctor's Associates v. Casarotto

116 S.Ct. 1652 (U.S. Sup. Ct. 1996)

FACTS   Doctor's Associates is the national franchisor of Subway sandwich shops. It entered a franchise agreement with Paul Casarotto that permitted Casarotto to open a Subway shop in Great Falls, Montana. The franchise agreement stated on page nine, and in ordinary type: "Any controversy or claim arising out of or relating to this contract or the breach thereof shall be settled by Arbitration." Later, when a dispute arose, Casarotto sued Doctor's Associates in a Montana state court. Doctor's Associates demanded arbitration of Casarotto's claims. However, Casarotto argued that the arbitration clause in the agreement was not enforceable because it violated a Montana statute. That statute provided that: *"Notice that a contract is subject to arbitration shall be typed in underlined capital letters on the first page of the contract; and unless such notice is displayed thereon, the contract may not be subject to arbitration."* Doctor's Associates claimed that the Montana statute was displaced by the *Federal Arbitration Act,* which declares written provisions for arbitration *"valid, irrevocable, and enforceable, save upon such grounds as exist at law or in equity for the revocation of any contract."*

ISSUE   Should the parties be required to arbitrate their dispute?

DECISION   Yes. States may regulate contracts, including arbitration clauses, under general contract law principles and they may invalidate an arbitration clause that violates such principles. What states may not do, however, is decide that a contract is fair enough to enforce all its basic terms (price, service, credit), but not fair enough to enforce its arbitration clause. Thus, generally applicable contract defenses, such as

continued

fraud, duress, or unconscionability, may be applied to invalidate arbitration agreements without violating federal law. Courts may not, however, invalidate arbitration agreements under state laws applicable *only* to arbitration provisions. Because Montana conditions the enforceability of arbitration agreements on compliance with a special notice requirement not applicable to contracts generally, the state law is preempted by the federal law.

http://www.law.vill.edu/Fed-Ct/fedcourt.html
http://supct.law.cornell.edu/supct/

Enforcing the Arbitral Award

After an arbitrator decides a case, he issues an **arbitral award**. If the losing party does not voluntarily comply with the decision, the winning party may have to petition a court to enforce the award. Courts seldom second-guess the decision made by the arbitrator. In fact, the *Uniform Arbitration Act*, which has been ratified by most states, makes both the agreement to arbitrate and the arbitral award enforceable in court. However, if it appears that the arbitrator failed to follow the rules stipulated in the arbitration agreement, acted in an arbitrary or discriminatory manner, or issued an award that violates state or federal law, a court will not enforce the arbitral award.

Preventive Law

Litigation can be confusing, time-consuming, and expensive. As important is the fact that by resorting to judicial remedies, people risk destroying what still could be a worthwhile relationship. For these reasons, many individuals prefer to explore less contentious alternatives before considering litigation. This section examines the importance of anticipating disputes and preparing for their smooth resolution.

Contracting partners might consider fashioning a flexible agreement that envisions regular renegotiation. Even when dealing with parties who insist upon certainty and predictability in their agreements, it is possible to craft a carefully worded contract that anticipates and defuses future conflicts.

Adjustment Provisions

Life holds so many surprises that conflicts and misunderstandings seem inevitable. Accordingly, it is essential that contracting partners (particularly in long-term agreements) maintain flexible attitudes at both the drafting and performance stages. Frequently, this flexibility can be incorporated into a contract through the use of some type of **adjustment provision**.

These clauses can take several forms. For instance, sometimes it is clear at the contract formation stage that some details need to be negotiated later. This might occur in a contract between a wholesaler and a retailer when the manufacturer has not yet given the wholesaler a firm price. At other times, the parties may anticipate that a key condition upon which the contract is based could change. For example, John may agree to remove waste materials from Paula's property at a fixed price. However, if he later uncovers hazardous wastes, he may have an entirely different conception of what constitutes a fair price. Finally, the parties often realize that events beyond their control (earthquakes, droughts, and other natural disasters) can render their original agreement exceedingly more difficult to perform. In anticipation of these events, a contract may include a wide variety of clauses calling for many courses of action, ranging from price escalation to renegotiation to cancellation.

Renegotiation

The time, expense, and uncertainty involved in litigation spur many disputing parties to seriously pursue contract **renegotiation.** As discussed above, sometimes the contract itself mandates renegotiation through an adjustment provision. However, even in the absence of such a requirement, the parties may find it to be in their best interest to voluntarily restructure their obligations.

Settlements

Even after disputants have become embroiled in litigation they may simultaneously pursue **settlement** efforts. In fact, some courts actively encourage litigants to consider that course of action. At the culmination of a successful settlement effort, the parties draft a formal agreement designed to terminate all or part of their legal dispute.

Because settlement agreements are meant to be legally binding, certain precautions should be taken in their negotiation and execution. First, in negotiations with a business, it is imperative that the discussions be conducted with a representative who is authorized to legally bind the company. Second, the settlement agreement must be carefully worded so that it resolves the key issues involved in the dispute without obligating the parties to additional, unintended responsibilities.

Key Contractual Provisions

The previous discussion introduced several ways of avoiding the costs and uncertainties associated with litigation. While the contract itself frequently calls for the use of those methods, they are most successful when the parties voluntarily pursue their ongoing relationship with cooperative spirits and flexible attitudes. The focus now shifts from an examination of attitudes to a look at several formal contractual provisions that permit people to renegotiate with a reasonable degree of certainty as to the costs and convenience of potential litigation.

Forum Selection Clause

Increasingly, business contracts include a **forum selection clause,** which specifies the place where any litigation must be brought. Most courts uphold a freely negotiated forum selection clause unless doing so is grossly unfair. Generally, there is no enforcement problem if the parties select the courts of either of their states or a third state that has some relationship to the contract.

Carnival Cruise Lines v. Shute

499 U.S. 585 (U.S. Sup. Ct. 1991)

FACTS   Eulala Shute purchased passage on a ship operated by Carnival Cruise Lines. Her ticket contained language informing her that the contract of passage was subject to certain terms and conditions. One such term was a forum selection clause stipulating that all disputes were to be litigated before a court located in the state of Florida. While the ship was in international waters off the Mexican coast, Shute was injured when she slipped and fell during a guided tour of the ship's galley. After returning to her home in Washington, Shute brought suit against Carnival in a federal district court in the state of Washington. When Carnival asked for a summary judgment on the grounds that the suit must be brought in Florida, Shute argued that the forum selection clause was unenforceable because it was not the product of negotiation between the parties.

ISSUE   Is the forum selection clause enforceable?

DECISION   Yes. Shute will not be permitted to sue in Washington. Including a forum selection clause in a form contract of this kind is permissible for several reasons: First, a cruise line has a special interest in limiting the forums in which it potentially could be subject to suit. Additionally, such a clause will eliminate in advance any confusion about where suits must be brought and defended, sparing the litigants and the courts much time and expense. Finally, it stands to reason that passengers who purchase tickets containing forum selection clauses benefit in the form of reduced fares reflecting the savings that the cruise line enjoys by limiting the forums in which it may be sued. It bears emphasis that forum selection clauses contained in form passage contracts are subject to judicial scrutiny for fundamental fairness. In this case there is no indication that Carnival set Florida as the forum for disputes as a means of discouraging passengers from pursuing legitimate claims. The company has its principal place of business in Florida and many of its cruises begin and end in that state. Similarly, there is no evidence that Carnival obtained Shute's consent to the clause by fraud or overreaching.

http://www.law.vill.edu/Fed-Ct/fedcourt.html
http://supct.law.cornell.edu/supct/

Choice of Law Clause

Contracting partners can eliminate a great deal of uncertainty by placing a **choice of law clause** in their agreement. Courts specifically require that the chosen law bear a *reasonable relation* to the transaction. Generally, this test is met if the parties select the law of either of their home states or that of a third state where the contract was negotiated or might be performed.

QUESTIONS AND PROBLEM CASES

1. Explain how the parties to an agreement can use their contract to minimize the confusion that might otherwise arise over the appropriate governing law or jurisdiction.
2. What is meant by *personal jurisdiction*?
3. What is the role of a pretrial conference?
4. How does negotiation differ from mediation? In what ways are they similar?
5. How do trial courts differ from appellate courts?
6. Rabbi Weiss, a resident of New York, traveled to Poland with six of his students to protest the continued use of a building on the outskirts of the Auschwitz concentration camp as a convent for an order of cloistered nuns. After staging a nonviolent protest on the grounds of the convent, Weiss and the students were forcibly ejected. A month later, Cardinal Glemp, a resident of Poland, delivered a sermon in Poland during which he stated that restraining Weiss prevented the nuns from being killed or the convent being destroyed. After Glemp's comments were published in several magazines with circulation in the state of Washington, Weiss filed a defamation action against Glemp in that state. While Glemp was making a three-day pastoral visit to Seattle, Weiss's process server tried to serve the summons and complaint at the rectory where Glemp was staying. Glemp, however, refused to meet with him. The process server waited until he could see Glemp through a large plate-glass window. He held the documents high and yelled, "Cardinal Glemp, official documents. You have been served." He then placed the documents on a concrete windowsill about four feet from where Glemp was sitting. The Washington service statute requires that *"The summons shall be served to the defendant personally or by leaving a copy of the summons at the house of his usual abode with some person of suitable age and discretion then resident therein."* When Glemp filed no answer to the complaint, Weiss moved for a default judgment. Glemp moved for a dismissal on the grounds that the service of process was insufficient. Was Glemp properly served?
7. OMS is a Canadian corporation with its principal place of business in Canada. Command-Aire is incorporated in Texas and has its principal place of business there. The OMS president met with Command-Aire representatives at a convention in Chicago and discussed the possible purchase of heat pump equipment manufactured by Command-Aire. At one point, OMS representatives traveled to Texas to deliver and discuss design specifications. Contract negotiations were conducted and the contract was finally consummated by use of telephonic and mail services. Although the initial sales agreement contemplated that Command-Aire would deliver the equipment in Canada, the parties ultimately agreed that OMS would take possession in Texas. OMS installed the pumps in Canadian condominiums. Later, when the heating pumps proved to be defective, OMS refused to make further payments. Command-Aire filed suit in a federal court in Texas, and OMS moved to dismiss for lack of personal jurisdiction. Does the Texas court have personal jurisdiction over OMS?
8. Interpane Coatings, a Wisconsin corporation, delivered goods to McDowell Pacific, an Australian buyer. The parties utilized a documentary exchange whereby McDowell would receive the bills of lading covering the goods upon its acceptance of drafts promising payment to Interpane. To facilitate this documentary transfer, Interpane and McDowell enlisted the services of Australia & New Zealand Banking Group (ANZ), an Australian bank. Out of concern that McDowell might fail to honor its promise to pay on the drafts, Interpane instructed ANZ not to release the bills of lading unless the bank itself would guarantee the debt. ANZ misunderstood these instructions and delivered the bills of lading to McDowell. After taking possession of the goods, McDowell refused to honor its obligation to pay on the drafts.

Interpane filed suit against ANZ for negligence and breach of contract. It brought suit in an Illinois federal district court because ANZ maintained an office in Chicago and thus could easily be served with process there. ANZ asserted that the U.S. district court was a highly inconvenient forum in which to litigate Interpane's claims and that the suit should have been brought in Australia. Should the U.S. district court dismiss the case on the grounds of *forum non conveniens*?

9. Deborah Patterson became employed as a medical technologist at Columbia Regional Hospital. Several years later she received a copy of Columbia's employee handbook and signed an arbitration clause set forth on the last page of the handbook. The handbook page containing the arbitration clause was introduced by the heading, **"IMPORTANT! Acknowledgment Form.** Upon receipt, please sign and present the acknowledgment form of this **handbook** to the Human Resources Department." Her employer removed the page from the handbook after she signed it and stored it in a file. When Patterson later received treatment from Columbia which she believed to be discriminatory, she filed a lawsuit in the federal district court. Should Patterson be required to arbitrate her claims?

10. Mitsubishi, a Japanese corporation, distributed automobiles through Chrysler dealers outside of the continental United States. Soler, a Puerto Rican corporation, entered into a distributorship agreement with Mitsubishi that permitted Soler to sell cars in Puerto Rico. The agreement provided that disputes would be arbitrated in Japan in accordance with the rules and regulations of the Japan Commercial Arbitration Association. When the new car market slackened, Soler attempted to cancel several shipments of cars and also tried to tranship cars to Latin America and the continental United States. Mitsubishi denied these requests and sought to compel arbitration of the parties' resulting disputes. Soler filed an antitrust suit against Mitsubishi in a U.S. district court, arguing that the arbitration agreement was not enforceable since only U.S. courts could hear antitrust claims. Should the U.S. court enforce the parties' arbitration agreement despite Soler's antitrust claims?

CHAPTER 3

THE LEGAL PROFESSION

A fter New York City passed an ordinance requiring window guards for apartments with children under 10 years old, the cooperative board of an apartment in Manhattan ordered Alec Diacou to pay for the bars on his windows. The cost of the bars was $909. Diacou refused to pay, arguing the cooperative was responsible for the bill. When settlement efforts broke down, the cooperative instructed its lawyers to sue. After an initial hearing and several appeals that lasted more than six years, the cooperative finally won. The cost of its efforts? The cooperative's attorneys submitted a bill for $73,547. Diacou paid at least $30,000 to his lawyers.

The Wall Street Journal, March 23, 1994, p. A1.

How could reasonably intelligent individuals justify spending over $103,000 for a $909 dispute?

Should Diacou, as the losing party, have to pay the cooperative's legal fees?

How can you receive adequate legal representation without having to pay exorbitant legal fees?

Introduction

Because of the complex nature of modern life, people are confronted with legal questions and controversies on a daily basis. To survive in this regulatory environment, they must develop a basic understanding of our legal system. Lawyers no longer are necessary only when one is suing or being sued. They perform vital roles in assisting people in avoiding legal emergencies and in planning their affairs. It is vital that each of us becomes aware of the roles that attorneys perform in the legal system.

Chapter Overview

The chapter opens with an overview of the fundamental characteristics of the attorney-client relationship. It examines the role of lawyers in the American legal system as well as the fundamental duties they owe their clients. This is followed by a brief discussion of the process of hiring and, in some cases, firing a lawyer. The chapter closes with a section exploring legal careers.

The Attorney-Client Relationship

http://
*www.law.cornell.edu/
topics/professional_
responsibility.html*
provides links to professional conduct and ethics sites for several states.

In the earliest years of colonial America, lawyers played an extremely limited role in the process of resolving disputes. Mediation and arbitration, rather than litigation, were common methods of resolving disputes. By the early 20th century, as a result of technological growth, business concentration, and urbanization, lawyers began to dominate the legal system. Their control remained largely unchecked until the 1960s and 1970s, when it became obvious that the legal profession was unaffordable to most middle- and lower-class Americans. At this same time, a general disrespect for lawyers and the legal profession began to develop.

Today, the legal profession is priced out of the reach of many Americans. Yet, because of the pervasive influence of legal rules, people still need timely and specific legal advice. As a result, we are witnessing growing interest in legal self-help books and paralegals as ways to gain cheaper access to legal knowledge. But there are limits to the effectiveness of these more affordable alternatives. It is essential for people to better understand the workings of a successful attorney-client relationship so they may more efficiently (and affordably) take advantage of the services offered by legal professionals.

The Adversary System

The **adversary system** lies at the core of the American judicial process. Lawyers are key actors in this system. Each attorney is required to present the strongest possible legal argument for her client. It is believed that through this advocacy, truth and justice will be uncovered. Of course, in persuading the jury, an attorney is not given free rein. She may be sanctioned for presenting her client's position in a dishonest way.

Role of the Judge

Theoretically, judges serve a fairly passive role in the adversary system. They oversee the presentation of evidence and the examination of witnesses to make certain that neither attorney behaves improperly. Of course, judges are not totally passive actors. They ultimately must decide the proper rule of law and communicate that information to the jury.

Problems with the Adversary System

The adversary system is not without its critics. The quest for truth and justice may be thwarted when the opposing lawyers are not of equal skill. In fact, large businesses and wealthy individuals may have a distinct advantage since they generally can afford to be represented by the very best attorneys.

The Florida Bar v. Machin

635 So.2d 938 (Sup. Ct. Fla. 1994)

FACTS   Nelson Gonzalez pled guilty to second-degree murder after being charged with the first-degree murder of Samuel Sierra and the kidnapping of Sierra's girlfriend, Susan Schultz. At the time of the murder, Schultz was pregnant with Sierra's child. Manuel A. Machin served as Gonzalez's attorney. At various times prior to the sentencing hearing, Machin offered, on behalf of his client, to set up a trust fund for Ms. Schultz's child in amounts up to $30,000. The trust fund would be set up for the child only if Ms. Schultz and Sierra's family did not speak in aggravation at Gonzalez's sentencing hearing. Machin feared that if the victim's family spoke in aggravation, the sentencing judge would impose a more severe sentence or reject the plea agreement entirely. The victim's family rejected the offer and reported Machin to the Florida Bar. He was suspended from the practice of law for 90 days for engaging in conduct prejudicial to the administration of justice. Machin appealed the finding of guilt and the suspension.

ISSUE   Should the attorney's suspension be upheld?

DECISION   Yes. A lawyer who tries to buy a victim's silence at sentencing prejudices the administration of justice. It does not matter that the attempt was unsuccessful. Each time such an attempt is made, confidence in the legal system is lost. The fair and proper administration of justice requires that the rich and the poor receive equal treatment before the court. A wealthy defendant cannot be allowed to buy silence and thereby gain a chance at a lesser sentence than that received by one unable to pay for silence. This is because when justice can be bought by the highest bidder, there is no justice. An attorney's involvement in the transaction only serves to accentuate the prejudicial effect on the system. When one charged with the special responsibility of upholding the quality of justice attempts to buy a more favorable sentence for a criminal defendant, doubt is cast on our entire system of justice.

Professional Qualifications

In most instances, a person may represent himself in a legal proceeding. No special qualifications are required. However, in other than small claims matters, the wisdom of representing oneself is questionable. Even a licensed attorney is unlikely to represent herself in a lawsuit because of the need for an advocate who possesses an objective view of the matter.

Only licensed attorneys may actually engage in the **practice of law** on behalf of another. Each state defines exactly what constitutes the practice of law. While *paralegals* and other professionals may help people complete legal forms, they may not counsel or provide specific information or advice concerning a client's legal affairs. Practicing attorneys generally must graduate from an accredited law school, pass a state bar examination, and possess good moral character.

Professional Responsibilities

http://
www.abanet.org/cpr/
home.html contains
information on ethics
rules.

A **fiduciary relationship** exists between a lawyer and his client. This means the attorney must act in the best interests of his client rather than pursue his own interests. Basically, the attorney-client relationship is grounded in the law of agency. (Agency principles are discussed in Chapter 12.) However, unlike most employees, because of his special training and skills, the attorney is permitted a great deal of latitude in determining how best to represent his client.

Confidentiality

A fundamental feature of the legal profession is the **attorney-client privilege.** This prevents a lawyer from disclosing confidential communications made by the client for the purpose of retaining the lawyer or securing legal service or advice from her in her professional capacity. The privilege is based on the notion that the proper and orderly functioning of the judicial system depends on a confidential relationship between the lawyer and the client. Unless a client makes a full disclosure to his attorney, the advice and representation he receives may be inadequate.

The attorney-client privilege does not require that the lawyer actually be retained, since a person may need to reveal confidential information while trying to persuade an attorney to provide legal representation. Further, the privilege also extends to the subordinates (secretaries, paralegals) of the lawyer during the course of the attorney-client relationship. However, the privilege does not cover statements made in the presence of people other than the lawyer or her subordinates. And a lawyer has a duty to report a client's statement that he intends to commit a crime.

People v. Gionis

892 P.2d 1119 (Sup. Ct. Cal. 1995)

FACTS   Aissa Marie Wayne, the daughter of late movie actor John Wayne, was divorced from Thomas Gionis, a doctor. After their breakup, Gionis threatened to kill Wayne on several occasions. After receiving an urgent telephone call from Gionis, John Lueck, an attorney who referred clients to Gionis for medical evaluations, visited his home. Gionis was in tears because he had just been served with divorce papers. Lueck made it clear that he would not represent Gionis because he knew both Gionis and Wayne. During their ensuing conversation, Gionis displayed wide mood swings, alternating between tears and anger. While in one of his angry moods, he showed Lueck some holes in a wall and said the altercation that caused that damage was nothing compared to what he was capable of doing. He also told Lueck how easy it would be for him to pay somebody to really take care of her. He finally commented that he was too smart to do something like that at a time when it would be obvious it was his responsibility. He said that if he were to do something, it would be at a more opportune time. One year later, Wayne and her boyfriend were brutally attacked by two gunmen. Gionis was convicted of hiring the attackers and sentenced to five years in prison. He argued his convictions should be reversed because the court admitted testimony from Lueck as to the statements Gionis had made during the earlier visit to his home.

ISSUE   Did Lueck's testimony violate the attorney-client privilege?

DECISION   No. Lueck, an attorney, was Gionis's friend and had been to his home approximately 15 times. The two also shared a business relationship in which Lueck referred between 100 and 200 clients to Gionis. Before Gionis made any incriminating disclosure, Lueck specifically stated he would not represent Gionis in the divorce proceeding. Lueck was very clear that he in no way wanted to be involved in the dispute between Gionis and Wayne. The attorney-client privilege does not apply each time issues touching upon legal matters are discussed with an attorney. A communication is not privileged, even though it may involve a legal matter, if it has no relation to any professional relationship of the attorney with the client. This was not a situation in which Gionis disclosed information while exploring the possibility of retaining Lueck as his lawyer. His insistence on talking with Lueck, despite Lueck's clear and reiterated unwillingness to act as his lawyer, gives rise to the reasonable inference that Gionis sought to speak with Lueck in his capacity as a friend, not as an attorney.

Ethical Issue

Both the adversary system and the attorney-client privilege may place a lawyer in a position where he knows he is defending a guilty person. Would you feel comfortable representing a person under those circumstances?

Loyalty

As a part of the lawyer's duty of loyalty to her client, she must avoid **conflicts of interest.** This imposes a responsibility to be faithful to the client's legal needs. The lawyer must avoid outside pressures that distract from her duty to protect and further her client's interests to the utmost. Further, she must avoid representing other individuals when their interests conflict with those of her client. There are two dimensions to the attorney's duty to avoid dividing her loyalties: conflicts that arise from successive representation of clients and those arising from simultaneous representation.

Successive Representation

Sometimes a former client seeks to have an attorney disqualified from representing a new client in litigation that conflicts with the former client's interests. The concern here is that in fully serving the needs of the new client, the lawyer may be forced to divulge confidences revealed by the former client to the attorney or some other member of her law firm.

http://
*www.legalethics.
com/* contains more
issues on legal
ethics.

When disputes over successive representation arise, the courts use a *substantial relationship test* to determine if the lawyer may represent the new client. Under this test, the former client may not prevent the attorney from representing a new client unless he can demonstrate a substantial relationship between the subjects of the former and the new representations. If such a relationship does exist, it is presumed that the attorney will use confidences revealed by the former client to fully represent the new client. Accordingly, the lawyer will be disqualified from representing the new client.

Simultaneous Representations

The duty of loyalty, rather than a concern for confidentiality, is at issue when an attorney or her law firm simultaneously represents two opposing clients. At its greatest extreme, this notion of divided loyalties exists when a lawyer tries to represent both the plaintiff and the defendant in a lawsuit. Such a case of dual representations runs counter to the underlying logic of the adversary system.

Even though the simultaneous representations may have nothing in common, and there is no risk of the attorney revealing confidences, disqualification still may be required. In fact, in most instances, disqualification under such circumstances is automatic. This is because a client who learns that his attorney or her firm is also representing a litigation adversary, even in a wholly unrelated matter, cannot be expected to sustain confidence and trust in the attorney. Even when the representations have nothing to do with each other, the client could reasonably question the lawyer's sense of loyalty.

Flatt v. Superior Court

885 P.2D 950 (SUP. CT. CAL. 1994)

FACTS   William Daniel was unhappy with the performance of his attorney, Donald Hinkle. Accordingly, he met with another lawyer, Gail Flatt, to discuss filing a malpractice lawsuit against Hinkle. During the course of this meeting, Daniel disclosed confidential information to Flatt concerning the conduct of Hinkle. Flatt told him he "definitely" had a claim for legal malpractice against Hinkle. One week after that meeting, Flatt returned Daniel's documents and advised him she could not represent him in an action against Hinkle because she had discovered that her law firm was representing Hinkle in an unrelated matter. Two years later, Daniel filed a malpractice claim against Hinkle. However, when it appeared that his claim against Hinkle might be barred by statute of limitations because it was not filed in a timely manner, Daniel sued Flatt. Specifically, he claimed that Flatt had committed legal malpractice because she did not advise him of the statute of limitations governing his claim against Hinkle.

ISSUE   Did Flatt have a duty to inform Daniel of the statute of limitations?

DECISION   No. An attorney's duty of loyalty to a client is not one that is capable of being divided, at least under circumstances where the ethical obligation to withdraw from further representation of one of the parties is mandatory. This conclusion is motivated by an appreciation of the damage done to the existing client's sense of trust and security—features essential to the effective functioning of the fiduciary relationship—likely to follow from a conclusion that Flatt had a duty to advise Daniel under the facts of this case. It is an attorney's duty to protect her client in every possible way, and it is a violation of that duty for her to assume a position adverse to her client. Flatt clearly had no duty to give Daniel advice that would have aided in advancing his contemplated lawsuit against Hinkle, her firm's existing client. Any advice to Daniel regarding the statute of limitations governing his claim against Hinkle would have run counter to the interests of Hinkle, an existing client, and her firm's obligation of undivided loyalty to him. Therefore, she had no duty to give Daniel any such advice.

Competence and Care

By accepting employment as the client's lawyer, an attorney agrees to exercise the skill, prudence, and diligence expected of lawyers of ordinary skill and competence in the community. The lawyer does not guarantee that the client will win a lawsuit. Thus, he is not necessarily liable for **malpractice** when the client loses. In fact, a lawyer is not liable for every mistake he might make. Lawyers are given a great deal of discretion in selecting an appropriate strategy for handling a legal dispute. As long as an attorney has a rational basis for the strategy he chooses, the courts are not likely to second-guess his professional judgment.

However, a client may successfully bring a malpractice claim when his attorney fails to draft court-related documents properly or in a timely manner, appear at a hearing, or assert a possible claim or defense. And important tactical decisions should be made only after the lawyer consults with his client.

Generally, to recover compensatory damages, the client must prove both injury and proximate causation (foreseeability). However, the client may recover any compensation he paid to the attorney without showing injury or causation in cases where the lawyer has breached a duty of loyalty.

Liability to Non-Clients

At common law, lawyers were not liable for professional malpractice to anyone other than their clients. Part of the justification for this restrictive rule was concern over the potential liability attorneys would face if they owed legal duties to an unforeseeable and unlimited number of third parties each time they failed to exercise professional competence. Over time, however, the rule was relaxed to permit third-party liability when the lawyer engaged in fraudulent or maliciously harmful conduct.

Today, two trends have emerged that impose third-party liability on attorneys in negligence cases. The first, the *third-party beneficiary test*, might arise when the attorney performs faulty legal work for the benefit of a non-client. For instance, by improperly drawing up a will for his client, a lawyer might be liable to the intended beneficiary who suffers economic loss when the will is unenforceable.

Some courts follow a *multicriteria test* in extending malpractice liability to non-clients. They balance various factors, including the extent to which the transaction was intended to benefit the non-client, the foreseeability of harm to the non-client, the degree of certainty that the non-client suffered injury, the closeness of the connection between the lawyer's conduct and the non-client's injury, and the moral blame attached to the lawyer's performance. Consider the following case where the court applies a multicriteria test in finding an attorney liable to a non-client.

Meighan v. Shore

40 Cal.Rptr. 744 (Cal. App. 2 Dist. 1995)

FACTS   Clement Meighan suffered chest pains and was taken to a hospital. While in the hospital, doctors did not immediately diagnose his condition as a heart attack. Meighan and his wife, Joan, later believed that he had been the victim of medical malpractice. They visited Samuel Shore, an attorney, to discuss their claims. Shore agreed to take their case; however, he stated that he would be representing Clement and not Joan. Nothing was said during the interview about Joan's right to pursue a claim in her own right for loss of consortium, and neither of the Meighans had any idea that there was such a tort. More than a year later, after the Meighans had substituted a new lawyer for Shore, they learned of Joan's entitlement to pursue an action for loss of consortium. However, by this time, the right had become barred by the statute of limitations. Joan sued Shore for legal malpractice for failing to inform them of her potential cause of action for loss of consortium.

ISSUE   Did the attorney have a legal duty to advise his client's wife of her potential claim for loss of consortium?

DECISION   Yes. It is significant that Shore's client, Clement, had a community property interest in his wife's recovery for loss of consortium, just as Joan had an interest in his recovery of damages for medical malpractice. The consortium tort is closely interwoven with the personal injury action. Thus, Shore had an obligation to advise Clement of those rights because the marital property would benefit by any recovery of damages by either spouse. Further, it was entirely foreseeable that Joan would lose her right to recover for loss of consortium unless Shore at least alerted her to its existence. Joan's injuries are certain in that it was inevitable that her cause of action would become barred upon the running of the statute of limitations. Her failure to file a claim in a timely manner was a direct consequence of Shore's failure to advise her of such a right. Under these circumstances, Shore had a duty to inform the Meighans of the existence of their rights under the consortium tort.

Immunity from Civil Liability

Judges, prosecutors, and public defenders may be administratively sanctioned (termination, disbarment) for their wrongdoings in regard to legal proceedings. However, they generally are immune from civil liability for such misconduct or malpractice. Each has a function which is essential to the working of the judicial system. Immunity aids in the recruitment of qualified individuals to perform such services. Private attorneys are not extended this immunity because they are not burdened by the same constraints as are judges, prosecutors, and public defenders. A private attorney is free to reject a case or client if her caseload is too great or the legal issues are too difficult. Judges, prosecutors, and public defenders do not have this discretion.

Solicitation

Despite the tremendous number of lawyers in this country, the most lucrative legal work—representing banks, insurance companies, and other large corporations—

is carried out by a small circle of law firms. They are sometimes challenged by an equally small group of plaintiff's law firms representing interests adverse to the corporate clients. A very large percentage of the solo practitioners, on the other hand, are struggling to earn a living.

Historically, struggling attorneys could not drum up business through the active solicitation of clients. It was argued that such advertising would interfere with the attorney-client relationship, since it would promote economic ends, rather than justice. However, in the mid-1970s, the Supreme Court recognized that commercial advertising was entitled to First Amendment protection. Accordingly, lawyers were permitted to advertise in the newspapers and other media. However, a state could prohibit lawyer advertising that was false, deceptive, or misleading, and it could place reasonable restrictions on the time, place, and manner of advertising.

In reviewing the constitutionality of a governmental regulation of truthful advertising, the courts use a three-part analysis. First, does the government have a substantial interest in regulating the speech? Second, does the regulation directly advance the governmental interest? Third, is the restriction on advertising no more extensive than necessary to serve the governmental interest? (Governmental regulation of commercial speech is examined in Chapter 5.) Consider the following case in which the Supreme Court upholds a restriction on client solicitations.

http:// www.abanet.org/ legalserv/lanews. *html* is the site for *Lawyer Advertising News,* with brief articles of interest on solicitation and internet advertising.

Florida Bar v. Went For It, Inc.

515 U.S. 618 (U.S. Sup. Ct. 618 1995)

FACTS   The Florida Bar conducted a two-year study of the effects of lawyer advertising on public opinion. The results indicated that lawyers mailed 700,000 direct solicitations in Florida annually, 40 percent of which were aimed at accident victims or their survivors. A survey of Florida adults demonstrated that Floridians have negative feelings about those attorneys who use direct mail advertising. Fifty-four percent of the population believed contacting persons concerning accidents or similar events is an invasion of privacy. A random sampling of persons who received direct-mail advertising from lawyers revealed that 45 percent believed that direct-mail solicitation is designed to take advantage of gullible or unstable people. In response to this study, the Florida Bar rules were amended to prohibit personal-injury lawyers from sending targeted direct-mail solicitations to victims and their relatives for 30 days following an accident or disaster. G. Stewart McHenry and his wholly owned lawyer referral service, Went For It, Inc., argued that the restrictions on direct-mail solicitations violated the First Amendment. He claimed that he routinely sent targeted solicitations to accident victims or their survivors within 30 days after accidents and that he wished to continue doing so in the future.

ISSUE   Does the Florida restriction on direct-mail solicitations violate the First Amendment?

DECISION   No. Commercial speech, like the advertising at issue here may be regulated if the government (1) has a substantial interest in support of the regulation, (2) demonstrates that the restriction directly and materially advances that interest, and (3) narrowly draws the regulation. Because direct-mail solicitations in the wake of

continued

accidents are perceived by the public as intrusive, the reputation of the legal profession in the eyes of Floridians has suffered commensurately. The regulation, then, is an effort to protect the flagging reputations of Florida lawyers by preventing them from engaging in conduct that is universally regarded as deplorable and beneath common decency because of its intrusion upon the special vulnerability and private grief of victims or their families. This is a substantial state interest. In light of the results of the extensive study conducted by the Florida Bar, we conclude that the state has demonstrated that its restriction of commercial speech directly and materially advances the substantial interests in protecting the privacy of accident victims and their families and in preventing erosion of public confidence in the legal profession. The purpose of the 30-day targeted direct-mail ban is to forestall the outrage and irritation with state-licensed legal professionals that the practice of direct solicitation only days after accidents has engendered. The regulation is reasonably well-tailored to achieve its objectives. Moreover, it is limited to 30 days and also affords lawyers a great deal of leeway to devise innovative ways to attract new business. They may advertise on television and radio as well as in newspapers and other media.

http://www.law.vill.edu/Fed-Ct/fedcourt.html
http://supct.law.cornell.edu/supct/

Ethical Issue

More and more we are witnessing lawyers advertising for clients on television and in the newspapers. Many people consider such solicitation to be highly unprofessional. Is this appropriate behavior for attorneys?

Professional Skills

A lawyer provides a variety of legal services for his clients. However, he generally is called upon either to prevent a legal problem from arising or to resolve a legal problem once it has arisen. To successfully fulfill either of these objectives, the attorney must be skilled at problem identification, legal research, and persuasion.

Problem Identification

An attorney must possess refined interview skills in order to uncover the facts necessary to identify potential legal problems. Without the ability to carefully screen and ascertain the relevant facts, neither the attorney nor a judge and jury can clearly understand the precise nature of a legal dispute or problem. The best lawyers are thorough interrogators as well as resourceful investigators.

Legal Research

http://
www.law.cornell.edu/ topics/legal_research. html provides a brief discussion of legal research.

Once the relevant facts have been identified, the lawyer determines the precise legal issues that are implicated. When more than one point of law is involved, he must discover how they interrelate. This aspect of a lawyer's responsibilities requires proficiency in methods of legal research. The lawyer must search for authoritative statements of the law. This involves the discovery of **mandatory**

Figure 3–1:   Legal Research

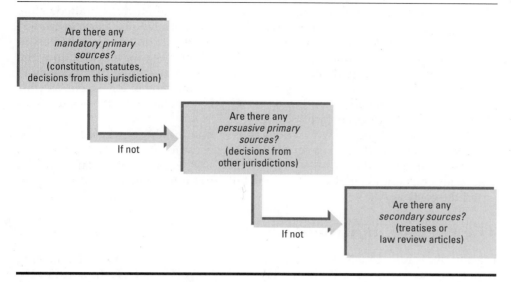

primary sources of law, such as constitutional provisions, statutes, or court decisions from the jurisdiction where the problem is to be resolved. When they are not available, he seeks **persuasive primary sources** (court decisions from other jurisdictions). If there are no primary sources addressing a particular point, the lawyer must fall back on **secondary sources,** like treatises and law review articles. A skilled attorney is able to uncover and fully comprehend the legal significance of these sources of law. (See Figure 3–1.)

Persuasion

An attorney must go beyond merely discovering the law; he must communicate this knowledge to others. If a business client does not fully understand the legal advice she is given, it is of greatly reduced value to her. Further, in our adversary system the lawyer plays an integral role in the courtroom. He must clearly inform the jury of the essential facts supporting his client's claim and tactfully educate the judge as to the correct interpretation of the relevant legal rules. Unless he can clearly and concisely communicate the correct application of the law to the facts, his client's chances of winning are reduced.

Hiring a Lawyer

Most people know little about the actual operation of the legal system and, accordingly, are uncertain about how to find a good lawyer. Friends and relatives often offer advice, but one must be careful before accepting such recommendations at face value. For instance, the fact that a lawyer recently lost a case does not necessarily make her a bad lawyer. It may have been a losing case. Likewise, the winning lawyer may have had a winning case. Further, a lawyer who successfully defends criminal suspects may not be experienced in handling divorces.

http://
www.wld.com is the
site of *West's Legal
Dictionary* for assis-
tance in finding a
lawyer.

*www.attorneyfind.
com* will assist you
in locating an attor-
ney by areas of
specialty.

Finding a Lawyer

Most bar associations provide referral services, but they often are of limited value. There may be little or no screening required for an attorney to be listed in the service. Referrals from acquaintances should be carefully scrutinized. Ask the person making the recommendation specific questions about her advice. How does she know of the attorney's qualifications? If the attorney represented that individual, find out the nature of the case to see if it was the same type of legal issue as your problem. You should look for a lawyer who is familiar with the legal issues involved in your particular case.

You also need someone with whom you can comfortably work. Ask questions designed to discover if that lawyer will be responsive to your needs. For instance, how responsive was the attorney to questions? Did he carefully explain how the case would be handled and why? Did the bill fairly reflect what the attorney projected the costs would be?

The First Appointment

It generally is wise to telephone and make an appointment for an initial meeting with a prospective lawyer. While on the telephone, you might ask the attorney for a free consultation to discuss the merits of your problem and to determine if legal action is prudent. Many lawyers give a free consultation if a potential client requests it. If the initial appointment is not free, find out in advance how much it will cost.

At the initial meeting, be prepared to give a clear explanation of your legal problem and your desired solution. Question the lawyer about her experience in such matters, as well as how she suggests the case be handled. Observe how attentive the lawyer is to you and your questions. Is she taking the time to carefully explain the strategy she would recommend?

Attorneys' Fees

Don't hesitate to ask about costs. Get an estimate of how long the case should take and what fees you are expected to pay. Each time you visit your attorney, have a clear list of the questions you need answered. Have the attorney explain each step of the case and estimate the time that will be involved. Find out when the attorney plans on meeting with you again and what she expects to report at that time. By wisely managing your attorney, it is possible to hold down your legal expenses.

Lawyers generally are not cheap. And, under the prevailing rules in this country, each party to a lawsuit generally must pay his own attorneys' fees. Thus, even if another person sues you and loses, you must pay the cost of defending yourself. However, there are several exceptions to this rule. First, some statutes provide that the losing party must pay the winner's attorneys' fees. The Civil Rights laws have such a provision. Second, some contracts contain provisions requiring the breaching party to pay the attorneys' fees of the nonbreaching party. In the case that opened this chapter, the lease between the cooperative and Diacou required that Diacou, as the losing party, must pay the cooperative's legal fees. However, the court felt the bill for $73,547 was excessive in light of the amount at issue. Diacou was ordered to pay $30,000 of the cooperatives attorneys' fees, and the cooperative had to pay the remainder.

Finally, courts have carved out certain exceptions to the general rules regarding responsibility for the payment of attorneys' fees. For instance, the *bad faith exception* often is applied when the losing party engaged in bad faith conduct during the course of the litigation. This rule is explained in the following case.

Towerridge v. T.A.O.

111 F.3D 758 (10TH CIR. 1997)

FACTS   Towerridge subcontracted with T.A.O. to perform most of the concrete and asphalt paving work for a construction project T.A.O. was building for the Oklahoma Air National Guard. T.A.O. was to make monthly progress payments to Towerridge for work satisfactorily completed. However, nearly from the beginning of Towerridge's performance, Towerridge and T.A.O. disagreed over whether Towerridge was working sufficiently productively and efficiently to complete its work on schedule. Towerridge asserted it was at all times ready and able to meet its obligations under the subcontract, and that any delays in its performance were caused by T.A.O. Additionally, it claimed T.A.O. failed to properly schedule, supervise, and coordinate the project, and that any defects in its work were the result of T.A.O.'s inadequate project management rather than the fault of Towerridge. After T.A.O. terminated Towerridge, Towerridge brought suit for the sums it claimed were due and owing for work allegedly performed. It also demanded that T.A.O. pay its attorneys' fees of $43,195 on the grounds that T.A.O. acted in bad faith in terminating Towerridge and in failing to fully pay for the work actually performed. T.A.O. argued that an award of attorneys' fees cannot be premised solely on prelitigation conduct.

ISSUE   Is Towerridge entitled to an award of attorneys' fees based on T.A.O.'s prelitigation bad faith?

DECISION   No. The longstanding "American Rule" generally bars prevailing parties from recovering attorneys' fees in the absence of a statute or enforceable contract providing for such an award. The rationale underlying this rule, which often operates to prevent full compensation to injured parties, is that because litigation is at best uncertain one should not be penalized for merely defending or prosecuting a lawsuit. Further, the poor might be unjustly discouraged from instituting actions to vindicate their rights if the penalty for losing included the fees of their opponents' lawyer. However, the federal judiciary has recognized several exceptions to the general principle that each party should bear the costs of its own legal representation. One such exception allows the courts the inherent power to assess attorneys' fees when the losing party has acted in bad faith or for oppressive reasons. This "bad faith" exception to the American Rule derives from the inherent power of the federal courts to sanction conduct that abuses the judicial process. Thus, fees awarded under the bad faith exception are punitive in nature, but are designed to punish the abuse of judicial process rather than the original wrong underlying the action. The exception does not reach bad faith conduct not occurring during the course of the litigation itself. It is helpful to categorize and distinguish three forms of bad faith conduct, one of which is not a basis for fee shifting though the other two lie within the bad faith exception to the American Rule. First, bad faith occurring during the course of litigation that is abusive of the judicial process warrants sanction through the charging of fees. The second category is bad faith in bringing an action or in causing an action to be brought. Where a party institutes an unfounded action wantonly or for oppressive

continued

reasons, or necessitates an action be filed or defends an action through the assertion of a colorless defense, that constitutes bad faith which is grounds for an award of attorneys' fees as well. However, this second form of bad faith must be distinguished from the third category, bad faith in the acts giving rise to the substantive claim. Such bad faith does not fall within the bad faith exception. Even assuming that T.A.O. acted in bad faith, its conduct was not abusive of the judicial process. Any bad faith occurred solely in T.A.O.'s prelitigation acts which gave rise to Towerridge's substantive claim. Thus, the bad faith conduct was not of either of the types which are within the scope of the bad faith exception.

Billing Methods

Attorneys may bill for their legal services in a number of ways. Accordingly, the client should inquire as to the precise method during his first meeting with the attorney. At that time, he also should request an estimate of the total costs that are likely to be incurred. Most states require that the particular fee arrangement be written in a **fee agreement.** Three of the most common methods of billing clients—flat fees, hourly fees, and contingency fees—are discussed below. Many lawyers employ some combination of these billing methods.

Flat Fees

Sometimes a lawyer agrees to perform a legal service for a **flat fee.** For instance, an attorney may advertise that he handles uncontested divorces that do not involve custody issues for $500. Or he may establish a set amount to draft a will.

Hourly Fees

A lawyer may charge her client an **hourly fee** for all the time she actually spends working on the client's case. This may include consultations with the client, legal research, and discussions with opposing counsel. Hourly billing is common for lawyers handling business law matters or civil litigation.

Contingent Fees

An attorney may be compensated by collecting a percentage of the amount she recovers for her client. For instance, Paul hires Janet, an attorney, to help him recover from a driver who collided with his car. Janet agrees to perform the legal work and to retain 33 percent of any amount she recovers from the other driver. If she recovers nothing, she will be paid nothing. Lawyers commonly charge such a **contingency fee** when handling civil matters. Contingency fee relationships generally are prohibited in criminal or divorce cases.

Retainers

Most lawyers require clients to pay an initial fee, called a **retainer,** when they first agree to perform the legal services. The lawyer's actual compensation is then offset against this amount. If the retainer exceeds the actual amount billable for the legal services, the attorney is obligated to return the surplus to the client. However, attorneys generally require their clients to pay all of the costs associated with the legal matter. For instance, filing fees, service of process charges, expert witness fees, and travel expenses generally are the client's responsibility. (Most states require clients to pay the litigation costs.)

Firing a Lawyer

Clients generally are free to dismiss an attorney for any reason. Certainly, an attorney who regularly misses deadlines, fails to keep a client informed as to the progress of a case, or disregards the legitimate expectations of a client should be dismissed. However, the attorney is entitled to compensation for the reasonable value of her services up to the point of the discharge. In some states, the lawyer may retain the client's file until such fees are paid. The client should make it clear, in a writing, that the lawyer's services have been terminated. Otherwise, it is conceivable that the lawyer will continue working and billing the client on the case.

Careers in Law

This final section provides a glimpse of the legal profession for those who may have an interest in pursuing a career in law. It first explores the role that lawyers perform in modern society. This is followed by a look at the law school admission process and the essential features of a legal education. The section (and the chapter) closes with a review of how law school graduates are admitted to the practice of law and the various careers they pursue.

The Lawyer's Role

Historically, lawyers have assumed a leading role in the evolution of American society from helping draft the Declaration of Independence to articulating and developing this country's common law tradition. Further, they have played key roles in the drafting, interpretation, and application of statutory law. Lawyers have regularly served in each of the three branches of government at both the state and federal level. And, of course, they perform integral advocacy and adjudicatory functions in the administrative, civil, and criminal law systems.

Law School

Contrary to popular myth, there really is no formal "pre-law" course of study. All that is required is that students graduate from a four-year college or university. Generally, it is recommended that undergraduate students take a wide range of college courses so they may enter law school with a broader base of knowledge and interests.

Gaining Admission

Most law schools pay little attention to an applicant's undergraduate major. Instead, they primarily focus on a student's Law School Admission Test (LSAT) score and his grade point average. The LSAT is extremely important since this standardized test is administered to all prospective law students. Prior to the test, candidates are urged to at least familiarize themselves with the mechanics of the test and the nature of the questions so they may use their time efficiently and effectively.

Some law schools scrutinize the rigors of an applicant's undergraduate course of study and weigh his grade point average accordingly. However, many others do not make such distinctions. Likewise, many law schools only use letters of recommendation and personal statements to distinguish among candidates with the same LSAT scores and grade point averages. To be safe, applicants should take time and care in crafting the personal statement and should seek recommendations from professors and employers who can frankly evaluate their aptitude for the study of law.

Legal Education

Beginning law students often are stunned to discover that the study techniques that worked for them as undergraduates are not effective in law school. Particularly during the first year, law students are immersed into an extremely stressful and demanding environment where they must learn to "think like a lawyer." Under the Socratic method, the role of the professor is to pose questions while students must learn to analyze the appropriate legal principles for resolving any number of real cases. Many professors conduct their classes in a confrontational style which forces students to think and persuade under a great deal of pressure.

During the first year, students generally have little choice over the classes they take. Most schools require that they take courses in Contracts, Torts, Constitutional Law, Property Law, Civil Procedure, Criminal Law, and Legal Research and Writing. During the second and third years of study, they usually have greater flexibility in course selection. In fact, at that time many students are able to supplement their theoretical education with part-time work at nearby law firms or legal clinics.

Admission to Practice

Fulltime students generally graduate after three years of law school. However, they still must overcome one more hurdle before they may practice law. Each state establishes licensing requirements a law school graduate must meet before she may practice law. These usually include proof of good moral character and the successful completion of a bar examination.

The Bar Exam

The bar exam normally lasts two days and consists of standardized multiple choice and essay questions requiring the applicant to apply legal principles and demonstrate a familiarity with state law. Some states also administer a multiple choice ethics exam. Requirements to sit for the bar exam, the nature of the questions, and the pass rates may vary greatly from state to state.

The License to Practice Law

After passing the bar exam, a lawyer is licensed to practice law in that particular state. She may appear before a U.S. District Court located there as well. After three years she is permitted to practice before the U.S. Supreme Court. An attorney may be licensed to practice law in more than one state. This may occur because the lawyer has passed a bar exam in each state or because the second state recognizes the qualifications of a licensed attorney who has practiced law in a neighboring state for a prescribed number of years. Further, some states allow an out-of-state attorney to make a brief appearance before a state court or tribunal for a particular case. However, as a general rule, no one may practice law for another in any state unless she is licensed in that state.

Birbrower v. Superior Court

949 P.2d 1 (Sup. Ct. Cal. 1998)

FACTS Birbrower, Montalbano, Condon & Frank is a professional law corporation incorporated in New York, with its principal place of business in New York. Birbrower attorneys, Kenneth Hobbs and Thomas Condon, performed substantial work in California relating to the law firm's representation of ESQ Business Services. ESQ is a California corporation with its principal place of business in California. Neither Hobbs nor Condon has ever been licensed to practice law in California and none of Birbrower's other attorneys was licensed to practice law in California during Birbrower's ESQ representation. The parties negotiated and executed a fee agreement in New York, providing that Birbrower would perform legal services for ESQ, including "All matters pertaining to the investigation of and prosecution of all claims and causes of action against Tandem Computers Incorporated." Tandem is a Delaware corporation with its principal place of business in California. While representing ESQ, Hobbs and Condon traveled to California on several occasions. During these visits they discussed various matters relating to ESQ's dispute with Tandem. They also visited California to interview potential arbitrators, to discuss a proposed settlement offer, and to negotiate with Tandem over possible changes in the proposed agreement. After ESQ settled the Tandem dispute it refused to pay Birbrower the more than $1 million called for in the fee agreement. ESQ argued that by practicing law without a license in California, Birbrower violated state law which rendered the fee agreement unenforceable.

ISSUE Is Birbrower entitled to compensation for the legal services it provided in California?

DECISION No. Section 6125 of the California Code states: *"No person shall practice law in California unless the person is an active member of the State Bar."* Section 6126 holds that: *"No one may recover compensation for services as an attorney at law in this state unless [the person] was at the time the services were performed a member of the State Bar."* The practice of law in California entails sufficient contact with the California client to render the nature of the legal service a clear legal representation. Mere fortuitous or attenuated contacts will not sustain a finding that the unlicensed lawyer engaged in sufficient activities in the state, or created a continuing relationship with the California client that included legal duties and obligations. This definition does not necessarily depend on or require the unlicensed lawyer's physical presence in the state. Physical presence here is one factor we may consider in deciding whether the unlicensed lawyer has violated Section 6125, but it is by no means exclusive. For example, one may practice law in the state in violation of Section 6125 although not physically present here by advising a California client on California law in connection with a California legal dispute by telephone, fax, computer, or other modern technological means. Regulation of the practice of law is accomplished principally by the respective states. Authority to engage in the practice of law conferred in any jurisdiction is not per se a grant of the right to practice elsewhere, and it is improper for a lawyer to engage in practice where he is not permitted by law or by court order to do so. Exceptions to Section 6125 do exist, but are generally limited to allowing out-of-state attorneys to make brief appearance before a state court or tribunal. They are narrowly drawn and strictly interpreted. Birbrower engaged in unauthorized law practice in California on more than a limited basis, and no firm attorney engaged in that practice was an active member of the California State Bar.

continued

Accordingly, Birbrower's fee agreement with ESQ is invalid to the extent it authorizes payment for the substantial legal services Birbrower performed in California. However, Birbrower may be able to recover some fees under the fee agreement for the limited legal services it performed for ESQ in New York to the extent they did not constitute practicing law in California, even though those services were performed for a California client.

Employment Options

There are at least 900,000 lawyers in this country with as many as 40,000 new attorneys licensed to practice each year. Approximately 60 percent of them find jobs in private practice. Many others serve in capacities such as public law practice, corporate work, or teaching. However, societal changes are rapidly altering the nature of the legal profession and, as a result, the nature of employment opportunities in law is likely to undergo substantial change as well.

Private Practice

A declining percentage of the attorneys in private practice work as solo practitioners. In part, this is because the high cost of doing business gives larger firms a distinct competitive advantage. Small firms are predominant in small towns and rural areas where they generally handle family matters (i.e., estate planning, domestic relations). The large firms, which often have more than 100 partners, are found in large urban areas. They tend to be segmented into specialty areas (i.e., litigation, corporate law, antitrust) and practice law on a national and international level. The large firms generally depend on large institutional clients for their revenue.

Medium-sized firms are found in both small and large cities. They share with their larger counterparts a tendency to departmentalize their attorneys into specialty areas and often focus on business law, real estate, estate planning, criminal defense, and personal injury suits. Finally, some attorneys practice law with legal clinics. Some of these clinics are parts of chain operations that provide routine legal services (i.e., wills, divorces, traffic offenses, and bankruptcies). They frequently rely heavily on the use of paralegals.

Many new attorneys engaged in private practice are unprepared for the stresses that can accompany work in a law firm. Law firms often place a great deal of pressure on new associates to increase their billable hours. Further, new attorneys frequently are surprised to discover that they are expected to generate new business by courting new clients. And recent graduates often are stunned and greatly dissatisfied with the "office politics" that characterizes many law firms.

Bohatch v. Butler & Binion

1998 TEX. LEXIS 13 (SUP. CT. TEX. 1998)

FACTS   Collette Bohatch became a partner in the law firm of Butler & Binion after serving as an associate for four years. John McDonald, the managing partner of the office, and Richard Powers, a partner, were the only other attorneys working with her in the firm's Washington office. The office did work for Pennzoil almost exclusively. After becoming a partner, Bohatch began receiving internal firm reports showing the number of hours each attorney worked, billed, and collected. From her review of these reports, she became concerned that McDonald was overbilling Pennzoil. She discussed this matter with Powers and together they reviewed and copied portions of McDonald's time diary. Bohatch then met with Louis Paine, the firm's managing partner, to report her concern that McDonald was overbilling Pennzoil. Paine said he would investigate. Later that day, Bohatch told Powers about her conversation with Paine. The following day, McDonald met with Bohatch and informed her that Pennzoil was not satisfied with her work and wanted her work to be supervised. This was the first time she had ever heard criticism of her work for Pennzoil. After Bohatch repeated her concerns to Paine in a telephone conversation, Paine and two other members of the firm's management committee investigated her complaint. They then discussed the allegations with Pennzoil's in-house counsel, John Chapman, who was the firm's primary contact with Pennzoil. Chapman, who had a long-standing relationship with McDonald, responded that Pennzoil was satisfied that the bills were reasonable. One month later, Paine met with Bohatch and told her that the firm's investigation revealed no basis for her contentions. He added that she should begin looking for other employment. After this meeting, she received no further work assignments from the firm. The firm denied her any further partnership distribution and, one year later, told her to vacate her office. Bohatch sued the law firm, claiming that a partnership has a duty not to expel a partner for reporting suspected overbilling by another partner.

ISSUE   Could the law firm lawfully expel Bohatch from the partnership?

DECISION   Yes. The relationship between partners imposes upon all participants the obligation of loyalty to the joint concern and of the utmost good faith, fairness, and honesty in their dealings with each other with respect to matters pertaining to the enterprise. Yet, partners have no obligation to remain partners. At the heart of the partnership concept is the principle that partners may choose with whom they wish to be associated. Courts have held that a partnership may expel a partner for purely business reasons. Further, courts recognize that a law firm can expel a partner to protect relationships both within the firms and with clients. Finally, many courts have held that a partnership can expel a partner without breaching any duty in order to resolve a fundamental schism. The duty that partners owe one another does not encompass a duty to remain partners or else answer in tort damages. Nevertheless, Bohatch argues the court should recognize that public policy requires a limited duty to remain partners (i.e., a partnership must retain a whistleblower partner). She argues that such an extension of a partner's duty is necessary because permitting a law firm to retaliate against a partner who in good faith reports suspected overbilling would discourage compliance with rules of professional conduct and thereby harm clients. While this argument is not without some force, we must reject it. A partnership exists solely because the partners choose to place personal confidence and trust in one another. Once one partner accuses another partner of impropriety, the partners may find it impossible to continue to work together to their mutual benefit and the benefit of their clients.

―――――――――――――――――― Ethical Issue ――――――――――――――――――

The court in *Bohatch v. Butler & Binion* went on to say that a lawyer still has a duty to report violations by her colleagues even though it may cost the honest attorney her job. Is the court placing an unfair burden on ethical lawyers? Now that you know the result of this case, what would you do if you discovered that one of your law partners was overbilling clients?

Public Law Practice

As many as 10 percent of this country's lawyers practice law for some governmental body. The federal government is the largest employer. It hires attorneys for all of the major departments (i.e., Justice, Treasury) both in Washington, D.C. and in their regional offices. Many other attorneys work for the Judge Advocate General's Corp. within each military service. And, within the judicial branch of government, attorneys are employed as judges and law clerks.

State governments also hire law graduates to serve in their executive and judicial branches. Further, the local governments employ lawyers in numerous capacities. Each county in the United States has a prosecutor's office which prosecutes criminal violations. And public defenders offices are established to provide legal representation for indigent criminal defendants.

Public law practice seldom provides the financial rewards that can be reaped in private practice. However, it does offer several attractive benefits. For instance, government practice usually has better working hours and greater job security than private practice. Further, many new lawyers enter public law service to gain expertise and contacts in a specialty area and then successfully move into a more lucrative position in private practice or in private industry.

Private Industry

Another 10 percent of the nation's active lawyers work for private corporations. In fact, some large organizations have corporate legal staffs which employ several hundred lawyers. Corporate attorneys, known as **in-house counsel,** may work in tax departments or become specialists on key regulatory issues affecting the company. In smaller corporations, the attorney may also perform some management functions.

While the lawyers' salaries in private industry are competitive, they seldom reach the levels of salaries at the largest law firms. However, the job benefits often are better and job mobility is likely to be greater. Many corporations, however, are hesitant to hire new law school graduates. Instead they recruit attorneys who already have practical experience in their industry.

Academic Careers

A small group of law school graduates teach law and law-related topics in law schools, universities, colleges, junior colleges, and high schools. Entry into this profession can be extremely difficult. Employers generally look for applicants who distinguished themselves in law school and/or private practice. While salaries in the academic field may be less than in private practice, the job benefits and working environment in academia may be excellent.

Nonlegal Options

Each year a large number of practicing attorneys change careers and pursue nonlegal job opportunities. There are a number of reasons for this. As was mentioned earlier, the stresses associated with generating new business, office politics, and increasing billable hours can be tremendous. This is becoming more and more evident as a growing pool of practicing attorneys compete for legal business. Many attorneys are reacting to this increased competitiveness by exhibiting greater contentiousness when dealing with opposing counsel. Combined with the public scorn for the legal profession and reduced job security in law firms and private industry, many practicing lawyers are experiencing declining job satisfaction. They are discovering that the skills developed in law school and professional practice frequently are marketable outside of the legal profession.

QUESTIONS AND PROBLEM CASES

1. Explain when a court is likely to award attorneys' fees to the winning party in a lawsuit.
2. Explain the role of the judge in the adversary system.
3. What problems can arise when a client fires her attorney?
4. What are three fundamental skills a good lawyer should possess?
5. Shortly after Teri Sowers's arrest by federal agents, Frank Swan telephoned Assistant United States Attorney Elana Artson and identified himself as Sowers's attorney. Because Swan also was representing Sowers's parents in a related criminal matter, Artson argued that Swan's representation of both Sowers and her parents amounted to a conflict of interest. She moved to disqualify Swan from representing Sowers. The court granted the motion, finding that a serious potential for conflict of interest existed. Later, Artson received a letter from Swan, claiming that her actions were neither just nor fair to Sowers and her family. Appended to the letter was a sheet of paper with the following words: "Male lawyers play by the rules, discover the truth and restore order. Female lawyers are outside the law, cloud the truth and destroy order." Artson filed a motion asking the district court to punish Swan for violating a rule which provides that *"no*

attorney shall engage in any conduct which degrades or impugns the integrity of the Court." Swan argued that his conduct did not violate the rule. Should Swan be punished?

6. Alice Gaylard contracted with Oxford Healthcare to provide home healthcare services, which included periodically bathing her. On December 16th, Dorothy Taylor gave Ms. Gaylard a bath and allegedly caused her to be burned with hot water. Ms. Gaylard was subsequently hospitalized. She filed suit against Oxford for her injuries. Before Ms. Gaylard filed suit against Oxford, her lawyer telephoned Dorothy Taylor and recorded the conversation. Initially, Ms. Taylor refused to discuss the bath and burns and told the lawyer to contact her supervisor at Oxford. However, after the lawyer persisted, Ms. Taylor began answering questions. The court later ruled that Ms. Taylor's recorded statements could not be used in court. It based this finding on a state rule that prevents a lawyer representing a client from communicating with a party the lawyer knows to be represented by another attorney without first obtaining the consent of that attorney. A comment to that rule extends its coverage to similar communications with employees of any organization represented by another attorney. Did the questioning of Ms. Taylor violate this rule?

7. Joseph Mrozek and Danette Ritz had been in a sometimes stormy relationship. One evening, after Mrozek and Ritz had been seen together, she was found dead with two gunshot wounds in her head. On the day after the murder, Mrozek telephoned an attorney, Sam Davis, who had represented him in previous matters. The phone was answered by Davis's secretary, Melissa Shupe. She told Mrozek that Davis was unable to speak with him because he was meeting with another client. Mrozek finally stated, "Honey, I don't think you understand. I've just committed a homicide. I have to talk with Sam." During a trial in which Mrozek was charged with murdering Ritz, the prosecutor subpoenaed Shupe to testify as to the telephone conversation she had with Mrozek. Davis argued that the conversation was inadmissible because of the attorney-client privilege. Should Shupe be ordered to testify against Mrozek?

8. Five members of the Hendry family—the mother, her son and daughter, and the daughter's two infant children—owned a historic 25-acre parcel of land in Virginia. They signed an agreement to sell the property for $4.5 million to a developer who planned to build a retirement home on the land. According to the agreement, if county officials failed to approve zoning changes needed to build the retirement home, the parties would undertake "good-faith" negotiations to restructure the transaction. When county officials turned down the retirement home project, the developer proposed amending the agreement to provide for the construction of a 56-unit residential development. Although the son told the developer that he objected to the proposed amendment, his mother and the developer signed an amendment while the son was away on vacation. Discovering what his mother had done, the son retained Francis Pelland, a lawyer. The son explained to the lawyer that he was opposed to the residential development and concerned about his mother's mental capacity. Ultimately, the county approved the plan for the residential development. However, all the owners—now including the mother— refused to sell. When the developer sued them for breach of contract, Pelland represented all the owners in defending the lawsuit. The mother was anxious to reach a settlement with the developer if it would allow her to keep a house on the land. The son, however, was opposed to the residential development because it would destroy the trees on the property. Following Pelland's advice, the family settled with the developer for $1.5 million. Unhappy with this result, the family members sued Pelland for breach of his fiduciary duty since he represented multiple clients with conflicting interests. Did Pelland engage in a conflict of interest? Explain.

9. Richard Dziubak pled guilty to second-degree manslaughter in the death of his mother. After serving 15 months in prison, he petitioned the court to vacate his guilty plea when it was discovered that Dziubak's defense expert had misread the toxicology report, which indicated fatal levels of antidepressant's in the decedent's blood. Dziubak was then retried and acquitted of the murder. Dziubak brought a malpractice suit against Thomas Mott, his public defender in the original criminal trial, for failing to properly interpret the toxicology report. Will Dziubak recover from Mott? Explain.

10. After Jerome Wagshal sued Charles Sheetz, the judge, pursuant to court rules, required the parties to participate in mediation. Mark Foster was appointed as the mediator for the confidential mediation proceedings. After the first session, Wagshal questioned Foster's neutrality and asked that he step down. Foster wrote a letter to the judge indicating that the case was one that should be settled and asking to be excused from his role as mediator. He specifically noted that Wagshal should be ordered to engage in a good-faith attempt to mediate. After the judge appointed another mediator, the parties settled their dispute. However, Wagshal then sued Foster, claiming Foster's letter to the judge forced him to settle the case against his will. Foster moved to dismiss the suit, arguing that, as a mediator, he was immune from civil liability. Is Foster correct?

4

GOVERNMENTAL POWER

N ew York passed a statute making it a felony to distribute to children, through any computer communications system, material of a sexual nature that is harmful to minors. However, a federal district court struck down the law, ruling that it was an unconstitutional burden on interstate commerce.

American Library Association v. Pataki, 969 F.Supp. 160 (S.D.N.Y. 1997).

As you read this chapter, consider this statute as well as the following questions.

What is interstate commerce?
What is the relationship between the power of the states and the federal government?
From where does the national government derive its power to legislate?
From where do the states derive their authority?

Introduction

The nature of American society is changing at an alarming pace. Expanding scientific knowledge and technological breakthroughs are creating new forms of human activity on a daily basis. While these advances promise many benefits, they simultaneously threaten to overwhelm us. In response to the increasing complexities of modern life, people are making greater and greater demands on governmental institutions to oversee and manage the many forces affecting (and sometimes threatening) their lives.

Of course, many people do not view the increasing governmental involvement in their lives as a blessing. There is considerable public dissatisfaction with the growth of governmental regulation. However, it probably is fair to say that such regulation is here to stay. The growing interrelationships among people make it necessary.

Chapter Overview

This chapter surveys the constitutional issues involved in the exercise of governmental power. Specifically, it examines the regulatory authority of Congress, the states, and the administrative agencies. The discussion begins with an exploration of the constitutional sources for congressional power to legislate. This is followed by a look at the legislative power of the states, with a special focus on the constitutional friction that arises when state and federal powers conflict. Attention is then turned to the power of government to take private property for public purposes. The chapter closes with an overview of the role of administrative agencies in the modern regulatory environment. (The discussion of the individual rights safeguarded from governmental abuse is reserved for Chapter 5.)

Congressional Power

The framers of the U.S. Constitution rejected a broad grant of authority to Congress, opting instead for more narrowly defined powers. The Supreme Court quickly seized upon this fact to insist that Congress can only exercise the powers granted to it by the Constitution. This often is called the doctrine of **enumerated powers** (or *delegated powers*).

Most of the powers conferred upon Congress are found in Article I, section 8, of the U.S. Constitution. These include, among others, the powers to coin money, establish uniform laws on the subject of bankruptcies, and declare war. However, of all the enumerated powers, four provide the basis for most congressional regulations. They are the commerce, taxing, and spending powers, and the necessary and proper clause. Each is discussed below.

http://
law.house.gov/4.htm
is the House of Representatives page that provides links to various CFR sites.

Commerce Power

The third clause of Article I, section 3, confers upon Congress the power *"To regulate Commerce . . . among the several States."* Throughout the country's history, courts have wrestled with the precise meaning of these words because the commerce power serves two important purposes. First, it provides an important source of congressional regulatory power. Second, it places limitations on the regulatory power of the state governments. (This is discussed later in this chapter.)

http://
www.doc.gov is the home page of the Department of Commerce.

Defining "Commerce"

Although the Constitution provides no real guidance as to what is meant by "commerce," the Supreme Court has long defined the word very broadly. The only real restriction placed on it has been to limit congressional regulation to "commercial" activities. But, for the most part, this has not been much of a limitation. For instance, in the case cited at the beginning of the chapter involving a New York statute regulating the distribution of sexual material on the Internet, the judge held that Internet communications constitute commerce within the meaning of the commerce clause. She noted that railroads, trucks, and highways are themselves "instruments of commerce" because they serve as conduits for the transport of goods and services. In her mind, the Internet is more than a means of communication; it also serves as a conduit for the transport of digitized goods throughout the country.

Defining "Among the Several States"

Courts have long interpreted commerce "among the several states" as creating a distinction between **interstate commerce** and **intrastate commerce.** Interstate commerce may be regulated by Congress. However, things that fall completely within the internal commerce of a state are classified as intrastate commerce and may be regulated only by that state.

Since the 1930s, courts generally have permitted Congress to regulate most commercial activities, even those physically confined within a single state. The case that follows marks the first time in 60 years that the Supreme Court has struck down a federal law on the ground that Congress exceeded its power under the commerce clause.

United States v. Lopez

514 U.S. 549 (U.S. Sup. Ct. 1995)

FACTS   On March 10, 1992, a 12th-grade student arrived at Edison High School carrying a concealed .38-caliber handgun and five bullets. Acting on an anonymous tip, school authorities confronted him. After admitting that he was carrying the weapon, he was arrested and charged with firearm possession on school premises in violation of the *Gun-Free School Zones Act.* Under that statute, Congress made it a federal offense *"for any individual knowingly to possess a firearm at a place that the individual knows, or has reasonable cause to believe, is a school zone."* The student argued that the federal statute was unconstitutional since it is beyond the power of Congress to legislate control over our public schools. The government claimed that the statute was a constitutional exercise of Congress's well-defined power to regulate activities in and affecting commerce, and that the "business" of elementary, middle, and high schools affects commerce.

ISSUE   Does this statute exceed congressional authority to regulate under the commerce clause?

DECISION   Yes. We start with first principles. The Constitution creates a federal government of enumerated powers. The powers delegated by the Constitution to the federal government are few and defined. Those which are to remain in the state governments are numerous and indefinite. This constitutionally mandated division of authority was adopted by the Framers to ensure protection of fundamental liberties. Just as the separation and independence of the coordinate branches of the federal government serve to prevent the accumulation of excessive power in any one branch, a healthy balance of power between the states and the federal government reduces the risk of tyranny and abuse from either front. The Constitution delegates to Congress the power *"to regulate Commerce . . . among the several States."* Throughout history this Court's interpretations of the commerce clause have increasingly recognized that the effects of many kinds of intrastate activity upon interstate commerce were such as to make them a proper subject of federal regulation. But even our modern-era precedents which have expanded congressional power under the commerce clause confirm that this power is subject to outer limits. The Court has heeded that warning and undertaken to decide whether a rational basis existed for concluding that a regulated activity sufficiently affects interstate commerce. Consistent with this structure, we have identified three broad categories of activity that Congress may regulate under its commerce power. First, Congress may regulate the use of the channels of interstate commerce. Second, Congress is empowered to regulate and protect the instrumentalities of interstate commerce, or persons or things in interstate commerce, even though the threat may come only from intrastate activities. Third, Congress's commerce authority includes the power to regulate those activities that "substantially affect" interstate commerce. The *Gun-Free School Zones Act* does not fall within either of the first two categories open to federal regulation. Thus, if it is to be sustained it must be an activity that substantially affects interstate commerce. Yet this statute is a criminal law that by its terms has nothing to do with commerce or any sort of economic enterprise, however broadly one might define those terms. It is not a larger regulation of economic activity, in which the regulatory scheme would be undercut unless the intrastate activity were regulated. It cannot, therefore, be sustained under our cases upholding regulations of activities that arise out of or are connected with a commercial transaction, which viewed in the aggregate, substantially affects interstate commerce. Further, the statute contains no jurisdictional element which would ensure, through case-by-case inquiry, that the firearm possession in question affects interstate commerce. It lacks a mechanism which might limit its reach to a discrete set of firearm possessions that additionally have an explicit connection with or effect on interstate commerce. We do not doubt that Congress has authority under the commerce clause to regulate numerous commercial activities that substantially affect interstate commerce and also affect the educational process. That authority, though broad, does not include the authority to regulate each and every aspect of local schools.

http://www.law.vill.edu/Fed-Ct/fedcourt.html
http://supct.law.cornell.edu.supct/

Taxing Power

The first clause of Article I, section 8, gives Congress the power *"To lay and collect Taxes."* Throughout history the courts have construed this language quite broadly and permitted Congress to assess a wide range of taxes. Certainly, the main reason behind the **taxing power** is to enable the federal government to raise revenue to finance its various functions. However, the judiciary regularly permits

Congress to use its taxing power to promote nonrevenue objectives as well. Thus, the government may discourage disfavored activities by imposing heavy taxes on them. As long as the nonrevenue objective could be legislated under one of Congress's enumerated powers, it may be regulated through federal taxation.

Spending Power

Besides containing the taxing power, the first clause of Article I, section 8, authorizes Congress to *"provide for the general Welfare of the United States."* The Supreme Court has not read this provision as a grant of broad authority to legislate for the general welfare. Instead, the phrase has been read, in combination with the taxing power, as permitting the government to spend the revenue it raises. Thus, while the taxing power provides a means of discouraging certain activities, the **spending power** may be broadly used to encourage activities. For instance, Congress might condition the availability of federal funds for highway maintenance on a state establishing a particular speed limit. Or it might provide disaster relief for flood victims. As long as the spending is for the benefit of the general welfare, rather than merely for a select few, it is likely to be upheld by the courts.

Necessary and Proper Clause

The **necessary and proper clause** appears at the end of Article I, section 8. It gives Congress the power *"To make all Laws which shall be necessary and proper for carrying into execution"* its enumerated powers. The Supreme Court has interpreted this clause as granting Congress broad discretion over how it exercises federal policy. Thus, once the legislature demonstrates that it is acting pursuant to a delegated power, it has wide latitude over how to address the problem.

For instance, Congress possesses authority under the enumerated powers of the commerce clause to stabilize agricultural production. As a result, it also has the power to regulate the production of crops, including wheat grown and consumed entirely on a single farm. While the effect on interstate commerce of a single farmer's crop may be trivial, combined with that of all other farmers, it has a substantial effect on the stabilization of agricultural production. As long as Congress can rationally believe it is necessary to regulate each farmer's wheat production to carry out its objective of stabilizing agricultural production, it has the power to do so.

United States v. Bishop

66 F.3D 569 (3RD CIR. 1995)

FACTS   A federal carjacking statute criminalizes the armed theft of any motor vehicle that has been transported, shipped, or received in interstate commerce. Congress believed that auto theft is an interstate problem that imposes substantial costs on society. It perceived a need for a comprehensive, national response addressing the many different aspects of the auto theft problem.

ISSUE   By enacting the statute, did Congress exceed its authority under the commerce clause?

DECISION   No. Congress could have rationally believed that it needed to regulate carjacking as one aspect of its comprehensive response to the national business of criminal auto theft. Carjacking costs consumers both through the direct economic losses caused by having their property taken away from them and through increased insurance costs. Congress could have rationally believed that carjacking is both economically motivated and part of greater economic activity. Further, motor vehicles are instrumentalities of modern interstate commerce. Congress may regulate threats to these instrumentalities even though the threat may come only from intrastate activities.

http://www.law.vill.edu/Fed-Ct/fedcourt.html

Implied Powers

The *necessary and proper clause* refers to more than the powers expressly delegated to Congress in Article I, section 8 of the Constitution. It also grants the legislative branch **implied powers,** as long as such powers do not conflict with any express restrictions imposed by the Bill of Rights or the concept of federalism. It was under its implied powers that Congress was able to establish a national bank. In upholding this exercise of power, the Supreme Court recognized the existence of broad congressional power to act within the letter and the spirit of the Constitution.

State Power

There are three basic domains for the exercise of regulatory power: the federal government, state and local governments, and a combination of the two. Activities that may be regulated only by the federal government include things like the coining of money and the regulation of foreign commerce that the Constitution reserves exclusively for Congress. The states also are excluded from regulating an area when there is a need for national uniformity. Refer to the case at the beginning of the chapter involving the New York statute regulating sexual materials on the Internet. The court struck down this state law because the Internet, like rail and highway traffic, requires a cohesive national scheme of regulation so that users are reasonably able to determine their obligations.

There also exists a narrow range of activities that fall outside of the Constitution's enumerated powers and, as a result, are subject only to state and local regulation. The *United States v. Lopez* case, discussed earlier, provided an example of one such activity (the regulation of handguns in public schools) that is off-limits to federal regulators because it is purely local in nature.

Finally, the broadest range of activities fall within the concurrent domain. Activities in this category generally may be regulated by both the federal and the state governments.

http:// lcweb.loc.gov/global/ state/stategov.html is the site of the Library of Congress resource page for state and local government, with links to articles, maps, state statutes, and other items of interest.

State Sovereignty

The state governments have very broad regulatory powers. States have the power to tax, to own and operate businesses, and to take private property for public purposes. (The "taking" power is examined in Chapter 16.) They also have broad **police powers** to pass laws to protect the health, safety, and general welfare of their citizens. Under our constitutional scheme, states possess all of the powers not delegated to the federal government. This view is reinforced by the Tenth Amendment, which holds: *"The powers not delegated to the United States by the Constitution . . . are reserved to the States."* Consider the *Printz* case, which struck down a federal law for unconstitutionally interfering with state sovereignty.

Printz v. United States
65 L.W. 4731 (U.S. Sup. Ct. 1997)

FACTS   The *Brady Handgun Violence Prevention Act* was part of a detailed federal scheme governing the distribution of firearms. Specifically, it required the U.S. Attorney General to establish a national instant background check system by November 30, 1998. As an interim measure, until the national system became fully operative, the *Brady Act* commanded the chief law enforcement officer of each local jurisdiction to conduct background checks on applicants for the purchase of handguns. Several local law enforcement officials objected to being pressed into federal service. They argued that congressional action compelling state officers to execute federal laws is unconstitutional.

ISSUE   May Congress constitutionally require state officers to execute federal laws?

DECISION   No. It is incontestable that the Constitution established a system of "dual sovereignty." Although the states surrendered many of their powers to the new federal government, they retained "a residuary and inviolable sovereignty." The Framers rejected the concept of a central government that would act upon and through the states, and instead designed a system in which the state and federal governments would exercise concurrent authority over the people. The great innovation of this design was that the citizens would have two political capacities, one state and one federal, each protected from incursion by the other. The Constitution thus contemplates that a state's government will represent and remain accountable to its own citizens. Even the *necessary and proper clause* does not justify this legislation for the simple reason that the *Brady Act* violates the principle of state sovereignty. Even where Congress has the authority under the Constitution to pass laws requiring or prohibiting certain acts, it lacks the power directly to compel the states to require or prohibit those acts. It is an essential attribute of the states' retained sovereignty that they remain independent and autonomous within their proper sphere of authority. The federal government may not compel the states to enact or administer a federal regulatory program.

http://supct.law.cornell.edu/supct/
http://www.law.vill.edu/Fed-Ct/fedcourt.html

Federal Preemption

Problems arise when state regulations conflict with congressional authority. Article VI, section 2, of the Constitution provides that the *"Constitution, and the Laws of the United States . . . shall be the supreme Law of the Land."* Known as the **supremacy clause,** this constitutional provision dictates that state laws that conflict with valid federal laws are unconstitutional. This is the doctrine of **preemption.**

A state statute may be preempted under three circumstances. First, there may be **express preemption** because the federal law explicitly asserts that it will be the exclusive source of regulation. Second, there may be **implied preemption** because federal regulation is so pervasive that it is not reasonable to believe that Congress intended for the states to also regulate the activity. Third, the state law may be preempted because it is in **actual conflict** with a federal law. This type of implicit preemption occurs because either it is impossible to comply with both state and federal requirements or the state law is an obstacle to the accomplishment of the full objectives of the federal law.

Gustafson v. Lake Angelus

76 F.3D 778 (6TH CIR. 1996)

FACTS   The city of Lake Angelus, Michigan, passed an ordinance prohibiting the operation of seaplanes on the surface of the lake. Gustafson, a seaplane pilot who owns a waterfront home on Lake Angelus, asserted that the ordinance was preempted by federal law. He conceded that Congress had not expressly spoken on the issue, but argued instead that the city ordinance was impliedly preempted because the *Federal Aviation Act* has pervasively occupied the field of aircraft regulation.

ISSUE   Is the city ordinance preempted by federal law?

DECISION   No. A state or local statute may be preempted in three ways. First, Congress may express a clear intent to preempt state or local law. Second, federal law may have an implied preemptive effect if Congress revealed this intent by occupying the field of regulation. Third, state or local law that actually conflicts with federal law is preempted. An examination of the *Federal Aviation Act* and the regulations concerning seaplanes and aircraft landing sites indicates that the designation of plane landing sites is not pervasively regulated by federal law. Instead, the matter is left primarily to local control. The plain language of the federal act's preemption provision expressly prohibits states from regulating aviation rates, routes, or services. This city ordinance does not infringe on these expressly preempted fields. In fact, the Federal Aviation Administration has acknowledged that land use matters within the federal aviation framework are intrinsically local. Water and land use compatibility are matters of local control. Finally, nothing in the city's ordinance conflicts with or impedes the objectives of federal law under the third prong of the preemption doctrine. Policy concerns support our conclusion. It is not feasible for Congress to determine how local land or bodies of water within a municipality are to be used in regard to the location of aircraft landing sites. The needs of each state are different, and this difference requires local, not national, regulation. If the Congress meant to preempt we believe there would be a mass of federal regulations concerning seaplane landing sites.

http://www.law.emory.edu/6circuit/

The Dormant Commerce Clause

We have seen how the commerce clause acts as an affirmative grant of regulatory power to Congress. It also impliedly restrains the federal government by prohibiting Congress from regulating purely intrastate activities. Further, the commerce clause prohibits state regulations that unreasonably interfere with interstate commerce. This negative aspect of the commerce clause, known as the **dormant commerce clause,** prevents the states from enacting protectionist measures designed to benefit in-state economic interests by burdening out-of-state competitors.

The Dormant Commerce Clause Test

Recent cases have formulated a four-part test to determine the validity of a state statute under dormant commerce clause analysis. In order to be constitutional, the state law must:

1. further a legitimate local interest;
2. not discriminate against interstate commerce in favor of local interests;
3. allow only incidental, not direct, regulation of interstate commerce; and
4. not create an **undue burden** on commerce by imposing costs on interstate commerce that are more excessive than necessary to bring about the local benefits.

This chapter opened with a description of a New York statute that, in banning certain sexual materials on the Internet, violated the dormant commerce clause. The statute was struck down for two reasons. First, it was a direct, rather than an incidental regulation of conduct that occurs entirely outside New York. Second, it was held to pose an undue burden on interstate commerce because it would achieve only limited local benefits while imposing excessive costs on out-of-state users.

Types of Effects on Commerce

State and local laws affecting commerce may be put into one of three categories. The first includes laws that explicitly discriminate against interstate commerce. Florida might, for example, forbid the sale of fruit grown in other states. Because such laws expressly create **disparate treatment,** they are *per se* unconstitutional.

The second category creates a type of **disparate impact.** It includes laws that appear to be neutral among states but actually bear more heavily on interstate commerce than on local commerce. Iowa's law setting a 55-foot limit for truck trailers, when all nearby states permit 65-foot trailers, bears more heavily on vehicles from other states. The out-of-state trucks are precluded from driving in Iowa, while Iowa trucks may move freely into the surrounding states. If such legislation creates an embargo on interstate commerce without hindering intrastate business, courts treat it as equivalent to a statute that expressly discriminates. However, if the discriminatory effect is weak, courts generally permit the law to stand if it is supported by legitimate reasons unrelated to the suppression of interstate commerce.

The third category includes state laws that affect interstate commerce without giving in-state firms any competitive advantage over those located elsewhere. Those statutes generally are upheld if they further legitimate local interests and do not impose excessive costs on interstate commerce.

Tolchin v. New Jersey Supreme Court

11 F.3D 1099 (3RD CIR. 1997)

FACTS To practice law in New Jersey, an otherwise qualified attorney must maintain an office and attend continuing legal education courses in the state. Tolchin, a resident of New York, argued that these requirements violate the commerce clause. He contended that the requirements favor New Jersey economic interests. As such, they amount to economic protectionism that offends the dormant commerce clause.

ISSUE Do the New Jersey requirements violate the dormant commerce clause?

DECISION No. The dormant aspect of the commerce clause prohibits economic protectionism. Where a statute regulates even-handedly to effectuate a legitimate local public interest, and its effects on interstate commerce are only incidental, it will be upheld unless the burden on such commerce is clearly excessive in relation to the local benefits. If a legitimate local purpose is found, then the question becomes one of degree. When a state statute directly regulates or discriminates against interstate commerce, or when its effect is to favor in-state economic interests over out-of-state interests, it may generally be struck down without further inquiry. On its face, New Jersey's bona fide office requirement does not discriminate against out-of-state attorneys. All attorneys who wish to practice in New Jersey must have a bona fide office there. The requirement's intent was to prevent occasional practice in New Jersey by an attorney once admitted, but who now practices primarily in another state and could have lost familiarity with New Jersey law and its development. New Jersey's mandatory attendance requirement also applies equally on its face to residents and nonresidents and does not effectively favor resident attorneys. Because the challenged requirements do not directly regulate or discriminate against interstate commerce, we must only compare the local benefits to the incidental burden to ensure that those burdens are not clearly excessive. The bona fide office requirement increases attorney accessibility. While it limits the mobility of some lawyers and reduces the options for consumers of the service they provide, these burdens do not outweigh the benefits. Likewise, the mandatory attendance benefits the public by ensuring that attorneys hear those topics thought to be important by the state bar. At the same time it imposes relatively small burdens on interstate commerce.

http://www.law.vill.edu/Fed-Ct/fedcourt.html

The State as a Market Participant

Some actions by state and local governments are not regulatory in nature. This situation occurs when the government becomes a participant in the market, rather than a regulator of the market. For instance, a city may operate a physical fitness center or provide garbage removal services in competition with private companies. Courts refer to such market participant behavior as **proprietary**, rather than governmental, action. When state and local governments are acting as regulators, they are subject to the limits of the dormant commerce clause. But when they are serving in a proprietary role, as participants in the market, they are free from its constraints. Consider the following case involving the dormant commerce clause and a state acting in a proprietary manner.

Chance Management v. South Dakota

97 F.3d 1107 (8th Cir. 1996)

FACTS   A South Dakota statute permits corporations to obtain a license as a video lottery machine operator for the South Dakota lottery only if residents of the state own a majority interest in the corporation. Chance Management was denied a license because its majority owner was not a South Dakota resident. It argued that the licensing requirement violated the dormant commerce clause.

ISSUE   Does the South Dakota statute violate the dormant commerce clause?

DECISION   No. The U.S. Supreme Court has recognized a distinction between the state "regulation of" a market and state "participation in" a market. A state acting as a market participant is free from the strictures of the commerce clause because there is no indication that the clause was intended to limit the ability of the states themselves to operate in the free market. South Dakota's video lottery law, including its residency requirement, falls within the market participant exception. The statute created a state business within the gaming market. South Dakota invested substantial sums of money to get the state lottery off the ground. The state is actively running a business in the gaming market. In furtherance of its money-making enterprise, the state has created a business relationship with its video lottery machine operators much akin to a partnership between private parties. The state, like any private gaming company, is free to choose those with whom it will deal.

http://www.wulaw.wustl.edu/8th.Cir/

Ethical Issue

When the state is acting in a proprietary role, it may constitutionally discriminate against commerce by favoring its own residents. Should states engage in such discriminatory behavior? What if the out-of-state participant could provide better services?

Local Government

http://
www.law.cornell.
*edu/topics/local_*
government.html will
take you to a Cornell
University site with
links to state and
local government
resources.

The U.S. Constitution recognizes only two sources of legislative power—Congress and the states. Cities and counties are considered to be subdivisions of the states for constitutional purposes. These municipal bodies derive their authority from the state. Their powers are of two types: those **expressly granted** to them by the state and those that may be **implied** as incidental to the express powers.

The express powers are similar to the enumerated powers the Constitution gives to Congress. They can only be determined by examining the state document creating the municipal body. Implied powers naturally follow from the local government's express authority. For instance, if a city is empowered to collect and dispose of garbage and other household waste, it might have the implied power to assess a fee on each household for garbage collection.

Figure 4–1: Federal versus State Power

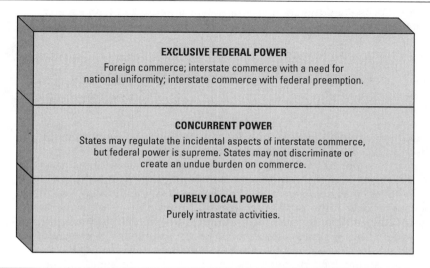

EXCLUSIVE FEDERAL POWER
Foreign commerce; interstate commerce with a need for
national uniformity; interstate commerce with federal preemption.

CONCURRENT POWER
States may regulate the incidental aspects of interstate commerce,
but federal power is supreme. States may not discriminate or
create an undue burden on commerce.

PURELY LOCAL POWER
Purely intrastate activities.

The Takings Clause

The Fifth and Fourteenth Amendments to the Constitution prohibit all levels of government (federal, state, and local) from taking property for public use without paying just compensation. The *takings clause* comes into play when the government, under its power of **eminent domain,** forces private landowners to sell their property so it may be dedicated to some public use. However, the Constitution places limits on the exercise of this power. Specifically, the *takings clause* requires that when a taking occurs, it must be for a public purpose and the private property owner is entitled to just compensation.

Taking

Not all governmental interference with property rights rises to the level of a **taking.** For instance, local governments frequently enact zoning ordinances that restrict the uses of private property. When these ordinances place only limited interference on the rights of the property owner, no compensation is required. However, if the government physically invades the property or severely limits its value, a taking has occurred and compensation must be paid. Thus, when an owner is denied all economically beneficial uses of her land, a compensable taking has occurred.

Lucas v. South Carolina Coastal Council

505 U.S. 1003 (U.S. Sup. Ct. 1992)

FACTS David Lucas paid $975,000 for two residential lots on the Isle of Palms in Charleston County, South Carolina. He intended to build single-family homes on the lots. However, two years later the state legislature enacted the *Beachfront Management Act.* This legislation prevented Lucas from erecting any permanent habitable structures on the lots. Lucas sued the state, claiming that it had taken his property without paying just compensation.

ISSUE   Has the state taken Lucas's property?

DECISION   Maybe. While property may be regulated to a certain extent, if regulation goes too far it will be recognized as a taking. There are at least two categories of regulatory action where compensation is required. The first encompasses regulations that compel the property owner to suffer a physical invasion of his property. In general, no matter how minute the intrusion or how weighty the public purpose behind it, compensation is required. The second category in which compensation is required occurs when a property owner has been called upon to sacrifice all economically beneficial uses of the property in the name of the common good. Where the state seeks to sustain regulation that deprives land of all economically beneficial use, it may resist compensation only if the prohibited uses were not part of the owner's lawful expectations when he first purchased the property. It seems unlikely that common-law principles would have prevented the erection of any habitable or productive improvements on Lucas's land when he first purchased the lots. However, the case must be returned to the state courts to determine this issue. Thus, to avoid paying compensation, South Carolina must identify background principles of nuisance and property law that prohibit the uses Lucas now intends for the lots. Only by making such a showing can the state fairly claim that, in prohibiting all such beneficial uses, the *Beachfront Management Act* is taking nothing.

Public Use

Only the government may force persons to sell their property. Similarly, when the government takes someone's property, it must be for a **public purpose** such as when the government takes private property for the development of highways, water control projects, and public buildings. However, sometimes an avowed public use is not so readily apparent. For instance, suppose a city takes private property in order to carry out an urban renewal project. If the property is resold to private developers, a court may well find the taking to be unconstitutional.

Just Compensation

When property is taken for a public use, the government still must pay the property owner **just compensation.** This means paying the fair market value at the time of the taking. However, not all landowners are happy with such compensation. They argue that the fair market value fails to consider the loss of goodwill in the case of commercial property, or the emotional attachment in the case of private homes.

Administrative Agencies

With the explosion of government regulation in this century has come an equally important phenomenon: the creation and widespread use of administrative agencies. Courts and legislatures often cannot deal with the complex problems continually arising in our rapidly changing environment. Administrative agencies, on the other hand, can develop a reservoir of expertise in various areas of regulation. They are better equipped to bring about a continuous and rapid development of regulatory policy without being hindered by the slower, case-by-case approach followed by the courts and legislatures. Allowing such agencies to hear and judge disputes speeds up problem solving and reduces the burdens placed on an already overworked judicial system. While there are numerous administrative agencies at both the state and federal levels, our discussion focuses on federal regulatory agencies.

Breadth of Agency Regulation

The goods we buy, the advertising of those goods, the interest rates we pay on loans, the rates we pay for utilities, and the availability and cost of public transportation are only a few of the many aspects of our lives that administrative agencies regulate. In the workplace, agencies regulate wages and hours of work, working conditions, unemployment and retirement benefits, and workers' compensation. (These regulations are discussed in Chapter 13.) Most people will never enter a courtroom but the actions of administrative agencies directly affect all our lives on a daily basis.

Characteristics of Agencies

Administrative agencies are, in theory, part of the executive branch of government. However, they may also perform legislative and judicial functions. In addition to investigating and prosecuting violations of statutes and regulations, many agencies have the power to issue regulations that have the force of law. They may also adjudicate disputes involving alleged violations of their regulations and the statutes they are charged with enforcing. There are two primary types of agencies: executive and independent.

Executive Agencies

Some administrative agencies reside exclusively within the executive branch of government. The Occupational Safety and Health Administration (OSHA), the Food and Drug Administration (FDA), and the Internal Revenue Service (IRS) are examples of these **executive agencies.** The president appoints the heads of the executive agencies and may remove them at will.

Independent Agencies

Some agencies are called **independent agencies** because they are not really part of the executive branch of the government and under the control of the president. Instead, they are headed by a board or commission. Although the members are nominated by the president, approximately half of them must be from each major political party and their appointment is confirmed by the Senate for fixed terms.

This type of regulatory agency is given authority by Congress to both make rules and enforce them. Congress grants rule-making power to the agency instead of establishing detailed rules in statutes. It is believed that the independent agency members and staff have greater expertise than Congress and will develop it further through regulatory experience. In addition, it is hoped that continuous regulatory supervision by the agency can be more adaptive to specific needs than reliance on legislation.

Agency Powers

http://
www.law.cornell.edu/
uscode/5/ch3.html is
a Cornell University
site where you can
examine the extent
of agency powers.

The authority of some agencies is confined to the performance of largely routine duties. However, the independent agencies frequently are granted wide-ranging authority to act. There are three primary powers that fall within this broad discretion: investigative power, rule-making power, and adjudicatory power.

Investigative Power

Agencies often are given broad **investigative power** so they can effectively regulate. They need to uncover much information about various practices so they can detect and prosecute regulatory violations. Because many people will not voluntarily cooperate with information requests, these agencies often exercise a *subpoena power* to gain access to witnesses and documentary evidence.

Courts place limits on the subpoena power in order to protect individual privacy interests. Investigations are not permitted unless they are authorized by law and conducted for a legitimate agency purpose. Even then, subpoena requests must be specific and not unreasonably burdensome.

Commodity Futures Trading Commission v. Collins

997 F.2D 1230 (7TH CIR. 1993)

FACTS The Commodity Futures Trading Commission (CFTC) suspected that Thomas Collins was violating the *Commodity Exchange Act*. It initiated an investigation to determine if he was making spurious trades for the purpose of reallocating losses to persons who could reap maximum tax benefits from the losses. As part of its investigation, the CFTC issued a subpoena directing Collins to produce copies of his federal income tax returns. Collins refused to comply with the subpoena on the ground that it would force him to incriminate himself since the tax returns contained information that might be used as evidence of felony violations of federal law.

ISSUE Should Collins be required to comply with the subpoena?

DECISION No. This subpoena should not be enforced. Income tax returns are highly sensitive documents; that is why federal law provides that agencies such as CFTC cannot get Collins's tax returns directly from the Internal Revenue Service. The self-reporting, self-assessing character of the income tax system would be compromised were they freely disclosed to agencies enforcing regulatory programs unrelated to tax collection itself. We are not experts in the investigation of violations of the commodity laws, so we may have overlooked reasons why, despite appearances, the effectiveness of the CFTC's investigation of Collins depends on its having access to his tax returns. The CFTC has not advanced any such reason. It asked for enforcement of the subpoena as a matter of rote, upon its bare representation that the tax returns might contain information germane to the investigation. That is not enough, if an appropriate balance is to be struck between the privacy of income tax returns and the needs of law enforcement.

http://www.kentlaw.edu/7circuit/

Rule-making Power

An agency's **rule-making power** is derived from the enabling legislation enacted by Congress for the creation of the agency. That statute must set out adequate guidelines for agency action. In some cases, agency actions may be attacked as being outside the jurisdiction of the agency as defined by the enabling statute. However, when an agency's rule-making does not exceed its regulatory authority, the courts generally do not substitute their judgment for that of an agency, even if they believe an agency's rules to be unwise. Only agency decisions that are *"arbitrary and capricious"* are overturned by the courts.

Adjudicatory Power

A number of agencies also exercise **adjudicatory powers** by deciding cases. Agency hearings are much less formal than court trials, since they never involve juries, and rules of evidence are less strictly observed. Those who are unhappy with an agency's decision must exhaust all administrative remedies before appealing the decision to a court of law. On appeal, the scope of judicial review of administrative agencies' actions is fairly limited.

When an agency decides a case, it is carrying out a judicial function. It is also, in effect, the prosecutor, since the agency staff decides whether or not to begin an enforcement action. Further, the agency serves a legislative role when making a rule and performs an executive function when enforcing it. This concentration of functions in a single agency was much criticized until passage of the *Administrative Procedure Act of 1946,* which requires a separation of the functions within the agency. Now, independent **administrative law judges** (ALJs) hear the evidence and make *preliminary decisions.* The agency board or commission then issues a *final order.* Such orders are appealable to, and enforced by, the federal courts.

Constitutional Limits

Administrative agencies are governmental bodies. Their activities are state (governmental) action that is subject to the constitutional restraints imposed by the Bill of Rights. (The limits on state action are discussed in Chapter 5.) Administrative agencies also give rise to concerns over the doctrine of **separation of powers,** which allocates power among the executive, legislative, and judicial branches of government. Since administrative agencies frequently exercise power traditionally associated with each of those branches of government, they often are criticized for violating the separation of powers principles. However, in recent years courts have been reluctant to sustain such challenges to agency action. As long as Congress clarifies the boundaries within which an agency must act, the delegation of power is likely to be approved.

Judicial Review

Persons aggrieved by agency actions sometimes bring lawsuits demanding redress. Normally, administrative actions are reviewable by the courts. But even reviewable agency actions can only be challenged in court by an aggrieved party whose interests have been substantially affected by the agency action. And even when an aggrieved person has such *standing,* she is precluded from suing in court if she has not fully exhausted any available administrative remedies.

Luan v. Defenders of Wildlife

112 S.Ct. 2130 (U.S. Sup. Ct. 1992)

FACTS A provision in the *Endangered Species Act* divides responsibility for the protection of endangered species between the Secretary of the Interior and the Secretary of Commerce. It also requires each federal agency to consult with the relevant secretary to ensure that any action funded by the agency is unlikely to jeopardize the existence or habitat of an endangered or threatened species. The two secretaries issued a joint resolution stating that the obligations imposed by the act did not apply to actions taken in foreign nations. Defenders of Wildlife (DOW), an organization dedicated to wildlife conservation and other environmental causes, sued the Secretary of the Interior, seeking a declaratory judgment that the joint resolution erroneously interpreted the geographic scope of the act.

ISSUE Does DOW have standing to bring this suit?

DECISION No. The constitutional minimum of standing has three elements. First, the plaintiff must have suffered an injury in fact—an invasion of a legally-protected interest which is (a) concrete and particularized, and (b) actual or imminent, not conjectural or hypothetical. Second, there must be a causal connection between the injury and the conduct complained of. Third, it must be likely, as opposed to merely speculative, that the injury will be redressed by a favorable decision. When the suit is one challenging the legality of administrative action or inaction, the nature and extent of facts necessary to establish standing depends considerably upon whether the plaintiff is himself an object of the action (or inaction) at issue. If he is, there is ordinarily little question that the action or inaction has caused him injury, and that a judgment preventing or requiring the action will redress it. When, however, as in this case, a plaintiff's asserted injury arises from the agency's allegedly unlawful regulation (or lack of regulation) of *someone else,* standing is not precluded, but it is ordinarily substantially more difficult to establish. DOW's claim to injury is that the lack of consultation with respect to certain funded activities abroad increases the rate of extinction of endangered and threatened species. Of course, the desire to use or observe an animal species, even for purely aesthetic purposes, is undeniably a cognizable interest for purpose of standing. But the "injury in fact" test requires more than an injury to a cognizable interest. It requires that the party seeking review be himself among the injured. DOW lacks standing because it does not meet this concrete injury requirement.

http://supct.law.cornell.edu/supct/

Ethical Issue

Did these two secretaries violate an ethical duty by not extending the reach of the *Endangered Species Act* to actions taken in foreign nations?

The Federal Trade Commission

In 1914, Congress enacted the *Federal Trade Commission Act*, which, in turn, created the Federal Trade Commission (FTC). This independent agency is charged with preventing unfair competitive practices in the marketplace. Section 5 of the act gives the FTC broad powers to deal with "unfair methods of competition"and "unfair or deceptive acts or practices in commerce." Under the act, the FTC has successfully attacked business practices ranging from false advertising to the wrongful use of coercion in contracting.

The FTC has the power to police the act by using the **cease and desist order,** an administrative order similar to an injunction. Such orders become final unless they are appealed to the courts, and their violation is punishable by fines of up to $10,000 per day. The FTC also has the power to issue **trade regulation rules,** most of which have been in the area of consumer protection. Violations of these rules are also punishable by fines of up to $10,000 per day.

h t t p : / / *www.ftc.gov* is the home page for the Federal Trade Commission.

QUESTIONS AND PROBLEM CASES

1. What is preemption? Explain how courts determine if a law is preempted.
2. What is meant by an undue burden on interstate commerce?
3. What is the doctrine of enumerated powers?
4. Congress passed the *Agricultural Adjustment Act* in an attempt to stabilize agricultural production and assure farmers of reasonable minimum prices for their produce. Wickard, the secretary of agriculture, announced annually a national acreage allotment for various farm products such as wheat. The allotment was apportioned to the states and, ultimately, to individual farms. Filburn operated a small farm on which he raised dairy cattle and chickens and grew a small amount of winter wheat. He sold some of the wheat, but used most of it on his farm as livestock feed and as food for his family. Although his federally established allotment for wheat was 11.1 acres, Filburn sowed and harvested 23 acres. When the Department of Agriculture assessed a penalty against him, he challenged the constitutionality of the regulation. Does Congress have authority to regulate local wheat production?
5. An 18-wheel tractor-trailer attempted to brake suddenly and ended up jackknifing into oncoming traffic. The truck was not equipped with an antilock braking system (ABS). Ben Myrick was the driver of the oncoming vehicle and was left permanently paraplegic and brain damaged after being hit by the truck, which was manufactured by Freightliner. Myrick sued Freightliner under state tort law, alleging that the absence of ABS was a negligent design that rendered the truck defective. Freightliner argued the tort suit was preempted by the *National Traffic and Motor Vehicle Safety Act.* That federal statute was enacted to reduce traffic accidents as well as deaths and injuries caused by traffic accidents. It requires the Secretary of Transportation to establish appropriate federal motor vehicle safety standards. The statute expressly states that whenever a federal safety standard is in effect, the states cannot establish or enforce a safety standard covering the same aspect of performance if it is not identical to the federal standard. However, the law also contained a clause stating that compliance with any federal motor vehicle safety standard does not exempt any persons from liability under the common law. At the time of the accident, no federal motor vehicle safety regulation addressed stopping

distances or vehicle stability for trucks or trailers. Is Myrick's tort lawsuit preempted by the federal statute?

6. The domestic retail price of beer in Connecticut was consistently higher than the price of beer in the three bordering states and, as a result, Connecticut residents living in border areas frequently crossed state lines to purchase beer at lower prices. Accordingly, Connecticut enacted a statute that required out-of-state shippers of beer to affirm that their posted prices for products sold to Connecticut wholesalers were, as of the moment of posting, no higher than the prices at which those products were sold in the bordering states. A brewers' trade association and several major producers and importers of beer challenged the statute's constitutionality, contending that it violated the commerce clause. Is the statute unconstitutional as a violation of the commerce clause?

7. Graffiti covers more than five million square feet of walls, signs, windows, and other public surfaces in Chicago. Full-time crews patrol the streets removing paint, but they are losing ground. Vandalism and trespassing are crimes, but prosecution has not sufficed. Chicago finally decided to do something more: to lump spray paint, the principal tool of the graffiti "artist," with burglars' tools and other criminal implements as contraband. A city ordinance forbids the sale of spray paint within the city limits. A consortium of makers, wholesalers, and retailers of spray paint challenged the ordinance as an unconstitutional violation of the commerce clause. They contended that the ordinance creates an undue burden on commerce by achieving its ends at an excessive price to interstate commerce since most of the spray paint sold in Chicago comes from outside of Illinois. Does the city ordinance violate the dormant commerce clause?

8. Bankers Trust New York, a bank holding company, sought the approval of the Board of Governors of the Federal Reserve System for an investment management subsidiary, BT Investment Managers, Inc. (BTIM), to operate in Florida. The application was rejected on the grounds that it violated a Florida statute that prohibited out-of-state banks, bank holding companies, and trust companies from owning or controlling a business that sold investment advisory services within the state. Does the Florida statute violate the dormant commerce clause?

9. Mississippi enacted a statute prohibiting the sale of milk and milk products from another state unless the other state accepted milk produced and processed in Mississippi on a reciprocal basis. When the state ordered A&P not to distribute in Mississippi milk processed in A&P's Louisiana plant, the company filed suit. Mississippi argued that the statute was a reasonable exercise of its police power, designed to assure the distribution of healthful milk products to its citizens. Has Mississippi violated the dormant commerce clause?

10. Christy Brzonkala, a female student at Virginia Polytechnic & State University, allegedly was raped by two male students, Antonio Morrison and James Crawford. She claimed that the two men's acts were motivated wholly by discriminatory animus toward her gender and were not random acts of violence. Brzonkala argued that their actions violated a federal statute, the *Violence Against Women Act*. That law makes those who commit a crime of violence motivated by gender animus liable to their victim for compensatory and punitive damages. Morrison and Crawford contend that Congress lacked the constitutional authority to enact such a statute. Does the *Violence Against Women Act* fall within the congressional authority to regulate interstate commerce?

CHAPTER 5

INDIVIDUAL RIGHTS

S anta Ana, California, passed an ordinance prohibiting people from camping and/or storing personal possessions on public streets and other public property. The law was challenged as a denial of equal protection because it punished people merely because of their involuntary status of being homeless. The California supreme court, using rational basis analysis rather than strict scrutiny, upheld the ordinance.

Tobe v. Santa Ana, 892 P.2d 1145 (Cal. Sup. Ct. 1995).

What protections are provided by the Equal Protection Clause?

How does rational basis analysis differ from strict scrutiny?

How do courts determine which type of constitutional analysis to use?

Introduction

Our political system has been described as a democratic republic. Basically, this means our lawmaking institutions are comprised of representatives of the people. In theory, then, this country's laws reflect the will of the majority of its citizens. For the most part, this is a satisfactory situation. However, it is not without its problems. What happens when the majority rejects or fails to consider interests vital to the well-being of individuals or minority groups?

This chapter explores the constitutional limitations placed on the power of the majority. Specifically, it examines the procedural and substantive rights reserved to individuals by the U.S. Constitution. It rounds out the discussion of governmental power presented in Chapter 4. After reading both chapters, students should come away with a better understanding of how the Constitution is both an instrument of power and a symbol of restraint.

Chapter Overview

The chapter opens with an overview of the analysis employed by courts when the government interferes with individual rights. This is followed by two sections exploring the special constitutional status of expression. The first looks at forms of speech and expressive conduct that are protected by the First Amendment. The second introduces several types of expression deemed unworthy of constitutional protection. The final two sections of the chapter examine two more important constitutional rights: the right to privacy and freedom of religion.

Constitutional Rights Analysis

http://
www.law.cornell.edu:
80/constitution/
constitution.
billofrights.html pro-
vides links to Articles
of the Constitution
and the Bill of Rights.

This section introduces the analysis employed by courts when balancing the power of the majority against the rights of individuals. It starts with an examination of the concept of state action, since the Constitution's individual rights safeguards operate only against governmental abuse. Next, it looks at perhaps the two most important checks on the arbitrary exercise of governmental power—the Due Process Clause and the Equal Protection Clause. The section closes with a review of the three basic methods of judicial scrutiny in individual rights cases.

State Action

The Constitution places limits on the arbitrary exercise of governmental power. These safeguards are included in the various amendments to the Constitution. However, many people fail to understand that the Constitution does not protect against everyone who might threaten their rights. It only protects individuals against "governmental" activity, usually called **state action.** Private individuals do not owe one another constitutional rights, unless some type of statute creates such a duty.

When traditional governmental bodies (legislatures, government agencies, etc.) are involved, there is no difficulty in finding state action and, therefore, a duty to preserve constitutional rights. However, sometimes the line between private action and state action is not so clear. In those cases, courts consider the degree of governmental involvement in the challenged activity. And, when private entities assume functions traditionally reserved for the government (private police protection) or when a governmental body compels private behavior, state action may be found.

Yeo v. Town of Lexington

1997 U.S. App. LEXIS 13198 (1st Cir. 1997)

FACTS   The Lexington School Committee decided to distribute condoms and informational packets about their proper use as a part of "safe sex" education to high school students without parental consent. This became an extremely divisive issue in the community. The local high school newspaper took a strong editorial position in favor of making condoms freely available at the school. Douglas Yeo was among the Lexington parents who opposed the new policy. He helped organize a group, LEXNET, whose stated purpose was to help inform Lexington parents about public school issues. Yeo attempted to run ads in the school newspaper encouraging students to practice sexual abstinence and providing an address for LEXNET, but the newspaper refused to print the ad. After Yeo complained, school administrators urged the student editors to carefully reconsider their position. However, they also made it clear that they supported the students' right to decide. After the students again rejected the ad, Yeo sued on the ground that the refusal violated his constitutional right to free speech. The officials contended that Yeo's claim was without merit because there was no state action. Specifically, they asserted that the decision to reject Yeo's ad was made by the student editors and that they are not governmental actors.

ISSUE   Was the decision to reject the ad state action?

DECISION   Yes. The importance of the state action requirement in this case is clear; Yeo simply cannot prevail on his constitutional claims if the school newspaper's refusal to print the LEXNET ads is not fairly attributable to the Town of Lexington. A basic principle of our constitutional framework is that the constitutional guarantee of free speech is a guarantee only against abridgment by government, federal or state. The Constitution does not protect individuals from the acts of private parties. Nothing in the record suggests that the newspaper escapes the reasonable perception that it bore the imprimatur of the school. School-paid faculty supervised the newspaper and it was at least partly designed to impart knowledge about journalism and publishing to the student participants. The newspaper may fairly be characterized as part of the school curriculum. This was not the students' private publication. First and foremost, it was the school newspaper. The student editors cannot properly be viewed as wholly private actors when they act as representatives of a public school publication. Because Lexington High School is a public secondary school, the refusals by the student newspaper to print the LEXNET abstinence ads constituted actions attributable to the state.

http://www.law.vill.edu/Fed-Ct/fedcourt.html

Ethical Issue

The Constitution does not require private entities to respect people's individual rights. Is it ethical for private entities to treat people with less deference and respect than the Constitution requires of the government?

Due Process

http://
*www.law.cornell.edu:
80/constitution/
constitution.
billofrights.html*
provides the text of
the Fifth Amendment.

The **Due Process Clause** has historically been among the most important checks on abusive governmental power. The Fifth Amendment prohibits the federal government from depriving any person of *"life, liberty, or property, without due process of law."* The Fourteenth Amendment applies the same standard to the states.

The level of constitutional safeguards people receive varies with the interest that is threatened. Life and fundamental liberty interests are highly protected while property interests receive much less attention. Due process has both a procedural and a substantive component.

Procedural Due Process

At a minimum, the Due Process Clause insists that the government pursue its objectives by establishing and following fair procedures. This protection against arbitrary governmental action is known as **procedural due process.** Reasonable notice, a reasonable opportunity to respond, and adherence to any established procedures are required whenever the government interferes with people's rights (see Figure 5–1).

Thus, unduly vague statutes violate procedural due process because they do not give people reasonable notice of what type of behavior is expected of them. However, the degree of procedural protection people receive depends on the severity of the deprivation they are facing. For instance, criminal procedures must be very elaborate because of the serious consequences of being convicted of a crime. A disciplinary hearing for student misconduct in a dormitory, on the other hand, may be less elaborate because university sanctions are less severe than criminal convictions.

Courts employ a three-factor test when evaluating the sufficiency of procedural safeguards. It requires examination and balancing of:

1. the nature of the private interest affected by the state action;
2. the risk of error and the effect of additional procedural safeguards; and
3. the corresponding governmental interest.

Figure 5–1:   Procedural Due Process

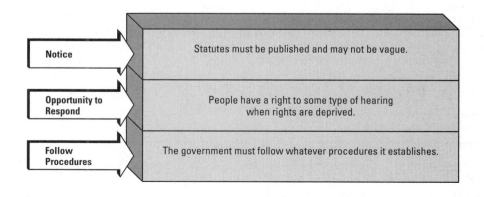

Substantive Due Process

Even when the government provides procedural due process, a court still may find its actions to be unconstitutional because they are substantively unfair. This notion, called **substantive due process,** safeguards people's rights against arbitrary or unreasonable governmental interference. However, when regulations burden only economic rights (property), the substantive due process analysis is largely neglected. In those cases, as long as the government accords procedural due process, its actions are constitutional. But when highly valued liberty interests are burdened, the governmental action must pass rigorous judicial scrutiny. (The manner in which courts review substantive due process cases is examined later in this chapter.)

Equal Protection

The **Equal Protection Clause** of the Fourteenth Amendment prohibits any state from arbitrarily discriminating against persons. The courts have interpreted the Fifth Amendment Due Process Clause as including a similar equal protection component. Thus, neither the states nor the federal government may unfairly discriminate. No substantive rights are created by the Equal Protection Clause. Instead, it holds that states must treat like cases alike. However, there are many times when the government provides benefits to, or imposes burdens on, some groups and not others. The constitutionality of such discrimination turns on the nature of the disfavored group and the government's reasons for making the distinction. This analysis is explained below.

http:// www.law.cornell. edu/topics/equal_ protection.html provides information on equal protection, as well as links to related sites.

Judicial Scrutiny

Most regulatory programs either discriminate in some manner or otherwise restrict the exercise of individual rights. When this occurs, the courts are called upon to decide if there has been a constitutional violation. In making this determination, courts balance the individual rights that are restricted against the governmental purposes served by the regulation.

There are a variety of judicial tests for examining due process and equal protection challenges. However, they share a common premise. When the government interferes with highly valued rights or discriminates on the basis of highly suspicious classifications, it must have an extremely important reason. But when the threat to individual rights is slight, judicial interference is minimal. There are three general types of analysis employed by the courts in due process and equal protection cases: rational basis, strict scrutiny, and intermediate scrutiny. (See Figure 5–2 on page 94.)

Rational Basis Analysis

Legislation restricting economic interests (property), or discriminating on the basis of nonsuspect classifications (categories other than race, national origin, gender, or illegitimacy), undergoes **rational basis** analysis. This is an extremely lenient level of scrutiny that presumes the regulation is constitutional. As long as the governmental action has a reasonable relationship to the achievement of a legitimate purpose, it is declared constitutional. Courts almost always find the existence of a rational relationship. (*Vacco v. Quill,* appearing later in this chapter, provides an example of rational basis analysis in an equal protection case.)

Figure 5–2:   Levels of Constitutional Scrutiny

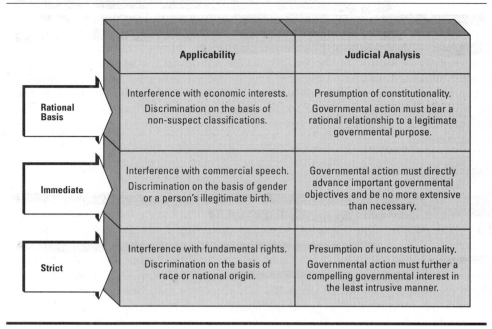

	Applicability	Judicial Analysis
Rational Basis	Interference with economic interests. Discrimination on the basis of non-suspect classifications.	Presumption of constitutionality. Governmental action must bear a rational relationship to a legitimate governmental purpose.
Immediate	Interference with commercial speech. Discrimination on the basis of gender or a person's illegitimate birth.	Governmental action must directly advance important governmental objectives and be no more extensive than necessary.
Strict	Interference with fundamental rights. Discrimination on the basis of race or national origin.	Presumption of unconstitutionality. Governmental action must further a compelling governmental interest in the least intrusive manner.

Strict Scrutiny Analysis

When state action denies people their fundamental constitutional rights, the courts initially presume that the restriction is unconstitutional. Similarly, when the government discriminates on the basis of certain **suspect classifications** (race or national origin), courts presume the governmental action is unlawful. In determining whether a **fundamental right** exists, the inquiry is whether the right involved is such that it cannot be denied without violating the fundamental principles of liberty and justice. Courts reserve this status for liberties that are deeply rooted in the nation's history and tradition. Accordingly, the fundamental rights generally are those liberties spelled out for protection in the Bill of Rights (speech, religion, association, right to vote, privacy, etc.).

When the government restricts the exercise of fundamental rights or discriminates on the basis of a suspect class, courts require more than a mere rational relationship between the statutory ends and means. Instead, the legislation is reviewed under **strict scrutiny.** Under this analysis, the statute is unconstitutional unless the government demonstrates that it is pursuing a *compelling governmental interest* in the *least intrusive manner.*

The case that opened this chapter implicated both due process and equal protection issues. Specifically, it was argued that the Santa Ana ordinance discriminated against poor people and interfered with their right to travel. If the court had used strict scrutiny analysis, it is conceivable the ordinance would have been declared unconstitutional. However, it used rational basis analysis because it did not find there to be a fundamental right to travel. Further, the Court noted that statutes that impose burdens on the homeless do not implicate a suspect classification. Thus, under rational basis analysis, the court upheld the ordinance because there was a rational relationship between the city's goal of maintaining its streets and public areas and its prohibition against camping in those streets and public areas. (The *McIntyre v. Ohio Elections Commission* case, appearing later in this chapter, provides an example of full strict scrutiny.)

Intermediate Scrutiny Analysis

Courts also recognize several types of **intermediate scrutiny** lying somewhere between rational basis and strict scrutiny analysis. This test generally is used to evaluate restrictions on commercial speech or discrimination on the basis of certain suspect classifications (gender or a person's illegitimate birth). This level of scrutiny generally requires that the classification serve important governmental objectives and are substantially related to the achievement of those objectives. (The intermediate scrutiny used for restrictions on commercial speech is discussed later in the chapter.) Consider the following case involving gender discrimination.

United States v. Virginia

116 S.Ct. 2264 (U.S. Sup. Ct. 1996)

FACTS   Virginia Military Institute (VMI) was a single-sex university whose distinctive mission was to produce citizen-soldiers, men prepared for leadership in civilian life and in military service. It pursued this mission through pervasive training of a kind not available anywhere else in Virginia. The state of Virginia offered women no opportunity anywhere to gain the benefits of the system of education at VMI. The state asserted two justifications in defense of VMI's exclusion of women: (1) that single-sex education contributes to diversity in educational approaches, and (2) VMI's adversarial approach would have to be modified and thereby undermined if VMI admitted women. A female high school student seeking admission to VMI complained that VMI's exclusively male admission policy violated the Equal Protection Clause. In response, the state of Virginia proposed a parallel program for women: Virginia Women's Institute for Leadership (VWIL) at Mary Baldwin College, a private liberal arts school for women. However, although VWIL would share VMI's mission—to produce citizen-soldiers—the VWIL program would differ, as does Mary Baldwin College, from VMI in academic offerings, methods of education, and financial resources.

ISSUE   Is VMI's men-only admission policy a denial of Equal Protection?

DECISION   Yes. Parties who seek to defend gender-based government action must demonstrate an exceedingly persuasive justification for that action. The burden of justification is demanding and rests entirely on the state. It must show at least that the gender-based classification serves important governmental objectives and the discriminatory means employed are substantially related to the achievement of those objectives. Virginia has shown no exceedingly persuasive justification for excluding all women from the citizen-soldier training afforded by VMI. The state has not shown that VMI was established, or has been maintained, with a view to diversifying educational opportunities within the state. However liberally this program serves the state's sons, it made no equivalent provision for her daughters. That is not *equal* protection.

continued

Further, women's successful entry into the federal military academies, and their participation in the military forces, indicate that Virginia's fears for the future of VMI are not solidly grounded. Virginia's solution to this problem—creation of the VWIL program—is not satisfactory. The state proposed a separate program, different in kind from VMI and unequal in tangible and intangible facilities. Virginia's generalizations about "the way women are," estimates of what is appropriate for *most women,* no longer justify denying opportunity to women whose talent and capacity place them outside the average description.

http://www.law.vill.edu/Fed-Ct/fedcourt.html
http://supct.law.cornell.edu/supct/

Freedom of Expression

http://
www.law.cornell.edu/
topics/first_
amendment.html
discusses the First
Amendment. For
more information,
choose the links on
this site.

Our freedom of speech is protected by the Constitution. However, like all rights, freedom of expression is not absolute. The government may restrict speech when it has a proper justification and furthers its objective in a proper manner. Judicial scrutiny of restrictions on expression take different forms, depending on the nature of the speech as well as the type of regulation. For instance, noncommercial speech is given full strict scrutiny, while commercial speech receives only intermediate scrutiny. The courts have devised special tests for determining the constitutionality of time, place, and manner regulations as well as restrictions on symbolic speech. However, each of the tests has one thing in common—the government may not restrict speech because it does not agree with the speaker's viewpoint. This section reviews these limitations on the freedom of expression.

Noncommercial Speech

The courts have consistently given the highest degree of constitutional protection to **noncommercial speech** (also known as pure or political speech). Thus, governmental restrictions on noncommercial speech must undergo strict scrutiny analysis. As such, they are upheld only if the government shows that (1) the regulation is furthering a *compelling governmental interest,* and (2) the regulation is no broader than absolutely necessary (*least intrusive means*) to promote that governmental interest (see Figure 5–3 on page 98).

McIntyre v. Ohio Elections Commission
514 U.S. 334 (U.S. Sup. Ct. 1995)

FACTS   Margaret McIntyre distributed leaflets to persons attending a public meeting at the Blendon Middle School in Westerville, Ohio. At this meeting, the superintendent of schools planned to discuss an imminent referendum on a proposed school tax levy. The leaflets expressed Mrs. McIntyre's opposition to the levy. Some of the handbills identified her as the author; others merely purported to express the views of "CONCERNED PARENTS AND TAX PAYERS." While Mrs. McIntyre distributed her handbills, an official of the school district, who supported the tax proposal, advised her that the unsigned leaflets did not conform to the Ohio election laws. Undeterred, Mrs. McIntyre appeared at another meeting on the next evening and handed out more of the handbills. Later, the school official filed an official complaint with the Ohio Elections Commission charging that Mrs. McIntyre's distribution of unsigned leaflets violated the Ohio Code. The Commission agreed and imposed a fine of $100. Mrs. McIntyre challenged the constitutionality of the ban on anonymous leafletting.

ISSUE Does the ordinance prohibiting all anonymous leafletting violate the First Amendment?

DECISION Yes. This is a regulation of pure speech. Moreover, even though this provision applies evenhandedly to advocates of differing viewpoints, it is a direct regulation of the content of speech. Indeed, the speech in which Mrs. McIntyre engaged—handing out leaflets in the advocacy of a politically controversial viewpoint—is the essence of First Amendment expression. That this advocacy occurred in the heat of a controversial referendum vote only strengthens the protection afforded to Mrs. McIntyre's expression. No form of speech is entitled to greater constitutional protection than Mrs. McIntyre's. When a law burdens core political speech, we apply "exacting scrutiny," and we uphold the restriction only if it is narrowly tailored to serve an overriding state interest. Ohio claims that the disclosure requirement is supported by the need to provide the electorate with relevant information. This informational interest plainly is insufficient to support the constitutionality of the disclosure requirement. In the case of a handbill written by a private citizen who is not known to the recipient, the name and address of the author adds little, if anything, to the reader's ability to evaluate the document's message. The state's interest in preventing fraud and libel stands on a different footing. We agree that this interest carries special weight during election campaigns when false statements, if credited, may have serious adverse consequences for the public at large. However, Ohio's prohibition of anonymous leaflets plainly is not its principal weapon against fraud. While it offers ancillary benefits to the state's more direct restrictions on fraud, we are not persuaded that they justify this restriction on core First Amendment rights. As this case demonstrates, the prohibition encompasses documents that are not even arguably false or misleading. A written election-related document—particularly a leaflet—is often a personally crafted statement of a political viewpoint. Mrs. McIntyre's handbills surely fit that description. As such, identification of the author against her will is particularly intrusive; it reveals unmistakably the content of her thoughts on a controversial issue. Under our Constitution, anonymous pamphleteering is not a pernicious, fraudulent practice, but an honorable tradition of advocacy and of dissent. Anonymity is a shield from the tyranny of the majority. The right to remain anonymous may be abused when it shields fraudulent conduct. But political speech by its nature will sometimes have unpalatable consequences, and, in general, our society accords greater weight to the value of free speech than to the dangers of its misuse. Ohio has not shown that its interest in preventing the misuse of anonymous election-related speech justifies a prohibition of all uses of that speech. The state may, and does, punish fraud directly. But it cannot seek to punish fraud indirectly by indiscriminately outlawing a category of speech, based on its content, with no necessary relationship to the danger sought to be prevented.

http://www.law.vill.edu/Fed-Ct/fedcourt.html
http://supct.law.cornell.edu/supct/

Figure 5–3:   Restrictions on Noncommercial Speech

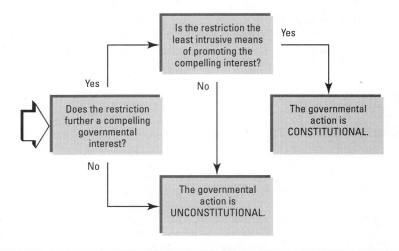

Commercial Speech

While constitutional safeguards have always been extended to noncommercial speech, it was long thought that **commercial speech,** such as advertising, enjoyed no First Amendment protection. However, in the mid-1970s the Supreme Court held that purely commercial speech was entitled to some constitutional protection. This protection was justified primarily by the public's interest in the free flow of accurate commercial information. Therefore, only truthful commercial speech is accorded First Amendment protection. (There is no such restriction on the constitutional protection for noncommercial speech.) False, misleading, or deceptive advertising may be lawfully suppressed.

Courts analyze governmental restrictions on commercial speech with an intermediate level of scrutiny. This requires the government to establish that it has a *substantial interest* (something less than a compelling interest) and that it is *directly advancing* that interest in a manner *no more extensive than necessary* to serve that interest (see Figure 5–4). (See *Florida Bar v. Went For It* in Chapter 3 for an application of the commercial speech test.)

Time, Place, or Manner Restrictions

Constitutional questions arise when people seek access to public property for the purpose of communicating with others. The government generally may impose reasonable restrictions on the **time, place, or manner** of such expression. For instance, a city may prohibit the use of loudspeakers in residential neighborhoods if the restriction applies equally to all types of expression (music, political speech, advertising). Courts employ a three-part test in deciding whether a law is a reasonable time, place, and manner restriction. First, they ask whether the speech restrictions are content neutral. Second, they must be narrowly tailored to serve a significant government interest. Finally, such laws must leave open ample alternative channels for the communication of information.

Figure 5–4:   Restrictions on Commercial Speech

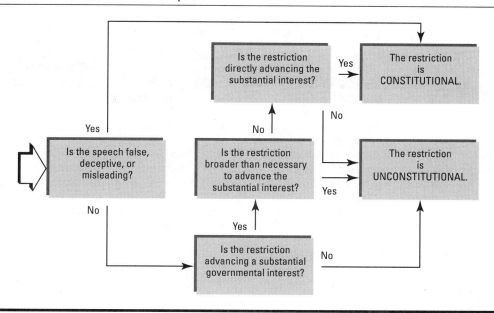

In a traditional *public forum* (streets or parks), the government may not discriminate against any segment of society when permitting access for speech purposes. However, in some instances, the government may restrict public use of a forum to certain classes of speakers. For instance, a local school may be designated as a *limited public forum*, which allows the government to limit access to only certain types of speakers (student groups) or certain topics (school business). As long as such restrictions are reasonable and not an effort to suppress expression merely because public officials oppose the speaker's viewpoint, they are constitutional.

Nunez v. San Diego

114 F.3d 935 (9th Cir. 1997)

FACTS   The City of San Diego enacted a juvenile curfew ordinance making it unlawful for *"any minor under the age of 18 years to loiter, wander, stroll or play in or upon public places or other unsupervised places after 10:00 p.m."* It made exceptions for a minor accompanied by an adult, conducting emergency errands for an adult, or returning home from an event sponsored by local education authorities or traveling from work. The law was passed to protect children from nighttime dangers, to reduce juvenile crime, and to involve parents in control of their children. Gabriel Nunez, a minor, challenged the ordinance as an unconstitutional restriction on the time, place, and manner of expression. He argued that the ordinance restricts minors from many otherwise lawful activities after curfew, such as studying with

continued

other students, meeting friends at their homes, practicing astronomy, attending concerts, and stopping at a restaurant to eat a late dinner.

ISSUE   Is the ordinance constitutional?

DECISION   No. We apply the traditional three-part test to determine whether the ordinance is a reasonable time, place, and manner restriction: (1) it must be content neutral; (2) it must be narrowly tailored to a significant government interest; and (3) it must leave open alternative channels for legitimate expression. It is undisputed that the regulation is content neutral. And, for First Amendment purposes, the physical and psychological well-being of minors is a compelling interest. But the ordinance is not narrowly tailored because it does not sufficiently exempt legitimate First Amendment activities from the curfew. It does not create even minimal exceptions to permit minors to express themselves during curfew hours without the supervision of a parent or guardian, preferring instead to have no First Amendment exception at all. This is not narrow tailoring. The ordinance is not a reasonable time, place, and manner restriction under the First Amendment. Clearly, San Diego could have enacted a narrower curfew ordinance that would pass constitutional muster.

http://www.law.vill.edu/Fed-Ct/fedcourt.html

Symbolic Speech

Expression does not have to be written or oral to receive constitutional protection. The First Amendment also safeguards various types of conduct that have expressive qualities. For instance, the courts have recognized flag burning as a form of expression protected against unreasonable governmental interference. Likewise, wearing a black armband, displaying a swastika, dancing nude, and burning a cross are forms of **symbolic speech.**

Courts have formulated a four-part test for examining the constitutionality of regulations that restrict expressive conduct. Such regulation is permitted if:

1. it is within the constitutional power of the government;
2. it furthers an important or substantial governmental interest;
3. the governmental interest is unrelated to the suppression of free expression; and
4. the incidental restriction of First Amendment freedoms is no greater than is essential to the furtherance of that interest.

Barnes v. Glen Theatre

501 U.S. 560 (1991).

FACTS   The Kitty Kat Lounge, located in South Bend, desired to present "totally nude dancing," but an applicable Indiana statute regulating public nudity required that dancers wear "pasties" and a "G-string" when they dance. Similarly, Glen Theatre, an adult bookstore in South Bend, provided nude performances and showings of the female body through glass panels. Both businesses claimed that non-obscene nude dancing performed for entertainment is expression protected by the First Amendment. They argued the public nudity statute was unconstitutional because its purpose was to prevent the message of eroticism and sexuality conveyed by the dancers.

ISSUE   Is the statute prohibiting nude dancing constitutional?

DECISION   Yes. Nude dancing of the kind sought to be performed here is expressive conduct within the outer perimeters of the First Amendment, though we view it as only marginally so. This does not end our inquiry. We must determine the level of protection afforded the expressive conduct at issue and determine whether the Indiana statute is an impermissible infringement of that protected activity. Indiana has not banned nude dancing as such, but has proscribed public nudity across the board. The public indecency statute is clearly within the constitutional power of the State of Indiana. The traditional police power of the states gives them authority to provide for the public health, safety, and morals. Further, Indiana's goal of protecting order and morality is a substantial governmental interest. This interest is unrelated to the suppression of free expression. Indiana is not proscribing nudity because of the erotic message conveyed by the dancers. The perceived evil that Indiana seeks to address is not erotic dancing, but public nudity. The statute also is "narrowly tailored." Indiana's requirement that the dancers wear at least pasties and a G-string is modest, and the bare minimum necessary to achieve the state's purpose.

http://www.law.vill.edu/Fed-Ct/fedcourt.html
http://supct.law.cornell.edu/supct/

Expression Outside the First Amendment

Some forms of expression are not constitutionally protected. Both obscenity and fighting words traditionally have been denied First Amendment protection. And today, an emerging type of expression—hate speech—has been the subject of constitutional confusion.

Obscenity

The protection of the First Amendment does not extend to obscene speech. The basic guidelines for deciding if expression violates a state **obscenity** statute is:

1. whether "the average person, applying contemporary community standards," would find that the work, taken as a whole, appeals to the prurient interest;
2. whether the work depicts or describes, in a patently offensive way, sexual conduct specifically defined by the applicable law; and
3. whether the work, taken as a whole, lacks serious literary, artistic, political, or scientific value.

http://
krusty.eecs.umich. edu/people/pjswan/ Baker/legal/ obscenity.html is the site of the Supreme Court's obscenity definition.

Problems with the Obscenity Test

The obscenity test has created a great deal of controversy. First, it is not very clear what actually constitutes obscenity. The courts allow juries to make this determination on a case-by-case basis. This can be confusing since sexually explicit messages that are indecent but not obscene are protected by the First Amendment. Second, each community is free to determine whether a particular message is obscene. This poses problems for the broadcast media and the Internet, whose messages frequently are received by unknown people in diverse communities throughout the country.

Indecency and the Broadcast Media

Of all the types of expressive media, the broadcast media receives the most limited First Amendment protection. There are two reasons for this distinction. First, the broadcast media have a uniquely pervasive presence in the lives of all Americans. Second, broadcasting is uniquely accessible to children. In light of these differences, radio and television broadcasts generally are subject to different—and often more restrictive—regulation than is permissible for other media under the First Amendment. Accordingly, courts generally uphold time restrictions on when indecent programs may be broadcast in order to limit what children may see and hear. (Speech issues and the Internet are discussed in Chapter 23.)

Fighting Words

Some speech causes an immediate violent response by the person to whom it is directed. These **fighting words** generally have been denied constitutional protection for two reasons. First, like obscenity, they are considered to be lacking in any intellectual or artistic value. Second, they pose an immediate threat to social order and public safety. However, consider the Supreme Court's protection of "symbolic" fighting words in the following case.

R.A.V. v. City of St. Paul

505 U.S. 377 (U.S. Sup. Ct. 1992)

FACTS In the predawn hours, several teenagers allegedly assembled a crudely made cross by taping together broken chair legs. They then allegedly burned the cross inside the fenced yard of a black family that lived in the neighborhood where one of the teenagers was staying. Although this conduct could have been punished under any of a number of laws, the city of St. Paul chose to charge the juveniles under the *St. Paul Bias-Motivated Crime Ordinance,* which proscribes placing "a symbol, object, appellation, characterization or graffiti, including, but not limited to, a burning cross or Nazi swastika, which one knows or has reasonable grounds to know arouses anger, alarm or resentment in others on the basis of race, color, creed, religion, or gender." The Minnesota Supreme Court upheld the constitutionality of the ordinance because it restricted only "fighting words" (conduct that itself inflicts injury or tends to incite immediate violence). It believed the ordinance reached only expression the First Amendment does not protect. The court also ruled that the ordinance was not impermissibly content-based because it was a narrowly tailored means of accomplishing the compelling governmental interest in protecting the community against bias-motivated threats to public safety and order.

ISSUE   Does this prohibition of "fighting words" violate the First Amendment?

DECISION   Yes. Even if this ordinance restricts no more than fighting words, it still is unconstitutional in that it prohibits otherwise permitted expression solely on the basis of the subjects the speech addresses. The First Amendment generally prevents the government from prohibiting speech or expressive conduct because of disapproval of the ideas expressed. However, we have sometimes said that some categories of expression (obscenity, defamation, fighting words) are not within the area of constitutionally protected speech. Such statements must be taken in context. What we mean is that these areas of speech can, consistently with the First Amendment, be regulated because of their constitutionally proscribable content. They are not categories of speech entirely invisible to the Constitution such that they may be made vehicles to content discrimination unrelated to their distinctively proscribable content. Thus, the government may proscribe libel; but it may not make the further content discrimination of prohibiting *only* libel critical of the government. It is clear that the St. Paul ordinance applies only to "fighting words" that insult, or provoke violence, "on the basis of race, color, creed, religion, or gender." Displays containing abusive invective, no matter how vicious or severe, are permissible unless they are addressed to one of the specified disfavored topics. Those who wish to use "fighting words" in connection with other ideas—to express hostility on the basis of political affiliation—are not covered. The First Amendment does not permit St. Paul to impose special prohibitions on those speakers who express views on disfavored subjects. St. Paul has not singled out an especially offensive mode of expression. It has not, for example, selected for prohibition only those "fighting words" that communicate ideas in a threatening (as opposed to a merely obnoxious) manner. Rather, it has prohibited "fighting words" of whatever manner that communicate messages of racial, gender, or religious intolerance. Selectivity of this sort creates the possibility that the city is seeking to handicap the expression of particular ideas. We do not doubt that St. Paul has compelling reasons for enacting this ordinance. Specifically, the ordinance helps to ensure the basic human rights of members of groups that have historically been subjected to discrimination. However, content discrimination plainly is not reasonably necessary to achieve St. Paul's compelling interest. An ordinance not limited to the favored topics would have precisely the same beneficial effect. In fact, the only interest distinctively served by the content limitation is that of displaying the city council's special hostility toward the particular biases thus singled out. That is precisely what the First Amendment forbids. The politicians of St. Paul are entitled to express that hostility; but not through the means of imposing unique limitations upon speakers who disagree. Let there be no mistake about our belief that burning a cross in someone's front yard is reprehensible. But St. Paul has sufficient means at its disposal to prevent such behavior without adding the First Amendment to the fire.

http://www.law.vill.edu/Fed-Ct/fedcourt.html
http://supct.law.cornell.edu/supct/

Hate Speech

The fighting words in the previous case demonstrate a type of **hate speech** that seems more and more pervasive today. Numerous college campuses and local communities have developed antiharassment codes and policies to encourage diversity and silence sexual, racial, and religious insults. As illustrated in *R.A.V. v. City of St. Paul,* these efforts at promoting multiculturalism may run afoul of the First Amendment to the extent that they attempt to suppress unpopular viewpoints. However, their constitutionality still is uncertain. Consider the following case where the court distinguishes *R.A.V.*'s "hate speech" ordinance from a law directed at racially motivated conduct.

Wisconsin v. Mitchell

508 U.S. 476 (U.S. Sup. Ct. 1993)

FACTS   A group of young black men and boys, including Todd Mitchell, gathered at an apartment complex. Several members of the group discussed a scene from the motion picture *Mississippi Burning,* in which a white man beat a young black boy who was praying. The group moved outside and Mitchell asked them, "Do you all feel hyped up to move on some white people?" Shortly thereafter, as a young white boy walked by, Mitchell said, "There goes a white boy; go get him." Mitchell counted to three and pointed in the boy's direction. The group ran toward the boy, beat him severely, and stole his tennis shoes. The boy was rendered unconscious and remained in a coma for four days. Mitchell was convicted of aggravated battery. That offense ordinarily carries a maximum sentence of two years imprisonment. However, because the jury found that Mitchell had intentionally selected his victim because of the boy's race, the maximum penalty for Mitchell's offense was increased to seven years under a penalty-enhancement provision enacted by the Wisconsin legislature. That provision increases the maximum penalty for an offense whenever the defendant "intentionally selects the person against whom the crime is committed because of the race, religion, color, disability, sexual orientation, national origin, or ancestry of that person." The state supreme court held that the penalty-enhancement provision violated the First Amendment directly by punishing what the legislature has deemed to be offensive thought.

ISSUE   Does the penalty-enhancement provision violate the First Amendment?

DECISION   No. Under the Wisconsin statute the same criminal conduct may be more heavily punished if the victim is selected because of his race than if no such motive was involved. Thus, although the statute punishes criminal conduct, it enhances the maximum penalty for conduct motivated by a discriminatory point of view. But motive plays the same role under the Wisconsin statute as it does under antidiscrimination laws, which we have previously upheld against constitutional challenge. Nothing in our *R.A.V.* decision compels a different result here. That case involved a First Amendment challenge to an ordinance prohibiting the use of "fighting words" that insult or provoke violence on the basis of race, color, creed, religion, or gender. Because the ordinance only prohibited a class of "fighting words" deemed particularly offensive by the city, we held that it violated the rule against content-based discrimination. But whereas the ordinance struck down in *R.A.V.* was explicitly directed at expression, the statute in this case is aimed at conduct unprotected by the First Amendment. Moreover, the Wisconsin statute singles out for enhancement bias-inspired conduct because this conduct is thought to inflict greater individual and societal harm. For example, bias-motivated crimes are more likely to provoke retaliatory crimes, inflict distinct emotional harms on their victims, and incite community unrest. The state's desire to redress these perceived harms provides an adequate explanation for its penalty-enhancement provision over and above mere disagreement with the offenders' beliefs or biases. It is but reasonable that among crimes of different natures those should be most severely punished, which are the most destructive of the public safety and happiness.

http://www.law.vill.edu/Fed-Ct/fedcourt.html
http://supct.law.cornell.edu/supct/

Ethical Issue

What role should universities and local governments play in dealing with hate speech? Should they issue policies and codes designed to restrain it or merely encourage others to offset its harsh effects with counter-speech?

Right to Privacy

The Constitution does not expressly provide a right of **privacy.** However, privacy is considered to be a fundamental right because the Supreme Court has interpreted the language of the Bill of Rights to bestow such a right on people. Courts construe the Constitution as providing two types of privacy protection. One form of privacy focuses on governmental intrusions, while the other concerns personal decisions or conduct. Courts use strict scrutiny to analyze the constitutionality of governmental interference with either form of privacy.

This section examines the two fundamental aspects of the right to privacy: the freedom from governmental intrusions and the right to make important personal decisions without government interference. The section closes with a brief look at a potential extension of the right to make personal decisions—the right to die.

Governmental Intrusions

People have a basic right to be left alone. This privacy interest protects against unnecessary **governmental intrusions** by strictly regulating the personal information the government may demand or publicly disclose. This right is implicated in criminal investigations when the police attempt to search a person or her possessions. Generally, police must first secure a search warrant based on probable cause. The warrant itself protects against unnecessary intrusions by carefully defining the scope of the search. This illustrates an application of the strict scrutiny requirements of a compelling interest and least intrusive means that are triggered when the fundamental right of privacy is restricted. (See Chapter 6 for further discussion.)

http://
www.law.cornell.edu/
topics/publicity.html
discusses publicity/
privacy issues, with
links to the *Lanham
Act* and intellectual
property sites.

Personal Decisions

http://
www.law.cornell.edu/
uscode/42/ch21A.
html#l is the site of
the U.S. Code section
on privacy protection.

The second fundamental privacy interest preserves to individuals a limited right to make important **personal decisions** and engage in certain kinds of conduct without unnecessary governmental interference. The courts have included within this category of privacy only decisions or conduct relating to marriage, procreation, contraception, family relationships, child rearing, and education.

City of Sherman v. Hodges

928 S.W.2D 464 (SUP. CT. TEX. 1996)

FACTS   The City of Sherman police chief denied Patrolman Otis Henry a promotion to the rank of sergeant because Henry was having a sexual affair with the wife of a fellow police officer. Henry ranked first on the city's civil servant list of eligible candidates for promotion to the sergeant's position. In fact, absent a valid reason to the contrary, he was entitled to the promotion. Henry maintained that the police chief did not have a valid reason for denying the promotion because his conduct was protected by the right of privacy.

ISSUE   Does the promotion denial violate Henry's right of privacy?

DECISION   No. Henry does not claim the police chief invaded his right to be left alone. Similarly, he does not complain that the government's method of obtaining information regarding his sexual affair constituted any type of intrusion into his personal life. Instead, Henry urges that the basis of the promotion denial violated his right to make certain fundamental decisions and engage in certain conduct without state interference. However, his adulterous affair with another officer's wife is unlike the recognized privacy rights concerning child rearing, family relationships, procreation, marriage, contraception, and abortion that are afforded special constitutional protection. Indeed, adultery is the very antithesis of marriage and family. Adultery, by its very nature, undermines the marital relationship and often tears apart families. Moreover, sexual relations with the spouse of another is not a right that is implicit in the concept of ordered liberty or deeply rooted in this Nation's history and tradition. Prohibitions against adultery have ancient roots. The right to privacy under the Constitution does not include the right to maintain a sexual relationship with the spouse of someone else.

Right to Die

In recent years we have witnessed a great deal of controversy over the possible emergence of a fundamentally protected **right to die.** Some would find such a right within the fundamental privacy right to make certain important decisions without government interference. And, in fact, the Supreme Court has strongly suggested that the Due Process Clause protects the traditional right to refuse unwanted lifesaving medical treatment. Not surprisingly, most states have laws safeguarding this right.

As a logical extension of the right to refuse lifesaving medical treatment, many terminally ill patients and doctors have asserted the existence of a right to a *physician-assisted suicide.* However, the Supreme Court has resisted formulation of such a right because it is not deeply rooted in the nation's history and tradition. At the same time, the Court has not rejected the constitutionality of statutes legalizing such assistance. An overwhelming majority of the states have outlawed assisting another person's suicide. Consider the following case where the Supreme Court upholds a ban on assisting suicide.

Vacco v. Quill

117 S .CT. 2293 (U.S. SUP. CT. 1997)

FACTS   The state of New York makes it a crime to aid another to commit or attempt suicide. However, it allows patients to refuse lifesaving medical treatment. Several doctors, and three gravely ill patients who have since died, challenged the constitutionality of the prohibition. They urged that because New York permits a competent person to refuse life-sustaining medical treatment, and because the refusal of such treatment is essentially the same thing as physician-assisted suicide, the state's assisted-suicide ban violates the Equal Protection Clause.

ISSUE   Does the ban on assisted-suicides violate the Equal Protection Clause?

DECISION   No. New York's laws outlawing assisted suicide affect and address matters of profound significance to all New Yorkers alike. They neither infringe fundamental rights nor involve suspect classifications. These laws are therefore entitled to a strong presumption of validity. Neither New York's ban on assisting suicide nor its statutes permitting patients to refuse medical treatment treat anyone differently than anyone else or draw any distinctions between persons. *Everyone,* regardless of physical condition, is entitled, if competent, to refuse unwanted lifesaving medical treatment. *No one* is permitted to assist a suicide. Generally speaking, laws that apply evenhandedly to all unquestionably comply with the Equal Protection Clause. We think the distinction between assisting suicide and withdrawing life-sustaining treatment, a distinction widely recognized and endorsed in the medical profession and in our legal traditions, is both important and logical. It is certainly logical.

http://www.law.vill.edu/Fed-Ct/fedcourt.html
http://supct.law.cornell.edu/supct/

Freedom of Religion

The First Amendment has two clauses offering constitutional protection for religion: the Establishment Clause and the Free Exercise Clause. The first prohibits governmental sponsorship of religion, while the second prohibits governmental interference with religion. As you might suspect, in our heavily regulated society, conflicts often arise between the simultaneous commands to neither help nor hinder religion. The courts generally resolve this dilemma by insisting only that governmental regulations be neutral toward religion.

Establishment Clause

The **Establishment Clause** states that the government *"shall make no law respecting an establishment of religion."* Specifically, it limits the ability of the government to engage in or support religion. Thus, state laws mandating school prayer violate this constitutional provision. However, problems arise in our complex society where governmental subsidies and other programs benefit a wide variety of interests, including religious institutions. For instance, many schools and cities freely provide access to their governmental buildings to private groups hoping to gain wider access to the local community. Establishment Clause issues arise when religious groups request similar access.

Courts have regularly held that tolerance of religious activities does not necessarily confer any imprimatur of state approval on religious sects or practices. In fact, they have devised a three-part test for analyzing the constitutionality of a statute or governmental practice that touches upon religion: (1) it must have a secular purpose; (2) it must neither advance nor inhibit religion in its principal or primary effect; and (3) it must not foster an excessive entanglement with religion. Under the first step the government may not convey a message of endorsement or disapproval of religion. The second step strikes down regulations that have an effect that encourages or discourages religious practice. It asks whether, despite the government's actual purpose, the practice under review in fact conveys a message of endorsement or disapproval. Finally, the prohibition against excessive entanglements prevents the government from excessive administration, monitoring, or surveillance of religious activities, institutions, or personnel. For instance, if school officials were required to lead prayers or review the content of prayers at pre-football game invocations, there would be excessive entanglement.

Bown v. Gwinnett County School District

112 F.3D 1464 (11TH CIR. 1997)

FACTS   The state of Georgia enacted the *Moment of Quiet Reflection in Schools Act* as an amendment to an earlier law allowing teachers to conduct a brief period of silent prayer or meditation. The amended version of the statute authorized public schools to conduct a brief period of quiet reflection for not more than 60 seconds at the beginning of each school day. The statute specifically stated that it was not intended to be and shall not be conducted as a religious experience or exercise. Instead, it was to be construed as an opportunity for a moment of silent reflection on the anticipated activities of the day. Brian Bown, a South Gwinnett High School teacher, expressed reservations regarding the implementation of the act. At the beginning of the school day, the following announcement was made over the school intercom system: "As we begin another day, let us take a few moments to reflect quietly on our day, our activities, and what we hope to accomplish." At the end of the announcement, Bown told his class, "You may do as you wish. That's your option. But I'm going to continue with my lesson." He continued teaching his lesson during the moment of quiet reflection. Because Bown repeatedly refused to comply with the moment of quiet reflection, he was terminated from his employment with the school. He argued the termination was unlawful because the moment of quiet reflection violates the Establishment Clause.

ISSUE   Does the moment of quiet reflection violate the Establishment Clause?

DECISION   No. Governmental action violates the Establishment Clause if it is entirely motivated by a purpose to advance religion. However, this act has a clearly secular purpose. Further, the act, as implemented by Gwinnett High School, does not have the primary effect of either advancing or inhibiting religion. The intercom announcement in no way suggested that students should or should not pray silently during the moment of quiet reflection. All students may use the moment of quiet reflection as they wish, so long as they remain silent. This case does not involve impermissible government coercion of students to engage in religious activity. The facts in no way indicate the state has created a situation in which students are faced with public pressure or peer pressure to participate in religious activity. Finally, the statute does not foster an excessive government entanglement with religion. Teachers are not asked to participate in, lead, or monitor prayers. In fact, this case involves no prayer for the teacher to monitor. All the act requires is that the students and the teacher in charge remain silent during the moment of quiet reflection.

http://www.law.vill.edu/Fed-Ct/fedcourt.html

Free Exercise Clause

The government is prevented from opposing religion by the **Free Exercise Clause**. Specifically, the Constitution requires that the government *"shall make no law . . . prohibiting the free exercise"* of religion. Of course, many laws and governmental policies place burdens on religious practices. For instance, a city's designation of an old church building as a historic landmark might prevent a congregation from substantially enlarging the building. However, this burden on the church would not violate the Free Exercise Clause if the ordinance did not single out religion or religious buildings. As long as it was a neutral law of general applicability, it would be constitutional. However, a policy denying the extension of governmental benefits to people who practiced religion or a particular religion would be struck down.

QUESTIONS AND PROBLEM CASES

1. What is state action? What is its relevance to due process analysis?
2. What is strict scrutiny? How does it differ from rational basis analysis in equal protection cases?
3. How do courts distinguish between commercial speech and political speech in terms of the degree of constitutional protection they are given?
4. The Maryland Department of Human Resources revoked a childcare center's license on findings that a number of preschool age children were victims of physical and sexual abuse while in the center's care. None of the alleged victims of child abuse testified in either of the two protracted hearings. Instead, the agency acted entirely on hearsay through the parents and others who had spoken with the children. The childcare center requested an opportunity to

conduct psychological examinations of the alleged victims prior to the hearing. This request was denied out of a desire to protect the children from experiencing further anxiety. The childcare center argued that the decision to revoke its license in the absence of such an examination was a denial of procedural due process. Was it?

5. Congress established Amtrak in order to avert the threatened extinction of passenger trains in the United States. The statute creating Amtrak provides for a board of nine members, six of whom are appointed directly by the President of the United States. The holders of Amtrak's preferred stock select two more directors and those eight select the ninth member, who serves as chairman of the board. Amtrak is not unique; it is one of many corporations created and participated in by the United States for the achievement of governmental objectives. Michael Lebron, a creator of billboard displays that involve commentary on public issues, tried to display an advertisement on a colossal billboard in Amtrak's Pennsylvania Station in New York City. The ad criticized the Coors family, owners of Coors beer, for its support of right-wing causes. When Amtrak refused to lease the space because it disapproved of the advertisement, Lebron filed suit against the railway, claiming the refusal violated his First Amendment rights. Amtrak argued that, whatever its relationship with the federal government, there was no state action because its charter specifically disclaims its status as a governmental agency. Is there state action? Explain.

6. Nebraska voters adopted an article to their state constitution that prohibited non-family farm corporations from owning and operating Nebraska farmland. Supporters of the Nebraska initiative contended that the measure was intended to address the social and economic evils perceived to be related to corporate farming. It was believed that a rise in corporate farming would result in a decline of the family farmer, who would be unable to compete with the ability of corporations to raise capital and benefit from tax

laws. It was also maintained that corporate farming would lead to absentee landowners, which would adversely affect the rural social and economic structure. MSM Farms, a Nebraska corporation with unrelated shareholders, challenged the family farm measure. Specifically, MSM Farms argued that the state's prohibition of non-family corporate farming denied it equal protection because it was not rationally related to achieving any legitimate state purpose. Further, MSM Farms felt the law was irrational because it does nothing to prevent the concentration of ownership of farmlands in corporations owned or controlled by families. Does the family farm measure discriminate in violation of the Equal Protection Clause?

7. Coors Brewing Company applied to the Bureau of Alcohol, Tobacco and Firearms (BATF) for approval of proposed labels and advertisements that disclosed the alcohol content of its beer. BATF rejected the application on the ground that the Federal Alcohol Administration Act prohibited disclosure of the alcohol content of beer on labels or in advertising. The labeling regulations also prohibited the use of descriptive terms that suggest high alcohol content, such as "strong," "full strength," or "extra strength." While the laws governing labeling prohibit the disclosure of alcohol content unless required by state law, federal regulations apply a contrary policy to beer advertising. Like the labeling restrictions, they prohibit statements of alcohol content in advertising, but they only apply in states that affirmatively prohibit such advertisements. Only 18 states prohibit such disclosure in beer advertisements. Thus, brewers remain free to disclose alcohol content in advertisements, but not on labels, in much of the country. Further, while the government bans the disclosure of alcohol content on beer labels, it requires such disclosure on the labels of wines and spirits. Coors claimed the labeling restrictions violated its First Amendment rights. The government responded that the ban was necessary to suppress the threat of "strength wars" among brewers, who,

without the regulation, would seek to compete in the marketplace based on the potency of beer. Does the labeling restriction infringe brewers' First Amendment rights?

8. Erznoznik, the manager of a drive-in theater, was charged with violating a municipal code for exhibiting a motion picture, visible from public streets, in which female buttocks and bare breasts were shown. The movie, *Class of '74*, had been rated "R" by the Motion Picture Association of America. An "R" rating indicates that youths may be admitted only when accompanied by a parent or guardian. The screen of the theater was visible from two adjacent public streets and a nearby church parking lot. People had been observed watching films while sitting outside the theater in parked cars and in the grass. The city acknowledged that its ordinance swept far beyond the permissible restraints on obscenity and thus applied to films that are protected by the First Amendment. Nevertheless, it maintained that any movie containing nudity that is visible from a public place may be suppressed as a nuisance. Specifically, the city claimed the ordinance was needed to prevent significant intrusions on the privacy of passersby who might see offensive scenes and as an exercise of the city's power to

protect children. Does the ordinance violate Erznoznik's First Amendment rights?

9. In 1992, a Florida state court permanently enjoined abortion protesters from blocking or interfering with public access to an abortion clinic in Melbourne, Florida, and from physically abusing persons entering or leaving the clinic. Six months later, in response to continued interference by abortion protesters, the state court amended its original order, enjoining a broader array of activities. The new injunction excluded demonstrators from a 36-foot buffer zone around the clinic's entrances and driveway. It also prohibited excessive noise levels and the displaying of antiabortion images in the area surrounding the clinic. Is the injunction a constitutional time, place, and manner restriction?

10. Section 16(c) of the *Public Telecommunications Act of 1992* seeks to protect the well-being of minors by restricting the hours within which indecent radio and television programs may be broadcast. The statute provides that indecent materials may only be broadcast between the hours of midnight and 6:00 a.m. Are section 16(a)'s restrictions on indecent radio and television broadcasts constitutional?

CRIMINAL WRONGS

Police obtained a warrant to search Albert Foster's home and automobile. The warrant authorized the search for the presence of marijuana and four specific firearms. After the police found marijuana and the firearms, they contacted the Drug Enforcement Agency (DEA) for assistance. While waiting for the DEA agents, the officers continued to search Foster's residence, where they uncovered several video-tapes that contained footage of sexual acts involving Foster and his stepdaughter. The search lasted more than seven hours despite the fact that the items listed in the warrant were discovered during the first hour of the search.

United States v. Foster, 100 F.3d 846 (10th Cir. 1996).

When must the police obtain a search warrant before conducting a search?
Was this a legal search?
What happens when police conduct an unlawful search?

Introduction

A crime occurs when a person intentionally commits an act prohibited by the government. When a person is suspected of criminal conduct, he may be investigated and arrested by the police and charged by a prosecutor. Because of the serious intrusions accompanying a criminal investigation, arrest, and conviction, accused persons are granted substantial constitutional protections. These safeguards are part of the body of law known as **criminal procedure.** This chapter examines the nature of criminal law as well as the rules of criminal procedure governing the criminal justice system.

Chapter Overview

The chapter begins with a look at the basic elements common to criminal behavior. This is followed by an examination of the procedural rules governing police searches, seizures, and arrests. Attention then is shifted to the basic features of criminal trials and criminal defenses. The chapter closes by exploring the imposition of criminal sanctions.

http:// www.law.cornell.edu/ topics/criminal_ procedure.html provides a brief overview of criminal procedure with links to other relevant sites.

The Nature of a Crime

Serious offenses (murder, rape, or kidnapping) are classified as **felonies.** Convicted felons may be fined, imprisoned, or even executed. Less serious criminal violations (check deception, possession of small amounts of marijuana, or disorderly conduct) may be **misdemeanors.** People convicted of misdemeanors are subjected to lesser fines or shorter jail terms than those who commit felonies. The least serious offenses are called **infractions.** They are not technically a crime; thus they cannot result in imprisonment. Instead, these violations (speeding, running a red light, or using false identification to purchase alcoholic beverages) generally result in noncriminal sanctions like fines.

There generally are three elements common to all criminal behavior. First, for a crime to occur, a person usually must violate a statute. Second, for most serious crimes, the person must have had criminal intent. Finally, the accused person is presumed innocent until the government meets its burden of proving his guilt beyond a reasonable doubt. (See Figure 6–1 on page 114.)

http:// www.law.cornell.edu/ topics/criminal.html provides a brief overview of criminal law information. Select "State Criminal Codes" for state-specific information.

http:// www.law.cornell.edu/ uscode/18/ is the site of an index of specific crimes, mainly against the federal government.

Statutory Violation

Behavior generally is not considered to be criminal unless it violates a **criminal statute.** Both the national and state government may enact such laws. However, there are limits on the government's power to enact criminal laws. Both the due process clause and the ex post facto clauses of the U.S. Constitution provide such constraints.

Some jurisdictions permit courts to treat outrageous conduct as criminal in the absence of a statute. Such behavior is known as a **common-law crime.** However, there is a distinct trend toward abolishing common law crimes in many states and they no longer exist in the federal jurisdiction.

Figure 6–1:   The Criminal Case

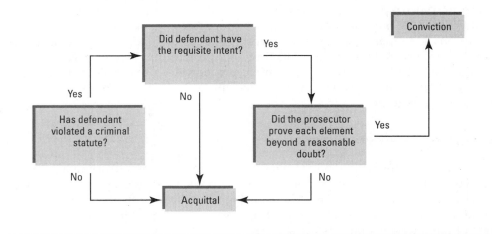

Due Process Limitations

Procedural due process requires that the language of a statute be sufficiently clear to give people adequate notice of what types of behavior are considered criminal. Vague statutes threaten to delegate basic policy matters to policemen, judges, and juries for resolution on a subjective basis. This creates a danger of arbitrary and discriminatory application of the criminal law. Thus, a city ordinance preventing people from "acting in a manner which others may find offensive" is too vague to be enforced.

   Substantive due process limits the government's authority to outlaw the exercise of people's fundamental constitutional rights. For example, a rule criminalizing flag burning is invalid because it unduly interferes with people's freedom of expression. The government may not restrict fundamental rights unless it has a compelling reason for doing so. And, with our flag-burning example, censorship of expression because it offends the public is not supported by a compelling governmental interest. (These due process limits on governmental power are explored in Chapter 5.)

Ex Post Facto Limitations

A person cannot be convicted of a crime unless the statute was in existence at the time when the behavior occurred. This is because the Constitution prohibits **ex post facto** laws—statutes that punish people for acts that occurred before the law was passed. A law is *ex post facto* if it punishes as a crime an act previously committed that was innocent when done, makes more burdensome the punishment for a crime after its commission, or deprives one charged with a crime of any defenses available according to the law at the time the act was committed. Consider the following case.

Gwong v. Singletary

683 So.2d 109 (Sup. Ct. Fla. 1996)

FACTS   Richard Gwong was convicted of second-degree murder and sentenced in 1989 to 22 years in prison. On the date that Gwong committed his offense, Florida law provided that he was eligible to earn incentive gain-time. That meant that for each month in which he engaged in positive activities, the Department of Corrections could grant up to 20 days of incentive gain-time, which would result in his receiving an early release from prison. However, in 1996, the Florida Department of Corrections issued an administrative rule that denied the ability to earn incentive gain-time to prisoners who were convicted of crimes such as murder and sex crimes, and who had 85 percent or less of their prison sentences remaining. More than 20,000 inmates, including Gwong, were immediately impacted by this rule. Gwong argued that the administrative rule violated the *ex post facto* clause.

ISSUE   Is the state rule revoking incentive gain-time an unconstitutional *ex post facto* law?

DECISION   Yes. In evaluating whether a law violates the *ex post facto* clause, a two-prong test must be applied: whether the law is retrospective in its effect, and whether the law alters the definition of criminal conduct or increases the penalty by which a crime is punishable. Even though a prisoner has but a mere expectancy in the availability of incentive gain-time, the prisoner's eligibility for reduced imprisonment is a significant factor entering into both the defendant's decision to plea bargain and the judge's calculation of the sentence to be imposed. This state rule applies to a class of inmates who committed their offenses before the rule's effective date and acts to enhance the measure of punishment because it eliminates the ability of an inmate to earn incentive gain-time. Here, the procedure for implementing the award of gain-time has not merely been altered; it has been changed to completely eliminate the ability of certain classes of inmates to receive gain-time even if they carry out their work in an outstanding manner.

Criminal Intent

Another essential element for most criminal violations is that the defendant possess **mens rea** (criminal intent) when she violates that statute. The actual wording of each law defines the level of intent necessary for a criminal violation to occur. In fact, criminal statutes may be categorized according to the type of intent they require: (1) specific intent, (2) general intent, or (3) strict liability.

Specific Intent

Courts define **specific intent** as a particular criminal intent beyond merely performing some action that happens to violate a statute. For instance, first degree murder requires a conscious or specific intent to take the life of another. Thus, an accidental killing would not qualify as first degree murder because the specific intent requirement would not be met.

General Intent

Other criminal statutes criminalize certain conduct even though the defendant had no specific intent to violate the law. Under these **general intent** statutes it is not necessary that the defendant actually know that her behavior violates the law. As long as she intended to perform the act that violated the terms of the statute, a court will infer a criminal intent from her behavior. This judicial trend toward implying intent makes it essential that people familiarize themselves with society's laws.

Strict Liability Crimes

Finally, in some instances, recklessness or mere negligence may be enough to trigger liability. For such a **strict liability crime,** the state need only prove that the defendant performed a wrongful act, irrespective of whether he intended to perform it. Strict liability crimes generally are public welfare statutes where the penalty is not too severe (i.e., motor vehicle statutes). However, consider the following case.

Collins v. State

691 So.2d 918 (Sup. Ct. Miss. 1997)

FACTS　James Lee Collins had sexual relations with LaQuita Sessom. At the time of the incident, James was 24 years old and LaQuita was 13. However, James consistently maintained that the sexual activity was consensual and that LaQuita told him she was 19 years old. LaQuita denied both of these assertions. In Mississippi capital rape requires rape of a child under the age of 14. If the perpetrator is over the age of 18, a sentence of death or life imprisonment may be imposed. However, if the perpetrator is between the ages of 13 and 18, the court in its discretion may determine an appropriate sentence. Statutory rape, on the other hand, requires carnal knowledge of an unmarried person of previously chaste character younger than the perpetrator and over 14 and under 18 years of age. After being convicted of capital rape, James argued that the trial court erred in not instructing the jury on his "mistake of age" defense.

ISSUE　Should the jury have been permitted to consider James's mistake of age defense?

DECISION　No. Crimes such as statutory rape and capital rape are defined by the ages of the persons involved. While age serves as a line of demarcation for purposes of the potential penalty for capital rape, age is the defining characteristic of statutory rape, be it forcible or not. The clear intent underlying the crime of statutory rape is that females under the age of 18 are legally unable to consent to sexual relations with another. Intent or mistake as to the age of the child is irrelevant. Historically, there have been two basic rationales for statutory rape laws. The first rationale is the need for strict accountability to protect young girls. The second rationale is the premise that the defendant's intent to commit statutory rape can be derived from his intent to commit the morally or legally wrongful act of fornication. The weight of authority in this country indicates that statutory rape has traditionally been viewed as a strict liability offense. Despite this fact, a few states permit a "mistake of age" defense in statutory rape cases. However, this defense remains the minority view and this court believes it is inconsistent with the two basic rationales for statutory rape laws. The states which recognize the defendant's mistake of age as a defense do so in large part because criminal offenses generally require the critical element of mens rea or criminal intent. Thus, the defendant's mistake is allowed as a defense to negate this element of the crime. However, the U.S. Supreme Court has expressly recognized that sex offenses, such as rape, in which the victim's actual age is at issue are exceptions to the general rule that criminal statutes require the state to establish intent. The capital rape statute appears to have the same purpose as does the statutory rape law. Accordingly, mistake of age is not a valid defense to the crime of capital rape as well.

Incapacity and Intent

The *mens rea* requirement is designed to punish conscious wrongdoers. For that reason, the law provides a defense for people who are unable to form criminal intent. There are three general types of incapacity recognized by the criminal law: intoxication, infancy, and insanity.

Intoxication and Intent

Suppose Joe serves Elena a punch containing alcohol. Elena was unaware that the drink contained alcohol and drove home in an intoxicated condition. Her **involuntary intoxication** may be a complete defense to the charge of driving while intoxicated because she had no intent to consume alcohol and drive.

American courts originally did not permit **voluntary intoxication** as an excuse for criminal behavior. However, by the end of the 19th century, most jurisdictions would consider voluntary intoxication in determining whether a defendant was capable of forming the specific intent required for some criminal offenses. For instance, if Marie commits murder while voluntarily drunk, she may avoid liability for first-degree murder because that crime requires a conscious intent to kill (premeditation). Still, she probably has violated some other type of homicide statute that does not require premeditation.

In recent years many state legislatures have enacted laws precluding consideration of voluntary intoxication in the determination of *mens rea*. These laws are part of an increased commitment to "law and order" and a response to studies indicating that a large number of violent crimes are committed by intoxicated offenders.

Infancy and Intent

Courts historically presumed that children were incapable of forming criminal intent. The idea behind this **infancy** defense has carried over into modern criminal law as most states have established a separate criminal justice system for juvenile offenders. For instance, some states have a separate juvenile code that deals with crimes committed by people less than 18 years of age. These states may provide special juvenile courts as well as separate detention facilities. However, a juvenile who is a repeat offender or who commits an extremely serious crime such as murder may be treated as an adult.

Insanity and Intent

Insanity may provide a complete defense to criminal liability. In some states, an offender is not criminally liable if, when the offense occurred, he did not comprehend the nature of his actions or realize that what he was doing was wrong. Other states follow an *irresistible impulse rule,* which excuses otherwise criminal behavior if the offender suffered from a mental disease that rendered her unable to control her actions and thereby resist committing the crime.

In recent years there has been a public outcry against insanity defenses. This has resulted in many jurisdictions limiting its availability. States also have responded by enacting procedural rules making it more difficult for a defendant to establish her insanity. For instance, criminal defendants are presumed to be sane, and in many jurisdictions they bear the burden of proving any insanity.

Some states have provided an alternative to a verdict that a defendant is "not guilty by reason of insanity." They permit juries to find an offender "guilty, but mentally ill." This allows a criminal conviction while still assuring that the defendant will receive medical treatment. This is consistent with the criminal justice procedures that delay a criminal trial for insane defendants who are incapable of assisting in their defense until they regain their sanity. Further, defendants who become insane after conviction may have their sentencing or execution delayed until their sanity returns.

Burden of Proof

Because an individual accused of a crime is faced with the threat of losing her life or liberty, the Constitution provides important safeguards against wrongful convictions. One of the most fundamental protections available to the accused is the *presumption of innocence.* The government (the prosecutor) may overcome this presumption only by proving **beyond a reasonable doubt** each element of the charged offense.

Although the reasonable doubt standard is a requirement of due process, the Constitution does not require that any particular form of words be used in advising the jury of this burden of proof. A common jury instruction might state: *The burden of proof is upon the prosecutor. All the presumptions of law independent of evidence are in favor of innocence; and every person is presumed to be innocent until he is proved guilty. If upon such proof there is reasonable doubt remaining, the accused is entitled to the benefit of it by an acquittal.* Reasonable doubt, itself, might be defined as *such a doubt as would cause a reasonable and prudent person in one of the graver and more important transactions of life, to pause and hesitate before taking the represented facts as true and relying and taking action thereon.* This standard does not require absolute or mathematical certainty. It permits findings of guilt based upon the strong probabilities of the case as long as they exclude any doubt that is actual and substantial, as distinguished from doubt arising from mere possibility or bare imagination.

Search and Seizure

The activities of government investigators are limited by the Fourth Amendment's prohibition of unreasonable searches and seizures. Throughout the years the courts have been forced to give meaning to this constitutional limitation. This section explores the basic rules governing police searches.

Search Warrants

Courts generally require that police obtain a **search warrant** before they may search either a criminal suspect or the things she owns. A judge or magistrate is not to issue such a warrant unless the prosecutor demonstrates that **probable cause** (good reason) exists to believe the search will uncover contraband or evidence of a crime. Even then, the warrant prevents against unreasonable intrusions by defining the scope of the search. (See Figure 6–2.)

Remember the case that opened this chapter? There, the police officers continued to search Foster's residence even after they had found all of the items listed

http://
www.law.cornell.edu/ topics/criminal.html provides a brief overview of criminal law information. Select "Amendment IV: Search and Seizures" for the text of the Bill of Rights amendment regarding unreasonable search and seizure.

Figure 6–2: A Search Warrant

| STATE OF INDIANA | SS: | IN THE MONROE CIRCUIT COURT |
| COUNTY OF MONROE | | MC: 53C0 > MC |

SEARCH WARRANT

To the <u>Monroe County Sheriff's Department</u>. You are authorized and Ordered, in the name of the State of Indiana, with the necessary and proper assistance to enter unto or upon <u>3810 South Market Street, Apartment #10, Bloomington, IN 47401</u>, and diligently search for <u>marijuana (cannabis sativa) and any and all controlled substances whose possession is illegal under the laws of Indiana</u>. You are ordered to seize such property, or any part thereof, found on such search.

Dated this 15th of May, 1998 at the hour 9:00 A.M./P.M.

_____
Robert Young, Judge
Monroe Circuit Court

Executed this _____ day of _____ , at the hour of _____ a.m./p.m.

_____
Law Enforcement Officer

RETURN

To the Judge of the Monroe Circuit Court: This warrant was served at _____ a.m./p.m. on the _____ day of _____ , and:

_____ The items on the attached property list were seized:

_____ The following items were seized:

_____
Law Enforcement Officer

in the search warrant. The court held that the police deliberately and flagrantly exceeded the terms of the search warrant. Accordingly, all of the evidence, even that which was properly seized, was ruled inadmissible in the criminal trial against Foster. Such a *blanket suppression* is used in cases where the police flagrantly disregard the terms of a search warrant.

Exceptions to the Warrant Requirement

Despite the Fourth Amendment's protection of the rights of criminal suspects, there are several important exceptions to the warrant requirement. First, not all observations by the police are considered to be searches. A person's reasonable expectation of privacy must be examined to determine if a search has occurred. Second, a warrant may not be needed if a person consents to a search. Further, police may perform a patdown search when it is necessary for their own protection. Finally, there may be special emergency occasions when it is not reasonable to expect a criminal investigator to secure a search warrant.

Expectation of Privacy

Police may use evidence or seize contraband without a warrant when it is in the *plain view* of the officers. This is because people have no reasonable **expectation of privacy** under such circumstances. Thus, police have been permitted to search garbage bags placed in a trash dumpster, conduct aerial surveillance from public airspace, and use as evidence conversations between suspects and government informants. Similarly, sobriety checkpoints are permitted on public highways, and police may expose airline travelers' luggage to drug-sniffing dogs. This is because such investigative techniques are felt to impose only minimal intrusions into peoples' privacy.

Consensual Searches

Searches that would otherwise require a warrant may be legal if they are *consensual.* Such consent may be express or implied. For instance, police often ask if they may conduct a search. If the suspect gives an affirmative response, the consent is express. The consent is implied in a case where a police officer asks a motorist to open his trunk and the motorist does so without objection.

A tenant's roommate may consent to a police search of those parts of an apartment that are accessible to all roommates. Suppose Elaine and Gloria share a two-bedroom apartment. Elaine may permit the police to search the kitchen, living room, and bathroom since both tenants share those spaces. However, she has no right to grant access to Gloria's bedroom.

Roommates in college dormitories also may give police permission to conduct searches. However, in the absence of an emergency, university officials generally may not permit police to search a dormitory room without first securing a search warrant.

Patdown Searches

Where a police officer observes unusual conduct that leads her to reasonably conclude that criminal activity may be occurring, she may briefly detain the suspicious person and make reasonable inquiries aimed at confirming or dispelling her suspicions. If the police officer reasonably believes the criminal suspect is armed and dangerous, she may conduct a warrantless **patdown search** to determine if the suspect is carrying a weapon. However, the purpose of this search is not to discover evidence of a crime, but to allow the officer to pursue her investigation without fear of violence. If the patdown search goes beyond what is necessary to determine if the suspect is armed, it is no longer valid.

Minnesota v. Dickerson

508 U.S. 366 (U.S. Sup. Ct. 1993)

FACTS   Two Minneapolis police officers were patrolling in a marked squad car when they observed Timothy Dickerson leaving a building considered to be a notorious "crack house." Dickerson began walking toward the police but, upon spotting the squad car and making eye contact with one of the officers, he abruptly halted and began walking in the opposite direction. The officers ordered Dickerson to stop and submit to a patdown search. The search revealed no weapons, but the officer conducting the search did take an interest in a small lump in Dickerson's nylon jacket. After examining it with his fingers and believing it to be a lump of crack cocaine in cellophane, the officer reached into Dickerson's pocket and retrieved a small plastic bag containing crack cocaine. Dickerson claimed the officers' seizure of the cocaine violated his Fourth Amendment rights.

ISSUE   Was the seizure of the cocaine unconstitutional?

DECISION   Yes. Dickerson has not claimed that the police were not justified in stopping him and frisking him for weapons. Thus, the question before this Court is whether the officer who conducted the patdown search was acting within lawful bounds when he determined that the lump in Dickerson's jacket was cocaine. Police officers may seize nonthreatening contraband detected during a protective patdown search so long as they stay within the bounds marked by the patdown exception to the warrant requirement. If a police officer lawfully pats down a suspect's outer clothing and feels an object whose contour or mass makes its identity immediately apparent, there has been no invasion of the suspect's privacy beyond that already authorized by the officer's search for weapons. If the object is contraband, its warrantless seizure would be justified by the same practical considerations that inhere in the plain view doctrine context. Here, however, the officer determined that the lump was contraband only after squeezing, sliding and otherwise manipulating the contents of Dickerson's pocket—a pocket which the officer already knew contained no weapon. His continued exploration of the pocket after having concluded it contained no weapon was unrelated to the sole justification for the patdown search (the protection of the officer and others nearby). Because the further search of Dickerson's pocket was constitutionally invalid, the seizure of the cocaine was likewise unconstitutional.

http://www.law.vill.edu/Fed-Ct/fedcourt.html
http://supct.law.cornell.edu/supct/

Other Warrantless Searches

There are other exceptions to warrant requirement as well. For instance, if someone is arrested, the police may search her and the area within her immediate control. However, the search must take place after the arrest. Police also may conduct a warrantless inventory search of property in an arrestee's possession. Courts give police wide latitude in searching motor vehicles when they have been lawfully stopped. (Automobile searches are discussed in Chapter 22.) And when police are in *hot pursuit* of a suspect, they may search any premises he might enter. In emergency circumstances, where there could be serious injury or a loss of life, a warrantless search may be conducted. Further, courts have permitted customs agents to carry out warrantless searches.

Unreasonable Searches and Seizures

Evidence obtained as a result of an unreasonable search and seizure is subject to the **exclusionary rule.** This judicially created rule provides that such evidence may not be used in a criminal trial against the accused. The U.S. Supreme Court believed the rule was necessary to deter criminal investigators from violating people's constitutional rights. However, it has long been a source of controversy as it sometimes allows criminals to go free merely because of negligence or unconscious wrongdoing by a police officer.

Perhaps in response to these criticisms, courts have made exceptions to the exclusionary rule. For instance, the prosecutor may present illegally obtained evidence if she can convince the court that it would have eventually been discovered by lawful means. And the Supreme Court carved out a "good-faith" exception in cases where police officers acted in reasonable reliance on a search warrant that later turned out to be invalid. The following case, *Arizona v. Evans,* further extends this "good-faith" exception.

Arizona v. Evans

514 U.S. 1 (U.S. Sup. Ct. 1995)

FACTS A police officer stopped Evans after he drove the wrong way on a one-way street. When the officer entered Evans's name into a computer data terminal located in his patrol car, the computer revealed that there was an outstanding misdemeanor warrant for Evans's arrest. Accordingly, the officer placed Evans under arrest. While Evans was being handcuffed, he dropped a hand-rolled cigarette the police officer believed smelled of marijuana. The officer's search of Evans's car revealed a bag of marijuana under the front seat. Evans was charged with possession of marijuana. It was later revealed that the outstanding misdemeanor warrant listed in the computer records was erroneous. It had been canceled (quashed) by the court 17 days prior to the traffic stop. Evans filed a motion asking the court to exclude the seized marijuana from evidence on the theory that the search was unreasonable because the arrest was unlawful.

ISSUE Should the marijuana be excluded from evidence?

DECISION   No. The arresting officer acted in objectively reasonable reliance on a police record indicating the existence of an outstanding arrest warrant. This case presents the question whether the evidence seized pursuant to that arrest should be excluded after the arrest warrant is determined to be erroneous regardless of the source of the error. The exclusionary rule operates as a judicially created remedy designed to safeguard against future violations of Fourth Amendment rights through the rule's general deterrent effect. In the context of a police search where the officers acted in objectively reasonable reliance on a search warrant, mistakenly issued by a neutral and detached magistrate, we previously held there to be no sound reason to apply the exclusionary rule as a means of deterring misconduct on the part of judicial officers who are responsible for issuing warrants. In such cases, suppressing the evidence would not further the ends of the exclusionary rule in any appreciable way. Excluding the evidence could in no way affect the magistrate's future conduct unless it was to make him less willing to do his duty. First, the exclusionary rule was historically designed as a means of deterring police misconduct, not mistakes by court employees. Second, there is no evidence that court employees are inclined to ignore or subvert the Fourth Amendment or that lawlessness among these actors requires application of the extreme sanction of exclusion. Finally, and most important, there is no basis for believing that application of the exclusionary rule in these circumstances will have a significant effect on court employees responsible for informing the police that a warrant has been quashed (canceled). Because court clerks are not adjuncts to the law enforcement team engaged in the often competitive enterprise of ferreting out crime, they have no stake in the outcome of particular criminal cases. The threat of exclusion of evidence could not be expected to deter such individuals from failing to inform police officers that a warrant had been quashed.

http://www.law.vill.edu/Fed-Ct/fedcourt.html
http://supct.law.cornell.edu/supct/

No-Knock Entries

Even with a valid search warrant, a police officer generally must knock and announce his presence and authority before entering a dwelling. This **knock-and-announce rule** is designed to decrease the potential for violence that might result from unannounced breakings and enterings into private property. It also seeks to protect privacy as much as possible by giving occupants notice of an impending intrusion by police. Another purpose of the rule is to avoid the unnecessary destruction that might result from a forcible entry.

No-knock entries may be permitted under certain circumstances. For instance, a police officer need not announce his presence when he has a reasonable belief that an occupant will use a firearm against him. The rule may also be dispensed with when there is a reason to believe that evidence will be destroyed if advance notice is given. When such events are likely, a judge or magistrate may issue a search warrant specifically authorizing a no-knock entry. However, state statutes providing blanket exceptions to the knock-and-announce rule generally violate the Fourth Amendment's prohibition against unreasonable searches.

Arrests

http://
*www.ojp.usdoj.
gov/bjs/* will take
you to the Web site
of the Department
of Justice Bureau
of Statistics, which
provides statistics
on crime and law
enforcement.

The criminal justice system affords the government a great deal of discretion in determining if a suspect should be arrested. However, an arrest is considered to be a seizure and, accordingly, is subject to the Fourth Amendment's prohibition against unreasonable governmental action. Courts often are called upon to review the actions taken by police officers in the course of making an arrest.

Arrest Warrants

Police normally must obtain an **arrest warrant** before they may arrest a criminal suspect. The arrest warrant is similar to a search warrant in that a judge issues it only after the police demonstrate probable cause that the person named in the warrant has committed a crime. (See Figure 6–3.)

No warrant is required to arrest a suspected felon in a public place. However, a warrantless arrest generally may not occur in a nonpublic place unless there are *exigent circumstances* that make immediate action by the police imperative. These circumstances arise when a reasonable person would believe that entry was necessary to prevent physical harm to the police officers or other persons. It may also occur if there is a substantial risk that relevant evidence will be destroyed or that the suspect will escape.

The arrest warrant requirement extends to attempts by police to enter private residences to arrest a nonresident who may be hiding there. In fact, under those circumstances the police also must obtain a search warrant unless a resident consents to the search or exigent circumstances dictate that the officer enter immediately.

United States v. Gooch

6 F. 3D 673 (9TH CIR. 1993)

FACTS   At about 3:50 a.m., police were called and told that Kenneth Gooch had shot at Marc Cole at a state campground. Upon entering the campground, Cole informed the officers that Gooch had fired a shot in his direction after a fight in which Gooch tried to stick Cole's head into the fire. These incidents occurred between midnight and 2:00 a.m. Sometime after 5:00 a.m., the three officers observed that the campsite was quiet and determined that Gooch was asleep in his closed tent. The officers, without seeking an arrest warrant, ordered Gooch out of the tent, patted him down, and arrested him. Gooch argued that the warrantless arrest violated his Fourth Amendment rights.

ISSUE   Was the arrest unlawful?

DECISION   Yes. The threshold issue is whether the Fourth Amendment protects a person's privacy interests in a tent located on a public campground. Gooch must have had both a subjectively and objectively reasonable expectation of privacy in the tent. The Fourth Amendment protects people, not places. What a citizen seeks to preserve as private, even in an area accessible to the public, may be constitutionally protected. Gooch had such a reasonable expectation of privacy in his tent. Absent exigent circumstances, a warrantless arrest is unconstitutional in a "non-public" place, even when that place is not one's residence. Although Gooch's tent was pitched on public property, the closed tent was a "non-public" place for purposes of

Fourth Amendment analysis. Further, there were no exigencies that justified a warrantless arrest. Although Gooch was intoxicated and had recently discharged a firearm, there was no ongoing threat. The officers arrived during daylight hours and the fight and discharge had occurred several hours before the arrest. The officers could not have reasonably believed there was a present danger to others. Because there was no ongoing threat and Gooch's tent was a "non-public" place, the warrantless arrest was not lawful.

Figure 6–3:   Arrest Warrant

AGENCY: MONROE COUNTY SHERIFF'S DEPARTMENT

WARRANT

IN THE MONROE CIRCUIT COURT
CAUSE NUMBER: 53C0 >

STATE OF INDIANA, COUNTY OF MONROE, SS:

State of Indiana, to the Sheriff of Monroe County, Greetings:

You are hereby commanded to arrest:

CARL DEAN WILLIAMS	SEX: MALE
132 N. MAPLE STREET	RACE: CAUCASIAN
BLOOMINGTON, IN 47401	HT: 5 ft. 6 inches
DOB: January 14, 1972	WT: 142 lbs.
SSN: 222-33-4444	EYES: Blue
HAIR: Brown	

if HE may be found in your bailiwick, so that you have HIS body before the Judge of the Monroe Circuit Court, instanter, then and there to answer the State of Indiana, on a charge of

CHARGES: RAPE

and abide the order of the court thereon and return this writ.

BOND: $ WITNESS, the Clerk and seal of said Court, this 9th day of July, 1998.

Beverly L. Taylor
Clerk, Monroe County

Copy:
Served this _____ day of _____, 199 .

_____ IN JAIL   Sheriff, _____.
IN. _____
BONDED _____
_____ NOT IN JAIL   By: _____
                                       (Deputy Sheriff)

Summons

In cases involving certain misdemeanors (shoplifting) and other petty offenses (traffic violations), where the suspect is unlikely to flee or injure anyone, an arrest may not be necessary. Instead, the suspect receives a **summons** ordering her to appear before the court. This process permits the accused to avoid incarceration prior to the trial and, if the charges are later dismissed or there is no conviction, she does not have an arrest on her record.

Arrest Procedures

Upon making an arrest, it is standard procedure for police to handcuff the accused and subject her to a thorough search. She is then taken to the police station for the **booking** process. This administrative procedure requires the accused to provide the police with personal information. She also will be fingerprinted and photographed.

Those charged with misdemeanors frequently are released immediately after the booking if they post **bail** (pay a fixed sum of money), which is returnable on the day of the trial. In some instances, an individual may be released merely by signing a statement promising to appear in court. This is known as **release on recognizance.**

Initial Appearance

People charged with felonies generally are taken before a judge or magistrate for an **initial appearance.** This usually occurs within 48 hours, although it may be even longer if the arrest is made on a weekend. At this time, the accused is advised of the charges against her, informed of her constitutional rights, and given an opportunity to plead guilty or not guilty. (This step is also called an **arraignment.**) The judge also establishes bail unless the accused is a flight risk, a continued threat to society, or already was free on bail, probation, or parole when the alleged crime occurred. When the amount of bail is high, criminal defendants often contract with a *bail bondsman,* who pays the state the specified sum of money if the accused fails to appear in court. For this service, the bail bondsman generally charges the defendant 10 percent of the bail. (Figure 6–4.)

Preliminary Hearing

Many states require that persons accused of felonies be provided a **preliminary hearing.** This additional procedural step is an evidentiary proceeding where the prosecutor must persuade the judge or magistrate there is *probable cause* to believe the accused committed a felony. If this burden is met, the formal charges against the defendant are filed with the trial court. The charges are called an *information* if filed by a prosecutor, or an *indictment* if returned by a grand jury. About half of the states require that grand juries (composed of citizens) approve of a decision to charge a person with a felony. (See Figure 6–5 on page 129.)

Interrogations

Criminal investigators often interrogate a suspect after taking him into custody. However, such questioning may raise constitutional issues because the Fifth Amendment provides that no person shall be compelled to testify against himself

---

Figure 6–4: Waiver of Initial Hearing

STATE OF INDIANA	SS:	**IN THE MONROE CIRCUIT COURT**
COUNTY OF MONROE		**MC: 53C0 > MC**

STATE OF INDIANA

      V.

CARL DEAN WILLIAMS

DEFENDANT'S WAIVER OF INITIAL HEARING

    Comes now the Defendant, by counsel, and would waive any reading of the charging Information, plead **not guilty**, and acknowledge an understanding of all applicable state and federal constitutional rights for purposes of initial hearing.

RONALD V. DURKEE
Attorney for Defendant

CERTIFICATE OF SERVICE

    I verify that a copy of the foregoing was delivered/mailed on ___July 10,___ 199<u>8</u>, to opposing counsel of record, pursuant to Ind. T.R.5.

RONALD V. DURKEE
Attorney for Defendant

---

in a criminal case. To safeguard this right, the courts require police to issue a **Miranda warning** to criminal defendants before beginning a custodial interrogation. Basically, the police must inform the defendant that: *he has the right to remain silent; any statements he makes can be used as evidence against him in a court of law; he has the right to an attorney; and if he cannot afford an attorney one will be appointed to represent him.*

    Any incriminating statements a criminal defendant makes before receiving a *Miranda warning* may not be admitted as evidence. Further, once a suspect in police custody demands an attorney, the interrogation must end. Investigators may not threaten to penalize an individual who invokes his right to remain silent. But the police still may seek personal information unrelated to the crime during the booking process. And they may continue gathering nontestimonial evidence like blood samples, fingerprints, and hair.

    The *Miranda warning* is required only when a suspect interrogated by the police is "in custody." The Supreme Court has defined a **custodial interrogation** as questioning initiated by law enforcement officers after a person has been taken into custody or otherwise deprived of freedom of action in any significant way. And there are other limitations on its protection. For instance, statements the accused makes to cellmates while incarcerated may be used as evidence. Further, the Supreme Court permitted an undercover police officer to pose as a cellmate and ask incriminating questions without first giving a *Miranda warning.*

Stewart v. United States

688 A. 2D 857 (CT. APP. D.C. 1995)

FACTS   Shawn M. Stewart was arrested for second-degree murder. After he was advised of his *Miranda* rights, Stewart invoked his right to remain silent at approximately 12:45 p.m. At about 3:30 p.m., Detective Treadwell escorted Stewart to a cellblock. Treadwell had known Stewart since he was a little boy, and both men had belonged to the same church all of their lives. During a private conversation at the cellblock, Treadwell told Stewart that he had made mistakes but neither Treadwell nor other church members would judge him. He told him further that Stewart was not standing alone because the church was still his support group. Treadwell then gave Stewart a picture of their bishop and asked if he was interested in talking any more with him. Stewart replied that he was. Treadwell departed on another assignment and did not return until late that evening. In the meantime, Stewart remained in the central cellblock without access to his parents or consultation with an attorney. When Treadwell returned, he immediately asked Stewart, "What happened?" Stewart then confessed to the crime. Later, other detectives took over the questioning and began transcribing the confession. Stewart signed a form signifying that he waived his right to remain silent.

ISSUE   Is Stewart's confession admissible as evidence?

DECISION   No. The admissibility of statements made after a suspect has invoked his right to remain silent depends on whether his right to terminate questioning was "scrupulously honored." Four factors need to be considered in determining whether a defendant's rights have been scrupulously honored: (1) was the suspect orally advised of his rights and did he orally acknowledge them, (2) did the police immediately cease questioning and make no attempts to resume or ask him to reconsider, (3) was there a sufficient break between the first and second interrogations and was the second performed at a different location by a different officer about a different crime, and (4) were *Miranda* warnings given before the second questioning session? Treadwell's cellblock conversation with Stewart was an interrogation and violated constitutional standards. Interrogation refers not only to express questioning, but also to any words or actions on the part of the police that officers should know are reasonably likely to elicit an incriminating response from the suspect. Treadwell knew that his words of inspiration were likely to elicit an incriminating response. The conversation cannot properly be characterized as spontaneous, casual, or personal. The cellblock conversation was not a proper restart of questioning because Stewart did not initiate the conversation and there had been only a short time since Stewart's invocation of his right to remain silent. Further, it concerned the same crime and Treadwell did not readvise Stewart of his right to remain silent, nor did Stewart waive it. Finally, the cellblock conversation induced Stewart's confession later that evening. Stewart's later waiver is not binding because the police did not scrupulously honor his earlier request to cut off questioning.

http://www.law.vill.edu/Fed-Ct/fedcourt.html

Figure 6–5: Information

STATE OF INDIANA	**SS:**	**IN THE MONROE CIRCUIT COURT**
COUNTY OF MONROE		**MC: 53C0 > MC**

STATE OF INDIANA

      V.

CARL DEAN WILLIAMS

DOB: January 14, 1972
SSN: 222-333-4444

                              INFORMATION:

                              RAPE

                              CLASS A FELONY

Affiant, DONALD E. JACOBSON, being duly sworn, says:

On or about 3:14 a.m., July 8, 1998, in Monroe County, Indiana, CARL DEAN WILLIAMS did knowingly or intentionally have sexual intercourse with STELLA MAY HUNSICKER, a member of the opposite sex, by using FORCE, to-wit: a KNIFE to compel STELLA MAY HUNSICKER to have sexual intercourse with CARL DEAN WILLIAMS, in violation of I.C. 35-42-4-1.

                             _____

                             DONALD E. JACOBSON, Affiant

Subscribed and sworn to before me and approved by me this 8th day of July, 1998.

                             _____

                             Rupert P. Brisbane

                             Deputy Prosecuting Attorney

STATE WITNESSES:

STELLA MAY HUNSICKER

MIRIAM DENISE JENKINS

Ethical Issue

During interrogations, police investigators sometimes lie to the suspect to induce him to make a voluntary confession. Is this ethical conduct?

Criminal Trials

If the defendant pleads not guilty at the arraignment, the court generally establishes a trial date. The defendant may then select the type of trial. For serious offenses where incarceration of more than six months is likely, the defendant may insist on a jury trial. However, the defendant may waive this right and opt for a *bench trial* in which the judge decides the outcome. A defendant may withdraw a

http://
*www.law.cornell.
edu/uscode/18/* con-
tains information
discussed in this
section. Choose
relevant topics from
the U.S. Code, Title
18, Part II–Criminal
Procedure.

request for a jury trial at any time before the actual trial date. During the course of the trial, the defendant has the right to confront and cross-examine any witnesses against him.

Plea Bargaining

Although a defense attorney is likely to charge much more for a jury trial, it sometimes is desirable because it gives the defendant greater leverage in **plea bargaining.** Because prosecutors often are overwhelmed with cases and are working on a limited budget, they may be willing to reduce the charges against a defendant in order to avoid the burden created by a jury trial. The vast majority of criminal cases are resolved by the defendant pleading guilty, often in exchange for a more lenient sentence.

Discovery

The federal government and most of the states have special **discovery** rules governing the gathering of evidence prior to a criminal trial. One of the major purposes of these rules is to uncover all material facts before the trial. Discovery also allows all parties access to the same information, thereby avoiding surprise at the trial.

Prosecutors have an affirmative duty to disclose all evidence favorable to the defendant. They must permit a defendant to inspect and copy all evidence within their possession that is material to the preparation of a defense or that the government intends to introduce at trial. This includes evidence that might assist the defendant in impeaching the testimony of witnesses for the prosecution.

An important component of the discovery process is the taking of **depositions,** whereby the prosecutor and defense attorneys interview witnesses prior to the trial. Depositions serve the major purposes of discovery and also record a witness's testimony before her memory fades or is altered by subsequent events.

Ethical Issue

Prosecutors have a duty to disclose to the defense attorney all evidence that supports the defendant's case. Is it ethical for a prosecutor to delay disclosing this information until the last possible moment?

Double Jeopardy

The Fifth Amendment prohibits the government from prosecuting a person more than once for the same crime. This rule against **double jeopardy** prevents a second criminal trial for an offense if the defendant has already been acquitted or convicted of that crime. However, it does not preclude multiple prosecutions by different governmental bodies. For instance, a murder may violate both federal and state law. Thus, both sovereigns could bring criminal actions against the defendant. Further, a single action may violate more than one criminal statute. Thus, a kidnapper also may be charged with violating statutes prohibiting assault and battery.

The Double Jeopardy Clause is not violated when a criminal defendant is also sued in a civil case. For example, O. J. Simpson was acquitted of the murder charges against him in a criminal trial. However, this did not prevent the murder victims' families from suing and recovering from him in a civil trial. This is because the bar against double jeopardy applies only to instances where a defendant is tried more than once for the same *crime*. An action for civil damages is not a criminal trial.

Criminal Defenses

More than 40 million people are victimized each year, with about one-third of that number classified as violent crimes. However, the actual arrest and conviction rate for criminal defendants is less than 20 percent. This is despite the fact that the criminal justice system employs almost two million people in a variety of jobs (police, corrections, courts, etc.) and spends about $100 billion each year.

This section looks at several common defenses against criminal liability. These include entrapment, mistake, and self-defense. In general, they arise in situations where the defendant lacked the knowingness and/or voluntariness to freely comply with the law.

Entrapment

Some crimes (drug dealing, money laundering) are uncovered through undercover police investigations. However, the conduct of these investigations sometimes raises ethical and legal problems. For instance, courts widely agree that criminal law is designed to regulate potentially harmful conduct for the protection of society. It is not meant to guarantee that all individuals possess pure minds and perfect character. Thus, courts will not convict an otherwise law-abiding person who is persuaded to commit a crime by undercover investigators.

In cases where there is evidence that the government induced an individual to break the law, the defendant may raise the defense of **entrapment.** The burden then shifts to the prosecutor to prove beyond a reasonable doubt either that the government did not induce the defendant to commit the crime or, if it did, that he was ready and willing to commit the crime in the absence of government encouragement. If the prosecutor cannot make this showing, the defendant must be found not guilty. According to some courts, a criminal predisposition is shown if the defendant was mentally willing to commit the crime in the absence of the governmental inducement. However, other courts, like in the decision below, require the prosecutor also to demonstrate that the defendant was in the position to commit the crime without governmental assistance.

United States v. Knox

112 F. 3D 802 (5TH CIR. 1997)

FACTS   Reverend David Brace was pastor of the Faith Metro Church in Wichita, Kansas. The church had financial difficulties and was heavily in debt. In an effort to raise money, Brace hired a financial consulting firm that employed Shannon Knox. At the time Knox was seeking financing for Faith Metro, undercover federal agents were running an elaborate sting operation designed to catch money launderers. The undercover agents met with Brace and Knox and told Brace they would be able to loan him $10 million. They then informed Brace that the money came from the sale of cocaine, and that he was being asked to launder it. Brace stated that he was not troubled by the money's source and that he was ready to start. After several test transfers of $100,000 that Brace laundered to designated accounts, the undercover agents gave him three canvas bags purportedly containing $10 million. The bags actually contained newspaper clippings. Brace was arrested as he left the parking lot where the transfer took place. After a jury trial, Brace was convicted of money laundering and sentenced to 175 months imprisonment. He appealed, arguing that he was entrapped.

ISSUE   Should the conviction be reversed because Brace was entrapped?

DECISION   Yes. Where the government has induced an individual to break the law, and the defense of entrapment is at issue, the prosecution must prove beyond a reasonable doubt that the defendant was predisposed to commit the criminal act prior to first being approached by government agents. The government conceded that Brace was induced; therefore, the evidence must prove beyond a reasonable doubt that Brace was predisposed to launder money. In determining predisposition we are to ask what the defendant would have done absent government involvement. This requires that we look not only to the defendant's mental state (his disposition), but also to whether he was able and likely, based on experience, training, and contacts, to actually commit the crime (his position). While the evidence of Brace's mental disposition to launder money is close, we must reverse because the government failed to prove that Brace, absent government involvement, was in a position to launder money. He had never committed a crime worse than speeding before he met the undercover agents. Brace certainly had never laundered money before, and knew little, if anything, about the subject. In fact, he had to send an associate to the library to figure out the mechanics of laundering money. When we ask the question of what Brace would have done if he had never met the undercover agents, we cannot answer "launder money for real drug dealers." Thus, the evidence is insufficient to prove predisposition. Accordingly, we hold that Brace was entrapped and his conviction must be reversed.

http://www.law.vill.edu/Fed-Ct/fedcourt.html
http://www.law.utexas.edu/us5th/us5th.html

Mistake

A defendant's **mistake** as to an issue of fact or law may be an effective defense if it deprives her of the intent required by a criminal statute. Of course, this defense generally would not be available for strict liability crimes or those requiring only general intent. However, for crimes in which a specific intent is needed a reasonable mistake may prevent criminal liability. For instance, suppose Bob and Helen each own a blue backpack and Bob mistakenly takes Helen's backpack under the honest belief that it is his. Bob has a valid defense to a charge of larceny if that state's larceny statute specifically requires that the defendant take property with the knowledge that it belongs to another.

Self-Defense

A potential defense to criminal liability arises when the defendant is coerced into committing an otherwise unlawful act. For instance, if Heather threatens Mark at gunpoint to steal a car, Mark has a valid defense because he did not voluntarily take the vehicle. Similarly, **self-defense** may amount to a legal justification for using force against another individual. States commonly permit a person to use reasonable force against an unlawful attack when such a response is necessary to prevent personal injury.

Statutory law and court decisions seldom allow the defense of self-defense unless the defendant was responding to an immediate threat of harm. Further, the defendant may only use deadly force in response to an imminent threat of deadly force. And some jurisdictions require that a defendant not use deadly force if he could have safely retreated from the threatening encounter.

Most jurisdictions also permit a person to resort to force in order to protect another from immediate harm. Likewise, nondeadly force is permissible when it is necessary to protect one's property from an immediate danger. However, deadly force generally is not permitted when protecting property unless the threat to the property is accompanied by a threat of deadly force.

Sentencing

Persons found guilty of criminal conduct generally are subject to criminal fines, imprisonment and, in extremely serious cases, death. It is common for courts to order both a fine and incarceration. This final section examines four components of criminal sentencing. First, it explores the reasons for criminal sanctions. Second, it looks at the constitutional prohibition against cruel and unusual punishment. Third, it introduces several forms of alternative sentencing. Fourth, it examines the trend toward placing nonpunitive restrictions on dangerous sex offenders.

Purposes of Criminal Punishment

There are four commonly recognized purposes for criminal sanctions: deterrence, rehabilitation, incapacitation, and retribution. Criminal punishment serves a **deterrence** function in two ways. First, *special deterrence* is furthered through punishment because a convicted offender may be less likely to commit further crimes after receiving a criminal sentence. Second, *general deterrence* also may occur because other members of society may be discouraged from committing similar crimes when they learn of the punishment inflicted on convicted criminals.

Criminal punishment also is viewed as a means of **rehabilitation.** Some argue that criminal fines and incarceration may positively reform the values and attitudes of criminal offenders so they may become productive members of society. And even if rehabilitation does not occur, incarceration serves an **incapacitation** function. During the time a criminal is imprisoned, he is prevented from committing further crimes against society. Finally, some people view **retribution** as a fundamental basis for criminal punishment. They believe that criminal sanctions, even if they do not further deterrence and rehabilitation goals, satisfy a societal desire for revenge against serious wrongdoers.

Cruel and Unusual Punishment

The Eighth Amendment's prohibition of **cruel and unusual punishment** limits the types and severity of penalties the government may impose. Punishment may be considered cruel and unusual when a person is subjected to cruel abuse, when a sentence is disproportionate to the offense, or when punishment is arbitrary.

Cruel Abuse

Prison officials must provide humane conditions of confinement. This includes adequate food, clothing, shelter, and medical care. Further, they must take reasonable precautions to guarantee the safety of inmates. Further, courts have held that the infliction of unnecessary pain in the execution of a death sentence constitutes cruel and unusual punishment.

Disproportionate Sentences

The courts follow a three-pronged approach in determining if a particular punishment is unconstitutionally disproportionate to the offense. First, they examine the nature of the offense and the offender. Next, they compare the challenged punishment with sentences given for more serious offenses. Finally, they compare the sentence with the punishment imposed for similar offenses in other jurisdictions.

Arbitrary Punishment

The courts have held the death penalty to constitute cruel and unusual punishment when is it arbitrarily used. Accordingly, a capital sentencing scheme must limit the sentencer's discretion in a way that minimizes the risk of arbitrary application. This requires the government to establish clear and objective standards that channel the sentencer's discretion. The standards must provide specific and detailed guidance that allows the sentencing process to be rationally reviewable.

Alternative Sentencing

Most states have established levels of fines and periods of confinement for various criminal offenses. It is extremely common for jail sentences to be shortened for good conduct. As one would expect, those convicted of a misdemeanor generally face less severe penalties than those who have committed felonies. Many states have implemented alternative sentencing programs for minor offenses.

Pretrial Diversion

In many states, first-time offenders who have committed a misdemeanor may be eligible for **pretrial diversion.** It generally is available if there are no other charges pending against the defendant. After paying certain program costs, the defendant may be eligible to have the charges dismissed if he is not arrested for any other offenses during the following year. If the defendant was arrested for the misdemeanor, only that arrest will show on his record after the successful completion of the pretrial diversion.

Earned Dismissal

Many states also provide **earned dismissal** as an option for first-time misdemeanor offenders and, in some instances, first-time felony offenders. Prosecutors often propose this program to defendants as part of a plea bargain. Under the terms of an earned dismissal, the defendant pleads guilty and then must complete the terms of the court's sentence. When the sentence is completed, the case is dismissed. The defendant's criminal record will then show only the arrest and not the conviction. In cases where the defendant appeared in court by summons rather than arrest, her record will show neither an arrest nor a conviction.

Nonpunitive Restrictions

In recent years, the state and federal legislatures have placed nonpunitive restrictions on criminal offenders in order to protect society from potentially dangerous individuals. These statutory schemes have been enacted in response to public outcries against child molesters and other sexual offenders. For instance, in 1994 Megan Kanka, a seven-year-old child, was abducted, raped, and murdered near her home in New Jersey. The man who confessed to her murder lived in a house across the street from the Kanka family and had twice before been convicted of sex offenses involving young girls. The Kanka family, the local police, and community members were unaware of the murderer's history.

In response to the intense public reaction, New Jersey enacted a *registration* and community *notification* law, known as **Megan's Law.** It required registration by those who had committed designated crimes involving sexual assault and provided for dissemination of this information to local police, schools, and, in certain instances, community members. Congress passed a statute requiring each state to enact similar programs as a condition of receiving certain federal funds. By 1996, 49 states had adopted sex offender registration and 32 had community notification requirements.

The courts have consistently upheld these statutes despite attacks on double jeopardy and *ex post facto* grounds. Specifically, the courts have ruled that these measures are reasonable regulations designed to protect the public welfare. Since they do not constitute punishment, they do not violate the double jeopardy and *ex post facto* clauses. Consider the following case involving a civil confinement procedure for persons determined to be sexually violent predators.

Kansas v. Hendricks

117 S.Ct. 2072 (U.S. Sup. Ct. 1997)

FACTS   The Kansas legislature enacted the *Sexually Violent Predator Act* in 1994 to grapple with the problem of managing repeat sexual offenders. The statute established a civil commitment procedure for the long-term care and treatment of sexually violent predators. It applied to (1) a presently confined person who had been convicted of a sexually violent offense, (2) a person charged with a sexually violent offense who was incompetent to stand trial, (3) a person found not guilty by reason of insanity of a sexually violent offense, and (4) a person found not guilty of a sexually violent offense because of a mental disease or defect. Leroy Hendricks was serving a prison sentence for taking indecent liberties with two 13-year-old boys. He had a long history of repeated child sexual molestation and abuse beginning in 1955. Shortly before his scheduled release from prison, the State filed a petition seeking Hendricks's civil confinement as a sexually violent predator. Under the terms of the Kansas statute, if it was determined that Hendricks was a sexually violent predator, he could be confined to a mental health care facility for control, care, and treatment until it was safe to release him to the public. Hendricks argued that the application of the statute to him violated the double jeopardy and *ex post facto* clauses of the U.S. Constitution.

ISSUE   Is it constitutional for the state to confine Hendricks as a violent sexual predator after his release from prison?

DECISION   Yes. The thrust of Hendricks's argument is that the statute establishes criminal proceedings; hence confinement under it necessarily constitutes punishment. But the state's objective was to create a civil proceeding instead of criminal confinement. As a threshold matter, commitment under the statute does not implicate either of the two primary objectives of criminal punishment: retribution or deterrence. Its purpose is not retributive because it does not affix culpability for prior criminal conduct. Instead, such conduct is used solely for evidentiary purposes, either to demonstrate that a mental abnormality exists or to support a finding of future dangerousness. In addition, the Kansas law does not make a criminal conviction a prerequisite for commitment—persons absolved of criminal responsibility may nonetheless be subject to confinement. An absence of the necessary criminal responsibility suggests that the state is not seeking retribution for a past misdeed. Nor can it be said that the legislature intended the statute to function as a deterrent. Those persons committed under the statute are, by definition, suffering from a mental abnormality or a personality disorder that prevents them from exercising adequate control over their behavior. Such persons are therefore unlikely to be deterred by the threat of confinement. A state may take measures to restrict the freedom of the dangerously mentally ill. This is a legitimate nonpunitive governmental objective. If, at any time, the confined person is adjudged safe to be at large, he is statutorily entitled to immediate release. The conclusion that the statute is nonpunitive removes an essential prerequisite for both the double jeopardy and *ex post facto* claims. There is no double jeopardy because the statute is civil in nature. Therefore, initiation of its commitment proceedings does not constitute a second prosecution. Further, commitment under the statute is not tantamount to punishment. Hendricks' *ex post facto* claim is similarly flawed. The statute does not impose punishment; thus, its application does not raise *ex post facto* concerns. Moreover, the statute clearly does not have a retroactive effect. To the extent that past behavior is taken into account, it is used only to establish that a person currently suffers from a mental abnormality or personality disorder and is likely to pose a future danger to the public.

http://www.law.vill.edu/Fed-Ct/fedcourt.html
http://supct.law.cornell.edu/supct/

The following illustration depicts the sequence of events that take place from the point at which a charge is filed to the sentencing of an offender. (See Figure 6–6.)

Figure 6–6:   Order of Events Once Charge Is Filed

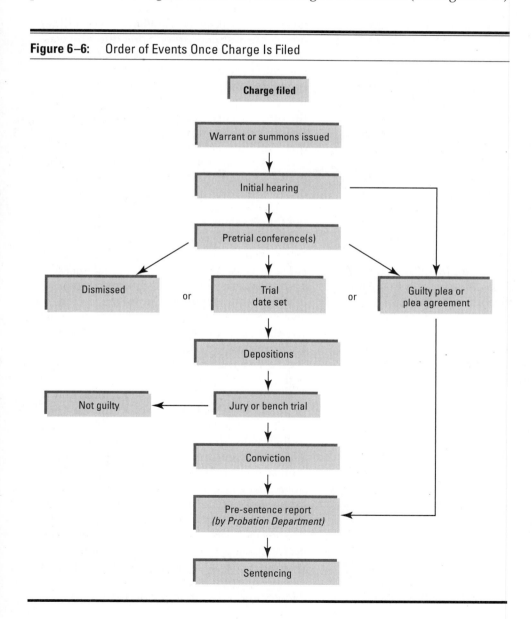

QUESTIONS AND PROBLEM CASES

1. List and describe the three types of statutory violations.
2. Describe the three elements common to all criminal behavior.
3. What is entrapment? What must the government show to avoid a finding of entrapment?
4. What course of action do the courts follow when police officers illegally gather evidence?
5. Police officers obtained a warrant to search Steiney Richards's hotel room for drugs and related paraphernalia. The police requested a warrant that would have given advance authorization of a "no-knock" entry into the hotel room, but the magistrate explicitly deleted those portions of the warrant. When the officers knocked on the hotel room door at 3:40 a.m., Richards cracked the door open with the chain still on the door. Upon seeing a uniformed police officer, Richards quickly slammed the door closed. After waiting two or three seconds, the officers began kicking and ramming the door to gain entry to the locked room. When they finally did break into the room, the officers caught Richards trying to escape through the window. They discovered cash and cocaine hidden in plastic bags above the bathroom ceiling tiles. Richards sought to have the evidence from his hotel room excluded on the ground that the officers had failed to knock and announce their presence prior to forcing entry into the room. Should the evidence be excluded? Explain.
6. Matthew C. Fuller was convicted of three counts of attempted sexual assault. However, the court suspended his sentence on the condition that he enroll in an outpatient Sex Offender Treatment Program and follow all policies of the program. Patients were not accepted into the program if they were in denial or did not honestly disclose evidence of past offenses they had committed. During his treatment Fuller disclosed to his treatment group three past offenses. In accordance with its statutory duty, the treatment center reported those prior offenses to the police.

Based on this evidence, Fuller was charged with three counts of sexual assault. Fuller argued that the evidence derived from his admissions should not be admissible as evidence. Is Fuller correct? Explain.

7. David Rowland was convicted of violating a city ordinance prohibiting *"Loitering for the Purpose of Engaging in Drug-Related Activity."* Police officers testified that, during evening hours, they witnessed Rowland several times on the same street corner. Sometimes he was leaning against a car. On other occasions, he was talking with a group of people. Every time Rowland saw the police, he retreated into a convenience store on the corner. When the officers learned Rowland had a prior drug arrest and conviction, they decided to question him. He fled when the police ordered him to approach their car. When the officers caught and arrested Rowland, they did not find any drugs or drug paraphernalia. However, he was charged with violating the loitering ordinance. The ordinance provided that: *"No person shall loiter in or near any thoroughfare, place open to the public, or near any public or private place in a manner and under circumstances manifesting the purpose to engage in drug-related activity."* Among the circumstances police could consider in determining whether such a purpose was manifest was if an individual was known to police to have been convicted of a drug offense in the past. Is the city ordinance constitutional?

8. The Cook County Jail assigned female guards to monitor male prisoners' movements. This resulted in the females observing men naked in their cells, the shower, and the toilet. Albert Johnson, a prisoner in the jail, brought suit, arguing that a policy allowing female guards to watch nude male prisoners amounted to cruel and unusual punishment. Cross-sex surveillance has been defended by prisons as necessary to avoid discrimination on the basis of sex when hiring prison guards. It also is more expensive for a prison to have a group of guards dedicated to shower and toilet monitoring than to have

guards all of whom can serve each role in the prison. Does the policy of cross-sexual monitoring impose cruel and unusual punishment on the prison population?

9. In the early morning hours, police officers received a complaint of loud noise emanating from the residence of Donald P. Rohrig. As the officers approached within a block of Rohrig's home in their squad car, they began to hear loud music. Shortly after the police arrived on the scene at 1:39 a.m., between four and eight pajama-clad neighbors emerged from their homes to complain about the noise. The officers banged repeatedly on the front door of the Rohrig's home, but received no response. They also walked around the outside of the two-story residence, all the while tapping to no avail on its first-floor windows. The back door was open, with only an unlocked screen door preventing access into the house. After knocking and yelling to announce their presence, the police entered the residence through the back door. Because there was a light on in the basement, the officers went there in the hope of finding an occupant who could turn the music down. Upon reaching the basement, they discovered wall-to-wall marijuana plants. Rohrig was eventually found in an upstairs bedroom. He filed a motion to have the evidence of the marijuana excluded from evidence because of the police officers' warrantless entry into his home. Should Rohrig's motion be granted? Explain.

10. Gerry La-Keith Brown called the police, his neighbor, and his sister-in-law with news that he had just found his wife dead in the garage. He asked the police dispatcher to send a squad car and an ambulance to the crime scene, which also was his home. He also volunteered that someone had robbed his wife because her purse was missing. Brown appeared very upset, and an officer escorted him to a patrol unit to calm down and stay warm until the investigators could speak with him. A detective unsuccessfully searched outside the residence for the missing purse. After noticing that the back door of the house leading to the garage was open, he went into the house. He discovered no evidence of the home being ransacked and noted blood splatters on the wall in a bedroom. The detective also discovered a cash register receipt from restaurant, which later would be used to disprove Browns assertion that he had remained home all evening. Brown argued that the evidence discovered by the detective was inadmissible in court because the police entered the home without a search warrant. Was the detective's warrantless search lawful? Explain.

CIVIL WRONGS

T y Slagle, who was 16 years old, worked the 11:00 p.m. to 7:00 a.m. shift at a White Castle restaurant. Because Ty's parents were concerned about his safety, a White Castle supervisor assured them he would not be allowed to leave the restaurant during the night shift. However, after becoming ill several hours into a shift, he was permitted to walk home at 3:15 a.m. Several blocks from the restaurant, Ty was robbed and assaulted by unknown assailants.

Slagle v. White Castle Systems, 607 N.E.2d 45 (Ohio App. 10 Dist. 1992).

Can Ty recover tort damages from White Castle?
Is Ty entitled to workers' compensation benefits?
How does tort law differ from workers' compensation?

Introduction

One basic function of our legal system is to establish and enforce the standards of conduct valued by society. **Tort** law actively promotes this goal by requiring persons who fail to adhere to accepted norms to pay for any resulting harm they cause to others. (A *tort* is defined as a "private wrong against persons or their property.") Today, because of the growing complexity of society and the increasing interaction among people, tort law is growing in importance. Accordingly, it is essential that each of us understands our rights and obligations under the tort law system.

Chapter Overview

This chapter introduces the three fundamental types of torts. It begins with a brief review of intentional torts, behavior that intentionally injures people or property. The focus then shifts to an examination of negligence law, a fault-based system that attaches liability for unintentional harms that arise when people fail to behave in a reasonable manner. Next is a look at strict liability, a tort theory that assesses liability on persons who engage in ultrahazardous activities. The chapter closes with a discussion of workers' compensation, a special type of strict liability governing work-related injuries.

Intentional Torts

An **intentional tort** occurs when a person consciously chooses to harm another. The victim of the intentional behavior is likely to receive compensatory damages for the direct and immediate harms she suffers. These include physical injuries, medical expenses, and lost wages. Courts may award punitive damages when the defendant's actions are especially outrageous.

Conduct that constitutes an intentional tort may also be a crime if it violates a statute. When this occurs, the defendant may face two trials—one criminal and one civil. For instance, despite O. J. Simpson's acquittal on murder charges relating to the deaths of Ron Goldman and Nicole Brown Simpson, he later was sued in intentional tort for their deaths. While these civil suits carry no threat of imprisonment, they require that the defendant compensate the victims' families for their losses.

This section briefly examines three classes of intentional torts: interference with personal interests, interference with property interests, and interference with business interests. Each of these types of tortious conduct has at least one element in common—the defendant's behavior must have been *intentional*.

Interference with Personal Interests

This type of intentional tort occurs when the defendant wrongfully interferes with the personal privacy, reputation, or physical or emotional welfare of the plaintiff. Because courts highly value these personal rights, a winning plaintiff is likely to recover punitive, as well as compensatory, damages.

http://
www.westbuslaw. com/topic_torts.html provides numerous briefed torts cases.

http://
www.ca.gov/s/govt/ govcode.html is an example of a state site, from which you can choose Government and Regulations, and begin a search for the topics discussed in this chapter.

Assault

When a person intentionally places another in apprehension of immediate harm, she has committed the intentional tort of **assault.** It is not necessary for any physical contact to have occurred. Thus, if Mary raises a stick and threatens to strike Paul, she has committed an assault. There is no assault, however, if Mary threatens to hit Paul sometime in the future. The threat must be of immediate harm.

Battery

The intentional touching of another in a harmful or offensive way without consent is **battery.** This intentional tort does not require the defendant to personally touch the plaintiff. Thus, if Mary strikes Paul with her stick, she has committed a battery. If Paul saw Mary swinging the stick before it struck him, Mary has committed assault and battery. In recent years, courts in several states have ruled that battery can apply to smoke from cigarettes, cigars, or pipes. Accordingly, they have held that exposing someone to secondhand smoke can constitute a battery.

Defamation

People who intentionally publish false statements that injure another's reputation may be liable for **defamation.** When the defamation is written, it is called *libel.* When it is spoken, it is called *slander.* Publication occurs when the defendant communicates the false statements to someone other than the plaintiff.

If the published statements are true, no matter how damaging, the defendant cannot be liable for defamation. Truth is a complete defense to a defamation claim. Further, in order to encourage people to speak freely, many individuals are given a broad *privilege* (defense) against defamation liability. Thus, the media cannot be held liable for defaming public figures (famous people) unless they knew their statements were false or they acted with reckless disregard for the truth.

False Imprisonment

The intentional tort of **false imprisonment** occurs when the defendant intentionally confines a person for an unreasonable period of time without consent. Generally, the plaintiff is confined if she cannot escape without the risk of harm or an affront to her dignity. False-imprisonment cases commonly arise when store owners stop suspected shoplifters. Most states give store owners a limited privilege to stop suspected shoplifters for a reasonable period of time to determine their identity or to hold them until the police arrive.

Intentional Infliction of Emotional Distress

The tort of **intentional infliction of emotional distress** occurs when the defendant engages in extreme and outrageous conduct that intentionally or recklessly causes the plaintiff to suffer severe emotional distress. The requirement of outrageousness is not an easy one to meet. It is aimed at limiting frivolous suits and avoiding litigation in situations where only rude behavior and hurt feelings are involved. Only conduct that offends against generally accepted standards of decency and morality qualify.

Courts traditionally would not recognize a claim for emotional injuries when physical injuries did not occur. However, more and more states allow plaintiffs to recover for purely emotional injuries, especially in cases where the defendant's conduct is particularly outrageous. Often the courts require that emotional distress, unaccompanied by physical harm, is compensable only when the defendant had the specific purpose of inflicting the emotional distress or knew that his conduct was likely to cause the emotional distress.

Drejza v. Vaccaro
650 A.2D 1308 (D.C. APP. 1994)

FACTS   Donna Drejza was assaulted, raped, and sodomized in her apartment by Jeffrey Smith, a former boyfriend with whom she had terminated a romantic relationship a few months earlier, but with whom she had remained friendly. She suffered bruises, swellings, and broken blood vessels around her eyes. Shortly after Smith left her apartment, Ms. Drejza called 911 to report the rape. She was taken to police headquarters where her case was assigned to Detective Michael Vaccaro, a member of the police department's Sex Offense Branch. Detective Vaccaro showed little interest in her story or in taking a detailed statement from her. Instead, he suggested that she simply forget about the incident. Throughout her interview, he acted in an obnoxious manner, snickered at her account, and generally treated her with derision and scorn, apparently because her assailant was someone she knew and because she had had voluntary sexual relations with him in the past. Although she had taken her torn underwear to police headquarters with her as she had been instructed to do, Detective Vaccaro threw them back at her and told her to "take your little panties home with you." He also joked and snickered at a reference in a medical report to her "marital hymen," remarking that this "means you are not a virgin." When Ms. Drejza later sued Detective Vaccaro for intentional infliction of emotional distress, the trial court held that, although Detective Vaccaro's conduct was obnoxious and boorish, it was insufficiently extreme to entitle her to any relief.

ISSUE   Has Ms. Drejza stated a claim upon which she can recover for intentional infliction of emotional distress?

DECISION   Yes. The dispositive issue in this case is whether Detective Vaccaro's conduct was sufficiently extreme or outrageous. The outrageous and extreme nature of conduct should not be considered in a sterile setting, detached from the milieu in which it took place. There were special circumstances in this case which profoundly affect the outrageousness calculus. We refer to Ms. Drejza's emotional state immediately following the dehumanizing sexual assault on her, to Detective Vaccaro's knowledge of her susceptibility and to the position of authority and trust which he occupied during his interaction with her. Detective Vaccaro was dealing with a woman who was in an extraordinarily vulnerable condition. Acts which are not generally considered outrageous may become so when the actor knows the other person is peculiarly susceptible to emotional distress. Further, Detective Vaccaro was a police detective and a member of the Sex Offense Branch. He was an official she could reasonably suppose could be trusted to assist her and investigate her complaint in a professional and helpful manner. Detective Vaccaro abused the authority of his office to ridicule, bully, humiliate, and insult her. Such alleged conduct, directed at a woman whose world has just been turned upside down as a result of a shattering and dehumanizing experience, was not merely obnoxious and insensitive. It was extreme and outrageous.

Invasion of Privacy

In recent years, courts have begun to recognize the intentional tort of **invasion of privacy.** It stems from people's right to some degree of solitude or escape from public scrutiny. Although publishing embarrassing facts (even if they are true) or pictures of people may create tort liability, publication of newsworthy items or matters of public record (police reports) do not support a claim of invasion of privacy. For instance, a Georgia newspaper was not liable for invasion of privacy when it published the name of a rape victim despite the existence of a statute prohibiting the media from reporting the names of sexual assault victims. The court ruled that because the woman shot and killed her attacker, she became the object of legitimate public interest. However, obscene telephone calls, illegal searches, and telephone harassment by bill collectors have resulted in tort recoveries.

Interference with Property Interests

Property owners have two fundamental property rights. First, they have a right of *quiet enjoyment*—to maintain their property free from interference by others. Second, they have a right to actively use or develop their property. The torts of interference with property rights often arise when one person's developmental rights conflict with another's right of quiet enjoyment. Three particular actions are worth noting: nuisance, trespass, and conversion.

Nuisance

Generally, a **nuisance** occurs when someone interferes with another's rights to use and quietly enjoy property, rather than causing substantial physical damage to the property itself. Loud parties, barking dogs, and obnoxious smells all are classic examples of actions that might constitute a nuisance. For a nuisance to occur, it is not necessary for there to be an actual physical invasion of the property.

Trespass

The intentional tort of **trespass** comes in two varieties. First, *trespass to land* arises when the defendant intentionally and unlawfully enters land possessed by another. It may also occur when the defendant causes some substance (smoke or other pollutants) to enter the land and create substantial damage to the property itself. Second, *trespass to personal property* entails intentional interference with the personal property of another. Thus, if Michael damages Trisha's laptop computer or hides it from her for an unreasonable period of time, he has committed a trespass to personal property.

Conversion

When someone deprives another of her personal property for an unreasonable period of time, he may be liable for the intentional tort of **conversion.** Trespass and conversion are similar. The major difference is that the interference in a conversion generally is much greater and, as a result, more likely to result in the defendant having to pay damages equal to the full value of the property.

Interference with Business Interests

Potential tort liability arises when people intentionally interfere with the economic rights of another. Designed to protect business interests, these *competitive torts* come in a variety of forms. Three such torts are discussed here:

1. injurious falsehood,
2. interference with contractual relations, and
3. interference with economic expectations.

Injurious Falsehood

The tort of **injurious falsehood,** also known as *disparagement,* is similar to defamation. However, instead of requiring the publication of false statements about a person, it involves making false statements about a business product or service. Liability normally does not result unless the defendant made the false statements knowingly or with reckless disregard for the truth. Further, the plaintiff is unlikely to recover damages unless he can prove that he lost business as a result of the false statements.

Interference with Contractual Relations

A person who intentionally induces someone to breach a contract with another may be sued for **interference with contractual relations.** In order to recover, the plaintiff must establish that she had an enforceable contract and, as a result of the defendant's *improper* behavior, the agreement was repudiated. For example, Norm is contractually obligated to sell widgets to Sharon. If Francis, one of Sharon's competitors, bribes Norm and convinces him to boycott Sharon, Francis has committed an intentional tort. Suppose instead that Francis, unaware of the contract between Sharon and Norm, contracts with Norm to deal exclusively with her. In this case, Francis did not have an improper purpose and, therefore, has not committed a tort.

Interference with Economic Expectations

An intentional tort also may arise in cases where the defendant improperly attempts to discourage people from contracting with someone. This is known as **intentional interference with economic expectations.** However, when the defendant and the plaintiff are competitors, courts are unlikely to assess tort liability if the defendant merely lured potential customers away by offering a better product, service, or price.

Negligence

The law of **negligence** is designed to ensure that each member of society behaves in a reasonable manner when interacting with others. Despite the fact that negligent behavior is unintentional (accidental), legal liability attaches when the defendant's behavior falls below the standards imposed by society. There are four fundamental steps a plaintiff must prove before she can recover in negligence:

1. the defendant owed her a duty,
2. the duty was breached,

3. the breach was both the actual and proximate cause of her injuries, and
4. the plaintiff suffered compensable injuries.

Even when negligence has been established, the defendant might avoid liability by proving the existence of any one of several defenses. They are assumption of risk, contributory negligence, and comparative negligence. First we will examine the basic elements of a negligence case. (See Figure 7–1.)

Duty

Each member of society is expected to behave in a manner that does not subject others to an unreasonable risk of harm. However, negligence law does not make each individual guarantee the welfare of all others. Instead, negligence liability is possible only when a defendant owes a **duty** to another. There is no duty unless there exists a reasonable expectation that the defendant will care for the welfare of the plaintiff. There are three basic ways this expectation arises: undertakings, relationships, and statutes.

Duties Created by Undertakings

A duty can also arise when someone engages in an *undertaking* that results in interaction with another person. Suppose Jane is walking down the street and notices a stranger, Daniel, lying in an alley. From the way Daniel is lying, it appears quite likely that he is in need of immediate medical attention. If Jane ignores the situation and Daniel dies, she is unlikely to have any negligence liability because

Figure 7–1:   The Plaintiff's Negligence Case

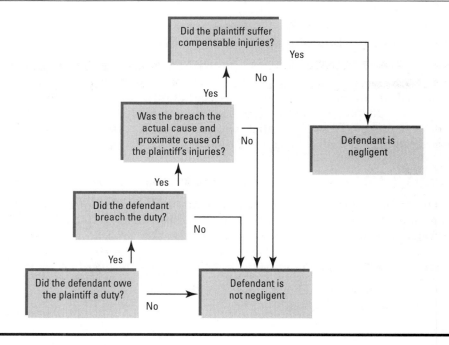

she owes him no legal duty. However, if she stops and renders assistance, a duty to act with care will arise.

In order to encourage people to lend assistance to those in need, most states have enacted *Good Samaritan* statutes. These laws provide various forms of immunity from negligence liability for people who voluntarily help others. For example, in Pennsylvania any person who renders emergency care or rescue will not be liable, except for intentional harms or gross negligence, if the rescuer is certified to provide first aid or advanced lifesaving.

Duties Created by Relationships

Duties often arise when there is a special *relationship* between the defendant and the plaintiff. For instance, when a patient visits the doctor, he places his health and well-being under the care of the doctor. Thus, negligence law imposes a duty on the doctor to behave in a responsible manner toward the patient. Similarly, in a wide range of contractual relationships, duties are imposed on people to care for others. Thus, an accountant must look out for the interests of his clients, and teachers owe duties to their students.

In the case that opened this chapter, Ty was unable to recover in negligence from White Castle because the restaurant did not have a duty to protect him from the criminal conduct of his assailants. The court ruled that an employer generally does not have a duty to protect its employees from injuries that occur while traveling to and from work. Further, despite Ty's youth, the court did not believe the restaurant assumed custody of him.

A special relationship sufficient to create a duty also exists between landowners and people who enter the land. Historically, many courts examined the nature of this relationship not only to create a duty but also to define the extent of the duty. *Business invitees*—people who visited the land in connection with a business interest of the property owner—were owed the greatest standard of care. *Licensees*—people who entered the land for their own purposes but with the consent of the landowner—were owed a lesser level of care. *Trespassers*—people who were on the property without the consent of the landowner—were owed the lowest standard of care. Over time the courts have blurred these formalistic distinctions and today are more likely to determine the level of care based on how much the landowner should have expected the presence of the plaintiff on the property.

Smithkline Beecham Corporation v. Doe

903 S.W.2d 347 (Sup. Ct. Tex. 1995)

FACTS Jane Doe, a 24-year-old graduate student studying for a master's degree in business administration, was offered employment by Quaker Oats as a marketing assistant. One of the conditions of Quaker's written offer was Doe's satisfactory completion of a drug-screening examination. Quaker contracted with SmithKline Beecham Clinical Laboratories to perform its drug testing. At a health center where a urine specimen was taken, Doe completed a medical history form on which she was to list all medications recently used. The only item Doe listed on the form was birth control pills, for which she had a prescription. She was not asked what foods she had

continued

eaten. After analyzing the urine sample, SmithKline reported to Quaker that it had detected the presence of opiates in Doe's urine. Doe then learned through her own research that eating poppy seeds can cause a drug test to reveal the existence of opiates. She informed Quaker of this and said that in the days before the test she had eaten several poppy seed muffins, which must have caused her positive test result. Quaker nevertheless withdrew Doe's offer of employment. Doe sued SmithKline for negligence for failing to warn her or Quaker how eating poppy seeds might affect a person's drug test.

ISSUE   Did SmithKline have a duty to warn Doe or Quaker about the effects of eating poppy seeds on drug test results?

DECISION   No. There is no dispute that a person's ingestion of poppy seeds in sufficient quantities will result in the presence of morphine and codeine in her urine. SmithKline was aware of this and knew that its test could not distinguish between poppy seed ingestion and drug use. It did not convey this information to Quaker or Doe. However, SmithKline merely performed a urinalysis and reported the presence of certain drugs or their metabolites. It neither created nor controlled the use to which its test results would be put. It might have given Quaker advice that Quaker would have followed, but it was under no obligation to Doe to do so. While SmithKline could and did foresee that a person will have a positive drug test due to having eaten poppy seeds, foreseeability alone is not sufficient to create a duty. The duty Doe seeks cannot be readily defined. It would require SmithKline to inform each test subject not only of the possible effect of poppy seeds but of all possible causes of positive results other than using drugs. Moreover, the duty Doe seeks would charge SmithKline with responsibility that belongs to its clients. SmithKline should be allowed to perform only the service it chose to offer and Quaker chose to procure—testing for the presence of drugs in the body.

http://
www.law.cornell.edu/ states/index.html provides access to some states' statutes. From here, choose a state, for example, New York. Next select "Statutes," and then choose "Civil Practice Law and Rules." Once at this site, you can select any of the specific topics discussed, such as "Article 2, Section 208, Infancy, Insanity" or "Article 16, Section 1600, Definitions." Another example is South Dakota, where you can choose "Government, Legislative," and finally "South Dakota Codified Laws." Some states do not provide access to their statutes.

Duties Created by Statutes

Duties also can be created by *statutes*. When a statute imposes a duty on a person for the protection of others, it is considered a *public safety statute*. Violation of a public safety statute creates a special brand of negligence, known as **negligence per se.** However, not every plaintiff benefits from negligence per se. First, the plaintiff must be a *member of the class* of people protected by the public safety statute. Second, the statute must have been designed to prevent the *type of harm* actually suffered by the victim.

Suppose Larry, a 23-year-old college student, held a party at which he served alcoholic beverages. Among those drinking at the party was Wyatt, a 17-year-old. By serving alcohol to Wyatt, Larry has violated a statute prohibiting the furnishing of alcoholic beverages to anyone under the age of 21. If Wyatt later drives home drunk and has a traffic accident, Wyatt and anyone he injures may have a negligence per se claim against Larry. This statute probably was designed to protect minors and third persons injured by intoxicated minors from the inability of minors to handle the consumption of alcohol responsibly. The fact that Larry might have reasonably believed Wyatt would drink responsibly is irrelevant since Larry's exercise of reasonable care is not a factor in negligence per se analysis.

Most states impose negligence per se liability on adults who provide alcohol to minors for the subsequent injuries suffered by the minor or any third persons.

Tort liability rarely is found in cases where private social hosts serve alcohol to intoxicated adults who then injure themselves or others. And most states have rejected the idea of holding minors liable in tort when they provide alcohol to other minors. Licensed alcohol vendors (liquor stores and taverns) that sell alcohol to intoxicated adults generally are liable to third persons injured by the intoxicated customer, but not to the customer himself.

Breach

The mere existence of a duty does not automatically make the defendant legally responsible for any injuries suffered by the plaintiff. The defendant will not be liable unless she has breached the duty she owed the plaintiff. A **breach** occurs when the defendant behaves in an unreasonable manner.

The Breach Equation

The determination of whether a breach has occurred depends on the surrounding circumstances. A doctor performing surgery in a fully equipped operating room is held to a higher standard of care than is a farmer who finds an accident victim bleeding to death in his field. A balancing process is utilized to determine if a defendant's action or inaction is unreasonable. On one side of the equation the courts consider the likelihood of harm, coupled with the potential for catastrophic results. These factors are balanced against the costs of protecting against harm. When the likelihood of harm is high and the costs of prevention are low, a breach normally is found if the defendant took no precautions. However, when the likelihood of harm is low and the costs of prevention are high, few safeguards are demanded.

Miller v. National Association of Realtors

648 N.E.2d 98 (App. 1 Dist. Ill. 1994)

FACTS Theodore Miller worked as a delivery man for a beer distributor. While making a regular delivery of beer kegs to the Billy Goat Inn, a tavern located in Chicago, Miller slipped on a piece of cardboard and seriously injured himself. Miller made deliveries to the tavern about twice a week, which required him to descend the loading ramp behind a two-wheeled hand truck loaded with two 160-pound barrels of beer. In order to avoid losing control of the kegs, Miller had to tip the hand truck back toward himself while descending the ramp. An open dumpster was kept at the top of the ramp for at least three months. The dumpster, which remained open continuously, faced the ramp and was filled with various types of debris. Miller testified that people working in the building used the dumpster and there was always some type of debris or dirt present on the ramp. The ramp was the only means of entry or exit for delivery men. Miller stated that he knew of other delivery men who had complained of the loading ramp area's condition prior to the date of his injury. On that day, the lighting was dim and Miller did not observe the condition of the ramp. The trial court dismissed Miller's negligence suit because he failed to prove the tavern owner knew of the dangerous condition.

ISSUE Could a jury reasonably believe the tavern owner breached a duty to Miller?

continued

DECISION   Yes. It is undisputed that Miller was a business invitee on the defendant's property at the time he was injured. Where a business invitee is injured by slipping on a foreign substance on the premises, a breach may be shown if the substance was placed there by the negligence of the proprietor or his servants. If the substance was on the premises through the acts of third persons or there is no showing of how it got there, a breach may be shown if it appears the proprietor or his servant actually knew of its presence, or if the substance was there a sufficient length of time so that it reasonably should have been discovered. A jury could reasonably determine that a breach has occurred here. The dim lighting, perpetual dirt and debris, and the complaints of other delivery men suggest the tavern owner may have failed to exercise due care. Further, a jury could reasonably infer that the cardboard was left on the ramp by one of the tavern's employees.

Res Ipsa Loquitur

Circumstances sometimes prevent a plaintiff from proving a defendant breached a duty. For example, when a passenger plane crashes, it often is difficult to determine precisely why the accident occurred. Under traditional negligence analysis, if the injured passengers cannot prove a breach occurred because the plane was serviced or operated in an unreasonable manner, they would lose any negligence suit. To avoid the harshness of this result, the doctrine of **res ipsa loquitur** ("the thing speaks for itself") was created. The plaintiff must prove two things before a court will apply res ipsa loquitur: (1) the defendant was in exclusive control of the instrumentality of harm; and (2) the harm that resulted normally would not occur in the absence of negligence by the defendant. When this occurs, most courts infer that the defendant was negligent. This places a substantial burden on the defendant to investigate the accident and avoid liability by proving that it was not negligent.

Negligent Product Liability

Product sellers and manufacturers often are sued in negligence for placing harmful products on the market. There are four fundamental ways in which sellers and manufacturers are accused of breaching their duty to purchasers and users. First, *improper manufacture* claims arise when products are improperly assembled or packaged. Second, even when products are assembled according to the manufacturer's blueprints, plaintiffs may claim that there are *design defects.* These lawsuits allege that the product could have been engineered in a safer manner. Third, manufacturers and sellers who prepare, install, or repair goods have a duty to inspect goods to detect dangerous defects. Failure to do so may give rise to liability under *improper inspection.* Fourth, negligence suits may be based on a *failure to warn.* These claims are premised on the idea that manufacturers and sellers have a duty to warn the public about products that pose a foreseeable risk of harm.

Causation

The law of negligence, unlike criminal law, does not impose a sanction on people whenever they breach a duty. In negligence the obligation to compensate occurs only when the duty that has been breached causes injury to a person or property.

This **causation** requirement has two elements both of which must be met before negligence liability arises: actual causation and proximate causation.

Actual Causation

When a person breaches a duty, he generally must compensate others for any damages they suffered as a result of his unreasonable behavior. He is not liable for things that would have happened even if he had performed his duty in a reasonable manner. Thus, the **actual causation** requirement is met when it can be shown that the plaintiff's injuries would not have occurred if the defendant had not breached his duty.

In many cases, the defendant's unreasonable conduct was not the only cause of the plaintiff's injuries. For example, after Catherine strikes a bicyclist with her car, he is run over by a speeding truck approaching from the opposite direction. Assuming both Catherine and the truck driver were negligent, the bicyclist probably could recover from either since each was a *substantial factor* in his injuries.

Suppose instead that the bicyclist saw Catherine approaching at a high rate of speed and swerved into the path of the speeding truck to avoid being struck by Catherine's car. Catherine might try to avoid negligence liability by arguing the truck was an *intervening* (superseding) *cause* that relieves her of liability. However, a court is unlikely to accept this argument since it is reasonable to expect speeding vehicles to be on the highway.

General Motors v. Saenz

873 S.W.2D 353 (Sup. Ct. Tex. 1993)

FACTS   Ricardo Saenz was driving his employer's water tank truck when a rear tire blew out, causing the vehicle to overturn and kill Saenz. The truck was designed and built by General Motors (GM) so it could be modified for a wide variety of uses. The 2,000 gallon water tank was added to the truck after GM sold it. However, when the water tank was full, the truck greatly exceeded the maximum safe weight for the entire vehicle. This safe weight was imprinted on a metal plate which GM had attached to the doorjamb on the driver's side at eye level. The plate stated that overloading could void the warranty and made reference to the owner's manual for additional information. The manual warned that overloading could create serious potential safety hazards. Neither Saenz's employer nor the company that installed the water tank ever checked the doorplate or the owner's manual to ascertain the vehicle's maximum safe weight. Saenz's beneficiaries claimed the accident occurred because the truck was overloaded and sued GM for failing to provide adequate warnings against overloading. The trial court found the warnings inadequate because they were not clear and did not list rolling the truck as one of the risks of overloading. GM argued its failure to give adequate warnings did not actually cause Saenz's injuries because no attention was paid to the warnings it did give.

ISSUE   Were General Motors' inadequate warnings the actual cause of Saenz's injuries?

DECISION   No. GM does not dispute that it had a duty to warn all users of the truck against overloading. However, to recover Saenz's beneficiaries must show that but

continued

for GM's failure to provide clear and more detailed warnings this accident would not have occurred. There is no reason to think that a clearer instruction would have been heeded. No one was misled by GM's warnings because no one read them. GM's failure to give a different warning could not have actually caused the accident when no one paid any attention to the warnings it did give. Thus, there is no evidence that the inadequacies in GM's warning caused the accident. Therefore, the plaintiffs are not entitled to compensation.

Proximate Causation

Courts frequently are unwilling to make defendants liable for all of the damages actually caused by their negligence. In part, this is because such unlimited liability could be catastrophic. However, it also stems from the problem we have in tracing actual causation over a long period of time or distance. An oil spill in Alaska may destroy fishing grounds and deprive fishermen in the region of jobs for several years. This may cause some of them to rob banks. If it were not for the oil spill, those crimes might not have occurred. Thus, the oil company is an actual cause of the robberies. However, courts will not take negligence liability this far. **Proximate causation** is the device courts use to confine negligence liability to manageable proportions. There is much confusion over what actually constitutes a proximate cause. However, many courts suggest that defendants are liable only for the outcomes they should have reasonably foreseen at the time the duty was breached.

Injury

After proving duty, breach, and causation, a plaintiff still must convince a court she suffered compensable injuries. For example, when Alice stops her car at a stoplight, she is struck by a vehicle that has been tailgating her. Even though the trailing driver breached a duty to her, unless Alice can show actual damage to her car (or to herself), she will not be compensated.

Problems often arise when the victim claims injuries of an emotional nature. Courts hesitate to compensate for emotional injuries, in part, out of concern that they may not be genuine. Recovery is even more difficult when it is sought by third persons claiming emotional injury after witnessing negligently caused harm to another.

Heiner v. Moretuzzo

652 N.E.2d 664 (Sup. Ct. Ohio 1995)

FACTS   Patricia Heiner was interested in conceiving a child through artificial insemination. Dr. Richard Moretuzzo, a gynecologist, requested that she undergo blood tests for rubella, hepatitis, and the human immunodeficiency (HIV) virus. After her preliminary blood test indicated Heiner was HIV positive, Dr. Moretuzzo administered a second test. The doctor informed Heiner the second test also was HIV positive and referred her to an infectious disease specialist. Two subsequent tests administered

by the specialist confirmed that, in fact, Heiner was HIV negative. She sued Dr. Moretuzzo for negligent infliction of emotional distress.

ISSUE   Should Heiner be permitted to recover for her emotional injuries?

DECISION   No. The claimed negligent diagnosis never placed Heiner or any other
person in real physical peril, since she was, in fact, HIV negative. Thus, this case differs significantly from those instances in which courts recognized a right to recover
for negligent infliction of emotional distress. We do not in any way dispute the legitimacy of Heiner's claims that she suffered serious emotional injuries when diagnosed
HIV positive. We have no doubt that the emotional damages suffered by Heiner were
real and debilitating. However, the facts of this case remind us that not every wrong
is deserving of a legal remedy. Heiner was not HIV positive and never faced an actual
physical peril as a result of her doctor's alleged negligence. While we remain vigilant
in our efforts to ensure an individual's right to emotional tranquility, we decline to
expand the law to permit recovery on the facts of this case.

http://www.courts.net/

The Negligence Defenses

After the plaintiff establishes the existence of the duty, breach, causation, and
injury requirements, he will recover unless the defendant presents a valid defense.
Negligence law recognizes three defenses: assumption of risk, contributory negligence, and comparative negligence.

Assumption of Risk

If the plaintiff *knowingly* and *voluntarily* exposes herself to a risk of harm, she cannot later recover in negligence for the injuries she suffered. Suppose Bill borrows
Michael's stepladder, despite knowing that several of the wooden rungs are
cracked. If Bill breaks an ankle when a rung collapses, he will lose any negligence
lawsuit against Michael because of his **assumption of risk.**

Smokers have historically lost lawsuits against cigarette manufacturers, in
part, because courts believe that smokers knowingly assume the risk of ill health
when they choose to smoke. However, recent revelations that tobacco companies
manipulated nicotine to addict smokers may override the assumption of risk
defense. Further, people who suffer from the effects of secondhand smoke have
not assumed the risk.

Many contracts contain *exculpatory clauses* that attempt to create an assumption of risk defense. For instance, a martial arts school may refuse to offer karate
lessons unless students first sign an agreement promising to waive their right to
sue for any injuries they suffer as a result of negligent instruction. Courts generally uphold these "waiver of claims" provisions when they are entered into knowingly and voluntarily. However, exculpatory clauses that attempt to relieve a
defendant from liability for intentional or reckless behavior are not enforceable.

Contributory Negligence

Traditionally, a plaintiff was denied any negligence recovery if her own negligence was a substantial contributing factor in producing her injury. Thus, if Robert

sped through a red light and struck Hannah with his car, Hannah could not recover if she had negligently darted into the street outside of the crosswalk. Her recovery would be barred under the doctrine of **contributory negligence.**

Many courts, unhappy with the harsh results that often arose when a plaintiff was only slightly contributorily negligent, applied the *last clear chance* doctrine to moderate its effect. Under last clear chance, Hannah might still recover from Robert if she can convince the court that he was aware of her negligent conduct and could have slowed his vehicle. Basically, she would be arguing that Robert should be liable because he had the last opportunity to avoid the accident.

Comparative Negligence

Most states have replaced the contributory negligence doctrine with a system of **comparative negligence.** Under comparative negligence, the court determines the degree of fault attributable to each party and then apportions damages based on their relative responsibilities. Thus, a court might rule that Robert was 75 percent responsible and Hannah 25 percent responsible for their accident. Under these circumstances, Robert would be required to pay for 75 percent of the cost incurred by Hannah's injuries.

The precise details of the comparative fault systems vary from state to state. For instance, in some states a plaintiff is entitled to no recovery when she is more at fault than the defendant. Other states don't make such a distinction. Some states have even replaced the assumption of risk defense with comparative negligence.

Strict Liability

Negligence liability is grounded in the idea that because the defendant was at fault, she should be responsible for compensating the victim for his loss. Tort liability may also arise in cases where the defendant was without fault because she exercised the utmost care. This notion of liability without fault is known as **strict liability.** It arises in instances where the defendant:

1. engages in abnormally dangerous activities, or
2. manufactures defective and unreasonably dangerous products.

Abnormally Dangerous Activities

People who engage in *abnormally dangerous* activities are strictly liable for the injuries they actually cause regardless of how much care they exercise. Strict liability flows from the idea that the defendant voluntarily undertook the ultrahazardous activity and, accordingly, should have insured against potential injuries to others.

Courts decide if an activity is abnormally dangerous after balancing its dangerousness against its social utility. There are six specific factors that courts generally consider:

1. a high likelihood of harm;
2. the likelihood that resulting harm will be great;
3. the inability to eliminate the risk by the exercise of reasonable care;
4. the extent to which the activity is not a matter of common usage;

5. the inappropriateness of the activity to the place where it is carried on; and
6. the extent to which the value to the community outweighs the activity's dangerous attributes.

After employing this balancing test, numerous activities have been classified as abnormally dangerous and, therefore, subject to strict liability. They include blasting, fireworks displays, crop dusting, and stunt flying. People who keep wild animals also have been held strictly liable for the damages the animals cause.

Strict Product Liability

Strict liability also attaches to people who sell *defective and unreasonably dangerous products*. A product is considered defective when it does not meet the reasonable expectations of the average consumer. It is unreasonably dangerous if it is more hazardous than a reasonable consumer would expect it to be. Generally, strict product liability only applies to persons in the business of selling the harmful product. Thus, it could be used against the manufacturer of a defective chain saw but not against a person who resold it at a garage sale.

Moss v. Wolohan Lumber Company

1995 U.S. Dist. LEXIS 7857 (N.D. Ill. 1995)

FACTS While engaging in a BB gun war, 16-year-old Tom Beilke intentionally shot 14-year-old Jason Moss. The BB struck Moss's safety goggles and rendered him permanently blind in his left eye. Both Beilke and Moss admitted they knew the dangers and risks associated with shooting each other with BB guns. Moss filed a strict product liability suit against the Coleman Company, the manufacturer of the BB gun fired by Beilke. The lawsuit claimed the BB gun was defective in that it contained improper warnings and was an inherently dangerous instrumentality.

ISSUE Should the manufacturer be liable under strict product liability?

DECISION No. In this case, it is undisputed that there is no design or manufacturing defect in the product. In fact, the BB gun worked as the boys expected. Beilke fully intended to perform the physical actions necessary to fire the gun. It operated as it was supposed to operate and as it was designed. The ordinary consumer would expect that a BB gun would cause harm when aimed at a person. The fact that such harm results from the gun's design and manufacture does not make the product, in the legal sense, defective and unreasonably dangerous to the ordinary consumer. The BB gun, if accompanied by adequate warnings, is not designed or manufactured in such a way as to be dangerous to an extent beyond that which would be contemplated by the ordinary consumer. Because the BB gun operated exactly as it was intended and its dangers were well known to the users, it was not unreasonably dangerous. Moreover, we are not willing to hold that this BB gun is an inherently dangerous instrumentality. It only became dangerous because it was used improperly. Both the BB gun itself and the box in which it was sold contained special warnings concerning its use. These warnings were simply disregarded by Beilke and Moss.

Effect of Strict Liability

If an activity is adjudged abnormally dangerous or a product is considered defective and unreasonably dangerous, the victim's chances of recovery are greater than they would be in a negligence case. There are three reasons for this. First, the plaintiff does not have to prove the defendant breached a duty. With strict liability, the actual degree of care the defendant exercised is not relevant in assessing liability. Second, proximate cause is not an element in a strict liability case. The plaintiff need merely prove that the abnormally dangerous activity or the defective and unreasonably dangerous product actually caused injury. Finally, the plaintiff's contributory negligence is not a defense to a strict liability case. The only defense available to the defendant is the plaintiff's knowing and voluntary assumption of risk. (In strict product liability suits, the defendant also may avoid liability by showing that the plaintiff substantially modified the product in a way that made it more hazardous.)

─────────────────────── Ethical Issue ───────────────────────

When a person engages in an abnormally dangerous activity, she should realize that, despite taking reasonable precautions, at some point in time she is likely to injure somebody. Because she will be liable in strict liability, she should purchase liability insurance. Is it ethical to engage in behavior that is likely to injure or kill someone?

Workers' Compensation

Each of the 50 states has enacted **workers' compensation** legislation making employers strictly liable for the workplace injuries suffered by their employees. These statutes guarantee compensation for most work-related accidents by eliminating the traditional tort law defenses of assumption of risk, contributory negligence, and the fellow servant rule. Workers' compensation should be viewed as a social program that basically forces employers to participate in a liability insurance system that covers most full-time employees.

Background

Historically, employees who suffered workplace injuries had an extremely difficult time recovering in negligence suits against their employers. First, employees often could not prove the employer was negligent and, therefore, legally liable for their claims. Second, courts routinely ruled that employees assumed the risk of employment-related hazards when they accepted employment. This *assumption of risk* defense bars an employee's tort law recovery. Third, if it could be shown that an injured employee's carelessness contributed to her injuries in any way, her claim was blocked by the doctrine of *contributory negligence*. Fourth, in cases where a co-employee's negligence contributed to the injury, the employer was shielded under the *fellow servant rule*. Finally, employees who filed negligence lawsuits against their employers were likely to be fired.

Purpose

The workers' compensation statutes are designed to eliminate the need for injured employees to sue their employers. They provide employees with a prompt and certain recovery by removing the need to prove employer fault. In exchange, the employee is likely to receive much less than might be recovered in a negligence lawsuit. In a sense, workers' compensation is a social compromise designed to provide accident insurance for employees, maintain workplace harmony, and protect the courts from a flood of workplace injury suits.

Benefits

The workers' compensation laws provide a variety of benefits to eligible employees. Injured employees who cannot work may be entitled to *disability benefits* based on a percentage of their weekly wages. They also may receive *medical benefits* that pay for hospitalization and other medical treatments. If an employee's disability prevents him from returning to his old job, some states provide *rehabilitation benefits* that cover the cost of training the employee for a new occupation. Workers' compensation also includes *specified injury benefits* that pay cash for the loss of specified body parts. A schedule of compensation makes clear the amount of money available for the loss of any particular part of the body. Finally, *death benefits* are paid to the surviving spouse and/or children of an employee who dies in a workplace accident.

Legal Effect

Certain basic features are common to the workers' compensation laws of most states. Generally, unless an employer has intentionally injured the employee, the employee is not permitted to sue the employer. In other words, workers' compensation is the *exclusive remedy* against the employer. For instance, Bill lost his left hand when it was smashed by the press he was operating at work. Because his injuries were covered by workers' compensation, he is precluded from suing his employer. However, many states permit Bill to sue a third person who was responsible for the injuries. Thus, Bill might sue the manufacturer of the press in the hope that a jury will award him more than he received under workers' compensation.

Administration of Claims

Most states have set up a governmental agency that administers its workers' compensation system. This board initially determines if an employee is entitled to workers' compensation benefits. Its decisions may be appealed to a state court. Two things must be shown before the board will award workers' compensation benefits. First, the person suffering the injuries must be a qualified employee. Second, the injuries must be work-related. (See Figure 7–2 on page 158.)

Figure 7–2:   Workers' Compensation

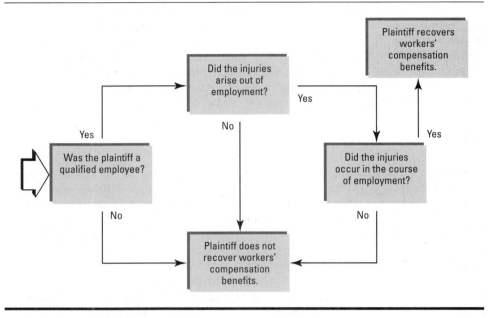

The Qualified Employee Test

Only **qualified employees** are entitled to workers' compensation benefits. Independent contractors are not covered. An individual generally is not considered to be an employee unless the employer controls the day-to-day details of her work. Further, the statutory schemes in many states do not cover part-time, agricultural, and domestic employees. Some states also exclude coverage for businesses that have less than three employees.

The Work-Related Injury Test

Workers' compensation covers only **work-related injuries.** There are two requirements that must be satisfied before an injury meets the work-related test. First, the injury must arise out of the employment. Second, the injury must have occurred in the course of employment.

Injuries do not *arise out of employment* unless they are somehow related to the nature of the job. Most courts use a "positional risk" analysis to make this determination. Under this approach, the injuries are likely to be covered by workers' compensation if the job placed the employee in the position where he was injured. However, some courts use the more restrictive, "increased risk" test when deciding if injuries arise out of employment. Under this approach, workers' compensation benefits are not available unless the employment actually increased the risk that the employee would suffer the type of injury that occurred.

The requirement that injuries be work-related also requires that they occur in the *course of employment.* When the employee is injured in the "time, place, and circumstances" of the job, the course of employment test is met. Employees who are injured while traveling to or from work generally fail to meet this requirement.

However, employees who are running errands for their employer or whose job otherwise requires travel may be within the course of employment.

In the case at the beginning of the chapter, Ty was unable to recover in workers' compensation because his injuries arose during the time he was traveling home from work. The court recognized that exceptions sometimes may be made when the employment creates a special hazard or risk. However, the special-risk exception did not apply in Ty's case because White Castle employees were no more susceptible to criminal assault than members of the general public walking down the same street.

Defenses Against Liability

As noted above, the traditional tort defenses (assumption of risk, contributory negligence, and the fellow servant rule) do not block a workers' compensation recovery. However, the employee cannot recover for self-inflicted injuries. And many states deny workers' compensation to employees who were intoxicated or under the influence of drugs when they were injured. Some states bar recoveries by employees who were engaged in horseplay if such behavior constituted a *substantial deviation* from their employment responsibilities.

Darco Transportation v. Dulen

1996 Okla Lexis 54 (Sup. Ct. Okla. 1996)

FACTS   Elmer Dulen was severely injured when a tractor-trailer rig, which he was driving, entered a railroad crossing and was struck by an oncoming train. Dulen and Polly Freeman, his codriver, were hired by Darco Transportation to transport goods cross-country. On the night of the accident, Dulen stopped his rig behind another truck when the signal arms at a railroad crossing lowered. The arms malfunctioned and came up before the train had reached the intersection. The first truck proceeded across the tracks and Dulen followed. His rig was struck by the train. The traffic investigator at the scene of the accident reported that Freeman was clad only in a T-shirt. Dulen's pants were unbuttoned, unzipped, and resting mid-hip when he was readied for transportation to the hospital. At the hospital, Dulen told the investigating officer that when the accident occurred, Freeman was sitting on his lap facing him and they were having sex.

ISSUE   Is Dulen entitled to workers' compensation benefits?

DECISION   Yes. We must be mindful that in this case we are applying workers' compensation law. The concept of a worker's contributory fault, which the workers' compensation statute discarded, must not be allowed to diminish the employer's liability. Compensable work-related injury must both (1) occur in the course of and (2) arise out of the worker's employment. If Dulen, when injured, was performing work in furtherance of his employer's business, he was acting in the course of employment. The fact that he and Freeman were having sex at the critical time does not negate his entitlement to workers' compensation benefits unless his conduct is deemed to be "horseplay," a complete departure from or abandonment of his employment.

continued

However, his having sex constituted no more than a careless, negligent or forbidden genre of performance. It did not amount to pure frolic which constituted a total abandonment of his employer's business. When Dulen was injured he occupied his assigned work station—the driver's seat behind the steering wheel of Darco's truck. No matter how morally reprehensible Dulen's conduct, he had not deviated from or abandoned Darco's mission. Dulen's injuries also arose out of his employment because they were caused by a risk to which Darco employees were subjected by their work. Dulen's job required his presence on the highways. A causal connection between the act in which he was engaged, when injured, and his job description is clear. Because the perils of Dulen's travel for Darco are co-extensive with the risks of employment, his injuries undeniably arose out of his work.

Ethical Issue

Notwithstanding the rules governing eligibility for workers' compensation, how do you feel about Dulen's recovery in this case?

QUESTIONS AND PROBLEM CASES

1. What is *res ipsa loquitur*? How does it modify traditional negligence analysis?
2. Explain how workers' compensation alters the traditional tort approach for workplace accidents.
3. Explain the fundamental difference between nuisance and trespass to land.
4. Richard Kapres, a 19-year-old student at Clarion University, attended three parties hosted by students. He consumed alcohol at each of the parties. While walking away from the last party, Richard was struck by an automobile and suffered various injuries. He claimed his intoxicated condition was a cause of his accident and sued the student hosts for negligently serving him alcohol. The defendants asserted that they owed no duty to Richard since they also were minors. Should a minor be held liable for furnishing alcohol to another minor?
5. Deborah Tolbert, a secretary employed by Martin Marietta Corporation, was raped by a janitor while on her way to lunch within the secured defense facility where she worked. She sued Martin Marietta, alleging that it had negligently hired the janitor and had negligently failed to make its premises safe for employees. Martin Marietta argued that Tolbert could not sue in negligence because workers' compensation was her exclusive remedy. Is Martin Marietta correct?
6. While Waterson was driving her car without wearing her seat belt, the vehicle went out of control and struck a telephone pole. It later was discovered that the accident occurred because the car had a defective axle. When Waterson sued General Motors in negligence, General Motors argued that Waterson's failure to wear her seat belt should reduce the amount of damages she might receive. Is General Motors correct?
7. After meeting in late 1979, Ted Fletcher and Patty Ruth dated frequently and developed a relationship that involved sexual relations. During that same time, Patty also engaged in sexual relations with a bartender at the nightclub where she worked as a waitress. When Patty got pregnant in October 1980, she told the bartender he was the father and he agreed to give her money for an abortion.

Within one week, however, the bartender left town with no forwarding address. Patty then told Ted about the baby and, while admitting to a single sexual encounter with the bartender, assured Ted that the baby was Ted's. Ted attended childbirth classes and stayed with Patty throughout labor and delivery. On numerous occasions thereafter, Patty assured Ted he was the father of the child. Over the next several years, Ted provided financial support and developed a deep, loving relationship with the child. However, in 1983, Patty had a chance encounter with the bartender and, one year later, married him. She then informed Ted that she and the baby no longer needed his financial support and informed him that he could no longer have visitation rights with the child. Medical tests confirmed that the bartender, not Ted, was the father of the child, and the court terminated Ted's visitation rights. Ted sued Patty for intentional infliction of emotional distress. Is Ted likely to prevail?

8. Ludmila Hresil was shopping in a Sears self-service store when she slipped on "phlegm-like" substance and fell. As a result of her fall, she had two operations on her leg and now is permanently injured. In her negligence lawsuit against Sears, Hresil testified that preceding her fall, there were no other shoppers in that area of the store for over 10 minutes. From this evidence, she inferred that the foreign substance was on the floor for at least 10 minutes prior to her fall. She argued that 10 minutes gave Sears sufficient time to notice the "gob" and clean it up. Has Hresil proven that Sears breached the duty it owed her?

9. Early one evening a man abducted a 10-year-old girl from the sidewalk in front of her home, dragged her across the street to a vacant apartment, and raped her. The vacant apartment had glass broken from its windows, and the front door was off its hinges. A city ordinance established minimum standards for property owners, requiring them to "keep the doors and windows of a vacant structure or vacant portion of a structure securely closed to prevent unauthorized entry." The child's mother sued the apartment owner for the injuries suffered by her daughter. Carefully explain how a court will analyze this lawsuit.

10. Three employees of Equitable Life Assurance Company were sent to Pittsburgh on company business. None had traveled for the company before and they were not given copies of the company's travel expense policies. After returning from the trip, a dispute arose because the verbal instructions the employees were given regarding allowable expenses differed from the company's written policies. Ultimately, each of the employees was ordered to return $200 to Equitable Life. When they refused to do so, arguing their expenses were honestly incurred, the company fired them for "gross insubordination." In seeking new jobs, the former employees were asked why they left Equitable Life and each said she was terminated for gross insubordination and attempted to explain the situation. After they had trouble finding new jobs, they sued Equitable Life for defamation. Do the former employees have a strong claim for damages under the intentional tort of defamation?

MAKING CONTRACTS

INTRODUCTION TO CONTRACTS

After buying a book at a Computer City outlet, Robert Bekin watched a clerk type his address into a computer. When Bekin asked if he would be placed on a mailing list, the clerk assured him that he would not be. As a precaution, Bekin wrote on the back of his check, *"Computer City agrees NOT to place Robert Bekin on any mailing list or send him any advertisements or mailings. . . . Computer City agrees that . . . damages for the first breach are $1,000. The deposit of this check for payment is agreement with these terms and conditions."* Soon after the check was cashed, Bekin received several flyers from the retail chain. After filing a breach of contract suit against Computer City, Bekin was awarded $1,000.

The Wall Street Journal, February 7, 1996, p. B1.

How was the contract between Bekin and Computer City created?

What were the terms of the contract between Bekin and Computer City?

What are the essential elements of a contract?

Introduction ▪▬▬▬▬▬▬▬▬▬▬▬▬▬

Contract law elevates private agreements between two or more persons or business entities into legally binding obligations. In essence, contracts are laws created by private parties and enforced by public institutions (courts). Because of contract law, people may enter relationships with a high level of confidence that their contracting partners will honor the promises they have made. This certainty facilitates the planning essential for complex business deals and provides peace of mind for participants in day-to-day consumer transactions.

Chapter Overview

Contract disputes involve either one or both of the following questions:

1. Do the parties have a contract?
2. If they have a contract, what rights and obligations does it create?

Prudent people try to structure agreements to maximize the likelihood that these questions are answered in a manner that carries out their original intent. Attainment of this goal generally requires an understanding of the legal rules governing the formation, performance, and enforcement of contracts.

This chapter examines the rules governing the formation of contracts. (Performance and enforcement issues are discussed in Chapter 9.) It begins by identifying the two bodies of law regulating contracts in the United States: the common law and the Uniform Commercial Code. This is followed by a brief survey of the basic kinds of contracts recognized by our legal system. Next is an explanation of equity and how it may offset the harshness that sometimes results from too strict an application of the contract rules. The chapter's final three sections explore the primary elements of a contract: offer, acceptance, and consideration.

The Law Governing Contracts ▪▬▬▬▬▬▬▬▬

After the American Revolution, most U.S. courts continued to follow British legal precedents. This included the common law contract rules. However, over the years, the U.S. laws governing contracts have split into two overlapping branches: the common law rules and the Uniform Commercial Code. (See Figure 8–1 on page 166.)

Common Law Rules

The common law of contracts has evolved gradually over time. When a new case arose, the judge declared the applicable rule of law. However, whenever the facts were similar to those in a previous case, the judge followed that earlier decision. After thousands of disputes were resolved in this manner, a large body of common law came into being. Today these common-law rules govern service contracts and agreements for the sale of land, stocks and bonds, and intangible property.

The discussion that follows introduces three common-law approaches: classical, modern, and a hybrid of the two. Which approach governs any particular contract is dependent on the philosophy of the judge or jurisdiction where the contract dispute is being heard.

Figure 8–1:   Choice of Law

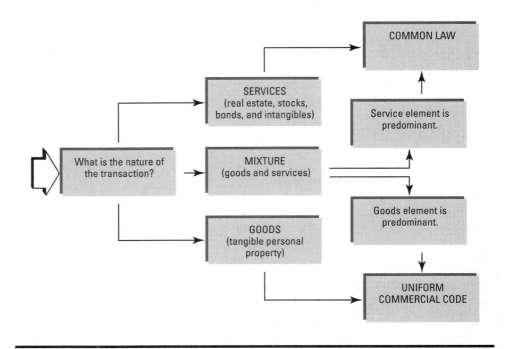

Classical Common Law

Early common-law contract rules were tailored for face-to-face agreements between parties with relatively equal bargaining strength. Under the *classical common law* approach, courts strongly favor the notion of freedom of contract. Accordingly, they maintain a hands-off approach that gives private parties a great deal of control over the terms of their agreements. While this sometimes results in people making bad deals, the courts believe freedom of contract includes the risk that bad bargains may occasionally occur. As long as the parties clearly demonstrated an intent to contract by carefully and definitely identifying the terms of their agreement, the courts will strictly enforce their contract. This approach to contractual relations provides predictable results that facilitated private planning.

Modern Common Law

With industrialization and modernization, the complexity of contractual relations increased tremendously. Today, many contracting parties (particularly consumers) frequently have much less knowledge and bargaining power than the business organizations with whom they are forced to deal. Contract rules have evolved over time to reflect these changing conditions. More and more courts are willing to assume a hands-on posture in order to protect weaker parties. While this *modern common law* approach lacks the clarity and predictability of classical contract theory, it permits judges to avoid the harsh results that might otherwise occur.

Hybrid Approach

The common-law rules applied by many courts today combine the principles of both the modern and the classical approaches. When both parties possess relatively equal knowledge and bargaining power (business versus business), one might expect the courts to apply the classical, hands-off rules. However, when there is a great disparity in the knowledge and the power of the parties (business versus consumer), courts are more likely to assume the modern, interventionist posture.

Uniform Commercial Code

Perhaps the greatest reform in American contract law has been the adoption of the **Uniform Commercial Code** (UCC) by all the states except Louisiana (which has adopted some of its provisions). The UCC contains a partial codification of the U.S. law governing contracts for the sale of goods. In part, it was designed to establish a uniform contract law for goods transactions; although it should be remembered that some of its language and interpretations vary from state to state within the United States. While the UCC is domestic U.S. law, its effect has extended well beyond the United States, since global businesses often select it as the governing law for their international contracts.

http:// www.law.cornell.edu/ ucc/1/overview.html, a Web site of the Legal Information Institute, provides an index of topics for the General Provisions of the UCC.

Application of the UCC

The UCC governs contracts for the **sale of goods.** (It defines "goods" as tangible, movable, personal property.) Thus, agreements to buy or sell cars, food, animals, or lumber are subject to the UCC. Service contracts (painting a house or mowing a yard) and agreements for the sale of land, stocks, and bonds are governed by the common-law rules.

http:// www.law.cornell. edu/ucc/ucc.table. html provides links to Articles 1–9 of the UCC.

While the UCC theoretically only applies to contracts for the sale of goods, in reality it enjoys a wider application for two fundamental reasons. First, many contracts involve elements of both goods and services. When this occurs, the UCC is the governing law if the goods provide the *predominant purpose* of the transaction. For example, the UCC governs a contract where a business agrees to buy lawn mowers from a manufacturer. While the contract involves both goods (the lawn mowers) and services (the manufacture and assembly processes), the predominant purpose of the contract is the acquisition of the goods. A contract to have lawn mowers repaired, on the other hand, falls within the common law.

Second, since its adoption the UCC has had a tremendous influence on the evolution of the general body of common-law contract rules. Many courts liberally apply UCC concepts and standards by analogy to contracts that technically fall outside its scope. Thus, a court may refuse to enforce a grossly unfair services contract on the grounds that it is unconscionable even though the rule prohibiting enforcement of unconscionable contracts technically is part of the UCC.

Nature of the UCC

The UCC has not completely replaced the common law for sale-of-goods contracts. Instead, it provides codified rules for only selected situations. In circumstances where there is no specific UCC provision, courts apply the common law. In general, the UCC has adopted rules that reflect the actual practices of contracting parties. It also attempts to promote fair dealing by imposing a duty of *good faith* on all contracting parties and, in certain situations, requiring that *merchants* (businesspersons) follow a higher standard of conduct.

Types Of Contracts

Contracts can be classified in a variety of ways. For instance, the manner in which the parties have formed the agreement might be considered. Or agreements can be grouped according to whether one or both of the parties made a promise. Sometimes, contractual agreements are distinguished by the extent to which their terms have been performed. Finally, contracts can be classified based on their level of enforceability.

Manner of Formation

In order to have a contract, there must be some type of agreement. The agreement is **express** if the parties explicitly describe their basic obligations when creating the agreement. For instance, Cathy might promise to mow David's lawn tomorrow afternoon in exchange for his promise to pay her $15 when she completes the job. If both promises are made, Cathy and David have formed an express contract. It does not matter if their promises are oral or in writing.

Contracts frequently are formed under circumstances where the terms are not explicitly stated. Thus, if Aaron orders a pizza, he is obligated to pay for it even though payment terms were never discussed. There is an **implied** agreement that the restaurant will deliver an edible pizza within a reasonable period of time and that, in return, Aaron will pay a reasonable price.

Providence Hospital v. Dorsey

634 A.2D 1216 (APP. D.C. 1993)

FACTS   Debra Dorsey admitted herself to Providence Hospital on May 5, 1989, and received treatment from that date until May 22, 1989. The hospital charged her $7,714.74 for its services. Debra's insurance paid $2,500 of the bill, and the charges were reduced further by $2,014.25 due to an allowance agreement between the hospital and Debra's insurance company. Debra never made any payments on the balance of $3,200.49. When the hospital sued, Debra responded that upon her admittance she gave the hospital information about her insurance company and it was her understanding that the insurance company would be responsible for paying the bill in full. The trial court ruled in favor of Debra, finding the hospital failed to prove Debra ever agreed to personally pay any of the hospital charges beyond what her insurance company would pay. The hospital argued on appeal that such an agreement could be implied.

ISSUE   Did Debra make an implied contract to pay the hospital?

DECISION   Yes. There is no dispute that Debra voluntarily came to the hospital and personally sought and received the services the hospital provided. Generally, gifts are not presumed in the law, and a person who both requests and receives valuable services impliedly has the obligation to pay reasonable compensation for them. A contrary understanding or expectation may of course be shown. This might be done by introducing evidence that Debra had informed the hospital she expected her insurance company to cover the entire costs at the time of her admittance.

Number of Promisors

Contracts also can be classified on the basis of whether one or both of the parties has promised to perform. In an earlier example, Cathy promised to mow David's lawn in exchange for his promise to pay her $15. Since each party promised something to the other, they created a **bilateral contract.** If Cathy failed to mow the lawn, David could recover from her for breach of contract. Likewise, if David prevented Cathy from mowing his lawn or failed to pay when she completed the job, she could recover from him.

Suppose instead that David told Cathy he would pay her $15 if she mowed his lawn. Under these circumstances, Cathy never promised to mow the lawn. If she does the work, David must pay her the money. However, if she decides against doing the job, David cannot recover from her for breach of contract. Since only one party (David) made a promise, David and Cathy have a **unilateral contract.** David can avoid any obligation to Cathy by revoking his promise before she begins mowing the lawn or begins substantial preparation to mow it.

Extent of Performance

Courts also describe contracts based on the extent to which they have been performed. When all of the parties have fully completed all of their contractual obligations, the contract is **executed.** If Cathy mows the lawn and David pays her the $15, their contract is executed.

An agreement is **executory** if it has not been fully performed. Thus, immediately after Cathy and David made their promises, but before the work was done, they had an executory contract. If Cathy finishes mowing the lawn and David has not yet paid, the contract is *partially executory.* This is because one party's (Cathy's) performance is completed while the other's (David's) is not.

Level of Enforceability

Courts do not enforce every type of agreement. And, in some instances, an agreement may be enforceable only at the option of one of the parties. If all of the legal requirements imposed by contract law are met, the parties have a **valid contract.** Courts enforce valid contracts. A **void contract** exists if the parties failed to comply with the basic contract requirements. For instance, an agreement to commit murder for money violates the requirement that contracts not be formed for illegal purposes. As a result, courts will not enforce the agreement.

A **voidable contract** is an agreement that could be canceled by one of the parties. It is enforceable unless the party with the right to cancel exercises that right. Suppose Alice persuaded Mark to buy her car by fraudulently turning back the odometer and misrepresenting the number of miles it was driven. Mark can cancel the contract if he chooses. However, if he still thinks the contract is a good deal, he can forfeit his right to cancel and force Alice to sell the car.

Sometimes an agreement fulfills the basic requirements for a contract but overlooks another legal rule. For instance, a contract for the sale of land is supposed to be in writing. If John orally agrees to buy Audrey's farm, their agreement may be an **unenforceable contract.** (Enforceability issues are discussed in the next chapter.)

Equitable Concepts

Historically, the British common law was procedurally oriented, and failure to strictly comply with its technical requirements often resulted in otherwise deserving parties being denied judicial relief. Over time, separate **equity** courts were created to minimize injustice. These tribunals were more flexible in their approach and, unlike the common-law courts, focused on achieving fair results.

The U.S. courts inherited these equitable principles from their British ancestors. However, today most states have abolished separate equity courts. Instead, each judge possesses equitable powers to deviate from a strict application of the common law when she believes such action is necessary to prevent injustice. Two equitable principles that often arise in contract formation disputes are quasi contract and promissory estoppel.

Quasi Contract

Let's go back to our earlier example where Cathy agreed to mow David's lawn in exchange for his promise to pay $15. They had an express, bilateral contract. (Note: it also was executory and enforceable.) Suppose, however, that Cathy misunderstood the directions to David's house and mowed Wayne's lawn by mistake. When she completed the job, David would not have to pay because she failed to comply with the terms of their contract.

Should Wayne be required to pay for her effort? Under a strict application of contract law, Wayne would not have to pay because he never contracted with Cathy. Yet if Wayne knew Cathy was mowing his lawn, it would be unjust for him not to pay for the benefit she bestowed upon him. Thus, under **quasi contract** a court could order Wayne to pay Cathy the reasonable value of her work.

Courts employ quasi contract to avoid situations where no contract exists, yet one person might be *unjustly enriched* at the expense of another. To recover under quasi contract, a plaintiff must prove three things:

1. she conferred a *benefit* on the defendant;
2. the defendant *knowingly accepted* the benefit; and
3. it would be *unjust* for the defendant to retain the benefit without paying its reasonable value.

Promissory Estoppel

Because contract law was developed to protect the *bargains* people make, courts seldom enforce gratuitous (gift) promises. Suppose Jack promised to buy Holly a new watch. If she did not pay Jack some price in return, a court will not require Jack to honor his promise. This is because there is no "bargained-for exchange." (This concept is discussed in a later section.)

Let's change the facts. After learning of Jack's intention to buy her a new watch, Holly gave her old watch to Karen. Assume further that Jack observed Holly making this gift in reliance on his promise. Under these circumstances, a court may require Jack to honor his promise even though there still was no "bargained-for exchange." By using the doctrine of **promissory estoppel,** the court can avoid the injustice that otherwise would result from Holly's reasonable reliance on Jack's promise.

Unlike traditional contract law, which protects bargains, the equitable concept of promissory estoppel protects *reliance*. Courts enforce promises under the doctrine of promissory estoppel when the promisee proves the following elements:

1. the promisor made a *promise* which he knew or should have known would induce reliance;
2. the promisee *reasonably relied* on the promise; and
3. the promisee will suffer a *detriment* if the promise is not enforced.

Hansen v. Gab Business Services, Inc.

876 P.2D 112 (App. Colo. 1994)

FACTS   Donald Hansen was employed as a branch manager by GAB Business Services. GAB voluntarily implemented a written incentive compensation plan. It stated that branch managers would be eligible for bonuses if they met the company's budget goals. However, the plan also stated that nothing in its provisions established any right or contractual obligation for payment to any individual or class of employees. Although Donald claimed to have met the company's budget goals, the company denied his eligibility for an incentive bonus. Hansen sued the company under theories of breach of contract, promissory estoppel, and quasi contract.

ISSUE   Is Donald entitled to the bonus under any of his legal theories?

DECISION   No. GAB clearly did not intend to establish a contract. A voluntary promise to pay an employee a bonus which does not obligate the employee to do something he was not otherwise obligated to do is a mere gratuity and is unenforceable. To recover under promissory estoppel, Donald must show there was a clear and unambiguous promise, upon which he reasonably and foreseeably relied, and that he sustained injury because of that reliance. The plan clearly indicated the company was not obligated to make any bonus payment. Therefore, Donald's reliance on some perceived promise was not reasonable. In order to recover under quasi contract, Donald needed to show he rendered services in good faith to the company, the company knowingly accepted the services, and it would be unjust not to compensate him for the reasonable value of the services. There is no evidence indicating the value of Donald's services exceeded his base salary.

Ethical Issue

How do you feel about GAB's refusal to give Hansen the bonus? Was its behavior ethical?

Offer

Contract law was designed to protect bargains. And the essence of an enforceable bargain under the common law is the *mutual agreement* of the contracting partners. By definition, the existence of an agreement is dependent on the consent of the parties. Courts do not believe there is sufficient consent to form a legally binding agreement unless they find evidence of an offer matched by an acceptance. This section examines the fundamental attributes of an offer. Acceptance is discussed in the following section.

Elements of an Offer

The first step in creating a contract is for one party to make an offer to the other. If the terms of the offer are accepted, the parties have created an agreement. There are three fundamental components to an **offer:** intent, definiteness, and communication.

Intent

In the course of their lives people are likely to make (and break) a variety of promises. Those of a social nature ("I'll meet you outside the library at 6:45 p.m.") seldom are enforceable, while those of a business nature ("I'll deliver the goods before Friday.") often are enforceable. Courts are reluctant to enforce any promise unless they find a clear indication of the parties' **intent to enter a legal obligation.**

Modern courts use an *objective standard* when looking for intent. A variety of points come into play when measuring someone's objective intent. For instance, the circumstances under which a promise was made might be important. If both individuals have frequently contracted in the past, a court may easily find they intend to contract again. On the other hand, if the parties were interacting in a social setting and had never contracted business with each other before, a court might demand a much stronger showing of intent.

Definiteness

A strong measure of whether people intend to contract is the specificity with which they have discussed the terms of the agreement. When their negotiations have not proceeded past a superficial level, courts generally assume they are not yet willing to create a contract. However, if they have ironed out most of the details involved in the transaction, they have met the objective standard of contractual intent. Thus, most courts will not find an offer (and hence a contract) unless the terms are stated with a fair degree of **definiteness.**

The actual level of specificity required depends on several factors. First, definiteness is necessary to help establish the parties' intent to be bound. If there already exist strong manifestations of intent (payment has been accepted or documents have been signed), a court permits greater indefiniteness. Second, definiteness tells the court what terms to enforce. When the parties have contracted with each other many times before, a court may feel free to look to their past dealings to fill in missing terms.

The law governing the contract also may affect the required level of specificity. Under the *classical common law,* courts regard themselves as "contract enforcers" rather than "contract makers." Thus, they demand a great deal of definiteness before recognizing an offer. The UCC rules governing sale-of-goods contracts, on the other hand, will find an offer as long as there is a reasonably certain basis for giving a remedy. In fact, the UCC contains a series of **gap fillers** that enable courts to fill in terms for price, quantity, delivery, and time of payment when such terms have been left open by the parties. Most courts that follow the *modern common law* interpret definiteness in a manner similar to the UCC.

Kiley v. First National Bank

649 A.2D 1145 (APP. MD. 1994)

FACTS   In July 1986, First National Bank acquired all checking and savings accounts held by the now-defunct Baltimore Federal Financial. Mr. Kiley had an account with Baltimore Federal at that time. This account had several features that were important to him: it was interest-bearing; it had no minimum balance requirement; and Baltimore Federal did not charge service fees. As part of the acquisition, First National continued those features. After acquiring Baltimore Federal, First National sent a letter to its customers that stated: "We're excited about having you as a new First National customer and want to assure you that any change to your accounts will be to your benefit." In October 1990, First National attempted to change Mr. Kiley's account and sought to impose a $15 monthly service charge. After Mr. Kiley complained, the bank dropped the charge and reinstated the original Baltimore Federal terms. However, on February 1, 1992, First National announced it was implementing minimum balance requirements and service fees on all its customers' accounts. Mr. Kiley objected; however, this time the bank refused to reinstate the original terms. When Mr. Kiley and the bank were unable to resolve their differences, First National requested that he close his account. Mr. Kiley refused to close his account and, instead, sued the bank for breach of contract. Specifically, he claimed the bank's 1986 letter to the Baltimore Federal customers created an enforceable contract promising them a lifetime interest-bearing, no-minimum-balance, no-service-fee checking account with First National.

ISSUE   Did the letter create a contract between the bank and its customers?

DECISION   No. It is well established that an enforceable contract must express with definiteness and certainty the nature and extent of the parties' obligations. If an offer is too vague with respect to essential terms, it may be invalid. In fact, even when a person intends to make an offer, it cannot be accepted so as to form a contract unless its essential terms are reasonably certain. Vague and indefinite offers cannot create enforceable agreements because the court cannot make a contract for the parties. For an agreement to be legally enforceable, its language must be sufficiently definite to clearly inform the parties of what they may be called upon to do. It also must be sufficiently clear and definite so the court, which may be required to enforce it, is able to know the purpose and intention of the parties. First National's letter obviously does not contain any essential terms. It is quite a stretch to construe the letter as a contract. At most, it is a mere expression of intent to do an act. A mere expression of intention to do an act is not an offer to do it. However, even assuming the bank's letter did create contractual rights, it was silent as to its duration. First National continued Baltimore Federal's terms for over five years; such a lengthy period was certainly reasonable.

Communication

An offer is not valid until it has been communicated to the offeree by the offeror. Absent this **communication,** a court is unlikely to believe the offeror has manifested an objective intent to enter a contract. A failure to communicate the terms of the offer would seem to suggest the offeror is not yet certain she wishes to go through with the deal.

Advertisements

Advertisements, price lists, and catalogs are seldom considered to be offers. They are treated instead as *invitations to make an offer.* When a buyer reads these materials and requests the listed goods, he is making an offer to buy them. The seller is then free to accept or reject the buyer's offer.

However, advertisements are treated as offers under certain circumstances. If the advertisement describes the goods with a high level of definiteness **and** requires some special performance by the buyer, many courts will find it to be an offer. For instance, suppose a store runs the following advertisement: *"Lawn chairs, a $29.99 value, yours for only $12.99. Limit one per customer. Offer available to first 100 customers."* Because this advertisement is likely to encourage people to rush to the store, a court may well find it to be an offer.

Duration of Offers

Although an offer has been made, it cannot be transformed into an agreement unless it still exists at the time of acceptance. Thus, it is important to recognize what actions terminate an offer.

Terms of the Offer

The terms of the offer itself may spell out its duration. For instance, the lawn chair advertisement in the previous section stated that the offer was available only to the first 100 customers. Another offer might tell the offeree it must be accepted within 10 days. On the 11th day, the offer will expire.

Lapse of Time

If the offer fails to state its duration, it will remain open for a reasonable time period. What is reasonable depends on the circumstances. If the offer concerns perishable goods, it may lapse within a matter of hours. An offer that is made during the course of a telephone call may lapse at the end of the conversation. Courts often look to industry standards and past dealings between the parties when trying to determine how long a specific offer will remain open.

Death or Insanity

An offer automatically ends if either party dies or is rendered insane before acceptance occurs. This is because there can be no mutual consent if one of the parties no longer is able to manifest an intent to contract.

Destruction of Subject Matter

An offer also ends if the subject matter of the contract is destroyed before acceptance occurs. A key assumption of an offer is that the goods are in existence. Once this assumption is no longer true, the offer is terminated.

Intervening Illegality

An offer automatically terminates if after it is made, but before it is accepted, the performance required in the contract becomes illegal. Suppose Ames offered to sell computers to a Chinese buyer. Before the buyer accepted the offer, the United States decided to prohibit all trade in high-technology goods with China. The offer would terminate once the government implemented the new policy.

Rejection

An offeree's **rejection** of an offer terminates the offer. It does not matter how the rejection occurs. For instance, Anne offered to sell Bob 30 widgets at $10 per widget. Bob responded that he would not pay more than $9.50 per widget. Bob made a **counteroffer** which impliedly rejected and terminated Anne's original offer. Rejections are effective when they are actually received by the offeror.

Revocation

An offeror generally may revoke her offer anytime prior to acceptance. She usually may do this even if the **revocation** contradicts an earlier promise to hold the offer open. Thus, if an offer stated it would remain open for 10 days, the offeror may revoke it sooner than that by notifying the offeree of her intent to terminate. Revocations are effective when they are actually received by the offeree. However, in instances where an advertisement is treated as an offer to the general public, the revocation is effective when it is published in the same manner as the original offer was communicated.

There are three basic exceptions to the rule that an offer may be revoked anytime prior to acceptance. First, under an **option** an offer cannot be revoked if the offeree has paid the offeror to hold it open for a specified time period. Second, in a sale-of-goods transaction, the UCC prevents the revocation of a **firm offer**. A firm offer is a promise by a *merchant* in a *signed writing* giving *assurances* it will be held open. If the firm offer does not state a specific time period, it must be held open for a reasonable amount of time. However, the time period cannot exceed three months. Third, under the doctrine of **promissory estoppel**, the offeror cannot revoke if the offeree has reasonably relied to his detriment on a promise to hold the offer open. (See Figure 8–2 on page 177.)

I. R. Kirk Farms, Inc. v. Pointer
897 S.W.2D 183 (APP. W.D. MO. 1995)

FACTS In March 1980, Kirk borrowed $10,000 and offered a farm as security for the loan. The Kirk family both occupied and worked the farm, which had been in the family for some time. In early 1988, when Kirk defaulted on the loan, an agreement was made to transfer the farm to W. L. Pointer. Under the terms of this arrangement, Pointer would lease the farm back to Kirk for two years. The deal also included an option agreement that offered to sell the farm back to Kirk for $10,000 at any time prior to February 1990. It contained language that made this offer irrevocable in consideration of $50. At the time this arrangement was created, Kirk did not actually pay the $50, nor was payment requested by Pointer. In the fall of 1988, when Kirk tried to pay the $50, Pointer refused to accept and stated the payment was not necessary. In February 1989, Kirk decided to exercise the option and tendered a check for $10,000

continued

to Pointer. Included was a letter of intent directing Pointer to convey title to the farm back to Kirk. Pointer refused to accept the tendered amount or to execute the deed to the farm, stating the option was unenforceable because the $50 had not been paid. Kirk sued Pointer.

ISSUE   Is Pointer required to sell the farm back to Kirk?

DECISION   Yes. Contract law clearly holds consideration is only necessary in an option situation to make the offer irrevocable. Even if consideration is not tendered, the offer, though not irrevocable, is a continuing offer to sell. The offer remains open until it has been accepted, withdrawn, or a reasonable time has passed. Without the option the offeror is free to revoke his offer at any time prior to acceptance. However, the offeror must communicate the revocation before the offeree has accepted. In this case, the offer to sell the farm, by its terms, would remain open until February of 1990. It would not terminate any earlier as long as Pointer failed to give Kirk notice of his intent to revoke. Pointer did not do this until after Kirk accepted by tendering the $10,000 check for repurchase of the farm. Even if Pointer had notified Kirk of his intent to revoke before the acceptance occurred, he is estopped from revoking. Kirk reasonably relied on the words of Pointer, who assured Kirk the $50 option payment was not necessary.

Acceptance

Mutual agreement is the essence of contract law. And the offeror, as the master of the offer, defines the substance of the contract. The actual agreement does not arise until the moment when those terms have been accepted. However, the offeror has the power to dictate when and how an acceptance may occur. This section examines the basic legal issues that arise in the acceptance context.

Intent to Accept

An **acceptance** occurs when the offeree manifests the *intent to enter into the same legal obligation* spelled out in the offer. Attempts by the offeree to change the terms of the offer or condition acceptance in any material way, generally are held to be counteroffers that terminate the original offer. However, as we shall now see, there are exceptions to this rule.

Mirror Image Rule

The *classical common law* insists that offerees follow the **mirror image rule,** which requires the acceptance to match precisely the terms of the offer. Accordingly, if an offeree responds to an offer by proposing additional or different terms that *materially alter* the terms of the original offer, the reply is treated as a conditional acceptance (rejection) that automatically terminates the offer. The offeree's response is a **counteroffer** that the original offeror is then free to accept or reject.

The *modern common law* is more flexible in its application of the mirror image rule. In cases where the offeree proposes additional or different terms that do not materially alter the original offer, that reply constitutes an acceptance unless the original offeror immediately objects. If the offeror does not object, the parties have a contract containing the offeree's additions or changes. However, if the offeror objects in a timely manner, there is no contract at all.

Figure 8–2: Exceptions to Offeror's Power to Revoke

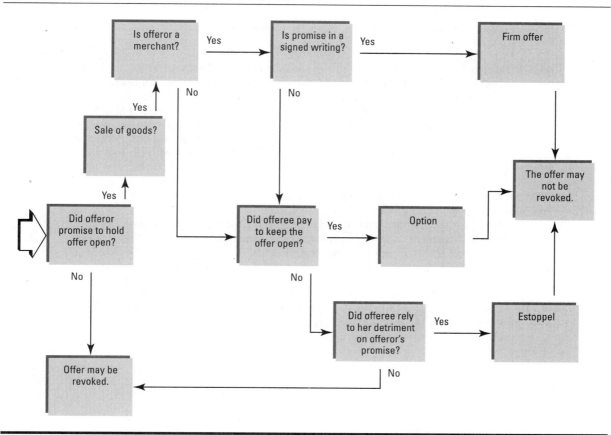

Safeco Insurance Co. v.
City of White House, Tennessee
36 F.3RD 540 (6TH CIR. 1994)

FACTS In 1987, the City of White House solicited bids from contractors to build a municipal wastewater treatment facility. The city made clear that the project was funded by the Environmental Protection Agency, which required contractors to make an effort to ensure that small, minority, and women's businesses were employed as sources for supplies, equipment, and services. The bid specifications also stated that the low bidder must forward to the city, no later than 10 days after the bid opening, documents reflecting compliance with the EPA's equal opportunity policy. Eatherly Construction submitted the lowest bid, which the city accepted on March 19, 1987. Eatherly understood that the city's acceptance was contingent upon approval by the EPA. However, Eatherly failed to provide the documents necessary for EPA approval. On June 8, 1987, the city reminded Eatherly that it must comply with the EPA's requirements. Eatherly responded that there was no binding agreement because the

continued

city had made a conditional acceptance. It then withdrew (revoked) its bid (offer). The city hired the next lowest bidder and sued Eatherly for breach of contract.

ISSUE Was a legally enforceable agreement formed when the city accepted Eatherly's bid?

DECISION Yes. For an agreement to be enforceable as a contract, there must be mutual assent. One party must accept the other party's offer. Unless an acceptance mirrors the offeror's terms, neither omitting nor adding terms, it has no legal effect as an acceptance and operates as a rejection and a counteroffer. A conditional acceptance does not bind the offeror. A nice distinction may be taken here between a conditional acceptance and a conditional contract. A conditional acceptance is a counteroffer and a rejection of the original offer. However, an enforceable agreement may arise if there is an unconditional acceptance of an offer for a conditional contract. In the second case, there is an acceptance. The city's invitation to bid specifically required bidders to make their bids (offers) subject to the EPA's minority business enterprise requirements. Thus, the condition of satisfying the EPA of compliance with its requirement was incorporated into the bid itself. When the city accepted the bid, subject to EPA approval, a binding contract between the city and Eatherly was formed. An acceptance may be unconditional even though the acceptor makes a conditional promise. Since Eatherly's offer included the condition of EPA approval and was accepted by the city, both parties became bound with their mutual assent. The city accepted Eatherly's bid unconditionally, and thus this is a classic case of an unconditional acceptance of a conditional promise. A contract was formed when the city accepted Eatherly's offer on Eatherly's terms—one of those terms rendered the contract subject to EPA approval. Eatherly was obligated to seek that approval in good faith.

Battle of the Forms

The UCC deviates from the mirror image rule in sale-of-goods contracts where the parties transact business through the use of competing standardized forms. The likelihood that these preprinted forms will agree in every detail is extremely slight. Accordingly, the UCC has devised a **battle of the forms** provision that makes it easier for the court to find an enforceable agreement. When the offeree's form indicates the intent to accept but also includes terms additional to those stated in the offer, the additional terms are treated as proposals for addition to the contract. When *both parties are merchants,* the additional terms become part of the contract unless: the offer made clear no such proposals could be included, the additional terms materially alter the contract, or the offeror objects to their inclusion within a reasonable time. If any of these three things occur, or if one or both of the parties are not merchants, there still is a contract, but it does not include the additional terms.

Manner of Acceptance

Acceptance occurs when the offeree communicates to the offeror the intent to be bound to the terms of the offer. The precise words or actions needed to indicate this intent vary. For instance, the offeror has the power to **stipulate** the manner of acceptance. If the offeror does this, acceptance does not occur unless the offeree communicates her acceptance in the specified manner. What is required to accept an offer also may depend on the type of contract anticipated: unilateral or bilateral.

Bilateral Contracts

Acceptance in a bilateral contract generally is an express *promise* (written or oral) to do whatever the offer requests. However, an acceptance also may be implied from the offeree's *behavior*. For instance, suppose Paul offered to rent Sarah a boat for $20. If Sarah climbed into the boat and rowed away, a court easily could imply an acceptance because her behavior communicated an intent to be bound to Paul's terms.

As a general rule, *silence* by an offeree does not operate as an acceptance. Consider the following situation. Adam mailed an offer to Ellen advising her that if she fails to reject within 72 hours, she will be bound to the terms of the offer. Ellen has no responsibility to respond and her silence will not create a contract. However, if Adam and Ellen regularly conducted business together on those terms in the past, her silence would constitute an acceptance.

Unilateral Contracts

Remember our earlier discussion of unilateral contracts? David promised to pay Cathy $15 if she mowed his lawn. This was a unilateral contract because Cathy was not asked to promise to mow the lawn. She was told she would be paid if she mowed it. Cathy can accept this offer by performing the requested act (mowing the lawn).

Time of Acceptance

Because the offeror generally has the power to revoke an offer anytime prior to acceptance, the time of acceptance can be critical. In face-to-face dealings, such problems seldom arise because the acceptance often occurs immediately after communication of the offer. However, when there is a time lag between receipt of the offer and communication of the acceptance, problems can arise.

Mailbox Rule

Under the *classical common law,* most courts apply the **mailbox rule.** This holds that an agreement is made at the instant the offeree *dispatches* the acceptance if he uses an **authorized means** of acceptance. This may be any means suggested by the offeror, the same means the offeror used, or any means as fast or faster than the means the offeror used. Acceptances sent by nonauthorized means are not effective until they are actually received by the offeror.

Under the mailbox rule, the risk of lost or delayed letters falls on the offeror. (Of course, the offeree would have to convince the court that the acceptance letter actually was dispatched.) The offeror may avoid this situation by stipulating that acceptance is not effective until actually received.

Reasonable Means Rule

Both the *modern common law* and the UCC suggest that an offer that fails to stipulate a means of acceptance authorizes acceptance by any **reasonable means.** The definition of what constitutes a reasonable means depends on the speed and reliability of the means, the nature of the contract (perishable goods), past dealings

http://
www.law.cornell.edu/
topics/commercial.
html lists a menu
of commercial law
topics.

between the parties, and industry standards. Acceptances transmitted by reasonable means are effective upon dispatch. However, an acceptance sent by an unreasonable means also is effective upon dispatch if it is received by the offeror within the same time that a reasonable means would arrive.

Cantu v. Central Education Agency
884 S.W.2D 565 (App. Tex. 1994)

FACTS   Maria Diosel Cantu was hired as a special-education teacher by the San Benito School District under a one-year contract for the 1990–91 school year. On Saturday, August 18, 1990, shortly before the start of the new school year, Maria hand-delivered to her supervisor a letter of resignation, effective August 17, 1990. In this letter, Maria requested that her final paycheck for the previous year be forwarded to an address some 50 miles away from San Benito. The superintendent of schools received the resignation on Monday, August 20. He wrote a letter accepting her resignation the same day and deposited it, properly stamped and addressed, in the mail at 5:15 p.m. that afternoon. At about 8:00 a.m. the next morning, August 21, Maria hand-delivered to the superintendent's office a letter withdrawing her resignation. This letter contained a San Benito address. In response, the superintendent hand-delivered that same day a copy of his letter mailed the previous day informing Maria that her resignation had been accepted and could not be withdrawn. When Maria sued, the trial court concluded that, because the school district's acceptance of Maria's resignation was effective when mailed, an agreement to rescind her employment contract was in force when she attempted to withdraw her offer of resignation. Maria appealed, contending a mailed acceptance is effective on dispatch only if the offeror sent the offer by mail or expressly authorized acceptance by mail. She argued that there was no express authorization to accept by mail.

ISSUE   Was the school district's acceptance of the offer of resignation effective when mailed?

DECISION   Yes. The expression that the offeror is the "master of her offer" reflects the power of the offeror to impose conditions on acceptance of the offer or specify the manner of acceptance. However, more often than not, an offeror does not expressly authorize a particular mode, medium, or manner of acceptance. In such cases, courts could have adopted a rule that no acceptance is effective until received. Instead, they created the mailbox rule, which makes acceptance effective upon dispatch. The modern common law adopts this approach: an acceptance by any medium reasonable under the circumstances is effective on dispatch, absent a contrary indication in the offer. The request or authorization to communicate the acceptance by mail is implied in two cases: (1) where the offer itself was communicated by mail and (2) where the circumstances are such that it must have been within the contemplation of the parties that the mails might be used as a means of communicating the acceptance. It was reasonable for the superintendent to accept Maria's offer of resignation by mail. She tendered her resignation shortly before the start of the school year—at a time when both parties could not fail to appreciate the need for immediate action to find a replacement. Further, her request that her final paycheck be forwarded to an address some 50 miles away indicated she could no longer be reached in San Benito.

Contradictory Responses

Sometimes an offeree changes her mind after responding to an offer. In a face-to-face encounter, the first response controls. However, when the parties are dealing over great distances, the rules must be more flexible. For instance, the offeree may first mail a rejection and then, after further reflection, telegram an acceptance. Because a rejection is not effective until it is actually received, the first reply received by the offeror governs. If the rejection arrives first, there is no agreement. (The acceptance is not effective on dispatch because the offeror may rely on the rejection.) If the acceptance arrives first, there is an agreement.

If the offeree first mailed an acceptance and then telegrammed a rejection, the acceptance normally would control because it was effective on dispatch. Thus, if the acceptance is received first, there still is an agreement. However, if the rejection arrives first, there is a contract unless the offeror relied to his detriment on the rejection by selling the goods to someone else. (This is an application of estoppel.)

Consideration ▬▬▬▬▬▬▬▬▬▬▬

Courts seldom enforce gratuitous promises. As a result, a person generally is not legally obligated to honor a promise unless the promisee paid some price for it. Suppose George offered to help Ingrid move to a new apartment. Although George and Ingrid have an agreement (she accepted his offer to help), he may legally renege on the promise unless Ingrid gave something in exchange for it. This price is known as **consideration.**

Definition of Consideration

Consideration may be defined as *legal value, bargained for and given in exchange for an act or a promise.* There are two dimensions to this definition: legal value and a bargained-for exchange. Each component is discussed below.

Legal Value

The consideration requirement means a person must pay a price for any promise she wishes to have enforced. However, the price she pays must have **legal value.** There are four ways for this to occur:

1. she *does something* she was not already legally obligated to do;
2. she *promises to do something* she was not already legally obligated to do;
3. she *refrains from doing something* she legally could have done; or
4. she *promises to refrain from doing something* she legally could have done.

To constitute legal value, the price paid must be legal. The following case illustrates a limitation on what the court will accept as legal value.

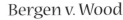

Bergen v. Wood
18 Cal.Rptr.2d 75 (App. 2 Dist. Cal. 1993)

FACTS   Duane Wood, a Bel-Air resident, was a former president of Lockheed and a widower. He met Birgit Bergen, a German actress, in Monte Carlo in the summer of 1981. At that time Wood was 65 and Bergen was 45. Although they developed an intimate relationship, the couple never cohabited. Bergen maintained her apartment in Munich, Germany. While she was in California she kept a room at the Beverly Pavilion Hotel in Beverly Hills. Bergen was Wood's traveling companion and accompanied him to social events. He provided her with money, and paid for her travel expenses and hotel accommodations. The relationship ended after seven years in late 1988. Bergen then sued Wood for breach of contract. She alleged that in 1982 they entered into an oral agreement whereby she agreed to be Wood's companion, his confidante, homemaker, and assist with his business affairs by acting as a social hostess. In return, Wood would provide for her financial support in accordance with her needs and his ability to pay. The trial court awarded Bergen $3,500 per month for 48 months. Wood appealed, arguing there was no consideration to support the alleged agreement because sexual services do not constitute legal value.

ISSUE   Was this agreement supported by consideration?

DECISION   No. Unmarried adults who live together and engage in sexual relations are competent to contract respecting their earning and property rights as long as the agreement does not rest upon illicit sexual activities. Cohabitation normally is a necessary condition of these property agreements because from cohabitation flows the rendition of domestic services, services which amount to lawful consideration for a contract between the parties. Further, if cohabitation were not a prerequisite to recovery, every dating relationship would have the potential for giving rise to such claims. This agreement is unenforceable because the parties did not cohabit and therefore no consideration was paid by Bergen severable from the sexual relationship. In addition to rendering sexual services, Bergen acted as Wood's social companion and hostess. Because services as a social companion and hostess normally are not compensated and are inextricably intertwined with the sexual relationship, Bergen failed to show any consideration independent of the sexual aspect of the relationship.

Legal value need not have actual value to the person requesting the promise, act, or forbearance. For instance, Eileen promised to give Richard a watch if he stayed on a strict vegetarian diet for three months. If Richard sticks to the diet, he has paid legal value because he had no prior legal obligation to be a vegetarian. Although Richard's diet may not benefit Eileen in any way, she still must give him the watch since he did what she requested.

Courts seldom look into the *adequacy of consideration*. That is, they generally do not worry about whether the promisee's price was worth the promisor's promise. However, there are exceptions to this rule. First, if the inadequacy is glaringly apparent ("I will give $30 for $3,000."), the agreement may be unenforceable. Second, if the court suspects fraud, duress, or undue influence (these concepts are discussed in the next chapter), it may look into the adequacy of consideration.

Ethical Issue

A promise unsupported by consideration generally is not enforceable under contract law. Is it ethical to make such promises and then not carry them out?

Bargained-for Exchange

Merely paying a price is not enough to guarantee the enforceability of the promisor's promise. Instead, the promisee must pay the price the promisor requested. When an offeror makes an offer, he describes what his obligations will be in the contract. His offer also indicates what legal value the offeree must pay in return. In essence, the offer describes the consideration each contracting party must pay.

Contract Modifications

During contract negotiations, the parties frequently are unable to foresee everything that might affect the actual performance or profitability of their agreement. Accordingly, during the performance stage of the contract, one or both of the parties often desires to modify the original agreement. Consideration issues often arise when a modification is attempted. The common law and the UCC approach modifications differently.

Common-Law Modifications

Under the common law, an agreement to modify the original contract generally is not enforceable unless it is supported by new consideration. For instance, Tom promised to paint Carol's house for $1,000. Prior to completing the job, Tom told Carol he would not finish unless she agreed to pay him an additional $200. Even if Carol promised to pay the extra amount, she does not have to unless Tom paid something additional for her new promise.

Under some circumstances, however, Carol's new promise might be enforceable. Suppose Tom requested more money because vandals had destroyed much of his earlier work. If it is not clear from the original contract which party (Tom or Carol) is responsible for damages caused by vandalism, Tom may no longer have a preexisting duty to complete the job for $1,000. In that case, Carol's promise to pay the additional money would be enforceable.

UCC Modifications

The UCC does not require new consideration to modify contracts for the sale of goods as long as the request is made in *good faith*. The good-faith requirement has two components. First, the modification request must be consistent with reasonable commercial standards of fair dealing. This means that the reason for wanting to modify should be something that would cause an ordinary merchant to attempt to modify (increased costs, unexpected difficulty). Second, the person wishing to modify must demonstrate that she was acting honestly and not merely exercising superior bargaining power to pressure the other party to modify.

Figure 8–3:   Formation of a Contract

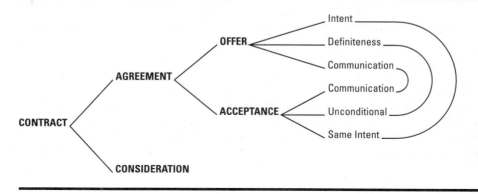

There are other limitations on modifications. For instance, if the original contract is in writing and contains a provision requiring modifications to be in writing, oral promises to modify are not enforceable. Further, a contracting party always has the right to reject a modification request.

QUESTIONS AND PROBLEM CASES

1. When is a contract governed by the Uniform Commercial Code rather than the common law?

2. Explain the general rule governing the offeror's power to revoke an offer. Describe the three exceptions to this rule.

3. How does implied contract differ from quasi contract?

4. Describe the difference between a bilateral contract and a unilateral contract.

5. Salamon agreed to buy two lots owned by Terra for $9,000 each. The agreement provided that Salamon would take possession of the lots by April, but would not have to pay the bulk of the purchase price ($8,500 per lot) until August. Salamon intended to build a house on each lot, sell the houses, and pay Terra with the proceeds of the sales. After partially completing the two houses, Salamon was unable to secure financing to finish the construction. Despite the fact that Terra extended the payment date several months beyond August, Salamon was unable to pay for the lots. Under the terms of the agreement, Terra retook possession of the lots. Salamon filed a quasi contract suit against Terra, seeking to recover the reasonable value of the partially constructed houses. Should Terra be required to pay?

6. Action Ads hired Judes as a salesman. The employment contract provided that: "Sixty days from your date of hire, Action Ads will provide a medical insurance program for you and your dependents." Judes was not a very successful salesman with the company, earning only $580 in commissions over a six-month period. In fact, during this time Judes filed for and received unemployment benefits from the government. Judes and Action Ads never discussed the details of the insurance coverage. The parties did not identify the insurance carrier, the risks insured against, or the amount of coverage. In reality, Action Ads never secured an insurance policy for Judes. When Judes was seriously burned in a gas explosion at his mobile home, he sued Action Ads to recover his medical expenses. Is Action Ads liable to Judes?

7. Robert Cagle went to Roy Buckner Chevrolet to discuss the purchase of a 1978 Limited Edition Corvette CP. General Motors produced only a small number of these cars, referred to as "Indy Vettes." Cagle talked to the used-car manager, who partially filled out a buyer's order form that was then presented to Joel Kelly, Buckner's new-car sales manager. After discussing the matter, Kelly agreed to sell Cagle an Indy Vette at list price. He wrote "list price" and signed his name on the partially completed form, signing in the middle of the page, rather than in the space provided for the signature. Cagle also signed the form and gave Kelly a $500 deposit. When the form was signed, Buckner did not have an Indy Vette in its possession. Two such cars were later received. However, because market demand for the cars had driven their value far above list price, Buckner refused to deliver either car to Cagle and attempted to return his deposit. When Cagle filed suit, Buckner argued the order form was too indefinite to create a contract. Is Buckner correct?

8. On September 24th, Benya presented Stevens and Thompson Paper Company (S&T) with an offer to purchase timberland owned by S&T for $605,000. S&T's lawyer made several modifications to the offer, raising the cash to be paid at closing from $5,000 to $10,000, raising the interest rate from 9 percent to 10 percent, and providing for quarterly rather than annual payments on the mortgage. S&T's vice president then initialed each change and signed the document, which was mailed back to Benya. In early November, S&T received a new offer from Benya that differed from the two previous versions in a number of ways. S&T neither signed this offer nor responded to it in any way. On November 7th, S&T sold the timberland to someone else. Benya sued for breach of contract. He argued that the September 24th offer formed an enforceable agreement since both Benya and S&T signed it. Is Benya correct?

9. Carroccia contracted to have Todd build a log home. Todd built the home, but it had numerous structural problems resulting from the inadequate construction techniques he used. Carroccia promised to pay Todd additional compensation if he would install tie-rods to correct the structural problems. When Carroccia failed to pay Todd for the tie-rod installation, Todd sued for breach of contract. Will Todd recover?

10. On June 19th, Berryman signed an option agreement giving Kmoch, a real estate agent, a 120-day option to purchase 960 acres of Berryman's land. Although the option agreement called for the payment of $10, Kmoch never paid any money to Berryman. In the latter part of July, Berryman telephoned Kmoch and asked to be released from the option agreement. Nothing definite was agreed to, and Berryman later sold the land to another person. In August, Kmoch decided to exercise the option and contacted the Federal Land Bank to make arrangements to buy the land. After being told by a bank representative that Berryman had sold the land, Kmoch sent Berryman a letter attempting to exercise the option. Berryman argued that there was no contract with Kmoch because his offer to sell was revoked prior to Kmoch's acceptance. Is Berryman correct?

ENFORCING CONTRACTS

America Online and other service providers filled magazines and mailboxes with diskettes allowing free trials to browse the Internet. People only needed to provide a credit-card number to get started. However, many trial users later discovered it was not so easy to stop. Credit-card accounts were billed automatically unless the user explicitly canceled. Yet the cancellation requirements often were a series of tricky procedures buried deep in lengthy contracts. America Online did not allow electronic cancellations because there were too many of them.

The Wall Street Journal, January 20, 1997, p. B1.

Think about this situation and consider these questions as you read this chapter.

Are these cancellation procedures fair?
Do contracts need to be fair?
How do we determine if a contract is fair?

Introduction

The previous chapter discussed how private agreements may become contracts. Through contract law, people are able to make plans, confident that their contracting partners will honor the promises they have made. However, Chapter 8 was merely a basic introduction on how to create a contract with a focus on the concepts of offer, acceptance, and consideration. This chapter takes a closer look at the procedural and substantive aspects of contract law by exploring the additional requirements that must be met before a contract will be enforced by the courts.

Chapter Overview

The chapter begins by examining capacity and real consent. These two concepts are integral aspects of the notion of consent underlying enforceable contractual agreements. This is followed by a discussion of illegality, since courts are unlikely to enforce agreements that are illegal or otherwise violate fundamental public policies. Next is a look at the types of contracts that generally must be in writing, followed by a quick look at how courts interpret such agreements. The chapter closes with a brief survey of the remedies available to someone who is injured by her contracting partner's failure to fully honor his contractual promises.

Capacity

The essence of a contractual agreement is the **mutual consent** of the parties. But real consent is not possible unless both contracting partners comprehend the significance of the legal obligation they are entering. Some individuals are presumed by law to lack the **capacity** to fully comprehend their legal rights and obligations. The legal system protects these individuals from falling prey to unscrupulous people by allowing them to cancel most of the contracts they enter. There are two classes of people generally presumed to lack capacity to contract: minors and the mentally impaired.

Contracts with Minors

In most states, a person is considered to be a **minor** (for contracting purposes) until she is 18 years old. Generally, minors do not have the capacity to contract and, therefore, they are given the right to cancel the agreements they enter anytime during their minority. Only the minor possesses this right. Thus, if an adult sells a car to a 16-year-old minor, the minor may return the car and demand his money back at anytime before he reaches the age of majority. (However, some courts may require the minor to pay for any wear and tear on the car, especially if he has lied about his age.)

Ratification

If the minor does not cancel his agreement within a reasonable time after reaching the age of majority, he forfeits the right. The courts presume that after reaching the age of majority, the minor has become an adult with the capacity to **ratify** the contract.

Necessaries

Despite lacking capacity to contract, minors must pay the reasonable value of any necessaries they have purchased. A necessary is anything essential to the minor's continued existence and general welfare (i.e., food, clothing, medical care). However, a minor may cancel a contract for necessaries without any penalty if she cancels before actually receiving the necessary. (See Figure 9–1.)

Contracts with the Mentally Impaired

The mentally impaired may also lack the capacity to contract. In some states, intoxicated people are treated as being mentally impaired if they are intoxicated at the time of contracting. The test for mental impairment is whether the person lacked sufficient mental capacity to understand the nature and effect of the agreement when the transaction was made. The rules regarding right to cancel, ratification, and necessaries basically are the same as the corresponding rules for minors.

Adams v. Adams

607 A.2D 1116 (Sup. Ct. Pa. 1992)

FACTS   After raising her four children, Karen Adams had a secret five-year homosexual relationship with another woman. Following the termination of this affair, she began psychological therapy in an attempt to salvage her marriage. Even after she and her husband separated, she continued her therapy. During one therapy session which her husband attended, he asked Karen, "What do you want?" She responded by writing on a piece of paper that she wanted the house, the car she was driving, their joint bank accounts, and a computer. Her husband took the note to his attorney, who drafted a property settlement agreement based on its terms. Karen signed the agreement despite her psychologist's advice that she seek her own legal counsel. She later tried to cancel the agreement, claiming that she lacked capacity to enter the agreement because of her mental impairment.

ISSUE   Did Karen's psychological problems deprive her of capacity to contract?

DECISION   No. There is no evidence that Karen suffered from emotional impairment of a nature that deprived her of the ability to comprehend the nature of the agreement. She was an intelligent person and was aware of her husband's and the family's resources. She chose to sign the agreement despite her psychologist's urging that she retain her own attorney. Karen sufficiently understood what she was doing and is bound by the settlement agreement.

Real Consent

The premise underlying capacity is that some people are unable to comprehend their legal rights and must be protected from others. However, there are other individuals who do have capacity to contract, but still are vulnerable to overreaching

Figure 9–1:   The Minority Defense

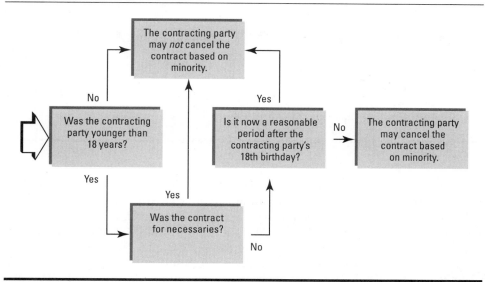

by individuals with superior knowledge or bargaining power. More and more courts are willing to intercede on behalf of people who lack the *knowingness* and/or *voluntariness* necessary to achieve **real consent.** When they find real consent to be lacking, these courts grant the injured party the right to cancel the agreement.

In cases of misrepresentation, fraud, or mistake, a contract may be voidable because one or both parties lacks the knowledge required for real consent. With duress, one party may lack sufficient voluntariness. When there is undue influence or unconscionability, the innocent person may lack knowingness and voluntariness. (See Figure 9–2.)

Misrepresentation

Sometimes a person gives her contracting partner a false impression about an important aspect of the contract. If the partner relies on this false statement, he may enter into an agreement he would not have accepted if he had known the truth. When the victim of the misstatement discovers the truth, he may cancel the contract under a theory of **misrepresentation.**

For instance, Jessica offered to sell her car to Paul for $7,500. She told him the car never had any major mechanical problems when, in reality, its transmission was replaced twice. Upon discovering the truth, Paul probably could return the car and demand his money back.

Elements of Misrepresentation

Misrepresentation occurs when someone makes a *false statement* of a *material fact* that is *reasonably relied on* and causes *harm* to another. Jessica made a false statement about the car and this statement gives rise to an action for misrepresentation even if she did not realize it was false (i.e., the transmission was replaced before she bought the car). Jessica's statement probably is material because Paul would

Figure 9–2:   Real Consent

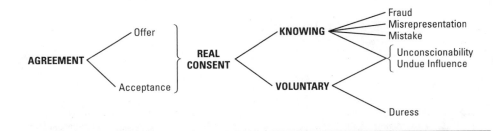

not have bought the car if he knew it had a history of transmission problems. Her statement was more than a mere opinion; she was stating a fact. Opinions (like "This is a great car.") do not give rise to misrepresentation claims. However, Paul cannot cancel the contract unless his reliance was reasonable. If he could have discovered that the transmission had been replaced through a reasonable inspection, he would have no right to cancel. Finally, Paul cannot cancel unless he actually suffered some harm. The court must believe a car without transmission problems is worth more than one with a history of such problems.

Fraud

If Paul could prove that Jessica knew or should have known her statements about the car were false, she could be liable for **fraud.** Paul's cause of action for fraud requires that he show that Jessica made a *misrepresentation* (the elements are listed above) *knowingly* and with an *intent to deceive.* Jessica's statements were knowingly made if she actually was aware of the car's transmission troubles or if she made the statements recklessly because she knew she did not have enough information to know if they were true. She had an intent to deceive if she should have realized that Paul would rely on her misstatement.

Fraudulent Behavior

Fraud normally arises from an express statement made by a promisor. However, silence may also give rise to an action for fraud. Particularly with important consumer transactions (like the sale of a home), a seller may have a **duty to disclose** material facts that the buyer could not have discovered through a reasonable investigation. And in cases where the seller realizes the buyer is mistaken as to an important aspect of the contract, there may be a duty to disclose the truth.

Remedies for Fraud

A defrauded party has a choice of remedies. First, he may treat the false statements as a misrepresentation and cancel the contract. Or, second, he may affirm (not cancel) the contract and sue the dishonest party for the tort of *deceit.* Because deceit is an intentional tort, the dishonest party may be required to pay both compensatory and punitive damages to the victim of her fraud.

Mistake

As with misrepresentation and fraud, a person may lack the knowingness essential for real consent when she is mistaken as to material terms in the contract. However, **mistake** differs from misrepresentation and fraud in that the mistaken belief is not the result of misstatements by the other party. The contract rules regarding mistake often turn on whether the mistake is mutual or unilateral.

Mutual Mistakes

When both parties to a contract are mistaken as to a material term, either may cancel the agreement upon learning the truth. This rule for **mutual mistakes** is premised on the idea that there is no real consent when both parties are mistaken. For instance, Sarah told Michael she wished to buy a cow for her dairy herd. Together they selected an animal without realizing it was barren; it could not bear young or give milk. Because both parties are mistaken, either may cancel the contract when it is discovered the cow is not suitable for a dairy herd.

Gould v. Board of Education
599 N.Y.S.2d 787 (Ct. App. N.Y. 1993)

FACTS Susan Gould achieved tenure as an elementary school teacher in New York City and indicated this fact on her application at a New York City high school. Gould was appointed to a three-year probationary position at the high school. Six months before the expiration of her three-year probationary term, Gould was notified that she would be terminated. However, the superintendent advised her that no information regarding the tenure denial would go in her file if she submitted her resignation. To avoid having the negative tenure recommendation appear in her file, Gould submitted her resignation the next day. When the resignation was submitted and accepted, Gould and the school board assumed that she was resigning as a probationary teacher. Neither was aware that her earlier tenure at the elementary school entitled her to a reduction in her probationary term from three to two years. And, under state law, because the school system had retained her beyond the two-year period, she was a tenured teacher.

ISSUE Is Gould entitled to cancel her resignation?

DECISION Yes. Generally, a contract entered into under a mutual mistake of fact is voidable and subject to cancellation. The mutual mistake must exist at the time the contract is entered into and must be substantial. The idea is that the agreement as expressed, in some material respect, does not represent the "meeting of the minds" of the parties. The discussion between Gould and the superintendent, the subsequent actions of Gould in submitting her resignation, and the school board in accepting it were all premised on a mutual mistake of fact as to a critical element: that Gould was a probationary employee. This misconception concerning a critical aspect of her employment pervades the entire transaction and provides a sound basis for treating the resignation as a nullity.

Unilateral Mistakes

Generally, when only one party is mistaken, he may not cancel the agreement. This forces people to exercise reasonable care before entering into contracts. However, there are two exceptions to this rule for **unilateral mistakes.** First, if the non-mistaken party knew or should have known of the other person's mistaken belief, he has a duty to disclose the truth. If he fails to do so, the mistaken party may cancel the agreement.

Second, some courts permit a mistaken party to cancel a contract when there is a reasonable *business computation error.* Suppose Reed, wishing to buy four thousand labels, typed an order form requesting "4mm labels." The industry term for a thousand labels was "m." By mistakenly requesting "4mm," Reed was ordering four million. If Reed informs the seller of the mistake before it relies to its detriment (produces four million labels for Reed), he may be able to cancel the contract.

Ethical Issue

Is it ethical to remain silent when you suspect that your contracting partner may be mistaken about an important aspect of the contract?

Duress

If someone is unreasonably coerced into entering a contract, he lacks the voluntariness essential to real consent. As a result, the coerced party may cancel the agreement under the theory of **duress.** There are two elements to an action based on duress: the agreement was induced by an *unreasonable threat,* and the victim had no *effective choice* but to enter the contract. For a threat to be unreasonable, it generally must involve something the individual is not legally entitled to do. Courts have found threats of a physical, emotional, or economic nature to constitute duress.

Undue Influence

Courts do not allow unscrupulous individuals to impose unfavorable agreements on persons with whom they have a confidential relationship. The victims of such **undue influence** may cancel their agreements because they generally lack both the knowingness and voluntariness elements of real consent. These cases generally involve old, sick, or very young persons who are the victims of overreaching by friends, relatives, or longtime advisors (doctors or lawyers).

Three things must be shown to establish undue influence: (1) a *relationship of trust and confidence* (2) in which *one person dominates* the other (3) with *unfair persuasion.* Courts are likely to find persuasion to be unfair when the vulnerable person was rushed into a decision without access to outside advice or time to consider the alternatives.

Johnson v. International Business Machines

891 F.Supp. 522 (N.D. Cal. 1995)

FACTS   Ronald D. Johnson was laid off from his position at IBM after working there for over 20 years. Johnson, an African-American, suspected his termination was based on his race and age in violation of federal employment law. After giving Johnson two-months notice of the layoff, IBM offered him a severance package, which would pay him 26 weeks of separation pay ($19,852.64). However, to receive this money he was required to sign a release in which he promised to never institute any legal claims against IBM. The release provided in bold print: **"IBM ADVISES YOU TO CONSULT AN ATTORNEY BEFORE YOU SIGN THIS RELEASE."** If Johnson did not sign the release, he would have received a separation allowance representing only two weeks pay ($1,527.20). Whether or not he signed the release, Johnson would have been involuntarily terminated by IBM. However, even if he refused to sign the release, IBM would permit Johnson to apply for a lower-paying manufacturing position. Johnson described his situation to an attorney, who advised him that if he signed the release, he would have difficulty pursuing discrimination charges against IBM. Despite this advice, Johnson signed the release. He then sued IBM for race and age discrimination. He argued that he was not bound by the terms of the release because it was procured by economic duress and undue influence.

ISSUE   Is Johnson bound by the terms of the release?

DECISION   Yes. In order to establish his claim for economic duress, Johnson needed to prove that (i) IBM engaged in a sufficiently coercive wrongful act; (ii) a reasonably prudent person in Johnson's economic position would have no reasonable alternative but to succumb to IBM's coercion; (iii) IBM knew of Johnson's economic vulnerability; and (iv) IBM's coercive wrongful act actually induced Johnson to sign the release. IBM did not commit a wrongful act by requiring Johnson to choose between the two weeks severance pay or signing the release and receiving 26 weeks severance pay. When he signed the release, Johnson was not facing imminent bankruptcy or financial ruin. He had objectively reasonable alternatives to signing. For instance, he could have applied for the lower paying manufacturing position. While most cases of undue influence involve persons who bear a confidential relationship to one another, a confidential relationship need not be present when the undue influence involves unfair advantage of another's weakness or distress. To establish his claim for undue influence, Johnson was required to prove (1) that IBM applied *excessive pressure* to induce him to sign the release; and (ii) that Johnson was *unduly* susceptible to such extraordinary persuasion. IBM did not employ excessive pressure or overpersuasion to induce Johnson to sign the release. Indeed, IBM exerted no pressure or persuasion whatsoever. Further, at the time he signed, Johnson did not suffer from a total weakness of mind which left him entirely without understanding, nor was he with a lesser weakness which destroyed his capacity to make a contract. Johnson, instead, had a mere weakness of spirit caused by his dismay at losing his job which he had held over the preceding 20 years and his anger and frustration in believing he had been racially discriminated against by IBM. This lesser weakness, whatever its medical diagnosis, was legally insufficient for rescission of a contract for undue influence.

Unconscionability

A person may lack both knowingness and voluntariness in cases of **unconscionability.** The Uniform Commercial Code, which governs contracts for the sale of goods, grants courts the power to refuse enforcement of unconscionable contracts. However, the concept of unconscionability is not confined to sale-of-goods transactions. Most courts refuse to enforce unconscionable agreements in all types of consumer transactions.

Unfortunately, there is no precise definition of unconscionability. However, it is more than a remedy for people who happened to enter into a bad bargain. Instead, it is designed to protect people from oppression and unfair surprise. Unconscionability may be found when there is an *absence of meaningful choice* (procedural unconscionability) combined with *terms unreasonably advantageous* to one of the contracting parties (substantive unconscionability). Generally, both must be found.

Procedural Unconscionability

Procedural unconscionability focuses on the manner in which the contract was negotiated as well as the relative circumstances of the parties. Courts look to see if each party had a reasonable opportunity to understand the terms and conditions of the agreement. Procedural unconscionability is more likely to be found where the agreement is embodied in one party's preprinted form, the weaker party had no meaningful choice, or the stronger party used deceptive practices to secure agreement. Consumers dealing with merchants are the parties most likely to be protected by the doctrine of procedural unconscionability. Businesspeople are less likely to be protected unless they are small businesses dealing with large corporations.

Substantive Unconscionability

The arguments for and against substantive unconscionability focus on the contents of the agreement. This involves examining the relative fairness of the obligations assumed by the parties. Substantive unconscionability is likely to be found if the terms are oppressive, unreasonably one-sided, or unjustifiably harsh.

Sosa v. Paulos

924 P.2d 357 (Sup. Ct. Utah 1996)

FACTS   Dr. Lonnie Paulos performed reconstructive knee surgery on Doncene Sosa. Less than one hour prior to the surgery, after Ms. Sosa was undressed and in her surgical clothing, someone from Dr. Paulos's office gave her three documents and asked her to sign them. One of them was an arbitration agreement in which Sosa agreed that any dispute would be resolved by arbitration and that she would be obligated to pay Dr. Paulos's arbitration fees (attorney's fees plus $150 per hour for his personal time spent on the matter) if the arbitrators agreed that he committed malpractice but she was awarded less than one-half of the amount she claimed. Ms. Sosa signed all three documents without reading them. Further, neither Dr. Paulos nor any member of his staff discussed the arbitration agreement with her at any time, either when she signed it or during any of her prior office visits. Immediately after awakening from anesthesia, Ms. Sosa became aware that there were surgical complications. She filed a complaint for medical malpractice. She also argued that the provision requiring her to pay Dr. Sosa's arbitration fees was unenforceable because it was unconscionable.

ISSUE   Is the provision unconscionable?

DECISION   Yes. A majority of courts divide unconscionability doctrine into two branches: procedural unconscionability, which focuses on the formation of the agreement, and substantive unconscionability, which focuses on the agreement's contents. When determining whether a contract is substantively unconscionable, we consider whether its terms are so one-sided as to oppress or unfairly surprise an innocent party. A provision requiring payment of costs by a patient who wins less than half the amount of damages sought in arbitration is substantively unconscionable. Under these terms, a patient must pay Dr. Paulos's attorney's fees and costs even in situations where it is established that he committed medical malpractice. There also are elements of procedural unconscionability surrounding the negotiation of this agreement. Ms. Sosa was not given a copy of the agreement until minutes away from surgery. She was rushed and hurried to sign and thus did not read them. The agreement was on a printed form and was drafted by Dr. Paulos, who was in a much stronger bargaining position considering the time of the delivery of the agreement to Ms. Sosa. We cannot conclude that the agreement was negotiated in a fair manner and that the parties had a knowing and voluntary meeting of the minds. Nor can we conclude that Ms. Sosa had a meaningful choice with respect to signing the agreement.

Illegality

Courts do not enforce agreements that violate the law or are contrary to important public policies. When a court finds **illegality** it generally takes a *"hands-off"* approach. For instance, suppose that Jack sells cocaine to Ellen on the condition that she pay him in one week. Even if Ellen consumes all of the cocaine, a court is not likely to make her pay Jack.

However, there are several exceptions to this "hands-off" approach. Sometimes courts allow a person to recover the value of her efforts when she unknowingly enters into an illegal agreement. Thus, if Donna cut Stuart's hair without realizing she needed a license, Stuart might be required to pay. Or if Doug is treated by an unlicensed physician, he probably could recover any money he had paid if he did not realize the doctor was unlicensed. This is because the licensing statute was designed to protect people like Doug. Finally, some courts allow a person to recover money he has spent if he cancels the agreement before any illegal acts have taken place. Thus, in our earlier example, suppose Ellen had paid Jack in advance for the cocaine. If she calls off the deal before Jack delivers the cocaine, a court might require Jack to return her money.

Al-Ibrahim v. Edde

897 F.Supp. 620 (D.D.C. 1995)

FACTS   George Edde was employed by the Sheikh Al-Ibrahim. As part of his employment, Edde was the Sheikh's constant companion. Because the Sheikh was a frequent high-stakes gambler, the job required Edde to accompany him on numerous visits to casinos in the United States. The Sheikh required that Edde sign for the Sheikh's winnings on documents that were submitted to the Internal Revenue Service. After leaving the Sheikh's employ, Edde began negotiations with the IRS by which he would pay past obligations, interest, and penalties on the gambling winnings he had claimed as his own. Edde never informed the IRS that the gambling winnings actually were won by and retained by Sheikh Al-Ibrahim. When the Sheikh failed to honor his promise to reimburse Edde for the more than $400,000 Edde had paid the IRS, Edde sued for recovery.

ISSUE   Should the Sheikh be required to reimburse Edde?

DECISION   No. Contracts to perform an illegal act, such as the contract between Edde and the Sheikh, normally are void and unenforceable. The purpose of this rule is to prevent wrongdoers from using or abusing the legitimate judicial process to resolve disputes over their illegal undertakings. As a U.S. citizen, Edde made false statements to the IRS in an effort to frustrate the lawful and timely collection of taxes. The fact that he ultimately paid the IRS does not excuse his behavior. He broke the law. To enforce the contract between Edde and the Sheikh would be to excuse Edde's conduct, to enforce a contract that had as its purpose the commission of illegal acts, and to permit the judicial process to be used in violation of public policy.

Statutory Violations

There are many statutes regulating peoples' behavior, and agreements in violation of these laws are unenforceable. These **regulatory statutes** often include the numerous licensing provisions that people must meet before they may sell goods or perform services. They were enacted to protect the public. People who do business without securing the necessary licenses generally are unable to receive compensation for the goods they have sold or the services they have performed.

The illegality rules governing regulatory statutes do not apply to **revenue-raising statutes.** While regulatory statutes were passed to protect the public welfare, revenue-raising measures are merely designed to raise money for the government. If a license is available to anyone who pays a fee, regardless of her qualifications, it is merely revenue raising. A person who fails to secure a license required by a revenue-raising statute may be subject to a fine, but can still insist on compensation for her goods or services.

Public-Policy Violations

Some agreements may not violate any specific statute, but still may be unenforceable because they are contrary to a fundamentally important **public policy.** Unfortunately, there is no precise definition for public policy, and the policies supported by some courts may be rejected by others. In fact, some judges reject the very idea that courts should insist that contracts remain consistent with any unlegislated idea of public policy. Other judges may use both unconscionability and public-policy analysis in deciding a case without identifying either by name.

Some courts do not enforce surrogacy agreements (carrying another person's child to term for a fee) because they are contrary to the judge's notion of public policy. (Surrogacy agreements are discussed in Chapter 19.) Others reject cohabitation agreements between unmarried couples because the judge opposes sexual relations between unmarried persons. (Cohabitation agreements are discussed in Chapter 18.)

Exculpatory Clauses

Many courts carefully scrutinize **exculpatory clauses** in contracts. These provisions attempt to relieve one person from liability for the consequences of his actions. If the waiver is freely bargained for and only limits a person's liability for negligence, most courts will enforce it. However, if it seeks to prevent liability for willful or reckless behavior or is unfairly imposed on the other party, it is not likely to be enforced.

Writing

As a general rule, oral contracts are just as enforceable as written agreements. Of course, it usually is wise to memorialize a contract in writing. The writing not only provides strong evidence of what was agreed upon, but it also makes it more likely that both parties have fully considered the legal significance of their promises. Each state has adopted a **statute of frauds** that requires that certain contracts generally must be in writing to be enforceable. (See Figure 9–3.) These are:

1. contracts for a transfer of land,
2. contracts to guarantee the debts of another,
3. contracts that cannot be performed within one year, and
4. contracts for the sale of goods for $500 or more.

http://www.moga.state.mo.us/statutes/c400-499/4000201.002 contains the revised statute of frauds for the state of Missouri.

Figure 9–3:   The Statute of Frauds

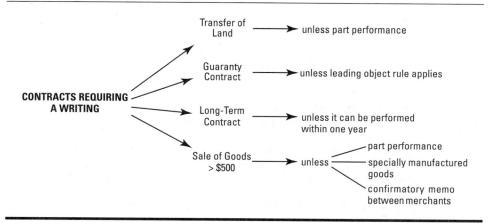

CONTRACTS REQUIRING A WRITING

Transfer of Land —— unless part performance

Guaranty Contract —— unless leading object rule applies

Long-Term Contract —— unless it can be performed within one year

Sale of Goods > $500 —— unless — part performance / specially manufactured goods / confirmatory memo between merchants

Transfers of Land

http://
www.law.cornell.edu/
ucc contains the text
of the UCC.

Contracts transferring ownership rights in real property generally must be in writing to be enforceable. Real property is defined as the earth's crust and everything firmly attached to it. Thus, the sale or mortgage of a house or other building, the sale or granting of an easement in land, or the sale of mineral rights requires a written agreement. (Mortgages and easements are discussed in Chapter 16.) Leases, on the other hand, are treated as personal property and do not require a writing unless they are long-term agreements. (Leases are discussed in Chapter 17.) Further, contracts to construct a house or other building do not fall within this statute of frauds provision. This is because they are a service (construction) rather than a transfer of ownership rights.

Some courts still enforce oral agreements transferring an ownership interest in land when the buyer has substantially relied on the transaction. Ordinarily, this reliance must take the form of **part performance** by the buyer. To demonstrate sufficient part performance, the buyer usually must have taken possession of the property, made substantial improvements, and made substantial payments.

Guaranty Contracts

A secondary promise to pay the debts of another requires a writing under the statute of frauds. Suppose Bank One threatens to repossess John's car because he has not been making timely payments. To prevent the repossession, John's father promises the bank that he will make future payments if John fails to do so. This is a **guaranty contract,** and John's father is a **guarantor** of John's debt. He has made a secondary promise (John made the primary promise) to pay the debt on the condition that John fails to pay. (Guaranty contracts are discussed further in Chapter 10.) The statute of fraud requires that secondary promises be in writing.

Under certain circumstances courts enforce oral guaranty contracts. This happens under the **leading object** (or main purpose) exception. In essence, when the guarantor's primary motive for making the guaranty promise was to benefit his own economic welfare, the promise may be oral. Suppose in our earlier example that John and his father used John's car in a delivery business they both operated. Since avoiding the repossession would benefit John's father economically, his promise to pay John's debt could be oral under the leading-object exception.

Sebaly, Shillito & Dyer v. Bakers Equipment

597 N.E.2d 1144 (Ct. App. Ohio 1991)

FACTS   Bakers Equipment/Wholesalers (BE/W) retained the law firm of Sebaly, Shillito & Dyer to handle legal action against several individuals. Eugene Stoller owned 100 percent of the voting stock of BE/W and was its president and chief executive officer. With the company in an insolvent condition and still owing $42,544.41 in legal fees, the law firm informed Stoller that it would withdraw its representation unless he personally guaranteed payment. In a telephone conversation, Stoller promised to pay the legal fees incurred by BE/W. Stoller later refused to pay, arguing that his oral guaranty promise was not enforceable under the statute of frauds.

ISSUE Is Stoller's oral promise to pay BE/W's legal fees enforceable?

DECISION Yes. When the leading object of the promisor is not to answer for another's debt but to pursue some economic or business purpose benefitting himself, his promise need not be in writing. Stoller's oral promise to guarantee BE/W's legal fees was outside of the statute of frauds. He was an officer of the corporation, the corporation owed him substantial amounts of money, he was employed by the corporation, and he was the sole shareholder. The proceeds from any legal action brought on behalf of BE/W by the law firm would directly benefit Stoller. Thus, his leading object when making the guaranty was to further his personal economic interest.

Long-Term Contracts

The statute of frauds requires that contracts that cannot be performed within one year of their formation must be in writing. This rule is premised on the idea that over long time periods memories are likely to fade, creating a need for written evidence of the contractual terms. Thus, a contract to work for two years must be in writing. But a contract to work until retirement or to work for life does not require a writing. Since a person could retire or die within one year, these agreements could possibly be performed within one year of formation.

Of course, if one party has performed on an oral contract that cannot be performed within one year, she is entitled to compensation for that performance. Thus, if Alice orally agrees to serve as ABC's computer consultant for three years, she is entitled to compensation for the time she has actually worked.

Sale of Goods for $500 or More

The Uniform Commercial Code has its own statute of frauds provision for sale-of-goods transactions. It requires that contracts for the sale of goods for $500 or more must be in writing. Therefore, if Francine orally promises to buy a television for $750, her promise is not enforceable. But if the price of the television had been $450, the seller could require her to make the purchase.

There are three exceptions to this writing requirement. They cover partial performance, specially manufactured goods, and confirmatory memos between merchants.

http://
www.law.cornell.edu/ ucc/2/2-201.html. contains information about the Uniform Commercial Code §2-201, Formal Requirements; Statute of Frauds.

Partial Performance

Oral contracts for goods costing more than $500 are enforceable to the extent that one party has made payment or delivered the goods. This **partial performance** exception protects against one party unfairly benefitting at the other's expense. Suppose Brett orally agreed to buy 100 karate uniforms from Century Martial Arts for $15 each. Because the contract is for $1,500, a writing is required. However, if Century had already delivered 20 uniforms, Brett would be required to pay $300.

Specially Manufactured Goods

The Uniform Commercial Code also provides an exception to its writing requirement when the contract involves the sale of **specially manufactured goods.** To meet this exception, the goods must be specially manufactured and not suitable for sale to others in the ordinary course of the seller's business. Further, the seller must have made a substantial beginning of their manufacture, or committed itself for their purchase, before learning that the buyer no longer wants them.

Suppose that the karate uniforms Brett orally promised to buy from Century Martial Arts were to be custom tailored with several colors and imprints used exclusively by Brett's karate school. Once Century has contracted to buy the uniforms from its manufacturer, or begun manufacturing the uniforms itself, it is too late for Brett to cancel the oral agreement. This exception is designed to protect Century from an undue hardship, since it would be unable to sell the uniforms to anyone else.

Confirmatory Memos

Sometimes only one party to the contract has signed a writing. Suppose after a telephone call from Brett, Century sent him a confirmatory memo acknowledging the contract for the uniforms. Because Century has signed a writing, it cannot back out of the contract. But Brett cannot be forced to buy any uniforms because he has not signed an agreement. This can pose a great hardship on Century if the goods are not specially manufactured because it cannot be certain that Brett will accept delivery of the uniforms.

However, the Uniform Commercial Code provides relief in cases like this where there is a **confirmatory memo** between merchants. (Century is a professional seller of karate uniforms and Brett is a professional buyer of them; so they both are merchants.) Century sent a memo to Brett confirming its obligation to sell the uniforms. If Brett does not reject the contract within 10 days of receiving the memorandum, he must honor his oral promise to buy.

--- Ethical Issue ---

Suppose Cheryl orally agreed to buy a $900 stereo from Tom. Two days later, before the stereo was delivered, Cheryl found a better deal somewhere else. She then refused to buy the stereo from Tom, arguing that her oral contact was unenforceable. The law allows her to do this. Is Cheryl behaving in an ethical manner?

Contract Interpretation

Disputes over the parties' respective rights and obligations in a contract are quite common. Whether the terms are written or oral, reasonable disagreements are still likely to occur. In most cases, the contracting parties privately work out their differences without the aid of an attorney or a lawsuit. However, sometimes they insist on litigating the matter. To handle these situations, the courts follow fairly predictable rules governing contract interpretation.

Rules of Interpretation

Courts give an agreement the meaning a reasonable person would give it in light of the circumstances surrounding the transaction. This generally entails determining the primary objective of the parties and interpreting the language in a manner that brings about that result. Ordinary words are given their ordinary meaning and technical terms are given their technical meaning unless the parties clearly indicate another intent.

Past Dealings and Industry Standards

When ambiguities arise, courts look to past dealings between the parties and to industry standards for guidance. However, express language governs past dealings and past dealings override industry standards unless the parties indicate otherwise. Thus, a person can make certain that past dealings or industry standards do not control the contract by clearly rejecting them in the agreement.

Form Contracts

A great number of day-to-day contracts involve the use of one party's preprinted forms. Two important rules govern the use of these forms. First, when the form is partly printed and partly written, the written terms override inconsistent preprinted terms. This is because the written terms would seem to more genuinely reflect the wishes of both parties. Second, any ambiguities in a printed contract are to be construed against the party who drafted the agreement. This is designed to prevent a party from intentionally using ambiguous language to defraud its contracting partner.

The Parol Evidence Rule

The **parol evidence rule** is one of the most important contract rules for people to remember. It holds that a person cannot use evidence of statements made before or at the same time as a writing to contradict any of the written terms. Suppose Robert was about to sign a lease for an apartment when he noticed a clause that required him to pay a $10-per-day late fee for rental payments made after the first day of the month. Robert refused to sign the lease until the landlord assured him that he could wait as long as the tenth day of the month before a late fee would arise. If the landlord later charges Robert a $10 penalty for a payment made on the second day of the month, the parol evidence rule precludes Robert from offering evidence of the landlord's oral statements. Robert should have insisted the writing reflect the terms orally promised by the landlord before signing the lease.

http:// www.law.cornell.edu/ ucc/2/2-202.html is the site of UCC Article 2, §2-202, "Final Written Expression: Parol or Extrinsic Evidence."

Campbell v. Machias Savings Bank

865 F.Supp. 26 (D. Me. 1994)

FACTS   Lisa Campbell applied for a loan from Machias Savings Bank to finance the purchase of a mobile home. At that time, the bank's loan officer informed Campbell that she would have to provide a down payment of 5 percent of the purchase price. Campbell told the loan officer that she did not wish to provide a security interest in her land and was told that no lien on her land would be necessary. Machias then purchased a house lot for $2,900. The documents Campbell signed at the closing included a security agreement granting the bank a first-mortgage lien on the mobile home and on Campbell's house lot. It also required that she pay $1,695.25 toward the

continued

$21,678.75 sales price of the mobile home, which was a 7.8 percent down payment. Later, Campbell had difficulty making her payments and the bank threatened foreclosure. Campbell argued that the bank breached its contractual obligations to her by deviating from the loan officer's original representations and obligating her to a security agreement that placed a lien on her land and required more than a 5 percent down payment.

ISSUE   Should the loan officer's original representations override the terms of the security agreement?

DECISION   No. Campbell claimed that by accepting her loan application, the bank offered her a loan in compliance with the loan officer's representations (5 percent down payment and no lien on her land). She argued that the bank has breached this oral agreement. Under the parol evidence rule, however, prior statements inconsistent with the terms of a signed writing are not admissible. Because the lien and down payment requirements discussed with the loan officer are inconsistent with the terms of the written security agreement, they are disallowed.

Exceptions to the Rule

Statements made before, or contemporaneously with, the signing of the written contract can be used to *clarify ambiguities* in the writing. If Robert's lease stated a $10-per-day late fee would apply to all unreasonably late rent payments, Robert could argue that, based on the landlord's oral statements, a payment was not "unreasonably late" until after the tenth of the month. Oral statements made *after* a writing is signed may also be admitted to show that a written contract has been orally modified. But if the writing clearly states that all modifications must be in writing, such oral evidence is not admissible. (See Figure 9–4.)

Remedies

If one party does not honor the terms of the contract, the injured party generally is entitled to a **remedy**. When fashioning a remedy, courts try to put the non-breaching party in the same position he would have been in if the contract had been performed according to its terms. This normally is done by requiring the breaching party to pay monetary damages. However, in special instances, equitable remedies may be available.

Figure 9–4:   Parol Evidence Timeline

PRE-SIGNING PERIOD	POST-SIGNING PERIOD
Negotiations Begin .... Written Contract Signed	Written Contract Signed .... Contract Fully Performed
Statements may not be used to contradict the terms of the signed writing. They may be used to clarify ambiguities.	Oral statements may be used to show that the signed writing was modified.

Monetary Damages

Suppose Ace Auto Sales agreed to sell Jeff a car for $7,300. However, one of its salespeople mistakenly sold it to another customer before Jeff arrived to complete the transaction. Ace is liable to Jeff for breach of contract. If the car was worth $8,000 to Jeff, Ace must pay Jeff $700 in **compensatory damages.** This is calculated by subtracting what Jeff was supposed to pay ($7,300) from the value of the car to him ($8,000). Generally, a breaching party is only liable for damages that should have been foreseeable at the time of contracting.

Courts often permit **liquidated damages** provisions in contracts. Remember our earlier example where the landlord charged tenants $10 a day for late rental payments? That is a liquidated damages provision. As long as the amount is reasonable and the situation is such that actual damages would be difficult to calculate, these provisions are enforceable.

Equitable Remedies

In limited circumstances, monetary damages would not be sufficient to make the nonbreaching party whole. In those special cases a court may permit an equitable remedy. Generally, when someone breaches a contract to sell land, courts provide the equitable remedy of **specific performance** to the nonbreaching party. This requires the seller to actually deliver the deed and possession of the land rather than merely pay compensatory damages. Courts tend to permit specific performance with land contracts as well as sales involving extremely unique personal property. However, specific performance is seldom available in personal service contracts because of the problems inherent in making people work with each other.

A court may provide an **injunction** preventing someone from doing something in cases where the nonbreaching party would otherwise suffer irreparable harm. Suppose one of Margaret's key salespersons attempted to work for a competing business in spite of a term in her original employment contract preventing her from competing with Margaret. The former employee might be enjoined (prevented) from working for the competitor.

http://
www.law.cornell.edu/ ucc/2/2-719.html, contains the text of UCC §2-719 regarding remedies.

Substantial Performance

With some contracts, a person may have difficulty performing exactly as was specified in the contract. For instance, when constructing a building, a shortage of materials may require the builder to deviate slightly from the original plans. In these cases, if the breach is only minor, the builder is entitled to compensation for **substantial performance.** This means the nonbreaching party should pay him the agreed-upon contract price minus the damages he suffered from the incomplete performance.

Excuses for Nonperformance

A person who fails to honor her contractual obligations may be able to avoid paying monetary damages to her contracting partner if she has a *legal excuse* for nonperformance. For instance, if events unforeseeable at the time of contracting and out of the control of the parties prevent performance, no damages are owed. This

impossibility defense may arise from death or serious illness of the promisor in a personal service contract. Or it can occur if the government enacts a statute outlawing the promisor's performance. With sale-of-goods contracts, courts merely ask that the performance be *commercially impracticable* rather than impossible.

Luminous Neon v. Parscale

836 P.2D 1201 (CT. APP. KAN. 1992)

FACTS   Rita Parscale leased two custom-designed outdoor advertising signs from Luminous Neon. Parscale used the signs for her recently opened business in Topeka. Under the terms of the lease, Parscale was to pay $191.75 plus tax each month for five years. However, soon after she leased the signs, the City of Topeka began street construction that severely limited access to Parscale's business. The enterprise subsequently closed and Parscale stopped making payments on the sign after 19 months. Under the liquidated damages provision of the lease, Parscale was liable to Luminous Neon for damages equal to 80 percent of the remaining payments due. That figure represented Luminous Neon's expenses incurred in manufacturing, financing, and installing the signs, as well as profit. The 20 percent of the payments that was not included as liquidated damages was for maintenance and service expenses that would not be incurred due to Parscale's breach. Luminous Neon demanded $6,951.04, which represented 80 percent of the remaining 41 payments plus a $300 sign removal fee. Parscale contended that she was excused from the performing on the contract under the doctrine of commercial impracticability and, in the alternative, that the liquidated damages provision was unreasonable because she originally could have bought the signs for $5,600.

ISSUE   Should the court order Parscale to pay the liquidated damages?

DECISION   Yes. As a general rule, difficulty or improbability of accomplishment without financial loss will not release a party from a contract under the doctrines of impossibility or impracticability. Though compliance may become a hardship, that will not excuse a party from contractual obligations that are possible and lawful. To excuse performance, impracticability must be objective rather than subjective. Subjective impracticability being, "I cannot do it" and objective impracticability being, "The thing cannot be done." Parscale's problem was merely subjective impracticability. In addition, it cannot be said that road construction is an unforeseeable event. Parscale should have safeguarded against this possibility in the lease. Her liquidated damages argument also fails. The general rule is that courts will not enforce a liquidated damages provision which fixes damages in an amount grossly disproportionate to the harm actually sustained or likely to be sustained. However, the contention that the original sales price of the signs constitutes reasonable damages is not persuasive. When one chooses to lease an item and then breaches that lease, it is unreasonable to believe damages should be based upon values attendant to a purchase of the item. By leasing rather than buying, Parscale avoided financing charges, insurance, repair, and maintenance expenses.

QUESTIONS AND PROBLEM CASES

1. Parties to contracts often run afoul of the *parol evidence rule*. Carefully explain this rule, giving an example of how it might create problems for someone entering into a contract.

2. What is meant by the term *necessaries*? What effect do necessaries have on a contract with a minor?

3. Under what circumstances will a court allow a contract to be canceled for a unilateral mistake?

4. What is the difference between a regulatory statute and a revenue-raising measure? For the purposes of contract law, why does this difference matter?

5. For several years prior to her husband's death, Florence Goldman cared for him at home. During much of her husband's illnesses (Alzheimer's and Parkinson's diseases) and some time thereafter, Goldman herself was under the care of a psychiatrist, who treated her for the depression stemming from the strain and grief she experienced because of her husband's declining health. As part of this therapy Goldman was treated with antidepressant drugs, which had a negative effect on her cognitive processes. August Bequai was a longtime friend whom Goldman regarded as almost a member of her family. He was an attorney and, during her husband's illness and death, Goldman looked to Bequai as her advisor and attorney. Three months after her husband's death, Goldman conveyed a condominium and another piece of property to Bequai for $10. Bequai told her the property transfers were merely temporary and were necessary for Bequai to set up a business for himself and Goldman. Can Goldman cancel the property transfers under the doctrine of undue influence?

6. Allegheny International hired Remcor, a company specializing in hazardous waste remediation, to remove radioactive material from property owned by Allegheny. The parties' contract specified that there was an estimated 3,200 cubic feet of contaminated materials and that they would be excavated by using a small mechanical excavator and hand tools. This is an expensive process, called *guided excavation,* that is appropriate for removal of small quantities of waste. The agreement called for a lump sum price of $351,500 for the estimated 3,200 cubic feet with a unit price of $109.75 per cubic foot for the removal of any additional materials in excess of the original estimate. After beginning work, Remcor reported that the amount of waste was well in excess of its early estimates. There actually was more than 50,000 cubic feet of radioactive material, and at the original contract price it would cost more than several million dollars to remove it. By this time, Remcor had abandoned the guided excavation method and replaced it with a mass excavation process that was more economically efficient for excavating huge amounts. Allegheny insisted that its original promise to pay $109.75 for removal in excess of 3,200 be canceled and reduced to a lower amount to reflect the lower costs of the mass excavation process. Should the original agreement be canceled?

7. Sherwood met with Walker, an importer and breeder of Angus cattle, for the purchase of some livestock. After several days, Sherwood contracted to buy a cow, known as "Rose 2d of Aberlone," for approximately $80. Walker confirmed the sale in writing. Later that month, when Sherwood attempted to take possession of the cow, Walker refused to accept Sherwood's payment or deliver the cow. When Sherwood sued for possession of the cow, Walker argued that at the time of the sale it was believed by both parties that the cow was barren and would not breed. Walker originally had paid $850 for the cow and, if not barren, she would be worth from $750 to $1,000. Walker decided not to deliver the cow to Sherwood after he discovered that she was with calf. Should Walker be required to deliver the cow to Sherwood?

8. American Oil Company presented to Weaver, a filling station operator, a printed form contract as a lease. The rental agreement

contained, in addition to the normal leasing provisions, a "hold harmless" clause which provided that Weaver (the lessee) would hold harmless and also indemnify American Oil (the lessor) for any negligence of American Oil occurring on the leased premises. The clause in this lease was in fine print and contained no title heading which would have identified it as an indemnity clause. Weaver had left high school after one-and-a-half years and spent his time, prior to leasing the service station, working at various skilled and unskilled labor-oriented jobs. The signing of the lease consisted of nothing more than the agent of American Oil placing the lease in front of Weaver and saying "sign," which Weaver did. Later, an American Oil Company employee negligently sprayed gasoline over Weaver and his assistant, causing them to be burned and injured. American Oil Company argued that the "hold harmless" clause in the lease relieved it of all liability for its employee's negligence. Did the "hold harmless" clause relieve American Oil from liability for negligence?

9. Griess purchased insurance from Farm Bureau that protected his livestock against "loss by windstorms." Although, the insurance policy included several exclusions, "loss by infectious diseases" was not specifically listed as an exclusion. Griess's swine herd later became infected by a virus carried downwind by a tornado. He filed a claim with Farm Bureau for his $149,000 loss. Farm Bureau refused to pay because the loss was caused by a virus rather than a windstorm. Should the insurance contract be interpreted to cover Greiss's loss?

10. Walker owned property in Alaska which he listed for sale. The listing agreement described the property as having 580 feet of highway frontage and stated, "ENGINEER REPORT SAYS OVER 1 MILLION IN GRAVEL ON PROP." A later listing described the property as having 580 feet of highway frontage, but listed the gravel content as "minimum 80,000 cubic yds. of gravel." Cousineau, a contractor who was also in the gravel extraction business, offered to purchase the property. He had tried to determine the lot's highway frontage, but was unable to do so because the property was covered with snow. After the sale was completed, Cousineau learned that the highway frontage was only 410 feet. At about the same time, the gravel ran out after Cousineau had removed only 6,000 cubic yards. Cousineau stopped making payments and attempted to cancel the contract. Should the contract be canceled?

CHAPTER 10

BORROWING MONEY

Marianne Driscol received annoying telephone calls at all hours of the day, interrupting her sleep and disrupting her work. The callers made a death threat and telephoned a bomb threat to her workplace. All the calls were made by collection agents pressuring Marianne to pay on a $2,000 credit card debt she owed. A jury ruled that Household Credit Services, the credit card issuer that hired the collection agents, owed Marianne $11 million in actual and punitive damages.

Bloomington Herald-Times, August 25, 1995, p. A5.

Consider Marianne Driscol's case against Household Credit and the various issues it raises, such as:

> What is a credit transaction? What rights and obligations does it trigger for lenders and borrowers?
>
> What can lenders do to guard against the risk that borrowers will fail to repay a loan?
>
> What are the rights and obligations of borrowers and lenders when a debt is not repaid in a timely manner?

Introduction

Increasingly, people are purchasing goods and services without cash or checks by deferring payment through the use of loans or credit cards. In fact, from 1991 through 1996, consumer debt increased over 39 percent and now exceeds $1 trillion. As the country moves further toward being a cashless society, it becomes imperative that each of us understands our rights and obligations when loaning or borrowing money.

Chapter Overview

The chapter begins with an introduction to the nature of credit, including a look at the specific issues that arise in credit card transactions. Next is a description of the special regulatory protections afforded consumers trying to obtain credit. After a brief examination of the law of suretyship, the focus shifts to Article 9 of the Uniform Commercial Code and its special rules governing secured credit in personal property. The chapter closes with a discussion of the options available to a lender when the borrower fails to repay, followed by a brief survey of the law of bankruptcy.

Credit Transactions

In this chapter the term **credit** refers to a transaction where a borrower obtains money, goods, or services in exchange for a promise to make payment at some future date. In general, this repayment includes the value of the money, goods, or services at the time the credit was extended (**principal**), plus an additional charge to compensate the lender for extending the credit (**interest**).

The amount of interest the borrower pays generally is determined by the *rate of interest* (a percentage rate multiplied times the balance due on the loan) and the length of time required to pay back the debt. However, it may also include other charges connected with the credit extension such as: numerical periodic rates, late fees, not sufficient funds (NSF) fees, overlimit fees, annual fees, cash advance fees, and membership fees. When borrowing money, you should be clear as to the amount of interest you are obligated to pay. In many credit transactions the rate of interest is *variable* rather than *fixed*. This means a general rise in interest rates in the country may trigger a correspondingly higher repayment obligation for the borrower.

Types of Credit

There are two basic types of credit: unsecured and secured. If the risk of nonpayment by the borrower seems low, the creditor may opt for an unsecured credit transaction. However, when the risk of nonpayment is high, secured credit may be a more prudent course for the creditor to follow.

Unsecured Credit

We engage in **unsecured credit** transactions on a regular basis. Perhaps you have recently visited the doctor and, rather than pay at the time of the service, you have the doctor's office bill you for payment. This is unsecured credit. The doctor is relying on your promise (express or implied) to make payment in a timely manner. Most credit card transactions also are a form of unsecured credit.

When extending unsecured credit, the creditor assumes a great risk. If the borrower is unable or refuses to repay the loan, the creditor's only legal recourse is to bring a civil lawsuit seeking repayment. In this suit, the creditor may ask the court to seize certain property of the debtor to satisfy its claim. Or if the borrower is working, the court may *garnish the wages* the borrower earns. However, in many instances, the borrower will have no available property and will not be earning enough money for the court to find garnishment to be appropriate. In those cases, the debtor may be **judgment proof.** This means the lender may have no practical means of forcing the borrower to repay.

The interest rates on unsecured loans often are quite high to compensate the lender for the greater risk of nonpayment. Many unsecured creditors also purchase credit insurance to cover unpaid loans. The cost of this insurance coverage generally is passed on to borrowers in the form of higher interest rates.

Secured Credit

Lenders may minimize the risk of nonpayment by insisting on **secured credit.** While this may take several forms, the most basic is for the debtor and creditor to identify a specific item of the debtor's property that the creditor may claim in the event of nonpayment. For instance, the bank loans Jane $10,000 in return for her promise to repay the debt in monthly payments for a period of three years. As a term of their contract, Jane gives the bank the right to seize her car if she fails to make payments in a timely manner. The bank could then sell the car and apply the proceeds of the sale to the balance due on the loan. Because secured credit reduces the creditor's risks, the rate of interest on secured loans often is lower.

Credit Cards

By 1996, credit card debt in the United States reached $360 billion. That is more than double its 1990 level. During that same period the average credit card balance per household doubled to almost $5,000. In fact, credit cards have become so commonplace that people often fail to realize that credit card purchases are loans.

Credit cards generally are easy to obtain and their convenience has encouraged widespread use for a variety of transactions ranging from purchases of groceries and gasoline to paying tax bills to the Internal Revenue Service. The 70 percent of credit card users who fail to pay off their balance each month often are spending between 15 and 18 percent interest on those purchases. Although credit card interest rates are regulated by state law, banks may charge out-of-state credit card customers the interest rate allowed by the bank's home state, even when that rate is higher that what is permitted by the state where the cardholder resides.

The Nature of Credit Card Debt

Most credit card transactions are unsecured loans from the credit card issuer to the cardholder. This explains the high interest rate that accompanies most credit cards. However, credit card purchases also may create secured credit if the sales slip adequately describes the goods purchased and acknowledges that the credit card issuer is retaining a security interest in them. For instance, Sears Roebuck has incorporated a security agreement with its Sears charge card. If Jimmy buys a videocassette recorder with his Sears charge card and fails to make timely payments, Sears may repossess the videocassette recorder. American Express, on the

http:// www.law.cornell.edu/ ucc/9/overview.html is the site of the contents list of Article 9 of the UCC. Select a topic for informatin on secured credit.

http:// www.law.cornell.edu/ topics/consumer_ credit.html, contains links to various federal statutes on credit and lending, as well as links to state sites.

other hand, is an unsecured creditor. If Jimmy had purchased the videocassette recorder on his American Express card, the creditor would have no special claim to the recorder if Jimmy failed to pay his monthly bill.

Unauthorized Charges

In order to provide credit card users with special protections, Congress enacted the *Fair Credit Billing Act* (FCBA). This legislation limits a cardholder's liability to $50 per credit card for unauthorized charges. Thus, if a thief stole Emily's Master-Card and made purchases totaling $700, Emily would be liable for only $50 of that amount.

Consumer advocates long complained that credit card companies made it extremely difficult for cardholders to remove unauthorized charges from their accounts. Issuers often placed unreasonable burdens on cardholders by requiring them to sign notarized affidavits, submit copies of police reports, appear in company offices to answer questions, and agree to testify in court. To address these concerns, the Federal Reserve Board set new guidelines for card issuers to follow when investigating claims of unauthorized charges. Specifically, issuers are required to conduct a "reasonable investigation" and are prohibited from dismissing a claim solely because the holder failed to comply with a "particular request" (such as filing a police report).

Minskoff v. American Express Travel Services
98 F.3d 703 (2nd Cir. 1996)

FACTS Equities, Inc., opened an American Express corporate charge account in the name of Edward Minskoff, the company's president and chief executive officer. Several years later, Equities hired Susan Schrader Blumenfeld as assistant to president/office manager. She was responsible for both the personal and business affairs of Minskoff as well as screening his mail and reviewing credit card statements. Minskoff stopped personally reviewing his corporate charge card statements after Blumenfeld was hired. In March 1992, American Express mailed a preaddressed application for an additional credit card to be issued from Minskoff's corporate account to Minskoff's business address. Blumenfeld completed the form, requesting a supplemental card in her name, without Minskoff's knowledge or consent. From April 1992 to March 1993, she wrongfully made charges on the card. During this period, American Express sent 12 monthly billing statements listing both Minskoff and Blumenfeld as cardholders, and itemizing the charges made by each. Minskoff reviewed none of these statements and Equities paid each monthly bill in full. In July 1992, American Express sent Minskoff an unsolicited invitation to apply for a platinum card. Blumenfeld accepted the invitation on behalf of Minskoff, again without his knowledge. She also requested a supplemental card to issue from this new account in her name. After receiving her platinum card, Blumenfeld wrongfully charged personal purchases to it between July 1992 and November 1993. During this period, American Express mailed 16 monthly statements, and the company paid each bill without reviewing the itemized charges. In November 1993, Minskoff discovered Blumenfeld's fraudulent activities and sought to recover the $276,334.06 that had been paid to American Express for Blumenfeld's charges. He argued that because Blumenfeld obtained each credit card through forgery and fraud, her use of them was unauthorized, and his liability was limited to $50 per card.

ISSUE   Is Minskoff's liability limited to $50 for each card?

DECISION   No. The term "unauthorized use" is defined as "a use of a credit card by a person other than the cardholder who does not have actual, implied, or apparent authority for such use and from which the cardholder receives no benefit." Blumenfeld clearly acted without actual or implied authority when she forged the supplemental card applications. Accordingly, Minskoff cannot be held liable for her initial possession of them. This result is consistent with the underlying legislative policy to protect cardholders against losses due to theft or fraudulent use of credit cards on the theory that the card issuer is in a better position to prevent such losses. However, while we accept the proposition that the acquisition of a credit card through fraud or theft does not create an authorized use, this does not preclude a finding that subsequent use of the card was authorized. To hold otherwise would permit an unscrupulous cardholder to allow another to charge hundreds of dollars in goods and services and then attempt to limit its liability to $50. We therefore find that the negligent acts or omissions of a cardholder may create apparent authority to use the card in a person who obtained it through theft or fraud. Minskoff's failure to examine the credit card statements that would have revealed Blumenfeld's fraudulent use constitutes a negligent omission that created apparent authority for the charges that otherwise would have been considered unauthorized. By repeatedly making payments without objection, Minskoff fortified American Express' continuing impression that nothing was amiss. Accordingly, Minskoff is liable for only $50 per card for Blumenfeld's purchases from the time each card was issued until he received the first statement listing her fraudulent use plus a reasonable time to examine those two statements. Minskoff is liable for all of her fraudulent charges after that time.

http://www.tourolaw.edu/2ndcircuit

Billing Errors

The FCBA also prescribes procedures the card issuer must follow when a cardholder believes there is a mistake on her billing statement. The holder is given 60 days from the date of the statement to report the error in writing. (See Figure 10–1 on page 212.) The issuer then has 30 days to notify the holder it has received the report. Within either 90 days or two billing cycles, the issuer must either correct the account, or, after an investigation, explain why the original statement was accurate.

While an investigation is ongoing, the credit card company may not report unpaid but contested amounts to credit reporting agencies as late payments. Even when the issuer denies the holder's complaint, the FCBA requires that the cardholder be given an opportunity to pay the contested amount before the issuer may report the payment as delinquent. The card issuer must then notify the cardholder of the identity of entities to whom it sends a credit report. Failure to comply with these requirements may result in the card issuer forfeiting the right to collect up to $50 from the cardholder.

Figure 10–1:   Verifying Credit Card Billing

_____
_____
_____, __ ____

Date: _____

_____
_____
_____, __ ____

Account: _____
Cardholder: _____

Dear Sir or Madam:

Please send a copy of the charge slip or other evidence of the above charges for my review.

I have enclosed a copy of my statement with the transaction in question highlighted and a copy of the charge slip for the transaction in question. Please contact me if you have any questions or need additional information.

Thank you for your attention to this matter.

Sincerely,

_____

--- Ethical Issue ---

In recent years, credit card companies have been scrambling to get new customers with offers to consolidate bills on a single credit card account. Yet credit card debt is a major cause of many people's credit woes. Is it ethical to encourage people to use credit cards?

Obtaining Credit

http://
http://www.law. cornell.edu/uscode/ 15/1601.shtml contains the text of the _Truth-in-Lending Act._

The importance of credit in this society should not be underestimated. Both the federal government and the states have enacted many laws regulating credit transactions. This section examines several federal regulations designed to protect the rights of borrowers.

Truth-in-Lending Act

To ensure that borrowers are well informed as to the important credit terms before securing a loan, Congress passed the _Truth-in-Lending Act_ (TILA). The purpose of this law is to give potential borrowers enough information to find the best deal possible among competing creditors. The statute also helps borrowers more fully understand all of their repayment obligations.

Disclosure Obligations

The TILA forces creditors to clearly state interest rates in terms of an *annual percentage rate*. This disclosure must include all costs required for the extension of credit within the listed **finance charge.** This includes charges imposed on the borrower by someone other than the lender for services required by the lender even when the lender does not retain the charges. Thus, if a lender required the borrower to pay the amounts billed by the lender's lawyer for drawing up the credit agreement, that amount would have to be listed as a finance charge.

Courts insist that creditors strictly comply with the TILA's disclosure requirements and liberally construe them in favor of the borrower. For instance, a creditor's disclosures must be in the proper technical form and in the proper locations on the contract or they violate the statute. Even minor deviations trigger liability, and consumers may sue for enforcement even when they have not actually been deceived or harmed.

Gibson v. Bob Watson Chevrolet-Geo

112 F. 3D 283 (7TH CIR. 1997)

FACTS   Ruthie Gibson bought a used car from Bob Watson Chevrolet on credit. The dealer gave her a statement captioned *"Itemization of Amount Financed"* that contained a category referred to as *"Amounts Paid to Others on Your Behalf."* Under that category was an entry that read: *"To North American for Extended Warranty $800.00."* The dealer later admitted that a substantial amount of the $800 was retained by him rather than paid over to the warranty provider (North American).

ISSUE   Does a dealer violate the TILA by failing to specifically disclose the amount of the warranty charge it retains?

DECISION   Yes. There are two possible violations of the TILA. First, when the dealer sold cars for cash rather than credit, it marked up the warranty less and hence retained a smaller amount of the warranty charge. Thus, the dealer is levying an additional charge on its credit customers that constitutes a "finance charge" that must be disclosed to the customer. Even if the amount of mark-up is the same for both cash and credit customers, there is a second violation of the TILA. The statute requires the lender to provide a *"written itemization of the amount financed"* including *"each amount that is paid to third persons by the creditor on the consumer's behalf."* This dealer has committed a TILA violation by not stating correctly in the written itemization the amount that North American actually received. Gibson would have had a greater incentive to shop around for an extended warranty, rather than the one offered by the dealer, if she realized the dealer was charging a "commission" for procuring the warranty from North American. Or she might have been more prone to haggle over the warranty price if she realized part of the amount was controlled by Bob Watson Chevrolet. Finally, she might have gone to another dealer in search of a lower mark-up on the warranty charges if she had been fully disclosed as to the dealer's share.

http://www.kentlaw.edu/7circuit/

The TILA statute also provides borrowers with a three-day cancellation period on credit transactions when the creditor takes a secured interest in a borrower's home. When a creditor fails to make all required credit disclosures, this cancellation period may be extended up to three years. Note, however, that this right of rescission is limited to things like home repairs or other types of home equity loans. It does not apply to mortgage loans in which the borrower takes out the loan to actually purchase the home. The TILA's three-day cooling-off period is more fully described in Chapter 16's discussion of home ownership.

Credit Advertising

Under the TILA, advertisers are precluded from listing only a few selected credit terms. If any terms are included in the advertisement, the lender is obligated to disclose all credit terms. Thus, a car dealer who states that a car can be purchased for only "$299 per month" must include all other credit terms.

Consumer Leases

An amendment to the TILA, known as the *Consumer Leasing Act* (CLA), extends the statute's disclosure obligations to certain consumer leasing transactions. It applies to leases for more than four months where the total financial obligation is less than $25,000. Specifically, the CLA requires the disclosure of all of the leasing costs as well as a clear statement of the lessee's financial obligations when the lease ends.

Fair Credit Reporting Act

http://
www.law.cornell.edu/
uscode/15/1681.shtml
provides the text for
the *Fair Credit
Reporting Act*.

By the mid-1990s, the three national credit reporting systems in this country were maintaining over 180 million credit files, with those files growing by almost two billion items of information each month. With that kind of volume, it is not surprising that almost 20 percent of the country's credit reports contain major mistakes. Because these reports frequently are used by prospective creditors, employers, landlords, and insurers, it is important for consumers to guard against inaccuracies.

To assist people in reviewing and correcting personal credit information, Congress passed the *Fair Credit Reporting Act* (FCRA). This legislation was also designed to protect against confidential information falling in the hands of persons with no legitimate right to it.

Reviewing Credit Reports

The FCRA permits people who have been denied credit because of information contained in a credit report to know the name and address of the **credit bureau** (credit reporting agency). (See Figure 10–2.)The consumer has 60 days from the date she learned of the denial to request a free copy of the report from the agency. That credit bureau may then be required to reinvestigate the information and delete inaccuracies. Even if the credit bureau does not believe there to be a mistake, it must allow the consumer to file a brief statement (up to 100 words) of her version of the disputed facts contained in the report. When information is deleted, the credit bureau must contact lenders and insurers who received the inaccurate

Figure 10–2:   Request for Reasons for Credit Denial

_____

_____

_____, __ ____

Date: _____

_____

_____

_____, __ ____

_____

My application for credit with you was made on _____ , for
_____. I was notified on _____ , that my
application has been denied.

Please advise if the adverse action was based in whole or in part on information contained in a
consumer credit report or on information obtained from a source other than a consumer reporting agency. If the adverse action was based on information from a source other than a consumer reporting agency, please indicate the nature of the adverse information, such as my
credit worthiness, credit standing, credit capacity, character, general reputation, or personal
characteristics.

I have been advised that an investigative report will be undertaken. Please provide a complete
and accurate description of the nature and scope of this investigation.

Your review of this matter would be appreciated. Please respond at your earliest convenience
regarding the results of your review.

Sincerely,

_____

information during the six-month period prior to its deletion. Any prospective
employer must be notified if it received the inaccurate information within the previous two years.

Even if a person has not been denied credit or a job because of a credit report,
he may check his credit file. However, there is likely to be a fee ranging from $2 to
$20. It generally is recommended that people review their credit report at least
every three years. Further, it is wise to check the report before applying for a job
or entering into a major credit transaction. (See Figure 10–3 on page 216.)

Unauthorized Disclosure

The FCRA prohibits the dissemination of consumer credit information to anyone
without a legitimate need for it. Further, a credit bureau generally may not report
most adverse information that is more than seven years old, except in the case of
bankruptcies. They may be reported for up to 10 years.

Figure 10–3:   Credit Report Request

_____

_____, __ ____

Date: _____

_____

_____

_____, __ ____

Re: Credit Report Request

_____

I would like to request a copy of my credit report file. I am providing the following information to obtain the report.

Current address:

     _____

     _____

     _____, __ ____

Additional previous address within the last five (5) years:

     _____

     _____, __ ____

As proof of my identity, enclosed _____

Enclosed is a check in the amount of $_____ to cover the cost of providing this report.

Please contact me if you have any questions or need additional information.

Sincerely,

_____

Source: Quicken Business Law Partner® 3.0 CD-ROM. Copyright © 1997 Parson's Technology, Inc. All rights reserved.

Enforcement of the FCRA

Consumers have private rights of action against credit bureaus that willfully or negligently fail to comply with any of the duties imposed by the FCRA. When such violations occur, the injured consumer may recover his actual damages, attorneys' fees, and court costs. Punitive damages are available in the case of willful noncompliance.

There are four elements to a case of *negligent noncompliance* of a credit bureau's duty to accurately report credit information. First, there must have been inaccurate information included in the credit report. Second, the inaccuracy was due to the credit bureau's failure to follow reasonable procedures to assure maximum possible accuracy. Third, the consumer suffered injury. Fourth, the consumer's injury was caused by the inclusion of the inaccurate entry in the credit report.

To show *willful noncompliance,* the consumer must produce evidence showing that the credit reporting agency "knowingly and intentionally" committed an act in "conscious disregard" for the rights of the consumer. Malice or an evil motive is not necessary.

Philbin v. Trans Union Corporation
101 F.3D 957 (3D CIR. 1996)

FACTS   Trans Union Corp. (TUC), a credit reporting service, prepared a credit report on James R. Philbin, Jr., that erroneously stated he was subject to a tax lien of approximately $9,500. Apparently, TUC had him confused with his father, James R. Philbin, Sr. After Philbin notified TUC of the error, it corrected the inaccuracy and added a notation to Philbin's credit report reading; *"Do not confuse with father, James Philbin Sr different address different social security number."* Over the next several years, Philbin was denied credit from numerous lenders. After receiving a copy of his credit report from TUC, he discovered that it erroneously stated that he had been released from a $9,580 tax lien. Despite immediately notifying TUC of the error, Philbin was denied credit one year later after the lender received another TUC credit report stating that he had been released from a $9,580 tax lien. That report also contained other incorrect information on delinquencies. This information apparently referred to Philbin's father, not to him. Philbin filed suit against TUC for violation of the FCRA.

ISSUE   Does Philbin have sufficient grounds for a case of negligent noncompliance with the FCRA?

DECISION   Yes. The FCRA was prompted by congressional concern over the abuses in the credit reporting industry. Its passage recognizes the crucial role credit reporting agencies play in collecting and transmitting consumer credit information as well as the detrimental effects inaccurate information can visit upon individual consumers. TUC does not dispute that its credit report contained inaccurate information. Nor is it contested that Philbin suffered emotional distress as a result of the inaccuracies. Further, other courts have held that allowing inaccurate information back onto a credit report after deleting it because it is inaccurate is negligent. Thus, a jury could easily infer that the reappearance of the inaccuracies was due to TUC's failure to follow reasonable procedures. Philbin's case, however, has not produced sufficient evidence to show willful noncompliance. After the first notification, TUC did remove the erroneous information for a period of time. Even though TUC failed to remove the errors after Philbin notified the company they had reappeared, this falls short of evidence of a willful violation.

http://www.law.vill.edu/Fed-Ct/fedcourt.html

Equal Credit Opportunity Act

Congress enacted the *Equal Credit Opportunity Act* (ECOA) to prevent discrimination in credit transactions on the basis of sex, marital status, race, color, religion, national origin, and age. Lenders also are prohibited from discriminating against

h t t p : / /
www.law.cornell.edu/
uscode/15/1691.shtml
contains the text for
the ECOA.

loan applicants because all or a portion of their income derives from public assistance programs. This law applies to a wide range of potential creditors (banks, finance companies, stores, credit card issuers) and covers all aspects of the credit transaction.

The ECOA does not guarantee credit to any of the protected classes of borrowers. Creditors still are free to establish their own standards for granting or denying credit as long as they do not discriminate against the protected classes. However, the statute requires that lenders either accept or reject a credit application within 30 days. When an application has been denied, the lender must either provide a specific reason or inform the applicant that she is entitled to request a specific reason.

Marital Status Protection

In formulating the ECOA, Congress recognized some of the special problems married women were confronting when seeking credit. As a result, the statute prevents lenders from refusing to give married women separate credit accounts or unnecessarily asking the applicant's marital status when an individual account is requested. Lenders also may not demand that a spouse co-sign a loan taken out by the other when the spouse seeking the loan is creditworthy. But a woman may demand that the credit history she and her husband created together also be treated as hers even though the credit was granted in his name alone. However, she may have unfavorable information from a joint account deleted from her individual credit history if it does not accurately reflect her credit standing. These reforms greatly assist recently widowed or divorced women in developing or maintaining a line of credit.

Calaska Partners v. Corson

672 A.2D 1099 (SUP. CT. ME. 1996)

FACTS   Inger and David Corson were a married couple. David was a practicing attorney and Inger was a homemaker. The couple jointly held title to the family residence. David applied to Maine Savings Bank (MSB) for a $200,000 line of credit to stabilize the cash flow of his law practice. At the time of the loan, David's individual share of real estate holdings exceeded $600,000. Despite the fact that Inger was not to receive any of the loan proceeds, MSB conditioned its extension of credit on obtaining both David's and Inger's signature on a note and mortgage encumbering the family residence. Richard Rummler, the MSB loan officer, explained that it was long-standing practice in the industry to obtain the signature of both spouses on the loan document even though only one spouse applied for the loan. After MSB became insolvent, Calaska Partners was assigned the right to collect on the loan. When David defaulted, Calaska sought to foreclose on the family residence. Inger argued that the foreclosure should not be permitted because the requirement that she co-sign the loan agreement violated the ECOA.

ISSUE   Did MSB violate the ECOA by requiring that Inger co-sign her husband's loan?

DECISION   Yes. David was individually creditworthy at the time he applied for the line of credit. His share of the real estate holdings ($600,000) was three times the amount of the line of credit ($200,000). MSB admitted that it was long-standing practice to require the signatures of both spouses. A court could reasonably find this to violate the spirit and the letter of the ECOA by requiring Inger's guaranty despite David's personal financial wherewithal. Because Inger's signature was obtained in violation of the ECOA, Calaska may not foreclose on the entire property. It only has rights to David's one-half interest in the family residence.

Suretyship

When a lender extends credit, there is always a risk of nonpayment. If this risk is great, the creditor may charge a higher rate of interest. However, a high rate of interest in no way guarantees payment of either the interest or the principal. For this reason, various mechanisms are available to lenders seeking to assure repayment of the debt. One such device, obtaining a security interest in some item of the debtor's personal property, is discussed later in this chapter. This section looks at another strategy for reducing risk: requiring either a surety or a guarantor.

Surety Versus Guarantor

A person who *co-signs* a borrower's loan also is liable for repayment of the debt. This cosigner is called a **surety.** Suppose Michelle (the *principal debtor*) sought a loan so she could afford to vacation in Florida over spring break. The bank (the *creditor*) loaned her the money, but only after her mother (the *surety*) co-signed the agreement. When the first payment falls due, both Michelle and her mother are immediately liable for that amount. (This is called *primary liability.*)

Sometimes the parties create *secondary liability* rather than primary liability. For instance, after Jeff had taken out an unsecured loan to pay for a scuba-diving trip to the Caribbean, he stopped making his scheduled payments. When his grandfather discovered the bank had filed a lawsuit against Jeff, he guaranteed payment of the debt if the bank would drop the lawsuit. Jeff's grandfather is a **guarantor** of his debt. Unlike the surety, who joins in the original promise to repay, the guarantor makes a separate promise to repay. A surety's promises may be oral, while a guarantor's promise must be in writing. (The guarantor's promise may be oral if the guaranty was made primarily to satisfy an economic interest of the guarantor. This is the "leading object" rule discussed in Chapter 9.) Otherwise, the rights and obligations of sureties and guarantors basically are the same.

Rights of the Surety

Even in debts secured by a surety, the principal debtor retains ultimate responsibility for repayment. Thus, anytime the surety pays the creditor, it possesses a **right of reimbursement** against the principal debtor. To assist the surety in recovering these amounts, the surety is given a **right of subrogation.** Under the right of subrogation, the surety acquires whatever rights the creditor had against the principal debtor. For instance, if the creditor had a security interest in some of the principal debtor's property as well as a surety relationship, the surety could repossess any of the secured property not already seized by the creditor.

Whenever there is more than one surety, each cosurety has a **right of contribution** against the others. Since most cosureties are *jointly and severally liable* for the debt, the creditor may seek full payment from any one of them. The surety who pays the creditor may then exercise the right of contribution to ensure that each cosurety pays its prorata share of the debt.

Obligations of the Surety

The surety generally is liable to the creditor the instant the debt falls due if the principal debtor fails to pay at that time. However, because suretyship relationships are contractual in nature, one must examine the parties' agreement to fully understand the extent of the surety's obligations. For instance, the agreement may stipulate that such liability does not begin until the creditor first gives notice and exhausts certain remedies against the principal debtor (i.e., attempts to collect payment through a lawsuit). This is called a *conditional guaranty*.

Defenses Available to the Surety

There are three basic restrictions on the surety's obligation to repay the debt. First, most of the contractual defenses against repayment that are available to the principal debtor also are available to the surety. Thus, if the principal debtor does not have to repay because the original contract lacked consideration, was induced by fraud, or is somehow breached by the creditor, the surety likewise is excused from performing. Second, the surety need not repay the debt if the creditor secures the surety's promise by fraud or otherwise fails to disclose material facts about the creditworthiness of the principal debtor. Third, a surety may be released from liability if the creditor makes agreements with the principal debtor without the surety's consent that increase the risk to the surety (e.g., agreeing that the principal debtor may sell collateral used to secure the loan).

There are two *personal defenses* available to the principal debtor that do not relieve the surety from liability. They are the principal debtor's lack of capacity (minority or insanity) and bankruptcy.

Secured Transactions

http://
www.law.cornell.edu/
ucc/9/overview.html
lists the contents of
Article 9 of the UCC.

This section examines Article 9 of the Uniform Commercial Code and its special rules governing secured interests in personal property. As was noted earlier, a lender in an unsecured credit transaction always faces the risk that the borrower will not repay the debt. Secured credit reduces this risk by providing the lender with some item of property it can seize in the event the debt is not repaid. Article 9 provides procedures for creating a security interest in personal property as well as a means for resolving conflicting claims among the borrower's various creditors.

There are three fundamental components to an Article 9 secured transaction. First, the lender and borrower must create a contractual relationship (called *attachment*) giving the lender a security interest in some item of the borrower's property.

Second, the lender must give notice (called *perfection*) of its security interest to the rest of the world. Third, the lender must carefully abide by the Article 9 rules in order to maintain a superior claim (called *priority*) in the face of competing claims by other individuals and creditors. (See Figure 10–4.)

Attachment

The act by which a borrower gives a lender a security interest in property is known as **attachment.** (That item of property often is called *collateral.*) Article 9 imposes two requirements on a lender wishing to attach an item of collateral. First, the lender must extend credit to the borrower. Unless a debt has arisen, there can be no attachment and, accordingly, no security interest. Second, the parties must enter into an agreement in which the borrower voluntarily gives a security interest in some item of the borrower's property. (See Figure 10–5 on page 222.)

A wide range of items can be attached. *Consumer goods* (cars, furniture, appliances, and other property intended for personal use) are common collateral for consumer loans. *Equipment, inventory,* and *accounts receivable* often serve as collateral for business loans. Items of collateral that become firmly attached to land or buildings are classified as *fixtures.* Many of the Article 9 rules vary depending on the particular type of collateral that has been attached.

The Security Agreement

The contract creating the attachment is known as a **security agreement.** Although it normally must be in writing and signed by the debtor, it may be oral in cases where the lender has taken possession of the collateral. Written security agreements must clearly describe the collateral so it may be readily identified. This description normally includes serial numbers or other identifying features. In essence, the security agreement is a contract between the lender and the borrower. Therefore, it must meet all the requirements for an enforceable contract.

Perfection

Although attachment creates a security interest, more is needed if the lender wishes to assert its rights against other people or lenders claiming rights to the same collateral. Article 9 requires that other claimants be notified of the lender's

---

Figure 10–4:   Secured Transactions: An Overview

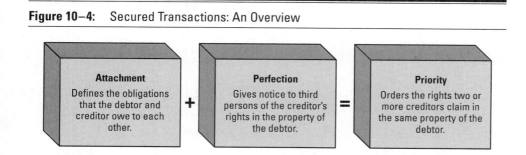

Attachment		Perfection		Priority
Defines the obligations that the debtor and creditor owe to each other.	**+**	Gives notice to third persons of the creditor's rights in the property of the debtor.	**=**	Orders the rights two or more creditors claim in the same property of the debtor.

security interest through an act called **perfection.** (See Figure 10–6.) There are four ways in which perfection occurs:

1. the lender takes possession of the collateral;
2. the lender files a finance statement;
3. automatic perfection; or
4. noting the security interest on a certificate of title.

Perfection by Possession

The requirements of perfection are met when the lender retains possession of the collateral. Suppose James borrowed $150 from Sarah and offered her a security interest in his television until the debt was repaid. If Sarah takes possession of the television at the time she loans the money, she does not need a written security agreement. She also need not do anything further to perfect her security interest. This is because the purpose of perfection is to notify the world that someone other

---

Figure 10–5:   Attaching a Security Interest

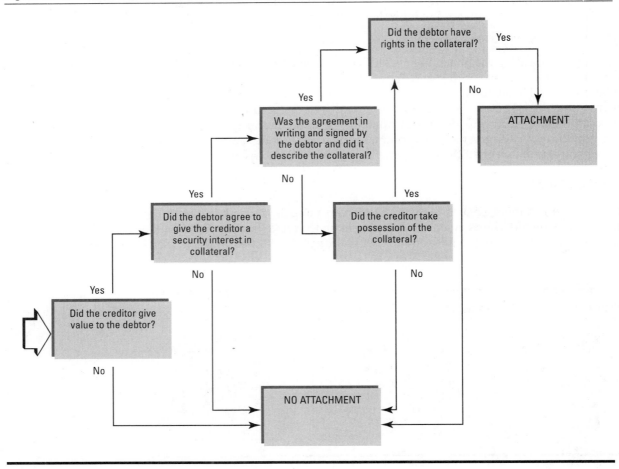

Figure 10–6: Perfection of a Security Interest

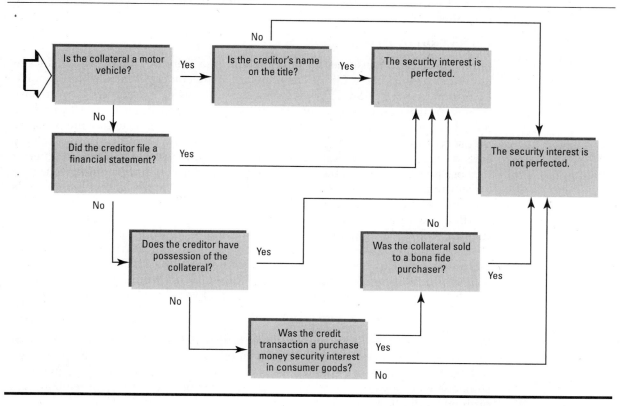

than James (the borrower) has rights to the collateral (the television). Sarah's possession provides a strong indication that she has rights to the television.

Perfection by Filing

Lenders usually perfect their security interest by filing a **finance statement** with a governmental office. In most states the filing site is the Secretary of State's office. However, for transactions with special local connections (i.e., farm products or farm equipment, fixtures), filing may be required in the county where the collateral is located.

To be valid, the finance statement must meet certain requirements. It must:

1. identify the borrower and the lender;
2. give mailing addresses for the borrower and the lender:
3. describe the collateral; and
4. be signed by the borrower.

If the finance statement states no expiration date, it is valid for five years. However, the lender may renew it by filing a *continuation statement* six months before the expiration date. After the debt is paid, the lender must file a *termination statement* within 10 days of a request by the borrower. Absent such a request, the lender is obligated to file a termination statement within 30 days of the debt's discharge for a consumer credit transaction. This automatic obligation does not apply to commercial loans.

Perfection by Attachment

For many secured consumer loans, the lender's security interest is perfected without either possession or filing. The mere act of attachment creates what is known as **automatic perfection.** This perfection by attachment is reserved for **purchase money security interests,** where the collateral is a consumer good. A purchase money security interest arises when the purpose of the loan is to buy the property that serves as the collateral. It occurs in either of two ways. First, a seller may extend credit on the goods she sells and retain a purchase money security interest in those goods. Second, a bank or some other lender may loan money so the borrower can buy goods. The lender's security interest in the newly purchased goods is a purchase money security interest.

Because a purchase money security interest in consumer goods is automatically perfected, the lender is spared the time and expense of filing finance and termination statements. However, automatic perfection generally is not available for motor vehicles. It also is of limited effectiveness when the collateral becomes a fixture or when a bona fide purchaser buys the collateral from the borrower. (Both fixtures and bona fide purchasers are discussed in the priority section below.)

Perfection by Certificate of Title

When the collateral is a motor vehicle for which state law requires a certificate of title (cars, trucks, and motorcycles), the lender must perfect its security interest by noting it on the title. If a creditor fails to do so, it may lose its security interest to someone who buys the car or loans money to the borrower without realizing the original lender had a security interest.

Priority

Often more than one person claims an interest in the same piece of property. Suppose Martin borrowed $1,450 from Finance Company and gave the lender a security interest in his boat. Before Finance's loan was repaid, First Bank loaned Martin $500 and retained a security interest in the same boat. If Martin fails to repay either of his loans, the court must decide which of the parties (Finance Company or First Bank) has first claim over the boat. It will use the Article 9 **priority** rules to make that determination.

The general priority rule is *first in time, first in right.* This means that when more than one lender has perfected a security interest in the same collateral, the first to perfect has priority. In our example above, Finance Company attached Martin's boat first. But if First Bank perfected before Finance Company, the bank would have priority. In cases where neither lender perfects its security interest, the first to attach prevails. There are several exceptions to the general priority rules. Four are discussed here:

1. bona fide purchasers,
2. buyers in the ordinary course of business,
3. fixtures, and
4. common-law liens.

Bona Fide Purchasers Exception

Remember from our earlier discussion that purchase money security interests in consumer goods are automatically perfected. However, automatic perfection is not effective when the borrower sells the collateral to a **bona fide purchaser**. A bona fide purchaser is someone who:

1. buys for personal, family, or household use,
2. pays value for the goods, and
3. has no knowledge of the security interest.

Suppose Appliance Store sold Maria a television on credit and retained a security interest in the television. As a purchase money security interest in consumer goods, it is automatically perfected. Thus, Appliance Store has a priority over any other lender who later attempts to take a security interest in the television. However, if Maria sells her television to Raymond at a garage sale, Raymond will take the television free and clear of Appliance Store's security interest. To defeat bona fide purchasers, lenders may not rely on automatic perfection. Instead they must perfect by filing, possession, or (with motor vehicles) placing their name on the certificate of title.

Buyers in the Ordinary Course of Business Exception

Consumers regularly purchase goods from retail stores without considering the fact that banks, manufacturers, and wholesalers may have perfected security interests in the store's inventory. Article 9 provides an exception to the priority rule for these customers in order to encourage people to freely buy goods from merchants. These consumers who make normal purchases from retail stores are called **buyers in the ordinary course of business.**

DBC Capital Fund v. Snodgrass

551 N.E.2d 475 (Ct. App. Ind. 1990)

FACTS   Devers Auto Sales borrowed money from DBC Capital Fund and gave DBC a security interest in its automobile inventory. DBC perfected this security interest by filing a finance statement with the Secretary of State on February 25, 1988. Cheryl Snodgrass bought a 1984 Oldsmobile from Devers on March 24, 1989. The automobile was taken from the inventory covered by DBC's perfected security interest. When Snodgrass took possession of the Oldsmobile, Devers told her the certificate of title would be mailed to her. However, one month later she was informed that DBC had possession of the title and considered itself to have a valid security interest on her automobile. In a telephone conversation, DBC told her that it would not release the title until she paid it $4,200. Snodgrass was unable to obtain proper licensing of the Oldsmobile without the certificate of title. Accordingly, she sued DBC for the title.

ISSUE   Is Snodgrass entitled to the certificate of title?

DECISION   Yes. Although DBC had a perfected security interest in the automobile, Snodgrass has a superior claim to the vehicle. As a buyer in the ordinary course of

continued

business she took the Oldsmobile free of the security interest created by Devers. After her purchase, DBC had no further claim to the automobile and must release the title. DBC's only recourse is against Devers for the proceeds the automobile dealer received from the sale to Snodgrass.

Fixtures Exception

Sometimes collateral is transformed into a **fixture** when it becomes firmly attached to a building or land. For instance, appliances that are later built into the wall of a kitchen would qualify as fixtures. It is quite likely that one lender would have a purchase money security interest in the appliances, while another would have a security interest in the home where they were installed. The lender with the purchase money security interest in the appliances (consumer goods) would not be able to rely on automatic perfection in such a case. Instead, Article 9 has devised special fixture filing rules that must be followed if that lender wishes to retain its priority. Fixtures are discussed in Chapter 15.

Common-Law Lien Exception

When a mechanic repairs your car, he is entitled to a **lien** on the vehicle to assure payment for the parts and services he has provided. Under both statutory and common law, a wide variety of parts and service providers are granted liens on the personal property they repair or improve. Two basic requirements must be met for someone to obtain a common-law or statutory lien over personal property. First, a debt must be created because of an improvement or provision of services relating to the personal property. Second, the improver or service provider must maintain possession of the personal property. (These security interests frequently are called *possessory liens.*) However, possession generally must have been entrusted to the improver or service provider. And once it voluntary relinquishes possession, it loses its lien.

Suppose the bank has a perfected security interest in Aaron's car. Despite the bank's security interest, it will not defeat the claims of a mechanic who repairs the car and maintains possession of it. Until the mechanic is paid for his repairs, his common-law lien over the car takes priority over the bank's prior perfected security interest. If Aaron fails to pay for the repairs, the mechanic may sell the car and pay off his bill. The bank is then entitled to any surplus to satisfy its claims against Aaron.

Default

In most credit transactions, the parties' loan agreement spells out what constitutes a **default** by the borrower. This act of default may trigger various collection efforts by the lender, including turning the account over to a debt collector. This section examines two aspects of the default issue. First, it discusses regulatory limits on debt collectors' activities. Second, it explores the various options available to lenders in secured credit transactions.

Regulatory Limits on Debt Collection

In response to numerous instances of abusive, deceptive, and unfair debt collection practices, Congress enacted the *Fair Debt Collection Practices Act* (FDCPA). Most states have followed suit and passed similar statutes. The federal statute encompasses only collection practices by debt collection agencies, including attorneys collecting on consumer credit transactions. However, it excludes collection efforts by actual lenders (stores, banks, etc.) attempting to collect on their own accounts.

Limits on Communications with Third Parties

The FDCPA regulates the manner in which debt collectors may contact third parties (i.e., the borrower's friends, relatives, or employer) when attempting to locate delinquent borrowers. A debt collector must identify himself and state that he is confirming or correcting location information on the borrower. He may not divulge that the borrower owes any debt, communicate by postcard, or use any language or symbol on an envelope that indicates he is in the debt collection business. In fact, he may only identify his employer if the third person expressly requests that information. Generally, the debt collector may not contact the third person more than once and, if he discovers that a borrower is represented by an attorney, may contact only the attorney.

Limits on Communications with the Borrower

A debt collector generally must avoid contacting a borrower at inconvenient times or places without the borrower's prior consent. (Absent special circumstances, the statute presumes a convenient time falls between 8:00 a.m. and 9:00 p.m. at the borrower's location.) The borrower may not be contacted at her place of employment when the debt collector knows the employer prohibits such communication. Further, if the borrower informs the debt collector in writing that she refuses to pay or wants the debt collector to stop contacting her, such communications must stop. This does not preclude the debt collector from informing the borrower that it is commencing some permitted legal action. However, any lawsuit may be filed only where the borrower signed the loan agreement or where the borrower currently resides.

Limits on Unfair Debt Collection Practices

A debt collector may not engage in conduct that might harass, oppress, or abuse the borrower. This section is violated by the use of threats of violence, the use of obscene or profane language, or allowing a telephone to ring repeatedly and continuously. False, deceptive, or misleading statements also must be avoided. This includes falsely stating the legal status or amount of the debt, falsely representing that the debt collector is an attorney, or threatening to take any action that cannot legally be taken or that the debt collector does not intend to take.

Required Disclosures

Within five days after first communicating with the borrower, the debt collector must accurately identify the amount of the debt and the name of the creditor to whom it is owed. This **validation notice** must include a statement that unless the borrower disputes the debt within 30 days, the debt collector will assume it is valid. This also must include a statement that if the borrower disputes the debt within the 30-day period, the debt collector will mail verification of the debt to the borrower. Until the borrower receives this verification, all collection efforts must cease.

Avila v. Rubin

84 F.3D 222 (7TH CIR. 1996)

FACTS   Raul Avila allegedly owed money on a student loan to his creditor, the Connecticut Student Loan Foundation. The foundation had a written contract with a collection agency, Van Ru Credit Corporation, and an oral agreement with an attorney, Albert Rubin, for debt collection services. Rubin and Van Ru were closely intertwined, with Rubin owning 80 percent of Van Ru and his son (who also served as Van Ru's president) owning the remaining 20 percent. Avila did not respond to two collection letters from Van Ru. The collection agency then referred Avila's account to Rubin, who sent letters under a letterhead identifying himself as an "Attorney at Law." The letters from Rubin and Van Ru told Avila of his *"right to dispute the validity of the debt within 30 days."* However, that information was immediately followed by the sentences: *"If the above does not apply to you, we shall expect payment or arrangement for payment within ten (10) days from the date of this letter. If payment is not received, a civil suit may be initiated against you by your creditor for repayment of your loan."* Although Rubin reviewed and approved the general form used on the collection letters, he never personally prepared, signed, or reviewed any letters sent to debtors. In fact, he sent out some 270,000 such letters each year. The letters actually were the product of nonattorney "legal assistant collectors" who directed a computer to generate the letters on Rubin's attorney letterhead. Avila claimed the letters: (1) violated the validation notice requirements of the FDCPA and (2) were false, deceptive, and misleading representations because they were not actually from an attorney as that term is defined by the FDCPA. The trial court agreed and entered a judgment of $84,983 against Rubin.

ISSUE   Should the judgment against Rubin be upheld?

DECISION   Yes. Claims against debt collectors under the FDCPA are to be viewed through the eyes of the "unsophisticated consumer." Telling a debtor he has 30 days to dispute the debt and following that with a statement that "[i]f the above does not apply" you have ten days to pay up or real trouble will start is entirely inconsistent and a failure to comply with the FDCPA. The unsophisticated consumer would be scratching his head upon receipt of such a letter. He wouldn't have a clue as to what he was supposed to do before real trouble begins. A debt validation notice to be valid must be effective, and it cannot be cleverly couched in such a way as to eviscerate its message. Further, the letters from Rubin were false and misleading because they were not from an attorney in any meaningful sense of the word. An attorney sending a collection letter must be directly and personally involved in their mailing. Rubin had no real involvement. An unsophisticated consumer, getting a letter from an "attorney," knows the price of poker has just gone up. If a debt collector wants to take advantage of the special connotation of the word "attorney" he should at least ensure that an attorney has become professionally involved in the debtor's file.

http://www.kentlaw.edu/7circuit/

—————————— Ethical Issue ——————————

Avila's alleged failure to pay on his student loans just netted him $84,983 because the debt collector did not comply with the FDCPA. What harm did these violations cause Avila? Could this law be encouraging defaults by debtors?

Secured Lender's Options

Article 9 does not define what constitutes an act of default in a secured credit transaction involving consumer goods. It leaves that up to the parties' security agreement. However, Article 9 does offer the lender several options when a default occurs. First, the lender may forget the collateral and sue the borrower as an unsecured creditor on the underlying promise to repay the loan. The lender will then hope the court can find some other property that can be sold to pay off the claim. Second, in some instances the lender may repossess the collateral and keep it in strict foreclosure. Third, the lender may repossess the collateral and sell it in foreclosure. Three important concepts—repossession, strict foreclosure, and foreclosure—are explored below.

Repossession

The basic nature of secured credit suggests that the lender has the right to **repossess** the collateral after the borrower defaults. Generally, the lender may personally seize the property if the repossession can be achieved without a *breach of the peace* (violence). In instances where such violence is likely to occur, the lender must petition a court to carry out the repossession.

Strict Foreclosure

In some consumer credit transactions the lender may opt to repossess the collateral and keep it in full satisfaction of the debt. However, this process, known as **strict foreclosure,** is subject to certain statutory restrictions. First, if the borrower has paid 60 percent or more of the purchase price or loan amount, the consumer goods may not be subject to a strict foreclosure unless the borrower agrees in writing. When less than 60 percent has been paid (or the collateral is not a consumer good), the lender may propose a strict foreclosure. This action will be permitted unless the borrower objects in writing within 21 days.

Foreclosure

The lender may opt to repossess the collateral, sell it, and apply the proceeds of the sale to the loan. This process, known as **foreclosure,** is subject to some important limitations. First, the borrower has a **right of redemption,** which allows her to recover the collateral by paying off the loan prior to the foreclosure sale. Second, the lender must sell the collateral in a *commercially reasonable manner* to ensure that it obtains the best price possible. Third, when there is a public sale (auction), the borrower must be informed of the time and place it is to occur. While a private sale is also possible, the borrower must be notified in advance so she has an opportunity to object.

Article 9 sets out the order in which the proceeds from the foreclosure sale are to be distributed. First, the lender is entitled to recover its costs of repossessing, storing, and selling the collateral. Next, the money is used to pay off the balance due on the debt (including interest charges). Any other creditors with a security interest in the collateral are then paid. The borrower is entitled to any of the remaining proceeds. If the sale does not bring in enough money to pay off the lender's claims, it is entitled to **deficiency judgment** against the borrower. This allows the lender to sue the borrower for the remaining balance as an unsecured creditor.

Bankruptcy

http://
www.law.cornell.edu/
topics/bankruptcy.
html provides infor-
mation and links on
U.S. bankruptcy law.

When borrowers are unable to pay their debts, there is a need to assure that some lenders do not obtain an unfair advantage over others. Likewise, lenders require protection against unscrupulous borrowers who may attempt to conceal assets that could otherwise be used to satisfy legitimate claims. Finally, borrowers require a means by which they may gain a fresh financial start so they can once again become productive members of society. The federal Bankruptcy Act addresses each of these objectives.

Types of Bankruptcy Proceedings

Bankruptcy cases initially are filed in the federal district courts. They may then be handed over to a special bankruptcy judge. There are four basic types of bankruptcy proceedings supervised by the courts:

1. liquidations,
2. reorganizations,
3. family farms, and
4. consumer debt adjustments.

Liquidations

Chapter 7 of the Bankruptcy Act governs **liquidations.** Under the liquidation proceeding, often called a *straight bankruptcy,* a bankruptcy trustee determines which of the borrower's assets are available for distribution to the various claimants. Creditors are paid in an order established by the Bankruptcy Act. Lenders with perfected security interests are in the most advantaged position since they have first priority to the proceeds of the sale of their collateral. Unsecured creditors who are lower in the order of distribution may be fortunate to receive a small percentage of their claim. Even though the distribution is unlikely to pay off all of the outstanding claims, it generally relieves the debtor from any further liability.

Reorganizations

The bankruptcy court supervises a **reorganization** of the debtor's business so its creditors can be paid under Chapter 11 of the Bankruptcy Act. This option is available to all forms of business (sole proprietorship, partnership, corporation) and avoids the need for a liquidation. The court appoints a committee of creditors and a trustee (who operates the business). The committee devises a plan for how the various classes of claimants are to be paid.

Family Farms

Chapter 12 of the Bankruptcy Act provides a special process for handling the bankruptcy of **family farms.** It only is available to farmers with a regular income who have accumulated most of their debt through their farming operations. Generally, the farmer retains possession of the property, but is supervised by a court-appointed trustee. The farmer is given 90 days to submit a plan for paying off creditors. The court will not confirm the plan unless the unsecured creditors receive at least the liquidation value of their claims. The farmer is discharged after fulfillment of the plan; although he may also be relieved from full compliance if subsequent hardships prevent total compliance.

Consumer Debt Adjustments

Debtors wishing to avoid the stigma of being declared bankrupt may seek a **consumer debt adjustment** under Chapter 13 of the Bankruptcy Act. This option is available only to individuals with regular income who have less than $250,000 in unsecured debts and $750,000 in secured debts. The process allows the debtor to request a reduction in the amount owed to each creditor, an extension of time to pay each creditor, or both a reduction and an extension. If the proposal is made in good faith and is approved by the secured creditors, the court appoints a trustee to administer it. Any unsecured creditor may veto the plan unless that creditor is paid in full or the debtor commits all of his disposable income for a three-year period to payment of his creditors. Generally, the plan must call for payments to be made over a period of three years or less, unless the court believes a longer period is needed. After the debtor completes the plan, he is discharged from further liability.

Bankruptcy Petitions

A debtor may file a **voluntary petition** for bankruptcy even though she is not actually insolvent. All that is necessary is that she is unable to pay her debts as they are due. Creditors may file an **involuntary petition** over the debtor's objections to force a distribution of the debtor's assets. When the debtor has 12 or more creditors, the involuntary petition must be supported by at least three creditors with at least $5,000 in unsecured claims. When there are less than 12 creditors, the petition could be forwarded by a single creditor with at least $5,000 in unsecured claims. (Chapter 12 and 13 proceedings are triggered only by voluntary petitions.)

A bankruptcy filing acts as an **automatic stay** on further collection efforts by creditors. This automatic stay is designed to prevent harassment of debtors but does not preclude all contact. Some courts have ruled that mere requests for repayment are not barred as long as they are not coercive or harassing.

Limits on Discharge

An honest debtor who complies with the terms of the bankruptcy proceeding generally is relieved from further liability on his debts. However, this **discharge** is not available to someone who already has received a bankruptcy discharge within the previous six years. And certain claims are *nondischargeable debts.* These include governmental taxes or fines; loans obtained under false pretenses;

damages owed due to willful or malicious injury; alimony or child support; educational loans due within five years of the filing; and debts that were not listed in the bankruptcy petition.

A discharge is reserved for honest debtors who make a good-faith effort to comply with the bankruptcy process. It is denied to dishonest debtors who have substantially abused the bankruptcy process. Thus, there are certain *acts that bar discharge.* These include falsifying or destroying financial records, making false statements or claims, transferring or concealing property to hinder or defraud legitimate claims, and failing to obey court orders.

Finally, the debtor may agree in writing to **reaffirm** a debt that would otherwise be discharged. Because a reaffirmation creates an exception to the "fresh start" principles of the bankruptcy laws, the Bankruptcy Act contains various safeguards to ensure that reaffirmations are genuine and not the product of abusive creditor practices. This promise to repay the lender must be made in writing before the discharge and generally must be approved by the court.

Anastas v. American Savings Bank
94 F.3d 1280 (9th Cir. 1996)

FACTS   Anastas held a VISA credit card from American Savings Bank, which he extended beyond its credit limit over a six-month period to make cash advances for gambling at Lake Tahoe casinos. During the same time period he extended several of his other credit cards to their credit limit to finance gambling activities. Although Anastas never failed to make the minimum monthly payments on his VISA card, he soon was unable to make the minimum monthly payment on all of his credit cards. He tried to work out an alternate payment schedule with his various creditors, but American Savings Bank was unwilling to do so. At the time of this voluntary bankruptcy petition, Anastas had a monthly take-home income of $3,465 and monthly expenditures of $3,535. He had assets of only $800 and credit card debt of over $40,000. He owed $6,624 to American Savings Bank on his VISA card. American Savings Bank argued the VISA debt was nondischargeable because Anastas knew he did not have the ability to repay the debt when he used the credit card.

ISSUE   Is the credit card debt dischargeable?

DECISION   Yes. For a credit card debt to be nondischargeable it must be shown that the cardholder lacked the intent to repay the debt at the time he made the charge. The focus should not be on whether the cardholder was hopelessly insolvent at the time he made the credit card charges. Instead, the express focus must be solely on whether the cardholder maliciously and in bad faith incurred credit card debt with the intention of filing bankruptcy and avoiding the debt. In this case there is no showing of an intent to defraud American Savings Bank. Anastas always made his monthly payments and he attempted to work out an alternate payment arrangement. Obviously, he had a serious gambling problem. However, there is no basis for finding the type of malicious and bad faith intent not to repay that is necessary to make this credit card debt nondischargeable.

QUESTIONS AND PROBLEM CASES

1. What is meant by attachment? How does it arise? How does attachment differ from perfection? (What is the function performed by each?)

2. What is the difference between secured credit and unsecured credit? What does it generally take for secured credit to arise?

3. What is a reaffirmation agreement?

4. When may a lender legally insist that a borrower's spouse co-sign a loan?

5. NCB Collection Services (NCB) issues debt collection letters to approximately one million debtors each year on behalf of American Family Publishers (AFP), an organization engaged in the business of selling magazine subscriptions. AFP provides NCB with computer tapes containing information about delinquent accounts, which NCB transfers to its own computer system. NCB's computers then generate form letters requesting payment of the debt. If the debtor does not respond to the initial collection letter, the computer automatically produces and mails additional letters according to a predetermined schedule. Although NCB maintains a program for assessing the reliability of its computer data, no employee of the agency reviews the file of any debtor until the debtor responds to NCB's demands for payment. Clomon received a series of form letters from NCB regarding her $9.42 debt to AFP. Five of the letters bore letterhead and signature lines indicating they were from "*P.D. Jackson, Attorney at Law, General Counsel, NCB Collection Services.*" This information was accurate in the sense that Jackson was employed as general counsel for NCB on a part-time basis. However, the letters were not actually signed by Jackson or any other person. (They bore a mechanically reproduced facsimile of Jackson's signature.) Jackson did not have any direct personal involvement in the mailing of the letters to Clomon and never reviewed her file. Did these letters violate the *Fair Debt Collection Practices Act's* prohibition of false and misleading communications?

6. Norma Wade financed the purchase of her Ford Thunderbird through Ford Motor Credit and gave the lender a security interest in the car. After Wade became delinquent on her loan, Ford Motor Credit contracted with the Kansas Recovery Bureau to repossess the car. When an employee of the Recovery Bureau first attempted this, he noticed a discrepancy between the serial number of the vehicle and the number listed in the loan papers. At that time, Wade told him that she had a gun, which she would use if he attempted to take the car. She then called Ford Motor Credit and said that she would shoot anybody who tried to take her car. One month later, at 2:00 a.m., an employee of the Recovery Bureau took the car from Wade's driveway. There was no confrontation with Wade, since the employee left the area before she discovered the vehicle was missing. Wade claimed the repossession was unlawful since it breached the peace. Is Wade correct?

7. Wiley pawned the title to his Toyota Tercel automobile to Eddie's Wholesale Jewelry & Pawn in exchange for $300. The pawn ticket that Wiley signed and received stated the terms of the arrangement, but failed to indicate the annual percentage rate of the transaction. Wiley later sued Eddie's, alleging that the omission of the annual percentage rate violated the disclosure requirements of the *Truth-in-Lending Act* (TILA). Eddie's argued that the TILA does not govern pawn transactions. Specifically, it asserted that pawnbrokers do not extend credit since they do not compel consumers to repay. Is Eddie's correct?

8. Hardage purchased a videocassette recorder and guitar board from Sears Roebuck & Company. For both purchases he used his Sears charge card. The sales slip Hardage signed at the time of purchase contained the following information: his account number, his name, the date of purchase, the amount purchased, a description of the goods, an invoice number, his address, and his

signature. The sales slip also stated that Sears retained a security interest in merchandise until the full purchase price was paid. Later, while there still remained a balance due on the Sears charge card, Hardage filed for a Chapter 7 bankruptcy. Sears claimed that it had a perfected security interest in the video-cassette recorder and guitar board. Is Sears correct?

9. On September 23, 1994, William Duke filed a Chapter 7 bankruptcy petition in which he listed Sears Roebuck & Company as one of his creditors. His filing triggered the automatic stay provision, which prohibits a creditor from engaging in any act to collect, assess, or recover a claim against the debtor that arose before commencement of the petition. After receiving notice of the automatic stay, Sears sent a letter to Duke's attorney, with a copy to Duke himself, which stated: *"There is a balance of $317.10 on this account. Should your client elect to reaffirm the Sears account upon liquidation of the outstanding balance in accordance with the Reaffirmation Agreement, charge privileges will be reinstated with a line of credit in the amount of $500.00. Enclosed are copies of the Reaffirmation Agreement."* Has Sears violated the automatic stay provision of the Bankruptcy Act?

10. When Rusty Jones, a used-car dealer, applied to First Financial Savings and Loan Association for a line of credit, Worth Camp agreed to co-sign the loan. The original loan for $25,000 was signed on August 2, 1984, and the parties intended that it would be repaid from the proceeds of sales of Jones's car inventory. By March 15, 1986, the amount had increased to $50,000. In August 1985, while Camp was considering whether to sign the new agreement increasing the loan amount to $50,000, he was told by First Financial's loan officer that the interest on the loan had been paid. In reality, the interest payments were four months delinquent. Further, as the $50,000 credit limit was approached, First Financial began making personal loans to Jones totaling almost $25,000, which were to be paid from the proceeds for his inventory. Camp was not aware of these loans. When Jones defaulted on the $50,000 loan, Camp argued that he was not liable because of First Financial's failure to disclose material facts to him. Is Camp correct?

CHAPTER 11

PAYING BY CHECK

W. T. Stringfellow Company (the Company) wrote a check to Julia Stringfellow for $20,774.99 from its checking account at First American Bank. However, after determining that it did not owe Stringfellow the money after all, the Company placed a stop payment order with the bank. That same day, Stringfellow presented the check for payment at First American Bank and requested that the bank issue her a cashier's check in its stead. The bank mistakenly overlooked the stop payment order and issued Stringfellow a cashier's check. She deposited the cashier's check in her account at Third National Bank. However, when Third National presented the check to First American Bank for payment, First American refused to pay.

Stringfellow v. First American National Bank,
878 S.W.2d 940 (Sup. Ct. Tenn. 1994).

How does a cashier's check differ from a personal check?
What is a bank's liability when it pays on a check in spite of a stop payment order?
What options were available to Third National Bank when First American Bank dishonored the cashier's check?
When may a bank refuse to honor a cashier's check?

Introduction

Consumer contracts generally involve one of three payment mechanisms: cash, credit, or check. The legal problems that arise in cash transactions generally involve situations where the buyer is later unhappy with the goods or services and seeks some remedy from the seller. Credit purchases usually involve a credit card or a promissory note. When buyers use credit cards, the problems they face when the seller's performance is deficient are similar to those that arise in a cash purchase. Promissory notes, on the other hand, may afford the buyer slightly greater leverage since he often may refuse to make further payments until any legal disputes are resolved. (Credit transactions are discussed in Chapter 10.)

Payment by check falls somewhere between cash and credit purchases. This chapter examines the legal issues involved when a buyer purchases goods or services with a check. In particular, it explores the rights and duties of check writers, payees, indorsers, and banks.

Chapter Overview

The chapter begins with an introduction to the various types of negotiable instruments. It then explains the concept of negotiability and the importance of becoming a holder in due course. This is followed by a look at how checks are negotiated. Attention is then turned to the various ways in which people may become liable for checks. The chapter closes by examining the check collection process and several important duties that banks owe their customers.

Kinds of Negotiable Instruments

http://
www.law.cornell.edu/
topics/negotiable.
html is a site on negotiable instruments, with links to banking law and the U.S. Treasury.

Checks are a form of commercial paper, known as **negotiable instruments,** that serve as a substitute for money. They are called negotiable instruments because of the ease with which they pass through the financial system. There are two basic types of negotiable instruments: (1) promises to pay money (promissory notes and certificates of deposit), and (2) orders to pay money (drafts and checks). This section briefly introduces each kind of negotiable instrument. However, throughout the remainder of the chapter, attention is primarily focused on checks.

Promissory Note

Historians estimate that commercial paper was used as long as four thousand years ago. It is thought that early trade was carried on with the use of a **promissory note.** When paying with a promissory note, one person (the *maker*) unconditionally promises to pay money to another person (the *payee*) or to someone specified by the payee, either on demand or at some particular time in the future. Most commercial and consumer loans (discussed in Chapter 10) make use of the promissory note. (See Figure 11–1.)

Certificate of Deposit

Banks and other credit institutions may issue a **certificate of deposit** when they accept the deposit of money. Specifically, the certificate of deposit contains (1) an

Figure 11–1:   A Promissory Note

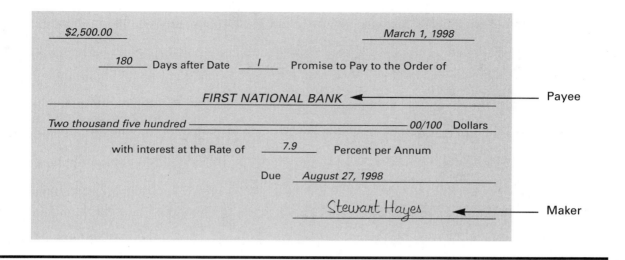

$2,500.00	March 1, 1998

___180___ Days after Date ___I___ Promise to Pay to the Order of

FIRST NATIONAL BANK ◄——————————— Payee

Two thousand five hundred ———————————— 00/100   Dollars

with interest at the Rate of ___7.9___ Percent per Annum

Due   _August 27, 1998_

Stewart Hayes ◄——————— Maker

---

acknowledgment that money has been deposited, and (2) a promise to repay the money on a particular date at a specified rate of interest. In short, a certificate of deposit is a note given by a bank. Today, many banks no longer issue certificates of deposit in paper form. Instead, they are handled electronically. When this occurs, the certificate of deposit does not qualify as a negotiable instrument.

Draft

While promissory notes and certificates of deposit are promises to pay money, a **draft** is an order to pay. With a draft, one person (the _drawer_) orders another person (the _drawee_) to pay money to a third individual (the _payee_) or to someone specified by the payee, either on demand or at a designated time in the future. The drawer is liable to the payee for the face amount of the draft. The drawee, on the other hand, is not liable to the payee unless it "accepts" the draft by signing it.

Check

A **check** is a special type of draft that is payable on demand. With a check, the drawee is the bank where the drawer has a checking account. Thus, when writing a check, the drawer orders its bank (the drawee) to pay on demand a certain amount of money to the payee or someone designated by the payee. For most day-to-day consumer purchases, people write _personal checks_ drawn on their personal checking accounts. (See Figure 11–2 on page 238.) However, there are several specialized types of checks.

Certified Check

In the earlier discussion of drafts, it was noted that a drawee does not become liable to the payee until the drawee "accepts" the draft by signing it. This is also

Figure 11–2:   A Personal Check

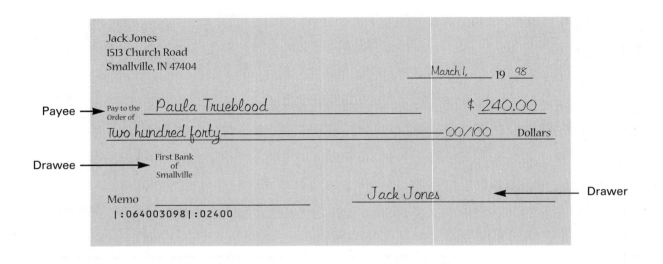

true with checks. Thus, when John writes a check to Mary, she has no guarantee that John's bank will honor the check when she presents it for payment. However, she can avoid this uncertainty by insisting that John make payment with a **certified check.** With a certified check, the bank immediately charges the funds against John's account at the time the check is issued. By certifying the check in advance, John's bank has accepted the negotiable instrument. This assures Mary that the check will be honored.

Cashier's Check

A **cashier's check** is a draft drawn by a bank upon itself and accepted in advance. By drawing the check upon itself, the bank guarantees it will honor the check when presented. Thus, a cashier's check is substantially equivalent to a certified check in that both contain guarantees from a bank that they will be honored when presented for payment. (See Figure 11–3).

In the case that opened the chapter, First American Bank issued a cashier's check to Stringfellow in exchange for the personal check she received from the Company. It did this after making certain the Company had sufficient funds in its checking account to cover the check. When issuing the cashier's check the bank charged Stringfellow a fee designed, in part, to compensate it for the risk of guaranteeing payment.

Money Order

A **money order** is a type of negotiable draft issued by banks, post offices, telegraph companies, and express companies. It often is used by purchasers as a

Figure 11–3: A Cashier's Check

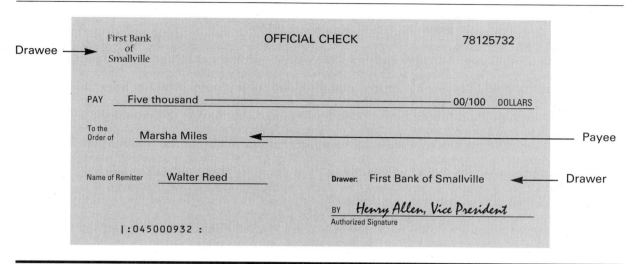

substitute for a check. While certified checks and cashier's checks contain the signature of a bank official, money orders frequently do not. This has caused some confusion about their use.

The most common form of money order sold by banks is that of an ordinary check drawn by the purchaser. It is no different than a personal check. The bank is a drawee and has no obligation to the payee to honor the money order. However, if the money order is drawn by the bank itself, it is treated like a certified check or cashier's check. Consider the following case in which the payee of a money order was not aware of this difference.

Trump Plaza Associates v. Haas
692 A.2D 86 (SUPER. A.D. N.J. 1997)

FACTS   James Haas deposited two checks in the amount of $20,000 and $22,000 in his checking account with Meridian Bank. Two days later, he purchased a $35,000 personal money order from Meridian. The bank's name and logo were printed on the upper left-hand side of the money order. It was made payable to the order of "Jim Haas." He signed the money order on the bottom right-hand corner of the document and presented the signed instrument to the Trump Plaza Hotel and Casino, where he was given $35,000 in cash to use at Trump's gaming tables. Meanwhile, the two checks Haas had earlier deposited in the bank were returned to Meridian unpaid, which resulted in a $38,584 overdraft in his account. Several days later, when Trump presented Haas' personal money order to Meridian for payment, the bank refused to pay. Meridian placed a "payment stopped" notation on the money order because Haas' account contained insufficient funds to cover the amount of the money order.

continued

Trump argued that Meridian unlawfully stopped payment on the money order and that it should not suffer due to Meridian's negligence in issuing the instrument.

ISSUE   May the bank lawfully refuse to pay on the money order?

DECISION   Yes. A personal money order has been described as an instrument for the convenience of anyone who does not have an ordinary checking account and needs a safe, inexpensive, and readily accepted means of transferring funds. There is a public perception that personal money orders are the equivalent of cash or have the credit of the issuing bank behind them. However, this perception is at odds with legal reality. A personal money order has the characteristic of a check in that it constitutes a draft drawn on a bank and payable on demand. Despite a payee's expectation that the drawee bank will pay a check, the bank has no obligation to pay it unless and until the bank has accepted it. Although acceptance of an instrument is generally manifested by such words as "accepted" in case of a draft, or "certified" in the case of a check, an acceptance may consist of the drawee's signature alone. However, it is essential that the instrument at least contain the signature of the drawee. This money order was not signed by any authorized representative of Meridian Bank, nor did it bear the signature of the bank. The mere fact that the printed name of the bank appeared on the face of the money order was not an acceptance.

http://www.meislik.com/recentnj.htm

Nature of Negotiable Instruments

Checks have special advantages that make them a highly desirable method of payment. When purchasing goods or paying bills, they are much safer than cash. There always is a possibility that cash may be lost or stolen. This is less of a problem with negotiable instruments. When a check is properly written, the drawer does not lose any money if it is lost or stolen.

Further, suppose Anne pays her electric bill with a check. Once the electric company presents the check to Anne's bank for payment, Anne has proof that the payment was made, which is helpful if the electric company neglects to record the payment. However, this is not a perfect way of verifying payment. For instance, if the electric company loses the check before presenting it for payment, Anne's canceled check may not reappear and she will have no proof of payment.

Negotiability

The safety and proof of payment aspects of checks are supplemented by another important attribute—they generally are accepted readily as a substitute for money. This is because of their **negotiability** feature. When commercial paper is negotiable, banks pay money for the instrument because they can become a holder in due course and take the instrument free of most contractual risks.

Suppose Sam Seller agreed to sell goods to Betty Buyer. Upon receiving the goods, Betty paid Sam by check. Sam then negotiated the instrument with his bank for cash. Later, even if the goods were defective, Betty must pay the full amount of the check to the bank. This is because the bank took the check free of Betty's defenses to her underlying contract with Sam.

This special protection provided to the bank by the negotiability feature of the check does not arise unless two conditions are met. First, the instrument must be in the proper form. Second, the bank must qualify as a holder in due course.

Proper Form

Commercial paper is not negotiable unless it meets certain requirements. It must:

1. Be in *writing*.
2. Be *signed* by the maker or drawer.
3. Contain an *unconditional promise or order to pay a sum certain in money*.
4. Be *payable on demand or at a definite time*.
5. Be *payable to order or to bearer*.

If Betty's check had not met these formal requirements, she still would owe money to Sam. However, the instrument she gave Sam would have been non-negotiable.

Paper that is nonnegotiable is governed by contract law rules. Accordingly, the bank would not have received any special protection when it paid Sam for the commercial paper. As a result, when Betty discovered that the goods were defective, she could legally withhold payment from the bank since she had that right against Sam. For this reason, banks are unlikely to give people like Sam full payment for commercial paper unless it is in the proper form and qualifies as a negotiable instrument.

Center Video v. Roadway Package System
90 F.3D 185 (7TH CIR. 1996)

FACTS Center Video Industrial sells video equipment to customers by mail order. It frequently contracted with Roadway Package Systems to ship its products. The contract between Center Video and Roadway required that Roadway collect "cash only" for COD shipments. That meant that Roadway could accept only "cash, cashier's check, certified check, or other similar instrument." Center Video arranged with Roadway to ship equipment valued at $13,530 to an address identified as the United States Peace Corps in Denver, Colorado. (It is not clear who actually ordered the goods or to whom they were delivered. All that is known is that the recipient was not the federal agency the United States Peace Corps.) Roadway released the goods to the recipient "Peace Corps," accepting as payment an instrument that resembled a check from the "United States Peace Corps" but that also had "certified funds" printed above a scribbled signature. Although "United States Peace Corps" was printed on the upper-left portion, which could cause a recipient to think a government agency stood behind the obligation, the instrument was drawn neither on a bank nor the U.S. Treasury and contained neither a routing nor account number. On the back, the instrument identified itself as a "purchase order," and instructed the payee to *"Send original proof of your federal identification number and routing code to Accounts Payable, United States Peace Corps. Allow 45 days for transfer and expect prime rate interest in addition."* Center Video was unable to collect on the instrument and demanded that Roadway pay $13,530 for the goods based on its failure to comply with the parties'

continued

agreement. Roadway contended that it was not liable because the document it accepted qualified as a "similar instrument" under the terms of its agreement with Center Video.

ISSUE   Is Roadway liable to Center Video for the price of the goods?

DECISION   Yes. This was a "cash only" transaction. Thus, Roadway's driver could accept only cash, a cashier's check, or a certified check. But he could not accept an ordinary check. An ordinary check does not qualify as a "similar instrument." What distinguishes the instruments specifically listed in Roadway's instructions from ordinary personal checks is that in addition to constituting demand instruments, each is an institutionally guaranteed instrument where money has already been paid or set aside, securing the instrument. An ordinary check, on the other hand, is "payable on demand" only if the account drawn upon has sufficient funds to cover the amount of the check at the time of demand. If funds are not sufficient, the institution can reject the demand. Most importantly, the "Peace Corps" instrument the Roadway driver accepted does not even reach the level of a demand instrument—an ordinary check—thus it certainly does not qualify as a "similar instrument." It was not an instrument payable on demand or when presented to a financial institution. While the face of the instrument was deceiving, drivers who collect payments upon delivery of goods should be wary of such instruments.

http://www.kentlaw.edu/7circuit/

Ambiguities

The amount to be paid on a check is indicated twice on the instrument—once in words and once in figures. Sometimes a person mistakenly writes an amount that differs from the figures. For instance, the words may say *"One hundred thirteen dollars and 00/100 cents,"* while the figures say *"$130.00."* When such ambiguities exist, there are special rules for interpreting the negotiable instrument. Typewritten terms override printed terms and handwritten terms override both typewritten and printed terms. The rules of interpretation also hold that written amounts prevail over figures. Thus, in our example, the check is worth $113.00 because the words override the figures.

Holder in Due Course

To qualify as a **holder in due course,** a person must:

1. Be a *holder* of a negotiable instrument.
2. Give *value* for the instrument.
3. Take the instrument in *good faith.*
4. Be *without notice* that the instrument is *overdue,* has been *dishonored,* or has any *defense* against it.

To qualify as a holder, the person must have possession of an instrument that is either payable to "bearer" or payable specifically to him. The value requirement is met when the holder pays a reasonable amount for the instrument. Good faith requires that the holder obtain the instrument honestly. The final requirement prevents a person from becoming a holder in due course if he is aware, before giving value for the instrument, of potential reasons why the drawer or maker may wish to stop payment.

A holder who does not meet all four requirements has only the rights of an assignee under contract law. As such, he is subject to any of the drawer's or maker's personal or real defenses against payment. A holder in due course, on the other hand, is entitled to payment unless the drawer or maker has a real defense. These two concepts (personal and real defenses) are explained below.

Personal Defenses

A holder in due course is entitled to full payment on a check even if the drawer has **personal defenses** to the underlying contract. Personal (or contractual) defenses include: fraud by a seller that induces a sale, defective goods or services, or nondelivery of goods or services. For instance, in our earlier example, Betty wished to stop payment on her check when Sam delivered defective goods. However, because Sam negotiated the check to a holder in due course (his bank), Betty may not stop payment. This is because her personal defense (defective goods) is not a valid defense against a holder in due course.

Real Defenses

Both holders and holders in due course are subject to a drawer's **real defenses.** Claims that go to the validity of the instrument qualify as real defenses. These include things like: a forged signature, the minority or incapacity of the drawer, duress that coerces the drawer to write the check, fraud in the essence (a person is tricked into signing a document without realizing it is a negotiable instrument), and a discharge in bankruptcy. If Betty could have proven any of these defenses, she could have refused payment on her check, even after it was negotiated to the bank.

Braden Corp. v. Citizens National Bank

661 N.E.2D 838 (CT. APP. IND. 1996)

FACTS Frank Splittorff was the president of two independent corporations, Braden Corporation and Polymer Technology Corporation. On November 26th, Splittorff wrote and signed a check on Braden's National Bank of Detroit (NBD) account in the amount of $5,000 payable to the order of Polymer Corporation. On the same day, Polymer presented the check for deposit into its checking account at Citizens National Bank. The proceeds of the check were immediately applied to pay several checks that Polymer had previously drawn on its account. Later that day, Citizens forwarded the check for collection to NBD. On December 3rd, NBD dishonored the check and returned it to Citizens because there were insufficient funds in Braden's account. Splittorff met with representatives of Citizens on January 3rd and advised them to present the check for payment at NBD the following day. However, on that same day, another officer of Braden ordered NBD to stop payment on the check. When Citizens sued Braden for payment, Braden denied liability on the check because Polymer had not paid consideration for it. Citizens argued that the personal defense of lack of consideration was not valid against it since it was a holder in due course. Braden

continued

asserted that Citizens did not qualify as a holder in due course because it did not give Polymer value for the check.

ISSUE   Is Citizens a holder in due course who is not subject to the personal defense of lack of consideration?

DECISION   Yes. A holder in due course is a holder who takes an instrument for value, in good faith, and without notice that it is overdue or has been dishonored, or of any defense against it. The record reveals that Citizens permitted Polymer to draw against the proceeds of the check. When Citizens allowed Polymer to draw against the credit given for Braden's check, it gave value for the check. Because Citizens is a holder in due course, it is not subject to Braden's defense of lack of consideration.

Limits on the Holder in Due Course Rule

The holder in due course rule can create a hardship on buyers who have purchased goods or services. Normally, if goods are defective or service is substandard, a buyer could withhold payment until the problem was corrected. However, if the buyer paid with a negotiable instrument, it could not stop payment for such personal defenses once the instrument was negotiated to a holder in due course.

To reduce this hardship, many states have eliminated the holder in due course rule when a consumer pays for goods with a promissory note. Further, the Federal Trade Commission has issued a regulation requiring persons who sell consumer goods on credit to state on the promissory note that holders of the note are subject to all of the buyer's claims and defenses. Sellers who fail to include such a notice may be fined as much as $10,000. (These limits on the holder in due course rule do not apply to checks.)

Transfer and Negotiation

After Jessica writes a check payable to Brian, he must transfer his rights to the instrument if he wishes to receive cash or other value for it. The process by which rights to checks and other negotiable instruments pass from one person to another is called **negotiation.** Generally, negotiation involves two steps: a physical transfer of the instrument to a holder and an indorsement. However, the actual requirements for negotiation depend on the type of paper to be negotiated. (See Figure 11–4.)

Types of Paper

For the purposes of negotiation, there are two basic types of checks: order paper and bearer paper. As is discussed below, the manner in which negotiation occurs depends, in part, on whether a check is order paper or bearer paper.

Order Paper

If an instrument is payable to a specifically identified person, it is called **order paper.** Thus, if Jessica writes a check "Pay to the order of Brian," the instrument is order paper because it specifically identifies the payee. Brian might then cash the

Figure 11–4:   A Simple Negotiation

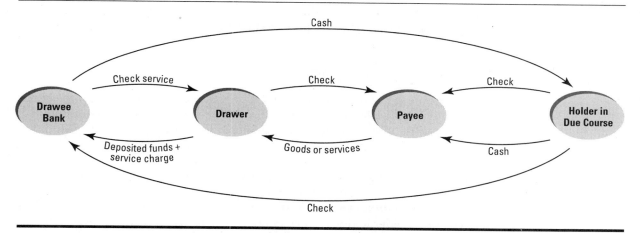

check at his bank and, above his signature on the back of the check, write the words, "Pay to the order of First Bank." The check continues to be order paper because it specifically identifies the bank as the indorsee (new payee) of the check.

Bearer Paper

An instrument is called **bearer paper** when it does not specifically identify the person to whom it is payable. For instance, Jessica could give Brian a check marked "Pay to the order of bearer" or "Pay to the order of cash." These both are examples of bearer paper because they do not specifically identify a particular payee.

Earlier we had an order paper example where Jessica wrote a check "Pay to the order of Brian." Suppose that Brian cashed the check at his bank merely by signing his name on the back. When this occurred, he did not specifically indicate a new payee (indorsee) for the check. This transformed the order paper into bearer paper. The legal significance of this transformation should become clearer later.

Holder

A person becomes a **holder** of a check when he physically possesses a check that is bearer paper. Or in the case of order paper, he is a holder if he possesses the instrument and is the specifically identified person to whom the check is payable. One's status as a holder is extremely important because negotiation does not occur unless the person seeking rights in the check is a holder.

When Jessica made a check "Pay to the order of Brian," he became a holder as soon as he took physical possession of the check. It was made payable to an identified person (Brian), and he was that person. If Brian merely signed his name on the back of the check (indorsed) and presented it to Bank One for cash, Bank One became a holder. This is because Brian's indorsement made the check bearer paper and the bank had possession of it.

Suppose that after Brian signed his name to the back of the check, Anna stole it from him. Anna would now be a holder. She is in possession of bearer paper. However, if Brian had written on the back of the check above his signature, "Pay to the order of Bank One," Anna would not have become a holder. She is in possession of order paper and is not the specifically identified person to whom the check is payable. Hopefully, this example demonstrates the wisdom of writing and indorsing checks as order paper rather than bearer paper to avoid unnecessary losses.

Nature of Indorsements

An **indorsement** occurs when a holder signs his name on the back of the check. Indorsements may also contain words restricting payment of the instrument (i.e., "For deposit only"). An indorsement is not legally necessary when negotiating bearer paper, although the recipient may refuse to accept a check without an indorsement.

Order paper may not be negotiated unless it is indorsed by the holder to whom the check is specifically payable. A person who takes possession of order paper without an indorsement does not become a holder and, consequently, cannot become a holder in due course. However, there is an exception when a holder deposits a check to his account with a bank but forgets to indorse it. In such cases, the bank may deposit the check without an indorsement.

Functions of Indorsements

There are three basic functions served by an indorsement. First, order paper generally cannot be negotiated without an indorsement. Second, the form of indorsement may affect future uses of the check. (This function is discussed below with the kinds of indorsements.) Third, by indorsing a check, the holder generally assumes liability on the instrument if the drawer does not pay. This is the reason that recipients of bearer paper may require their transferor to indorse the check. (Liabilities on checks are discussed later.)

Kinds of Indorsements

The future uses of a check may be affected by the kind of indorsement the holder used when negotiating the instrument. There are four basic types of indorsements:

1. special,
2. blank,
3. restrictive, and
4. qualified.

Special Indorsement

When a holder indorses a check with a **special indorsement,** she indicates that the instrument is to be order paper. A special indorsement contains the signature of the indorser as well as the identity of the person to whom the check is now payable. For instance, suppose Megan wishes to deposit a check she received from Bill that was written "Pay to the order of cash." Megan is a holder of bearer paper. If the check is stolen before she deposits it, the thief would be a holder who could negotiate the check. To protect against this risk, Megan might write a special indorsement such as "Pay to the order of Citizens Bank" above her signature on the back of the check. By doing this she has transformed the check into order paper, which could be negotiated only with the signature of Citizens Bank.

Similarly, Bill may have originally drawn the check as order paper by writing "Pay to the order of Megan." This requires Megan's signature before it can be negotiated. If she writes "Pay to the order of Citizens Bank" above her signature on the back of the check, Megan has insured that the check remains order paper by the use of her special indorsement.

Blank Indorsement

When an indorser uses a **blank indorsement,** she indicates that the check is to be bearer paper. This occurs if the indorser merely signs her name without identifying to whom the check is now payable. Suppose Megan received a check from Bill that stated "Pay to the order of Megan." If she merely signs her name on the back of the check, Megan has transformed the order paper into bearer paper.

Restrictive Indorsement

When a holder signs on the back of a check and indicates the purpose for which the instrument is to be used, she has signed with a **restrictive indorsement.** A restrictive indorsement obligates the next transferee to follow the instructions contained in the indorsement. Accordingly, the indorser can sue the immediate transferee in contract to recover any damages caused by the transferee's failure to follow the instructions.

Suppose Megan wishes to guarantee that the proceeds of her check from Bill are deposited in her account at Citizens Bank. She might place the restrictive indorsement *"For deposit only in Account #732-3893"* above her signature on the back of the check. Unless the bank deposits the money in her account, it is liable to Megan in conversion. Banks involved in the collection process (discussed later) frequently use the restrictive indorsement *"For collection only."*

State of Qatar v. First American Bank

885 F.Supp. 849 (E.D. Va. 1995)

FACTS   One of Qatar's employees, Bassam Salous, defrauded his employer by having checks drawn on Qatar's account in purported payment of false invoices he had created. Although all of the unauthorized checks were made payable to individuals other than Salous, he nonetheless successfully deposited the checks into his own personal account with First American Bank of Virginia. These checks all bear the forged indorsements of the payee named on the face of the check, along with a stamped "for deposit only" restriction. First American Bank argued that it fully complied with the restrictive indorsements on the checks when it deposited the proceeds in Salous's account. An indorsement in this form, the bank argued, is far less restrictive, as it merely directs that the check's proceeds be deposited in *an* account, not that they be deposited into a *particular* account.

ISSUE   Is the bank liable for handling the checks' proceeds in violation of the restrictive indorsements?

DECISION   Yes. The specific question presented here is whether a bank complies with the restrictive indorsement "for deposit only" when it deposits a check bearing

continued

that restriction into *any* person's account, or whether that restriction requires the bank to deposit the check's proceeds only into the account of the named payee. The law makes clear that the phrase "for deposit only" is a restrictive indorsement. But it does not define "for deposit only" or specify what bank conduct would be inconsistent with that restriction. Not surprisingly, however, most courts confronted with this issue have held that the restriction "for deposit only," without additional specification or directive, instructs banks to deposit the funds only into the payee's account. This construction of "for deposit only" is commercially sensible and is adopted here. The clear purpose of the restriction is to avoid the hazards of indorsing a check in blank. A person who indorses her check in blank runs the risk of having the check stolen and freely negotiated before the check reaches its intended destination. To protect against this vulnerability, the payee can add the restriction "for deposit only" to the indorsement, and the bank is required to handle the check in a manner consistent with that restriction. In so adding the restriction, the payee's intent plainly is to direct that the funds be deposited into her own account, not simply that they be deposited into some account. It is virtually impossible to imagine a scenario in which a payee cared that her check be deposited, but was indifferent with respect to the particular account to which the funds would be credited.

Qualified Indorsement

Suppose that Rebecca, an attorney for Michael, negotiated a settlement with Frank that required Frank to pay Michael $2,500. Rather than make the check payable to Michael, Frank wrote "Pay to the order of Rebecca." In order to negotiate this order paper to Michael, Rebecca must sign the back of the check. However, she does not wish to be liable on the instrument if Frank stops payment or his account has insufficient funds.

Rebecca may use a **qualified indorsement,** in which she disclaims such liability. This might take the form of writing *"Without recourse"* above her signature on the back of the check. In fact, she might combine the qualified indorsement with a special indorsement. She could write on the back of the check "Pay to the order of Michael, without recourse" immediately above her signature.

Ethical Issue

Suppose Paul accidentally dents Rhonda's car in the parking lot. Rhonda claims there is $600 worth of damage, while Paul, although admitting it was his fault, argues the damage does not exceed $400. Paul sends Rhonda a check for $400 and writes on the back, above where she must indorse, "In Full Settlement of All Claims." By cashing the check, Rhonda will be accepting Paul's assessment of the damage. Is it ethical for Paul to induce a settlement in this manner?

Liability on
Negotiable Instruments

It is important for people who write, as well as receive, checks to understand how they may become liable on a negotiable instrument. This section explores the various ways in which liability arises. It examines contractual liability, warranty liability, negligence liability, the imposter rule, and the fictitious payee rule. The section ends with a look at the comparative negligence rule that allocates liability between drawers and banks.

Contractual Liability

A person generally assumes **contractual liability** when she signs a check. Thus, drawers and indorsers are liable on a check if the bank on which it is drawn refuses to pay. Suppose Allen drew a check on his account with First Bank payable to the order of Brenda. She then signed it and cashed it at Second Bank. When Second Bank presented the check for payment, First Bank refused to pay. Because First Bank did not accept (sign) the check, it has no liability to Second Bank or Brenda. However, Second Bank may demand payment from either Brenda or Allen. And if Brenda repays Second Bank, she may recover from Allen.

Once First Bank accepts the check, Allen is no longer contractually liable to Brenda or Second Bank. Further, if the acceptance took place after Brenda indorsed the check, she would be excused from contractual liability once the acceptance occurred.

Warranty Liability

Even when a person has not signed a check, he may still assume **warranty liability** on the instrument. This might arise if the person violates either a transfer warranty or a presentment warranty.

Transfer Warranties

People who transfer a check to another person make certain implied *transfer warranties* that might trigger personal liability on the instrument. Specifically, the transferor promises that:

1. he is entitled to transfer the instrument;
2. all signatures are authentic or authorized;
3. the check has not been altered;
4. there are no defenses against the transferor's rights to the check; and
5. the transferor is not aware of insolvency proceedings against the drawer or acceptor of the check.

If the transferor breaches any of these warranties, he is liable to a transferee who took the instrument in good faith for her damages up to the amount of the check plus expenses and loss of interest.

Presentment Warranties

A person who presents a check for payment makes certain *presentment warranties*. Suppose Helen presents Bob's personal check drawn on Third Bank to Third Bank (the drawee) for payment. When Third Bank pays on the check, Helen impliedly promises that:

1. she was, at the time she presented the check, entitled to obtain payment;
2. the check was not altered; and
3. she had no knowledge that Bob's (the drawer's) signature was not authorized.

Violation of any of these presentment warranties permits Third Bank to recover its losses, up to the amount paid plus expenses and lost interest, from Helen.

Negligence Liability

The drawee bank normally may not charge a check against the drawer's checking account if the payee's signature is forged. Or if the amount of the check has been altered, the drawer is liable for no more than the amount for which it was originally drawn. However, under **negligence liability,** the drawer may be liable to a holder in due course if the drawer's negligence makes the alteration or unauthorized signature possible. This might occur when a company is grossly negligent in its audit procedures and thereby facilitates embezzlement.

Imposter Rule

Suppose Nancy convinces Robert that she is Andrea. Not realizing that Nancy is an imposter, Robert draws a check payable to Andrea and gives it to Nancy. When this occurs, under the **imposter rule,** any person may negotiate the check by indorsing it with Andrea's name. This rule is designed to place on the drawer the responsibility to determine the true identity of the payee. It is felt that drawers, like Robert, are in a better position than some later holder of the check to make this determination.

Fictitious Payee Rule

Under the **fictitious payee rule,** a dishonest employee of the drawer has a company check made payable to someone who does not exist. Or she may have the check written to someone who does business with her employer without ever intending to give him the check. If the dishonest employee is authorized, she signs the check on behalf of her employer. Otherwise, she tricks her employer into signing it. She then indorses the check in the name of the payee, presents it for payment, and keeps the proceeds. As with the imposter rule, any person may indorse the check in the name of a fictitious payee.

Golden Years Nursing Home v. Gabbard

640 N.E.2d 1186 (Ct. App. Ohio 1994)

FACTS   Nancy Gabbard was employed as the office manager at Golden Years Nursing Home and was responsible for handling the financial aspects of the business. Bud Angus, the administrator, was responsible for running the nursing home. He was the only person authorized to sign checks for Golden Years. For many years, Gabbard made false representations to Angus that certain employees desired loans. After Angus made the checks, Gabbard would take the checks, forge the employees' (payees') indorsements, and deposit or cash them at Star Bank, where she had a personal account. The employees whose names were on the checks never actually requested the loans. The entire scheme was concocted by Gabbard exclusively for the purpose of embezzling the money. When Golden Years discovered the embezzlement, it sued Star Bank to recover the value of the forged checks deposited or cashed by Gabbard.

ISSUE   Is the bank liable for the value of the forged checks?

DECISION   No. As a general rule, the forgery of a payee's indorsement on order paper, such as the Golden Years' checks, breaks the chain of title and no subsequent transferee of the instrument can qualify as a holder. As a result, anyone who pays on a check containing a forged indorsement is liable for the value of the check. However, the fictitious payee rule validates a forged payee's indorsement whenever the drawer or his employee has designated as payee someone who is not really intended to have an interest in the instrument. In such a case, good title passes to a subsequent transferee and the check is properly payable out of the drawer's/employer's bank account, despite a forged payee indorsement. The theory behind this rule is that the risk of loss caused by a dishonest employee should be placed on the employer rather than on the subsequent holder bank. This is because the employer is normally in a better position to prevent such forgeries by reasonable care in the selection or supervision of employees, or, if not, is at least in a better position to cover the loss by fidelity insurance. Gabbard, a Golden Years employee, provided her employer with names of employees who had not really requested loans. She did this for the specific purpose of embezzling money without ever intending that the employees have an interest in the checks. Accordingly, the fictitious payee rule precludes Golden Years from asserting the forged payee indorsements against Star Bank.

Comparative Negligence Rule

The harshness of negligence liability and the imposter and fictitious payee rules may be reduced when a bank that pays on the check could have detected the alteration or forgery if it had exercised reasonable care. Under this **comparative negligence rule,** the loss may be allocated between the drawer and the bank. A bank fails to exercise reasonable care in the processing of checks when it does not observe the reasonable commercial standards prevailing among other banks in the area.

The Bank's Duties to Customers

This chapter closes with a brief look at the duties a bank owes its checking account customers. While these duties are defined largely by the contract between the bank and the customer, the deposit agreement must be consistent with state law. This section discusses the basic duties owed by the bank; however, it first examines the fundamental nature of the check collection process.

http://
www.law.cornell.edu/
uscode/12 takes you
to the site of the U.S.
Code on banking.

Check Collection Process

The bank upon which a check is drawn and by which it is payable is known as the payor or **drawee bank.** After the drawer issues a check payable to the payee, that person generally submits the check to either the drawee bank or another bank. The first bank to which the check is submitted for collection (even if it also is the drawee bank) is the **depositary bank.** When the depositary bank is not the drawee bank, it presents the check to the drawee bank for payment either directly or through one or more **intermediary banks.**

If the drawee bank refuses to pay (dishonors) the check, the intermediary banks may reverse the transaction and recover from their immediate transferor. Ultimately, the depositary bank seeks payment from its customer or the drawer. If the drawee bank pays (honors) the check, it charges the amount of the check to the drawer's checking account.

Duty to Pay

Unless the drawee bank issues a cashier's check or a certified check, it owes no duty to payees or indorsees to honor the check. However, its failure to honor the check violates its contractual duty to the drawer when there are sufficient funds in her account at the time the check is presented for payment. Breach of this duty may subject the drawee bank to liability for the damages suffered by the drawer.

Overdrafts

When there are not sufficient funds to cover the check, the drawee bank may, at its discretion, honor the check. It then has the right to charge the amount of the overdraft to the customer's next deposit or any other accounts the drawer has with the drawee bank. Ultimately, the bank may sue the drawer for the overdraft. (See Figure 11–5.)

Stale Checks

When checks are more than six months old, the bank does not owe its customer a duty to honor them. However, it may pay on such a **stale check** when its actions are in accordance with sound banking practices and it is acting in good faith.

RPM Pizza v. Bank One Cambridge
869 F.Supp. 517 (E.D. Mich. 1994)

FACTS   RPM, a Domino's Pizza franchisee, erroneously issued a $96,000 check drawn on RPM's account with Bank One Cambridge payable to a computer broker, Systems Marketing. After realizing its error, RPM placed a stop payment order on the check. As stated in the terms of its account contract, written stop payment orders are effective for a period of six months. The stop payment order on the check expired on December 6th, and RPM failed to renew the order. On December 22nd, Systems Marketing deposited the check in its account at the Bank of Tampa. At that time the check was more than six months old and was, therefore, stale. Notwithstanding the check's staleness, Bank of Tampa credited the check to Systems Marketing's account and sent it to Bank One Cambridge. When Bank One Cambridge paid the check, RPM sued the bank for wrongfully honoring the check.

ISSUE   Did Bank One Cambridge violate its duty to RPM?

DECISION   No. When paying on a stale check, a drawer bank violates the duty of ordinary care owed to its customer (the drawer) unless it acted in accordance with sound banking practices. There was no such violation here. The law expressly permits payment of stale checks and this check was only stale by three weeks. Further, Bank One Cambridge made the payment in good faith. The term "good faith" is defined as "honesty in fact in the conduct or transaction." The good faith test requires an evaluation of the bank's intent, rather than its diligence. Indeed, a bank could act in good faith and still not follow accepted banking procedures. Here, there is not so much as one scintilla of evidence to demonstrate that the bank noted the stale date, the existence of the expired stop-payment order, or was in any respect less than completely unwitting when it paid the stale check.

Figure 11–5: Notice of Insufficient Funds

_____
_____
_____, _____ _____

October 27, 1997

_____
_____
_____, _____ _____

Bank: _____
_____

The subject _____, dated _____, drawn by you on _____, in the amount of $_____, and payable to _____, has been returned unpaid for the following reason:

  –Insufficient funds

You will be charged a returned check fee charge of $_____.

Please arrange to immediately replace this _____ with cash in the amount of $_____ no later than _____. If payment is not made immediately, your account will be charged $_____, and no further credit will be extended until the amount is paid in full. When you make the replacement payment, your old _____ will be returned to you.

Please forward your payment to:

_____
_____
_____, _____ _____

Please be advised that according to the terms of the _____, interest will begin to accrue on _____ at the rate of 0.00% per _____.

If you have any questions, please contact _____ at: _____

Your prompt attention to this matter is appreciated.

Sincerely,

_____

Postdated Checks

A person may write a check knowing that he does not have sufficient funds to cover the check at the present time. He then postdates the check to make certain it is not presented for payment until he is able to deposit sufficient funds in his checking account. However, when postdating checks, the drawer should notify both the payee and the drawee bank of this fact. Otherwise, the check may be presented for payment before the date on the check and dishonored by the drawee bank. Or the bank could honor the check and make the drawer liable for the overdraft.

Stop Payment Order

Suppose Doug issued a check payable to Paula in exchange for a used television. Soon after giving her the check, Doug discovered she had stolen the television from her neighbor. Since Doug must return the television to the neighbor, he wants his money back. He might telephone his bank and give it an oral **stop payment order.** If the bank receives the order before it has paid or certified the check and with enough time to notify its tellers, the bank must refuse payment. Oral stop payment orders are valid for 14 days. However, they are valid for six months if they are confirmed in writing. Further, Doug can extend the stop payment order for an additional six months by instructing the bank in writing to continue it. (See Figure 11–6 on page 256.)

If the bank mistakenly pays Paula in spite of Doug's stop payment order, it must recredit Doug's account for the amount of the check. However, that would not be true if Paula had negotiated the check to a holder in due course and the bank paid the holder in due course. Because Doug's defense against payment is only a personal defense, he is liable to a holder in due course. Thus, he would not suffer a compensable loss if the bank paid the holder in due course. Doug's only recourse would be to sue Paula.

David v. First National Bank
650 So.2d 1227 (Ct. App. La. 1995)

FACTS   Jackie Kehoe loaned money to Kim Moisant, a woman she met through a mutual friend. Because other checks given to her by Moisant for repayment of the loan had been returned for insufficient funds, Kehoe accompanied Moisant to First National Bank so Moisant could buy a cashier's check to repay the loan. Moisant's friend, Kristie Farrington, also went to the bank with them. While Moisant and Farrington went into the bank, Kehoe remained outside in her car. They emerged from the bank with a First National Bank check, clearly labeled "Official Check," drawn on Citicorp, for $5,011.85 payable to Kehoe. The check used to purchase the official check was drawn on the account of Clara Wolfrum and was made payable to Kristie Farrington. Soon after issuing the official check, First National Bank discovered that Wolfrum's check had been stolen and her signature was a forgery. The bank immediately stopped payment on the official check. Kehoe argued that the official check issued by First National Bank was a cashier's check on which payment cannot be stopped.

ISSUE   May the bank stop payment on the official check?

DECISION   Yes. A cashier's check is not susceptible to a stop payment order because its acceptance for payment is simultaneous with its issuance. That is, the fact that the drawer orders payment on itself represents immediate acceptance of the check and thus its payment cannot be stopped. But a cashier's check is a check drawn by a bank on itself. However, the official check issued by First National Bank was drawn on First National Bank's account at Citicorp. Thus, the drawee bank is different. Such a check is a "teller's check." Payment of a check drawn on another bank can be stopped at any time prior to acceptance by the drawee bank. Of course, once it is honored by the drawee bank, a stop payment order is too late. Here, First National Bank was free to stop payment anytime prior to the check being accepted by Citicorp. It did just that and Kehoe cannot complain.

Ethical Issue

When a person pays for goods with cash and then is dissatisfied with them, it is not possible to stop payment. The buyer's only recourse is to request a refund. Is it ethical for a buyer to pay with a check and then stop payment when she is dissatisfied with the goods?

Forgeries and Alterations

Generally, the drawee bank must recredit the drawer's account if it honors a forged check. And if the amount of the check has been altered, the bank may charge only the original (pre-alteration) amount against the drawer's account. Of course, as was discussed earlier, the bank may avoid or reduce liability if it can demonstrate the drawer's negligence, the imposter rule, or the fictitious payee rule.

In cases where an embezzler commits multiple forgeries or alterations, the drawer has a duty to notify the bank within a reasonable time. Once the drawer receives her bank statement showing the first forgery or alteration, she has 30 days to notify the bank. If she fails to do so, the bank is not liable for any such checks it pays in good faith after the 30-day period has elapsed. However, the bank must recredit the drawer's account for checks it honored after the 30-day period if she shows that the bank failed to exercise ordinary care when it paid the checks.

The drawer must discover and report to the bank any alteration or forgery of her signature within one year of the time her bank statement or the checks were made available to her. Otherwise, she loses any claim against the bank, even if it failed to exercise ordinary care when it honored the checks. In instances where the check contained unauthorized indorsements, the drawer has three years to discover and report the irregularity.

Figure 11–6:   Stop Payment Order

_____

_____

_____, _____ _____

Date: _____

_____

_____

_____, _____ _____

Re: Stop Payment on Check

_____

Please stop payment on the following check drawn on _____, account number
_____:

     Check drawn by: me

This stop payment is being requested because the check is presumed lost and is being replaced.

You are also directed to stop payment on the following check drawn on _____,
account number _____:

     Check drawn by: me

This stop payment is being requested because the check is presumed lost and is being replaced.

I agree to pay your customary amount as a service charge for this service.

Please deduct the service charge from my account.

I agree that the Bank will not be liable if the account number, amount, check number or payee,
as provided above, are incorrect.

I agree to hold the Bank harmless from any liability, costs and expenses, arising from the Bank's
refusal to pay this item. I further agree that the Bank is granted a reasonable time in which to act
after receipt, which shall in no event be less than the opening of business on the next business
day after this stop payment order is received. If this check is paid on the banking day this order
is received, the payment shall not constitute lack of good faith or failure to exercise ordinary care.

This written stop payment order is effective for _____ months unless renewed.

Please contact _____ if you have any questions or need additional information.

Sincerely,

_____

Source: Quicken Business Law Partner® 3.0 CD-ROM. Copyright © 1997 Parson's Technology, Inc. All rights reserved.

QUESTIONS AND PROBLEM CASES

1. When is a drawee bank not liable for honoring a check despite having received a stop payment order from its customer?

2. What is a cashier's check? What does it have in common with a certified check?

3. What is the importance of becoming a holder in due course?

4. Explain the difference between order paper and bearer paper.

5. Sana Travel Service drew a check on National Bank for $33,000 payable to Al-Bark. On the line on the face of the check that usually holds memoranda, Sana inserted the words: *"Just to hold for the security of future business."* This notation was meant to indicate that Sana was providing Al-Bark with a security deposit to guarantee that it would perform on a future contract between the two. After receiving the check, Al-Bark indorsed it and negotiated it to Carador for cash. When National Bank received the check, it telephoned Sana, who directed the bank not to pay on the instrument. Carador sued for the $33,000, alleging that Sana was liable to it because it was a holder in due course. Sana contended that the notation on the face of the check was a conditional promise to pay, thereby destroying the check's negotiability. Is Sana correct?

6. Louise Kalbe drew a check "pay to the order of cash" for $7,260 on her account at Pulaski State Bank. Although the check was lost or stolen, Kalbe never reported this fact to the bank nor did she stop payment on it. When the check ultimately was presented for payment, Kalbe had only $700 in her checking account. Despite this fact, the bank honored the check and created an overdraft in Kalbe's checking account. It then sued Kalbe to recover the amount of the overdraft. Is Kalbe liable to the bank?

7. Robert Griswold presented to a Vectra Bank teller a notarized power of attorney together with several United States savings bonds owned by Walter Noack. The power of attorney authorized Griswold to redeem the savings bonds. At Griswold's request, the teller issued a cashier's check payable to Noack for the value of the savings bonds. Griswold then presented the check to a Bank Western teller. It was indorsed "Walter Noack: pay to the order of Robert Griswold." The teller accepted the check for deposit, and Bank Western collected from Vectra the full amount of the check. Vectra later learned that Noack had died six years earlier and the purported signatures of Noack on the power of attorney and the check were forgeries. Vectra was required to reimburse the United States Department of the Treasury for its payment upon redemption of the bonds. Vectra then filed suit against Bank Western for breach of warranty of title. Is Bank Western liable to Vectra?

8. Louise Bradshaw worked as a bookkeeper for Gordon Neely. Her duties included preparing company checks for Neely's signature and reconciling the company checking account. She prepared several checks drawn on American National Bank that were made payable to herself and contained a large space to the left of the amount written on the designated line. Neely was aware of these gaps when he signed the checks. After Neely signed, Bradshaw altered the checks by adding one or more digits to the left of the original amount and cashed them at American National Bank. Is the bank liable to Neely for cashing the altered checks?

9. On December 10, 1993, Carriage House bought 13 automobiles from Rolls-Royce. Carriage House paid with checks drawn on its account with United Jersey Bank. Rolls-Royce agreed not to present the checks for payment until January 14, 1994, in reliance on assurances there would be sufficient funds in Carriage House's checking account to cover the checks on that date. On January 14th, Carriage House informed Rolls-Royce that its bank account did not hold sufficient funds to cover the checks. After more than one year of negotiations, Rolls-Royce finally presented the checks for payment to United Jersey Bank on March 7, 1995. Rolls-Royce sued Carriage

House when the checks were not honored. Carriage House argued the lawsuit should be dismissed because Rolls-Royce was not a holder in due course and because it did not present the checks for payment until over one year after they were delivered. Should the lawsuit be dismissed?

10. Clark Crapps established several checking accounts with Columbia County Bank and several other banks. Columbia allowed immediate credit on deposits made into these accounts. That is, Columbia allowed Crapps immediate access to the funds without waiting for the deposited items to clear. From the accounts in which deposits were made, Crapps would obtain cashier's checks and/or use those funds for deposit to other accounts at either Columbia or other financial institutions. Checks drawn upon the accounts in other banks were deposited into the Columbia account although insufficient funds were available in the other institutions to satisfy the deposited checks. The deposited checks were covered by depositing checks drawn on the Columbia account into the accounts maintained in the other financial institutions. By such activity, the insufficiency of the funds available to cover the checks in the Columbia account was hidden. Included in the deposits were checks drawn upon Crapps's account with First Railroad Credit Union. Columbia credited Crapps's account with the deposits without waiting for the deposited checks to clear. Crapps then obtained two cashier's checks from Columbia, each for $300,000, in return for checks in like amount drawn upon his account at Columbia. Crapps deposited the cashier's checks in his First Railroad account. At about this time, Columbia became aware of the check-kiting scheme. When First Railroad submitted the cashier's checks for payment, Columbia refused. Columbia argued that it does not have to pay First Railroad because it is not a holder in due course. Should Columbia be required to honor its cashier's checks?

Business Relationships

12 CHAPTER

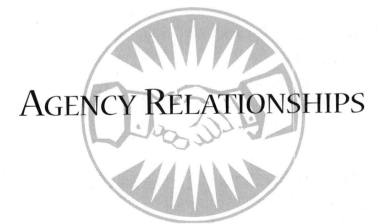

AGENCY RELATIONSHIPS

Victory Tabernacle Baptist Church hired Ladison, gave him keys to all of the church's doors, and permitted him to have frequent unsupervised contact with children. After it was discovered that Ladison had repeatedly raped the plaintiff's 10-year-old daughter both at the church and at other locations, the mother sued the church for damages. The church argued that it was not liable because the rapes did not occur within the scope of Ladison's agency.

J. v. Victory Tabernacle Baptist Church, 372 S.E.2d 391 (Sup. Ct. Va. 1988).

This case raises several issues that you should consider while reading this chapter:

> What is the legal significance of the fact that Ladison was an agent of the church?
> Under what circumstances will the church be liable for Ladison's behavior? (Does it matter that this tort occurred outside the scope of the agency?)
> What should principals (like the church) do to avoid being liable for the torts of their agents?

Introduction

It is quite likely that you have been involved in numerous agency relationships during your life. Perhaps you hired an attorney or made a purchase on behalf of a friend. Generally, when one person (the **agent**) acts *for the benefit of and under the direction of* another (the **principal**), an agency arises. Agency law deals with three essential issues:

1. What contractual duties do principals and agents owe each other?
2. What contractual liability do principals and agents have to third persons who deal with the agent?
3. When are principals liable for the torts or crimes of their agents?

Chapter Overview

The chapter begins with an investigation of how agency relationships are created. It then examines the three basic questions described above: the obligations principals and agents owe each other, the contractual liability owed to third persons, and the circumstances when the principal is liable for the agent's torts or crimes. The chapter concludes with a discussion of the proper ways of terminating an agency.

Creating an Agency

There are very few formalities required for the creation of an agency. For example, while agencies often are created by contract, they frequently exist in the absence of a contractual agreement. And, although a few agency agreements must be written (e.g. an agency formed for the purpose of selling land), oral agency agreements generally are upheld. Further, an agency may arise even though the agent is uncompensated. As long as Ann consents to Robert acting on her behalf and under her control, an agency will be found.

http://
www.law.cornell.edu/
topics/agency.html
provides brief information on agency laws.

Capacity

In law the word **capacity** describes the ability of a person to legally perform an act. There is a general concern that some classes of people (e.g., minors, mentally impaired) need to be protected in their dealings with others. Thus, in contract law, a person who lacks capacity to contract may be able to *avoid* (cancel) her contract with another.

Capacity of the Principal

People commonly act through agents. For instance, in a partnership, each partner acts as an agent for the other partners in the operation of the business. And corporations, as artificial persons, can act only through agents. As a general rule, an individual legally can do anything through an agent that he could do personally. Thus, the legal effect of an authorized agent's action will be the same as if the principal performed the act himself.

However, the law of capacity places an important limitation on the power of the agent to bind the principal. A principal is bound on a contract made by the agent only to the extent that the principal would have been bound if he had performed the act himself. This means that if the principal lacks capacity to contract, he can avoid contracts made in his name by his agent. (This should not be confused with situations where a court has appointed a guardian to act on behalf of someone lacking legal capacity.)

Capacity of the Agent

Agents do not need capacity to contract. As long as the principal has authorized the agent to create contracts on the principal's behalf, the agent may do so. Both partnerships and corporations may act as agents. Note, however, that marriage does not automatically establish an agency relationship. Thus, in the absence of some express, implied, or apparent consent on the part of Mary, her husband does not have authority to act as her agent.

Types of Agents

Our legal system recognizes a number of different relationships where one individual works on behalf of another. The motivation of the subordinate and the type of control exercised by the superior help define the legal consequences flowing from the relationship. This section looks at four types of agents: employees, independent contractors, apparent agents, and subagents. (See Figure 12–1.)

Employees

Persons who are under the control of the principal both as to the *objective* of their work and the *means* used to achieve that objective are known as **employees**. Employers often give detailed instructions to their employees about day-to-day performance. In general, employers are buying the time of their employees. Thus, while on the job, the employee is closely identified with the employer. For this reason, employers frequently are legally liable for the consequences of their employees' behavior.

Independent Contractors

A principal exercises much less control over the activities of an **independent contractor** and, accordingly, is less likely to be liable for her activities. Independent contractors work according to their own methods. The principal controls only the **objectives** the independent contractor is expected to achieve. The actual means used to accomplish those objectives are left to the discretion of the independent contractor.

Figure 12–1:   Employee versus Independent Contractor

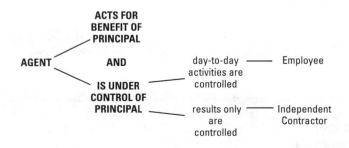

Apparent Agents

While words of the parties may provide strong evidence of the existence or non-existence of an agency, the parties' actions and the surrounding circumstances also are important. In fact, a court may find there to be an agency despite the fact that the parties expressly intended not to create one. In these instances the agent is known as an **apparent agent.** Consider the following case.

Gilbert v. Sycamore Municipal Hospital

622 N.E.2D 788 (SUP. CT. IL. 1993)

FACTS After suffering pain in his chest and left arm while lifting weights, Jack Gilbert visited the emergency room of Sycamore Municipal Hospital. Dr. Frank, the emergency room doctor, ran several tests and informed Gilbert that there was no evidence of heart disease. Gilbert was prescribed pain medication and discharged that day. He died later that evening. An autopsy revealed signs of heart disease. The hospital contended it was not liable for the doctor's alleged malpractice because he was not the hospital's agent. In fact, the doctors set their own fees, billed separately, kept their profits, and bore the losses from their practice. They determined their own work schedules, salaries, vacations, and maximum absences. However, the hospital does not advise emergency room patients of this fact.

ISSUE Was there a principal-agent relationship between the hospital and Dr. Frank?

DECISION Yes. A reality of modern hospital care involves the reasonable expectations of the public. Generally, people who seek medical help through the emergency room facilities are unaware of the status of the various professionals working there. Absent a situation where the patient is directed by his own physician or where the patient makes an independent selection as to which physician he will use while there, it is the reputation of the hospital itself upon which he would rely.

Subagents

If a corporation becomes an agent it must employ a **subagent** to carry out its agency responsibilities. In effect, a subagent is an agent of an agent. Both the principal and the agent are liable to third persons for the authorized actions of a subagent. However, between the principal and the agent, the agent ultimately is liable for the subagent's behavior. When the corporation is the agent, the authority to appoint a subagent is implied. In other instances, one must look to the agency agreement, past dealings, or industry standards to see if such an appointment is authorized.

In many circumstances, an agent is authorized to appoint an agent for the principal rather than a subagent. For example, a company's sales manager probably is authorized to hire salespersons for the business. These individuals are agents of the company rather than subagents. This means that the sales manager is not liable for their actions unless he was negligent in their hiring or supervision.

Duties of the Agent

http://
www.technorealtor.
com/agency.html has
descriptions of agent
duties, especially
relating to the most
well-known form,
real estate agency.

Agency law has developed primarily from the decisions of the courts. Accordingly, most agency rules, including the duties that agents owe their principals, are derived from the common law of agency. However, these common-law duties may be increased and, in some cases, decreased through an agreement between the principal and the agent.

When there is no agency contract or when any such contract does not discuss duties, the common law imposes the following duties on the agent:

1. duty of loyalty,
2. duty to obey,
3. duty to exercise care,
4. duty to communicate information, and
5. duty to account.

Duty of Loyalty

The **duty of loyalty** is the most important common-law duty an agent owes a principal. This is because the agent is a **fiduciary** of the principal. A fiduciary is a person who is legally required to act in the best interests of another rather than pursue her own personal interests.

There are several dimensions to the duty of loyalty. For instance, the agent generally must avoid *conflicts of interest* with the principal. This prevents the agent from selling to, or buying from, the agency without the advance approval of the principal. The agent also must avoid competing with the agency. However, such conflicts may be permissible if the agent fully discloses them to the principal and the principal does not object to them.

The duty of loyalty also demands *complete honesty* from the agency in all dealings with the principal. Further, the agent must safeguard *confidential information* he discovers in the course of the agency. This prevents the agent from using the principal's secrets for private gain or disclosing them to third persons. This might include trade secrets, customer lists, or special sales techniques. However, the duty of loyalty does not prevent the agent from using any general knowledge he acquires while working for the principal. And the agent may compete with the principal after termination of the agency unless he has agreed not to compete.

Chernow v. Reyes

570 A.2D 1282 (N.J. CT. APP. 1990)

FACTS Ronald Chernow is in the business of auditing telephone bills for customers. He determines whether the customer's phone equipment is in place, properly billed, and in working order. He also checks for overcharges and receives half of any overcharge refund the customer receives from the telephone company. Chernow hired Angelo Reyes as an auditor. During his employment, Reyes, without Chernow's knowledge, took various steps to establish a business that competed with Chernow's. He obtained three auditing contracts and performed work under those agreements while still employed by Chernow. He also solicited a fourth account, but did no work for that firm until after terminating his employment with Chernow. None of the businesses with whom Reyes contracted was one of Chernow's existing customers. Further, Reyes's personal soliciting and auditing activities did not take place during his regular working hours. He devoted that time to Chernow's business.

ISSUE   Did Reyes have a conflict of interest that breached his duty of loyalty to Chernow?

DECISION   Yes. An agent owes a duty of loyalty to his principal and must not, while employed, act contrary to the principal's interest. Unless otherwise agreed, the agent is subject to a duty not to compete with the principal concerning the subject matter of the agency. By engaging in a competitive enterprise, Reyes crossed the line between permissible preparation to change jobs and actionable conduct. Chernow was entitled to expect that a person on his payroll would not undertake to pursue competitive commercial opportunities. The protection accorded is not limited to the diversion of the principal's customers. It extends to pursuing and transacting business within the larger pool of potential customers who might have been solicited by the principal.

--- Ethical Issue ---

Is it ethical to work for an employer knowing that you are only trying to gain enough experience to open up your own competing business?

Duty to Obey

Agents have a fundamental **duty to obey** the instructions of their principals. They may not ignore instructions that seem unwise and are prohibited from substituting their personal judgment for that of their principals. When no instructions are given, the agent has a duty to act in the best interests of the principal. If an agent violates her duty to obey, she is liable for any losses her principal suffers. Of course, the agent would not be liable for refusing to commit an illegal act.

Duty to Exercise Care

The **duty to exercise care** requires the agent to carry out his responsibilities with the care and skill common for the kind of work he is performing. The expected level of care often depends on past dealings between the agent and the principal as well as customary practices in a particular trade or industry. It might also depend on the representations the agent has made about her level of expertise as well as on the level of compensation she is receiving.

Duty to Communicate Information

Under the **duty to communicate information,** an agent must promptly notify her principal of anything she discovers in the course of her agency responsibilities. This is because information received by an agent in the scope of the agency is considered to have been received by the principal. However, if the information does not relate to the scope of the agent's responsibilities, the principal is bound only if the information actually is passed on by the agent.

Duty to Account

When an agent receives money or property in the course of the agency, his **duty to account** requires him to either convey them to the principal or explain his inability to do so. This includes an obligation to turn over any gifts the agent receives from third persons in the course of the agency, unless the principal allows the agent to keep them. Payment to the agent of a debt owed to the principal discharges the debt if the agent has the authority to receive such payments. This is true even if the agent breaches the duty to account and steals the money.

When the agency contemplates the agent operating a business or receiving regular payments, the duty to account generally requires the agent to provide periodic records of receipts and expenditures. The timing and extent of these records often is established in an agency agreement. This report is known as an **accounting.**

Duties of the Principal

In the absence of a formal agency agreement, the common law imposes the following duties on the principal:

1. duty to compensate,
2. duty to reimburse and indemnify, and
3. duty to keep accounts.

Figure 12–2 illustrates the relationship of the agency duties of both the agent and the principal.

Figure 12–2: Agency Duties

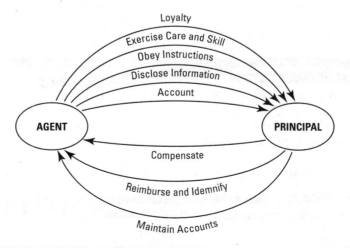

Duty to Compensate

Although agencies often are uncompensated, a **duty to compensate** exists unless it is established that the parties intended a gratuitous (unpaid) relationship. A well-drafted agency agreement should specify the amount and time of compensation. Absent a clear agreement on compensation, the courts look to customary compensation levels in the particular trade or industry.

As a general rule, the agent is not entitled to compensation for transactions that arise after the relationship has ended. However, in some instances, the former agent may collect commissions on sales if she was the **procuring cause** of the transaction. When the sale would not have occurred without the agent's efforts, the agent is the procuring cause. As such, she is entitled to payment even when somebody else actually completes the sale.

Duty to Reimburse and Indemnify

If an agent, while acting in the scope of the agency, makes monetary advances on behalf of the principal, she is entitled to reimbursement. Similarly, if she suffers financial losses while acting for the principal she should be indemnified. This is because of the principal's **duty to reimburse and indemnify.**

Of course, the principal is not required to pay for unauthorized expenses incurred by the agent. Further, he need not indemnify the agent for losses she suffers due to her own negligence.

Duty to Keep Accounts

In a compensated agency, the principal has a **duty to keep accounts** so the appropriate level of compensation can be readily determined. For example, an employer must keep and make available to a salesperson a record of the sales on which commissions have been earned.

The Principal's
Contractual Liability

An authorized agent is able to bind his principal to contracts with third persons. Even when the agent possesses no actual authority, a court may determine that apparent authority exists. If so, the outcome is the same: the principal is liable to the third person for any resulting contract. Finally, in instances where the agent had no authority at all, the principal might be liable on a contract with the third person if the principal ratifies the agent's actions.

This section explores the various ways in which an agent can contract on behalf of a principal. (See Figure 12–3 on page 268.) It requires an examination of the following agency concepts:

1. actual authority
   a. express authority
   b. implied authority
2. apparent authority
3. ratification

Figure 12–3: Contractual Liability

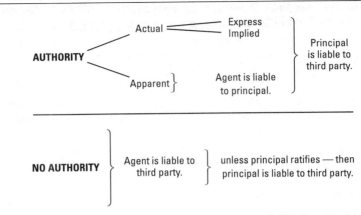

Actual Authority

When an agent acts with **actual authority,** she is acting within the confines of the agency agreement. Actual authority is proper authority in the sense that it is an exercise of what the principal and agent expressly or impliedly intended the agent to do. Thus, actual authority has two components: express authority and implied authority.

Express Authority

When the principal specifically describes the agent's power to act, he is giving the agent **express authority.** This may be done in writing or orally. The test for determining the existence of express authority is *the specific language the principal uses in granting the authority to act.*

Implied Authority

An agent also possesses **implied authority** to do whatever is reasonably required to carry out the objectives of the agency. Implied authority often is necessary because the principal seldom can foresee every contingency that might arise during the course of the agency. The agent may use this implied authority to fill in the gaps created by incomplete or ambiguous instructions from the principal.

Agents often have implied authority to act in emergencies when it is not reasonable to contact the principal for precise instructions. For instance, if a vehicle owned by Ace Delivery Service breaks down while its agent, Mark, is making a delivery, Mark probably has implied authority to contract on behalf of Ace Delivery to have the vehicle towed. The test for determining if implied authority exists is *the justifiable belief of the agent.* Remember, however, implied authority is limited by the express instructions of the principal. Thus, if Ace Delivery had cautioned that under no circumstances should Mark contract for repair services, he would have no implied authority to have the vehicle repaired.

Apparent Authority

In our previous example, it was determined that Mark had no actual authority (express or implied) to have the vehicle repaired when Ace Delivery had cautioned against such action. However, despite the absence of actual authority, Mark might still have **apparent authority** to bind Ace Delivery for the repairing service. This could occur if the mechanic reasonably believed Mark possessed authority to bind Ace Delivery because he had done so in the past.

The test for determining the existence of apparent authority is *the justifiable belief of the third person dealing with the agent.* However, the source of apparent authority (as for actual authority) is the principal. It arises when the principal's actions or failure to act induce or allow the third person to believe the agent has authority. The words or actions of the agent alone cannot create any type of authority.

Apparent authority often arises from past dealings with the third person or from customs in the trade. For this reason, whenever the principal wishes to limit an agent's authority in ways that deviate from customary or past practices, she should communicate such changes to the third person. Apparent authority may exist when the agency relationship has ended, but the principal never notifies third persons of this fact.

An agent acting with apparent (but not actual) authority binds the principal to the contract with the third person. However, the exercise of apparent authority is in violation of the agent's duty to obey, since the agent possesses no actual authority. Accordingly, the principal may sue the agent for damages for breaching the agency agreement.

Remember the *Gilbert v. Sycamore Municipal Hospital* case that appeared earlier in this chapter? There, an emergency room doctor was treated as an agent of the hospital despite the fact that the doctor and the hospital never intended to create an agency relationship. The doctor was an **apparent agent.** The following case provides another example of apparent authority.

American National Fire Insurance v. Kenealy

72 F.3d 264 (2d Cir. 1995)

FACTS   After purchasing a 41-foot boat, the *Fin Chaser,* Thomas and Diane Kenealy asked the Fitzpatrick Agency (Fitzpatrick) to make yacht insurance available to them. In September 1992, Fitzpatrick insured the *Fin Chaser* with American National Fire Insurance Company (American National). The policy stated there would be no coverage under the policy if the insured yacht was used or navigated outside the navigation limits specified in the policy. It established as navigation limits *"United States Atlantic coastwise and inland waters between Eastport, Maine and Cape Hatteras, North Carolina."* It further stated that there would be a *"lay-up period,"* a time when the boat was not in use, and that this period ran from December 1 to April 1. In August 1993, the Kenealys decided to take their boat to Florida and the Bahamas for the winter. They contacted Fitzpatrick and asked that the navigation limits be extended and that the lay-up provision be deleted. Fitzpatrick subsequently sent a fax

continued

to American National, requesting that the geographical limits be broadened to include Florida and the Bahamas until May 1994 (a date the Kenealys state they never knew about or wanted). After American National agreed by reply fax, Fitzpatrick sent the following letter to the Kenealys: *"This will serve to confirm that coverage has been bound to extend the navigation territory on your yacht policy through Florida and the Bahamas. The lay-up period on the policy has been deleted. You now have 12 months of wet navigation."* A few days later American National promulgated a change endorsement that extended the navigation limits and deleted the lay-up period, but made the changes operable from September 10, 1993, until May 1994. The Kenealys never received this document. On June 7, 1994, the *Fin Chaser* sank in Bahamian waters. American National denied liability because the boat was outside the policy's navigation limits when it sank. American National argued that the Kenealys could not rely on Fitzpatrick's letter because the original policy stated that there could be no changes in the policy except those expressly agreed to and endorsed by *"us."*

ISSUE   Did Fitzpatrick have apparent authority to change the policy?

DECISION   Yes. Fitzpatrick was a duly authorized agent who signed the declarations page of the original policy. A separate document sent to the Kenealys by American National stated that Fitzpatrick was the "agent or broker." Further, American National's premium bills stated that the Kenealys should *"contact the above producer [Fitzpatrick] with any questions or changes regarding your policy or premiums."* On the basis of these documents, the Kenealys could reasonably rely on Fitzpatrick's September 4, 1993 letter as an effective statement of the changes that had been made to the original policy. The clause in the original policy requiring that changes must be agreed to and endorsed by *"us"* is not an ironclad prohibition against agency representation. It does *not* say, for example, that changes made by an agent are not "agreed to and endorsed" by the company. The policy is totally silent on that question. American National had ample opportunity to inform its insureds of limits it wished to place on the authority of its agents. American National should have the burden of monitoring the apparent authority of its agents. This finding recognizes that using agents is often to the insurer's advantage. It, in effect, prohibits insurers from taking the benefits of agency representation while still strategically withholding information as to what authority the agent actually has, and whether the company is bound if an accident occurs.

http://www.tourolaw.edu/2ndcircuit

Ratification

When an agent exceeds her authority (both actual and apparent), the principal is not liable for any resulting contract with a third person. Similarly, one is not liable for the acts of someone who is not an agent. However, a person may become liable for these unauthorized actions through **ratification.**

By ratifying the unauthorized actions, an individual releases the agent from liability to both the principal and the third person for having exceeded her authority. The effect of ratification is to treat the act as if it had been actually authorized in the first place. As a result, the principal gains all the benefits of the contract, but also assumes all of its obligations.

In the clearest cases, the principal merely states that he is ratifying what would otherwise be an unauthorized action. However, such an expression is not necessary. Courts often infer ratification from the fact that a principal has accepted the benefits of an unauthorized agreement. And failure to repudiate an unauthorized action after it has been brought to the principal's attention can also constitute ratification.

The Agent's Contractual Liability

When an agent remains within the scope of his authority while contracting on behalf of the principal, generally only the principal and the third person are bound to the agreement. (Remember that an agent acting with only apparent authority would then be liable to the principal for exceeding his actual authority.) However, there are several special circumstances where the agent himself may become personally liable on the contract with a third person. The agent assumes such liability in the following situations:

1. unauthorized actions,
2. nonexistent or incompetent principal,
3. agreements to assume liability,
4. undisclosed agency, and
5. partially disclosed agency.

http://www.law.cornell.edu/topics/professional_responsibility.html links to sites about the professional responsibility of members of the legal profession.

Unauthorized Actions

Generally, when David represents that he is making a contract on behalf of Jill, he expressly or impliedly promises that he is authorized to do so. When such authority does not exist, David breaches an express or implied **warranty of authority**. For such breaches David is personally liable on the contract if Jill refuses to ratify. This liability exists in cases where David had no authority at all as well as when he exceeds the authority Jill has granted him. Of course, if the third person was aware of the fact that David had no authority when he made the contract, David would not be liable.

Nonexistent or Incompetent Principal

David also breaches the implied warranty if he represents a principal that has no legal existence. For instance, if David contracts on behalf of a corporation that has not yet been formed, he is personally liable on the contract. The same is true if he signs an agreement on behalf of a club that has no formal existence as a partnership or corporation. Finally, if David's principal lacks the capacity to contract (e.g., the principal is a minor or is otherwise adjudged legally incompetent), David is personally liable on the agreement. However, once again, if the third person is aware of the principal's lack of capacity, David can avoid personal liability.

Agreements to Assume Liability

Sometimes an agent intentionally becomes a party to the contract along with the principal. For instance, Daphne and Eric may work together in a joint venture, and

Eric may authorize her to purchase supplies for the venture. Daphne might sign a purchase agreement on behalf of both Eric and herself. Each would be jointly liable on this contract.

In other cases, the agent may intentionally sign a contract guaranteeing the principal's performance. Suppose that Jessica forms a corporation in which she is the sole shareholder. When loaning money to the corporation, the bank is likely to require that Jessica sign a special agreement promising that she will pay if her corporation is unable to do so.

Fully Disclosed and Undisclosed Agencies

When the third person is aware that the agent is representing another, and the third person also knows the identity of the principal, the agency is **fully disclosed.** By fully disclosing the agency, the agent generally may avoid personal liability on the contract with the third person. (Of course, the agent is liable if the principal is nonexistent, the principal lacks capacity, or the agent agrees to assume liability.)

When the agency is **undisclosed,** the third person not only does not know the identity of the principal, she doesn't even realize the agent is representing another. This might occur because the principal does not want its identity to be known. For instance, General Motors may wish to buy up several parcels of land. However, it fears that landowners will hold out for a higher price if they realize a major corporation intends to build a new facility. Accordingly, it will instruct its purchasing agents to act as if they are buying the land for themselves.

In an undisclosed agency, the agent is liable on any agreements with third persons. Of course, the agent may then seek indemnification from the principal. Because the contract was made for its benefit, the principal may enforce it. Likewise, if the third person learns the identity of the principal, she may recover from the principal instead of the agent.

You'll See Seafoods v. Gravois

520 So.2d 461 (Ct. App. La. 1988)

FACTS   James Gravois purchased The Captain's Raft restaurant and then sold it to Computer Tax Service, Inc., a corporation owned by him and his wife. Gravois never informed the managers, employees, or suppliers of The Captain's Raft that the restaurant was owned by the corporation. You'll See Seafoods supplied fresh seafood to the restaurant. You'll See's president, William Hayward, likewise thought that Gravois owned the restaurant as he was never informed otherwise and checks for seafood were signed by Gravois with no indication of a corporate capacity. The checks themselves as well as the menus were printed with the name "The Captain's Raft" with no indication that it was a corporate entity. You'll See sued Gravois to collect $24,161 owed for seafood delivered to the restaurant. Gravois denied liability, claiming that he was merely an agent and that Computer Tax Service, which by this time was bankrupt, was liable for the debt. You'll See argued that Gravois was personally liable as an agent for an undisclosed principal.

ISSUE Was Gravois liable as an agent for an undisclosed principal?

DECISION Yes. An agent is liable to those with whom he contracts on behalf of his principal when he fails to disclose the identity of his principal. Further, the agent has the burden of proving he disclosed his capacity and the identity of his principal if he wishes to avoid personal liability. Express notice of the agent's status and the principal's identity is not required if the facts and circumstances indicate a third party should have known or was put on notice of the principal-agent relationship. However, that was not the case here as the evidence clearly indicates that You'll See was unaware of the agency relationship that existed between Gravois and the corporation.

Ethical Issue

When the agent acts as an undisclosed agent, the third person does not realize she is contracting with the principal. Suppose the agent knows the third person would not want to contract with the principal. Is it unethical to serve as an undisclosed agent under such circumstances?

Partially Disclosed Agency

Sometimes when an agent signs a contract or check, she indicates her status as an agent but fails to identify her principal. This is known as a **partially disclosed** agency because the third person knows he is dealing with an agent but is unaware of the identity of the principal. Basically, partially disclosed agencies are treated like agencies that are undisclosed. The agent is liable on the contract but may seek indemnification from the principal.

Figure 12–4 illustrates the contractual liability of the agent and the principal in a fully disclosed, partially disclosed, or undisclosed agency.

Figure 12–4: Disclosing the Agency Relationship

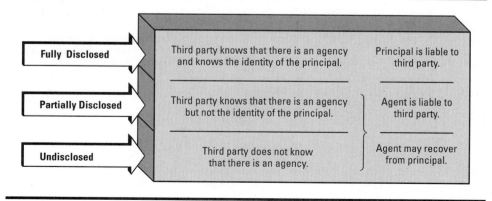

Fully Disclosed	Third party knows that there is an agency and knows the identity of the principal.	Principal is liable to third party.
Partially Disclosed	Third party knows that there is an agency but not the identity of the principal.	Agent is liable to third party.
Undisclosed	Third party does not know that there is an agency.	Agent may recover from principal.

Liability for Torts and Crimes

Remember the case that opened this chapter where the church employee sexually assaulted the little girl? The resulting lawsuit against the church raised the issue of when a principal is liable for the torts and crimes committed by its agents. Unfortunately, it is not always clear where and when such liability attaches. However, there are some agency rules that provide general guidance. (See Figure 12–5.)

Respondeat Superior

Principals often are liable for the torts of their agents under the doctrine of **respondeat superior,** which means "let the master answer." This theory of liability generally applies to situations where the agent is an employee, although it may sometimes occur with independent contractors. Respondeat superior makes the principal liable without regard to whether the employer was actually at fault. As long as the agent was acting within the **scope of employment** when the tort occurred, the principal is liable. Several factors are considered in deciding if the tort occurred within the scope of employment:

1. Was the act committed within the *time* and *space* limits of the employment? If it occurs after work hours and away from the workplace, respondeat superior is less likely to be found.
2. Did the employee intend to benefit the employer when committing the tort? If the agent is serving his own personal agenda without any motivation toward benefiting the principal, respondeat superior is unlikely.
3. Is the action leading to the tort incidental to, or of the same general nature as, responsibilities the agent is authorized to perform? If not, respondeat superior is not likely to be found.

Figure 12–5:   Principal's Tort/Crime Liability

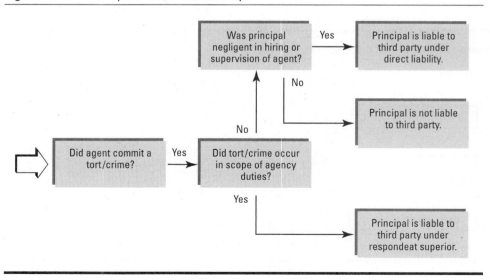

Respondeat superior liability is much more likely to be found when the agent commits negligence rather than an intentional tort. This is because intentional torts seldom fall within an agent's scope of employment.

Lisa M. v. Henry Mayo Newhall Memorial Hospital

907 P.2D 358 (Sup. Ct. Cal. 1995)

FACTS Lisa M. visited the hospital for an ultrasound examination. After conducting the ordered examination, the technician left the ultrasound room for about 10 minutes to develop the photographic results. On his return, he asked Lisa if she wanted to know the sex of the baby, and she said she did. He told her, falsely, that he would need to scan "much further down," and that it would be uncomfortable. With her cooperation, the technician inserted the ultrasound-generating wand in her vagina. After a while he put down the wand and fondled her with his fingers. While fondling her, the technician explained that he needed to excite her to get a good view of the baby. After discussing the examination with her regular obstetrician, Lisa discovered that the technician's actions were improper. She sued the technician and the hospital.

ISSUE Is the hospital vicariously liable under the theory of respondeat superior?

DECISION No. An employer is vicariously liable for the torts of its employees committed within the scope of their employment. The employee's willful, malicious, and criminal torts may fall within the scope of employment for purposes of respondeat superior even though the employee was not actually authorized to commit the intentional tort. California no longer follows the traditional rule that an employee's actions are within the scope of employment only if motivated, in whole or part, by a desire to serve the employer's interests. It is sufficient if the injury resulted from a dispute *"arising out of the employment."* Respondeat superior liability should apply only to the types of injuries that are as a practical matter sure to occur in the conduct of the employer's enterprise. Here, the technician simply took advantage of solitude with a naive patient to commit an assault for reasons unrelated to his work. His decision to engage in conscious exploitation of the patient did not arise out of the performance of the examination, although the circumstances of the examination made it possible.

Direct Liability

Again consider the case that opened the chapter. The church argued that it was not liable for its employee's intentional tort (sexually assaulting the child) because the action was outside of his scope of employment. The church was correct in the sense that it would not be liable under respondeat superior. However, it still was found liable under a theory of **direct liability.**

Under direct liability, the principal basically is liable because of its own tort. In this case, a thorough background check would have revealed that the employee had recently been convicted of aggravated sexual assault on another young girl. One condition of his probation was that he not be involved with children. Thus, the church committed an independent tort of *negligent hiring and supervision* by placing an unfit person in an employment situation involving unreasonable risk of harm to others. Consider what must be shown in the *Lisa M.* case for the patient to find the hospital directly liable for the actions of the ultrasound technician who molested her.

Liability of the Agent

Both Ladison, in the case that opened this chapter, and the ultrasound technician in the previous case are liable for their tortious acts. They would not be relieved of personal liability even if they had been acting within the scope of their employment. Agents are liable for their own behavior even when they are acting at the direction of their principal. An agent has no duty to comply with orders that are wrongful because he has a duty to society not to commit torts.

Of course, a third person who is injured through the tortious conduct of an agent can get only one recovery. Thus, the injured person is more likely to sue the principal since there is a greater likelihood that the principal will have liability insurance.

Criminal Liability

When a principal instructs her agent to commit a crime, the agent is under no legal obligation to do so. In fact, an agent who commits a criminal act under instruction from her principal is guilty of that crime. Originally, it was extremely difficult to convict a principal for the crimes committed by her agent. This was because the commission of a crime normally fell outside of the scope of employment unless the agent received specific orders to violate the law. Today, however, revised criminal codes have made it much easier to impose criminal liability on principals. As with the tort cases, the courts look to see if the agent's criminal behavior occurred within the scope of employment. Consider the following case.

State v. Smokey's Steakhouse, Inc.

478 N.W.2D 361 (Sup. Ct. N.D. 1991)

FACTS   During an inspection of Smokey's Steakhouse, a restaurant and bar, police officers arrested two 20-year-old women for being in the bar while underage. Neither woman had been asked for proof of age by any Smokey's employee, and both had been served alcoholic beverages. Smokey's Steakhouse was charged with commission of a criminal act for allowing a person under the age of 21 to remain on premises where alcoholic beverages were being sold. Smokey's contended that, as a corporate defendant, it could not be liable for the crime because its bartender was acting outside of the scope of her employment in serving the women. Specifically, it asserted that one of the women was the bartender's underage sister and that the bartender intentionally violated Smokey's company policy against serving underage patrons.

ISSUE   Is Smokey's criminally liable in spite of its employee's violation of company policy?

DECISION   Yes. A corporation can be convicted of a crime when the offense is committed by an employee acting within the scope of her employment. An employee is acting within the scope of her employment for criminal law purposes when: (1) she has authority to do the particular corporate business that was conducted illegally; and (2) she was acting, at least in part, in furtherance of the corporation's business interests. However, a corporation is not insulated from criminal liability merely because it published instructions and policies which are violated by its employee. The corporation must place the acts outside the scope of an employee's employment by adequately enforcing its rules. There is no evidence that Smokey's ever attempted to enforce its policy that employees not serve underage patrons. Accordingly, the bartender was acting within the scope of employment when she served the two underage women and allowed them to remain on the premises.

Terminating the Agency

Three important issues arise when the principal decides to terminate the agency relationship. First, does he have the power to terminate? Second, will he be required to pay damages to the agent for wrongful termination? Third, what should the principal do to end any apparent authority the former agent might still possess after termination of the agency?

Contractual Limits on Termination

Prudent persons discuss the method and manner of termination in an agency agreement. This contract may establish a fixed period of time for the agency to continue (e.g., one year). Or their agreement may require that either party give advance notice (e.g., 90 days) before ending the relationship. When no such time is specified, most courts treat the agency as automatically ending when the result for which the agency was created has been accomplished. If either party terminates the relationship in violation of an agency agreement, she is liable for breach of contract. Of course, both parties may mutually agree to modify their agency agreement and change the termination date.

Agency at Will

Notwithstanding their agency agreement, either party generally may terminate the agency at any time, since the relationship is based on mutual consent. This gives each party the *power to terminate* even if there is no contractual right to do so. This doctrine, known as **agency at will,** stems from the judicial reluctance to force people to continue personal relationships against their will. Of course, whenever one party exercises the power to terminate in violation of the *right to terminate,* the nonbreaching party may recover monetary damages in a breach of contract suit.

There are two important exceptions to the rule that one possesses the power to terminate the agency at any time. They are: agency coupled with an interest and public policy restrictions.

Agency Coupled with an Interest

An **agency coupled with an interest** arises when the agency relationship is created as a means of security for the agent. It is irrevocable without the consent of the agent. For example, suppose Michael borrows $2,000 from First National Bank. As a term of the loan, Michael gives the bank authority as his agent to repossess and sell his car if he fails to pay back the loan. Michael cannot revoke the bank's power to act as the agent at a repossession sale unless the loan is paid in full. Even his death does not terminate the agency as long as the debt remains unpaid.

Public Policy Restrictions

There are certain **public policy** exceptions that limit the parties' power to terminate the agency. For instance, termination based on race, color, sex, religion, national origin, and age generally are prohibited by state and federal legislation. Statutes also may prevent termination of an agent for engaging in labor union activities or reporting unsafe working conditions.

Industrial Representatives v. CP Clare Corporation

74 F.3D 128 (7TH CIR. 1996)

FACTS   CP Clare, a manufacturer of electrical components, engaged Industrial Representatives, Inc. (IRI) in April 1991 to solicit orders for its products. By Fall 1994, CP Clare's sales in IRI's territory exceeded $6 million annually, a tenfold increase since IRI's engagement. CP Clare decided to take promotion in-house and sent IRI a letter terminating the agency at the end of October 1994. CP Clare gave IRI 42 days notice (their agency agreement required only 30). The contract contained a further obligation: CP Clare had to pay IRI a commission for all products ordered before the termination date that were delivered in the next 90 days. CP Clare kept this promise. However, IRI believed it has not been paid enough for the work it did in boosting CP Clare's sales. IRI argued that the termination violated public policy because CP Clare was trying to take "opportunistic advantage" of the goodwill IRI's services created for CP Clare's products. In short, IRI felt that it had made a substantial investment in the product sales and that the anticipated future sales were now like an annuity that CP Clare wrongfully decided to capture.

ISSUE   Has CP Clare unlawfully terminated the agency relationship?

DECISION   No. No one, least of all IRI, could have thought that a contract permitting termination on 30 days' notice, with payment of commissions for deliveries within 90 days thereafter, entitled the agent to the entire future value of the goodwill built up by its work. The terms on which the parties would part ways were handled expressly in this contract, and IRI got what it bargained for. Contracts allocate risks and opportunities. If things turn out well, the party to whom the contract allocates the upper trail of outcomes is entitled to reap the benefits. This agreement provides explicitly for what has come to pass: termination with substantial outstanding business. IRI knew or should have recognized that the 90-day period created a risk; and it could have responded by demanding a higher commission rate to compensate.

http://www.kentlaw.edu/7circuit/

Termination by Operation of Law

The law terminates an agency if certain events occur. Among these are the death or insanity of either party and the bankruptcy of either party if it affects the agency. Termination also occurs if the objective of the agency becomes impossible or illegal, or if the subject matter of the agency is lost or destroyed. For example, a real estate broker may be hired as a rental agent for a house. If the house burns down, the agency ends.

Notice to Third Persons

Remember the earlier discussion of apparent authority? There it was noted that former agents may still possess apparent authority to bind the principal after termination of the agency relationship. For this reason, it is important that principals properly notify the world that former agents no longer possess the authority to bind them to contracts. **Actual notice** must be given to those third persons who have dealt with the agent in the past. This generally takes the form of a written notification because this makes it easier to prove that notice was given. **Constructive notice** is sufficient for persons who knew of the agency but never formally dealt with it. It might be given by posting a notice in a newspaper of general circulation in the area where the former agent worked. (See Figure 12–6.)

Figure 12–6:   Providing Notification of Termination of Agent's Authority

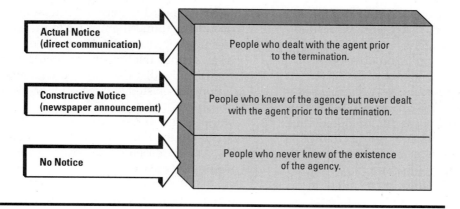

QUESTIONS AND PROBLEM CASES

1. When is information given to the agent by a third person treated as if it was given to the principal?

2. When might an agent legally engage in a conflict of interest with her principal?

3. Distinguish between the tests for implied and apparent authority. How does the liability of the agent exercising implied authority differ from the liability of the agent exercising apparent authority?

4. Why is the principal generally liable for the torts of an employee but not for the torts of an independent contractor?

5. Skyline Builders hired Graffice as manager for an apartment complex Skyline managed for K.M.S. This gave Graffice general supervision over 198 units and a passkey admitting him to all of the units. Prior to hiring Graffice, Skyline ran a credit check on him; however, it never checked his California references despite the fact that his application showed him as having worked in Minnesota for only the previous three months. In reality, Graffice had been imprisoned twice—once for receiving stolen property and once for armed robbery and burglary. His application had described these crimes as traffic tickets. Further, his two California job references turned out to be his mother and his sister. After he was hired by Skyline, Graffice used the passkey to enter the apartment of a female tenant whom he then raped at knifepoint. She sued Skyline for negligently hiring Graffice. Is Skyline directly liable for the intentional tort committed by Graffice? Explain.

6. Although Ingersoll indicated his intent to leave his employment with RTV by May, RTV persuaded him to stay until the end of August. Ingersoll launched a competing business, known as TransMedia, in July. In early August, while he was still with RTV, Ingersoll submitted a bid for a Department of Defense contract on behalf of TransMedia, despite the fact that the Department of Defense was one of RTV's major clients. After TransMedia won the contract, RTV learned that the company was operated by Ingersoll. RTV sued Ingersoll for breach of his fiduciary duties. Ingersoll argued that if RTV had not persuaded him to stay beyond his announced resignation date, this conflict never would have arisen. Did Ingersoll breach his duty of loyalty to RTV?

7. Consumers Insurance Service was Lang's insurance agent on a 1986 Toyota that was insured with Interstate Bankers Mutual Casualty Company. Lang later purchased a 1988 Toyota from Nugent Toyota, but before he was allowed to remove it from the dealership, the dealer's credit manager called Consumers to verify that the new car would be insured. A Consumers' employee indicated that the 1988 Toyota was insured by Interstate. Based on these assurances, Lang took delivery of the new car, started driving it, and paid the insurance premiums when they became due. Several months later Lang wrecked the 1988 Toyota and filed an insurance claim. Interstate denied coverage on the grounds that it had never agreed to insure the car. Lang sued Interstate, alleging that the agency relationship between Interstate and Consumers bound the insurer to the assurances made by its agent. Interstate denied that an agency relationship existed. Should Lang's suit be dismissed because no agency relationship existed between Interstate and Consumers?

8. Arthur Jensen, Inc., was a corporation engaged in the housing construction business. Arthur Jensen owned over half of the corporation's stock and served as its president. Alaska Valuation Service (AVS) conducted housing appraisals for Jensen on numerous occasions over the years. When AVS took the orders for appraisals, it was not aware that it was dealing with a corporation. It believed that it was dealing directly with Jensen. Jensen never specifically informed AVS of his status as an agent for Arthur Jensen, Inc. AVS attempted to hold Jensen personally liable for the appraisal services. Is Jensen personally liable as an agent for an undisclosed principal?

9. VIP Tours, Inc., arranged tours of central Florida attractions. Cynthia Hoogland conducted 29 such tours for VIP between July 1980 and March 1981. Both Hoogland and VIP considered Hoogland to be an independent contractor. She worked for VIP only when it needed her services, and she could reject particular assignments. She was free to work for other tour services and she did so. Once Hoogland accepted a job from VIP, she was told where to report and was given instructions about the job. She also had to use a VIP-furnished vehicle and wear a uniform with the VIP logo when conducting tours. Aside from ensuring that she departed on time, however, VIP did not tell her how long to stay or what kind of tour to conduct at each tourist location. Lastly, Hoogland was paid on a per-tour basis. When Hoogland later filed a claim for unemployment compensation benefits, the Florida Division of Labor denied her claim on the basis that she was an independent contractor rather than an employee. Is Hoogland an employee?

10. For approximately eight years, Van Matre was employed as an insurance agent for Prudential Insurance Company. During his employment, Van Matre sold several types of life insurance policies to various customers throughout the central Illinois area. He also serviced those policyholders as well as others assigned to him by Prudential. In the course of his employment, Van Matre was given access to information on each of the policyholders with whom he dealt. After terminating his employment with Prudential, Van Matre became an agent for Transamerica Insurance Company. He then succeeded in inducing several of his former customers to terminate their Prudential policies and to purchase instead policies issued by Transamerica. Prudential argued that Van Matre's postemployment use of information about policyholders obtained while he was employed by Prudential was a breach of his fiduciary duty to avoid using confidential information in competition with a former principal. Accordingly, it sued to enjoin his future interference with his former customers and for $100,000 in damages for the terminations he had already caused. Did Van Matre breach his fiduciary duty of loyalty?

GETTING A JOB

I n the wake of a tragic shooting spree carried out by a disgruntled postal worker, the U.S. Postal Service fired Thomas Lussier. His "erratic behavior and verbal outbursts" convinced Lussier's supervisor he was "mentally unbalanced" and capable of similar violence. However, an Oregon judge found the discharge to be unlawful because Lussier had a mental disability and was protected by antidiscrimination law.

The Wall Street Journal, April 5, 1995, p. B1.

As you read this chapter, consider the following issues:

> The catch-22 confronting employers who have growing concerns over safety on the job.
> The responsibilities employment law imposes on employers as well as the fundamental protections it reserves for employees.

Introduction ▬▬▬▬▬▬▬▬▬

As the example at the beginning of this chapter illustrates, employers today often are frustrated over the growing—and sometimes conflicting—demands placed on them by society. On the one hand, courts and legislatures are making employers more and more accountable for the actions of their employees. At the same time, employees are demanding, and often receiving, greater safeguards against intrusive and arbitrary treatment by their employers. For these reasons, it is vital that employers and employees alike understand the legal rules governing the employment relationship.

Chapter Overview

The chapter first introduces the nature of the employment relationship and the actual hiring process. After a summary of the basic protections available to labor unions, the focus shifts to the regulation of employees' wages and hours. Next is a discussion of privacy concerns and the limitations on employers' personnel policies. This is followed by a brief review of employers' responsibilities to provide for the health and safety of their workforce. The chapter closes with an analysis of the regulatory safeguards against discrimination in the workplace, and finally, an examination of the legal issues that arise when the employment relationship is terminated.

Creating the Employment Relationship ▬▬▬▬▬▬▬

Not all working situations create an employer/employee relationship. And since most workplace regulations protect only employees, special attention must be paid to the actual classification of each individual in the workforce. Accordingly, this section begins by investigating the criteria that give rise to an employment relationship. This is followed by a brief look at the legal issues that arise during the actual hiring process.

Employment Law Coverage

The first step in determining one's legal status under employment law requires a determination of whether the worker is an employee or an independent contractor. (Employees and independent contractors also are discussed in Chapter 12.) This distinction is of the utmost importance since employees are protected by a host of employment laws while independent contractors receive little statutory protection.

http://
www.law.cornell.edu/
topics/employment.
html provides information and links for this topic.

Employees

The majority of workers in this country are employees. In determining if a worker is an **employee**, and therefore protected by employment laws, the courts follow tests designed by the Internal Revenue Service. The IRS classifies a worker as a *common-law employee* when the employer retains *day-to-day control* over both the *objectives* and *methods* of the worker's activities.

The term "employee" also includes workers designated by the IRS as *statutory employees*. This category covers individuals like delivery persons and home workers who otherwise would not qualify as employees under the day-to-day control test. However, because of special legislation including them within the coverage of various employment laws, they are classified as employees. (See Figure 13–1.)

Independent Contractors

A worker who does not qualify as a statutory employee and is not under the day-to-day control of the employer usually is an **independent contractor.** With independent contractors, the employer controls the *objectives* of the work but defers to the worker's discretion over how that outcome is reached. Unlike most employees,

---

Figure 13–1:   Employment Agreement

This Employment Agreement (this "Agreement") is made effective as of October 27, 1997, by and between _____, ("_____"), of _____, _____, _____ and _____, ("_____"), of _____, _____, _____.

1. EMPLOYMENT. _____ shall employ _____ as a _____.

_____ accepts and agrees to such employment, subject to the general supervision, advice and direction of _____ and _____'s supervisory personnel. _____ agrees to perform faithfully, industriously and to the best of _____'s ability, experience, and talents, the services described on the attached Exhibit A, which is made part of this Agreement by reference. _____ shall also perform (i) such other duties as are customarily performed by an employee in a similar position, and (ii) such other and unrelated services and duties as may be assigned to _____ from time to time by _____.

2. COMPENSATION. As compensation for the services provided by _____ under this Agreement, _____ will pay _____ an annual salary of $_____ payable in monthly installments payable on the _____ day of each month.

3. ENTIRE AGREEMENT. This Agreement contains the entire agreement of the parties and there are no other promises or conditions in any other agreement whether oral or written. This Agreement supersedes any prior written or oral agreements between the parties. Amendments to this Agreement must be made in writing and signed by both parties.

Employer: _____

By: _____

_____

Date: _____

Employee: _____

_____

Date: _____

Source: Quicken Business Law Partner® 3.0 CD-ROM. Copyright © 1997 Parson's Technology, Inc. All rights reserved.

independent contractors generally offer their services to a variety of employers. Most employment laws do not govern the relationship between the employer and an independent contractor.

Strategies for Avoiding Employment Law Coverage

Many businesses pursue strategies to increase profits by avoiding the obligations owed to employees under the employment laws. Some contract with services that provide temporary workers for various functions. These workers are the employees of the services. Other companies label workers as independent contractors or partners in an attempt to circumvent the employment laws. However, as the following case indicates, courts look past these labels and classify workers according to the actual control exercised by the employer.

Simpson v. Ernst & Young

100 F.3D 436 (6TH CIR. 1996)

FACTS In 1989, the accounting firm of Arthur Young & Co. merged with Ernst & Whinney to form a mega-firm known as Ernst & Young. Despite premerger promises that there would be no staff reductions, Ernst & Young secretly planned to reduce its staff by 5 percent. Immediately after the merger, the company implemented this plan by systematically discharging older partners. By eliminating older partners, the accounting firm hoped to avoid substantial retirement liabilities. One discharged partner, Peyton Larue Simpson, sued Ernst & Young for age discrimination in violation of the *Age Discrimination in Employment Act* (ADEA). Ernst & Young defended on the ground that the ADEA did not apply because Simpson was a "partner" rather than an "employee."

ISSUE Is Simpson an employee of the accounting firm?

DECISION Yes. Whether Simpson is an "employee" within the meaning of the ADEA turns on his actual role in the management, control, and ownership of Ernst & Young. In approaching this subject it is significant to observe that bona fide independent contractors and partners are employers, not employees; and as employers, neither come within the entitlement protection of the ADEA. In resolving this dispute, we look to the particular circumstances of the case at hand and, in so doing, focus not on any label but on the actual role played by Simpson in the operation of the accounting firm. Ernst & Young's business, assets, and affairs were directed exclusively by a 10 to 14 member Management Committee and its chairman. That committee exercised exclusive control over the admission and discharge of all personnel, including Simpson. It unilaterally determined the compensation of all personnel, which authority was executed in total secrecy. Simpson and those similarly situated had no vote for the chairman or the members of the Management Committee. The characterization of "partner" was a title that carried no legal significance. Simpson and his similarly situated colleagues were relegated to the position of an employee subject to the virtually absolute, unilateral control of the Management Committee.

http://www.law.emory.edu/6circuit/

The Hiring Process

When making hiring decisions, employers should thoroughly investigate the qualifications of each prospective employee. Failure to do so may result in a tremendous waste of time, energy, and money. However, employers also must be careful that their background checks are not overly intrusive. Otherwise, they may violate state and federal laws safeguarding the applicants' privacy rights.

Advertising Job Openings

Most employers are prohibited from discriminating on the basis of race, religion, color, gender, national origin, physical disability, and age by state and federal law. Some states and localities also outlaw discrimination based on marital status and sexual orientation. (Antidiscrimination rules are more thoroughly discussed later in this chapter.) When advertising job openings, employers must be careful to comply with these laws. Unwitting violations are less likely to occur if employment opportunities are advertised in a wide range of places and all job qualifications are actually necessary to successful job performance.

Checking Job References

Failure to conduct a reasonable background check may expose employers to legal liability if their employees later harm customers or clients. Under the agency concept of direct liability (discussed in Chapter 19), employers can be liable for the crimes and intentional torts of their employees if a reasonable investigation would have revealed that the applicant posed a risk to others. The victims may sue the employer under the tort of **negligent hiring.**

Tort liability is reduced when the employer has documented that it conducted a reasonable background check of each job applicant. The more sensitive the job (working with children, having passkeys to apartments, etc.), the more thorough the investigation should be. It is reasonable to personally contact each previous employer as well as to check for felony convictions. And driving records should be checked if the job calls for the employee to drive a vehicle. Credit checks also may be reasonable if the employee is to have access to money or other valuables. Note, however, that the *Fair Credit Reporting Act* (discussed in Chapter 10) requires that job applicants be told if they are denied employment based on information appearing in a credit report.

Consent Forms

Care must be taken to ensure that the background check is not unnecessarily intrusive. For instance, a credit check probably is not relevant for an applicant for a house-painting position. Even inquiries about arrest records may be risky since many arrests do not lead to convictions. While felony convictions generally may be investigated, some states restrict questions about juvenile records or misdemeanor convictions more than five years old. More and more employers have prospective employees sign **consent forms** permitting a thorough background check as part of their application process. These documents limit the employer's potential liability and encourage job references to be more forthright with their recommendations. (The legal problems associated with employee references are discussed later in this chapter.)

Preemployment Testing

To ensure that applicants are qualified for the job, employers may conduct various types of preemployment testing. However, while such tests may be useful in measuring specific job skills (typing, computer programming, etc.), they may be illegal if they probe areas unrelated to the job. Thus, aptitude and personality tests may be either discriminatory or overly invasive.

Most employers are prevented from conducting applicant screening with mechanical lie detector tests by the *Employee Polygraph Protection Act*. It allows preemployment polygraph testing for only the most sensitive jobs (armed guards, workers in the pharmaceutical industry, etc.). It further restricts the right of employers to test current employees to situations where the employee is reasonably suspected of conducting some serious workplace wrong (theft, industrial espionage).

Preemployment medical exams as well as questions about an applicant's medical condition or history may violate the *Americans with Disabilities Act* (ADA). (The ADA is discussed later in this chapter.) However, it generally is permissible to make a job offer conditional upon the applicant passing a medical examination. The ADA specifically precludes an employer from conducting drug tests on job applicants until such a conditional offer has been made.

Labor Unions ▰▰▰▰▰▰▰▰

This country's labor movement came about because of perceived abuses of employees by their employers. By the mid-1950s, union membership rose to a high of almost 40 percent of the workforce. However, that number is projected to fall below 10 percent by the year 2001, perhaps due to the growing protection available to workers by modern employment laws. Although employees generally unionize because of dissatisfaction with their employer's workplace policies, unions have expanded their roles beyond merely negotiating employment contracts. They have assumed an active lobbying posture in both local and national politics and often provide extensive benefit programs in areas like insurance, healthcare, and pensions.

http:// *www.law.cornell.edu/ topics/labor.html* provides links to many labor law sites.

The Labor Laws

Early unionization attempts in this country met with harsh opposition. Union organizers often were prosecuted under federal laws prohibiting conspiracies that restrained trade. Further, employers regularly had new job applicants sign **yellow-dog contracts,** which required that they promise not to join unions. Finally, courts generally enjoined strikes because they might become violent. The tide began to turn in 1932 with passage of the *Norris-LaGuardia Act,* which prohibited the courts from enjoining lawful strikes and outlawed yellow-dog contracts.

The National Labor Relations Act

In 1935, the *National Labor Relations Act* (NLRA) recognized the right to organize and bargain collectively. Actions by employers that interfered with these rights were declared to be unfair labor practices. The NLRA also established the *National Labor Relations Board* (NLRB) to administer the act by conducting union elections and hearing charges of unfair labor practices. Certain groups are excluded from the NLRA's protections for union activities. These include farm workers, government workers, managers and supervisors, certain professionals (accountants), and the families of employers.

NLRB v. Town & Country Electric
116 S.Ct. 450 (U.S. Sup. Ct. 1995)

FACTS   Town & Country Electric, a nonunion electrical contractor, wanted to hire several licensed electricians for construction work. Town & Country advertised for job applicants, but refused to interview 10 union applicants who responded to the advertisement. The International Brotherhood of Electrical Workers filed a complaint with the NLRB claiming Town & Country committed an unfair labor practice because it refused to interview the applicants due to their union membership. Town & Country argued that the 10 job applicants were not employees protected by the NLRA because they were paid by the union to try to organize the company after they secured the advertised jobs.

ISSUE   Were the job applicants protected from unfair labor practices by the NLRA?

DECISION   Yes. It did not matter that the 10 union members were simply applicants who were never hired. The NLRA defines the term "employees" who are protected against discrimination based on union membership to include job applicants. The act also grants employees the rights to self-organization, to form, join, or assist labor organizations, to bargain collectively, and to engage in other concerted activities for the purpose of collective bargaining or other mutual aid or protection. The list of employees covered by the NLRA's protections should be read broadly to include workers who are also paid union organizers.

http://www.law.vill.edu/Fed-Ct/sct.html
http://supct.law.cornell.edu/supct/

The Labor-Management Relations Act

http://
*www.law.cornell.edu/
uscode/29/ch7.html*
is the site of the text
of the LMRA.

Twelve years after passage of the NLRA, Congress became concerned over the growing power exerted by unions in the workplace. In response, it enacted the *Labor-Management Relations Act* (LMRA) to protect both employees and employers from labor union abuses. The LMRA (also known as the *Taft-Hartley Act*) declares certain behavior by unions to be **unfair labor practices.** These include attempts to coerce employees to join a union, pressuring employers to discriminate against employees who are not union members, refusing to bargain in good faith with an employer, and charging excessive initiation fees.

The Labor-Management Reporting and Disclosure Act

In a further attempt to rein in union power, Congress enacted the *Labor-Management Reporting and Disclosure Act* in 1959. This statute creates a code of conduct to be followed by unions and employers to ensure honesty and fair dealing.

It was specifically designed to counter allegations of corruption and undemocratic procedures within the labor unions. The act requires unions to abide by constitutions and bylaws, establishes a bill of rights for employees, and mandates that unions disclose their financial affairs to the Secretary of Labor.

Right-to-Work Laws

The NLRA permits the states to enact laws that prohibit making membership or nonmembership in a union a condition of employment. Nearly half of the states have passed these **right-to-work laws.** These laws require unions to give fair and equal representation to all workers in their bargaining union regardless of whether they have joined the union or paid membership dues.

Union Elections

Employees who choose to unionize must be part of a **bargaining unit.** This is a group of employees who share similar job classifications and, accordingly, share similar concerns about the terms of employment. If at least 30 percent of the workers in a bargaining union signify a desire to unionize, the NLRB conducts a secret election to determine if the majority of them wish to be represented by a union. (A majority can also vote a union out of existence through a *decertification election.*)

After the union is formed, the bargaining unit is governed by majority rule. The representatives of the union then negotiate a contract with the employer covering work-related issues such as wages, benefits, vacations, etc. There are three basic types of contracts between unions and employers: the open shop, the agency shop, and the closed shop.

The Open Shop

Under an **open shop** arrangement, a union represents the bargaining unit but individual workers are not required to become members or pay dues. This situation is most common in the states that have enacted right-to-work laws.

The Agency Shop

With an **agency shop,** workers are free to decide whether or not they wish to become union members. However, even if they decide against membership, they must pay union dues to cover union activities that secure benefits for the workforce. Agency shop arrangements are not permitted in the states with right-to-work laws.

The Union Shop

With a **union shop,** workers are required to join the union at the expiration of a grace period after becoming an employee. There is some controversy over the legality of union shop contracts because they stipulate that the employee may be fired for failing to join the union. However, this usually is not an issue since unions have been reluctant to insist on such discharges.

Union Dues

Union contracts typically include a **check-off clause** that requires employers to withhold money from employees' paychecks to cover union dues. In recent years, the courts have held that unions may not, over the objections of dues-paying

h t t p : / /
www.dol.gov/dol/esa/
public/regs/statutes/
olms/lmrda.htm
provides the text of
the LMRDA.

nonmembers, spend funds on activities unrelated to the bargaining unit (political lobbying). This requires the union to inform nonmembers of their right to object and demand a reduction in fees when such activities are funded. The nonmembers must also be given adequate notice of such expenditures so they may intelligently decide whether to object.

Wages, Hours, and Pensions

http://
*www.law.cornell.edu/
uscode/29/ch8.html*
provides the index
of the FLSA.

In response to the workplace abuses prevalent during the Great Depression, the state and federal governments passed comprehensive rules regulating wages, hours, and other working conditions. Regulations also govern social security benefits. Finally, Congress has enacted special legislation designed to curb careless and dishonest management of private pension funds.

The Fair Labor Standard Act

Most employers with annual sales totalling $500,000 must comply with the wage and hour conditions imposed by the *Fair Labor Standards Act* (FLSA). In general, this comprehensive statute imposes a minimum wage of $5.15 per hour and guarantees pay of time-and-a-half for time worked over 40 hours per week. (Some states require higher minimum wages.) The FLSA also prohibits most employment of children under the age of 14 and places restrictions on the hours and working conditions of minors under the age of 18. Finally, the act outlaws sex discrimination in pay. (This provision is discussed later in the chapter.)

Exempt Employees

Certain classes of employees are not covered by the wage and hour provisions. For instance, executives, administrators, professionals, and outside salespeople are not protected by the act's wages and hours provisions. And when employees regularly earn at least $30 per month in tips, the FLSA allows employers to credit half of the tips toward the hourly wage and possibly pay no more than $2.58 per hour.

Wage and Hour Violations

Some employers attempt to skirt the wage and hour requirements by falsely labeling employees with titles like "assistant manager." However, in determining if a worker is exempt, the Labor Department focuses on the actual working relationship rather than the job label. Violations of the FLSA could result in fines up to $10,000 and imprisonment, although such penalties are rare. In most cases, the employer will be required to pay the unpaid wages or overtime compensation as well as a small fine.

Reich v. Circle C. Investments

998 F.2d 324 (5th Cir. 1993)

FACTS   Circle C. Investments operated the Crazy Horse Saloon and a similar night-club, Lipstick. Both clubs featured topless dancers. The dancers received no compensation from Circle C. Their pay was derived solely from the tips they received from customers for performing on stage and performing private "table dances" and "couch dances." At the end of each night, the dancers must pay Circle C. a "tip-out," which was set at $20. They were required to pay the "tip-out" regardless of how much they made in tips. Circle C. characterized the "tip-out" as stage rental and argued that the dancers were merely "tenants." According to Circle C., the dancers were not employees, but were businesswomen renting space, stages, music, dressing rooms, and lights from Circle C. The Secretary of Labor claimed the dancers were "employees" within the meaning of the *Fair Labor Standards Act* and, as such, Circle C. willfully violated the minimum wage and overtime provisions of the act.

ISSUE   Were the dancers employees subject to the protections of the *Fair Labor Standards Act?*

DECISION   Yes. To determine employee status under the FLSA, we focus on whether the dancers, as a matter of economic reality, were economically dependent upon Circle C. To gauge the degree of a worker's dependency, we consider five factors: (1) the degree of control exercised by the employer; (2) the extent of the relative investments of the worker and the alleged employer; (3) the degree to which the worker's opportunity for profit or loss is determined by the alleged employer; (4) the skill and initiative required in performing the job; and (5) the permanency of the relationship. These factors are merely aids in determining the underlying question of dependency; no single factor is determinative. Circle C. exercises significant control over the dancers. It imposes weekly work schedules and issues fines for absences or tardiness. A dancer's investment is limited to her costumes and a padlock while Circle C., on the other hand, owns the facilities, the liquor license, and the inventory at each nightclub. While a dancer's initiative, hustle, and costume significantly contribute to the amount of her tips, Circle C. is responsible for the advertising, location, business hours, aesthetics, and inventory of beverages and food. These greatly control a dancer's opportunity for profit. Many of the dancers had no prior experience with topless dancing before coming to work for Circle C. Thus, they do not exhibit the skill or initiative of persons in business for themselves. It does appear that the dancers are free to dance at other clubs. While this impermanent relationship between Circle C. and the dancers might indicate a non-employee status, it is overridden by the previous factors. Here, the economic reality is that the dancers are not in business for themselves but are dependent upon Circle C. for employment.

http://www.law.utexas.edu/us5th/us5th.html

Social Security Retirement Benefits

Federal law requires employers to withhold each employee's share of **social security** taxes as well as pay a matching employer's share. The social security program was implemented to provide regular compensation for retired workers. The amount an individual receives is dependent upon the *work credits* she has earned. Work credits are measured as the number of quarters (January–March, April–June, etc.) the employee has worked. Elderly spouses and disabled children may also be entitled to derivative benefits.

http://
www.ssa.gov
will take you to the
Web site for the
Social Security
Administration;
select a topic under
Social Security Law.

Private Pensions

Approximately half of today's workforce is covered by pension plans provided by employers or labor unions. However, for many years employees were lulled into a false sense of security by pension promises that were never fulfilled. Many of the private pension funds were raided by unscrupulous employers. In other instances, employees changed jobs or were fired just before retirement age and lost their pensions.

To address these injustices, Congress enacted the *Employment Retirement Income Security Act* (ERISA). This statute is designed to prevent the most outrageous abuses in the management of pension and benefit plans. However, it does not require employers to provide pension funds; it merely regulates their management once they have been offered. ERISA requires that employers make clear who is covered by a pension plan and supply basic information as to what is provided.

Personnel Practices and Employee Privacy

Employers have an understandable concern about the conduct of employees within the workplace. And the employment laws require employers to maintain a growing amount of information about employees. For these reasons, today's employers are more actively and pervasively monitoring the lives of their employees. However, when surveillance pries into employees' lives more than is reasonably necessary to further legitimate business objectives, it may unlawfully conflict with employees' privacy rights.

Personnel Records

Because most employers already are obligated by law to gather information on employees' wages, hours, and workplace injuries, it makes sense to regularly maintain individualized **employee files.** The U.S. Constitution and federal law limit the type of information that governmental employers may maintain in their personnel records. Private employers, on the other hand, have few restraints on the kinds of information they may gather. However, a growing number of states have begun granting employees access to their own employee files and providing means for employees to correct erroneous information. To avoid tort liability, employers should maintain the confidentiality of employee records. This is particularly important when files contain sensitive information like medical records.

Workplace Testing

Employers may have legitimate reasons for testing their employees. For instance, various skills tests may be necessary to be certain that employees are qualified to perform their tasks. And insurers may insist that employees undergo medical examinations as a requirement for insurance coverage. Drug and alcohol tests may be desired to protect against employee abuses that might harm fellow employees or customers. Finally, polygraph tests may be called for when an employee is suspected of committing a serious wrong in the workplace.

Medical Tests

Medical and psychological tests are permissible when it is reasonable to believe an employee is a safety hazard. Thus, in the case that opened this chapter, rather than give an immediate discharge, the U.S. Postal Service probably should have required Lussier to undergo testing. Drug and alcohol testing generally is permitted when the employee poses a threat to others or is in a safety-sensitive position (i.e., bus driver, airline pilot). Absent these circumstances (safety hazard, safety-sensitive position), employers generally should avoid such tests if they wish to minimize the threat of invasion of privacy suits.

Lie Detector Tests

The *Employee Polygraph Protection Act* (discussed earlier) only allows employers to request a lie detector test as part of an ongoing investigation when there is a reasonable suspicion that the employee was involved in the incident under investigation. The employee must be given reasonable notice of the test, informed of her right to an attorney, provided with a written statement setting out the basis of the employer's reasonable suspicion, and informed that she has a right to refuse the polygraph test.

http:// *www.law.cornell.edu/ uscode/29/ch22.html* is the site of USC Title 29, Chapter 22—"Employee Polygraph Protection."

Workplace Surveillance

Most forms of workplace surveillance are permitted by the courts. This is because business premises generally invite lesser expectations of privacy. Further, courts recognize that employers possess legitimate interests in the safe and efficient operation of the workplace.

Monitoring Telephone Calls

Employers generally may monitor telephone calls made to and by employees at the workplace. This may be justified to evaluate customer service. However, federal law does not permit monitoring personal calls without the employee's consent. Thus, as soon as an employer discovers that a call is personal rather than business related, the employer must hang up. (Some states do not allow any calls to be monitored unless both parties to the conversation have consented.)

Monitoring Mail

When mail addressed to an employee is delivered to the workplace, the employer may have a right to open it when it appears to be business related. But letters stamped "personal" or "confidential" generally should not be opened unless the employer has a compelling business reason. The rules concerning electronic mail are unclear. However, files and electronic messages on workplace computers probably are not protected from employer surveillance.

Video Surveillance

Under most circumstances, video surveillance of employees is permissible when it occurs in open workplace areas. And it may also occur in private offices and cubicles, especially when they are shared by more than one employee. Of course, expanding such surveillance into restrooms and locker rooms raises greater privacy concerns. However, even then the intrusion may be permissible in sensitive industries where security concerns are great. Employers can lessen the likelihood of legal liability for invasion of privacy by notifying employees of any video surveillance in advance.

Performance Reviews

Most employers periodically evaluate the performance of their employees. **Performance reviews** serve the important business purpose of documenting an employer's hiring, promotion, discipline, and firing practices. These evaluations also benefit employees by informing them of what management expects, how they measure up, and what needs to be done to gain wage increases or promotions.

For these reasons, courts give employers great latitude when evaluating employee performance. While employees may believe a review is false or misleading, they will have difficulty recovering tort damages as long as the employer exercised good faith when conducting the review.

Jensen v. Hewlett-Packard

18 CAL.RPTR.2D 83 (CAL. APP. 4TH DIST. 1993)

FACTS   After being hired by Hewlett-Packard, Sean Jensen regularly received favorable performance evaluations. However, when Hewlett-Packard offered him management of a newly created area project, he declined the position. His coworker, Hank Phelps, accepted the job and became Jensen's boss. One year later, Phelps gave Jensen a written evaluation stating that while his work was adequate in certain respects, he had been the subject of third-party complaints, was not carrying his weight, had a negative attitude in dealing with others, evidenced a lack of direction in his project activities, and was unwilling to take responsibility for the projects he oversaw. Jensen took exception to every comment in the evaluation in a letter distributed to other Hewlett-Packard managers. He then demanded Hewlett-Packard initiate an internal investigation and insisted the performance review be removed from his personnel file. After an investigation, Hewlett-Packard concluded Phelps's concerns were well founded and refused to remove the evaluation from Jensen's personnel file. Jensen filed suit for libel, claiming Phelps could not have had an honest and good-faith belief in the truth of the statements because they were without factual basis. He argued that Phelps, anticipating a poor review himself, was simply trying to cover up his own incompetence.

ISSUE   Should Jensen prevail in his libel suit?

DECISION   No. Libel is a false and unprivileged public statement of facts by writing which injures another person. As a prelude to this holding we must express our strong judicial disfavor for libel suits based on communications in employment performance reviews. Clearly, there is a legitimate reason for performance evaluations and management has an unquestioned obligation to keep them. We would therefore be loath to subject an employer to the threat of a libel suit in which a jury might decide, for instance, that the employee should have been given a rating of "average," rather than "needs improvement." Unless an employer's performance evaluation falsely accuses an employee of criminal conduct, lack of integrity, dishonesty, incompetence, or reprehensible personal characteristics or behavior, it cannot support a cause of action for libel. This is true even when the employer's perceptions about an employee's effort, attitude, performance, potential, or worth to the enterprise are objectively wrong and cannot be supported by reference to concrete, provable facts. In any event, even if Phelps's statements were made in bad faith, they could not provide a legitimate basis for a libel claim because they were statements of opinion, not false statements of fact.

Workplace Health and Safety

Modern businesses are actively concerned with workplace health and safety for a variety of reasons. Some employers tackle these issues out of humane concern for the welfare of their workforce. Others realize that health and safety measures help them retain productive workers, reduce absenteeism, and avoid legal liability. Further, today's state and federal employment laws impose special health and safety obligations on most employers. (Workers' compensation laws are discussed in Chapter 7.)

The Occupational Health and Safety Act

Congress passed the *Occupational Health and Safety Act* (OSHA) in 1970 to protect the safety of workers by requiring employers to eliminate most workplace hazards. This includes obligating companies to train their employees to safely deal with potential hazards, to follow OSHA safety regulations, to retain detailed safety records, and to notify OSHA officials when workplace injuries occur. The law applies to any business that affects interstate commerce, no matter how few workers it actually employs. The OSHA statute also allows each state to provide more comprehensive rules for businesses to follow.

http://
www.law.cornell.edu/
uscode/29/ch15.html
is the site of the OSHA. You can also see http://*www.osha. gov* for additional information.

OSHA Enforcement

OSHA officials generally may make unannounced inspections of worksites. However, if an employer objects to a visit, the inspector must obtain a search warrant before entering the premises. (Employers in relatively safe industries with less than 10 employees are exempt from unannounced inspections by federal OSHA officials.)

Most OSHA violations are detected as a result of employee complaints. The statute broadly protects this right to complain by prohibiting employers from penalizing employees who make complaints. In extremely unsafe situations, the employee has the right to refuse to work if doing so would threaten serious injury. It is an OSHA violation to penalize an employee who exercises this right.

Penalties for OSHA Violations

Penalties for OSHA violations usually depend on the seriousness of the infraction. OSHA also considers whether the employer has a history of violations and whether there has been a good-faith attempt to comply with the law. If a company retaliates against an employee who has exercised her rights under OSHA (filing a complaint or refusing to work in unsafe conditions), it may be ordered to pay damages to the employee.

While the federal OSHA rarely pursues criminal prosecutions against employers who maintain unsafe worksites, state OSHA officials are less reluctant to do so. State prosecutors have successfully brought criminal actions against both companies and their officers who have recklessly exposed employees to hazardous working conditions. The charges have ranged from reckless endangerment to murder.

Workplace Safety Teams

OSHA suggests that employers post *safety codes* to make clear their commitment to workplace safety. Some states, however, are taking this further and mandating that businesses establish **workplace safety teams.** These committees usually are composed of equal numbers of workers and managers who are to consult closely on ways to reduce workplace hazards. They also provide employees with an alternative to filing an OSHA complaint when they uncover unsafe working conditions. Some laws require that employers with poor safety records consult with state officials on how to improve their performance.

The Family and Medical Leave Act

http://
www.law.cornell.edu/
uscode/29/ch28.html
provides the index of
the FMLA.

An extremely controversial health and safety measure, the *Family and Medical Leave Act* (FMLA), was enacted in 1993. It provides that an employee who has worked for at least 12 months at a company with 50 or more workers may receive up to 12 weeks of **unpaid** family and medical leave each year. (Employees must work for at least 1,250 hours a year to qualify.)

Reasons for Leaves

Employees may use up to 12 weeks of unpaid leave for childbirth, adoption, their own serious illness or that of a spouse, child, or parent. Either women or men may take absences for the birth of a child or adoption. Leaves can be taken in increments of as little as one hour at a time. Employees who take a medical leave generally must be allowed to return to their same or an equivalent job, with the same pay and benefits.

Notice Requirements

Where the need for a leave is foreseeable, the employee must notify the employer at least 30 days in advance of when it is to begin. This is likely to occur in cases of childbirth, adoption, or planned surgeries. However, there may be medical emergencies where advance notice is not possible. In such cases, the regulations implementing the statute require that an employee give notice of the need for FMLA leave as soon as practicable under the facts and circumstances of the particular case.

Abuses of the Act

The FMLA has met with only grudging acceptance and, in many cases, flagrant disregard by employers across the country. It is estimated that at least 40 percent of employers refuse to comply with its terms. The Labor Department has substantiated this by reporting that 61 percent of the family-leave complaints uncover employer violations. (For most employment laws, only about 16 to 20 percent of the complaints result in relief being granted.) Employers who violate the statute by denying a leave, or retaliating against employees who take leave, are liable for compensatory damages. Wrongfully discharged employees may receive back pay and reinstatement.

To qualify for a medical leave, employees must have a serious health condition. This includes an illness that incapacitates someone for more than three days, requires at least one visit to a health professional, and leads to supervised, ongoing treatment such as a prescription drug. However, many employers complain that workers are widely abusing the FMLA provisions by taking leaves for relatively minor ailments. To reduce false claims, the FMLA allows employers to demand a **medical certificate** from a doctor indicating when the health condition began, the length of time it is likely to last, a diagnosis of the patient's condition, and whether hospitalization is required. The employer may request a second opinion from another doctor (not a company doctor), but the employer must pay for the opinion. When the first two doctors give conflicting reports, the employer and employee may select a third doctor whose opinion is binding.

Freemon v. Foley

911 F.Supp. 326 (N.D. Ill. 1995)

FACTS   Jimmye Freemon was employed as a nutritionist at Mount Sinai Hospital in Chicago. Her immediate supervisor was Gilda Ivy. Ivy reported to Steve Foley, whose direct supervisor was the Vice President for Human Resources, Steven Hulsh. None of these individuals were officers or directors of Mount Sinai. Freemon had been disciplined in the past for poor performance and absenteeism, and was on probation at the time this dispute arose. On May 29th, Freemon learned that her five-year-old son, Joseph, had contracted chicken pox. The next workday, she contacted Ivy and informed her she would not be in the office because of her son's illness. When she took Joseph to the doctor on June 2nd, Freemon learned that her other son, three-year old Joshua, had a contagious fungal infection. When she told Ivy of her need to remain at home with her children, Ivy told Freemon that her vacation time would cover her absence until June 13th, and that she should return to work at that time. However, on June 16th Freemon informed Ivy that Joshua had contracted chicken pox and she would not be back at work until June 21st after another visit to the doctor. Freemon returned to work on June 21st and provided a copy of a doctor's statement, but it covered only June 2nd. When Ivy called Freemon's doctor to verify the need for her lengthy absence, she was denied specific information about the childrens' medical condition because Freemon had not signed a medical release form. Ivy immediately complained to Foley about Freemon's poor performance and recommended her termination. Foley relayed this information to Hulsh and was told by Hulsh to suspend her. That same day, Foley suspended Freemon and told her to provide him with proper documentation or she would be discharged. After Freemon failed to comply with repeated demands that she either sign a release form or provide medical records verifying the need for her May 31st–June 21st absence, she was discharged. Freemon sued Ivy, Foley, and Hulsh, claiming violations of the *Family and Medical Leave Act*. They argued they could not be held liable for any alleged violations of the FMLA because they were not Freemon's "employer."

ISSUE   May supervisors be personally liable for FMLA violations?

continued

DECISION   Yes. The FMLA makes "employers" who violate the statute liable to the injured employee for compensatory damages, back pay, and equitable relief. It extends employer status to *"any person who acts, directly or indirectly, in the interest of an employer to any of the employees of such employer."* This tracks word for word the definition used in the *Fair Labor Standards Act,* which has extended liability to an individual who has supervisory authority over the complaining employee and was responsible in whole or in part for the alleged violation. Thus, even if an individual does not exercise exclusive control over all the day-to-day affairs of the employee, so long as he possesses control over the aspect of employment alleged to have been violated, he may be personally liable. From these facts, it is clear that Ivy, Foley, and Hulsh exercised sufficient control over Freemon's ability to take protected leave to qualify as "employers" under the FMLA.

Employment Discrimination ▬▬▬▬

This country's workplaces have long been plagued by both blatant and subtle discrimination. State and federal legislators, recognizing the harmful social and economic consequences of such behavior, have responded by enacting comprehensive laws prohibiting arbitrary employment discrimination. This section examines the major statutes designed to eliminate discriminatory practices in the workplace.

Title VII

http://
www.eeoc.gov/laws/
vii.html is the site of
Title VII of the Civil
Rights Act of 1964.

Title VII of the Civil Rights Act is the centerpiece of this country's workplace antidiscrimination efforts. It prohibits employers from discriminating on the basis of race, color, religion, sex, or national origin. Generally, an employer violates Title VII if it bases hiring, compensation, promotion, firing, or benefit decisions on any of these characteristics. Title VII applies to private employers with at least 15 employees, labor unions, employment agencies, and state and local governments.

Types of Discrimination

http://
www.eeoc.gov/
eeoinfo.html
provides links to
topics about employ-
ment discrinination.

Both the courts and the Equal Employment Opportunity Commission (EEOC), the agency that administers Title VII, have liberally construed the law's reach. Thus, employers violate the act not only when they engage in **intentional discrimination** (i.e., refusing to consider women for supervisory positions), but also violate when they make employment decisions that are neutral on their face but have a **discriminatory impact.** For instance, a company may require that security guards be at least six feet tall. This preemployment screening device, while appearing facially neutral, discriminates on the basis of sex and national origin despite it's neutral appearance, since it disqualifies a disproportionate number of women and certain ethnic minorities from qualifying for the job.

The *Pregnancy Discrimination Act,* an amendment to Title VII, provides that discrimination on the basis of sex includes discrimination on the basis of pregnancy, childbirth, or related medical conditions. This requires that pregnant employees and those recovering from abortions be treated no differently than any other temporarily disabled employees. But the prohibition against sex discrimination does not prevent discrimination based on *sexual orientation*. Thus, employers may legally refuse to hire an individual who is gay or lesbian without violating Title VII. However, at least eight states and over 100 cities have rules prohibiting discrimination based on sexual orientation.

Discrimination Defenses

Under limited circumstances an employer may lawfully discriminate on the basis of sex, religion, or national origin. This occurs when the job has special requirements making such discrimination necessary. This narrow defense is called a **bona fide occupational qualification** (BFOQ). For instance, a Catholic school could require that its theology instructors be Catholic. And an athletic club could hire only men as men's locker room attendants. However, stereotypical preferences (some customers don't want a female mechanic) are not valid defenses. And there are no BFOQ defenses for discrimination based on race or color. (See Figure 13–2.)

Sexual Harassment

The U.S. Supreme Court has declared workplace **sexual harassment** to be illegal discrimination based on sex. There are two basic types of sexual harassment. **Quid pro quo** harassment occurs when a term of employment is conditioned upon the employee submitting to unwelcome sexual advances. Thus, if Diane's supervisor tells her that she will not be promoted unless she sleeps with him, she has a cause

Figure 13–2:   Title VII of the Civil Rights Act

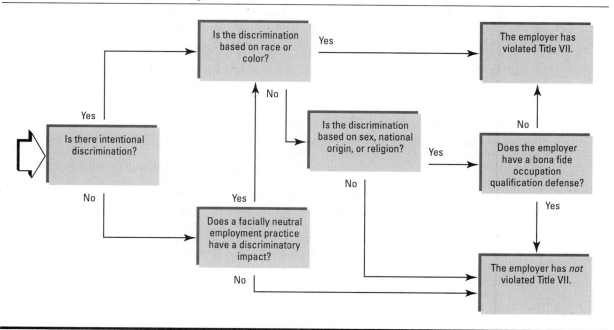

of action for quid pro quo sexual harassment. The other type of sexual harassment, **hostile environment,** is the subject of a great deal of litigation. It occurs when a supervisor or coworkers subject an employee to intimidation, ridicule, or insult based on the employee's gender.

Surprisingly, most sexual harassment complaints are lodged against coworkers rather than supervisors. And most complaints are brought by females. However, in recent years a growing number of lawsuits are brought by men or women alleging sexual harassment by members of the same sex. Initially, some courts would not hear same-sex claims. However, in 1998, the U.S. Supreme Court ruled that same-sex sexual harassment may be pursued under Title VII. (See Figure 13–3.)

Gary v. Long

59 F.3D 1391 (D.C. CIR. 1995)

FACTS   After Coramae Gary began working at the Washington Metropolitan Area Transit Authority (WMATA), James Long, her supervisor, began a pattern of sexual harassment. He first tried to entice her into having sexual relations with him by promising to make her job easier. When this failed, he repeatedly threatened her with adverse employment consequences, including termination, if she did not submit to his advances. Long made crude references to her body and threatened to "get" her when she refused to meet him. He also told her that he would have her fired if she told anybody of his sexual advances. Gary unfailingly rejected Long's overtures and made him aware that they were unwelcome. One year later, under the pretext of inspecting a construction site, Long drove Gary to a secluded storage facility where he allegedly raped her. He then threatened reprisals if she told anyone what had happened. Six months later, Gary filed a grievance with WMATA and filed suit for both quid pro quo and hostile environment sexual harassment. WMATA argued that it was not liable for Long's actions because it was unaware of the sexual harassment and at all relevant times had an active and firm company policy against sexual harassment.

ISSUE   Is the employer liable for the supervisor's sexual harassment?

DECISION   No. While an employer is strictly liable for the *quid pro quo* harassment of a supervisor, there was no *quid pro quo* harassment in this case. It takes more than saber rattling alone to impose *quid pro quo* liability on an employer. The supervisor must have wielded the authority entrusted to him to subject the victim to adverse job consequences as a result of her refusal to submit to unwelcome sexual advances. In this case, Gary should have realized that Long lacked the authority to fire or suspend her. There is no doubt that Long's alleged conduct was sufficiently severe and pervasive enough to create a hostile work environment. But an employer should not be liable for its supervisor's hostile environment harassment where, as here, the employer has established that it adopted policies and implemented measures such that the victimized employee knew or should have known that the employer would not tolerate such conduct and that she could report it to the employer without fear of adverse consequences. In this case, WMATA had sponsored seminars on the subject, distributed staff notices to all employees informing them that sexual harassment would not be tolerated, and made available to all employees the names and telephone numbers of EEO Counselors to whom they report acts of discrimination. It also had a detailed grievance procedure for the formal and informal processing and review of discrimination complaints. In fact, a WMATA attorney investigated Gary's complaint and, although he determined there was no corroborating evidence to support her claim, WMATA granted Gary's request to be transferred to another facility to avoid contact with Long.

http://www.ll.georgetown.edu/Fed-Ct/cadc.html

The Equal Pay Act

Congress passed the *Equal Pay Act* as an amendment to the *Fair Labor Standards Act* (discussed earlier). This measure requires employers to pay both sexes equally for work that requires equal skill, effort, and responsibility when it is performed under similar working conditions. When an employer is discovered paying one sex less than the other for the same job, it is required to raise the lower pay rate. Of course, an employer does not violate the *Equal Pay Act* if it can show that the pay differentials are based on some factor other than sex. For instance, different pay rates may be permitted when they are the result of seniority, merit, or incentive systems (like piecework).

http:// *www.eeoc.gov/laws/ epa.html* provides the text of the Equal Pay Act.

Figure 13–3:   Sexual Harassment

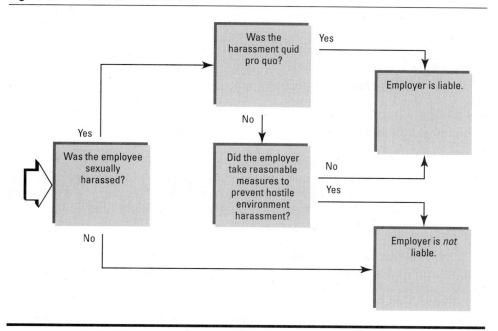

Age Discrimination

http://
www.eeoc.gov/laws/
adea.html provides
the text of the ADEA.

Companies with 20 or more employees are prohibited from discriminating on the basis of age by the *Age Discrimination in Employment Act* (ADEA). Under this statute, employees are not entitled to protection until they reach the age of 40. Aging employees may be discharged, however, if the employer can show that they no longer have the ability to perform their tasks. And top-level executives who are to receive high pension benefits may be forced to retire at age 65. Finally, employers may legally justify disparate treatment based on age if they can show that age is a valid bona fide occupational qualification.

Disabilities Discrimination

http://
www.law.cornell.
edu/uscode/42/ch126.
html provides links
to the sections of
the ADA.

The *Americans with Disabilities Act* (ADA) prohibits employment discrimination on the basis of disability. This comprehensive law is premised on the notion that it is wrong to keep a person with a disability out of the workforce when, with reasonable accommodation, he could become a productive member of society. To be protected by the ADA, a person must have a disability and be qualified to perform the job.

Persons with Disabilities

The ADA defines a person with a disability as someone who:

1. has a physical or mental impairment that substantially limits one or more major life activities,
2. has a record of being substantially limited, or
3. is regarded as being substantially limited.

Impairments like blindness or deafness would fall within the first category. A person with a history of cancer or heart disease, whose illness is now cured, would fall within the second category. The third category includes people who may have no impairment, but are falsely thought to have a disability by employers.

The ADA specifically includes people with AIDS or AIDS-related conditions within its coverage. However, homosexuality, bisexuality, and various sexual disorders like exhibitionism are excluded. Compulsive gambling, illegal drug use, and alcoholism also are not protected. However, substance abusers who are in treatment programs or people who now are rehabilitated may be protected.

Qualified Individuals

The ADA's protection is only available to individuals with disabilities who also are qualified to perform the essential functions of the job. This requires employers to carefully identify what functions are essential to the job and to determine if an applicant with a disability can perform those functions. Further, an individual who is unqualified due to a disability cannot be rejected outright if the employer could provide **reasonable accommodations** that would enable her to perform the job. Of course, accommodations need not be made if they would impose an undue hardship on the employer. In determining if an accommodation creates an undue hardship, courts consider: the size of the business and its financial resources, the cost of the accommodation, and the impact of the accommodation on business operations.

─────────────────────── Ethical Issue ───────────────────────

How do you feel about the responsibilities imposed on employers by the *Americans with Disabilities Act*? If the act were repealed, do you think employers should continue making accommodations for disabled employees?

Terminating the Employment Relationship

Most employees are shocked to learn how fragile their right to employment is in the United States. Under the **employment-at-will** doctrine, which predominates in this country, an employer generally may fire an employee at any time for any reason or for no reason. An employer may dismiss an at-will employee on a mere "whim." However, employers still must exercise caution when discharging workers. There are a number of legal pitfalls, ranging from exceptions to the employment-at-will doctrine to responsibility for unemployment compensation, waiting to trip the unwary.

Exceptions to Employment at Will

Employers may not freely discharge workers when doing so would violate the terms of an **employment contract.** Top executives and union members are likely to have agreements stipulating when and how a covered employee may be terminated. Some courts also infer promises that termination will only be for *good cause* from the language used in personnel handbooks and job interviews.

An employer may be prevented from discharging an employee if doing so violates **public policy.** Thus, terminations based on race, color, religion, sex, national origin, age, and disability or discharges in violation of other employment laws are prohibited. Likewise, employers are in violation of public policy when they discharge employees who refuse to violate the law, report their employer's illegal conduct (whistle-blowing), or exercise a constitutional right (voting) or duty (serving jury duty).

A few courts recognize a third exception to the employment-at-will doctrine based on an **implied covenant of good faith and fair dealing.** They prohibit firings that are made in *bad faith*. These generally involve instances where the discharge had nothing to do with job performance and was conducted in an extremely offensive manner.

─────────────────────── Ethical Issue ───────────────────────

Is it ethical for an employer to fire one employee and replace her with another person merely because the employer liked the second person better? Is it ethical for an employee to quit one job and take another merely because the employee liked the second employer better?

Right-to-Sue Waivers

A growing number of employers offer **severance pay** at the time they discharge an employee. This compensation (perhaps money and a limited extension of job benefits) may be required by contract. However, in most instances it is designed to minimize the likelihood of wrongful discharge lawsuits. In return for a severance package, the employer is likely to insist that the employee sign a **release** waiving his right to sue.

Courts frequently disregard releases if they are not knowingly and voluntarily executed. Factors that guide a court include: the employee's education and business experience; the amount of time the employee had to consider the release before signing it; the employee's opportunity to consult with an attorney; the clarity of the release; and the value of the consideration given in exchange for the release. Consider the following case.

Puentes v. United Parcel Service
86 F.3D 196 (11TH CIR. 1996)

FACTS   Lazaro Ginart and Sergio Balsinde were discharged from their jobs with United Parcel Service (UPS) after working for the company for 14 and 15 years, respectively. At the time of their terminations, both employees were offered substantial severance packages and the ability to "resign for personal reasons" on the condition that they sign releases waiving all employment discrimination claims arising out of their discharges. However, after signing the waivers, the men filed suit against UPS alleging they were unlawfully terminated as a result of discrimination on the basis of national origin and/or race as part of UPS's ongoing pattern of terminating management-level Hispanics and replacing them with non-Hispanics. Ginart and Balsinde argued that the releases were invalid because they were given only 24 hours to decide whether to sign.

ISSUE   Do the signed releases prevent the employees from suing their employer for unlawful discharge?

DECISION   No. Waivers of employees' rights must be carefully scrutinized. Here, the employees do not suggest that they lacked sufficient business experience to evaluate the releases or that the language was not clear. Further, the consideration UPS offered in exchange for the waivers was not unjust. However, the previous decisions evaluating the enforceability of such releases indicate that, absent some reason for urgency, 24 hours is too short a period for employees to adequately consider their options. Additionally, neither employee had any role in deciding the terms of the release. None of the terms were negotiated. In fact, when Ginart asked to take a copy of the release home overnight to think about it, UPS would not allow it. This, like the 24 hour time constraint may well have been motivated by a desire to impede the employees' ability to consult with an attorney.

http://www.law.emory.edu/11circuit

Covenants Not to Compete

Former employees frequently accept employment with a competitor or start up a competing business soon after leaving their current employment. To minimize this risk, many employers insist that new employees sign **covenants not to compete.** (See Figure 13–4 on page 306.) These agreements prohibit an employee from competing with her former employer after leaving her job. Courts are reluctant to enforce these contracts if they deprive the former employer of an opportunity to earn a living. However, they may be enforced if three conditions are met:

1. the former employer has a legitimate business reason for restricting the former employee's job opportunities;
2. the agreement is confined to a reasonable geographic area; and
3. the agreement is for no longer than is reasonably necessary.

Unemployment Compensation

The state and federal governments jointly administer an **unemployment compensation** program that provides financial support for many unemployed workers. A broad range of discharged employees are entitled to unemployment payments as long as they have worked for a reasonable time period and earned a minimum amount of wages. (These eligibility levels are established by state law.) Employees are not eligible unless they are available and qualified to return to their old job. However, workers who have quit their jobs without good reason or have been terminated due to **willful misconduct** are not entitled to compensation. Willful misconduct has been described as:

1. the wanton and willful disregard of the employer's interest;
2. the deliberate violation of rules;
3. the disregard of standards of behavior an employer can rightfully expect from its employers; or
4. negligence that demonstrates wrongful intent.

Employers contribute money to finance the unemployment compensation program. The amount each employer pays is determined by the size of the company payroll and the amount of unemployment claims made against the employer's account. Thus, companies with lower levels of unemployment generally pay fewer unemployment taxes.

Giving Employee References

Employers should maintain the confidentiality of performance reviews and other information they gather about their employees. Files should be locked up and generally made available only to supervisors with a legitimate business need to know the contents of a file. However, there are times when individuals outside of the business may be permitted access to such information. This is likely to occur when prospective employers request references on a company's former employees.

Former employees may sue for defamation or breach of privacy when unfavorable recommendations deprive them of a new job or otherwise injure their reputation. The threat of such legal action has persuaded many employers to refrain

http:// www.dol.gov/dol/esa/ welcome.html is the ESA home page.

Figure 13–4: Non-Compete Agreement

This Non-Compete Agreement (this "Agreement") is made effective as of October 27, 1997, by and between _____, of _____, _____, _____, and _____, of _____, _____, _____.

In this Agreement, the party who is requesting the non-competition from the other party shall be referred to as "_____," and the party who is agreeing not to compete shall be referred to as "_____."

1. NON-COMPETE COVENANT. For a period of _____ after the effective date of this Agreement, _____ will not directly or indirectly engage in any business that competes with _____. This covenant shall apply to the geographical area that includes all of the State of _____.

2. NON-SOLICITATION COVENANT. For a period of _____ after the effective date of this Agreement, _____ will not directly or indirectly solicit business from, or attempt to sell, license or provide the same or similar products or services as are now provided to, any customer or client of _____. Further, for a period of _____ after the effective date of this Agreement, _____ will not directly or indirectly solicit, induce or attempt to induce any employee of _____ to terminate his or her employment with _____.

3. PAYMENT. _____ will pay compensation to _____ for the covenants of _____ in the amount of $_____. This compensation shall be payable in a lump sum on _____.

4. CONFIDENTIALITY. _____ will not at any time or in any manner, either directly or indirectly, use for the personal benefit of _____, or divulge, disclose, or communicate in any manner any information that is proprietary to _____. _____ will protect such information and treat it as strictly confidential.

5. ENTIRE AGREEMENT. This Agreement contains the entire agreement of the parties regarding the subject matter of this Agreement, and there are no other promises or conditions in any other agreement whether oral or written.

6. SEVERABILITY. The parties have attempted to limit the non-compete provision so that it applies only to the extent necessary to protect legitimate business and property interests. If any provision of this Agreement shall be held to be invalid or unenforceable for any reason, the remaining provisions shall continue to be valid and enforceable. If a court finds that any provision of this Agreement is invalid or unenforceable, but that by limiting such provision it would become valid and enforceable, then such provision shall be deemed to be written, construed, and enforced as so limited.

7. INJUCTION. It is agreed that if _____ violates the terms of this Agreement irreparable harm will occur, and money damages will be insufficient to compensate _____. Therefore, _____ will be entitled to seek injunctive relief (i.e., a court order that requires _____ to comply with this Agreement) to enforce the terms of this Agreement.

Protected Party: _____

By: _____

_____

Non-Competing Party: _____

By: _____

Source: Quicken Business Law Partner® 3.0 CD-ROM. Copyright © 1997 Parson's Technology, Inc. All rights reserved.

from giving references other than stating the dates during which an individual was employed. However, most courts make tort liability unlikely when the statements:

1. were made in good faith;
2. were disclosed only to individuals with a legitimate need for the private information; and
3. disclosed no more than was necessary.

Consider the following case.

Randi W. v. Muroc Joint Unified School

929 P.2D 582 (SUP. CT. CAL. 1997)

FACTS Gilbert Rossette, a Mendota school official, wrote a strong recommendation for Robert Gadams despite Rossette's knowledge of Gadams's prior improper contacts with female students. These included hugging some female junior high students, giving them back massages, making "sexual remarks" to them, and being involved in "sexual situations" with them. However, Rossette's recommendation noted only positive aspects of Gadams's tenure in Mendota, including his "genuine concern" for students and his "outstanding rapport" with everyone. It concluded, "I wouldn't hesitate to recommend Mr. Gadams for any position." Richard Cole, an official at Tranquility High School, knew that Gadams had been the subject of various parents' complaints, including charges he led a panty raid and made sexual overtures to students. Despite the fact that Gadams was forced to resign under pressure due to sexual misconduct charges, Cole's recommendation listed only favorable qualities and stated Cole "would recommend him for almost any administrative position he wishes to pursue." David J. Malcolm, an official at Muroc Joint Unified School, provided a positive evaluation of Gadams despite his knowledge of disciplinary actions taken against him regarding sexual harassment allegations. This included a charge of "sexual touching" of female students that induced Muroc to force Gadams to resign. Malcolm described Gadams as "an upbeat, enthusiastic administrator who relates well to students" and who was "in large part" responsible for making the campus "a safe, orderly and clean environment for students and staff." The letter concluded by recommending Gadams "for an assistant principalship or equivalent position without reservation." Based on these recommendations, Livingston Middle School hired Gadams as a vice principal. In that capacity, he allegedly molested and engaged in sexual touching of a 13-year-old female student. She sued Rossette, Cole, Malcolm, and their school systems in tort for failing to use reasonable care in recommending Gadams for employment.

ISSUE May recommendation writers be legally liable for misrepresenting the qualifications and character of an individual?

DECISION Yes. A writer of a letter of recommendation owes to prospective employers and third persons a duty not to misrepresent the facts in describing the qualifications and character of a former employee, if making these misrepresentations would present a substantial foreseeable risk of physical injury to others. Based on the facts alleged in the complaint, the defendants could foresee that Livingston's officials would read and rely on their recommendation letters in deciding to hire Gadams. Likewise, they could see foresee that, had they not unqualifiedly recommended Gadams, Livingston would not have hired him. And they could foresee that Gadams,

continued

after being hired by Livingston, might molest or injure a Livingston student. It is certainly arguable that these unreserved recommendations of Gadams, together with the failure to disclose facts reasonably necessary to avoid or minimize the risk of further child molestation or abuse, could be characterized as morally blameworthy. However, we must be careful to avoid a conclusion that might discourage former employers from ever writing recommendations. Therefore, this duty of care should not extend to third persons unless there is resulting physical injury or some special relationship between the parties.

http://www.california.findlaw.com

QUESTIONS AND PROBLEM CASES

1. When may an employer require employees to take a lie detector test?
2. What kind of notice must an employee give in order to avail herself of a protected leave under the *Family and Medical Leave Act?*
3. What is meant by the term "qualified individual" under the *Americans with Disabilities Act?*
4. Overton had a long history of mental illness, which included bouts of depression. When he took a job, his employer knew of his condition and that he was on medication. His job description did not mention that he would be dealing with the public, and some employees in similar positions had no public contact. Soon after he started working, Overton began to have difficulties with his immediate supervisor because he sometimes fell asleep at his desk due to his medication. Later, he was told he would have to write permits, which would entail some contact with the public. Overton complained that his emotional problems made such contact difficult, if not impossible, and requested that his job be restructured so he could avoid this duty. His request was denied and Overton was eventually discharged. Was the discharge unlawful?
5. Microsoft employed a core staff of permanent employees. It categorized them as "regular employees" and offered them a wide variety of benefits, including paid vacations, sick leave, holidays, short-term disability, group health and life insurance, and pensions. The company supplemented its core staff of employees with a pool of individuals to whom it refused to pay any fringe benefits. They were classified as "independent contractors" or "freelancers." Freelancers were hired when Microsoft needed to expand its workforce to meet the demands of new product schedules. Although initially hired to work on specific projects, several of the freelancers had worked on successive projects for a minimum of two years. Microsoft fully integrated them into its workforce: they often worked on teams along with regular employees, sharing the same supervisors, performing identical functions, and working the same core hours. Because Microsoft required that they work on-site, they received admittance card keys, office equipment and supplies from the company. However, they wore badges of a different color, were not invited to official company functions, and were not paid overtime wages. In addition, they were not paid through Microsoft's payroll department. Instead, they submitted invoices for their services, documenting their hours and the projects on which they worked, and were paid through the accounts receivable department. Were the freelancers employees who qualified for the protections offered by the employment laws?
6. After beginning her employment with Westlake Polymers in 1986, June Manuel missed a substantial number of days of work each year. As a result, Westlake's supervisors advised Manuel that her employment would be in

jeopardy if her attendance did not improve. Despite the warning, she still missed a substantial number of workdays. In October 1993, two months after the *Family and Medical Leave Act* went into effect, Manuel was treated for an ingrown toenail. She notified Westlake of the recommended toenail removal procedure. With the understanding that she would return to work on Monday, she was given Friday off from work for the medical procedure. Over the weekend, the toe became infected and she ended up missing more than a month of work. When she returned to work, she was suspended for four days. Manuel claimed that Westlake violated the FMLA by punishing her for the absences for the ingrown toenail. The employer responded by claiming her absences for the ingrown toenail were not protected by the FMLA because Manuel did not specifically mention the FMLA when she sought time off for the infection. Must employees seeking medical leave for unforeseeable circumstances specifically mention the FMLA when giving notice of the need for time off?

7. Darrin Dougherty worked for Fair Acres Geriatric Care Center for approximately five-and-one-half months as a certified nursing assistant, working with eight geriatric patients. He was then reassigned to a unit that included three patients with AIDS. Dougherty told his employer that he would not work with AIDS patients because he feared getting the virus and transmitting it to his children. Fair Acres discharged Dougherty for refusing to accept the work assignment with the AIDS patients. Dougherty argued that his refusal was justified because his employer failed to provide him with any precautions other than rubber gloves. Fair Acres contended that Dougherty was not entitled to unemployment compensation because his discharge was for willful misconduct. Should Dougherty receive unemployment compensation?

8. Michael Bullard worked for Bigelow Holding Company. The business had adopted a policy of discriminating against African-Americans. For instance, Bigelow employees were instructed to use deception and subterfuge to prevent African-Americans from becoming tenants in Bigelow rental units. While Bullard was aware of this policy, there is no evidence that he ever refused to carry out any of his employer's racist practices. However, Bullard did remark to a fellow employee that "Blacks have rights too." When Donna Dallman, one of Bigelow's managers, learned of this comment, she fired Bullard because she allegedly did not want anyone who was sympathetic to African-Americans working for Bigelow. Was Bullard's firing unlawful as a violation of public policy?

9. Blocker was an auditor with AT&T. Prior to working with AT&T, she had worked as a staff auditor and accountant for several other companies. Blocker later complained that she was not receiving the same salary as a new male auditor, Bradshaw, even though she had been with the company longer and they were doing the same work. AT&T defended the pay difference by explaining that Bradshaw was brought in as a lateral transfer from a management position in another division. AT&T had a policy of laterally transferring personnel from eliminated positions in its other areas at the same salary rather than downgrading or demoting them. Has AT&T violated the *Equal Pay Act?*

10. During the time Mechelle Vinson worked for Meritor Savings Bank, she received regular pay raises and promotions. However, at that same time, her supervisor made repeated demands on her for sexual favors, fondled her in front of other employees, exposed himself to her, and raped her on several occasions. When Vinson sued the company for sexual harassment, it defended on the basis that she was not denied any job benefits. Does Vinson have a legitimate basis for claiming sexual harassment?

STARTING A BUSINESS

J oan Bingham, Mortimer Zuckerman, and Anne Peretz formed a corporation, PFP Inc., to explore the feasibility of publishing a weekly newspaper in Washington, D.C. They initially contributed $50,000 to the corporation, then added another $760,000 after it was determined that the newspaper would be feasible. One year later, a limited partnership, Washington Weekly Limited, was formed to raise additional capital for the newspaper. Initially, PFP Inc. was the sole general partner and Susan Greenberg was the sole limited partner, although Bingham was mistakenly listed as a general partner. When PFP Inc. was unable to pay for advertising and marketing services, suit was brought against PFP Inc., the limited partnership, and Bingham.

Bingham v. Goldberg Marchesano. Kohlman, 637 A.2d 81 (D.C. App. 1994).

When are shareholders liable for corporate debts?

How does a limited partnership differ from a partnership and a corporation?

Within a limited partnership, how do the rights and duties of limited partners differ from those of general partners?

Introduction ▬▬▬▬▬▬▬▬▬▬▬▬

The ease with which someone can start a business encourages millions of people to do so. However, the lack of legal formalities often is a trap for the unwary. Every year, thousands of new businesses fail, in part because their owners failed to recognize the major pitfalls on the road to success. While the marketplace offers lucrative opportunities for enterprising individuals, it also possesses a wide variety of hazards for the less sophisticated. Thus, it is unwise to start a venture without first fully exploring the legal implications of owning and operating a business.

Forms of Business Organization

Throughout the life of any business, the owners are faced with numerous operating choices, many of which are integral to the success of the enterprise. One of the most important decisions is the selection of the appropriate organizational structure. This determination can greatly affect the successful operation and resulting profitability of the business. The owner must choose from among the traditional types of business organization (sole proprietorship, general partnership, corporation, limited partnership), or from one of the emerging forms (limited liability partnership, limited liability company).

http:// www.law.cornell.edu/ topics/topic2.html# *enterprise law* provides information about corporations, partnerships, and joint ventures. Select a topic.

Each type of business structure possesses distinct advantages and disadvantages that must be fully considered. These include: limited liability, taxation, legal formalities, financing, management, continuity, and liquidity of investment. Rarely do all of the factors favor one form of business organization. For this reason, it is wise to consult an accountant and an attorney who can fully explain the fundamental features of each.

Chapter Overview

This chapter examines the legal forms of business organization. It introduces their basic features as well as the strengths and weaknesses of each. In this way, the reader may better understand how to make the best choice. Next is a discussion of the legal aspects of owning and operating a business franchise, since franchising is one of the most common ways of conducting business in this country. The chapter closes with a brief review of several regulatory matters that should be investigated before opening any type of business.

http:// www.sba.gov is the home page for the Small Business Administration, with links to resources, services, and regulations.

Sole Proprietorships ▬▬▬▬▬▬▬▬▬

The most basic form of business organization is the **sole proprietorship.** The owner may use a trade name, such as The Bait Shop, to identify the business to the public. However, for legal purposes, the enterprise is merely an extension of the owner. With the exception of the requirement that a sole proprietorship can have only one owner, there are no real legal restrictions on establishing a sole proprietorship.

Liability in Sole Proprietorships

Because the business and the owner are the same, the owner of a sole proprietorship is personally liable for all of the enterprise's obligations. Suppose Allen opened a computer consulting business. Starting the business was relatively easy. First, Allen signed a five-year lease to rent office space. Next, he borrowed several thousand dollars from the local bank to purchase office equipment. Finally, he hired several people to work in the office.

Because Allen is the sole owner of the enterprise and did not file for incorporation, his business is a sole proprietorship. As a result, the employees of the company are the personal employees of Allen. If the business does not make enough money to pay their salaries and wages, Allen is personally liable for those amounts. He also is personally liable to the landlord and the bank. If the business fails or is otherwise unable to pay the rent and loan payments, Allen must pay them out of his nonbusiness assets.

Managing the Sole Proprietorship

A sole proprietorship can be created without any legal formalities. Similarly, it can be terminated merely by closing the door or otherwise ceasing operations. A sole proprietor also is free, within the limits of the law, to unilaterally manage the business affairs. This ease of management is perhaps the greatest advantage of this form of business organization.

Sole Proprietorship Taxation

A sole proprietorship and its owner are treated as a single entity for taxation purposes. Thus, Allen will report his business income and losses on his individual state and federal income tax forms. He may deduct the amounts he pays as salaries and wages as well as any day-to-day business expenses. However, most of his personal (nonbusiness) expenses are not deductible. Thus, he should maintain two separate bank accounts: one for paying business expenses and one for personal expenditures. This makes it easier to document legitimate deductions.

General Partnerships

There are surprisingly few legal formalities involved in creating a **general partnership.** In fact, courts sometimes find people to be partners even though they never actually intended to form a partnership. This section examines the basic structure and fundamental features of the general partnership form of business.

Creating a General Partnership

A *partnership* is an association of two or more people who carry on as co-owners a business for profit. It does not require a writing and, in fact, does not require any express agreement. Thus, people sometimes unwittingly create partnerships when they jointly operate a business enterprise with the intention of earning a profit. (Nonprofit associations are not partnerships.) The key things a court looks at in determining if a partnership has been created is if the individuals are sharing in both the profits and the important management decisions of the venture.

Bass v. Bass

814 S.W.2D 38 (Sup. Ct. Tenn. 1991)

FACTS   During the six years prior to their marriage, Linda and William Bass lived together. After William bought a restaurant, Linda worked there for 17 hours a day while William was employed at a beer store. Later, they both worked 12-hours shifts in the restaurant so they could keep it open 24 hours a day. The couple pooled their money to pay bills and to lease the restaurant. Linda never was compensated for her efforts. William also started several other businesses that were quite successful. Those ventures were financed from the profits earned by the restaurant. Although the couple finally married, they divorced in the same year. Despite the divorce, they immediately began living and working together again. All of the businesses were listed exclusively in William's name. However, Linda wrote and signed most of the checks for the operations. Once again, she never was paid wages or salary. When William died, Linda claimed half of his assets as his business partner.

ISSUE   Were William and Linda partners?

DECISION   Yes. A partnership is an association of two or more persons to carry on as co-owners a business for profit. It is not essential that the parties actually intended to become partners. It is the intention to do the things that constitute a partnership that determines whether individuals are partners. There is no question that Linda and William carried on as co-owners of a business for profit. They pooled their money. Aside from her financial contributions, Linda invested a considerable amount of time and labor into operating the various ventures. Finally, when Linda's sister began working at the restaurant, unlike Linda, she was paid wages for her efforts. This establishes an intent to treat Linda as more than an employee.

The Partnership Agreement

While a written partnership agreement normally is not required, it is wise to formally draw up such a contract. This agreement, known as the **articles of partnership,** is useful when misunderstandings or disagreements arise. Legal disputes among partners are most likely to occur in partnerships that fail to draft a partnership agreement.

There are no legal rules governing what terms should be included in the articles of partnership. However, the agreements usually indicate how profits and losses are to be allocated among the partners. They often describe the authority of the partners, the term for which the partnership is to exist, and the type of business to be carried on.

Managing the Partnership

Unless the partnership agreement states otherwise, all partners have an equal voice in management. While most matters are decided by majority rule, it usually requires unanimous consent to deviate from the partnership agreement or to change the fundamental nature of the partnership business. Suppose David, Janet, and Terry form a partnership for the purpose of carrying on a landscaping business. The decision over where they should purchase supplies would require the consent of only two of the partners. However, if they were contemplating purchasing property for the purpose of renting out apartments, approval of all three would be necessary.

Problems may arise when the partners are evenly divided on a course of action. If their deadlock cannot be resolved, they may have to dissolve the partnership. To avoid this result, some partnership agreements stipulate a means of resolving deadlocks.

Authority of Partners

As agents for the partnership, partners have broad authority to bind one another on business contracts. Even when acting contrary to the articles of partnership, a partner may bind the partnership if she has apparent authority. Suppose the landscaping partnership discussed above stated in its partnership agreement that individual partners would not have authority to make purchases for more than $500. Despite this provision, Terry ordered a garden tractor costing $2,000 for the partnership. If it is customary in this area for businesses to make orders of this size and the seller was unaware of the limits on Terry's authority, the partnership would be liable on the contract. Of course, Terry would be liable to the partnership for having exceeded her actual authority.

Duties of Partners

Partners owe one another the same duties that agents owe their principals. This means they must not allow their self-interest to interfere with their duties to the partnership. They may buy from or sell to the partnership only with the advance approval of their partners. Further, unless otherwise agreed, each partner must devote her full time and best efforts to the partnership business.

Liability in General Partnerships

Like sole proprietors, partners in a general partnership are personally liable for the debts of the business. This means that if the partnership business is unprofitable, the individual partners may lose more than they invested in the business. They may be forced to pay partnership debts from their personal assets. However, some courts do not permit partnership creditors to sue individual partners on contract claims until the partnership assets have been exhausted. (See Figure 14–1.)

Liability of Outgoing Partners

Whenever a partner ends his association with the partnership, the enterprise is legally dissolved. However, the partners frequently agree to create a new partnership and continue the business. The continuing partners often agree to relieve the outgoing partner of further liability for the debts of the original partnership. But this agreement is not binding on the original partnership creditors unless they agree to release their claims against the outgoing partner. The outgoing partner generally is not liable for debts the new partnership incurs after his departure unless the continuing partners have apparent authority to bind him. This may occur if the creditors of the original partnership have not been notified of his departure.

Figure 14–1:   Creditors and a General Partnership

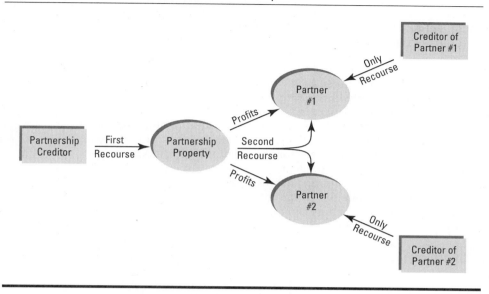

Liability of Incoming Partners

Someone who joins an existing partnership has a type of *limited liability* for the previous obligations of the partnership. This means she is liable for no more than her share of the partnership assets. She is fully liable for any debts incurred after she became a partner.

Citizens Bank v. Parham-Woodman Medical Associates

874 F.Supp. 705 (E.D. Va. 1995)

FACTS   Citizens Bank and Parham-Woodman Medical Associates, a general partnership, entered a construction loan agreement on April 30, 1995. The loan, in the principal amount of $2 million, was to fund construction of a medical office building for the partnership. Nilda Ante and Larry King were the only partners when the loan was extended. As contemplated by the agreement, the bank made advances from time to time during the construction of the building. Between April 1985 and June 1986, the advances totaled $1,457,123.15. On June 25, 1986, Nada Tas and her husband, Joseph Tas, joined the partnership. From that date until November 17, 1986, Citizens Bank made additional advances in the amount of $542,876.85. After the medical office building was built, the partnership defaulted on the loan. Ante and King went into bankruptcy and their personal liability was eliminated. The bank then sued Nada and Joseph Tas, claiming they were personally liable for the $542,876.85 in advances made after their admission to the partnership.

ISSUE   Are Nada and Joseph Tas personally liable for the advances made after their admission to the partnership?

continued

DECISION   No. Nada and Joseph Tas have personal liability only if the advances represent partnership debt that arose after they became partners. On April 30, 1985, the bank became obligated to lend the partnership the total sum of $2 million to be advanced from time to time upon satisfaction of contractually specified conditions. At the same time, the partnership agreed to borrow the $2 million from the bank. The loan agreement required the advances to be applied to the limited purpose of building construction and the partnership was obligated contractually to complete the construction. The bank was not free after April 1985 to impose additional conditions on its making future advances. Notwithstanding the somewhat contingent arrangement respecting disbursement of the loan, the debt arose on April 30, 1985. Partnership law makes an incoming partner liable for all obligations arising before his admission, but provides that this liability shall be satisfied only out of partnership property. Thus, existing and subsequent creditors have equal rights against partnership property and the separate property of all the previously existing partners, while only the subsequent creditors have rights against the separate estate of newly admitted partners. This rule enables potential creditors of the partnership to know that what they see of a partnership is what they can reach and it permits potential incoming partners to avoid surprise liabilities.

Compensation of Partners

Disputes often arise among partners over compensation. Therefore, compensation issues should be thoroughly discussed and included in the articles of partnership before beginning the partnership business. The agreement should clearly establish rules that govern:

1. the distribution of profits,
2. the allocation of losses, and
3. the right to salary or wages.

Distribution of Profits

In the absence of a contrary agreement, the partners are to equally share any profits earned by the business. This is the case even when the partners have made unequal capital contributions. Suppose Alice, Brittany, and Corey form a partnership to operate a restaurant. Alice contributes $20,000 and Brittany gives $20,000 to cover the start-up costs. Corey is able to supply only $10,000. If the business earns $30,000 in its first year, each of the partners is entitled to an equal share ($10,000). If they want their right to the profits to reflect their share of the capital contributions, they should indicate that desire in the partnership agreement.

Allocation of Losses

Unless the partnership agreement states otherwise, the sharing of losses is the same as the sharing of profits. Thus, if the restaurant loses $6,000, each partner is responsible for $2,000 despite the unequal contributions. If the articles of partnership stipulates that profits are to be distributed to reflect each partner's capital contribution, the losses would be allocated according to that same formula. Thus, Alice and Brittany are each liable for $2,400 and Corey must pay $1,200.

Right to Salaries and Wages

Partners ordinarily are not entitled to salaries or wages for their efforts unless the partnership agreement clearly gives such a right. Suppose Alice worked at the restaurant every day for a minimum of 12 hours a day. Brittany and Corey, on the other hand, were so involved in their other ventures that they seldom set foot in the restaurant. Despite this fact, Alice is not entitled to wages unless the partners agree to pay her a salary. In the absence of such an agreement, her share of the profits is the only compensation she will receive.

—————————————— Ethical Issue ——————————————

In the previous example, would it be fair for Brittany and Corey to refuse to pay Alice wages and simultaneously assert their right to an equal share of the partnership profits?

Partnership Taxation

A general partnership is similar to a sole proprietorship in that neither is a taxable entity. However, partnerships are required to file an informational return that reports the business's profits and losses for the year, as well as how much should be attributed to each partner. The individual partners then pay taxes on their pro rata share, even if the profits were not actually distributed during that taxable year.

The partnership form may offer tax advantages in early years of the business when profits are less likely to occur. If the partners have other sources of income, they can reduce their tax liability on that income by deducting their partnership losses.

Termination of the Partnership

Unless the partners have carefully drawn up a partnership agreement, the partnership may lack stability. For instance, **dissolution** occurs whenever a partner terminates her association with the partnership. The departing partner may then demand a **liquidation** of the partnership business, which forces the other partners to dismantle the enterprise and distribute its assets. Absent an agreement to maintain a partnership for a specific time period, any partner may compel a dissolution and liquidation at any time.

There is no automatic right to continue the business beyond the time stipulated in the articles of partnership. For this reason, the partnership agreement often has language limiting the right of a partner to force a liquidation. It may include a *buyout agreement* that allows ongoing partners to pay off any departing partner and thereby continue the business.

Corporations

Much of the dynamic economic development in this country is attributable to the emergence of the modern **corporation.** Because of its limited liability feature, a corporation encourages people to participate in business enterprises without fear of losing more than their investment. Further, as an entity separate and distinct from its shareholders (owners), the corporation can easily hold property over long periods of time since its existence is not automatically threatened by the death, bankruptcy, or retirement of an owner.

Types of Corporations

There are numerous kinds of corporations. However, their precise features cannot be fully understood without examining the incorporation statutes of each state. Four types of corporations are examined here: nonprofit corporations, professional corporations, publicly held corporations, and close corporations.

Nonprofit Corporations

The states permit private persons to create and operate *nonprofit corporations.* They may be formed for a variety of purposes including medical care, childcare, performing arts, and social clubs. While their founders and members are not permitted to make a profit from the venture, they may earn reasonable salaries or wages by acting as corporate officers or employees. Nonprofit corporations are not required to pay income taxes and those who contribute to the enterprise may deduct that amount from their personal taxes.

Professional Corporations

Many states permit professionals (doctors, lawyers, accountants) to incorporate only through a *professional corporation.* (Some states call them "professional service corporations.") Generally, the activities of the corporation are limited to the professionals' area of professional expertise, and all of the shareholders must be licensed members of that profession. Many professionals desire professional corporations so they can shelter their personal assets from the malpractice of their colleagues. Others desire the corporate form because they receive favorable tax treatment for the various fringe benefits (insurance, retirement plans) the corporation offers its employee/shareholders.

Publicly Held Corporations

Most of the largest business enterprises are *publicly held corporations.* The aim of these businesses is to make a profit that may be distributed to the shareholders in the form of dividends. A publicly held corporation sells shares to diverse groups of people who often have no interest in managing the business.

Close Corporations

Most incorporated businesses are *close corporations.* In fact, most publicly held corporations started out as close corporations and only "went public" after experiencing some degree of success. While there is no uniform definition of a close corporation, these enterprises generally share three characteristics:

1. they have few shareholders;
2. most of the shareholders knew each other before buying their shares; and
3. most shareholders are active in the business.

The remainder of this discussion primarily deals with close corporations.

Creating a Corporation

The legal formalities involved in creating a corporation are much stricter than they are for sole proprietorships and general partnerships. There are three fundamental steps that must be met:

1. preparation and signing of the articles of incorporation by one or more of the incorporators;
2. publicly filing the articles and paying all incorporation fees; and
3. receipt of a certificate of incorporation from the state.

The Articles of Incorporation

The **articles of incorporation** is the basic corporate document that outlines the powers of the corporation and the rights of the shareholders. It must include the name of the corporation, the number of shares the corporations can issue, and the name and address of each incorporator. (See Figure 14–2.)

http:// *www.law.cornell.edu/ topics/corporations. html* provides links to the SEC, securities acts, and other sites relevant to corporations.

Figure 14–2:   Articles of Incorporation

ARTICLES OF INCORPORATION
of

_____

The undersigned person(s), acting as incorporator(s) of a corporation organized under the laws of Delaware, hereby adopt(s) the following Articles of Incorporation:

ARTICLE I
CORPORATE NAME

The name of this corporation is _____.

ARTICLE II
SHARES

The total number of shares which the corporation shall have authority to issue is _____ shares of no par value stock.

ARTICLE III
REGISTERED OFFICE AND AGENT

The street address of the corporation's initial registered office and the name of its initial registered agent at such address is:

_____
_____
_____   County
_____, _____

ARTICLE IV
PURPOSE

The purpose of the corporation is to engage in any lawful activity permitted by the laws of this state.

continued

Figure 14–2:   continued

ARTICLE V
DIRECTORS

The names and residence addresses of the persons constituting the initial board of directors are:

_____

_____

_____ , _____

After the initial board of directors, the board shall consist of such number of directors as shall be determined by the shareholders from time to time at each annual meeting at which directors are to be elected.

The directors shall be divided into _____ classes, the number of directors to be allocated to each class to be as nearly equal as possible and with the term of office in one class expiring each year after the initital annual meeting of shareholders.

ARTICLE VI
LIABILITY OF DIRECTORS

To the fulles extent permitted by law, no director of this corporation shall be personally liable to the corporation or its shareholders for monetary damages for breach of any duty owed to the corporation or its shareholders, except that a director may be held personally liable for (i) breaches of the duty of loyalty, (ii) acts or omissions not in good faith or which involve intentional misconduct or a knowing violation of law, (iii) declaration of unlawful dividends or unlawful stock repurchases or redemptions, or (iv) a transaction from which the director derives an improper personal benefit.

Any director or officer who is involved in litigation or other proceeding by reason of his or her position as a director or officer of this corporation shall be indemnified and held harmless by the corporation to the fullest extent permitted by law.

Certification

I certify that I have read the above Articles of Incorporation and that they are true and correct to the best of my knowledge.

_____

_____ , Incorporator

_____ , _____

State of _____ , County of _____ , ss:

Subscribed and sworn to (or affirmed) before me this _____ day of _____ , 19 _____ .

_____

Notary Public

The Certificate of Incorporation

After the state reviews the articles of incorporation to ensure consistency with the state's incorporation laws, it issues a **certificate of incorporation.** This certifies that the corporation is in existence. Shareholders who knowingly conduct business on behalf of the corporation before the state issues the certificate of incorporation may be personally liable on the contracts.

Managing the Corporation

In publicly held corporations, the shareholders own the business but do not have authority to make management decisions. Instead, they elect a board of directors that selects a management team to conduct the corporation's day-to-day affairs. This governance model is not appropriate for close corporations. Accordingly, the various close corporation statutes generally dispense with these formalities and permit the shareholders to manage the business like a partnership.

Minority shareholders in a close corporation are particularly vulnerable because there is no ready market for their shares if they wish to leave the corporation. For example, Paul, Renee, and Doug each own a one-third interest in a close corporation. Paul and Renee vote to hire themselves as employees of the corporation and deny this privilege to Doug. They then pay themselves high salaries with expensive fringe benefits. As a result of these costs, the corporation does not show a profit and, accordingly, Doug is never paid any dividends.

Some courts actively intervene in these types of cases to protect the minority shareholders from oppression by the majority. However, at the time of incorporation, Doug could have protected himself by insisting that the articles of incorporation include a provision requiring unanimous consent for all hiring decisions.

─────────────────── Ethical Issue ───────────────────

Suppose Jack owned 51 percent of the shares in a corporation and Diane owned the other 49 percent. Using his majority control, Jack hired himself as an employee and paid himself a large salary. This salary reduced the amount of profit that could be distributed as dividends to Diane. Jack refused to hire Diane as an employee. Is this ethical?

Liability in Corporations

The principal reason that people choose the corporate form of business organization is to gain the advantages of **limited liability.** This means that shareholders are not personally liable for the debts of the corporation. The most they risk is the amount they have invested in the corporation.

There are several exceptions to this rule against personal liability. First, when loaning money to a close corporation, many creditors insist that one or more of the shareholders personally guarantee the corporation's payment. When that occurs, the guarantors are personally liable if the corporation does not repay the debt. Second, shareholders who actively manage the business may be personally liable when their negligence causes injury to third persons.

Third, courts sometimes hold shareholders personally liable for corporate debts under a concept known as **piercing the corporate veil.** Before piercing the veil, courts generally insist that two requirements be met:

1. There is *domination* of the corporation by one or more of the shareholders.
2. The domination results in an *improper purpose.*

Domination often occurs when corporate formalities are ignored and a shareholder/manager treats corporate property as her personal assets. (The corporation is viewed as the *alter ego* of the dominating shareholder/manager.) The improper purpose test generally is met when the corporation is *undercapitalized.* This occurs when the shareholders fail to give a corporation sufficient assets to meet expected claims. Or in many cases, the shareholders withdraw large amounts of corporate assets to prevent a corporate creditor from reaching them. (See Figure 14–3.)

N.L.R.B. v. Greater Kansas City Roofing
2 F.3d 1047 (10th Cir. 1993)

FACTS   Greater Kansas City Roofing (GKC) had been operated as a sole proprietorship owned by Judy Clarke and managed by her husband, Charlie Clarke. In 1983, because of numerous violations of the labor laws, the National Labor Relations Board (NLRB) ordered the business to pay a total of $133,742.47. Tina Clarke, Charlie's sister, began loaning money to GKC in 1984 to help it out of its financial difficulties. Finally, when the business was unable to pay Tina the more than $38,000 it owed her, she decided to set up a new corporation and run the business herself. Tina Clarke became the sole shareholder, officer, and director of The New Greater Kansas City Roofing Corporation (New GKC). She was unaware at the time this corporation was formed that GKC had committed labor law violations and that the NLRB had an outstanding judgement against the business. New GKC basically took over the assets of its predecessor and retained many of its former customers. New GKC's staff was comprised almost exclusively of the former employees of GKC, including Charlie Clarke, who was employed to manage the corporate business. Tina failed to adhere to corporate formalities in her dealings with New GKC. She used a trade name associated with the corporation, as well as its address and telephone number, to establish a credit card collection account and to open a checking account for her escort service, Affaire d'Amour. There is no evidence New GKC had bylaws, accounts, stock, corporate records, or held meetings. In 1988, the NLRB attempted to collect its outstanding judgment against GKC. It alleged that New GKC was the alter ego of GKC and that its corporate veil should be pierced so that Tina Clarke could be held personally liable on the claim.

ISSUE   Should the court pierce the veil and find Tina Clarke liable on the corporate debt?

DECISION   No. The corporate structure is an artificial construct of the law, a substantial purpose of which is to create an incentive for investment by limiting exposure to personal liability. Only in extreme circumstances will the corporate form be disregarded so the personal assets of a controlling shareholder may be attached to pay the debts of the corporation. However, the corporate veil should be pierced only in situations where it is essential to avoid impropriety or injustice. This is an alter ego case. That is, the NLRB seeks to pierce the corporate veil because Tina Clarke disregarded New GKC as a separate entity and operated the company as if it were her own personal activity. Under the alter ego theory a shareholder will have personal liability for corporate debts only if a two-prong test is met. First, the shareholder must disregard the corporation's separate identity. Second, adherence to the corporate fiction would sanction a fraud or promote an injustice. While Tina Clarke's sloppy manner of conducting business under New GKC might have disregarded the corporation's separate identity, there is no evidence that she committed fraud, either in the formation of the corporation or in the misuse of the corporate form. There is nothing to indicate New GKC was created to avoid the judgment since she was unaware of it when she formed the corporation. Further, there is no showing that Tina Clarke used the corporate form to work an injustice. She already had loaned GKC over $38,000 and, after incorporation, continued to loan her own money to the business.

Corporation Taxation

For tax paying purposes, a corporation normally is treated as a taxable entity. It must file a return and pay taxes on its profits. The shareholders do not automatically report corporate profits on their individual tax returns. They must wait until the profits are distributed to them through the payment of dividends or until they sell their shareholdings at a profit. This raises the specter of double taxation. Profits are taxed at the corporate level and then again at the shareholder level when dividends are distributed.

http:// *www.irs.ustreas.gov/ prod/bus_info/index. html* contains information on corporate taxation, with links to related sites.

Figure 14–3:   Piercing the Corporate Veil

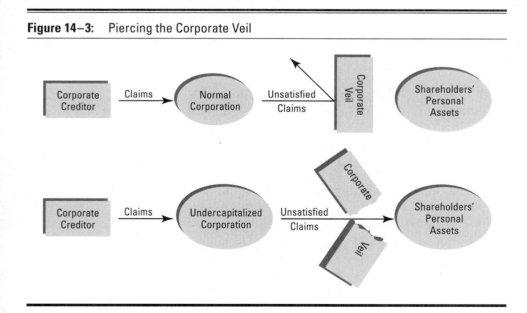

Subchapter S Corporations

The Internal Revenue Code permits corporations to avoid double taxation through the creation of a **Subchapter S Corporation.** When the shareholders elect this option, they are taxed like a partnership in that no corporate tax is paid. Corporate profits and losses are reported directly on the shareholders' individual tax returns. The corporation files only an informational return that indicates each shareholder's share of profits or losses. To qualify as a Subchapter S Corporation, there can be no more than 35 shareholders, all of whom must consent in writing to be taxed as a partnership.

Lessening the Corporate Tax Burden

In close corporations that don't qualify for Subchapter S treatment, shareholders who actively operate the business can lessen the burden of double taxation. As shareholder/employees they may receive salaries or wages. While the salaries are income to the shareholders, they are business deductions for the corporation. Further, fringe benefits like health insurance or retirement benefits can be provided to shareholder/employees if they are available to all employees. Their cost can be deducted by the corporation and their value is not immediately taxable to the shareholder/employees.

Transferability of Shares

Shareholders in close corporations seldom intend to have their shares sold to the public at large. They carefully selected their original business associates and have no wish to work with strangers in the future. As a result, shareholders of close corporations often insist on special restrictions on the transferability of shares. Courts normally enforce such restrictions if they are clear and reasonable. However, they are not enforceable against a shareholder unless she had notice of their existence. This normally is achieved by printing the terms of the restriction on the front or back of the stock certificate. Three of the more common restrictions on the transferability of shares are: option agreements, buyout agreements, and consent restraints.

Option Agreements

To maintain the balance of power and keep unwanted newcomers out of the corporation, the articles of incorporation may include an **option agreement.** Also known as a *right of first refusal,* this device gives the corporation or its shareholders (on a pro rata basis) the right to purchase shares offered for sale. The price may be whatever amount is offered by an outsider or a figure calculated by a preset formula measuring the fair market value of the stock.

Buyout Agreements

One concern with close corporations is that there is no ready market for the shares when a shareholder wishes to liquidate his holdings. Few people are interested in buying into a small business dominated by strangers. A **buyout agreement** addresses this problem by requiring the corporation or the remaining sharehold-

Rosiny v. Schmidt

587 N.Y.S.2d 929 (App. Div. N.Y. 1992)

FACTS   The Ched Corporation had a shareholders' agreement that provided that *"shareholders will not, during their lifetime, sell, assign, transfer, or pledge their stock unless it is first offered to the other shareholders. The price at which said stock shall be offered for sale shall be the book value thereof as of the last day of the month immediately preceding the date of said offer or $200 per share, whichever amount is greater. With regard to postmortem transfers, the surviving shareholders may buy the decedents' shares at the same price applicable to transfers during their lifetime."* When Priddy and McGuire died, their heirs claimed the right to inherit their shares of Ched stock. They claimed that the postmortem buyout provision in the shareholders' agreement was unenforceable because the other shareholder, Rosiny, was an attorney, while Priddy and McGuire were elderly and less educated.

ISSUE   Should the court enforce the buyout agreement?

DECISION   Yes. Priddy, a former bookkeeper who was later an office manager, agreed to return to a book value formula after her husband had signed an earlier agreement with a fair market value approach. McGuire, who ran a successful business for many years, had specifically rejected the fair market value approach when he signed the present buyout agreement. Any claim that Rosiny exerted deceptive or high-pressure tactics to induce Priddy and McGuire to sign is not borne out by the record. While the buyout formula now permits Rosiny to purchase the shares at a price considerably lower than their fair market value, the validity of the provision does not rest on any abstract notion of intrinsic fairness of price. To be invalid, more than mere disparity between the buyout price and the current value of the stock must be shown. However, the record fails to support the absence of meaningful choice on the part of Priddy and McGuire when they signed the agreement. It is true that in a close corporation shareholders must deal in good faith in conducting the affairs of the corporation. However, there is no dictate requiring one shareholder to explain a provision of a buyout agreement to another. No fiduciary agreement is created by a shareholders' agreement containing a mandatory buyout provision.

ers to purchase the shares upon the death or retirement of a shareholder. As with option agreements, the buyout agreement normally contains a predetermined formula for calculating the purchase price.

Consent Restraints

Close corporations can maintain the balance of power and keep out unwanted persons through the use of **consent restraints.** These devices are useful in controlling the number of shareholders, perhaps to preserve the entity's status as a Subchapter S Corporation. Consent restraints require shareholders to gain the permission of the other shareholders before they may sell shares to anyone other than the corporation or to the current shareholders on a pro rata basis.

Termination of the Corporation

Corporations may be dissolved upon the written consent of all of the shareholders. They may be involuntarily dissolved if they don't pay their annual franchise taxes or fail to file an annual report with the state. In instances where the majority shareholders are oppressing the minority shareholders or the shareholders are hopelessly deadlocked and can no longer transact business, the courts may dissolve a corporation. Finally, creditors may convince a court to dissolve a corporation if it is insolvent and unable to pay its debts.

Limited Partnerships

The **limited partnership** is a variation of the general partnership form of business structure. It often is selected by people interested in passive investments, like real estate. The limited partnership was designed to offer passive investors the limited liability feature available to corporate shareholders.

Creating a Limited Partnership

A limited partnership cannot be formed (or continued) unless it has at least one **general partner** and one **limited partner.** There also are precise legal rules governing its existence. For instance, the business must file a **limited partnership certificate** with the state. This document describes the nature of the business, the location of operations, and the duration of its existence.

The limited partnership certificate also must contain specific information about the partners. It must give their names, addresses, and the capital contributions each made. Further, it must make clear which of the individuals are general partners and which are limited partners. The certificate also must identify the circumstances that permit a partner to withdraw from the limited partnership.

Liability in Limited Partnerships

The rights and liabilities of general partners in a limited partnership essentially are the same as those of partners in a general partnership. However, the rules governing limited partners are different. First, unlike general partners, limited partners are not agents of the limited partnership. Thus, they have no automatic authority to bind the business on contracts and owe the enterprise no agency duties. Second, and most important, limited partners do not have personal liability on partnership debts. If the limited partnership's assets are insufficient to pay the claims of creditors, the limited partners need not fear losing their personal assets. General partners, on the other hand, have unlimited personal liability on business debts.

If the business fails to properly file a limited partnership certificate, the limited partners may lose their limited liability. Some states protect the limited partners who immediately renounce any interests in the business profits upon discovering the filing error. Others require them either to immediately file a proper certificate or stop accepting distributions of profits. However, they will have unlimited personal liability to creditors who contract with the business under the good-faith belief that it was a general partnership. (See Figure 14–4.)

8 Brookwood Fund v. Sloate

539 N.Y.S.2D 411 (APP. DIV. N.Y. 1989)

FACTS Brookwood was a limited partnership created for the purpose of trading investment securities. Although new limited partners were added to the limited partnership, the limited partnership certificate did not reflect this fact on October 19th when the stock market crashed and Brookwood was unable to pay all of its creditors. On October 23rd, Brookwood filed an amended certificate that properly identified the new limited partners. Brookwood's creditors claimed the failure to have a proper certificate on file at the time of the stock market crash stripped the limited partners of limited liability. As soon as Barbara Stein, one of the limited partners, learned of the lawsuit against her, she renounced all interests in the profits of the business.

ISSUE Is Barbara personally liable on Brookwood's debts?

DECISION No. The governing law holds that a person who erroneously believes she has become a limited partner is not bound by the obligations of the partnership if, upon discovering her mistake, she promptly renounces her interest in the profits of the business. As soon as Barbara learned of the action against her, she renounced her interests in the profits of Brookwood. To find Barbara personally liable on partnership debts that arose before her renunciation, the creditors must prove they did business with Brookwood in reliance on the belief that Barbara was a general partner. This was not the case.

Managing the Limited Partnership

Only the general partners may manage a limited partnership, although there are some limits on their control. For instance, the general partners are *fiduciaries* of the enterprise. As such, they must act in the best interests of the limited partnership

Figure 14–4: Rights of Limited Partnership Creditor

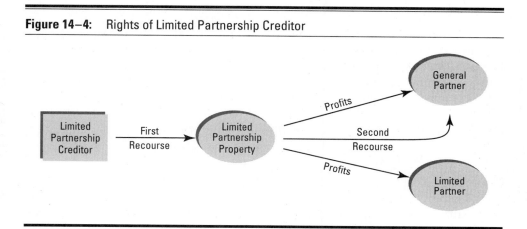

rather than pursuing their own personal interests. Further, they may not add new general partners without the unanimous consent of the limited partners. And they may not add new limited partners unless that power was reserved in the limited partnership certificate.

Limited partners who actively manage the business are treated as general partners. This does not prevent them from making suggestions to the general partners. They also may vote on major decisions such as dissolution, sale of all of the assets, or adding a general partner. However, limited partners must avoid participating in the day-to-day management decisions of the enterprise or they may lose their limited liability.

Limited Partnership Taxation

Limited partnerships share the tax advantages of general partnerships. However, they offer special advantages to limited partners who wish to make passive investments in real estate. The limited partner is entitled to deduct any business losses as well as any real estate deductions from his other sources of income.

Emerging Forms of Business Organization

In recent years, various states have enacted laws allowing the creation of hybrid forms of business organization. There are two particular forms that merit discussion here. They are limited liability companies and limited liability partnerships.

Limited Liability Companies

Limited liability companies (LLCs) combine the taxation characteristics of partnerships with the limited liability features of corporations. They differ from limited partnerships in that all of the investors in an LLC are able to participate in day-to-day management. And, unlike S Corporations, there are no limits on the number of members an LLC may have.

Creating an LLC

The formalities involved in creating an LLC are similar to the requirements for corporations and limited partnerships. The articles of the LLC must be filed with the state. The business name must include either the words "limited liability company" or some other indication of its limited liability feature. In many states, the LLC is required to publicly file an annual report. At least four states (California, Delaware, Oregon, and Rhode Island) do not permit professionals (doctors, lawyers, accountants, etc.) to operate their business as an LLC.

Managing the LLC

Members of an LLC may actively manage the business without fear of losing their limited liability. They may share in the management in proportion to their capital contributions. However, LLC members frequently elect a manager or a management team to operate the business.

LLC Taxation

The IRS treatment of LLCs depends on the nature of each state's LLC statute. Unless the LLC is set up so that it can easily be dissolved, the IRS will not afford it the single-tax treatment available to partnerships. For this reason, like partnerships, LLCs normally are dissolved upon the death, retirement, or bankruptcy of any member. However, the business need not be terminated if the other members unanimously agree on a continuation.

In S Corporations, profits and losses are apportioned for tax purposes based on each shareholder's investment in the corporation. Thus, a shareholder with 30 percent of the corporation's shares is allocated 30 percent of the corporation's profits or losses. The IRS allows LLCs more flexibility in the allocation of profits and losses. If the members agree, the LLC could pay 50 percent of its profits to a member who owned only a 30 percent interest but provided extensive services to the business.

Limited Liability Partnerships

Facing growing numbers of costly lawsuits, the major accounting firms sought a new kind of business structure to shield partners' personal assets from malpractice claims. The states responded by permitting the formation of **limited liability partnerships** (LLP). In recent years, many law firms have begun joining the accounting profession in making the switch from general partnerships and professional corporations to limited liability partnerships.

Creating an LLP

LLPs are relatively easy to organize around an existing partnership. The partners need merely file an LLP form with the state and then maintain an adequate amount of professional liability insurance. After this is done, the personal assets of partners not involved in wrongdoing by other members of the firm will be sheltered from malpractice claims against the firm. Partners who are directly involved in the litigation (those who actually committed the malpractice) still have unlimited personal liability.

Managing the LLP

As with general partnerships, all of the partners in an LLP have equal say in its management. Of course, this can be altered by agreement. New partners cannot join the LLP without the unanimous consent of the current partners.

LLP Taxation

LLPs are taxed like general partnerships. The LLP pays no income taxes. Instead, each partner reports her share of the LLP's profits and losses on her personal tax return.

Franchising

Some bright and well-motivated individuals would make outstanding business owners, but lack the vision and initiative to build a new business from the ground up. These people may be interested in **franchising.** The franchising relationship is contractual in nature. For a fee, the franchisor grants the right to sell an established product and, in the case of *business format franchising,* also provides a proven method to sell successfully.

Franchising may be the most common way of conducting business today. Look around and you will see franchises everywhere. Examples include gas stations, fast-food restaurants, motels, tax preparers, transmission shops, automobile dealers, and car washes. In fact, the success rate for franchisees has been estimated as three times greater than for starting up a business alone. While franchisees generally conduct business as corporations, they can use any of the forms of business organization discussed earlier.

The Franchise Agreement

The **franchise agreement** is the contract that lays out the basic terms governing the relationship. These include the franchise fee. For a successful franchise, the fee generally runs into six figures. The agreement is likely to require the franchisee to pay a percentage of its weekly or monthly sales in addition to the fixed fee. Franchise agreements should also spell out the length of the relationship. This may be for a five-year or longer time period. Most franchisors reserve the right to terminate a franchisee for good cause. However, franchisees should carefully review the agreement. For example, in recent years the Subway sandwich-shop chain has offered a standard franchise agreement that gives the franchisor the right to repurchase franchises at any time with only 30 days' notice.

Many inexperienced people have suffered financial ruin after believing the exaggerated claims of fraudulent franchisors. Others have suffered large financial losses after being unfairly terminated by their franchisor. Accordingly, people should consult a marketing consultant, an accountant, and a franchise attorney before signing a franchise agreement. They can assess market conditions, the financial stability of the franchisor, and the rights and obligations contained in the franchise agreement.

Protection of Franchisees

Some franchisees have lost their life savings to unscrupulous franchisors who grossly misrepresented the opportunities for success or the assistance the franchisor would provide. Others blindly sign the franchise agreement and later are shocked to discover how harsh its terms are. The Small Business Administration believed the termination provision in the Subway franchise agreements (discussed above) to be so restrictive that it refused to guarantee loans to franchisees who signed it. In response, Subway agreed to amend the agreement, but only for franchisees seeking Small Business Administration assistance.

Both the federal and state governments regulate franchising relationships. For instance, the Federal Trade Commission requires franchisors to provide prospective franchisees with copies of the franchise agreement. And franchisees must be given a **franchise offering circular,** which discloses important details about the franchise as well as the legal and financial background of the franchisor. Many states impose even stricter disclosure requirements. Finally, federal law establishes a 10-day "cooling-off" period during which a franchisee can change her mind about entering into the franchise agreement.

Sperau v. Ford Motor Company

674 So. 2d24 (Sup. Ct. Ala. 1995)

FACTS   Samuel Foster and Dee-Witt Sperau, both African-Americans, were engaged in the construction business when Ford Motor Company recruited them to open an Alabama dealership. Recruiting African-Americans as franchised dealers was part of Ford's nationwide minority dealer program. When they initially rejected Ford's overtures, the company reduced the capital required to operate the dealership from $632,000 to $535,000 and increased the estimated return on capital from 56 percent to 65.4 percent. Ford also told them the vast majority of black dealers were successful in making a profit. Ford did not disclose the substance of its equal-opportunity progress reports. This data made clear that the return on investment for black dealers was substantially lower than the average for all dealers. Further, a higher percentage of black dealers historically were in a loss position compared to the percentage of all dealers. Ford routinely withheld this information from black dealer candidates. When Foster's and Sperau's dealership went bankrupt after three years, they sued Ford for fraud and deceit for failing to disclose the substantial likelihood of failure of black franchisees.

ISSUE   Did Ford breach a duty to disclose the actual profitability performance and failure rates of its black franchisees?

DECISION   Yes. There was evidence from which the jury could find by a clear and convincing standard that Ford defrauded the two men. It used sales and profit forecasts and capitalization requirements which were deceptive based upon the actual facts known to Ford. At the same time the company was actively recruiting black franchisee candidates with sales and returns on profit forecasts of 65.4 percent, it was informing its Board of Directors that it expected those same new black dealers to suffer losses. Ford occupied a superior position with respect to this historical information. Foster and Sperau did not have this data at their disposal and, therefore, had to rely on Ford's statements. Even in a commercial setting involving educated, sophisticated businessmen like Foster and Sperau, Ford was under a duty to make a full and fair disclosure.

Franchisor Concerns

Franchising provides franchisors with an opportunity to expand by using the resources of the franchisees. Through a comprehensive franchise agreement, the franchisor still may maintain considerable control over the distribution of its products or services. However, if the control is too pervasive, courts may hold the franchisor liable for torts and crimes committed by the franchisee and its employees.

Regulatory Issues Affecting the Business

Up to this point we have focused on the structural aspects of starting a business. However, there are many other issues that must be considered regardless of the form of business organization. This final section explores three regulatory matters that should be investigated before setting up operations: licensing requirements, zoning restrictions, and naming the business.

Licensing Requirements

http://
osdbu.treas.gov is
the U.S. Treasury
site for registering
a business.

It is essential for prospective business owners to determine what types of permits are required before opening their doors, since all levels of government (federal, state, and local) may impose some type of licensing requirement. While it often is difficult to discover precisely what licenses are necessary, it is safe to assume there will be extensive licensing involved in particular occupations (restaurants, bars, and liquor stores). Business owners are advised to contact lawyers, accountants, the IRS, the state department of revenue, and the chamber of commerce for assistance.

Federal Requirements

Federal requirements are minimal for most small businesses. First, business owners should apply for an *employer identification number* from the Internal Revenue Service. Second, close corporations wishing to be taxed as partnerships must file for status as a Subchapter S Corporation. Otherwise, unless the business is engaged in transportation, alcohol, firearms, or communication, there probably are no federal permits required. (See Figure 14–5.)

State Requirements

There are several key areas where one should expect to find state licensing requirements. First, most states require businesses to obtain a license to collect sales taxes. They also may require an income tax registration similar to the federal employer identification number. People engaged in a broad range of occupations (doctors, accountants, hairdressers, real estate agents) probably need a state permit to practice their trade. Finally, businesses that use employees may need to register to ensure that they comply with workers' compensation and unemployment compensation requirements.

Local Requirements

The city or county planning department and the clerk's office may have useful information on any required local permits. Further, local governments often tax business equipment and, as a result, require a personal property filing each year. Many cities have a department that monitors the erection of new structures as well as the remodeling of existing buildings. It is likely to require any number of permits before any construction is permitted. Sometimes the local fire department is able to assist in contacting the appropriate governmental officials.

Zoning Restrictions

Imagine signing a long-term lease to run your new business at a particular location and then learning that a local zoning ordinance prohibits conducting business there. This could be financially devastating. For this reason, it is essential that you fully understand local regulations before settling on a business site.

Cities commonly regulate the type of business that may operate in a given area. And many communities only allow a business to open if it provides a set number of off-street parking spaces. To the frustration of new business owners,

Figure 14–5: Employer I.D. Number

APPLICATION FOR EMPLOYER IDENTIFICATION NUMBER

EIN _____

1.   Applicant Name: _____

2.   Trade Name, if different: _____

3.   "Care of" Name: _____

4a.   Address: _____

4b.   City, State, Zip: _____, _____ _____

5a.   Business Address, if different: _____

5b.   City, State, Zip: _____, _____ _____

6.   County, State: _____, _____

7.   Name of Principal Officer: _____ SSN: _____

8a.   Type of Entity (check only one): _____ SSN: _____

8b.   If corporation, State, Country of Incorporation: _____

9.   Reason for applying: Started new business: specify: _____

10.   Date business started or acquired: _____

11.   Closing month of accounting year: _____

12.   First date wages or annuities were or will be paid: _____

13.   Highest number or employees expected in the next twelve months:
       Non-Agricultural: _____   Agricultural: _____   Household: _____

14.   Principlal Activity: _____
       Will the Applicant's business involve the sale of alcohol? Yes

15.   Is the Applicant's principal activity manufacturing? Yes
       What is the principal product and raw material used? _____

16.   To whom are the products sold? Businesses

17a.   Has the Applicant applied for EIN previously? Yes

17b.   Enter the applicant's legal name on prior application: _____
        Enter the applicant's trade name on prior application: _____

17c.   Date on which previous application was filed: October 27, 1997
        City in which a previous application was filed: _____
        State in which a previous application was filed: _____
        Previous EIN: _____

Under the penalties of perjury, I declare that I have examined this application, and to the best of my knowledge and belief, it is true, correct, and complete.

Name: _____

Title: _____

Business Telephone Number: _____

Signature: _____

Date: _____

these restrictions often favor established enterprises. For example, after Randy bought a tavern from Isaac, he was shocked to discover that local rules prohibited smoking in his establishment. When the ordinance was enacted, Isaac's tavern and all other existing bars were exempted (grandfathered) from its effect. However, new businesses or purchasers of the current taverns were covered by the law.

There are two primary options open to someone confronted by crippling zoning rules. First, especially in cities that are actively courting new businesses, it may be possible to informally persuade local officials to interpret the ordinance in a way that less interferes with your operations. Second, the business may qualify for *variance* if it can be shown that the ordinance creates an undue hardship by depriving the owner of reasonable use of the property.

Naming the Business

Legal formalities may be involved in selecting a name for a new enterprise. If the business uses a name other than that of its owner, that name must be registered under the state's *fictitious name statute*. And, for a small fee, it is possible to have a statewide or national search conducted to ensure that this name is not the same as, or confusingly similar to, one used by another business. If it is not, the owner may decide to register the name on the federal register of trademarks to acquire exclusive rights to it.

QUESTIONS AND PROBLEM CASES

1. When is a limited partner liable for more than her investment in a limited partnership?

2. Why might a person elect to invest in a close corporation rather than a limited partnership?

3. In a general partnership, what is the importance of the articles of partnership? When are they required?

4. Explain the federal income tax liability of a general partnership.

5. Schymanski and Conventz became equal partners in a business for the purpose of building and operating a fishing lodge. Conventz was to supervise the construction of the lodge and handle the advertising in Alaska. Schymanski was to conduct a promotional campaign in Germany. After numerous delays and disagreements, Conventz demanded the partnership be dissolved. He also insisted on compensation for his architectural efforts, despite the fact that the oral partnership agreement was silent on that issue. Is Conventz entitled to compensation for his work?

6. After L. E. Ward's death, his widow, three children, and a grandson formed a corporation, Ward Farms, Inc., to hold the family farmlands. Leroy Ward controlled 50 percent of the corporation. Throughout the life of the corporation, numerous conflicts existed between Leroy and the other shareholders. Because they could never reach an agreement, a dividend was never declared. Several lawsuits were instituted among the shareholders concerning corporate affairs. Leroy petitioned the court to dissolve the corporation. Should the court dissolve Ward Farms?

7. Margo Neff is disabled and requires a wheelchair to gain mobility. She filed suit against American Dairy Queen Corporation alleging that the Dairy Queen retail outlets in San Antonio had numerous barriers that made those stores inaccessible to the disabled. The *Americans with Disabilities Act* requires an individual who "operates a place of public accommodation" to provide full and equal enjoyment of its facilities. American Dairy

Queen argued that it was not responsible for removing the barriers because it did not own, lease, or operate the stores. As evidence it offered copies of its franchise agreements with the local franchisees who ran the retail outlets. Neff contended that the terms of the franchise agreements supported her claim that American Dairy Queen retained sufficient control over the operation of the San Antonio stores to make it an operator of the stores for the purposes of the statute. Specifically, the franchise agreement gave American Dairy Queen the power to veto modifications to the stores' facilities. Does American Dairy Queen's veto power make it an "operator" of the restaurant and therefore responsible for compliance with the equal-access requirements of the federal statute?

8. Scott entered into a five-year employment contract with Baca Grande Corporation, a resort that was owned by AZL Resources, Inc. During Scott's employment, Baca Grande owned some assets; however, it maintained separate corporate and financial records at AZL's corporate offices. Baca Grande often operated with a "zero bank account" and frequently required loans from AZL; however, there was no evidence that it was undercapitalized when it was formed. When Scott was fired from his position, he sued AZL (Baca Grande's sole shareholder) for breach of contract. Is AZL liable for Baca Grande's financial obligations to Scott?

9. Paul Swanson owned 25 shares and Robert Shockley owned 75 shares in North Central Adjustment Co., Inc. Shockley, the majority shareholder, sold his shares to John Davis, who was not and never had been a shareholder in the corporation. Davis agreed to pay $90,000 for the stock in installments payable over a 10-year period. Swanson brought suit, alleging that the sale was in violation of a bylaw restricting sales of the shares. The bylaw permitted sale of the stock only after the corporation and the other shareholders had been given the right of first refusal to purchase the shares at a formula price. The formula price for Shockley's 75 shares at the time of the sale to Davis was $7,500. Shockley defended his sale to Davis on the grounds that eight months prior to the sale, the bylaw containing the right of first refusal was repealed. In that vote, Shockley voted his shares in favor of the repeal, while Swanson, the minority shareholder, abstained. Is Swanson entitled to buy Shockley's shares at the formula price under the right of first refusal?

10. After 15 years of operating as a sole proprietorship, Randy Braswell incorporated the business. He formed a close corporation, Worldwide Machinery Sales, Inc., of which he was president and sole owner. Later, a federal grand jury issued a subpoena requiring Braswell to produce the books and records of the corporation. Braswell resisted on the grounds that such a requirement forced him to incriminate himself. Can the government require Braswell to produce the documents?

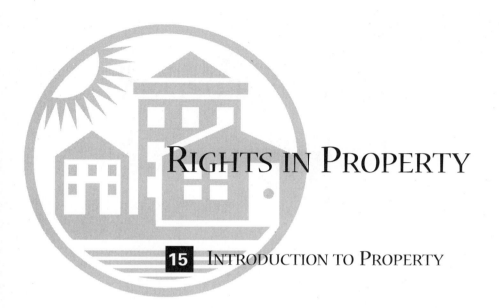

RIGHTS IN PROPERTY

INTRODUCTION TO PROPERTY

Steven York and Risa Adler-York could not achieve a pregnancy through normal coital reproduction. Accordingly, six eggs were removed from Risa and fertilized with Steven's sperm, creating six embryos. Five embryos were transferred to Risa's uterus and the sixth was cryogenically preserved at the Jones Institute for Reproductive Medicine. None of the fertilization efforts resulted in pregnancy. Because the Yorks were dissatisfied with the results of the efforts at the Jones Institute, they requested that the frozen pre-zygote be transferred to another institute. The Jones Institute refused to do this. The Yorks sued for possession of the pre-zygote, claiming the Jones Institute was violating the duties imposed by bailment law.

York v. Jones, 717 F.Supp. 421 (E.D. Va. 1989).

Did the Yorks have a property interest in the pre-zygote?
Was there a bailor-bailee relationship between the Yorks and the Jones Institute?
What are the rights and duties imposed by the law of bailments?

Introduction ▬▬▬▬▬▬▬▬▬▬▬▬▬▬▬

In this country, the concept of property is extremely important. The Constitution itself prohibits the government from taking a person's property without due process of law. Yet, despite the importance most people attach to their property rights, few fully understand the breadth of the term "property." It may refer to a car, a building, or a plot of land. It might also encompass some intangible notion such as a tenant's rights created by a lease with a landlord.

Legally, property ownership is considered to be a *bundle of rights recognized and enforced by society.* This definition recognizes that more than one person can have legal rights in the same property. The law of property was established to regulate these varied, and sometimes conflicting, rights.

Chapter Overview

This chapter focuses on personal property, bailments, wills, and trusts. A discussion of the real-property issues involved in buying a home is reserved for Chapter 16. Landlord-tenant law (renting apartments) is presented in Chapter 17.

The chapter begins by introducing the basic types of property recognized by the legal system. It next looks at various ways of legally acquiring ownership of personal property. This is followed by an examination of the law of bailments. The chapter closes with an overview of the rules governing inheritance and trusts.

Kinds of Property ▬▬▬▬▬▬▬▬▬▬

The law classifies property based on its general characteristics. This classification can be important because it may determine many of the rules governing acquisition and control of the property. As you should quickly discover, the same property frequently falls into more than one category.

Physical Characteristics Classifications

Property sometimes is categorized based on its physical characteristics. For instance, land, automobiles, and clothing all have a physical existence and therefore are classified as **tangible property.** Accounts receivable, patents, and easements, on the other hand, have no physical existence. They are classified as **intangible property.** Tangible property is taxed in the state where it is located, while intangibles are taxed in the state where their owner permanently resides.

Real Property

The earth's crust and all things firmly attached to it are known as **real property.** Thus, a plot of land is real property because it is part of the earth's crust. Similarly, a tree growing on the land or a house built on the parcel also are real property. They are firmly attached to the land. When a person dies without leaving a will, her real property is distributed according to the laws where the property was located.

http://
www.yahoo.com is the Internet address for Yahoo!, an online search engine. From here, initiate a search for "personal property" topics.

Personal Property

All things that are not real property (things other than the earth's crust and the objects firmly attached to it) are known as **personal property.** Thus, a car, clothing, and an umbrella all are personal property. Upon death, the laws of the state where a person permanently resides govern the disposition of the personal property. Sometimes an object may shift between the real and personal property classifications. For instance, when a tree is growing in the woods it is real property because it is firmly attached to the earth's crust. Once the tree is chopped down and cut into lumber, it is transformed into personal property. But if the lumber is used to build a house, it becomes real property because it is once again firmly attached to the earth's crust.

Fixtures

Personal property that is firmly attached to the earth's crust, and thereby becomes real property, is known as a **fixture.** Sometimes, however, it is not clear if the personal property is so firmly attached to the real property that it becomes part of the real property itself. As we have noted, that may be important in determining how the property is handled upon the death of the owner. But it is significant for other reasons as well. Suppose Brandon agrees to buy a house from Nicole. Part of Brandon's attraction to the house may have been the wet bar in the den. If the wet bar is not a fixture, Nicole may remove it upon selling the house. If it is a fixture, it must remain with the house. Whether or not an object becomes a fixture is dependent upon three primary factors: (1) intent, (2) attachment, and (3) appropriateness.

Intent

The parties to a contract generally may mutually decide whether an object is to be treated as a fixture. Thus, even if the wet bar was firmly attached to the house, Nicole and Brandon could have agreed in their contract that she had the right to remove it. Or if it was not clearly attached, Brandon still may have insisted that she agree to leave it behind as one of the terms of his offer to buy the house.

When a homeowner attaches personal property to a house, there is a presumption that it was intended to be a fixture. However, when personal property is attached to the real property in a business lease, it is treated as a *trade fixture.* At the termination of the lease, a trade fixture is treated as personal property unless its removal would substantially destroy the value of the real property. Further, if trade fixtures are not removed before the lease expires, they are treated as the property of the landlord.

Attachment

The intent of the parties often can be implied from the manner in which the personal property is attached to the real property. For instance, if removing the wet bar would leave a gaping hole in the wall or floor of the den, a court would presume that the parties intended that it remain. But if its removal would not be conspicuous or cause damage to the house, it would not be considered a fixture.

Appropriateness

Courts also consider the appropriateness of the personal property to the underlying real property when determining if it is a fixture. For instance, suppose a homeowner installed a dishwasher, oven, and refrigerator with matching colors and designs in his kitchen. The oven and dishwasher were permanently installed into the walls, while the refrigerator was standing freely in a corner of the kitchen. A court may well treat the refrigerator as a fixture even though it was not firmly attached to the house. This is because its use was so consistent with the other appliances that a reasonable buyer might expect it to remain with the house.

In Re Sheetz
657 A.2d 1011 (Cmwlth. Ct. Pa. 1995)

FACTS   Sheetz, Inc., owns and operates convenience stores in Pennsylvania. Each store consists of a one-story building, gasoline pumps, a parking area, and a lighted canopy over the pumps. The canopies are used to protect the pumps and its customers from inclement weather. They are large metal structures with poured concrete foundations. The canopies are fabricated off the premises and can be and have been relocated with relative ease from one store to another. Weighing between 20 and 35 tons each, the canopies are mounted on pillars attached to the ground by bolts sunk in poured concrete foundations that, in turn, are also covered with concrete. For tax purposes, Sheetz classified the canopies as personal property. However, the Pennsylvania Board of Tax Assessment determined that the canopies were real property. Sheetz argued that because the canopies could be removed with little damage to the land, they are personal, rather than real, property.

ISSUE   Are the canopies real property?

DECISION   Yes. A fixture is an article in the nature of personal property which has been so attached to the realty that it is regarded as part and parcel of the land. The considerations to be made in determining whether or not personal property becomes a fixture include (1) the manner in which it is physically attached or installed, (2) the extent to which it is essential to the permanent use of the building, and (3) the intention of the parties who attached or installed it. As to the first consideration—the manner in which the article has been installed—while a canopy can be removed with little damage to the real property, to remove it would require significant effort. As to the second factor—whether it is essential to the use of the improvement—canopies are a customary and usual part of a gasoline station to protect customers and pumps from the elements. Sheetz's chief financial officer testified the canopies were needed to improve Sheetz's overall image or customer perception of product quality. Further, they provided significant improvement in lighting the sales area and customer parking lots to offer a safer environment. Finally, of paramount importance is the intention of the parties when they attach property and whether they want it to be a permanent part of the real property. The prior considerations—the manner in which the property is attached and the reason it is done in the particular situation—can be looked at as merely objective manifestations that aid in determining the intention of the parties. Just because the canopies can and have been removed does not mean the intention was not to make them permanent. Nothing in the record indicated that anyone intended to remove them as long as the property was being used as a convenience store selling gasoline. They are an integral part of Sheetz's property and will be attached until worn out or Sheetz no longer occupies the premises. As such, they are part of the real property and are taxable as such.

Acquisition of Personal Property

http://
tenant.net/Other_
Areas/Oklahoma/
ocsa10.html contains
a sample personal
property inventory
worksheet.

This section examines the various ways in which a person may acquire ownership rights in personal property. The discussion of acquisition by will or inheritance is reserved until later in the chapter. The means of acquiring ownership of homes and other real property is discussed in Chapter 16, while the acquisition of lease-hold interests is explained in Chapter 17.

Production

People generally own the property they produce. However, this right can be waived if they have agreed to produce items for someone else. This sometimes causes disputes when workers discover new inventions and seek to profit from their creativity. When an employee produces property with her employer's equipment and is acting within the time, space, and scope of her employment, there is a strong presumption that the property belongs to the employer. However, in all such cases, the employment agreement between the parties should be examined to determine who possesses the property.

Purchase

An extremely common method of gaining ownership of personal property is by purchase. Acquisition of tangible, personal property (goods) by purchase is governed by sales law—a special branch of contract law. (The law of sales is introduced in Chapter 8.)

A general rule of property and sales law is that a purchaser can obtain no greater rights than were possessed by his seller. Suppose Tom steals a guitar from Owen and sells it to Beth. Because Tom's rights to the guitar were inferior to Owen's, Owen also has greater rights than Beth. Thus, if Owen discovers that Beth has the guitar, he can recover it from her and she will have to sue Tom for the return of her money. (See Figure 15–1.) There are two important exceptions to this rule: transfers of voidable title and the entrusting rule.

Figure 15–1:   Purchasing Stolen Property

A = original owner
B = thief
C = purchaser

Where goods are forcibly stolen and sold	Where goods are taken by fraud or entrusted to a merchant
A > B	A > B
B = C	B < C
A > C	A < C
A regains possession of the goods	C retains possession of the goods

Voidable Title

Suppose Tom stole some checks from Aaron. He then impersonated Aaron and bought the guitar from Owen, paying for the guitar by forging one of Aaron's checks. Under these circumstances, Tom has **voidable title** to the guitar. Tom later sold the guitar to Beth. Under sales law, a seller with voidable title can pass good title to a **good-faith purchaser for value.** If Beth paid a fair price for the guitar and was unaware of Tom's fraud, she will have acquired good title and need not return the guitar to Owen. He will have to sue Tom for damages.

Alsafi Oriental Rugs v. American Loan Company

864 S.W.2d 41 (Ct. App. Tenn. 1993)

FACTS   Arlene Bradley convinced the owner of Alsafi Oriental Rugs that she was an interior decorator who wanted to sell some of his rugs to one of her customers. Despite never having met or done business with Bradley before, the owner allowed her to take three rugs on the condition that she would return them if her customer did not wish to buy them. In reality, Bradley worked for a rug dealer, Walid Salaam, who had convinced her to "check out" rugs on approval from other rug dealers in town. Bradley turned the three rugs over to Salaam, who took them to a pawnshop operated by the American Loan Company. He received $5,000 for them. When Alsafi discovered that the rugs were at the pawnshop, he brought suit to recover possession of them.

ISSUE   Is the pawnshop required to return the rugs to Alsafi?

DECISION   No. A person with voidable title has the power to transfer good title to a good-faith purchaser who pays value for the goods. Here, Bradley obtained the rugs through a voluntary transfer of possession and not through any wrongful nonpermissive taking of the goods. As such, she had voidable title to them and was empowered to pass title to Salaam. He in turn passed title to American Loan Company. It was a good-faith purchaser for value since it had no actual knowledge or reason to believe that Salaam was not the true owner of the rugs.

Entrusting Rule

Sales law also has an **entrusting rule** that acts as a major exception to the notion that a person can transfer no greater rights in property than he possesses. Suppose Owen had left his guitar in Tom's guitar store to have it repaired. If Tom fraudulently sold it to Beth, who was a normal customer (buyer in the ordinary course of business), she would acquire good title to the guitar. Owen will have to sue Tom for monetary damages. The entrusting rule holds that anyone who entrusts goods to a merchant who regularly deals in goods of that type gives the merchant the power to transfer good title to a buyer in the ordinary course of business.

Unowned Property

The first person who takes possession of unowned property generally becomes its owner. For instance, Karen becomes the owner of a wild animal if she exercises enough control over it to deprive it of its freedom. For this reason, the first hunter to trap or kill a wild animal owns it. Of course, state and federal laws may govern when or if wild animals may be acquired. And if a trespasser catches or kills a wild animal on someone else's land, the land owner generally owns the animal. Today, the only major category of unowned property, other than wild animals, is abandoned property (discussed below).

Found Property

When a person finds property, questions arise over the rights and duties of the finder. Those rights and responsibilities depend on how the found property is classified. There are four categories of found property: (1) abandoned property, (2) lost property, (3) mislaid property, and (4) treasure trove. (See Figure 15–2.)

Abandoned Property

When an owner no longer wants to possess property, it is considered to be **abandoned property.** When the original owner intentionally discards property in such a way as to indicate he is voluntarily relinquishing all right, title, and interest in it, the property is abandoned. It then becomes a type of unowned property and belongs to its finder. However, if abandoned property is embedded in the soil, it belongs to the owner of the land where it is located.

Lost Property

Property is lost when its owner unintentionally and involuntarily parts with its possession and does not know where it is. Stolen property that is found by someone who did not participate in the theft is considered to be **lost property.** However, if a finder of lost property discovers the identity of the owner and fails to return the property, she has committed the crime and intentional tort of conversion. This may also be true if she knows of a reasonable means of discovering the identity of the owner and fails to try. Many states have statutes requiring finders of lost property to place a notice in a local newspaper. Then if the owner does not appear within a prescribed period (often one year), the finder becomes the owner of the lost property.

Mislaid Property

Sometimes a person voluntarily puts property in a particular place and then overlooks or forgets where it is. This is known as **mislaid property.** It differs from lost property in that its owner voluntarily and intentionally placed the mislaid property in the location where it was eventually found by another. In contrast, property is not considered lost unless the owner parts with it involuntarily.

The finder of mislaid property does not own it. Instead, the right of possession to mislaid property belongs to the owner of the premises where it was found. He is expected to hold the property until its true owner returns for it. This rule was created because it is likely that the true owner may someday remember where

Figure 15–2:   Found Property

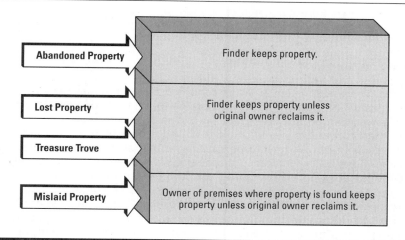

the property was mislaid and return for it. However, each state has enacted laws that require the true owner to claim it within a certain time period (frequently one year). Otherwise, the owner of the premises becomes the owner.

Treasure Trove

Some found property is classified as **treasure trove.** It consists of coins and currency that were concealed by their owner. It becomes treasure trove if the property must have been hidden or concealed for such a length of time that its true owner is probably dead or undiscoverable. Like lost property, treasure trove belongs to the finder unless the true owner appears within a statutorily prescribed time.

Benjamin v. Lindner Aviation
534 N.W.2D 400 (SUP. CT. IOWA 1995)

FACTS   In April 1992, State Central Bank became the owner of an airplane when the bank repossessed it from its prior owner who had defaulted on a loan. In August 1992, the bank took the plane to Lindner Aviation for a routine annual inspection. Heath Benjamin, an employee of Lindner, conducted the inspection. As part of the inspection, he removed panels from the underside of the wings. Although these panels were to be removed annually as part of the routine inspection, a couple of screws holding the panel on the left wing were so rusty that Benjamin had to use a drill to remove it. Inside the left wing, he discovered two packets wrapped in aluminum foil. Inside the foil was over $18,000 in currency, tied in string and wrapped in handkerchiefs. The money was predominately twenty-dollar bills with mint dates before the 1960s, primarily in the 1950s. The money, which smelled musty, was turned over to the police. After nobody came forward within 12 months, a dispute arose over who was entitled to it. Benjamin claimed it was his since the money was treasure trove or

continued

was lost or abandoned. Lindner argued the money was mislaid and, as the owner of the premises on which the money was found (the hangar where the plane was parked), it now owned the money. State Central Bank also contended that the money was mislaid. However, it asserted that the plane was the premises where it was found and, as owner of the plane, it now owned the money.

ISSUE   Is the bank the owner of the money?

DECISION   Yes. There is substantial evidence to find that the money discovered by Benjamin was mislaid property. The place where he found the money and the manner in which it was hidden are important here. The bills were carefully tied and wrapped and then concealed in a location that was accessible only by removing screws and a panel. These circumstances support an inference that the money was placed there intentionally. This inference supports the conclusion that the money was mislaid. The money does not appear to be lost. The circumstances do not indicate that it was placed in the wing unintentionally. And there is no evidence suggesting the money was placed in the wing by someone other than the owner. It is not abandoned because both logic and common sense suggest that it is unlikely someone would voluntarily part with over $18,000 with the intention of terminating his ownership. The location where the money was found is much more consistent with the conclusion that the owner was placing the money there for safekeeping. The mint dates, the musty odor, and the rusty condition of the screws indicate that the money must have been hidden for some time. However, the money was no older than 35 years. And the airplane had a well-documented ownership history. Under these circumstances, we cannot say that the money meets the antiquity requirement or that it is probable that its owner is not discoverable. Thus, it is not treasure trove. The money is mislaid property and the premises where it was found are the airplane, not Lindner Aviation's hangar. The policy behind giving ownership of mislaid property to the owner of the premises where the property was found supports this conclusion. If the true owner of the money attempts to locate it, he would initially look for the plane. It is unlikely he would begin his search by contacting businesses where the airplane might have been inspected.

http://www.findlaw.com/

———————————————————————— Ethical Issue ————————————————————————

Did the bank have a moral obligation to share this money with Benjamin or Lindner Aviation?

Gifts

h t t p ://
www.law.cornell.edu/
*topics/estate_gift_*
tax.html provides
information and links
on gift taxes.

Another means of acquiring property, both real and personal, is by gift. A gift occurs when the donor voluntarily transfers the property to the donee without receiving any consideration (payment) in return. The donee bears the burden of proving three elements when she claims to have received a gift: (1) intent, (2) delivery, and (3) acceptance.

The *intent* requirement is met if the donor wished to voluntarily transfer title of the property without contemplating any payment in return. However, merely desiring or promising to make a gift is not enough. There also must be actual or constructive *delivery*. This element occurs when the donor transfers dominion and control over the property. Actual delivery occurs when the donee or her agent takes physical possession of the property. Constructive delivery might arise if the donor gave the donee the contents of his safe-deposit box by handing her the key. The final requirement for a gift, *acceptance*, generally does not pose a problem. However, it might arise in defeating a gift if the donee shows that she rejected delivery of an unwanted gift.

—————————————————— Ethical Issue ——————————————————

A promise to make a gift is not enforceable; it must be delivered to be binding. Is it ethical to make such a promise and then not deliver the gift?

Kinds of Gifts

Most gifts are unconditional. That is, once the gift has been delivered, the donor cannot revoke it. Such a gift is called a gift **inter vivos**. There are two major exceptions to the notion that a gift is unconditional. The first arises with engagement rings and other gifts made in contemplation of marriage. Many states permit their revocation if the marriage does not take place. (These gifts are discussed in Chapter 18.)

Second, a gift made in contemplation of the donor's death may be conditional. This is known as a gift **causa mortis**. For instance, believing he will not survive a serious operation, Mark gives his cat to Susan and tells her to take care of it if he dies. Mark may revoke this gift *causa mortis* and regain the cat if (1) he recovers from the operation; (2) he changes his mind before he dies; or (3) Susan dies before Mark does. Figure 15–3 on page 348 illustrates the factors involved in acquiring property by gift.

Dastugue v. Fernan

662 So.2d 538 (Ct. App. La. 1995)

FACTS   When Paul Dastugue and Sharon Fernan were married, Dastugue gave her an engagement/wedding ring he had purchased from Aucoin Hart Jewelers for $10,730. Soon thereafter, the couple were divorced. At that time, Dastugue still owed Aucoin Hart $5,365.01 on the ring. Fernan returned the ring to the jeweler and was offered a store credit for the amount of the partial payment that had been made toward the purchase price. When she refused the credit, Aucoin Hart gave her a receipt indicating it was holding the ring. Later, Dastugue sent Fernan a poem lamenting the end of their marriage. It contained a passage which stated: *"So now it is my move and I fast agree—the ring is yours and I am free but you the one now bound."* Fernan took the letter to Aucoin Hart, who concurred with her belief that Dastugue was abandoning his claim to the ring. She traded the ring to the jeweler in return for a $5,000 credit. Dastugue claimed ownership in the ring.

continued

ISSUE   Does Dastugue own the ring?

DECISION   No. Whether the original donation of the ring was in contemplation of marriage is no longer relevant. This is because Dastugue made a second valid donation of the ring after the marriage ended. When the donor's will to give and the donee's physical possession of the movable property operate simultaneously, there is sufficient delivery to constitute a valid gift *inter vivos.* Delivery is defined as relinquishing control or dominion over property and placing it within the dominion of the donee. Fernan presented the ring to Aucoin Hart and possessed the receipt for its return. This demonstrated her dominion at the time she received the poem from Dastugue. The words of the poem clearly state, "the ring is yours." This expresses a clear intent to donate the ring to Fernan. By transferring the ring to the jeweler in return for $5,000 credit, Fernan demonstrated her acceptance of the gift.

Gifts to Minors

Each state has adopted some form of the *Uniform Gifts to Minors Act,* which establishes simplified means of donating money and securities to minors. Money may be deposited in an account in the donor's name, in an account in the name of

Figure 15–3:   Acquiring Property by Gift

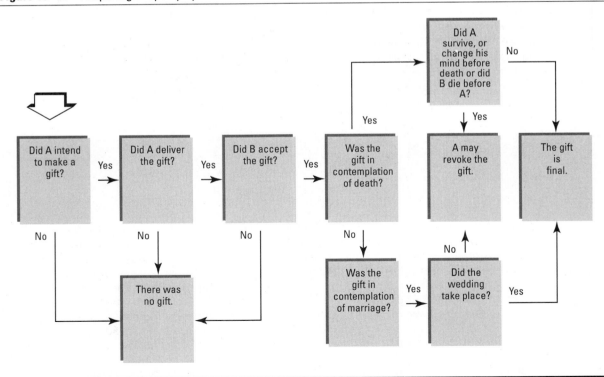

another adult, or with a bank with trust powers. Securities may be registered in the name of another adult, a bank trustee, or a broker who is to serve as custodian for the minor. Unregistered securities may be placed in the possession of an adult, trustee, or broker who is to serve as custodian in return for a written acknowledgment from the custodian.

Bailments

The law of bailments is a specialized branch of property law that also contains elements of contract and tort law. A **bailment** arises when the *bailor* delivers personal property to the *bailee* with the understanding that the property is to be returned to the bailor or someone else designated by the bailor. For instance, if Karen loans her car to Larry, she is a bailor and he is a bailee. Any specific agreement between Karen and Larry, as well as the general law of bailments, will determine the rights and duties of the parties.

http:// *www.ornl.gov/patent/* *bailments.html* provides links to sites about bailments.

Creation

Bailments may be created by either express or implied contract. They are distinguished from cases where an owner delivers *custody* rather than *possession* of his property to another. For instance, when you leave your car in a pay parking lot and receive a claim check, you may or may not have created a bailment. If you parked the car yourself and retained the keys, the parking lot owner probably has only custody and no bailment is created. But if a parking lot attendant parks the car for you and keeps your keys until he returns the car to you, he has taken possession and a bailment has arisen. The three fundamental elements to a bailment are listed below and illustrated in Figure 15–4.:

1. The bailor owns or has the right to possess the bailed property.
2. The bailor delivers exclusive possession and control (but not title) of the property to the bailee.
3. The bailee knowingly accepts possession of the property and agrees to return or transfer it pursuant to the bailor's instructions.

Figure 15–4: Creation of a Bailment

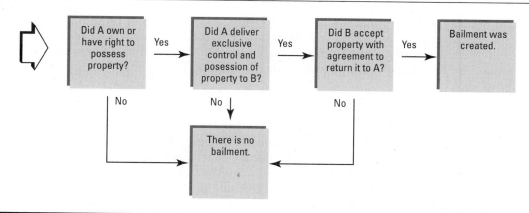

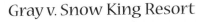

Gray v. Snow King Resort

889 F.Supp. 1473 (D. Wyo. 1995)

FACTS   Richard Gray purchased a ticket for an amusement ride known as the "Alpine Slide," which was owned and operated by the Snow King Resort. The ride involved navigating a wheeled bobsled down a winding trough-shaped slide built of fiber-reinforced concrete. Snow King personnel directed Gray to select a sled from a supply maintained by Snow King. The sled's downhill speed was controlled by a brake lever, but Gray alleges he was never given adequate instructions on how to keep the sled at a safe speed. As he began to go down the slide, his sled gathered momentum, hit a dip in the slide, and launched into the air. The force of the landing caused him to suffer serious back injuries. Gray argues that Snow King's furnishing the sled to him constituted a bailment, which triggered its liability for his personal injuries.

ISSUE   Was a bailment created when Snow King gave the sled to Gray?

DECISION   Yes. A bailment constitutes the delivery of property by one person (the bailor) to another (the bailee) in trust for a specific purpose, with an express or implied contract that the property will be returned or duly accounted for when the special purpose is accomplished. In a bailment, the bailor transfers possession of property, but retains title. The transaction in this case constituted a bailment. Snow King, as bailor, transferred possession of the sled to Gray for the specific purpose of descending the Alpine Slide. Clearly, at least an implied agreement existed that when Gray reached the bottom of the slide, having accomplished the specific purpose for which the sled was entrusted to him, he would return the sled to Snow King. We reject the argument that Mr. Gray's purchase of a ticket to ride the Alpine Slide created a mere license. Had the Alpine Slide been a roller coaster or a ferris wheel, where control of speed, direction and operation was under the complete control of Snow King, the license argument would have been more persuasive. Here, however, Gray took possession and control of the bobsled and the accompanying control of its direction and speed. The events in this case are more analogous to the lease or bailment of a rental car than the purchase of a license (ticket) to attend a movie.

In the case that opened this chapter, the Yorks claimed that a bailor-bailee relationship existed and the court agreed. It held that even though the parties did not specifically intend to create a bailment, the elements of a bailment were present. Accordingly, when the Yorks ended the relationship, the Jones Institute, as a bailee, had a duty to return the pre-zygote.

Bailee's Duty of Care

One of the bailee's fundamental duties is to take reasonable care of the bailed property while it is in her possession. Of course, what constitutes reasonable care may vary depending on the particular circumstances. Many courts consider the type of bailment when determining if the bailee has met her duty. There are three basic types of bailments: (1) sole benefit of the bailor, (2) sole benefit of the bailee, and (3) mutual benefit.

Sole Benefit of the Bailor

Suppose Ann had visited her neighbor, Stewart, and accidentally left her watch on his patio while swimming in his pool. As the owner of the premises where the property was mislaid, Stewart has a duty to care for the watch until Ann returns for it. This is a bailment for the *sole benefit of the bailor* because Stewart receives no benefit for caring for the watch. Accordingly, courts may be more lenient in the level of care to which Stewart is held because the bailment may be somewhat of a burden on him.

Benefit of the Bailee

Suppose instead that Ann had loaned her watch to Roger. This is a bailment for the *sole benefit of the bailee.* Roger benefits from this bailment, while Ann receives nothing in return. Roger may be held liable for even slight negligence because a court is likely to hold him to a much higher standard of care.

Mutual Benefit

When both the bailor and bailee benefit from the bailment, it is a *mutual benefit* bailment. Thus, in the previous case (*Gray v. Snow King Resort*), the bailment was for the mutual benefit because both Gray and Snow King benefited from Gray's use of the bobsled. Gray was able to use the sled, and Snow King was paid for allowing him temporary possession of it. In mutual benefit bailments, the bailee must exercise the ordinary care one would expect someone to use in caring for her own property.

When the bailee is a retail business, the mutual benefit is not always so apparent. For instance, suppose Ann accidentally mislaid her watch in the shower room of her health club. After a member turned the watch over to the club's lost-and-found department, a court might construe it as a mutual benefit bailment. The health club would have a duty to care for the watch until she returns for it and has benefited by her continued membership.

Institute of London v. Eagle Boats

918 F.Supp. 297 (E.D. Mo. 1996)

FACTS　William Seebold, the president of Eagle Boats, was approached by a boating magazine that wished to do a feature on a motorboat manufactured by the company. The boat was a 1991 Seebold Eagle 265 Limited Edition and was considered to be the "Cadillac" of motorboats in its class. The magazine feature would include a written article and photographs of the boat on Grand Lake, near Ketchum, Oklahoma. Seebold called Paul Hopkins, a marina owner, and arranged to use one of Hopkins's boats for the article. The arrangement was for Seebold to transport the boat to Ketchum. It was loaded on a trailer owned by Hopkins and hooked to Seebold's truck. The trailer did not have a locking device on it (a device capable of locking the trailer to the truck). At about 9:30 p.m. Seebold parked the truck, boat, and trailer on a motel parking lot at the end of the lot, facing away from the highway. There was one dusk-to-dawn light shining in front of the motel. Of all the boats parked on the lot, Hopkins's boat was

continued

parked closest to the road. His boat was also the most expensive one on the lot. When Seebold awoke at around 5:00 a.m., the boat and trailer were missing. At the time of the theft, the boat and trailer had a fair market value of more than $60,000.

ISSUE   Is Seebold liable for the loss of the boat and trailer?

DECISION   Yes. There is no dispute that Hopkins and Seebold entered into a bailment relationship. In a mutual benefit bailment, such as this, the duty of the bailee is to exercise ordinary care in the handling and safekeeping of the bailed property. This includes using ordinary care to prevent theft of the bailed property. The parking spot Seebold chose was the closest parking space to the roadway. In reality, he took no affirmative steps to insure the safety of the boat/trailer. The boat/trailer could have been stolen with relative ease because Seebold failed to take any appropriate measures, such as a locking device or overnight supervision, to deter theft. Seebold has failed to show that he exercised ordinary care in the safekeeping of the boat while it was in his possession.

Disclaimers

Bailees sometimes try to limit their liability for the bailed property through the use of **disclaimers.** These might take the form of a notice on a claim check or a sign on a wall stating, "Not liable for lost, stolen, or damaged items." Courts are reluctant to enforce these limits unless the terms were clearly communicated to the bailor. Thus, if the disclaimer has not been specifically pointed out to the bailor, it may be invalid. Further, any attempt to disclaim liability for the bailee's intentional wrongdoing is unenforceable. Professional bailees sometimes limit their liability to a set amount, but permit the bailor to pay an additional charge if she wishes to insure the property for a higher value.

Bailor's Duty of Care

Bailors make an implied warranty that the bailed property is fit for the purposes for which it is intended. This includes a promise that there are no hidden defects that make its use unsafe for the bailee. For instance, in *Gray v. Snow King* (discussed earlier), Snow King breached this duty when it permitted Gray to rent a bobsled that could not be safely operated on the slide. Many courts also impose strict liability on commercial bailors who rent out abnormally dangerous property. The court in *Gray v. Snow King* also found Snow King to be strictly liable for Gray's injuries.

Special Bailments

Airlines, railroads, ships, busses, and trucks frequently are bailees. Those that are regulated by the government as *common carriers* are held to an extremely high standard of care. They are absolute insurers of the goods they carry. They may only avoid liability by showing that a loss was caused by (1) an act of God, (2) an act of a public enemy, (3) an act of the government, (4) an act of the bailor, or (5) the nature of the goods. Common carriers normally may limit their liability to a fixed amount unless the bailor pays for higher coverage.

Hotels, motels, and other providers of food and lodging are considered to be *hotelkeepers*. Although they technically are not bailees because they seldom maintain exclusive possession of their customers' property, they are treated like common carriers for liability purposes. Most states permit hotelkeepers to limit their liability for property that is kept in a guest's room. To receive full protection, the guest must check her valuables into the hotel safe.

Inheritance

Ownership of property is transferred upon the death of the property owner. The property may pass according to the terms of a validly executed will or, in its absence, under the terms of a state's intestacy laws. Thus, a **will** is an extremely important document since it provides instructions for how and to whom your property is to be distributed.

http://
*www.law.net/~usala
w* provides information and documents on wills.

Administration of Estates

When someone dies, each state provides a procedure for collecting the decedent's assets, settling his debts, and distributing the remaining property to the appropriate people. All of this is done under the supervision of a probate court. With a will, a person (the **testator**) may designate a **personal representative** to administer his estate. Absent a will, the court selects the administrator. In his will, the decedent could have avoided a potentially timely and cumbersome judicial process by indicating in advance how his property should be distributed.

If there is a will, it should immediately be filed with the probate court so it may be approved as a valid document by the judge. The personal representative then prepares an inventory of the decedent's assets and liabilities. At this time, his unpaid creditors may file claims against the estate. Only after these claims and any appropriate taxes are paid may property be distributed to his **beneficiaries** (if there is a will) or his **heirs** (if there is no will).

Hecht v. Superior Court

59 CAL.RPTR.2D 222 (CT. APP. CAL. 1996)

FACTS   For five years prior to his death, William Kane had been living with Deborah Hecht. He was survived by two college-aged children of his former wife. In October 1991, Hecht deposited 15 vials of his sperm at a Los Angeles sperm bank and instructed it to release the vials to Hecht. That year he also executed a valid will in which he bequeathed all right, title, and interest in the sperm to Hecht. A portion of the will entitled "Statement of Wishes" provided, "It being my intention that samples of my sperm will be stored at a sperm bank for the use of Deborah Ellen Hecht, should she so desire . . . [to] become impregnated with my sperm." At about the same time, he wrote his children a letter expressing his hope that Hecht would use the sperm to have a child by him after his death. Nine days later, Kane took his own life. His children then began a prolonged battle to frustrate Hecht from conceiving a child using his sperm. In order to end three years of litigation over Kane's will, Hecht

continued

and his children reached a settlement in which Hecht was to be given 20 percent of the estate's assets. As a result, she received three vials of the frozen sperm. When her attempts to conceive with this sperm proved unsuccessful, she sued for the remaining 12 vials.

ISSUE   Is Hecht entitled to the remaining vials of sperm?

DECISION   Yes. This case involves a conflict between the decedent's clear intent to donate sperm to Hecht for the purposes of procreation and a property settlement purporting to distribute all assets of the estate. The genetic material involved here is a unique form of property. It is not subject to division through an agreement among the decedent's potential beneficiaries which is inconsistent with decedent's manifest intent about its disposition. A man's sperm or a woman's ova or a couple's embryos are not the same as a quarter of land, a cache of cash, or a favorite limousine. Rules appropriate to the disposition of the latter are not necessarily appropriate for the former. If we are to honor decedent's intent as expressed in several written documents, his sperm can only be used by and thus are of value to only Hecht. Even she lacks legal entitlement to give, sell, or otherwise dispose of decedent's sperm. Thus, in a very real sense, to the extent that this sperm is "property" it is only "property" for Hecht. As such it is not an "asset" of the estate subject to allocation, in whole or in part, to any other person whether through agreement or otherwise.

Formalities

A person must have **testamentary capacity** to dispose of property by will. This requires that he is of *sound mind* and *legal age* at the time the will was made. If this capacity was lacking, or if the will was procured by fraud or undue influence, it is not valid.

Although the formalities for drafting a will vary from state to state, they are similar. First, the will generally must be in **writing.** However, some states permit soldiers in active service or sailors at sea to make an oral will disposing of the property in their immediate possession. Second, it must be **witnessed** by two (some states require three) disinterested witnesses. These are people who are not receiving property under the will. Third, it must be **signed** by the testator. Fourth, the will must be **published** by the testator. This generally is accomplished merely by declaring when signing that the document is his will. Fifth, the testator and the witnesses must all sign in the **presence and sight** of one another. Wills generally include an **attestation clause** after the testator's signature reciting the formalities that have been followed.

Some states relax these formalities if the will is written and signed *entirely* in the testator's own handwriting. Thus, it would not be valid if any part of it was typed. Many states also require that such a will be dated and clearly indicate that it is meant to be a will.

Living Wills

http://
www.senioralternatives. com/897/livingwills. html provides information on living wills.

Courts have long recognized the right of adults to control the decisions relating to their own medical care, including the decision to have medical or surgical means calculated to prolong their lives provided, withheld, or withdrawn. One manner in which a competent adult may guarantee that these wishes be followed, in the event she later is incompetent and in a vegetative state, is to execute a **living will.** In this document she can specify that life-sustaining treatment be withheld or discontinued when there is no likelihood of recovery.

Some lawyers recommend drafting a *health-care power of attorney* at the same time the living will is executed. This document authorizes a designated person to make medical decisions when an individual is temporarily or permanently unable to do so.

Intestacy

A person has died **intestate** if she dies without a valid will. When this occurs, her real property is distributed under the laws of the state where it is located and her personal property is distributed under the laws of the state where she maintains her permanent residence. While these laws may vary, they generally look first to see if the decedent is survived by a spouse, children, or grandchildren and distribute the property to them. When there are no such heirs, they look for parents or siblings. Heirs like grandparents, cousins, aunts, or uncles are next in line. When there are no living heirs, the property is given to the state.

Trusts

A **trust** arises when a person with legal rights to property (the *trustee*) is under a duty to hold it for the benefit of another (the *beneficiary*). The individual who creates the trust is the *settlor* (or donor). The same person generally may hold several of these positions; however, if there is only one beneficiary, the beneficiary may not be the trustee. *Inter vivos trusts* are effective during the settlor's life, while *testamentary trusts* are created by will and become effective after the settlor's death.

Trustee's Duties

The trustee is a fiduciary, who owes a duty of loyalty to administer the trust for the benefit of the beneficiary. As a fiduciary, she must avoid conflicts of interest and must exercise reasonable skill, judgment, and care in the administering of her duties. These duties normally are spelled out in the trust agreement.

Beneficiaries' Rights

Unless the trust agreement permits it, the settlor may not revoke or modify the trust without the unanimous consent of the beneficiaries. If the settlor is dead, the beneficiaries may agree to modify the agreement's terms only if doing so would not frustrate a material purpose of the trust. Courts sometimes permit modifications when changes in circumstances threaten to undermine the settlor's intent in establishing the trust.

Beneficiaries normally may assign their rights to the principal or income from the trust. Thus, if Carl, as beneficiary of trust, is to receive $5,000 a month for the next six years, he may pledge this as collateral for a loan. If he defaults on the loan, his creditor would be entitled to Carl's payments until the debt is fully paid. However, a settlor sometimes places a **spendthrift clause** in a trust. This provision prevents creditors or other assignees from gaining access to the beneficiaries' interests.

1 – 800 –
Choice In Dying, Inc.
(800) 989-9455

http://
www.law.cornell.edu/
topics/estates_trusts.
html provides links
to federal Web sites
on estates and trusts.

There are several limitations on the enforceability of spendthrift clauses. First, the settlor cannot make himself a beneficiary and put his own property beyond the reach of his creditors. Second, a spendthrift clause is not effective against a claim for alimony or child support. Third, a spendthrift clause is not effective against a creditor who has supplied necessaries to the beneficiary. Fourth, after principal or interest has been distributed to a beneficiary, her creditors can reach it.

Many states currently are considering a fifth exception for creditors that preserved or benefited an interest in the trust. For example, an attorney who performed legal work that increased the holdings of the trust might be able to sue the trust for payment.

QUESTIONS AND PROBLEM CASES

1. How do the duties of a common carrier differ from those of a normal bailee?
2. What is a fixture? How does a court determine if property is a fixture?
3. What is a gift *causa mortis*? When may it be revoked?
4. What is meant by the term "dying intestate"?
5. Cray Valley Products installed heavy machinery and equipment in a building owned by Chittenden Falls Realty. Cray Valley was leasing the building as a site for the production of resins and micronized products. When Cray Valley opted not to renew the lease and made arrangements to remove the machinery and equipment, Chittenden objected. Cray Valley argued that it had the right to the machinery and equipment because it paid for it, paid for its installation, and used it to carry on its business. It admitted that the removal would be a substantial undertaking and would entail the removal of sections of the roof and sections of both interior and exterior walls. Despite the magnitude of the project, however, the structural integrity of the premises would not be compromised and the damage to the building would be repaired as part of the removal process. Chittenden asserted that since the machinery and equipment would be damaged during removal, they must remain as permanent fixtures. May Cray Valley legally remove the machinery and equipment?
6. Coradina Rivera leased a car to James McEnroe, who Rivera knew owned an auto dealership. McEnroe later fraudulently obtained title to the car in the name of his dealership and sold it to Expo Rent-a-Car. Expo sold it to Marlin Imports, who in turn sold the car to Marvin Carlsen. Rivera sued Carlsen to regain possession of the car. Will Carlsen be required to return the car to Rivera?
7. Kenneth Hotarek and Suzanne Benson were divorced two years after their son, Paul, was born. Paul was killed in an automobile accident at the age of 15. For the 13 years before Paul died, Suzanne had absolutely no contact with him and provided him with no financial support. Paul had no will and his estate at the time of his death totaled over $500,000 in uninsured motorist's benefits. After locating Suzanne, the probate court awarded her half of Paul's estate in accordance with state law. The relevant statute provided that when a person dies intestate leaving no spouse or children, the estate should be distributed equally to the decedent's parents. Kenneth objected to the distribution to Suzanne on the grounds that she had abandoned Paul during his life. Is Suzanne entitled to half of Paul's estate?
8. Sports Complex owns and operates a multi-attraction family amusement park. The Pacer 3000 go-cart attraction consists of a track and go-carts. One ticket allows a patron to drive around the track for one lap in a go-cart. If the patron wishes to continue after the first

lap, she must stop and present another ticket. Attendants regulate when drivers begin their first lap, the direction of the go-cart, and go-cart speed. They also enforce the track rules, including a prohibition on bumping or cutting off, by ejecting drivers who engage in these activities. However, once a go-cart driver is on the track, the attendants have no immediate way of retaking the go-cart. Tabitha Golt purchased and used tickets to drive a go-cart. On her second lap, she had traveled a short distance when another go-cart ran into her go-cart from behind. She suffered severe injuries to her eye and head. Her parents claimed that Sports Complex was strictly liable for Tabitha's injuries under bailment law. Sports Complex argued there was no bailment because the requisite transfer of possession and control did not occur with respect to the go-cart. It pointed out that its employees supervised the facilities and controlled the conduct of drivers on the track. Was there a bailor-bailee relationship in this case?

9. Crella Magee agreed to store her furs for the summer with Mysel Furs. The company arranged to have UPS deliver three boxes to Magee. She inserted one fur in each box, and UPS, after giving her a delivery ticket for each, picked them up for delivery to Mysel. Six weeks later Mysel issued Magee a storage receipt that listed just two furs. When she called the company, Magee was assured that all three furs were in storage. However, when she went to pick them up, one fur, worth $3,400, was missing. The storage receipts that Mysel sent to Magee limited the company's liability to $100. Was the company's liability limited to $100?

10. In 1985, a few weeks after Jesse Ford's wife died, his only son died in an automobile accident. He began to drink heavily after those losses. Jean Stinson, Ford's daughter, attempted to care for him during this period by cooking and cleaning for him. Stinson claimed that in 1988, when Ford received $280,000 in settlement of a wrongful death action filed after his son's death, he said that he wanted to give her $100,000 as a gift. He already had placed $100,000 in a savings account owned by his other daughter, Marlene, which she alone spent. Stinson indicated that she wanted her money placed in a certificate of deposit. Ford then had his bank issue a certificate deposit listed in the names of "Jean Stinson or Jesse Ford." It listed her address and she regularly received the monthly interest checks from 1988 through 1994. In 1994, Ford cashed the certificate of deposit and placed the $100,000 in his personal checking account. Stinson sued her father, claiming the money belonged to her. Is Stinson correct?

BUYING A HOME

Jeffrey Stambovksy bought a house from Helen Ackley. However, at the time of the sale, Stambovsky did not know that the house was reputed to be possessed by poltergeists, which Ackley and members of her family had reportedly seen. When Stambovsky learned of the house's reputation, he demanded his money back. The court canceled the contract because Ackley breached her duty to disclose the existence of the ghosts to Stambovsky before selling him the house.

Stambovsky v. Ackley, 572 N.Y.S.2d 672 (App. Div. N.Y. 1991).

What duties does a seller owe a prospective home buyer?
What is the role of a real estate broker?
What processes are available to protect home buyers from unscrupulous sellers?

These and other issues are discussed in this chapter.

Introduction

At least two out of every three American families own their own home. That percentage would be even higher except that many people cannot afford the minimum down payment and closing costs associated with a home purchase. There are many reasons that home ownership is so attractive, but perhaps the most important is that a home tends to be a fairly secure investment. Most housing is a good hedge against inflation, and the mortgage interest rates associated with financing a home purchase generally are among the lowest of all types of loans. Further, many of the costs associated with buying a home are tax deductible.

Buying a home is one of the most important financial transactions most people ever make. The costs are high and, as a result, a poor decision can be financially crippling. Wise buyers do not purchase a home without first arming themselves with a basic knowledge of the legal and practical implications of home ownership. The goal of this chapter, then, is to provide readers with an overview of **real estate law** so they may better understand the rights and duties associated with home ownership.

Chapter Overview

This chapter explores the basic steps involved in the purchase of a home and home ownership. It begins with an examination of the basic contract to buy residential property, including various types of agreements with real estate brokers. Next is a discussion of the concepts of home ownership and joint ownership of real estate. This is followed by an investigation of the primary methods of financing residential real estate transactions. The focus then shifts to various governmental regulations governing home purchases and ownership. The chapter closes with a review of public and private restrictions on home ownership.

Real Estate Contracts

The basic rules of contract law (discussed in Chapters 8 and 9) govern the residential real estate transaction. However, each state has its own set of real estate laws, and each community may have developed "local customs" that are incorporated into that body of law. For these reasons, prudent home buyers generally seek the assistance of an attorney experienced in real estate law before completing a purchase. Further, sellers often engage a real estate broker to simplify the selling process. This section examines the contracting process, including the special rules governing real estate brokers.

http:// www.law.cornell.edu/ topics/real_estate. html is the site of information on real estate transactions, with links to state sites.

Real Estate Brokers

Although a person may sell her house without professional assistance, many sellers (and some buyers) engage the services of a **real estate broker.** Every state requires that real estate brokers be licensed and imposes standards of conduct that must be followed. In addition, real estate brokers are agents of the party that has retained them and, accordingly, owe fiduciary duties to that person. (Agency duties are discussed in Chapter 12.)

Generally, a real estate broker who has been hired by a seller is entitled to compensation when he procures a buyer who is *ready, willing, and able* to buy the

http://
*www.law.cornell.edu/
topics/state_statutes.
html#property* con-
tains state-specific
information on real
estate laws. Access
the site and choose a
state—for example,
Georgia—and key in
"broker" for informa-
tion on state regula-
tions on brokers. It
may be necessary to
search through your
specific state site.

property. If the seller refuses to go through with the sale, the broker still is entitled to compensation. The broker's right to compensation is spelled out in the **listing contract** between the seller and the broker. There are four basic types of listing contracts:

1. open listing,
2. exclusive agency,
3. exclusive right to sell, and
4. multiple listings.

Open Listing

With an **open listing,** the seller reserves the right to engage other brokers to sell the property. The seller then owes a commission only to the first broker who finds a ready, willing, and able buyer. If the seller finds the buyer herself, she is not required to pay any commissions.

Exclusive Agency

An **exclusive agency** listing protects the real estate broker from competing brokers but not from the seller. Under its terms, the broker earns his commission if he or any other real estate broker finds a ready, willing, and able buyer during the time designated in the listing contract. However, if the seller finds a buyer herself, she is not required to pay a commission to the broker.

Exclusive Right to Sell

With an **exclusive right to sell** listing, the broker is entitled to a commission anytime a ready, willing, and able buyer appears during the time the listing contract is in effect. It does not matter who procured the buyer (the seller, the broker, or a competing broker); the real estate broker who signed the listing contract receives the commission.

Multiple Listings

In recent years, more and more brokers have opted to sell homes under a **multiple listing.** This requires the real estate brokers in a particular area to pool their listed properties. When a ready, willing, and able buyer appears, the broker who listed the house and the broker who procured the buyer share the commission. Under the rules of multiple-listing organizations, member brokers must share their listings within a specified time period, notwithstanding the nature of the listing agreement with the seller.

In Re Opinion No. 26 of Committee on Unauthorized Practice
654 A.2d 1344 (Sup. Ct. 1995)

FACTS   The local custom in South Jersey typically involves residential real estate closings in which neither the buyer nor the seller is represented by an attorney. About 60 percent of buyers and 65 percent of sellers are not represented by a lawyer. This contrasts sharply with the North Jersey practice where only one-half of 1 percent of buyers and 14 percent of sellers proceed without legal counsel. In North Jersey, when both seller and buyer are represented by legal counsel, they sign nothing, agree to nothing, and expend nothing without advice of competent counsel. If they are initially without counsel when they sign a contract of sale prepared by the broker, they ordinarily then retain counsel who can revoke that contract in accordance with a three-day attorney review clause. The typical South Jersey transaction starts with the seller engaging a broker who is ordinarily a member of the multiple-listing system. The first broker to find an apparently willing buyer gets in touch with the seller and ultimately negotiates a sale price agreeable to both. The potential buyer requires financing arrangements, which are often made by the broker. Before the execution of any sales contract, the broker puts the buyer in touch with a mortgage company to determine if the buyer qualifies for the needed loan. Assuming the preliminary understanding between the seller and buyer remains in effect, the broker will present the seller with the standard form contract used in that area. If they sign the contract, both parties will have become legally bound to perform numerous obligations without the benefit of any legal advice whatsoever. At that point, the broker, who represents only the seller and clearly has an interest in conflict with that of the buyer, performs a series of acts on behalf of the buyer, and is the only person available as a practical matter to explain their significance to the buyer. The New Jersey State Bar Association sought a determination that the South Jersey practice constituted the unauthorized practice of law by real estate brokers.

ISSUE   Are the South Jersey brokers engaged in the unauthorized practice of law?

DECISION   No. We find it necessary to state the Court's view of the matter at the outset. The Court strongly believes that both parties should retain counsel for their own protection and that the savings in lawyers fees are not worth the risks involved in proceeding without counsel. All that we decide is that the public interest does not require that the parties be deprived of the right to choose without a lawyer. They should, of course, be informed of the risks. Specifically, we rule as follows: a real estate broker may order a title search and abstract and the practice of conducting closings or settlements without the presence of attorneys shall not constitute the unauthorized practice of law. However, we attach a condition to this ruling that is designed to assure that the decision to not retain an attorney is an informed one. If that condition is not met, the brokers are engaged in the unauthorized practice of law, and attorneys with knowledge of that fact who participate are guilty of ethical misconduct. We require that brokers extend to buyers and sellers advance written notice of their right to retain counsel and the risk of not doing so.

Sales Contract

Although the precise content of the **sales contract** varies depending on the parties' negotiations, certain terms ordinarily can be expected. For instance, both the seller and the buyer should sign the contract. There should be a legal description of the property to be sold, including the lot and block or survey description and any fixtures or personal property being sold with it (refrigerator, stove, and other appliances). There should be language evidencing the buyer's promise to buy and the seller's promise to sell, as well as a statement of the purchase price and other financial details. This agreement also should indicate the date on which the buyer may take possession of the home.

Writing Requirements

The statute of frauds requires that contracts for the sale of an interest in real property be evidenced by a writing. (The writing requirement and its exceptions are discussed in Chapter 9.) It is important for the parties to carefully draw up their sales contract, making certain that it contains all material terms. This is because the **parol evidence rule** (discussed in Chapter 9) holds that the written terms override any contradictory oral promises made prior to the writing. Suppose that during negotiations the seller promised to pay the prior year's property taxes, but the written contract placed that responsibility on the buyer. Under the parol evidence rule, the buyer is now obligated to pay the taxes.

Earnest Money

Immediately after the seller signs an acceptance of the buyer's offer, the buyer is expected to provide the seller with **earnest money.** When the seller engages a real estate broker, the broker generally holds the earnest money. This money evidences the buyer's good-faith intention to complete the transaction and is retained by the seller if the buyer wrongfully fails to complete the transaction. If the sale is completed, the earnest money is applied toward the purchase price of the home. The actual amount of earnest money required for a particular transaction often is determined by local custom, although the buyer and seller are free to negotiate whatever amount they choose.

In some localities, buyers and sellers sign a special agreement, called a **binder,** when the seller accepts the buyer's offer to purchase. This preliminary agreement outlines the general terms of their understanding, but does not legally bind them until a formal contract is drawn up.

Mortgage Contingency Clause

Buyers generally are reluctant to make a large earnest money deposit in the absence of a **mortgage contingency clause.** This provision relieves the buyer from the obligation to purchase (and permits the return of the earnest money) if he is unable to obtain suitable financing. A mortgage contingency clause is of great importance since most buyers do not know if they will qualify for a loan at the time they make an offer to buy a particular house. This is because a financial institution's willingness to lend generally is based both on the creditworthiness of the buyer and an appraisal of the property. The clause generally states the amount of financing the buyer is seeking and the maximum interest rate he is willing to pay.

Subject-to-Sale Contingency Clause

Many buyers are attempting to sell their present home at the same time they are seeking to purchase a new house. Because of the high cost of housing, most of these buyers insist that the sales contract contain a **subject-to-sale contingency clause.** This provision relieves the buyer from having to purchase the new house (and permits return of the earnest money) if her old residence is not sold within a designated period (e.g., 45 days).

Duty to Disclose

Traditionally, under the concept of *caveat emptor* ("let the buyer beware"), sellers or their brokers had no duty to disclose hidden defects to a buyer. Today, however, most states impose on sellers and real estate brokers a **duty to disclose** defects that materially affect the value of the residence when they are not readily observable to the buyer. Failure to make such disclosure may result in the buyer having a right to cancel the contract or recover monetary damages.

Remember the haunted house case that opened the chapter? There, the court canceled the contract because the seller had a duty to disclose the stories of the hauntings to the buyer. It stated that fairness and common sense sometimes dictate that an exception to caveat emptor be made. The impact of the reputation of the house went to the very essence of the bargain between the parties. As a newcomer to this particular town, the buyer could not have been expected to have any familiarity with its folklore. He acted reasonably in inspecting the premises and doing a title search. The most thorough search, however, would not unearth the property's ghoulish reputation. Where a material condition is peculiarly within the knowledge of the seller and unlikely to be discovered by the prudent buyer, a contract cancellation generally is permitted.

Consider the following case, where the court considers whether to expand the seller's duty to disclose.

Strawn v. Canuso

657 A.2d 420 (Sup. Ct. N.J. 1995)

FACTS   Canuso Management Corporation built and marketed homes in two subdivisions in close proximity to a closed, hazardous-waste dump site, known as Buzby Landfill. None of the more than 150 families who purchased homes in the subdivisions knew of the existence of the landfill when they bought their homes. Canuso, on the other hand, allegedly knew about the landfill when it was still operational before the homes were built. The home buyers claimed that Canuso was aware that toxic wastes dumped in the landfill began to escape and were contaminating the groundwater and surrounding lakes with hazardous waste. Despite this fact, Canuso's sales agents were instructed never to disclose the existence of the Buzby Landfill, even when asked about odors from gases released from the site. Canuso argued that it had no duty to disclose to prospective buyers the conditions of somebody else's property.

ISSUE   Did the seller have a duty to disclose the off-site physical conditions?

DECISION   Yes. For many years courts continued to cling to the notion that a seller had no duty to disclose anything to a home buyer. That attitude endured even though the purchase of a home is almost always the most important transaction consumers will ever undertake. However, *caveat emptor* has not retained its original vitality and no longer prevails in New Jersey. Sellers generally need disclose only matters of which they have some degree of personal knowledge. Moreover, they need only disclose matters not reasonably ascertainable by the buyer. This case stretches the boundaries of the seller's duty to disclose since it involves a duty to disclose off-site

continued

conditions that materially affect the value of the property. The principal factors shaping the duty to disclose have been the difference in bargaining power between the professional seller of residential real estate and the purchaser of such property and the difference in access to information between the seller and the buyer. The first factor causes us to limit our holding to professional sellers of residential housing and the brokers representing them. The reseller of residential property has the same advantage in the bargaining process. Regarding the second factor, professional sellers of residential housing and their brokers enjoy markedly superior access to information. Hence, it is reasonable to extend to such professionals a similar duty to disclose off-site conditions that materially affect the value or desirability of the property.

http://www.camlaw.rutgers.edu/library/search.html

Ethical Issue

Sally listed her house for sale for $120,000 (its present appraised value). Howard has made an offer to purchase at that price. However, he knows that the city council is planning major improvements in the area that should greatly increase the property value in the very near future. Does Howard (the buyer) have an ethical duty to disclose this information to Sally?

Transferring Ownership Rights

After the buyer and seller have reached an agreement on the material terms of the real estate contract, they designate a date and time to complete their legal obligations to each other. The process where these mutual obligations are performed is known as the real estate **closing.** At that time, the buyer generally pays the purchase price and the seller conveys possession and, perhaps, title to the property. Buyers have several processes and legal theories at their disposal to assure that the purchased property is as promised by the seller.

Title

When discussing a home or any other type of real property, the concept of **title** does not refer to a physical document but rather to the right to possession and control of the premises. In a real estate transaction, the buyer is purchasing these ownership interests from the seller. At the closing, the seller generally is obligated to convey **merchantable title** to the buyer. This means that the property does not have any claims against it that would unreasonably interfere with the buyer's future possession and control.

Protecting Against Defects in Title

In many states, the seller presents the buyer with an **abstract of title.** This provides a history of the chain of title up to the date of closing. However, it does not guarantee that the title is good. Buyers often protect against the risk of defects in title (other people with claims to the property) by purchasing **title insurance.** Lenders generally require that buyers secure title insurance as a condition to granting a mortgage loan. When a buyer has title insurance, he is compensated by the insurer if the title is defective. Prudent buyers retain an attorney, a professional abstractor, or a title company to perform a comprehensive search to uncover any defects in the seller's title.

Deed

Ownership interests in real estate (title) generally are transferred by signing and delivering a **deed.** Each state has its own procedures for how this transfer is to occur. The basic procedures are discussed here.

Requirements of the Deed

A deed is not valid unless it

1. is in writing,
2. describes the property,
3. recites the name of the buyer,
4. recites the name of the seller,
5. is signed by the seller, and
6. states the price paid for the property.

It is not necessary to include the actual price of the property since property owners usually wish to keep that confidential. Instead, the deed may describe the purchase price as: *"one dollar and other valuable consideration."*

Most states require that a notary public make an **acknowledgment** after witnessing the seller's signature. This is a formal declaration that the notary knows the seller and that the signature was made in the notary's presence. Finally, a transfer by deed is not valid unless the deed is actually delivered to the buyer or someone who holds it for the buyer's benefit (e.g., the lender who finances the buyer's purchase).

Types of Deeds

There are two types of deeds that are used in most states. The first, a **quitclaim deed,** conveys to the buyer whatever title (ownership rights) the seller has in the property. With this type of deed, the seller makes no promise as to what type of title that is. Thus, the seller is not guaranteeing there are no competing claims to the property. Quitclaim deeds normally are used for curing technical defects in the chain of title. For instance, after a divorce a man may convey a quitclaim deed to the family home to his ex-wife as part of the property settlement. (See Figure 16–1 on page 366.)

A second type of deed is the **warranty deed.** When a seller conveys a warranty deed, she is promising to transfer the property free and clear of any competing claims. Should such claims arise, the seller has a duty to defend the buyer against it. With a *general warranty deed,* the seller warrants against any defects in the title to the property. A *special warranty deed* guarantees only against defects that arose after the seller acquired the property herself. (See Figure 16–2 on page 367.)

Figure 16–1:   Quitclaim Deed

This indenture witnesseth that _____

of _____ *County in the State of* _____

Releases and quit claims to _____

of _____ *County in the State of* _____, *for and in consideration of* _____
the receipt whereof is hereby acknowledged, the following Real Estate in _____ *County*
in the State of Indiana, to wit:

State of Indiana, _____ **County, ss:**   Dated this _____ Day of _____, 19_____
Before me, the undersigned, a Notary
Public in and for said County and State,   _____ *Seal*
this _____ day of _____,
19 _____, personally appeared: _____ *Seal*

        _____ *Seal*

Source: *West's Indiana Practice* Volume 9, 2d.ed.

Recording the Deed

A properly executed deed may be valid when it is delivered, but delivery alone does not provide the buyer with adequate protection. It also is important to notify the world of the buyer's title to the property. Otherwise, a fraudulent seller may resell the property to another buyer, who may then assert her own rights over the house. To prevent such third-party claims, the buyer should immediately **record** the deed.

Each state has its own recording statute stipulating how and where the real estate deed must be recorded. Generally, these laws provide for the recording of deeds and mortgage interests in a public office where it gives notice to the rest of the world of the buyer's interest in the property.

Implied Warranty of Habitability

Traditional contract law did not make a builder, developer, or professional seller of new homes liable for structural defects unless the sales contract included specific language guaranteeing the condition of the premises. However, most states have abandoned this approach and now provide buyers of new homes with an **implied warranty of habitability** that guarantees the residence is free of hidden defects that would make it unsafe or unsuitable for human habitation. When a

Figure 16–2: Warranty Deed

This indenture witnesseth that _____

of _____ County in the State of _____

Conveys and warrants to _____

of _____ County in the State of _____ , for and in consideration of _____
the receipt whereof is hereby acknowledged, the following Real Estate in _____ County
in the State of Indiana, to wit:

State of Indiana, _____ County, ss: **Dated this _____ Day of _____ , 19_____**
Before me, the undersigned, a Notary
Public in and for said County and State,
this _____ day of _____ ,   _____ Seal
19 ____ , personally appeared:
                                                _____ Seal

                                                _____ Seal
And acknowledged the execution of the
foregoing deed. In witness whereof, I
have hereunto subscribed my name
and affixed my official seal. My commission expires _____ , 19 ____ .

_____
            Notary Public

Source: *West's Indiana Practice* Volume 9, 2d. ed.

builder, developer, or professional seller of a new home violates this implied warranty, it must compensate the buyer for the cost of repairs or for the loss in value
of the property. When the damage to the property is particularly severe, the buyer
may cancel the contract.

The implied warranty of habitability has been confined to builders, developers, and professional sellers of new homes. It does not extend to ordinary people
who are selling their homes, although they have a duty to disclose hidden defects
to their buyers. In recent years, some courts have extended the warranty of a
builder, developer, or professional seller to subsequent purchasers for a reasonable period of time. Suppose Mark bought a new house from Budget Builders and
one year later sold the property to Catherine. If she uncovers previously hidden
flaws in the structure after taking possession, Catherine probably can assert the
implied warranty of habitability against Budget Builders.

Strict Liability

Almost half of the states now recognize strict liability claims against builders and developers of new homes. Under strict liability, the developers must pay damages if a new home is proven to be defective. This liability attaches even when the developer was not negligent in constructing the building. In the case that follows, the court finds that developers may even be liable for the emotional distress suffered by the buyer of a home that is defectively built.

Salka v. Dean Homes of Beverly Hills

22 CAL.RPTR.2D 902 (CT. APP. CAL. 1993)

FACTS Robert and Nancy Salka purchased a new home from a builder, Dean Homes of Beverly Hills. Although the soils compaction report for the tract recommended houses be constructed on reinforced slabs, Dean Homes constructed the Salka home on a raised foundation with a subfloor of 18 to 24 inches below the exterior grade. This created a basin for the collection of both surface and groundwater. From the beginning of their occupancy, the Salkas experienced flooding, standing water, and ground saturation. Dampness resulted in the floor buckling, with condensation collecting in, under, and around the house causing the wallpaper to peel and producing a damp, dungy smell. Water accumulated by the front door, invaded the windows, and affected the French doors. After finding Dean Homes strictly liable for the faulty construction, the trial court awarded the Salkas $213,913 for the costs of repair and $50,000 for Nancy Salka's emotional distress.

ISSUE Should the builder be liable for the buyer's emotional distress?

DECISION Yes. Upon learning of the pooling of water in her home, Nancy Salka experienced tightening in her stomach and heart. She also became distressed and developed a feeling of despair. Her condition persisted over a seven-year period during which the water problem remained uncorrected. The parade of workmen advising her that the problems were monumental and possibly beyond repair added to her sense of despair. She found the musty, damp odor to be bothersome and embarrassing. Because of the odor and damp condition of her home, she stopped entertaining because she was embarrassed and humiliated over these circumstances. Here, Nancy Salka's claim for emotional distress is simply a component of the compensatory damages arising from Dean Homes's strict liability. Her claim is a direct result of the disruption flowing from the defective construction of her home. The Salkas reasonably relied on the skill and experience of Dean Homes to provide them with a home fit for its intended purpose. They are entitled to be compensated for all damages ensuing from the defective condition of the home. The determinative issues are whether Nancy Salka's emotional distress was foreseeable and whether this is the type of emotional harm that society should absorb without compensation. Dean Homes's construction of the foundation was contrary to the recommendation of the soils compaction report. A builder of homes should foresee that the construction of a defective foundation may not only result in significant property damages, but induce emotional distress as well. Given that home ownership is often referred to as the essence of the American dream, Nancy Salka's emotional distress is quite foreseeable. Moreover, this is not the type of emotional distress the homeowner should be expected to absorb. The buyer of a new home generally is not on an equal footing with the builder and is unable to protect herself. The purchase of a home is not only the largest investment most people will make in their lifetime, it also is a highly personal choice concerning how and where one lives her life. Generally, no other material acquisition is of equivalent personal importance.

Financing the Transaction

The high cost of housing guarantees that most buyers do not have the cash on hand to purchase a home outright. Instead, they generally seek credit from either a lending agency or the seller. This section looks at the three primary devices for financing the purchase of a home: the real estate mortgage, the land contract, and the deed of trust.

Real Estate Mortgage

Generally, a **mortgage** is a three-party transaction involving the **mortgagor** (the buyer/borrower), the **mortgagee** (the lender) and the seller. The mortgagee lends money to the mortgagor, who then uses the proceeds of the loan to pay the seller for the home. In return, the mortgagor promises to repay the loan and, as additional security, gives the mortgagee a security interest in the property.

http:// www.law.cornell.edu/ topics/mortgages. html provides brief information on mortgages, with links to state and other relevant sites.

Sometimes, when a buyer does not qualify for financing from a professional lender, the seller herself may finance the transaction. This is a two-party transaction whereby the seller/lender conveys the property to the buyer/borrower in return for his promise to make payments on the property. The seller is a mortgagee who retains a security interest in the property. The buyer is a mortgagor. The legal rules governing two-party mortgages are the same as those for three-party mortgages.

Foreclosure

Suppose Sally agrees to sell her house to Bob for $150,000. To finance the purchase, Bob makes a $30,000 down payment and borrows an additional $120,000 from National City Mortgage Company. Bob, the mortgagor, then will make payments to National City (the mortgagee) until the loan is fully paid. If he should default on the loan, National City may foreclose on the mortgage.

A **foreclosure** gives the lender the right to sell the property and apply the proceeds of the sale to Bob's debt. If the house sells for more than the balance due on the loan, that surplus is returned to Bob. If the proceeds are not sufficient to repay the loan, Bob may be personally liable for the deficiency. (However, some states do not permit a deficiency judgment against a mortgagor of residential property.) But most states would give Bob a **right of redemption,** usually for six months to one year after the default, during which time he could repay the loan and regain possession of the property.

Extinguishing the Seller's Mortgage

It is very likely that Sally, the seller, did not own the house outright. Suppose she was making mortgage payments to her lender, First Federal, and owed a balance of $105,000 at the time of her sale to Bob. In all likelihood, National City would pay Bob's $120,000 loan in two disbursements. A $105,000 check would be made to First Federal to pay off Sally's mortgage. The remaining $15,000 would be paid to Sally. Bob would then own the house **free and clear** of First Federal's mortgage interest. (See Figure 16–3.)

Taking Subject to the Seller's Mortgage

If First Federal's loan was not paid in full, Bob would be buying the property **subject to the mortgage.** This could be risky for both Bob and National City. If Sally later defaulted on her mortgage payments, First Federal could repossess and sell the property at a foreclosure sale even though Bob was now the owner. (See Figure 16–4.)

Assuming the Seller's Mortgage

If Sally's mortgage contract with First Federal was assignable, Bob might avoid borrowing from National City Mortgage and, instead, **assume the mortgage** with First Federal. This would require that he pay Sally $15,000 and take over her payments for the $105,000 balance on her mortgage. (See Figure 16–5.)

Land Contracts

A **land contract** (sometimes called an *installment real estate contract*) is another means of financing the purchase of a home. This is a contractual agreement whereby the seller sells the property and the buyer agrees to pay the purchase price plus interest over a period of time. Generally, the buyer also is required to make an agreed-upon down payment at the time the sale takes place. Although the buyer takes immediate possession of the property, the seller in a land contract retains title to the property and does not convey the deed until the purchase price is fully paid.

Forfeiture

Upon a buyer's default, the rights and responsibilities of the parties to a land contract generally depend on the precise terms of their agreement. During negotiations, the seller may press for procedures allowing him to easily retake possession, while the buyer negotiates for a long grace period within which she may come

---

Figure 16–3:   Buyer Extinguishing Seller's Mortgage

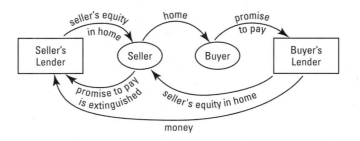

Figure 16–4:   Buyer Taking Subject to Seller's Mortgage

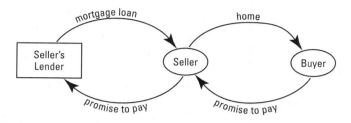

into compliance with the agreement. In most cases, the seller has two possible remedies: First, he may foreclose, sell the property, and return any surplus or sue if there is a deficiency. Second, he may declare a **forfeiture,** cancel the contract, and retake possession of the property. Any previous payments made by the buyer are treated like rent and retained by the seller.

Forfeitures create harsh results in instances where the buyer has made substantial payments toward the purchase price before defaulting. Suppose Amy bought a house from Jack for $90,000 on a land contract. After reducing the principal due on the loan to $50,000, she lost her job and stopped making house payments. If Jack declares a forfeiture, he may retain the $40,000 in principal plus the interest payments Amy has made as well as retake possession of a house that probably is now worth more than the original sales price. (Amy will lose all of the equity she built up on the home.)

In some states, land contract buyers are protected against unreasonable results. First, the seller generally must give the buyer notice of any default and provide a reasonable time period for the buyer to redeem the property by paying off the balance due. Second, in instances where the buyer has built up a great deal of equity in the property, some courts require that the seller use a foreclosure sale rather than a forfeiture. In that way, the buyer retains her equity by receiving the surplus earned at the foreclosure sale.

Figure 16–5:   Buyer Assuming Seller's Mortgage

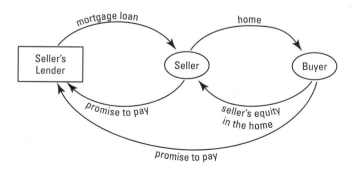

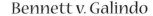

Bennett v. Galindo

1994 U.S. Dist. LEXIS 15726 (D. Kan. 1994)

FACTS   Harold and Karen Galindo purchased a house from Carl Bennett for $46,000 under a land contract. The contract called for a down payment of $12,000 and 180 monthly installments of $355.04 at a 9.5 percent fixed interest rate. The Galindos were to pay real estate taxes and insurance. They were given immediate possession of, but not legal title to, the premises. The title was not to be conveyed until the Galindos paid the entire purchase price. The land contract defined a default as failure to pay six monthly installments, real estate taxes, or insurance premiums. If the buyers defaulted, they were to forfeit all money previously paid to Bennett and were to surrender immediate possession of the premises. After the Galindos failed to pay monthly installments for April through June and September through December, and the property taxes for the last six months of the year, Bennett instituted forfeiture proceedings. The contract balance was $32,479 at the time Bennett demanded possession of the property. The buyers argued that they had a right of redemption that permitted them to pay off the loan and retain possession of the house.

ISSUE   Do the buyers have a right of redemption?

DECISION   Yes. It is well settled law that a statutory right of redemption has no place in the enforcement of land contracts unless the seller seeks a foreclosure rather than a forfeiture. However, the law does not favor a forfeiture. Therefore equity may, when deemed appropriate under all of the circumstances, provide an equitable period of redemption for the buyer to avoid the harshness of a forfeiture. This equitable remedy need not be expressly provided for in the land contract agreement. If the down payment by the buyers had been negligible, and the monthly payments had been but few, the contract ordinarily will be enforced according to its terms. But, as here, where the buyers have made substantial payments and improvements to the property, the buyers' rights should not be summarily extinguished. This court considers substantial the Galindos' payment of approximately $20,000 toward the purchase price. For this reason, the Galindo's are granted a six-month equitable redemption period.

Ethical Issue

When a seller executes a forfeiture in a land contract default, she may end up receiving more than the balance due on the contract if the buyer has built up any equity in the property. Is it fair for the seller to keep this surplus?

Deed of Trust

A few states permit a **deed of trust** to be used as a financing device for the purchase of a home. There are three parties to this transaction:

1. the buyer who borrows the purchase price,
2. the trustee who holds legal title to the property until the loan amount is fully paid, and
3. the lender who is the beneficiary of the trust.

Under a deed of trust, the buyer/borrower immediately takes possession of the property, but he conveys title to the trustee. The trust agreement spells out the parties' rights and obligations. These usually provide that the trustee is to foreclose and sell the property if it receives notice from the lender that the borrower has defaulted on the loan agreement. The proceeds of the foreclosure sale are given to the lender, with any surplus belonging to the borrower.

Lenders traditionally favored a deed of trust because it made it easy to liquidate the property of a defaulting borrower. The trustee could summarily sell the property and avoid a time-consuming foreclosure proceeding. Further, the borrower was not given a right of redemption. However, in recent years most states have undermined these benefits by providing borrowers with a fairly lengthy right to redeem their property.

Regulation of Real Estate Transactions

Recognizing the fundamental importance of home ownership, Congress has enacted several statutes specifically protecting home buyers and home owners. The purposes of these laws range from protecting buyers from discrimination to making certain that buyers are equipped with sufficient information to ascertain the wisdom of buying a home. Federal law also protects current home owners from repairpersons who seek to attach liens to residential property. Finally, home sales and home ownership often involve important tax considerations.

Fair Housing Act

The *Fair Housing Act* prohibits discrimination against home buyers based on race, color, religion, sex, national origin, handicap, and familial status. Its provisions apply to real estate brokers, lenders, appraisers, and sellers. (However, it does not apply to a private individual selling a single-family home without the assistance of a broker.) The protection against discrimination based on familial status is intended to protect pregnant women and families with children from being denied housing. However, it exempts from its coverage adult or senior citizen communities that place minimum age limits on residents.

*http://
www.law.cornell.edu/
uscode/42/ch45.html
is the site of the
index of the federal
Fair Housing Act.*

Real Estate Settlement Procedures Act

Home buyers are guaranteed access to important information related to the cost of a home by the *Real Estate Settlement Procedures Act*. This disclosure permits a buyer to comparison shop for the most favorable terms possible. Under this law, the buyer must receive advance notice of the settlement costs involved in the home purchase. These generally include: real estate broker's commissions, loan origination fees, loan discount points, appraisal fees, credit report fees, inspection fees, insurance premiums, prepaid interest and taxes, title search fees, survey fees, title insurance premiums, transfer and recording fees, escrow fees, and attorney's fees.

Interstate Land Sales Full Disclosure Act

Developers who subdivide property into 50 or more lots and use the mails or telephone to sell the property must comply with the *Interstate Land Sales Full Disclosure Act.* The statute was enacted in response to widespread cases of fraud by sellers of vacation and retirement homes. It requires developers to prepare property reports disclosing material information about the development so prospective buyers can make informed decisions.

Mortgage Disclosure

http://
www.law.cornell.edu/
uscode/15/1601.shtml
is the site of the
Truth-in-Lending Act.

The *Truth-in-Lending Act* (TILA) assists buyers in gaining complete and accurate information about the cost of credit when seeking financing for a home purchase. The law requires lenders to disclose the actual cost of credit. Specifically, this includes the finance charges and the annual percentage rate. (The TILA is discussed further in Chapter 10.) The disclosure must be made before the transaction is completed.

The TILA also provides special protection for home owners who borrow money for a consumer transaction and give the lender a security interest in their home. A home owner is given a three-day cooling-off period during which he may rescind the transaction by notifying the lender by mail, telegram, or another form of written communication. This three-day period is extended to three years if the lender fails to comply with the TILA's disclosure requirements or does not provide the home owner with rescission forms. Lenders also are prohibited from disbursing money, providing services, or delivering materials until the rescission period has expired.

The purpose of the three-day waiting period is to give the home owner an opportunity to reconsider any transaction that would have the serious consequences of encumbering the title to her home. However, the right of rescission is limited to credit extended for home repairs or other types of home equity loans. It does not apply to mortgage loans where the buyer borrows the money to actually purchase the residence.

Taylor v. Domestic Remodeling
97 F.3D 96 (5TH CIR. 1996)

FACTS   Domestic Remodeling approached Alberta Taylor about remodeling her home. Mrs. Taylor authorized the company to construct an addition onto the house and roof it. The total cash price was $17,500. At the same time, Mrs. Taylor signed a loan application to obtain financing for the remodeling through Green Tree Financial Corporation. Green Tree approved the loan on June 11th and Mrs. Taylor signed a deed of trust granting a security interest in her home to Green Tree. That same day, she also signed a Notice of Right to Cancel, which advised her that she had until midnight of June 14th (or three days from the date she received the Truth-in-Lending disclosures) to cancel the transaction. Neither Domestic Remodeling nor Green Tree gave Mrs. Taylor the Truth-In-Lending disclosures until June 27th. Several years later, Mrs. Taylor sued to rescind the transaction because of TILA violations.

ISSUE   Does Mrs. Taylor have the right to rescind the agreement?

DECISION   Yes. The TILA provides that in the case of any consumer credit transaction in which a security interest will attach to residential property, the consumer has a three-day cooling-off period. If the creditor fails to deliver forms, or fails to provide the required information, then the consumer's right of rescission is extended for three years after the date the transaction is consummated. No money shall be disbursed, no services shall be performed, and no materials delivered until the rescission period has expired. When a consumer rescinds a transaction, the security interest giving rise to the right of rescission becomes void and the consumer shall not be liable for any amount. In this case, Domestic Remodeling violated the TILA by constructing the addition to the house before the rescission period had expired. Further, the notice to rescind was misdated because three days after delivery of the disclosure forms would have been July 1st, not June 14th. Even if Mrs. Taylor should have been reasonably aware that the cooling-off period did not terminate until after she had received both the notice and the disclosures, by that time the construction was complete. The combination of these two violations resulted in a material failure to disclose to Mrs. Taylor her right to rescind. Accordingly, her right to rescind should have been extended to a three-year term.

http://www.law.utexas.edu/us5th/us5th.html

Tax Implications

Home ownership may give rise to various important tax implications. For instance, some localities impose a transfer tax when real property is sold to a new owner. And local governments often assess taxes against residential property as a means of funding schools and various other governmental functions. The state and federal governments generally permit these local taxes to be deducted from gross income for income tax purposes. Further, the interest paid on mortgage loans often is tax deductible.

Co-ownership of Real Estate

Frequently, more than one person may take title to residential real estate. For instance, Angela and David, a married couple, may buy a home and have it titled in both of their names. Or several families may buy units in a condominium complex and share access to certain common areas. Real estate law has established a set of procedures for dealing with conflicts among various co-owners of residential property.

Tenancy in Common

A **tenancy in common** arises when property is transferred to two or more persons with no indication of how they are to share it. It is likely to arise when a home owner wills her house to two or more heirs. Each of the tenants in common has an equal right to use and possess the property. None can exclude the others from exercising those ownership rights. Each tenant in common is responsible for all property expenses on an equal basis. Upon the death of any tenant in common, his ownership interest passes to his heirs.

When conflicts arise among tenants in common, they may request a court to *partition* the property. This could result in the court physically dividing the real estate among the co-owners. When such a division is not practical, a court may order the premises sold and divide the proceeds.

Joint Tenancy

A **joint tenancy** arises when property is equally transferred to two or more persons in a single transaction. Even then the document evidencing that transfer must specifically indicate the intent to create a joint tenancy. (Otherwise, the co-owners are tenants in common.) Upon the death of a joint tenant, her ownership rights are automatically transferred to the other co-owners on an equal basis. This is known as a *right of survivorship*. Joint tenants may not will their interest to anyone else. However, they may mortgage or sell it to someone else. When a sale occurs, the new buyer becomes a tenant in common. And, as with a tenancy in common, joint tenants may voluntarily divide the property or seek a court-ordered partition.

Tenancy by the Entirety

In many states, married couples may co-own real estate in a **tenancy by the entirety.** This form of co-ownership looks like a joint tenancy except that neither spouse may unilaterally transfer his or her property interest. Thus, in a tenancy by the entirety, a husband cannot sell his rights to the real estate unless his wife also signs the deed. Like the joint tenancy, neither spouse may transfer the property by will because of the right of survivorship. If the couple should later divorce, their property interests are transformed into a tenancy in common.

Community Property

Eight states treat property acquired by a spouse during marriage as **community property.** Each spouse has equal rights to real estate they acquire during the marriage. The fact that one spouse paid all or most of the purchase price is not relevant. However, if one spouse owned the home before the marriage, or acquired it by gift or will during the marriage, she would be the sole owner.

Cooperatives

With a **cooperative,** a group of people own an entire building and individual owners rent apartments within the premises. Only owners may rent and they generally need the consent of the others before they may sell their interest or sublease their apartments. The cooperative may be set up as a tenancy in common or a joint tenancy. However, it is more common for the people to establish a corporation that owns the building. The co-owners then become shareholders of the corporation.

Condominiums

A residential **condominium** is a multifamily structure. Unlike a cooperative, the separate units within the structure are individually owned. Each condominium owner has exclusive title to the particular unit she owns and usually may freely sell it to others without the consent of the other condominium owners. The hall-ways, elevators, swimming pools, and parking areas generally are owned by all of the co-owners as tenants in common.

Condominium buyers pay property taxes on their individual units and pay a monthly fee to the condominium association to maintain the common areas. Each owner, as well as anyone buying a unit from an owner, must comply with the bylaws governing the association. Condominium deeds generally make reference to bylaws to provide notice to buyers of the community obligations that attend condominium ownership.

Nahrstedt v.
Lakeside Village Condominium Association
878 P.2d 1275 (Sup. Ct. Cal. 1994)

FACTS Lakeside Village is a large condominium development consisting of 530 units spread throughout 12 separate three-story buildings. The residents share common lobbies and hallways, in addition to laundry and trash facilities. The project is subject to certain covenants, conditions, and restrictions (CC&Rs) that were included in the developer's declaration recorded with the county recorder at the inception of the development project. Included among the CC&Rs is a pet restriction, which provides in relevant part: *"No animals (which shall mean dogs and cats), livestock, reptiles or poultry shall be kept in any unit."* Ownership of a unit includes membership in the project's homeowners association, the Lakeside Condominium Association, the body that enforces the CC&Rs. Natore Nahrstedt purchased a Lakeside Village condominium and moved in with her three cats. When the Association learned of the cats' presence, it demanded their removal and assessed fines against Nahrstedt for each successive month she remained in violation of the pet restriction. Nahrstedt brought a lawsuit against the Association, challenging the enforceability of the pet restriction.

ISSUE Is the pet restriction enforceable against the condominium owner?

DECISION Yes. When creating a condominium project, the land developer must prepare a declaration that must be recorded prior to the sale of any unit in the county where the land is located. The declaration, which is the operative document for the creation of any common interest development, typically describes the real property and any structures on the property, delineates the common areas within the project as well as the individually held units, and sets forth restrictions pertaining to the use of the property. Use restrictions are an inherent part of any common interest development and are crucial to the stable, planned environment of any shared ownership arrangement. The restrictions on the use of property in any common interest development may limit activities in the common areas as well as in the confines of the home itself. Generally, courts uphold decisions made by the governing board of an owners association so long as they represent good faith efforts to further the purposes of the common interest development, are consistent with the development's governing documents, and comply with public policy. Subordination of individual property rights to the collective judgment of the owners association together with

continued

restrictions on the use of real property comprise the chief attributes of owning property in a common interest development. The recorded pet restriction of the Lakeside Village condominium development is not arbitrary, but is rationally related to health, sanitation, and noise concerns legitimately held by residents of a high-density condominium project. For many owners, the pet restriction may have been an important inducement to purchase into the development.

Restrictions on Home Ownership

Residential property owners have a variety of rights over their homes. However, those rights are not without limitations. A number of restrictions are placed on home owners by the common law, private agreements, and public land use controls. This final section examines some of the basic restrictions on land ownership.

Nuisance Law

Residential property owners possess a right of *quiet enjoyment* that entitles them to be free from unreasonable interference from others. If John engages in noisy or foul-smelling activities on his property, he may interfere with Amanda's quiet enjoyment of her own home. When his objectionable conduct is unreasonable, John's activities may constitute a **nuisance.** Amanda could sue for monetary damages or seek an injunction to force him to refrain from the undesirable use.

Mechanic's Liens

People who furnish labor or provide materials for the improvement of real estate may claim a **mechanic's lien** (or *materialman's lien*) on the property. Each state has its own laws defining how the lienholder may satisfy the lien. But in general, if the repairs or materials are not paid for, the lien may be foreclosed by selling the real estate and using the proceeds to pay the lienholder's claim. Thus, it is important for prospective home buyers to discover if the property is subject to any liens. The lienholder generally must record the lien in the office where the deed is recorded within a prescribed time period after the improvements were made (e.g., 30, 60, or 90 days, depending on the state).

Easements

Sometimes a person has the right to use the property of another, but cannot occupy it on a long-term basis. The right to make use of another's real property is known as an **affirmative easement.** If John has the right to use a private road over Amanda's property in order to reach his own house, he has an affirmative easement. A **negative easement** arises when a person has the right to prevent a neighbor from making certain uses of the neighbor's land. If Amanda is prohibited from erecting any structure that blocks John's view of the lake adjoining her property, John has a negative easement over Amanda's property.

Zoning Ordinances

Local governments generally have the authority to enact **zoning ordinances** that regulate the use of real estate. These regulations may restrict certain lots to only residential purposes or single-family dwellings. They also may control the size or nature (historic designs only) of a structure. New zoning ordinances may have only a prospective effect. This means they may not interfere with the uses of current home owners.

http:// www.capitol.state.tx. us/statutes/tocs/ lg021100toc.html is the site of local zoning statutes for the state of Texas.

Eminent Domain

Under its powers of **eminent domain,** the government may take *private property* for *public uses.* This sometimes is necessary for the construction of highways, public buildings, or urban renewal. However, when the government does take property for a public use, it must provide the private property owner with *just compensation.* Generally, this means the owner is entitled to the fair market value of his property.

Many disputes arise over whether a *taking* actually has occurred. For instance, many zoning ordinances deprive home owners of numerous uses of their property, but are not such a complete interference that they constitute a "taking" that requires compensation. When governmental action effectively denies a property owner the reasonable use of her land, she may file an **inverse condemnation** action to obtain compensation.

Restrictive Covenants

Home sellers may insist that prospective buyers agree to certain **restrictive covenants,** limiting the future use of the property. For instance, developers in residential subdivisions frequently place limits on the minimum size and cost of houses built on their lots. Or to maintain the beauty of a neighborhood, the developer may place a restriction in each deed prohibiting the erection of structures on certain portions of lots. However, restrictive covenants will not be enforced if they effectively prevent the transfer of the property to anyone else.

Citizens for Covenant Compliance v. Anderson

906 P.2D 1314 (SUP. CT. CAL. 1995)

FACTS Jared and Anne Anderson own two adjacent parcels of property that are part of two separate subdivisions in Woodside. One parcel was part of Skywood Acres. When Skywood Acres originally was subdivided, the developers recorded a declaration restricting property use to residential purposes only and limiting pet ownership to dogs, cats, hares, fowls, and fish. The second parcel was part of Friars subdivision. The declaration recorded for this subdivision restricted use to single-family residences and prohibited the keeping of animals other than household pets. The Andersons' deeds to their property made no mention of the recorded restric-

continued

tions. Soon after buying the lots, the Andersons contracted to operate a winery on the property. They also kept seven llamas there. Citizens for Covenant Compliance, an association representing both subdivisions, filed a lawsuit against the Andersons seeking to enforce the restrictions in the recorded declarations. The Andersons argued that the restrictions were unenforceable because they were never referenced in the deeds to the property.

ISSUE   Are the restrictive covenants enforceable?

DECISION   Yes. Modern subdivisions are often built according to a general plan containing restrictions that each owner must abide by for the benefit of all. By statute, any restrictive covenant may be recorded by the county recorder of the county in which the property is located. Recording consists of copying the restriction in the record book and indexing it under the names of the parties. Every conveyance of real property recorded as prescribed by law provides constructive notice of its contents to subsequent purchasers. Restrictive covenants have long been recorded under these provisions. These restrictions were recorded before any of the property was sold, thus giving the Andersons constructive notice of their existence. In essence, if the restrictions are recorded before the sale, later purchasers are deemed to agree to them.

QUESTIONS AND PROBLEM CASES

1. What is meant by the term *multiple listing?*
2. What is a mortgage contingency clause? Why is it important?
3. How does a quitclaim deed differ from a warranty deed?
4. Explain how a joint tenancy differs from a tenancy by the entirety.
5. Dorris Reed purchased a house from Robert King. Neither King nor his real estate agent told Reed that a woman and her four children had been murdered there 10 years earlier. Reed learned of the gruesome episode from a neighbor after the sale. Describe when a seller of a home has a duty to disclose information to the buyer. Did a duty to disclose arise in this particular case?
6. Bob Driggers sued Ken and Louann Locke for damages resulting from an automobile accident that occurred at an intersection. Driggers claimed that holly bushes growing on the Lockes's property at the intersection so impaired motorists' ability to see oncoming vehicles as to be the cause of the accident. Do the Lockes have a duty to trim their bushes so they do not obscure the view of oncoming traffic on the adjoining roadway?
7. Marvin Lewis held property sold by Christel Steinhoff pursuant to a land contract. When Lewis defaulted on his payments, Steinhoff sued to recover the remaining balance of the purchase price. Lewis claimed that the seller's only remedy upon default was a forfeiture. According to Lewis, this limited Steinhoff to retaking possession of the property and, therefore, precluded a suit for the balance due on the contract. Is the buyer correct?
8. On January 18th, Martha Rodash obtained a home equity mortgage of $102,000 on her house with AIB Mortgage Company to pay for medical treatment for her multiple sclerosis. On that same day, at the loan closing, the lender gave Rodash the following four documents: (1) a federal Truth-in-Lending Disclosure Statement; (2) a Mortgage Settlement Statement; (3) a Notice of Right to Cancel, which stated that Rodash had three

days to rescind the mortgage; and (4) an Acknowledgment of Receipt of Notice of Right to Cancel and Election Not to Cancel. Rodash signed the Election Not to Cancel at the closing. The loan proceeds were distributed on January 23rd. Rodash stopped making her mortgage payments on July 1st and, on December 26th, she notified the lender that she was rescinding the transaction under the Truth-in-Lending Act. Does Rodash have a right to rescind?

9. McCord purchased a farm from Looney on a land contract with the $250,000 purchase price to be paid over 20 years. Four years later, McCord received a $183,000 loan from the Farmers Home Administration (FmHA). In return he granted the FmHA a second mortgage on the farm. McCord subsequently defaulted on his obligation to Looney. At the time of the default, McCord had paid $123,000 to Looney but still owed $249,000 on the contract price. At that time, the property was worth $455,000. Looney sought a forfeiture of the contract. The FmHA objected to the proposed forfeiture, arguing that the court should order foreclosure proceedings. What is the difference between a forfeiture and a foreclosure? Why does it matter to the FmHA which one is used? Which procedure would McCord want?

10. David and Karen Binette bought residential property from the Dyer Library Association. At the time of the purchase, the Binettes were not aware of the existence of a 3,000-gallon underground oil tank on the property. They learned of its existence only after the closing. They later were forced to have it removed because it was corroded and allowed oil to leak into the ground and water to leak into their fuel oil, contaminating their property and destroying their heating system. State law imposed an absolute duty on property sellers to provide written notice of the existence of underground oil tanks prior to the sale or transfer of real estate. The Binettes sued the Dyer Library Association for negligent misrepresentation. The Library Association argued that liability for negligent misrepresentation requires the affirmative supplying of false information. Can the seller's silence make it liable for negligent misrepresentation?

RENTING AN APARTMENT

Andrew Noble and Stuart Odle signed a lease to rent an apartment from Linda Alis for one year. However, before taking possession they decided they did not want to live there. Although the apartment eventually was rented to someone else, the landlord sued Noble and Odle for the rent during the time it was vacant. The court rejected the landlord's claim and ordered her to return Noble's and Odle's security deposit because she had failed to obtain an occupancy permit as required by the city housing code.

Noble v. Alis, 474 N.E.2d 109 (Ct. App. Ind. 1985).

Consider this case, as well as the following questions, as you read this chapter.

What is the function of a lease?

What are each party's responsibilities after a tenant abandons an apartment or is evicted?

After the landlord/tenant relationship ends, under what circumstances may the landlord keep the security deposit?

What effect do local housing codes have on the landlord/tenant relationship?

Introduction

Renting a house or an apartment often is one of the first major decisions young adults make after leaving home. For some people this experience is trouble-free. The furnace never breaks, their roommates have no vices, the neighbors are quiet, and their landlord is kind and understanding when a rent check bounces. But many others are not quite as fortunate. They often learn the hard way that their lease provided them with much less protection, and far more responsibilities, than they anticipated.

Problems are less likely to occur and are more easily resolved when all of the involved parties understand their rights and duties before signing a rental agreement. Armed with a basic knowledge of landlord/tenant law, they can negotiate a contract that more fully meets their expectations and thereby avoid costly legal disputes.

http:// *www.law.cornell.edu/ uscode/42/3604.shtml* contains the U.S. Code on Fair Housing.

Chapter Overview

The chapter first introduces the basic nature of the landlord/tenant relationship. This includes a look at the fundamental document defining that relationship—the lease. The next two sections explore the corresponding rights and duties of landlord and tenants. The chapter closes with a review of the common ways in which the landlord/tenant relationship is terminated.

The Landlord/ Tenant Relationship

Under early English law, real property (land) could not be devised by will but personal property could. Leases were created as a means of avoiding this and other constraints. They were considered a form of personal property that was exempt from the many limits placed on the transfer of real property. Still, since they primarily anticipated a transfer of the underlying land, they were governed by property law, which offered little protection to tenants.

The Lease

The foundation of the landlord/tenant relationship is the **lease.** It is an agreement whereby the **landlord** (the *lessor*) grants the **tenant** (the *lessee*) the right to use a portion of his land for a period of time.

Today, most leases are less concerned with the underlying land than with the structures built on the property. As a result, modern landlord/tenant law draws heavily from contract law principles. Contract law more readily recognizes that tenants frequently have little knowledge or power when entering into leases. As we shall see, it provides special remedies to protect tenants from overreaching by their landlords. (See Figure 17–1 on pages 385-386.)

http:// *www.law.cornell.edu/ topics/landlord_ tenant.html* provides links to the *Uniform Residential Landlord-Tenant Act.*

Lease Formalities

Landlord/tenant relationships may be express or implied. Accordingly, no special words are needed to create a lease. But leases may be governed by the Statute of Frauds, which requires that certain contracts be in writing. (The writing requirements of the Statute of Frauds are discussed in Chapter 9.) Thus, many states require that leases for more than one year must be in writing. However, other states do not require a writing for a residential lease unless its term is for more than three years.

When a writing is required, the lease generally must include: (1) the names and signatures of the parties, (2) a description of the property to be rented, (3) the length of the lease, and (4) the amount of rent. Some states only require that the lease be signed by the party to be charged. Suppose Francine signs the lease but her landlord does not. Francine could not legally change her mind and refuse to honor the agreement. But her landlord could change his mind any time before Francine takes possession of the property. On the other hand, many other states require both signatures before a lease is binding on the parties. (The *Schultz* case on pages 388–389 illustrates the problems that may arise when only one party has signed a lease.)

Special Lease Clauses

Many landlords use lengthy written leases that are highly protective of the landlord's rights with little regard for the tenant's interests. Because many courts liberally enforce leases, each party should carefully read the document to avoid becoming saddled with unexpected and burdensome obligations. Four particular clauses that frequently appear in leases—savings clauses, acceleration clauses, late-fee clauses, and joint and several liability clauses—are discussed in later sections of the chapter. Another common provision—an attorneys' fees clause—is examined now.

Attorneys' Fees Clauses

Landlords frequently include an **attorneys' fees clause** in their leases. This provision requires that whenever the landlord hires an attorney to enforce any provision in the lease, the tenant must pay the attorney's fees if the landlord wins the case. This clause gives the landlord a great deal of leverage when legal disputes arise. If a tenant vigorously defends himself, the matter may end up in court. If the landlord wins, the tenant may have to pay both his lawyer and his landlord's attorney. In fact, some landlords bill tenants for the cost of an attorney even if they merely have their lawyer write a letter warning the tenant about a minor lease violation.

Side Agreements

Many friendships are destroyed by people trying to live together as roommates. This is particularly true of college students who may have met each other in a dormitory where a friend's study habits, drinking, drug use, girlfriend or boyfriend, and neatness never was an important issue. However, once people share close quarters, all of that frequently changes.

After carefully screening potential roommates, it may be wise to enter into both formal and informal **side agreements** governing the important aspects of living together. Issues like responsibility for utilities, cooking, and cleaning can be covered in these agreements. They also can be useful when one roommate leaves and attempts to rent her space to someone else. Should the remaining tenant have to accept a stranger or someone of the opposite sex as a roommate? These are important issues that should be anticipated in a side agreement.

Figure 17–1:   Real Estate Lease

This Lease Agreement (this "Lease") is made effective as of October 27, 199___, by and between

_____ ,

("Landlord"), and

_____ ,

("Tenant"). The parties agree as follows:

PREMISES.   Landlord, in consideration of the lease payments provided in this Lease, leases to Tenant _____ (the "Premises") located at

_____ , _____ , _____ .

TERM. The lease term will begin on April 1, 199___ and will terminate on _____ .

LEASE PAYMENTS.   Tenant shall pay to Landlord monthly payments of $_____ per month, payable in advance on the _____ day of each month, for a total annual lease payment of $_____ . Lease payments shall be made to the Landlord at _____ , _____ , _____ , which may be changed from time to time by Landlord.

POSSESSION.   Tenant shall be entitled to possession on the first day of the term of this Lease, and shall yield possession to Landlord on the last day of the term of this Lease, unless otherwise agreed by both parties in writing.

USE OF PREMISES/ABSENCES.   Tenant shall occupy and use the Premises as a dwelling unit. Tenant shall notify Landlord of any anticipated extended absence from the Premises not later than the first day of the extended absence.

KEYS.   The Tenant will be given _____ keys. If all keys are not returned to the Landlord at the end of the Lease, the Tenant shall be charged $_____ .

PROPERTY INSURANCE.   Landlord and Tenant shall each be responsible to maintain appropriate insurance for their respective interests in the Premises and property located on the Premises.

DEFAULTS.   Tenant shall be in default of this Lease, if Tenant fails to fulfill any lease obligation or term by which Tenant is bound. Subject to any governing provisions of law to the contrary, if Tenant fails to cure any financial obligation within _____ days (or any other obligation within _____ days) after written notice of such default is provided by Landlord to Tenant, Landlord may take possession of the Premises without further notice (to the extent permitted by law), and without prejudicing Landlord's rights to damages. In the alternative, Landlord may elect to cure any default and the cost of such action shall be added to Tenant's financial obligations under this Lease. Tenant shall pay all costs, damages, and expenses (including reasonable attorney fees and expenses) suffered by Landlord by reason of Tenant's defaults. All sums of money or charges required to be paid by Tenant under this Lease shall be additional rent, whether or not such sums or charges are designated as "additional rent."

HABITABILITY.   Tenant has inspected the Premises and fixtures (or has had the Premises inspected on behalf of Tenant), and acknowledges that the Premises are in a reasonable and acceptable condition of habitability for their intended use, and the agreed lease payments are fair and reasonable. If the condition changes so that, in Tenant's opinion, the habitability and rental value of the Premises are adversely affected, Tenant shall promptly provide reasonable notice to Landlord.

continued

Figure 17–1: continued

NOTICE. Notices under this Lease shall not be deemed valid unless given or served in writing and forwarded by mail, postage prepaid, addressed as follows:

LANDLORD:

Name: _____

Address: _____

_____, _____ _____

TENANT:

Name: _____

Address: _____

_____, _____ _____

Such addresses may be changed from time to time by either party by providing notice as set forth above.

ENTIRE AGREEMENT/AMENDMENT.   This Lease Agreement contains the entire agreement of the parties and there are no other promises or conditions in any other agreement whether oral or written.   This Lease may be modified or amended in writing, if the writing is signed by the party obligated under the amendment.

SEVERABILITY.   If any portion of this Lease shall be held to be invalid or unenforceable for any reason, the remaining provisions shall continue to be valid and enforceable.   If a court finds that any provision of this Lease is invalid or unenforceable, but that by limiting such provision it would become valid and enforceable, then such provision shall be deemed to be written, construed, and enforced as so limited.

CUMULATIVE RIGHTS.   The rights of the parties under this Lease are cumulative, and shall not be construed as exclusive unless otherwise required by law.

GOVERNING LAW.   This Lease shall be construed in accordance with the laws of the State of _____ .

LANDLORD:

_____

_____

_____

TENANT:

_____

_____

_____

Source: Quicken Business Law Partner® 3.0 CD-ROM. Copyright © 1997 Parson's Technology, Inc. All rights reserved.

Duration of the Lease

Landlord/tenant relationships generally are classified according to their duration and manner of termination. There are four fundamental categories of leases: (1) a term of years, (2) a periodic tenancy, (3) a tenancy at will, and (4) a tenancy at sufferance. (See Figure 17–2.) Each type is discussed below.

Term of Years

When a lease stipulates a fixed period of time that the landlord/tenant relationship is to last, it is called a **term of years.** The duration of this type of lease is expressly stated in either a written or an oral agreement. (Some states have laws limiting how long a lease may last.) A term-of-years lease automatically terminates at the expiration of the time period stated in the lease. But some leases may require that a tenant give advance notice of an intent to terminate or the lease is automatically renewed for an additional term.

Figure 17–2:   Lease Duration (Tenancies)

TYPE	DURATION	EXPIRATION
Term of Years	Fixed period established by lease.	Automatic unless lease requires notice.
Periodic Tenancy	No specific time period stated in lease. Duration often implied from when rent is due (i.e., month-to-month or year-to-year).	Month-to-month leases require one month notice. Year-to-year leases generally require between 30 days and 90 days notice.
Tenancy at Will	No fixed period. Either party may terminate by giving notice.	Many states require between 10 and 90 days' notice.
Tenancy at Sufferance	Continues until landlord demands posession or elects to treat relationship as a new tenancy.	Expires when landlord gives notice. If new tenancy is created, expiration is governed by type of tenancy.

Periodic Tenancy

When no specific duration is stated in the rental agreement, the parties have a **periodic tenancy.** The actual duration of the lease for termination purposes is determined by when the rent is due. Thus, if rent is paid monthly, the parties have a tenancy from month-to-month. When there is doubt as to the length of a tenancy, many courts presume that it is month-to-month. Periodic tenancies normally require advance notice of an intent to terminate by the landlord or tenant. Thus, with a month-to-month tenancy, either party must give one month's notice before she may legally end the relationship. Failure to give such notice triggers a renewal of the lease for another term (one month in this case). Under common-law rules, year-to-year tenancies required six months' notice of an intent to terminate. However, most states have laws reducing this notice period from between 30 and 90 days.

Tenancy at Will

With a **tenancy at will,** either the landlord or the tenant may freely terminate the landlord/tenant relationship. This tenancy arises when the landlord consents to a tenant taking possession without the parties ever agreeing upon a duration or stipulating a period for making rental payments. Under common law, the tenancy at will terminates as soon as one party receives the other's notice of an intent to terminate. However, some states have enacted laws requiring advance notice of between 10 and 90 days.

Schultz v. Wurdlow

1995 OHIO APP. LEXIS 333 (CT. APP. OHIO 1995)

FACTS   Emily Schultz and Kerri Minnich, students at Ohio State University, wished to rent an apartment from Earl Wurdlow. After the women submitted a "Rental Application and Agreement," Wurdlow informed them that they needed to have their parents complete and sign a "Parent Agreement." Contrary to his normal policy, Wurdlow allowed Schultz to move in before receiving the parental agreement because her mother promised to sign and return it. Minnich provided him a copy of the form; however, it included her signature rather than her mother's or father's signature. When Wurdlow realized that neither woman's parents were going to sign and return the form, he gave them 30 days' notice to move out. Although the women did so, Wurdlow claimed they also were responsible for his re-rental expenses and his loss of revenue while the apartment remained vacant.

ISSUE   Is the landlord entitled to retain the security deposit?

DECISION   No. Under this state's laws, a lease must be in writing and signed by the parties. While both tenants signed the "Rental Agreement," Wurdlow failed to do so. Accordingly, there was no properly executed lease. When an agreement purporting to be a lease has a defect and the tenant enters into possession and pays rent, a tenancy at will is created. The tenancy is subject to all other terms of the purported lease except duration. Duration is determined by the period covered by the expected rent payment. Because rent here was paid on a monthly basis, a month-to-month tenancy resulted and either party had the right to terminate the lease with one month's notice. Wurdlow gave such notice. When the women moved out of the apartment, Wurdlow's only claim was for re-rental expenses and loss of rent revenue; however, these are not recoverable under a properly terminated month-to-month tenancy. Therefore, the tenants are not liable for Wurdlow's losses.

Tenancy at Sufferance

Suppose that Andrew rented an apartment for 12 months. At the expiration of this term of years, he failed to move out as was required by his lease. Andrew has a **tenancy at sufferance.** This tenancy continues until the landlord either demands possession of the property or elects to treat the relationship as a new tenancy (term of years, periodic tenancy, or tenancy at will).

The Landlord's Rights and Duties

http:// *www.law.cornell.edu/ topics/landlord_ tenant.html* provides links to the *Uniform Residential Landlord-Tenant Act.*

Reference generally must be made to the lease to determine the specific rights and duties of the landlord. However, there are common-law and statutory rules that supplement, and sometimes override, the terms of the lease. This section explores the basic rights and responsibilities that most landlords have by virtue of the landlord/tenant relationship. Specifically, it examines rent, security deposits, duties to repair, warranties of habitability, housing codes, and the landlord's liability for personal injuries.

Rent

The compensation paid to the landlord in exchange for the tenant's right to possess the property is called **rent.** Normally, leases specify the amount and the time when rent is due. When the agreement fails to stipulate a particular amount, many courts rule that a landlord is entitled to the reasonable value of the property during the rental period. When there has been no agreement as to the time for payment, most courts hold that no rent is due until the end of the period covered by the lease. Thus, for a one-year lease, the landlord would not be entitled to payment until the end of that year.

Under traditional common-law rules, a landlord did not have the right to automatically terminate the lease when a tenant failed to pay rent. However, today most landlords reserve that right in their leases. Further, most states now have statutes giving landlords the right to summarily retake possession when rent is not paid in a timely manner. These rights are examined later in the chapter. At least half of the states give the landlord a lien on any of the tenant's personal property located at the premises to secure payment of the rent.

Late-Fee Clause

Most leases contain a **late-fee clause** that requires tenants to pay a preset amount if a rental payment is late. Courts routinely enforce these provisions if the amount of the late fee is reasonable. Late-fee charges of between $2 and $10 per day are likely to be upheld for most residential leases.

Joint and Several Liability Clause

In the *Nylen* case on pages 401–402, after one of three roommates moved out and stopped paying rent, the two remaining roommates were sued for the entire amount owed each month. Despite the fact that each of the three tenants probably believed she was liable for no more than one-third of the monthly rent, each was liable for the full amount. This is because most leases contain a **joint and several liability clause** that makes each tenant responsible for the other tenants' share of the rent. Thus, even though the two remaining tenants regularly paid their shares of the rent, they were evicted because they refused to pay the missing roommate's share. (Of course, if they had paid her share, they could sue her to recover that amount.)

Security Deposits

Leases usually permit landlords to retain a **security deposit** to assure payment of rent and to protect against a tenant's failure to return the premises in an undamaged condition. With residential leases the amount of the security deposit usually is equal to one month's rent. However, the parties generally may set the amount at any level they wish except in states that place a ceiling on the amount.

At the end of the lease term, the landlord is obligated to return the security deposit to the tenant subject to any damage claims the landlord may have. However, for many years landlords arbitrarily retained security deposits. As a result, many states have passed statutes governing their return. Some laws require that the deposit be held in a separate account and that the landlord pay interest on the money. Most statutes require that the security deposit be returned within a specified time period (e.g., 30 days) from the termination of the lease. If the landlord keeps any portion of the security deposit, he is required to notify the tenant in writing within the prescribed time period of his reasons for the retention. Failure to abide by these statutes may subject the landlord to damage claims by the tenant.

Duchon v. Ross

599 N.E.2D 621 (CT. APP. IND. 1992)

FACTS   Duchon rented an apartment from Ross and paid a $490 security deposit. The lease was to run for one year. After Ross notified Duchon that the lease would not be renewed when it expired, Duchon vacated the premises, sent Ross the keys, and informed her to send future correspondence to him at his business address. Several months later, Ross sent Duchon a letter stating a carpet needed to be shampooed, the locks had been rekeyed, a washer and dryer no longer were in the house, and the backyard was damaged because it had been used for vehicle parking and needed to be reseeded. The letter provided that once the costs associated with the damages were assessed, Duchon would receive a final accounting. Eventually, Duchon filed suit for return of his security deposit, reasonable attorneys' fees, and court costs.

ISSUE   Is Duchon entitled to his security deposit, attorneys' fees, and court costs?

DECISION Yes. Section 12 of the Indiana Code provides that "(a) upon termination of a rental agreement, all of the security deposit . . . *shall* be returned to the tenant, except for any amount applied to (a) the payment of accrued rent; (b) the amount of damages that the landlord has or will reasonably suffer by reason of the tenant's non-compliance with . . . the rental agreement; and (c) unpaid utility or sewer charges that the tenant is obligated to pay under the rental agreement; *all as itemized by the land-lord in a written notice delivered to the tenant together with the amount due within forty-five (45) days* after termination of the rental agreement and delivery of posses-sion. . . . (b) If the landlord fails to comply with subsection (a), the tenant may recover all of the security deposit due the tenant and reasonable attorneys' fees." Section 14 of the Indiana Code states: "In case of damage to the rental unit or other obligation against the security deposit, the landlord *shall* mail to the tenant, *within forty-five (45) days* after the termination of occupancy, *an itemized list of damages* claimed for which the security deposit may be used . . . , *including the estimated cost of repair for each damaged item . . . .* The list *must be accompanied by a check or money order for the difference between the damages claimed and the amount of the security deposit held by the landlord."* Section 15 provides: "Failure by the landlord to comply with the notice of damages requirement within the forty-five (45) days after the termination of occupancy *constitutes agreement by the landlord that no damages are due,* and the landlord *must* remit to the tenant immediately the *full* security deposit." Section 16 states that failure to abide by this 45-day rule makes the landlord *"liable* to the tenant . . . [for the amount of deposit] withheld by the landlord *plus* reasonable attorneys' fees and court costs." Section 14's direction is explicit and mandatory. Ross's letter is plainly inadequate under the statute as the letter provides that the costs for repairs had not been determined. Ross also is precluded from recovering other damages to which she may believe she is entitled. The clear intent of Section 15 is that if a landlord fails to provide the requisite notice within the 45-day period there are "no other dam-ages" to collect. A landlord can attempt to pursue a claim for "other damages" only if it returns the tenant's security deposit within 45 days or provides statutory notice.

Duty to Repair

Under the traditional common-law rules, the landlord had no duty to repair the rented property. The tenant, on the other hand, was required to ensure that premises were protected from the elements (rain, snow, etc.). However, there are several important exceptions to these common-law rules. First, when the landlord has a multiunit building and rents different units to different tenants, he is respon-sible for maintaining in good condition the **common areas** such as stairs, eleva-tors, hallways, sidewalks, and parking lots. Second, in the lease the parties may assign specific duties to repair to the landlord. Third, when the property has hid-den (latent) defects of which the landlord is aware but the tenant has not discov-ered, the landlord has a duty to repair. The landlord's duties to repair arising out of warranties of habitability and housing codes are discussed below.

Habitability

In the early years of landlord/tenant law, a landlord had no responsibility to guar-antee that the rented property was in a safe condition. This did not pose much of a problem when our country was an agrarian society and most leases involved farmland. Today, particularly with residential leases, judges are reluctant to follow that common-law rule. Modern courts regularly hold that a tenant's duty to pay rent is dependent upon the landlord's obligation to provide property that is suitable for human habitation (habitable). Accordingly, they impose on landlords who rent residential property an **implied warranty of habitability.**

The warranty of habitability first requires that the landlord provide the tenant with an apartment or house that is safe for dwelling at the beginning of the lease. Second, it requires the landlord to repair the premises if they should become unsafe at any time while the lease is in effect.

A landlord's breach of the implied warranty of habitability may provide the tenant with several remedies. Some states permit the tenant to recover a portion of her rent to compensate for the reduced value of the property. Other states allow a tenant to claim such a breach as a defense against an action brought by the landlord for the nonpayment of rent. It also may be possible for a tenant to repair the defect herself if the landlord does not do so within a reasonable time after learning of its existence. The tenant could then deduct the cost of the repairs from her rent. Finally, when an unrepaired defect causes a serious health hazard, a tenant might have grounds to move out and cancel the lease. (This type of constructive eviction is discussed later in the chapter.)

Dowler v. Boczkowski
691 A.2d 314 (Sup. Ct. N.J. 1997)

FACTS Ronald Boczkowski purchased a two-story, single-family dwelling that he used as rental property. Before renting the house, Boczkowski installed a smoke detector on the second-floor level where the bedrooms are located. Whenever the smoke detector was taken by an outgoing tenant, Boczkowski would install another one before the next tenant took possession of the home. William Dowler became a tenant on January 19th. His lease did not contain any provisions concerning a smoke detector. Prior to Dowler's taking possession, Boczkowski had relocated the smoke detector to a downstairs hallway. After Dowler took possession, neither he nor Boczkowski performed any maintenance on the smoke detector. On June 23rd, Dowler came home at about 5:30 p.m. after drinking a few beers. He took a shower and fell asleep. One of Dowler's partially extinguished cigarettes ignited a trash container while he was asleep. The fire spread and Dowler suffered serious burns because the smoke detector did not activate. Dowler sued Boczkowski, alleging that the implied warranty of habitability required that the landlord provide a reliable fire protection system to warn tenants of fire.

ISSUE Did the landlord breach an implied warranty of habitability?

DECISION No. There is an implied warranty of habitability and livability for residential dwellings. This gives a tenant an additional remedy of remaining in possession, making repairs, and deducting the cost of the repairs from future rents. A breach of this warranty may expose the landlord to liability for personal injuries caused by the breach. Here, the alleged negligent installation of the smoke detector in no way affected the habitability of the home. There can be no doubt that smoke detectors enhance the safety of a dwelling. But the absence of a smoke detector at a given location is readily apparent to a tenant. Dowler never complained to his landlord about the lack of smoke detectors or the placement of the existing smoke detector. Even if he thought additional smoke detectors were required, or the location should be changed, he elected not to make the change and deduct the costs from future rents.

http://www-camlaw.rutgers.edu/library/search.html

Housing Codes

In recent years, state and local governments have made substantial efforts to improve the quality of housing for low- and middle-income tenants. To carry out this task, they have enacted **housing codes** that impose various duties on landlords. For instance, in the case that opened this chapter, the landlord lost his right to recover damages from his tenants for abandoning their apartment because she failed to obtain an occupancy permit as was required by the city housing code.

Housing codes generally require landlords to maintain rental properties in a clean, safe, and sanitary condition. They may impose on the landlord the responsibility to make any structural repairs essential to the habitability of the building. Failure to comply with the code may subject the landlord to fines, loss of all or part of the agreed-upon rent, and even cancellation of the lease.

http://
www.cdc.gov/nceh/
pubcatns/1994/cdc/
books/housing/
housing.htm#top
contains text on housing codes and links to related sites.

Enforcement Agencies

Many communities have established enforcement agencies that inspect rental properties at the request of tenants. They can be useful in gathering evidence of code violations and in establishing that a building violates the warranty of habitability. Generally, after inspecting rental units, the inspectors provide the landlord with a list of defects that must be repaired within a reasonable period of time.

Expanded Roles for Codes

Modern housing codes often regulate many details of the landlord/tenant relationship. For instance, many cities have rent-control ordinances that place a ceiling on the amount of rent a landlord may charge. Other codes often contain **retaliatory eviction** provisions that prohibit landlords from evicting, or refusing to renew leases with, tenants in retaliation for the tenant complaining about code violations. Finally, many states and cities have enacted laws that prevent landlords from discriminating against people based on race, color, religion, national origin, age, marital status, or sexual orientation. (These laws often exempt people who rent a room in the landlord's house.) These statutes also make it unlawful for the landlord to make any oral or written inquiries concerning these protected classifications. For instance, in the case that follows, it would be illegal for the landlord to ask the prospective tenants if they were married to each other.

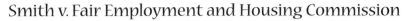

Smith v. Fair Employment and Housing Commission
913 P.2D 909 (Sup. Ct. Cal. 1996)

FACTS   Gail Randall and Kenneth Phillips, who were an unmarried cohabitating couple, applied to rent an apartment from Evelyn Smith. The landlord asked whether the couple was married and refused to rent to them because they were not. Smith's refusal to rent the premises to the couple violated the *California Fair Employment and Housing Act,* which makes it "unlawful . . . for the owner of any housing accommodation to discriminate against any person because of the . . . marital status . . . of that person." Smith argued that the act could not be enforced against her because it would violate her religious belief that sex outside of marriage is sinful and that it is a sin for her to rent her units to people who will engage in nonmarital sex on her property.

ISSUE   Is the state required to exempt the landlord from complying with the statute because of her religious beliefs?

DECISION   No. The first amendment does not support the landlord's claim. Her religion may not permit her to rent to unmarried cohabitants, but the right of free religious exercise does not relieve an individual of the obligation to comply with a valid and neutral law of general applicability on the ground that the law proscribes (or prescribes) conduct that her religion prescribes (or proscribes). This act's ban on marital status discrimination is a law both generally applicable and neutral towards religion. It prohibits all discrimination without reference to motivation, and its object is to prohibit discrimination irrespective of reason, not because it is undertaken for religious reasons. If this landlord does not wish to comply with an antidiscrimination law that conflicts with her religious beliefs, she could avoid the conflict without threatening her livelihood by selling her units and redeploying the capital to other investments. The exemption the landlord seeks can be granted only by completely sacrificing the rights of the prospective tenants not to be discriminated against by her in housing accommodations on account of marital status. To say that the prospective tenants may rent elsewhere is to deny them the full choice of available housing accommodations enjoyed by others in the rental market as well as the right to be treated equally by commercial enterprises.

Landlord's Liability for Injuries

Traditionally, landlords were not liable to tenants or third persons for injuries that occurred on the premises. This rule followed from the idea that since the tenant was in possession of the property, she was in a better position than the landlord to make necessary repairs. Of course, in those situations where the landlord has a duty to repair, his failure to reasonably carry out the duty may trigger tort liability. And there is a growing legal trend toward making landlords liable for some criminal conduct that occurs on their property.

Landlord's Tort Liability to Tenants

The growing influence of housing codes and judicial recognition of the implied warranty of habitability have resulted in an expanding duty on landlords to use reasonable care in maintaining rental units. Failure to comply with this duty may result in the landlord being liable in negligence for any resulting injuries suffered by a tenant. But liability usually does not occur unless the landlord had both notice of the defect and a reasonable opportunity to make the necessary repairs.

As a rule, courts do not make landlords liable in tort for **patent defects** (those that are readily observable), because the tenant should be able to see and avoid the danger. However, the landlord is liable for **latent defects** (hidden dangers) of which the landlord is aware when the tenant does not know of their existence. Consider the following case. (See Figure 17–3 on page 396.)

Howard v. Horn

810 P.2D 1387 (CT. APP. WASH. 1991)

FACTS   William Horn rented one unit of a duplex he owned to Larry Howard. Approximately two weeks after Howard moved onto the premises, he stumbled on the uneven cement walkway between the porch and the driveway. He fell across three steps leading to the front door and into the glass panel on the door, severely cutting his arm when the glass shattered. The accident occurred just after dusk while Howard was unloading groceries and carrying children from his car. The porch light was on and Howard admitted that the uneven edge of the cement was visible if you were looking for it. Howard sued Horn for negligence, contending that the uneven sidewalk and the failure to install a handrail along the front steps and safety glass in the window panel were evidence of the landlord's breach of a duty of care.

ISSUE   Should the landlord be liable in tort for the tenant's injuries?

DECISION   No. A landlord may be liable for personal injury to a tenant if the injury is caused by a latent defect known to the landlord. Here, the uneven cement and lack of a handrail were clearly observable patent defects. The failure to use safety glass was a latent defect that the landlord was not aware of until it was broken and he learned that it should be replaced with safety glass. Statutes providing a duty to repair base the landlord's duty upon notice and a reasonable time to repair. Moreover, the defects alleged here do not impact the livability of the dwelling so as to render it unfit for habitation.

Landlord's Tort Liability to Third Persons

Traditional landlord/tenant law held that after transfer of possession and control of leased property to the tenant, the landlord was not responsible to third persons on or off the premises. However, some jurisdictions have made an exception and extended a landlord's tort liability to third persons when two conditions are met. First, the landlord must have knowledge of the dangerous condition of the property. And second, the landlord must have retained some right to control the premises to protect against their dangerous condition. (See Figure 17–4 on page 397.)

Figure 17–3:   Landlord's Tort Liability to Tenant

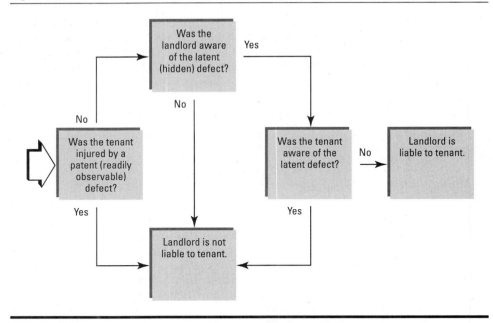

Landlord's Criminal Liability

Courts increasingly are finding that a landlord's duty to maintain the leased property in a safe condition includes the taking of minimal precautions to protect against reasonably foreseeable criminal acts. Such responsibility extends to crimes committed against both tenants and third persons who are on (and in rare cases, near) the property. However, this duty to control the wrongful acts of others is imposed only when such criminal conduct can be reasonably anticipated.

―――――――――――――――― Ethical Issue ――――――――――――――――

Suppose that in the past year several tenants have been assaulted in their apartments by an intruder who is still at large. Does the landlord have a duty to warn prospective tenants of this fact? Does he have a duty to hire security guards?

The Tenant's Rights and Duties

http://
www.law.cornell.
*edu/topics/landlord_*
tenant.html contains
text and links on
this topic.

The previous discussion of landlords' rights and duties implied certain corresponding rights and duties of tenants. For instance, the landlord's responsibility to provide and maintain a habitable dwelling supports the tenant's right to **quiet enjoyment** of the property. And the landlord's right to collect rent and receive a security deposit is balanced by the tenant's duty to provide the same. This section

Figure 17–4: Landlord's Tort Liability to Third Persons

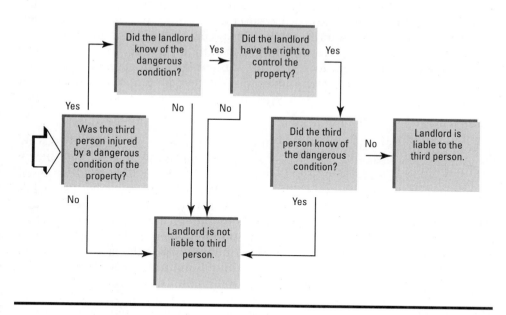

examines three other specific obligations imposed on tenants: (1) the duty not to commit waste; (2) certain duties that arise when tenants transfer their rights to the leased property; and (3) tenant liability for injuries that occur on the premises. Remember, however, that the lease must be examined to determine precisely which rights and duties a tenant has in any particular landlord/tenant relationship.

Waste

The tenant generally has the right to exclusive possession of the leased property. However, this right gives her a corresponding responsibility for the day-to-day care and upkeep of the premises. Her duty not to commit **waste** requires that the tenant make reasonable efforts to protect the property against harm. This may include a responsibility to perform ordinary repairs (i.e., replace a window, fix a dishwasher). But major repairs, particularly those of a structural nature like repairing a roof or replacing a furnace, generally are the responsibility of the landlord.

In the absence of lease terms governing use, the tenant may use the premises in any manner consistent with the purpose of the lease. Thus, a residential tenant might have an implied right to hang pictures and mirrors on the walls of their rented house or apartment. Further, the tenant has no legal liability for deterioration of the property resulting from ordinary wear and tear. However, a tenant who cuts trees, destroys the lawn, or knocks holes in walls has exceeded her rights to use the property. She may be required to compensate the landlord for violating her duty not to commit waste.

Transfers by the Tenant

Tenants with residential leases may freely transfer their right to possession of the premises unless the parties expressly restrict this right in their rental agreement. Modern leases regularly require tenants to obtain the landlord's permission before making such a transfer. However, courts generally do not permit a landlord to arbitrarily withhold consent for a transfer. It is common for leases to require the tenant to pay the landlord a fee to cover the administrative costs associated with the transfer. There are two common types of transfers: assignments and subleases.

Assignments

A tenant generally transfers his remaining rental interest to a third person by **assignment.** For instance, Jack leased an apartment for 12 months, but after 9 months he wanted to leave school for summer vacation. As a result, he assigned the remaining three months of his lease to Paula. As an assignee, Paula has assumed all of the rights and duties Jack possessed by virtue of the landlord/tenant relationship. However, this assignment does not automatically relieve Jack of his duties to the landlord. If Paula fails to pay rent, the landlord can recover it from Jack. To avoid continued liability, Jack must persuade the landlord to grant a *novation,* which is a new contract relieving him from further responsibility.

Subleases

When the transfer occurs through a **sublease,** the tenant transfers some, but not all, of her remaining right to possess the property. The original landlord/tenant relationship still exists. However, the tenant creates a new landlord/tenant relationship with the sublessee. Suppose that Jane rented an apartment for 12 months from Dunn Hill Apartments. With 8 months remaining on the lease, she persuaded Mark to sublease the apartment for four months while she studied overseas. Unlike in an assignment, she has not transferred all of her remaining rights to the property, since she will have another four months remaining on her lease when she returns from her overseas studies. And, as a sublessee, Mark does not acquire Jane's rights or duties under the lease with Dunn Hill. Instead, there still exists a landlord/tenant relationship between Dunn Hill and Jane, as well as another landlord/tenant relationship between Jane and Mark. Jane now is Mark's landlord.

Tenant's Liability for Injuries

Third persons who are injured as a result of unreasonably dangerous conditions on the rental property generally may recover in tort from the tenant. This is because the tenant is the person with possession of, and control over, the premises. Of course, when injuries arise from defects in the common areas, from a landlord's negligent repairs, or from sources over which the tenant had no control, the tenant is not liable.

Termination of the Landlord/Tenant Relationship

If all goes well, the landlord/tenant relationship will not end until the expiration of the term designated in the written or oral rental agreement. Our earlier examination of leases discussed how the duration is determined as well as the requirements for termination of each type of tenancy. Sometimes, however, a tenant surrenders the premises before the lease has expired. And, other times, a landlord may rightfully or wrongfully force a tenant off of the property. This final section examines these types of termination.

Surrender and Abandonment

The landlord/tenant relationship can be terminated prior to the time the lease normally would end if the parties mutually agree to a **surrender.** This agreement between the landlord and the tenant relieves the tenant of further liability, including the duty to pay rent, under the lease.

Abandonment occurs when a tenant wrongfully vacates the premises prior to expiration of the lease. It may be viewed as an offer of surrender by the tenant, which may be accepted by the landlord. As a general rule, a tenant is liable for all remaining rent under the lease if she abandons the property. However, if the landlord retakes possession of the premises or rerents them to someone else, he has accepted the offer of surrender and the tenant is relieved of any obligation to pay further rent.

Acceleration Clauses

With an **acceleration clause,** all of the rent owed for the remainder of the lease term immediately falls due if the tenant breaches the lease. Suppose Caroline signs a one-year lease that requires her to pay $400 in rent each month. However, after paying rent for two months, she loses her job, stops paying rent, and abandons the apartment. Despite the fact that the landlord retakes possession of the property, an acceleration clause in her lease would require her to pay the remaining balance of $4,000 (10 months x $400) to the landlord.

Many courts are suspicious of such clauses because they provide little encouragement to a landlord to try to rerent the apartment and minimize the amount of money a tenant might owe. But, as long as the landlord makes a reasonable effort to rent the premises, the acceleration clause is likely to be enforced. However, a court will reduce the amount Caroline owes by any amount the landlord collects if he rerents the apartment to other tenants during the remaining term of Caroline's lease. Consider the following case.

Aurora Business Park v. Albert

548 N.W.2D 153 (Sup. Ct. Iowa 1996)

FACTS Michael Albert agreed to rent property from Aurora Business Park on March 1, 1991. The lease was for five years, with rent to be paid on a monthly basis. Albert immediately took possession of the property after signing the lease, but abandoned the premises in June of 1993. Aurora was unable to rerent the property. The lease contained the following clause: *"In the event of termination of this Lease by reason of a violation of its terms by the Lessee, Lessor shall be entitled to prove claim for and obtain judgment against Lessee for the balance of the rent agreed to be paid*

continued

for the term herein provided, plus all expenses of Lessor in regaining possession of the premises and the reletting thereof, . . . crediting against such claim, however, any amount obtained by reason of any such reletting." Aurora retook the property and brought an action to recover past unpaid rent and the balance of rent for the remaining term of the lease. Albert asserted that an award of future rent would be improper because the acceleration clause constituted an unenforceable penalty and, alternatively, that the court was required to offset any future rent by the reasonable use of the premises to the landlord or a reasonable amount for rent the landlord would actually receive during the remaining term of the lease.

ISSUE   Is the tenant liable for the balance of rent for the remaining term of the lease?

DECISION   Yes. Albert breached the lease by abandoning the property and by defaulting on the rental payments. Some jurisdictions have held that provisions for the acceleration of payments of rent are invalid as unenforceable penalties. Other jurisdictions, however, find specific acceleration clauses to be valid and enforceable. In this state, a landlord and tenant may agree to the landlord's remedies if the tenant abandons the property and fails to pay rent, as long as the provision does not constitute a penalty. Lease clauses that set the amount of damages owed (liquidated damages clauses) are not a penalty when the amount of damages would be uncertain and the amount fixed is fair. In this case, when the lease was signed it was not possible to know if another suitable tenant could be found if a breach were to occur. Thus, there was a considerable amount of uncertainty as to actual amount of damages Aurora would suffer if Albert breached the agreement. It is fair for the landlord to recover damages equal to the amount of rent reserved in the lease, less any amounts received in rerenting the premises. The acceleration clause places Aurora in the position it would have occupied had Albert performed the entire lease. However, if Aurora is able to rerent the property during the remaining term of Albert's lease, it must credit this against the amount Albert owes.

Eviction

Landlords may have a right to **evict** tenants who breach the terms of the rental agreement. For instance, a tenant's failure to pay rent, waste of the property, or behavior that disrupts other tenants' right to quiet enjoyment may be grounds for eviction.

Summary Process Statutes

Most jurisdictions have **summary process statutes** that provide landlords with a quick judicial procedure for regaining possession of rented property. Each statute provides a list of circumstances that must be met before a landlord can avail herself of this accelerated process. A tenant's nonpayment of rent or holding over after expiration of the lease's terms generally permit use of the summary process.

Self-Help

Many states still permit landlords to use **self-help** to evict tenants who have violated the terms of their lease. But most states prohibit the landlord from using force when evicting a tenant. What constitutes a peaceable repossession of the property varies from jurisdiction to jurisdiction. Landlords who use unnecessary force may be liable to the tenant for damages and the tenant generally is able to regain possession of the property.

Savings Clauses

If the landlord evicts a tenant, the tenant generally is relieved of any obligation to pay further rent. This is because once the relation of landlord and tenant is annulled, the promise to pay rent also is extinguished. A **savings clause** creates an exception to this rule. This clause provides that termination of the landlord/tenant relationship does not affect the former tenant's liability for rent. Accordingly, if a tenant is evicted from her apartment for violating the terms of the lease, she still is liable for the rent for the full lease term. Of course, if the landlord rerents the property during the remaining time left on her lease, he must credit that rent against the amount the former tenant owes.

Nylen v. Park Doral Apartments

535 N.E.2D 178 (CT. APP. IND. 1989)

FACTS   Susan Nylen, Elizabeth Lewis, and Julie Reed, students at Indiana University, executed a rental agreement with Park Doral Apartments for a term from August 26, 1986, until August 19, 1987. Performance of the lease was secured by a deposit in the amount of $420, constituting prepayment of rent for the last month of the lease term. At the end of the fall semester, Julie Reed moved out of the apartment and in February 1987, she refused to pay any further rent. Susan Nylen and Elizabeth Lewis remained in possession of the apartment, paying only two-thirds of the total rent due for the month of February. Park Doral Apartments filed suit for ejectment of the tenants for failure to pay rent in full for the month of February. While the ejectment proceedings were pending, Susan Nylen and Elizabeth Lewis made a payment of $280 for the rent due in March. Subsequently, the court ordered Nylen and Lewis to pay full rent or vacate the premises. They vacated the premises pursuant to court order on March 13, 1987. At a final hearing on the issue of damages, the court awarded delinquent rent owed plus the balance of rent due under the lease from the time of Nylen and Lewis' eviction. The delinquent portion of the rent was $140 per month for February and March, and the balance for the remainder of the lease was $420 per month for April through July. The court also awarded $362 in late fees, $600 in attorney fees, and $75.24 in consequential damages. Total relief awarded by the court, set off by the $420 security deposit, was $2,577.24 plus the costs of the action. The tenants appealed this decision, arguing the award of future rents was contrary to law because the eviction terminated the lease and abrogated the duty to pay further rent. They also claimed the lease was unconscionable and therefore unenforceable.

ISSUE   Were the tenants liable for the rent due for the entire term of the lease?

DECISION   Yes. It is a general rule that a tenant will be relieved of any obligation to pay further rent if the landlord deprives the tenant of possession and beneficial use

continued

and enjoyment of any part of the premises by an actual eviction. However, an exception to the general rule exists when the lease includes a savings clause expressly providing that termination shall not affect the accrual of liability for rent. Park Doral's rental agreement with Nylen and Reed contained a savings clause that stated: *"Eviction of tenant for a breach of lease agreement shall not release tenant from liability for rent payment for the balance of the term of the lease."* The savings clause in the rental agreement is valid and enforceable. It is entirely consistent with existing case law. Park Doral's suit for ejectment did not operate as a denial of the rental agreement that barred recovery under the savings clause of the lease. A suit for ejectment does not constitute a denial that a lease agreement exists. It is a means of enforcing the lease. Thus, the ejectment action brought by Park Doral does not preclude recovery of future rents under the savings clause. The trial court's enforcement of the lease provision permitting the landlord to recover a $2 per day late fee also is correct. Where the nature of an agreement is such that a breach would result in damages which are uncertain and difficult to prove, and where the stipulated sum payable on breach is not greatly disproportionate to the loss likely to occur, that fixed sum will be accepted as liquidated damages and not as a penalty. While there was a disparity in bargaining power between Park Doral Apartments and the tenants, it cannot be said that this disparity led the tenants to sign the lease unwillingly and unaware of its terms. They were given an opportunity to read and did in fact read the rental agreement. They asked questions of the manager concerning the lease, although neither one objected to or sought modification of the lease terms. The rental agreement was a standardized form contract that strongly favored Park Doral Apartments. However, contracts are not unenforceable simply because one party enjoys an advantage over the other. The fact that the lease contained terms favorable to Park Doral did not render it unconscionable. It cannot be defined as one "such as no sensible man not under delusion, duress or in distress would make, and such as no honest and fair man would accept."

Ethical Issue

Many tenants do not understand the legal significance of lease provisions like savings clauses, acceleration clauses, and joint and several liability clauses. Does the landlord have an ethical duty to fully explain these clauses before a new tenant signs the lease?

Constructive Eviction

When a landlord substantially interferes with a tenant's quiet enjoyment of the property, he may have committed a **constructive eviction.** If the premises are uninhabitable because of a lack of heat or water, or they are otherwise unsafe, there may be grounds for constructive eviction. However, before making such a claim, a tenant normally must notify her landlord of the problem and allow a reasonable time for the defect to be repaired. Finally, she must abandon the premises within a reasonable time after it is obvious that the problem is not being repaired. (Some courts do not require the tenant to abandon the property.) When a constructive eviction occurs, the tenant is relieved of liability for rent since the lease is terminated.

Sam v. Beaird

685 So.2d 742 (Ct. App. Ala. 1996)

FACTS   Marlene Sam and James Beaird entered into a residential lease whereby Sam agreed to rent a house from Beaird. Under the lease agreement, Beaird was obligated to maintain the house at certain designated standards. Sam asserted that the house was not habitable on two occasions during her occupancy. First, she claimed that in November there were recurring problems with the heating system in the house. And during the following January, a pipe under the house froze, leaving Sam without water for six days. Sam sued Beaird under a theory of constructive eviction.

ISSUE   Did the landlord constructively evict this tenant?

DECISION   No. To constitute a constructive eviction resulting from the interference with the right of the tenant to quiet enjoyment, it is necessary that the conduct of the landlord manifest an intent to deprive the tenant of possession of the rented premises. The intent need not be actual, but may be presumptive, or inferable from the character of the landlord's interference. The evidence presented at trial did not indicate that Beaird intended to render the house uninhabitable. Although Sam testified that the property fell into disrepair at times during her occupancy, Beaird took steps to make the necessary repairs when notified that repairs were needed.

QUESTIONS AND PROBLEM CASES

1. Are oral leases enforceable? Explain.
2. What is the legal effect of a savings clause in a lease?
3. How does an assignment differ from a sublease?
4. Under what circumstances will a landlord be liable in tort for injuries suffered by a tenant on the premises of the rental property?
5. Burke and Maltbie, students at Indiana University, entered into a written lease with Breezewood for 12 months. Burke and Maltbie were joint lessees and were obligated to pay $235 per month; they had agreed between themselves that Burke would pay $122.50 and Maltbie would pay $112.50. The lease contained a provision that Breezewood would plaster and paint the bathroom, and repair the toilet and cold water pipes to a proper working condition. It also stated that the tenants had examined the premises and their taking possession was conclusive evidence of receipt of the apartment in good order and repair. Burke and Maltbie took possession and paid a $235 damage deposit. They immediately discovered numerous defects: rotting porch floorboards, broken and loose windows, an inoperable front door lock, leaks in the plumbing, a back door that would not close, a missing bathroom door, inadequate water pressure, falling plaster, exposed wiring over the bathtub, and a malfunctioning toilet. Later they discovered a leaking roof, cockroach infestation, the absence of heat and hot water, more leaks in the plumbing, and pigeons in the attic. The city had in effect a minimum housing code at that time. Complaints by persons other than Burke and Maltbie prompted code enforcement officials to

inspect the dwelling. They discovered 50 violations, 11 of which were hazardous to the health of the occupant. These conditions remained largely uncorrected after notice by the code officers and further complaints by Burke and Maltbie. Burke developed pneumonia and was hospitalized, the cause of which he attributed to inadequate heating of the apartment. Maltbie finally vacated the premises, notified Breezewood, and refused to pay further rent. Breezewood agreed to let Burke remain and pay $112.50 per month. Breezewood then filed suit against Burke and Maltbie for $610.75, which was the balance due under the written rental contract. Burke and Maltbie each filed counterclaims in which they contended there was an implied warranty of habitability that Breezewood had breached. They sought damages and a reduction in rent. Evidence presented by Burke and Maltbie showed that the reasonable rental value of the apartment was only $50 per month as it was during colder weather and $75 per month during warmer weather. Did Breezewood breach an implied warranty of habitability?

6. Charlene Thomas owned a house that she rented to her daughter, Julie Hoffard. There was no written rental agreement, but Hoffard paid rent on a month-to-month basis. On several occasions, when Hoffard acquired too many pets, Thomas instructed her to remove some of them from the property. Hoffard owned a large black labrador retriever, which was usually kept penned up. However, it was occasionally allowed to roam the surrounding premises. The dog had once been quarantined after several complaints that it had attacked people. Thomas was aware of these problems with the dog. Finally, the dog attacked and severely bit Rosa Park, a small child who was playing in a neighboring lot at the time of the attack. The child's parents sued Thomas, claiming that a landlord has a duty to control his tenant's pets. Is the landlord liable in tort for the dog's attack on the child?

7. Rivard Melson rented a residence from Mary Cook in October. Their oral lease required Melson to pay $400 per month in rent. In November, Cook informed Melson by letter that the rent would be increased to $525 per month, effective January 1st. On December 10th, Melson told Cook that he would not pay the increased rent. Melson gave Cook a check for $400, as rent for January, on January 2nd. Cook returned the check and stated that the rent was now $525. When Melson finally vacated the premises on February 1st, Cook sued him for $525 in unpaid rent. Is Melson liable for the increased rent?

8. Maria S. was raped by three unknown intruders in the apartment she shared with her brother and uncle. The apartment was owned and managed by Willow Enterprises. She testified that she was unable to identify her attackers, and was unaware of how they gained access to the building. Maria's uncle was employed as a security guard at the building six days a week. But the rape occurred on a Monday, the uncle's day off. Maria argued that the failure to provide a security guard on Mondays demonstrated that the landlord was negligent. However, she was unable to present adequate evidence of prior criminal activity at the premises. Should Willow Enterprises be liable to Maria in negligence?

9. John Marshall rented a two-bedroom apartment in his multiunit apartment building to Anita Hatfield on April 11th. Their written lease stated that the premises were *"to be used by LESSEE from the 11th day of April 1992 until the 30th day of April 1992.* The rent was $364 per month. A dispute arose the following month when Hatfield began paying rent in partial payments contrary to the terms of the lease. Marshall also received complaints that Hatfield's children were noisy and disturbing other tenants in the building. Approximately six weeks after the lease began, Marshall filed a court action seeking to evict Hatfield and claiming damages for back rent. Hatfield agreed to vacate the apartment by June 30th and paid all rental and late fees owing up to and including the month of June. However, Marshall also demanded rent for July because he was unable to find another tenant until August. He claimed she was liable for this

amount since they had a tenancy from year-to-year. Is Marshall correct?

10. Carl Duda rented a house to Randy Thompson for a term of two years. As that lease was nearing expiration, Thompson renewed for another two years for the period January 1, 1995, to December 31, 1996. The annual rent was $19,200, which could be paid in monthly installments for the convenience of the tenant only. The written lease provided that in case of default by the tenant, the landlord could automatically demand the annual amount (or balance of the amount). Thompson failed to pay his rent for November and December 1995. On January 10, 1996, Duda demanded that Thompson pay the two months' past-due rent plus the entire $19,200 for 1996. Should the court require that Thompson pay the entire amount?

Family Relationships

MARRIAGE AND COHABITATION

Mary and Ralph Lampus were married in Mexico on May 26, 1950, and lived together as husband and wife until he died on April 9, 1990. In reality, Ralph was never legally divorced from Caroline Lampus, his first wife. He concealed this fact from Mary for the 40 years they lived together. It was not until Ralph died that Mary learned from a hospital nurse that Ralph's prior marriage had not ended in divorce. She sued his estate for damages because of his failure to inform her that he already was married. The trial court dismissed her claim, ruling that it was blocked by the state's *heartbalm statute*.

Lampus v. Lampus, 660 A.2d 1308 (Sup. Ct. Pa. 1995).

What is the legal effect of the cohabitation between Ralph and Mary? Was it a marriage?

What is a common-law marriage? Did Ralph and Mary have a common-law marriage?

What is a "heartbalm statute"? Does it block Mary's lawsuit?

Introduction

What is marriage? To some it evokes a sense of belonging and emotional support. It suggests family and offers the vision of a safe haven in a vast universe threatening to overwhelm us. Others see marriage as a ceremony where two people legally intertwine their lives. Simultaneously, it may signify a physical and emotional bond between two individuals.

Courts have long considered marriage to be perhaps the most important relationship in civilized society. Yet a quick look around us makes clear that this institution is in great turmoil. Over half of all marriages end in divorce. And growing numbers of couples are, either by choice or by legal necessity, cohabitating rather than formally marrying. Still, the majority of people are not giving up on marriage. In fact, most divorced people remarry.

If the marital institution is to survive, it must keep pace with the rapid changes in peoples' expectations and lifestyles. This presents a tremendous challenge for a legal system that must effectively regulate the personal and property rights of married and cohabiting couples. The challenge is even greater for each of us as we attempt to understand the role of law in our personal relationships.

Chapter Overview

The chapter begins by examining the traditional concept of marriage and the regulatory requirements governing its creation. This is followed by a look at several alternatives to traditional marriage such as common-law marriage, cohabitation, and same-sex marriage. The discussion then turns to the various rights and obligations husbands and wives assume by virtue of their marital relationship. Attention is then focused on how couples can contractually arrange their rights and responsibilities through the use of prenuptial agreements. The chapter closes with a brief survey of the legal issues that arise when an engagement is broken.

Marriage Requirements

Because our legal system honors the *private bond* between marriage partners, they are given tremendous freedom to define the essential nature of their relationship. However, courts are not disinterested in what occurs within the marital relationship. They have characterized marriage as the most important relation in life and as the foundation of the family and of society. It has been described as fundamental to the very existence and survival of the human race. Due to this status as a vital *social institution,* many features of marriage long have been regulated in the name of the public interest.

There is no federal law of marriage. As with most family law matters, the authority to regulate the marital relationship is reserved exclusively to the states. This includes the power to determine the contractual requirements, the qualifications of the parties, the procedures necessary to solemnize the marriage, and the rights and obligations created by matrimony. Although the details vary from state to state, the most basic provisions are strikingly similar.

Procedural Steps

Most states refuse to recognize a marriage unless the prospective spouses meet certain consent, consanguinity, health, licensure, and ceremonial requirements. Failure to strictly comply with these procedural steps may result in a state annulling the purported marriage. (See Figure 18–1.)

Consent

The states view marriage as a *civil contract* between two persons, and the essence of this contract is the **consent** of the parties. It follows from the consensual nature of marriage that each partner must possess the mental capacity to understand the legal, economic, and emotional commitment he or she is making. Similarly, a marriage entered into on the basis of fraud or duress would be void.

Each state has established an *age of consent* as a prerequisite to marriage. In most states this is the age of majority, which generally is 18. However, the states also permit younger persons (usually no younger than 16) to marry with *parental consent*. The parental consent requirement sometimes is waived for pregnant teenagers. (In isolated cases a court may override the consent requirements.)

Consanguinity

The term **consanguinity** refers to blood relationships or common ancestry. All states prohibit marriages between very close relatives. Thus, it is unlawful to marry one's parents, children, grandparents, siblings, aunts, uncles, nieces, or nephews. Many states do not recognize marriages between first cousins. And some states disallow marriage between a stepparent and stepchild.

Figure 18–1: Marriage Requirements

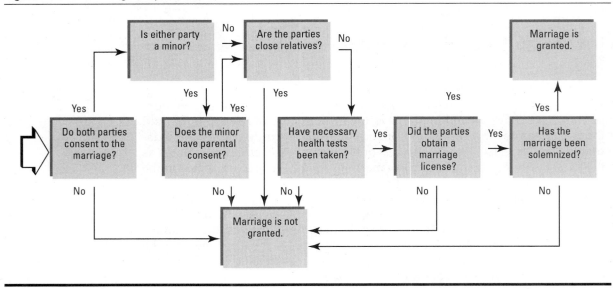

Health Examinations

Many states require blood tests or some other type of physical examination to ensure that both partners are not carrying a communicable disease. The number of states imposing these **health examinations** had been in decline. However, with the growing awareness of the AIDS epidemic, more and more states now are demanding a premarital HIV antibody test.

Licensure

Generally, both partners must apply for a **marriage license.** This permit will not be granted unless the consent, consanguinity, and health requirements, as well as any residency requirements, are met. Further, if it is discovered that one of the applicants is legally married to another, the license will be denied. Thus, in our chapter opener, Mary and Ralph were not married because of his failure to receive a divorce from Caroline. Finally, most states impose a **waiting period** so the prospective spouses can fully contemplate the action they are about to undertake.

http:// *www.idph.state.il.us/ vital/forms/marriage. htm* contains information on Illinois marriage license procedures.

Ceremonial Requirements

Most married couples participate in a ceremonial wedding, which involves having the license validated by someone authorized to perform marriages, such as a member of the clergy or a public official. The content of this ceremony is left to the discretion of the parties, except that they must **solemnize** their relationship. This usually involves exchanging vows verifying their matrimonial intent to the presiding official and, frequently, to one or more witnesses. The husband and wife then sign and record a *marriage certificate.*

Annulment

States sometimes deny the existence of a marital contract despite the couple having secured a license and solemnized their relationship in a marriage ceremony. This proceeding, known as an **annulment,** could occur if one of the partners never legally terminated his or her marriage to a prior spouse, if one of the partners was under age and did not obtain parental consent, or if one partner fraudulently induced the other to get married. This fraud also may be found when a partner conceals important information prior to the wedding (e.g., being pregnant, having children by a previous marriage, having been convicted of a felony, having an infectious venereal disease, or being sexually impotent). In our chapter opener, the purported marriage between Ralph and Mary must be annulled because he was already married.

An annulment is a declaration by a court that a legal marriage never took place. Thus, both partners are returned to the legal and financial status they were in prior to the faulty marriage. However, courts sometimes exercise their equitable powers to award temporary support and attorneys' fees to an innocent spouse who was fraudulently induced into marriage. To recover such an award, the defrauded spouse must demonstrate her need for emergency financial assistance as well as the other spouse's ability to pay. Courts have a great deal of discretion in making these determinations.

In Re Marriage of Johnston
22 CAL.RPTR.2D 253 (APP. 4 DIST. CAL. 1993)

FACTS   After 20 months of marriage, Brenda sought to have her marriage to Donald annulled on the grounds that her consent had been fraudulently obtained. At the trial, Brenda testified she was unaware of Donald's severe drinking problem until after the marriage and was upset to discover this and disappointed in his refusal to seek help. She knew before the ceremony that he was unemployed, but did not realize he would refuse to work thereafter. She stated their sex life after marriage was unsatisfactory and that he was dirty and unattractive. In short, he turned from a prince into a frog. During their marriage, Brenda transferred title to a home she owned prior to the marriage to her name and Donald's. If the marriage is annulled, the property transfer would be void and the home would belong to Brenda. However, if the marriage is terminated through divorce, Donald may share in a distribution of the property.

ISSUE   Should the marriage be annulled?

DECISION   No. A marriage is voidable and may be adjudged a nullity if the consent of either party was obtained by fraud, unless such party afterwards, with knowledge of the facts constituting the fraud, freely cohabited with the other as husband or wife. Brenda has presented insufficient grounds for an annulment. The concealment of incontinence, temper, idleness, extravagance, coldness or fortune inadequate to representations cannot be the basis for an annulment. The fraud must go to the *very essence* of the marital relationship before it is sufficient for an annulment.

Nontraditional Relationships

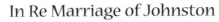

Many couples do not avail themselves of traditional marriages. There are numerous explanations for this. Some have had unhappy experiences with marriage, yet still wish to live with a companion for emotional, physical, or economic reasons. Others are uncertain of their commitment to one another and decide to live together on a trial basis. In a growing number of cases, the partners may be same-sex couples who are denied the right to marry. This section explores three examples of nontraditional relationships: common-law marriage, cohabitation, and same-sex marriage.

Common-Law Marriage

Some people, for a variety of reasons, live together as man and wife without ever obtaining a marriage license or taking part in a marriage ceremony. While the actual requirements of a **common-law marriage** vary among the states, there are three fundamental steps that must be met: a present intent to be married; a holding out as husband and wife to others; and cohabitation. Contrary to most people's belief, there is no minimum time period that couples must live together in order to create a common-law marriage. They are married the instant the three requirements are met. The key test is that the elements must be demonstrated with enough definiteness that neither party is surprised by the existence of the marriage.

In our chapter opener, Ralph and Mary Lampus lived together as man and wife for 40 years. At first glance, they certainly appear to have met the requirements for a common-law marriage. However, they would not be treated as common-law spouses even though they lived in a state, Pennsylvania, that accepts such marriages. This is because Ralph was already married to Caroline. Until that marriage ended by divorce, he could not marry anyone else under either a traditional or a common-law marriage.

Marriage Validation Statutes

Only 12 states continue to permit common-law marriages to take place within their borders. The other 38 states have withdrawn approval because of the fraud, confusion, and surprise that often accompany their recognition. However, many states have enacted *marriage validation statutes*, which provide that they will recognize a marriage that was validly contracted in another state. For instance, Pennsylvania permits common-law marriages while New York does not. If a couple become man and wife by common law while residing in Pennsylvania and then later move to New York, that state will treat them as man and wife out of deference to the laws of Pennsylvania.

Ram v. Ramharack

571 N.Y.S.2d (Sup. Ct. N.Y. 1991)

FACTS   Sylvie Ram and Bisram Ramharack began living together in 1978 while they were both married to other people. By 1984, they were divorced from their respective spouses and free to solemnize their relationship. Sylvie became pregnant by Bisram in 1984 and as soon as her divorce became final, they went to the marriage license bureau. When the clerk requested copies of their divorce papers, Bisram said they were locked in his safe-deposit box and he had lost the key. Subsequently, when his divorce papers became available, Sylvie asked him to go again with her to the marriage license bureau. He told her, "We are living happily together like husband and wife. It's no big deal not having a piece of paper." They never went back for a marriage license. Throughout their time together, Sylvie and Bisram held themselves out to numerous people as husband and wife. Both before and after 1984 (when they became legally able to marry), the couple visited relatives in Washington, D.C. (which recognizes common-law marriages), two to three times a year. During their stays, they cohabited together. When Sylvie filed for divorce in 1990, Bisram denied that they had ever been married. He claimed that there was no express mutual agreement to be husband and wife. While admitting the statement (quoted above), he argued that it took place in New York and was never repeated in Washington, D.C.

ISSUE   Did the couple have a common-law marriage?

continued

DECISION Yes. Common-law marriages in New York were outlawed by statute. However, a common-law marriage validly consummated in another state or jurisdiction (for example, Washington, D.C.) can be recognized in New York under the doctrine of full faith and credit if the other state recognizes the validation of the common-law marriage. Minimum contacts with a common-law marriage jurisdiction are sufficient to activate recognition if Sylvie can prove three things: (1) a present intent to be married; (2) a holding out as husband and wife to others in both New York and the other state; and (3) cohabitation. There is no dispute that steps (2) and (3) have been met. Bisram's entire defense rests on the legal contention that his "present tense" agreement to live with Sylvie "like husband and wife" took place in New York and not in Washington, D.C. However, this court does not adhere to a doctrine that flies in the face of reality. If the parties enter into an agreement to live "like husband and wife," that signifies an intention to be married without the formality of solemnization. If they then cohabit together and hold themselves out to others that they are husband and wife, should their original agreement have to be repeated in express terms? The answer obviously is, NO!

Marriage Evasion Statutes

Some states wish to closely regulate the activities of their residents even when they are outside of the state. These states have passed *marriage evasion statutes,* which prohibit recognition of marriages performed out-of-state by persons seeking to avoid the requirements of their state of residence. For example, Illinois refuses to recognize out-of-state common-law marriages by their own residents. Thus, if an Illinois resident travels to Pennsylvania for the purpose of creating a common-law marriage, it will not be recognized in Illinois. Other states do not recognize a common-law marriage obtained out-of-state by their own residents unless they first established significant contacts with the state permitting the common-law marriage. Figure 18–2 illustrates the criteria that must be met in order to establish a common-law marriage.

Cohabitation

A growing number of couples are choosing to live together outside of wedlock. Many do this as a trial before formalizing their relationship through marriage. (Curiously, several studies suggest that couples who cohabit prior to marriage actually are more likely to divorce.) For many years society treated unmarried couples quite harshly, making it difficult for them to secure housing, insurance, or credit. In fact, many states still have laws prohibiting sexual relations between unmarried persons. However, these laws seldom are enforced.

Still, **cohabitation** can raise legal problems. While states generally protect the rights of children born of unmarried couples, those children may have to overcome burdensome procedural requirements before they can obtain important legal rights. Further, upon termination of a cohabitation relationship, a father may have to establish paternity before he will be awarded child custody or visitation rights. And, as will be seen in Chapter 20, a divorced parent may risk losing custody of her children if she lives with a man out of wedlock.

Figure 18–2: Common-Law Marriage

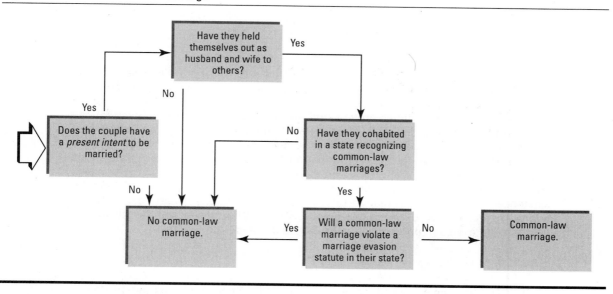

Society is becoming increasingly tolerant of cohabitation arrangements. Many communities have enacted legislation prohibiting discrimination based on marital status. Further, more and more businesses and governmental bodies are recognizing a status known as *domestic partnerships*. They extend to these cohabiting couples many of the same rights available to married couples. Some of these benefits include death benefits, parental and bereavement leaves, family insurance coverage, and eligibility for family discounts.

Same-Sex Marriage

For the same reasons that many heterosexual partners seek to formalize their bond through marriage, lesbian and gay couples are demanding societal recognition of their partnership. However, while the U.S. Supreme Court has declared that the right to marry is part of the fundamental right of privacy, no state currently permits **same-sex marriages.** (They are legal in Denmark and Norway, but only when at least one of the partners is Danish or Norwegian.) The courts generally have recognized the states' authority to restrict the right to marry to people of the opposite sex in order to foster the traditional concepts of marriage and family.

Advocates of same-sex marriage argue that these restrictions fail to recognize social realities. They claim that current marriage laws are based on a model (a working husband with a homemaker wife) that describes less than 10 percent of U.S. families. To a limited degree, the notion of domestic partnerships (described above) is addressing this flaw, as are the recent legislative and judicial trends prohibiting discrimination against same-sex partners in housing. In the landmark decision that follows, the Hawaiian Supreme Court opened the door for Hawaii to become the first state to legalize same-sex marriages.

Baehr v. Lewin

852 P.2D 44 (SUP. CT. HAW. 1993)

FACTS   Three same-sex couples filed applications for marriage licenses with the Hawaiian Department of Health, pursuant to the state marriage law. The couples' marriage license applications were denied solely on the ground that the couples were of the same sex. The couples argued that the ban on same-sex marriages violated their right to privacy and illegally discriminated on the basis of sex. The Department of Health claimed the marriage law's bias in favor of heterosexual marriages in no way burdened these couples' private relationships. It did not believe the state was under any obligation to grant official approval to homosexual unions since the state's marriage laws were enacted to protect and foster the basic family unit. It denied the existence of sexual discrimination because the law prohibited marriages between two women as well as between two men. The lower court dismissed the lawsuit for failure to state a claim upon which relief can be granted.

ISSUE   Should the lawsuit be dismissed?

DECISION   No. The constitutions of both the United States and the State of Hawaii recognize fundamental privacy rights with regard to procreation, childbirth, child rearing, and family relationships. It would make little sense to recognize a right to privacy with respect to other matters of family life and not with respect to the decision to enter the relationship that is the foundation of family in our society. However, we do not believe a right to same-sex marriage is so rooted in the traditions and collective conscience of our people that failure to recognize it would violate the fundamental principles of liberty and justice that lie at the basis of all our civil and political institutions. Neither do we believe that a right to same-sex marriage is implicit in the concept of ordered liberty, such that neither liberty nor justice would exist if it were sacrificed. Accordingly, we hold that these couples do not have a fundamental right to same-sex marriages arising out of the right to privacy. Our holding, however, does not leave them without a potential remedy in this case. Hawaii's refusal to allow them to marry on the basis that they are members of the same sex deprives them of access to a multiplicity of rights and benefits that are contingent upon marital status. Yet, the state constitution prohibits state-sanctioned discrimination against any person in the exercise of his or her civil rights on the basis of sex. Despite the fact that Hawaii's marriage law has equal application to male/male or female/female marriages, we find it to constitute sexual discrimination. The mere equal application of a statute containing sexual classifications is not enough to remove the classifications from the constitutional prohibitions against invidious discrimination. This case must therefore be remanded to the lower court. The burden will then rest on the state to overcome the presumption that this marriage statute is unconstitutional by demonstrating that it furthers a compelling state interest and is narrowly drawn to avoid unnecessary abridgment of constitutional rights.

http://hsba.org/Index/Court/CLALPM.htm

─────────────────── Ethical Issue ───────────────────

A Hawaii circuit court has since ruled that same-sex couples should be permitted to marry because the state did not have compelling reason to block such unions. However, the court stayed the ruling while the case is being reconsidered by the state supreme court. The U.S. government, in the meantime, has enacted legislation (the *Defense of Marriage Act*) allowing states to refuse to recognize same-sex marriages performed in other states. How do you feel about this legislation?

Marital Rights and Obligations ▬▬▬▬

The marital relationship entitles each spouse to a variety of legal rights and benefits. Each may receive income tax advantages (deductions, credits, exemptions), rights relating to inheritance upon the death of a spouse, and the right to bring wrongful-death claims. Certain obligations also attend the marriage institution, including the duty to provide financial support for the health and welfare of a dependent spouse.

Separate Property

As a general rule, a spouse may individually control the property he or she brings into the marriage. Those assets, as well as property acquired by gift or inheritance during the marriage, are considered to be **separate property.** Most states adhere to the common-law notion that property earned by one spouse during marriage is owned by that spouse unless she voluntarily shares it with her mate. (The community property states, on the other hand, treat it as owned by both spouses.) Creditors of one spouse have no automatic claim to the separate property of the other.

http:// orc.avv.com/title-31/ sec-3103/home.htm. contains information on the state code on spousal property rights for Ohio, a separate property state.

Marital Property

All states distinguish between property owned by the individual spouses and property owned by both spouses as married partners. **Marital property** refers to the property the spouses acquire together throughout the marriage. A growing number of courts allow individual creditors of either spouse to reach these assets. Separate property may be transformed into marital property if it is voluntarily joined with marital property or the spouses otherwise treat it as jointly owned. However, many courts rule that one spouse's creditors cannot reach marital property that is not in that spouses' name. When property is titled in both spouses' names, there may be a presumption that it is marital property.

http:// www.leginfo.ca.gov/ calaw.html contains information on spousal property rights for California, a community property state.

Bank One, Appleton, NA v. Reynolds

500 N.W.2D 337 (APP. WIS. 1993)

FACTS   Lynn Reynolds signed an agreement on March 1, 1989, that guaranteed a $23,000 loan that Bank One extended to his business, Reynolds Candys, Inc. The agreement contained a marital purpose clause that stated: "*Each Guarantor who*

continued

signs above and is married represents that this obligation is incurred in the interest of his or her marriage or family." Anne Reynolds, Lynn's wife, did not sign the agreement. When the business defaulted on the loan, Bank One sued Lynn on the guaranty. After the complaint was served, but before a judgment was awarded, Lynn and Anne entered into a marital property agreement, stating that all income earned by Anne was her individual property. After the bank won a monetary judgment against Lynn, it asked the court to garnish Anne's wages to help pay for the judgment. Anne objected, arguing the underlying debt was not a marital debt and her wages did not constitute marital property.

ISSUE   Is Anne personally liable on the debt?

DECISION   Yes. Under state law the marital purpose statement signed by Lynn is conclusive evidence that the debt the bank seeks to collect is a family obligation. Any debt incurred by a spouse in the interest of the marriage or the family may be satisfied only from *all marital property* and all other property of the incurring spouse. Thus, the obligation could be satisfied from all of the spouses' marital property and all of Lynn's separate property. Anne's argument that her wages are not marital property by virtue of the marital property agreement is not correct. No provision of a marital property agreement may adversely affect the interests of a creditor unless the creditor had actual knowledge of that provision when the underlying debt was incurred. Bank One extended its loan and Lynn signed the agreement designating the debt as a marital debt before the marital property agreement was made. Therefore, the bank had no actual notice of the marital property agreement when the underlying debt was incurred.

Liability on Debts

A spouse has a duty to provide food, shelter, clothing, and medical care for his or her disabled spouse. And both spouses have the same obligation to their minor children. Failure to live up to this responsibility is a crime. However, one spouse is not automatically liable for the debts of the other. Joint liability generally accompanies only those debts incurred for the benefit of both spouses or those instances where the spouses have otherwise indicated a willingness to assume joint liability (e.g., jointly held credit cards, a pattern of paying the bills of the other). (See Figure 18–3 on page 419.)

Necessaries

Historically, a woman lost the capacity to contract upon marriage. She was unable to purchase food, clothing, shelter, or medical care. Her husband was able to control her property and any income from it. However, he also had a legal duty to provide support for his wife. To offset the legal difficulties faced by women whose husbands shirked their spousal support obligations, the common law developed the **doctrine of necessaries.** This authorized a woman to purchase necessaries and charge them to her husband in instances where he failed to provide for her.

Scope of the Doctrine

The definition of what constitutes "necessaries" certainly encompasses those things essential for one's basic food, shelter, and medical needs. Beyond that, it

Figure 18–3:   Liability for Debts of a Spouse

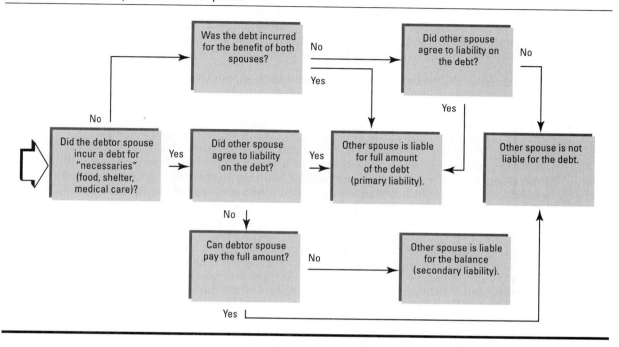

varies among married couples depending on their social and economic status. Expenditures that exceed the other spouse's financial means are not necessaries.

Nature of Liability

Courts now recognize the need for gender-neutrality and impose liability on each spouse for necessaries purchased by the other. It does not matter if the noncontracting spouse did not know of the purchases or never promised to pay for them. However, the liability generally is secondary. This means that the noncontracting spouse is liable only if the contracting spouse is unable to pay the debt.

Bartrom v. Adjustment Bureau, Inc.

618 N.E.2D 1 (Sup. Ct. Ind. 1993)

FACTS   Howard and Mary Bartrom were married on January 26, 1979. Ten years later, on June 24, 1989, Mary and her three children left because of Howard's abuse of alcohol and repeated acts of physical and mental violence toward his wife. On July 27, 1989, Mary filed for divorce. However, eight days later, before the divorce was finalized, Howard was involved in an automobile accident and rendered comatose. Soon after Howard's accident, representatives of the hospital contacted Mary requesting that she execute an agreement to pay for his treatment. She refused

continued

the request. Mary never visited Howard during his hospitalization and refused to participate in discussions regarding the withdrawal of his life support. Howard died on August 25, 1989, without ever regaining consciousness. When Howard's assets were insufficient to pay the $67,637.75 hospital bill, the debt was assigned to Adjustment Bureau for collection. Adjustment Bureau sought payment from Mary personally. Mary disclaimed liability because of her separation from Howard.

ISSUE Is Mary personally liable for her estranged husband's hospital bills?

DECISION Yes. The notion that the available resources of one spouse ought to be used to help support the other should the other become necessitous flows from the nature of the marital relationship. This duty of spousal support is clearly imbedded in the modern law of domestic relations. To a limited extent, this doctrine of necessaries transforms property, at least with respect to creditors, from separately owned to communally owned. We hold that each spouse is primarily liable for his or her independent debts. Typically, a creditor may look to a non-contracting spouse for satisfaction of the debts of the other only if the non-contracting spouse has otherwise agreed to contractual liability or can be said to have authorized the debt by implication. When, however, there is shortfall between a dependent spouse's necessary expenses and separate funds, the law will impose limited secondary liability upon the financially superior spouse by means of the doctrine of necessaries. We characterize the liability as limited because its outer boundaries are marked by the financially superior spouse's ability to pay at the time the debt was incurred. It is secondary in the sense that it exists only to the extent that the debtor spouse is unable to satisfy his or her own personal needs or obligations. The fact that these spouses were separated does not diminish this responsibility. The duty of spousal support continues at least until the marital relationship is terminated by divorce.

Interspousal Immunity

Suits between spouses originally were prohibited because they were inconsistent with the idea that a husband and wife were a single person in the eyes of the law. They also were perceived as destructive of the family institution. Accordingly, courts erected an **interspousal immunity** that prevented one spouse from bringing a negligence or intentional tort suit against the other. The only remedy available to an injured spouse was to sue for divorce or to have her husband criminally prosecuted.

Today, all states recognize that women have rights separate and distinct from their husbands. They also believe that physically and emotionally abusive behavior should not be protected in order to promote marital harmony. At least 39 states now permit one spouse to sue the other for physical injury, and a number permit suits for emotional distress. As a result, the legal profession is witnessing a growing legal specialty known as *domestic torts*. However, several states permit negligence lawsuits but not actions for intentional torts. They reason that spouses who are victims of an intentional tort should seek their remedy through divorce.

Marital Privilege

For the same reasons spouses were not permitted to sue one another, they historically could not testify against each other in criminal trials. This **marital privilege** has two dimensions: the marital confidence privilege and the spousal testimony privilege.

Marital Confidence Privilege

Like the attorney-client privilege, the *marital confidence privilege* requires spouses to keep confidential the statements or admissions made by one another during marriage. It applies only to confidential communications and can be asserted even after the couple's marriage has ended. A statement is considered confidential if it was made in reliance on the confidence of the marital relationship.

There is a strong presumption that communications privately made between spouses are confidential. However, communications made in the presence of a third person or actions that are injurious of the other spouse do not fall within the marital confidence privilege.

Spousal Testimony Privilege

There also is a marital privilege that covers adverse testimony against a spouse even when it does not meet the confidentiality test. This *spousal testimony privilege,* unlike the marital confidence privilege, applies only to criminal proceedings. Further, it is not available after a marriage has ended.

In most states the spousal testimony privilege only prevents a person from being compelled to testify against her spouse. She may voluntarily testify against her spouse if she wishes. Further, many states have created an exception to privilege when the spouse is charged with a crime against a minor child. They have determined that the public policy of protecting children against crime outweighs the policy of preserving the harmony and unity of marriage.

State v. Peters

444 S.E.2d 609 (App. Ga. 1994)

FACTS Randall Horace Peters was killed by shotgun blast in his home on March 19, 1992. The police officer who investigated concluded there had been no burglary, but furniture and other items had been arranged to make it appear that the killing resulted from burglary. Peters's wife, Linda Chapman Peters, gave inconsistent accounts of her whereabouts at the time of the murder, but eventually admitted she had seen Walter Sargent that evening. Upon further questioning, both Linda and Walter admitted they had been conducting an illicit affair for several years. A grand jury recommended that an indictment be issued accusing Linda of murdering Randall and that Walter be granted immunity to testify against her. A hearing was set for June 24. On June 23, Linda and Walter were married. Before the marriage took place, Linda told her daughters she probably would have to marry Walter so he would not testify against her. The district attorney stated that the investigation probably would not go forward without Walter's testimony. When Walter was served with a subpoena to testify before the grand jury, he argued he could not be compelled to testify because of the marital privilege. The trial court concluded that the time of the marriage was solely to afford Walter the protection of the marital privilege so he could avoid testifying against Linda.

continued

ISSUE   Can the court compel Walter to testify?

DECISION   No. State law provides that husbands and wives shall be competent but shall not be compellable to give evidence in any criminal proceeding for or against each other. The courts have applied this privilege based on the status of the husband and wife at the time testimony is sought or given. If the marriage is terminated by divorce at the time of testifying the privilege is lost. Courts have not questioned the viability of the privilege itself, even in a case where the witness divorced and remarried the defendant shortly before trial. The marital privilege has been criticized by the courts and by legal scholars for many years. However, allegations that a marriage contracted solely for the purpose of barring testimony have been considered by a number of courts and they have overwhelmingly declined to create such a judicial exception to the marital privilege. Many states have created such an exception by statute. The circumstances of this case amply demonstrate the potential for abuse of the far-reaching protection afforded by the marital testimonial privilege. However, the legislature has determined the limits of that privilege and we are not permitted to alter that determination by judicial amendment.

Name Change

Upon marriage there is no requirement that either spouse adopt the name of the other. Similarly, there generally is no rule preventing cohabiting couples from using the same last name. As long as people are not trying to defraud their creditors or illegally profit by using the name of a celebrity, they can call themselves anything they like.

An adult can change his or her name either by regularly using the desired name or by filing a petition with the court. The rules are more strict for children.

Changing an Adult's Surname

A certain amount of persistence may be necessary for people desiring to change their names without a court order. They generally find that legal and consumer encounters are smoother if they have changed their personal documents (driver's license, social security card, and credit cards) to reflect the new name.

The process of changing an adult's name by court order also is simple. Generally, the individual must fill out a short form and then publish a legal notice of the name change in a local newspaper. The state also may require the petitioner to attend a court hearing where a judge insures the change is not being made for fraudulent purposes.

Changing a Child's Surname

Conflicts over the surname of children frequently arise after a divorce. It then generally requires a court order to effect such a change. Courts resolve these parental disputes by considering the best interests of the child. Judges traditionally presumed the father's surname was in the child's best interests. However, today a wide range of factors are considered. These include the length of time the child has used one surname, the anxiety the child may suffer if the name is changed, and the personal preferences of older children.

Some courts impose a presumption in favor of the surname selected by the parent who has physical custody of the child. In fact, several states have laws delegating the choice of surname to the custodial parent. When there is joint custody and the parents disagree, New Jersey gives the child a hyphenated surname combining the parents' names in alphabetical order. (Custody rights and responsibilities are discussed in Chapter 20.)

Ethical Issue

Should a parent change a child's surname over the objections of the child?

Prenuptial Agreements

The high rate of marital failure (one divorce for every two marriages) and second marriages has made people more and more cautious. Many prospective spouses only will enter marriage if they can guarantee their money and other property will not be distributed to their partner in the event of a divorce. Accordingly, they insist that the other spouse sign a **prenuptial agreement** (also called an antenuptial agreement) prior to the marriage.

While the substance of prenuptial agreements varies widely, they tend to cover three subjects: (1) property and support rights (both during and after marriage), (2) the personal rights and responsibilities of the spouses during the marriage, and (3) custody and support obligations to children born during the marriage. (See Figure 18–4.)

http://
www.azleg.state.az.
us/ars/25/title25.htm
contains information
regarding Chapter 2,
Article 1—"Arizona
Uniform Premarital
Agreement Act."

http://
www.capitol.state.tx.
us/statutes/fatoc.html
is the site of Texas
Family Code topics.

Property and Support Rights

Agreements governing the distribution of property rights are of two basic types. Some confine themselves to distribution upon the death of a spouse, while others

---

Figure 18–4:   Prenuptial Agreements

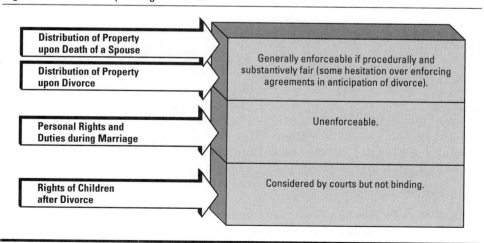

are executed in anticipation of divorce. Courts have shown a much greater reluctance to enforce agreements made in anticipation of divorce than those contemplating a distribution of property upon death. This hesitation results from the courts' fear that widespread enforcement of prenuptial agreements might encourage spouses to divorce.

Personal Rights and Responsibilities

Agreements concerning the rights and obligations of the spouses during marriage are not likely to be enforced by the courts. For instance, the couple may agree in advance to an allocation of responsibility over household and childcare chores. Or they might pledge to openly discuss certain types of issues (financial concerns, sexual desires or frustrations). And the contract may even establish a means of resolving marital conflicts (a pledge to participate in marriage counseling when disputes arise). However, because courts are reluctant to interfere with the private bond created by marriage, they are likely to treat these as moral, rather than legal, obligations.

Rights of Children

Prenuptial agreements involving the rights of children are not binding on the courts. In fact, many states have laws specifically prohibiting the enforcement of agreements that adversely affect children's support rights. And while courts consider the parents' wishes concerning childcare after divorce, judges retain great discretion in determining custody issues.

Drafting an Enforceable Agreement

A growing number of courts enforce prenuptial agreements that distribute property between the spouses. They are viewed as consistent with the public interest because they facilitate the orderly termination of marriage. However, courts still are worried that one spouse might be left in a position where she is dependent upon public assistance. Thus, these contracts are carefully reviewed to ensure their procedural and substantive fairness.

Procedural Fairness

An enforceable prenuptial agreement must guarantee *procedural fairness*. This requires that both parties enter the agreement voluntarily after making a full financial disclosure to each other. Thus, in cases where the agreement was presented to a bride minutes or hours before the wedding, courts often refuse to enforce its terms. Or when a party conceals the true extent of his property and resources, the agreements frequently are thrown out. While no state requires each partner to retain a separate attorney, that probably is the safest course toward guaranteeing the enforceability of the contract. Finally, most states require that prenuptial agreements be in writing and signed by the parties.

Substantive Fairness

Prenuptial agreements also must promote *substantive fairness*. This does not mean that the presence of unequal provisions will invalidate the agreement. Instead, courts focus on whether the contract is fair and reasonable under the circumstances.

Thus, in instances where the parties are entering a second marriage and both were gainfully employed prior to the marriage, courts generally presume the contract is valid. However, in a case of first marriage, where the wife is expected to be a homemaker, the court is not likely to enforce an agreement releasing the husband from a duty to provide support in the event of divorce.

States are divided on whether the substantive fairness of the agreement should be measured at the time the contract was drafted or at the time of enforcement. The trend seems to be to determine its fairness at the time of enforcement.

Pajak v. Pajak

385 S.E.2d 384 (Sup. Ct. W.Va. 1989)

FACTS   William Pajak, Sr., married Patricia Schmidt in 1949 and they were divorced in 1954. Pajak married again in 1963 and fathered two children, Clark and William, by his second wife. This marriage also ended in divorce in 1980. Pajak then married his third wife, Audrey, in 1982, after he and Audrey entered into a prenuptial agreement by which she waived all interests in his estate. When Pajak died without a will in 1985, Audrey argued the agreement was invalid and filed a claim for a wife's statutory share of his estate. Before his marriage to Audrey, Pajak was a man of considerable wealth who had a variety of active business interests. Audrey had been an employee at one of the businesses he owned. Their prenuptial agreement was drafted by Pajak's lawyer and presented to Audrey at the lawyer's office one day before the couple was married. She testified that the lawyer discussed the agreement with her briefly, and that she signed it without reading it. Audrey claimed that at the time she signed the prenuptial agreement, she was not fully informed of the extent of Pajak's wealth. She also maintained she did not know or understand the meaning of the words or clauses used in the agreement.

ISSUE   Should the court enforce the prenuptial agreement and deny Audrey a share of Pajak's estate?

DECISION   Yes. The prenuptial agreement was entered into willingly and intelligently and Audrey Pajak thereby is bound by its terms. This case involves a traditional prenuptial agreement designed to protect the inheritance rights of children from claims made by a new wife who is not the children's mother. Prenuptial agreements like this are favored by public policy because they enhance, rather than detract from, opportunities to form marriage relationships in middle-age and later. Without the ability to enter into enforceable prenuptial agreements that protect assets from the statutory entitlement of a second spouse, an older person with money acquired with the help of an earlier spouse would be reluctant to remarry. In this case, it is unlikely Pajak would have remarried if he had not been assured he could protect his assets for his children. Audrey should have been aware that Pajak owned a number of businesses and lived reasonably well. It is not necessary for both parties to execute a detailed, written financial statement such as is required for a bank loan. Further, Audrey made no effort to read the agreement nor did she ask to have it examined by her own lawyer. She cannot now claim it was induced by fraud, duress, or misrepresentation.

Cohabitation Agreements

Unmarried heterosexual and same-sex couples who choose to live together out of wedlock may wish to draft a domestic partnership contract. Like prenuptial agreements, these *cohabitation agreements* may cover property distributions, personal responsibilities, or childcare issues. The enforcement issues also are similar. However, the parties must be cautious because some courts are reluctant to recognize the legitimacy of sexual relations between unwed partners. Thus, courts refuse to enforce a cohabitation agreement if they believe it contains the promise of an exchange of money or property for sexual services.

Broken Engagements

A chapter on marriage would not be complete without some discussion of the legal issues arising when an engagement is broken. As this final section illustrates, the rights of the parties often vary depending on whether the decision to terminate the engagement was mutual or unilateral. Three specific topics are explored: (1) common-law actions for breach of promise, (2) statutory limitations on such lawsuits and, (3) the ownership of gifts made in contemplation of marriage.

Common-Law Recovery

Courts historically have allowed jilted lovers to recover monetary damages for *breach of a promise to marry.* The cause of action grew from the notion that marriage was a property transaction brought about by complex family negotiations. It simultaneously reinforced the view that marriage was necessary to secure a woman's social, financial, and legal security. Finally, promises of marriage often occasioned a loss of virginity and jilted women were socially stigmatized.

Parties who successfully litigate these breach-of-promise suits may recover both tort and contract damages. This includes emotional suffering, damage to reputation, and various out-of-pocket expenses (wedding clothes, transportation, catering). Punitive damages are available in particularly outrageous cases. And, perhaps most importantly, many successful plaintiffs are able to recover for the loss of the social position and economic standing they would have attained if the marriage had taken place. This last factor often leads to large damage awards because it permits jurors to closely examine the wealth of the person who broke the engagement.

Heartbalm Statutes

By the middle of the twentieth century, breach-of-promise-to-marry suits fell into disrepute for three primary reasons. First, there was serious concern that frivolous suits were being brought to extort out-of-court settlements from wealthy individuals. Second, jurors regularly awarded successful plaintiffs exorbitant amounts of money. And, third, as women's legal rights and status grew, there was less concern about the loss of a suitor destroying her social and economic prospects.

Today, 24 states have enacted **heartbalm statutes** that abolish or strictly limit the cause of action for breach of a promise to marry. For instance, the Florida law provides that promises to marry made in that state are not enforceable. Illinois, on the other hand, has erected very strict procedural requirements that must be precisely followed or the cause of action is lost. (The Illinois statute is discussed in the *Wildey* case that follows.) And Washington, by action of the state supreme court, prohibits plaintiffs from recovering for loss of expected social or financial position. Despite these statutes, a majority of states still recognize a cause of action for breach of promise to marry.

In our chapter opener, the court ruled that Mary's lawsuit against Ralph was not blocked by the state's heartbalm statute, which abolished all causes of action for breach of contract to marry. The Pennsylvania Supreme Court held that the statute was designed to block lawsuits based on sentimental bruises, wounded pride, and social humiliation. It was not intended to preclude an action to recover damages because of a failure to inform a purported spouse of a bigamous marriage.

Wildey v. Springs
47 F.3RD 1475 (7TH CIR. 1995)

FACTS   Sharon Wildey, a Chicago attorney, and Richard Springs, an Oregon rancher, enjoyed a relationship early in 1992. They carried on a long-distance romance by telephone and frequent visits during January and February. In March the couple took a five-day Florida vacation and, during that trip, Sharon suggested marriage. Despite Richard's initial reservations, they decided on a "commuter-type" marriage for a five-year time period, leading to an eventual relocation for both in Florida or the Caribbean. Later in March, Richard formally proposed and presented Sharon with an engagement ring. After several more visits, Richard began having second thoughts about the marriage. In April he composed a letter to Sharon explaining his doubts and breaking off the engagement. Sharon responded with several letters. In the first she explained the broken engagement had caused her to become extremely depressed and asked for financial help. Richard wrote back that he already had told her to keep the engagement ring and some money he had placed in a Chicago bank account. In her second letter, Sharon announced her intention to sue. That letter contained the date the parties had planned to get married and made references to several elements of damages (medical bills from counseling and lost income) Sharon believed she had suffered. However, it did not mention any of the dates on which the parties had exchanged marital promises. Illinois has a heartbalm statute that describes the type of notice a plaintiff must provide before bringing a breach-of-promise-to-marry suit. The law states that failure to give proper notice results in dismissal of the suit and bars any further cause of action. The required notice must be written, signed, and sent within three months of the date of the breach. Further, it must contain the date on which the promise or agreement to marry was made. The trial court, while acknowledging Sharon's failure to give proper notice, ruled she had substantially complied with the statute. Accordingly, it awarded her $118,000. Richard appealed.

ISSUE   Should the court uphold the damage award?

DECISION   No. Omission of the date the parties became engaged is fatal to Sharon's claim. The state's heartbalm statute requires plaintiffs to include several items in the notice that must be sent to the defendant. The date the parties became engaged is

continued

clearly one of those items. Although the strict construction we rely on may seem unwarranted, it is appropriate. The statute makes clear that failure to give proper notice results in the claim being dismissed. This plain language reflects the legislature's priorities. Further, the purpose behind the Illinois heartbalm statute was to make it *more* difficult for plaintiffs to bring suits of this nature. A liberal construction allowing substantial, rather than strict, compliance with the notice requirements undermines this legislative goal. Finally, Sharon is a seasoned attorney and she consulted with an attorney before sending the required notice. She should have understood the statute's requirements.

http://kentlaw.edu/7circuit/
http://law.vill.edu/Fed-Ct/fedcourt.html

Engagement Gifts

Engagement rings and other gifts made in contemplation of marriage generally are treated under personal property law as *conditional gifts*. As such, they may be recovered if the marriage is cancelled. However, the rules are not uniform in every state. (Note: the heartbalm statutes, discussed above, do not bar suits for return of engagement rings or other gifts in contemplation of marriage.)

Most courts hold the donor of an engagement ring can recover it if the engagement is broken by mutual agreement or if the donee unjustifiably refuses to marry. However, if the donor of the ring terminates the engagement without good cause, the donee may keep it. Some courts return the ring under any circumstances. They reason that a party should not be penalized for deciding not to go forward with a marriage when he or she has doubts about its wisdom.

QUESTIONS AND PROBLEM CASES

1. Generally, how long must a couple cohabit before a court will recognize a common-law marriage?
2. When is a wife legally liable for debts incurred by her husband?
3. What legal steps must be taken before a person legally can change his or her surname?
4. What must be shown before a court will enforce a prenuptial agreement?
5. In 1975, Kathleen and Joseph Gilvary were married in Kentucky. They obtained a marriage license, participated in a religious ceremony, and filed a marriage certificate. In 1984, Kathleen learned that Joseph had never obtained a divorce from his first wife. Based on Joseph's continuing promises that he

would divorce his first wife and then legally marry her, Kathleen remained with him. In 1992, Joseph obtained a divorce from his first wife but then abandoned Kathleen. She filed a petition for annulment of the marriage and distribution of their property. The trial court denied her additional request for temporary alimony and attorneys' fees, claiming that an annulment merely should place the partners in the position they were in prior to the marriage. Is the trial court correct?
6. Timothy Hamilton had sex with a 12-year-old female. She later gave birth to a child and claimed that Hamilton was the child's father. He was then charged with statutory rape for having sex with a minor who was not his

wife. Shortly before the trial, Hamilton and the victim were married. Can his wife be compelled to testify against him?

7. Elizabeth and Michael Anderson took part in a ceremonial marriage in Savannah, Georgia, on March 17, 1972. They were unaware that the dissolution of her previous marriage did not become final until April 5, 1972 (19 days after their wedding). After living together and holding themselves out as husband and wife in Georgia, the couple moved to Florida. Georgia recognizes common-law marriages while Florida does not. However, Florida will respect a common-law marriage when entered into in a state where they are legal. Are Elizabeth and Michael married? Explain.

8. Robert and Genevieve Crawford were married on December 8, 1968. He had been married once before and was substantially older than she. Three days before the wedding, Robert accompanied Genevieve to his attorney's office where she was presented with a prenuptial agreement to sign. She was unaware that an agreement had been drafted and was first advised of its existence on her arrival at the attorney's office. Genevieve spent less than 10 minutes at the office and did not understand the terms of the agreement before signing it. She was not given a copy of the document and, therefore, did not discuss it with an independent counsel. The prenuptial agreement gave Robert complete control over the property he brought into the marriage and stated that Genevieve would not assert any claim over the property by way of inheritance or divorce. The document failed to list the value of the property. Will a court enforce this prenuptial agreement?

9. Kathryn and Thomas Gentry were married on February 26, 1975. Each had been through protracted divorce proceedings prior to this marriage, and Kathy was aware that Tom's divorce and property settlement had been particularly bitter. A few days before their wedding, Tom and Kathy signed a prenuptial agreement drawn up by an attorney who was a mutual friend. In unambiguous terms the parties agreed that upon termination of the marriage, each would relinquish any rights in the property the other owned at the time of the marriage or at the time of dissolution. The agreement disclosed the nature and value of their respective assets. Tom's net worth was approximately $1.5 million, while Kathy's assets were valued at several thousand dollars. Kathy was not employed outside the home after the marriage, although she received an allowance from Tom each month. Their income was derived largely from Tom's business enterprises. While they were married they maintained separate bank accounts, and virtually all assets were purchased with funds from Tom's account. Kathy's name did not appear on any documents evidencing title to any assets acquired during the marriage, with the exception of a house in California that was purchased in both of their names. When the couple divorced in 1986, the court awarded to Tom all property titled in his name and to Kathy all property titled in her name, except the house in California. It awarded the house to Tom since it was purchased with funds from his separate account. Kathy argued she is entitled to one-half of the equity in the California house. Is she correct?

10. Marie Henriksen and Malcolm Cameron met in England in 1973 and were married in 1974. During the course of their marriage, Malcolm physically and emotionally abused Marie. This abuse ranged from accusing her of sleeping with his brother to raping and assaulting her on several occasions. The court granted the parties a divorce in 1988. In April 1989, Marie sued Malcolm for intentional infliction of emotional distress resulting from physical and psychological abuse. The jury awarded Marie $75,000 in compensatory damages and $40,000 in punitive damages. Malcolm appealed the judgment, arguing Marie's claim was barred by the interspousal immunity. Is Malcolm correct? Explain.

PARENTHOOD

Ruben Pena began dating Amanda Mattox when he was 19 and she was 15. After Amanda became pregnant by Ruben, her parents forbade her to continue seeing him. Although Amanda disobeyed their order, she never told Ruben she was pregnant. Amanda's parents arranged to have Ruben arrested and jailed for statutory rape for having sexual intercourse with a person who was younger than 16. They then spirited her off to Indiana, where she gave birth. The child was immediately placed for adoption. When Ruben learned of these events, he sued for monetary damages for loss of his parental rights.

Pena v. Mattox, 84 F.3d 894 (7th Cir. 1996).

Does Ruben legally have parental rights to the child?
What procedural steps must be met before a child may be placed for adoption?
Does an adopted child have the right to be informed of the identity of her biological parents?

Introduction ▬▬▬▬▬▬▬▬▬▬▬▬▬▬▬

Few parents would argue with the idea that good parenting is the most difficult responsibility they ever have undertaken. Think of the overwhelming influence that parents can and do have on the lives of their children. Throughout childhood most of us are emotionally, financially, and legally dependent on our parents. And it doesn't stop there. The attitudes and behaviors we exhibit throughout our adult lives largely reflect our family environment.

Despite the tremendous impact parenting has on the fabric of society, it is governed by very few legal rules. There are no entrance examinations or required training programs conditioning one's right to be a parent. In fact, except in cases of extreme abuse or neglect, the law does not regulate the quality of parenting at all. Instead, it primarily focuses on the division of rights and obligations between parents.

Still, every day people marry or cohabit with the idea of raising a family together. Too often, however, they are so blinded by their immediate emotional and physical attraction to each other that they overlook the serious emotional, financial, and legal responsibilities accompanying parenthood. This oversight has turned millions of dreams into nightmares.

Chapter Overview

The chapter begins with a look at several traditional parenthood issues. These include paternity disputes, the rights of stepparents, and the problems faced by children born to unmarried parents. The discussion then turns to the basic duties parents owe both to their children and to third persons who are injured by them. This is followed by an examination of several parental control issues (discipline, child abuse, and the right of children to sue their parents). Our attention is then focused on the issues that arise when people choose to adopt children. The chapter closes with a review of the legal aspects of creating a family through the use of artificial insemination, surrogacy, or egg donations.

http:// www.law.cornell.edu/ topics/state_statutes. html#family provides links to sites that provide information on specific state statutes that deal with families and parenting.

Establishing Parenthood ▬▬▬▬▬▬▬▬▬

Special problems exist when the identity of a child's biological father is in doubt. These situations often arise when married women engage in extramarital affairs or when cohabiting couples have children outside of traditional marriage. (Later sections examine the legal aspects of adoption, artificial insemination, surrogate motherhood, and egg donations.) Under these circumstances, courts may be called upon to clarify the rights and obligations of the parties. After examining the legal issues involved with establishing paternity, the discussion turns to a look at the rights of stepparents and the rights of children born out of wedlock.

Paternity

There are two basic types of disputes concerned with establishing the identity of a child's biological father. First, the mother or her child may initiate the claim in order to receive financial support from the father. In the second scenario, a man may argue that he is the biological father so he can gain custody or visitation rights.

Medical Tests

Courts generally accept the accuracy and dependability of blood tests or other scientific procedures designed to establish **paternity.** Under the DNA identification process, DNA specimens from the child, mother, and alleged father are compared. If the alleged father's sample does not contain a strand that matches the child's DNA, he cannot be the biological father of the child. If the strands do match, then a paternity index is calculated, which allows the tester to determine the statistical probability that the alleged father is the biological parent. Thus, these tests can definitely prove nonpaternity and can establish a high statistical probability of paternity.

State in Interest of Gray v. Hogan

613 So.2d 681 (5th Cir. La. 1993)

FACTS Lynette Gray applied for support enforcement services through the Louisiana Department of Health and Human Resources. Her application named Keith Hogan as the absent parent of her child, Sean Gray. Lynette testified that she met Hogan while she was walking and he was jogging. They exchanged pleasantries. A short time later, they accidentally met again and this time they exchanged telephone numbers. She claimed they dated a few times and had sexual relations three times at his apartment. Lynette knew many details about Hogan's family, employment and residence, including several details about the inside of his apartment. Lynette admitted she also had sexual relations with her ex-fiancé during the conception period, but she knew he was not Sean's father. Keith testified he did not know Lynette, had never seen her before, did not date her, and never had sexual relations with her. He was asked and agreed to submit to a blood test. The test was conducted and the results indicated a 99.99 percent probability he was Sean's father. After reviewing the test results and hearing the contradictory stories, the trial court ruled the state had not met its burden of establishing Keith's paternity by a preponderance of the evidence. On appeal, the state argued the trial court erred in dismissing the paternity action because the evidence weighed heavily in favor of a finding of paternity.

ISSUE Should the dismissal of the paternity action be overruled?

DECISION No. The determination of whether there has been sufficient proof of paternity is a question of fact. A petitioner's burden of proof in a paternity action is by a preponderance of the evidence. Scientific testing alone is not sufficient to prove paternity, but it is persuasive and objective proof that can help establish paternity. High paternity indices have been upheld as reliable where there was other sufficient corroborating evidence of paternity introduced at trial. Based on the totality of the evidence and in light of the trial judge's broad discretion in evaluating the credibility of witnesses and determining factual issues, we cannot say the trial judge was clearly wrong or manifestly erroneous in his finding that the state failed to meet its burden of proof.

Burden of Proof

Most states require the person trying to establish paternity to do so by a *preponderance of the evidence.* Some states impose even stricter burdens of proof ("clear and convincing evidence" or "beyond a reasonable doubt"). A husband normally is presumed to be the biological father of children born to his lawful wife during marriage unless he is sterile or impotent. The policies underlying this presumption are to preserve the integrity of the family unit, protect children from the legal and social stigma of illegitimacy, and promote individual rather than state responsibility for child support.

Many states have laws denying anyone other than the husband or wife the right to rebut this presumption. As a result, a man who fathers a child through an adulterous relationship with a married woman cannot legally claim paternity. Only the mother or her husband can pursue a paternity action. Not all states follow this approach. Some permit a married woman's extramarital partner to bring a paternity action in cases where he has established a "substantial parent relationship" with the child. (See Figure 19–1 on page 434.)

In Re Paternity of Baby Doe

558 N.W.2D 897 (CT. APP. WISC. 1996)

FACTS After Kimberly J. L. gave birth to a daughter, Thomas M. P. petitioned the court to order Kimberly and the child, Baby Doe, to submit to blood tests so he could establish his paternity. Thomas contends that he had a romantic relationship with Kimberly J. L. that lasted three or four months. He testified that during that time he and Kimberly had consensual sexual intercourse on many occasions. Kimberly testified that Thomas was not her boyfriend and they never had consensual sexual intercourse. Instead, she testified that she was raped by Thomas during the conception period and that she fears him for her own safety. Kimberly has never been married, but has a child with Lloyd P. Although she and Lloyd no longer reside together, he regularly keeps in touch with her and her two children, and both of the children refer to Lloyd as their father. Thomas has never had contact with Baby Doe. The court took judicial notice of the fact that a Minnesota court decided that Thomas engaged in sexually inappropriate behavior with his daughters and was an unfit parent. Additionally, the court found that if Baby Doe was Thomas's child, her conception was the result of a nonconsensual sexual assault of Kimberly by Thomas.

ISSUE Is Thomas entitled to a paternity determination?

DECISION Yes. State law expressly provides the alleged father of a child the right to a determination of paternity, regardless of the circumstances of the case or the circumstances out of which paternity may have arisen. Notwithstanding Kimberly's allegation of rape, the legislature has not provided that an alleged father has no standing in a paternity proceeding if he sexually assaulted the mother or that the court may dismiss paternity proceedings if it determines that conception resulted from a sexual assault. The legislature has provided that in cases where the mother was married to someone other than the man alleging paternity at the time of conception, a court may

continued

refuse a paternity determination if it is not in the best interests of the child. This exception is designed to protect children born into a marriage from the interference of another man with the existing marital father-child relationship, and to preserve family unity. However, it does not apply in this case since Kimberly was not married at the time of conception. Accordingly, Thomas has a statutory right to a paternity determination. We make no determination as to the fitness of Thomas to be a parent to Baby Doe because that is not the issue in this case. Instead, such an assessment is appropriate in the context of a proceeding to terminate Thomas's parental rights, and this decision in no way interferes with Kimberly's right to initiate or maintain such an action.

--- Ethical Issue ---

Suppose the paternity test establishes that Thomas is the father of Baby Doe. Should Kimberly try to conceal this fact from her daughter?

Rights of Stepparents

Biological parents generally have duties to support their children as well as rights to spend time with them. Even when the relationship between the partners ends, the legal relationship between each biological parent and the children continues

Figure 19–1: Establishing Paternity

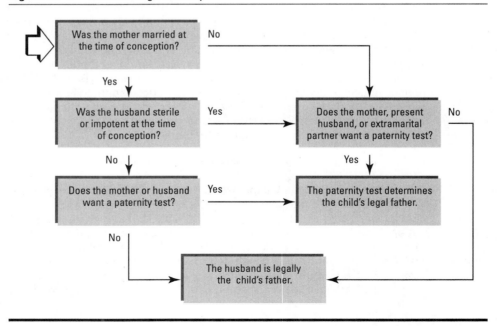

unless terminated by a court. Nonbiological parents (known as **stepparents**) frequently have no legal relationship with their mate's children. Thus, after providing emotional and economic support to their stepchildren for many years, a stepparent may be barred from further contact with them.

The high incidence of remarriage or cohabitation by divorced parents with children has made this situation very common today. Unless the stepparent legally adopts the children, his or her rights can be unilaterally terminated by the children's biological parent. This has occurred in cases where a stepparent has acted as a parent to a child for many years. When the biological parent (the stepparent's mate) dies, the other biological parent frequently is able to terminate all contact between the stepparent and the child.

Alison D. v. Virginia M.

572 N.E.2D 27 (CT. APP. N.Y. 1991)

FACTS   Alison D. and Virginia M. began living together in 1978. Two years later they decided to have a child and agreed Virginia would be artificially inseminated. Together, they planned for the conception and birth of the child and agreed to share jointly all rights and responsibilities of childrearing. Virginia gave birth to a son in 1981, and he was given Alison's last name as his middle name and Virginia's last name as his surname. Both women shared in all birthing expenses and provided for the boy's support. During his first two years, both women jointly cared for and made decisions for the child. When the boy was two years old, Alison and Virginia terminated their relationship and Alison moved out of their home. They agreed to a visitation schedule and Alison also agreed to pay support. The boy referred to both of the women as "mommy." In 1986 Virginia began to restrict Alison's visitation with the child, and in 1987 Alison moved to Ireland to pursue career opportunities. She continued her attempts to communicate with the child; however, Virginia terminated all contact between Alison and the boy, returning Alison's gifts and letters. Alison filed suit, seeking visitation rights.

ISSUE   Should the court award Alison visitation rights?

DECISION   No. New York law allows either parent to apply to the court to seek guardianship or custody of the parent's minor child. Although the court is mindful of Alison's understandable concern for the child and of her desire that her contact with him continue, under this law she has no right to seek visitation and, thereby, limit or diminish the right of the concededly fit biological parent to choose with whom her child associates. Alison is not a "parent" within the meaning of the New York statute. Alison concedes she is not the child's biological mother nor is she a legal parent by virtue of an adoption. Rather she claims to have acted as a "de facto" parent. However, this claim is not sufficient. It is the child's mother and father who, assuming fitness, have the right to the care and custody of their child, even in situations where the nonparent has exercised some control over the child with the parents' consent. It has long been recognized that, as between a parent and a third person, parental custody of a child may not be displaced absent grievous cause or necessity. To allow the courts to award visitation—a limited form of custody—to a third person would

continued

necessarily impair the parents' right to custody and control. Alison concedes that Virginia is a fit parent. Therefore she has no right to petition the court to displace the choice made by this fit parent in deciding what is in the child's best interests. We decline her invitation to read the term "parent" in the state law to include categories of nonparents who have developed a relationship with a child or who have had prior relationships with a child's parents and who wish to continue visitation with the child.

Same-sex couples who choose to have children are especially vulnerable to the threat of losing contact with children they have raised. Because only one of the same-sex partners can be the biological parent, the nonbiological parent must take great care to develop and preserve his or her parental rights. A growing number of states now recognize same-sex adoptions *(second-parent adoptions)*. Same-sex partners may also draft agreements to protect the parental rights of the nonbiological parent. However, the enforceability of these contracts is far from clear. The following case suggests that the courts may become more responsive to the special parenthood problems that arise in nontraditional families. However, most states that have considered this issue have ruled against the nonbiological parent.

In Re H.S.H-K

1995 WISC. LEXIS 75 (SUP. CT. WIS. 1995)

FACTS   Sandra Holtzman and Elsbeth Knott are two women who shared a close, committed relationship for more than 10 years. In 1983 they began living together in a home they jointly purchased. In 1994 they solemnized their commitment to each other, exchanging vows and rings in a private ceremony. They decided early in the relationship to rear a child together by having Elsbeth artificially inseminated with sperm from an anonymous donor. Sandra was present during labor and delivery and took three weeks off from work to stay with Elsbeth and the baby. The couple jointly selected the child's name, using first and middle names from each of their families and a surname that combined their last names. From 1988 until 1993, Sandra provided the primary financial support for Elsbeth, herself, and the child, and both women shared childcare responsibilities. In 1993 Elsbeth told Sandra their relationship was over; however, they continued living together for five months for the child's sake. On May 26, 1993, Elsbeth and the child moved out. When Sandra tried to maintain contact with the child, Elsbeth informed Sandra she was terminating Sandra's relationship with the child. Sandra filed a petition for visitation rights. The court reluctantly denied Sandra's request, concluding the state's visitation law ignores the welfare of children reared by adults in nontraditional relationships when those relationships terminate. It claimed it was prohibited from awarding Sandra visitation rights because the law does not recognize the alternative type of relationship that existed in this case. Sandra appealed.

ISSUE   Can the court award visitation rights to Sandra?

DECISION   Yes. While the state's visitation statute does not apply to Sandra's petition for visitation rights to Elsbeth's biological child, it does not preempt the courts' long recognized equitable power to protect the best interests of a child by ordering visitation. The court may determine whether visitation is in the child's best interests if Sandra first proves she has a parent-like relationship with the child and that a significant triggering event justifies state intervention in the child's relationship with his biological mother. To demonstrate the existence of the parent-like relationship with the child, Sandra must prove four elements: (1) that Elsbeth (the biological parent) consented to, and fostered, Sandra's formation and establishment of a parent-like relationship with the boy; (2) that Sandra and the boy lived together in the same household; (3) that Sandra assumed obligations of parenthood by taking significant responsibility for the child's care, education and development, including contribution towards the child's support, without expectation of financial compensation; and (4) that Sandra has been in a parental role for a length of time sufficient to have established with the boy a bonded, dependent relationship parental in nature. To establish a significant triggering event justifying state intervention in the child's relationship with his biological parent, Sandra must prove Elsbeth interfered substantially with Sandra's parent-like relationship with the boy, and that Sandra sought court ordered visitation within a reasonable time after the interference. If Sandra proves all of these things, the trial court may then consider whether visitation is in the best interest of the child. The proceedings must focus on the child. This boy needs and deserves the protection of the courts as much as a child of a dissolving traditional relationship.

Legitimacy

For many years the legal system discriminated against children who were born out of wedlock. Early laws deprived them of many benefits, including the right to inherit from either parent. During the last two decades, the U.S. Supreme Court has granted these children the right to inherit from both parents, to recover for the wrongful death of a parent, to receive workers' compensation and social security benefits after the injury or death of a parent, and to receive child support.

Children born outside the marital relationship still encounter problems not faced by the offspring of married couples. When a married woman gives birth to children, there is strong presumption they are the offspring of her husband. However, when an unmarried woman gives birth, she or her children must first establish paternity before the children are entitled to benefits connected to their father.

Parental Duties ▬▬▬▬▬▬▬▬

Every state demands that parents provide their children with adequate food, shelter, care, and education. In instances where parents fail to fulfill these responsibilities, their parental rights may be terminated. However, courts are reluctant to take children away from parents unless there are clear signs of severe neglect or abuse. And, even then, the parents must be accorded a full hearing before their parental rights can be permanently ended.

http:// www.capitol.state.tx. us/statutes/fatoc.html provides information concerning Title 2 of the Texas Family code.

Prenatal Care

A mother's legal duties to her children actually may begin prior to birth. Judicial decisions recognizing a woman's right to an abortion (discussed in Chapter 1 simultaneously have made clear that the government has a compelling interest in the welfare of unborn children. This concern has prompted increasing demands on pregnant women to behave responsibly and avoid recklessly endangering the health of their unborn children. For instance, courts have ruled a state's interest in protecting a fetus could override a mother's refusal to undergo prescribed medical treatment. In some instances courts have ordered caesarean sections or blood transfusions over the objections of the pregnant woman.

Due to a growing awareness of the harmful effects a pregnant woman's substance abuse can have on a fetus, prosecutors are increasingly charging women with crimes when they deliver babies who are addicted to drugs. However, courts have been reluctant to uphold these prosecutions. Several states are overcoming this judicial reluctance by enacting statutes specifically criminalizing drug use by pregnant women. Further, some courts have removed drug-exposed babies from the custody of their mothers immediately after birth.

Matter of Stefanel Tyesha C.

556 N.Y.S.2D 280 (A.D. 1 DEPT. N.Y. 1990)

FACTS   Stefanel Tyesha C. had a positive toxicology for cocaine when he was born on September 6, 1988. His mother admitted to hospital personnel and child welfare authorities that she had used cocaine during her pregnancy. The Commissioner of Social Services brought a neglect proceeding against her. After the petition was filed, the mother informed the court that she had enrolled in a drug rehabilitation program. However, she never completed the program. She then claimed the petition failed to state a cause of action because prenatal conduct cannot form the basis of a finding of neglect. When the family court agreed and dismissed the petitions, the commissioner appealed.

ISSUE   Should the neglect child petition be dismissed?

DECISION   No. A neglected child is a child less than 18 years of age whose physical, mental, or emotional condition has been impaired or is in imminent danger of becoming impaired as a result of the failure of his parent. Ordinarily, a child will not be found neglected because of parental drug use unless such use resulted in the parent's failure to exercise a minimum degree of care which caused the child's condition to be impaired or to be in imminent danger of becoming impaired. The mother argued there was no neglect because there was no impairment of the child's condition at birth nor has any misconduct occurred subsequent to the child's birth. Contrary to these contentions, we find a positive toxicology for cocaine in a newborn constitutes actual impairment. Although the mother alleges an isolated detrimental act committed during pregnancy cannot constitute neglect, she is wrong. Even a single act of misconduct can support such a finding. The mother's assertion that a cause of action for neglect cannot be maintained in the absence of allegations of continued drug use after the birth of her child also is not correct. A court cannot and should not await a broken bone or shattered psyche before extending its protective cloak around a child. The prenatal use of cocaine often causes miscarriages, stillbirths, premature, low-weight births or leaves the cocaine-exposed babies with various physical and neurological malfunctions. Living children have legal rights and interests in remaining alive, in being protected from physical injury, from disabling preventable illnesses and afflictions, and from psychological damage. Even if neglect is established, the child will not necessarily be removed from his mother's care. A dispositional hearing could allow for his release to his mother's custody under certain conditions and with agency supervision. However, sufficient facts have been stated which, if proven upon trial by a preponderance of the evidence, would warrant a finding of neglect.

Day-to-Day Care

Parents are obligated to provide their children with food, shelter, clothing, education, and medical attention. Failure to fulfill this obligation (known as **child neglect**) is a crime and can result in the parents losing custody of the children. However, except in extreme cases of neglect or when the parents file for divorce, courts seldom monitor the amount of financial support that children receive.

Duration of Duty

Parental support obligations generally end on a child's 18th birthday. However, they may be extended if the child is physically or emotionally disabled. Further, a growing number of courts require parents to pay a child's college expenses. This **postmajority support** usually occurs when the parents originally promised to pay for a college education and are financially able to do so.

Under the **emancipation** doctrine, parental support obligations may be terminated before children reach the age of majority. Emancipation arises when minor children remove themselves from their parents' care and assume the responsibilities of adults. Minors often become emancipated when they marry or enlist in the military. Figure 19–2 illustrates the three types of duties parents must fulfill toward their children.

Figure 19–2:   Parental Duties to Children

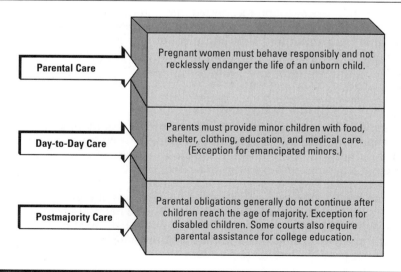

Parental Care	Pregnant women must behave responsibly and not recklessly endanger the life of an unborn child.
Day-to-Day Care	Parents must provide minor children with food, shelter, clothing, education, and medical care. (Exception for emancipated minors.)
Postmajority Care	Parental obligations generally do not continue after children reach the age of majority. Exception for disabled children. Some courts also require parental assistance for college education.

Duty to Third Persons

Traditionally, parents were liable for torts committed by their children only under very narrow circumstances. For instance, the parents might be held liable if they knew their son was a reckless driver, yet entrusted him with the family car without supervision. Parents also were liable for the negligent acts of children when the children were acting on behalf of their parents when the injuries arose. Thus, the parents would be liable if their daughter negligently struck a bicyclist while driving to the store at the request of her father.

Today, most states have enacted **parental liability statutes.** These laws impose financial responsibility on parents when their children commit *intentional torts* that injure people or property. Accordingly, parents are very likely to be legally liable for acts of vandalism carried out by their children. However, many of these laws place a ceiling on the amount of damages a parent may have to pay.

Fuller v. Studer

833 P.2D 109 (SUP. CT. IDA. 1992)

FACTS   Andy Studer and his father-in-law, Charles Seager, took Studer's three-year-old daughter, Barbara, and three other children snowmobiling. After giving the children rides on the snowmobiles, Studer and Seager began loading their two snowmobiles onto a trailer. While they were loading Studer's snowmobile, Seager moved his John Deere snowmobile ahead of the trailer where he left it with the motor running. Barbara then climbed upon the John Deere and pressed the throttle. The snowmobile took off and eventually went over an embankment and ran over seven-year-old Nina Fuller. Nina received severe and permanent injuries. Nina's parents filed a suit against Andy for negligent supervision of Barbara.

ISSUE   Should Andy be liable for the injuries inflicted on Nina by his daughter?

DECISION   No. The common law has long recognized that parents are not responsible for the torts of their children. While the state legislature enacted a law permitting some responsibility to third parties, it limited parental liability to economic losses caused by intentional torts (rather than negligence) and placed a $2,500 ceiling on any recovery. Although it could be argued that a suit based on negligent supervision violates the common law and legislative policy, this is not the case. Negligent supervision is an action based upon the independent act of negligence on the part of a parent in failing to exercise proper control of a minor child. A parent who has knowledge of his minor child's propensity for a particular type of harmful conduct is under an affirmative duty to guard against the foreseeable consequences of that specific propensity. Thus, this duty requires a two-step analysis. First, the court must look to see whether a parent has knowledge of a minor child's propensity for a specific harmful conduct. If the first step is answered affirmatively, then it must be determined whether the parent took reasonable steps to guard against the foreseeable consequences of the minor child's propensity for the specific harmful conduct. Because there was no evidence to show that Andy knew of any propensity of Barbara to climb upon and play on a snowmobile, he is not liable for the injuries she caused.

Parental Control ▰▰▰▰▰▰▰▰▰▰▰▰

Our legal system gives parents broad discretion over how to raise their children. It is only when parents are neglectful or abusive that the government is likely to interfere. This section begins by looking at the authority of parents to discipline their minor children. Attention is then turned to the special problems associated with child abuse. The section closes with a discussion of the parental immunity doctrine that limits the right of children to sue their parents.

1 – 800 –
Most states have social services hot lines. Missouri's Parental STRESS Helpline is 1-800-367-2543.

Discipline

As noted above, parents can be legally and financially liable for the activities of their children. In fact, their failure to know where their children are or what they are doing might well trigger parental liability for breaching the duty to reasonably supervise one's children. The law encourages parents to monitor their children's behavior. It allows them to establish broad rules governing behavior, association (choice of friends), dress, and curfew.

1 – 800 –
The New York State Child Abuse Hotline for the general public is 1-800-342-3720.

Parents may punish their children if in doing so they are not abusive. In general, the punishment must be "reasonable." This threshold is crossed when the parent no longer acts to correct or educate, but instead seeks to inflict pain or injury on her child. Courts treat this as a flexible standard that varies with a child's age, sex, size, and physical and mental condition. They also consider whether the punishment is proportionate to the offense and if it is likely to be particularly degrading or likely to cause serious or permanent injury.

Child Abuse

It is illegal for adults to intentionally and unreasonably inflict injury on children. **Child abuse** can be physical, psychological, or sexual. In many instances, a child will be tormented with all three types of abuse simultaneously.

Legal Process

Every state has legislation requiring childcare providers (e.g., teachers, doctors) to report their suspicion of child abuse. This usually triggers an investigation by the local child protective agency. If evidence of abuse is uncovered, the matter may proceed to a family court. In many cases the child will remain in the care of her parents pending the outcome of this hearing. However, when there are allegations of severe abuse, a child may be removed from the home immediately and placed in temporary *foster care.*

Judicial Relief

Parents accused of child abuse generally will be represented by an attorney. Further, most states will appoint an attorney to represent the interests of the child. If the family court determines by a *preponderance of the evidence* (some states use the *clear and convincing evidence* standard) that abuse has occurred, it may permanently remove the child from her parents. However, except for the most severe cases, courts frequently return the child to her parents on the condition the family undergoes regular counseling.

Criminal Sanctions

Family courts do not have authority to bring criminal sanctions against abusive parents. It is up to the local prosecuting attorney to decide if there is sufficient evidence to prove *beyond a reasonable doubt* that criminal abuse occurred. If there is, the abusive parent can be tried and, if convicted, sentenced to prison.

Parental Immunity

http://
www.azleg.state.az.
us/ars/8/title8.htm
contains the Arizona
codes on termination
of the parent-child
relationship.

Because early American courts viewed children as evil and in need of strict discipline, most forms of parental discipline were seen as necessary and proper. Accordingly, the courts crafted a **parental immunity** that greatly restricted the ability of children to sue their parents. Several policy reasons have been advanced in support of this immunity:

1. a child's suit against her parent would damage domestic tranquility;
2. such suits would create a danger of fraud and collusion;
3. requiring a parent to pay damages to his child would deplete family resources;
4. awarding damages to a child could benefit the parent if the child predeceased the parent; and
5. the threat of lawsuits might interfere with parental care, discipline, and control.

Today, most states have carved out exceptions to this doctrine. For instance, such suits often are allowed when a parent intentionally injures his child. Thus, in cases of child abuse or other intentional torts, children generally are free to sue their parents. Many states also permit children to sue their parents for negligence. However, these claims usually are prohibited if the parents' negligence arose out of the parental duty to provide food, shelter, or medical care. The discharge of these basic parental responsibilities involves matters of private choice that fall within parental discretion. Absent culpability beyond normal negligence, courts are reluctant to "second-guess" a parent's management of family affairs.

Courts are more likely to permit children to sue their parents when the negligence occurs outside the parental responsibility to nurture, care, or discipline. Thus, in many states the immunity does not apply to suits arising out of a parent's business activities. Others have found the doctrine inapplicable to automobile accidents. (The availability of liability insurance has much to do with this.) And many courts permit children to sue a parent when the parent violated a duty owed to the public at large, rather than exclusively to the child. Consider the following case where the Arizona Supreme Court abolishes the doctrine of parental immunity in that state.

Broadbent by Broadbent v. Broadbent

907 P.2D 43 (SUP. CT. ARIZ. 1995)

FACTS Christopher Broadbent was playing in and around his parents' swimming pool while his mother, Laura, watched him. No one else was home. At that time, Christopher was two and one-half years old and did not know how to swim. While he was in the water, the child wore inflatable vinyl rings on his upper arms to assist him in staying afloat. The child got out of the pool and removed the flotation rings. When the telephone inside the house rang, Laura went inside to answer it. She left Christopher unattended beside the pool while she talked on the telephone for five to ten minutes. While standing and talking on the telephone, Laura could not see the pool area. In addition, she previously had removed her contact lenses and could not see the outside area clearly. After being on the telephone at least five minutes, Laura checked on Christopher and saw him floating in the deep end of the pool. He was revived but suffered severe brain damage. A tort action in the name of the child was filed against Laura, alleging that her negligence caused his injuries. Laura admitted that she was negligent in her supervision of Christopher. However, she argued that doctrine of parental immunity prevented this lawsuit against her.

ISSUE   Should Christopher be permitted to sue his mother in negligence?

DECISION   Yes. The traditional justifications provide weak support for the continued existence of the parental immunity doctrine. The injury to the child, more than the lawsuit, disrupts family tranquility. In fact, if the child is not compensated for the tortious injury, then peace in the family is even less likely. Family tranquility is not disturbed when the parents have liability insurance. This fear of upsetting family tranquility also seems unrealistic when we consider how such a lawsuit generally is initiated. The parent most often makes the decision to sue herself, and she is in effect prepared to say that she was negligent. A damage award for the child will not deplete, or unfairly redistribute, the family's financial resources. These cases will generally not be brought if no insurance coverage is available. In fact, if a child has been seriously injured and needs expensive medical care, a successful lawsuit against the parent and subsequent recovery from the insurance company could ease the financial burden on the family. The justification that allowing children to sue their parents would undercut parental authority and discretion has more appeal than the other rationales. However, parents do not possess unfettered discretion in raising their children. We need to fashion an objective standard that does not result in second-guessing parents in the management of their family affairs. It should recognize that parents always owe a parental duty to their minor child. The issue of liability should revolve around whether the parents have breached this duty and, if so, whether the breach of duty caused the injury. The parent is not immune from liability for tortious conduct directed toward his child solely by reason of that relationship. A parent may avoid liability because there is no negligence, but not merely because of the status as parent. Laura Broadbent is not immune from liability in this case because of the doctrine of parental immunity, which we hereby abolish. Therefore, the trial court must determine if she acted as a reasonable and prudent parent would have in this situation.

AdZZZoption

Nonbiological parents may become permanent, legal parents of children through the **adoption** process. Stepparents and same-sex partners, as well as heterosexual couples, frequently seek to adopt children. Sometimes foster parents adopt children who have been permanently taken from abusive or neglectful parents.

http:// *www.law.indiana. edu/codes/in/31/art- 31-3.html* contains information on adoption laws in Indiana.

Methods of Adoption

There are five basic ways to adopt. (1) A *public agency* (the welfare department) may match abused or abandoned children with adoptive parents. (2) Other prospective parents pay a *private adoption agency* to locate a child. These private adoptions are strictly regulated by the states. (3) Under *foreign adoptions* it is possible to adopt a child living in another country. The U.S. immigration laws provide visas for foreign children who are adopted by U.S. citizens. (4) Some people opt for a *private adoption* whereby they personally locate a mother willing to place her child for adoption. While the adoptive parents may pay the mother's medical and legal expenses, it is illegal to pay her a fee for the child. (5) Finally, *stepparent adoptions* are very common. They arise when someone marries or cohabits with a parent who has had children by another partner. Through adoption the stepparent legally assumes the rights and obligations of the missing biological parent.

Adoption Procedure

After someone petitions for an adoption, courts often enter an *interim order* awarding temporary custody to the new parents. After a complete investigation and hearing, a *final decree* of adoption may be issued.

Each state has established precise rules that must be followed before an adoption will be legal. These procedures must be carefully followed because courts monitor them carefully. Although the adoption laws vary from state to state, there are certain basic rules they have in common. These include regulations governing parental qualifications, suitability, and consent. (See Figure 19–3.)

Parental Qualifications

Adoptive parents generally must be at least 21 years old. Many states also place a maximum age on the parents out of concern that elderly persons may not be suitable parents. Further, most states require the adoptive parents to be a certain number of years older (frequently at least 10 years) than the children they wish to adopt. It also is common for states to require that both the adoptive parents and the children be residents before they will consider an adoption. However, not all states have strict residency requirements.

Suitability

Some courts are reluctant to approve adoptions when the children's religion is different than that of the adoptive parents. Issues, such as religion, are part of the general inquiry into the **suitability** of the adoptive parents. Their health, education, and financial stability may also be considered. Some courts hesitate to permit unmarried couples, same-sex couples, or single parents to adopt. All of these things are investigated to determine if the adoption is in the *best interests of the children.*

Consent

Because adoption greatly affects the inheritance and support rights of adopted children, state laws often require that older children consent to the adoption.

Figure 19–3:   Adoption Procedures

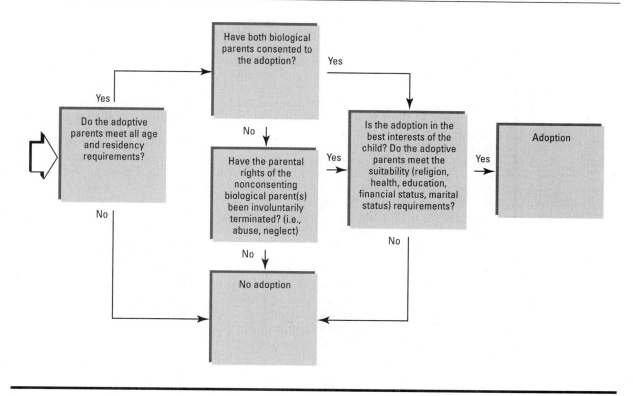

Further, unless parental rights previously have been terminated by a court, the biological parents also must consent to the adoption. (This is likely to occur if a parent has severely abused or neglected the children.) Some states waive the **parental consent** requirement if a parent has abandoned the children or failed to provide for their financial support.

In the case that opened this chapter, Ruben never consented to the adoption of his child. However, the adoption still was valid because Ruben had no enforceable parental rights since Amanda's pregnancy was the result of statutory rape. The court was concerned that if such criminals were given parental rights, they might be able to swap them for an agreement of the victim's family not to press criminal charges. (Does this reasoning seem consistent with our earlier case, *In Re Paternity of Baby Doe*?)

Depending on the state in which the adoption is granted, the biological parents may be given a *grace period* during which they may withdraw their consent. Most states also impose a *waiting period* before a new mother can consent to the adoption of her newborn child. As the following case illustrates, failure to comply fully with the consent requirement can have tragic consequences for the adoptive parents as well as the adopted children.

In Re Clausen

502 N.W.2D 649 (Sup. Ct. Mich. 1993)

FACTS On February 8, 1991, Cara Clausen gave birth to a baby girl in Iowa. Forty hours later, she signed a release of custody form, relinquishing her parental rights to the child. Clausen, who was unmarried at the time of the birth, had named Scott Seefeldt as the father. On February 14, 1991, he executed a release of custody form. On February 25, 1991, Roberta and Jan DeBoer, who are Michigan residents, filed a petition for adoption of the child in juvenile court in Iowa. A hearing was held the same day the parental rights of Cara Clausen and Seefeldt were terminated, and the DeBoers were awarded temporary custody of the child during the pendency of the proceeding. They returned to Michigan with the child, and she has lived there continuously with them since then. However, the prospective adoption never took place. On March 6, 1991, nine days after the filing of the adoption petition, Cara Clausen filed a motion in the Iowa Juvenile Court to revoke her release of custody. She stated she had lied when she named Seefeldt as the father of the child, and that the child's father actually was Daniel Schmidt. He filed an affidavit of paternity on March 27, 1991. On December 27, 1991, an Iowa district court held Schmidt had established he was the biological father of the child and that the DeBoers had failed to establish Schmidt had abandoned the child or that his parental rights should be terminated. It concluded a best interests of the child analysis was not appropriate and the DeBoers had no legal right or claim to the physical custody of the child. The DeBoers immediately petitioned the Michigan courts to enjoin enforcement of the Iowa custody order. During the more than two years of legal arguments, the Deboers retained physical custody of the child.

ISSUE Should the adoptive parents be required to return the child to her biological parents?

DECISION Yes. No one would seriously dispute that a deeply loving and interdependent relationship with an adult and a child in his or her care may exist even in the absence of a blood relationship. However, whatever emotional ties may develop between adoptive parents and children have their origins in an arrangement in which the state has been a partner from the onset. The DeBoers acquired temporary custody of this child, with whom they had no prior relationship, through the power of the state and knew their right to continue custody was contingent on completion of the Iowa adoption. Within nine days after assuming physical custody, the DeBoers learned of Cara Clausen's claim that her consent to adoption was unlawful because she had not been afforded the 72-hour waiting period required by Iowa law. Within two months of the child's birth, they learned of Daniel Schmidt's paternity claim. Iowa has not acted arbitrarily. Rather, its courts proceeded with the adoption petition of the DeBoers, and at the conclusion of the proceedings ruled there would be no adoption. The fact the DeBoers might now be the best parents for the child is not relevant. While a child has a constitutionally protected interest in family life, that interest is not independent of her parents' rights absent a showing they are unfit. The DeBoers were unable to prove Schmidt would not be a fit parent, and made no such claim as to Clausen. It is now time for the adults to move beyond saying their only concern is the welfare of the child. They must put those words into action by assuring the transfer of custody is accomplished promptly with minimum disruption of the life of the child.

————————— Ethical Issue —————————

The DeBoers were notified that their temporary custody was revoked nine days after they filed for adoption. Still, they defied the Iowa court and kept the child in Michigan for over two years. Clausen and Schmidt are legally entitled to their baby. Yet the child has known only the DeBoers as her parents for all but 40 hours of her life. Who are the villains in this case?

Legal Effect

Legal adoptions completely terminate the parental rights and duties of one or both of the children's biological parents and fully transfer them to the adoptive parent or parents. The adoptive parents have full legal and physical custody over the children and must provide for their food, shelter, care, and education. The adopted children frequently assume the family name of the new parents and are subject to their parental control.

Adoption Disclosure Statutes

For many years all adoption records were *sealed* to prevent the biological parents from interfering with the relationship between children and their adoptive parents. These laws also protected the biological parents from the unwanted presence of their children. Some states permitted the release of these records if both the children and their biological parents consent.

Modern courts have expressed skepticism that information concerning birth should be protected from disclosure, since the government has long kept records of when, where, and by whom babies are born. Accordingly, they have upheld **adoption disclosure statutes** that balance the interest of children in knowing the circumstances of their birth and the competing interest of some biological and adoptive parents in concealing the circumstances of birth.

A typical adoption disclosure statute makes adoption records available to an adopted person who is 21 years old or older. The information is released only to the parents, siblings, lineal descendants, or lineal ancestors, or the adopted person, and only with the express written consent of the adopted person. Such laws also have a **"contact veto,"** under which a parent, sibling, spouse, lineal ancestor, or lineal descendant of an adopted person may register to prevent contact by the adopted person. A violator of the contact veto provision is subject to civil and criminal liability. Before disclosing the identity of an adopted person's relatives, the state searches for the relatives to give them a chance to register for the veto. However, the relatives of an adopted person can veto only contact, not disclosure of their identities.

Nontraditional Pregnancies ▆▆▆▆▆▆

Adoption is not the only alternative for infertile couples and single people desiring to raise a family. Medical breakthroughs are providing opportunities for these people to have genetically related children. This final section examines the special legal issues accompanying the growing use of artificial insemination, surrogacy, and egg donations by prospective parents. (See Figure 19–4 on page 448.)

Figure 19–4:   Nontraditional Pregnancies

ALTERNATIVES	PROCEDURE	LEGAL RISK
Artificial Insemination	Woman is injected with the sperm of her husband or some other donor.	The sperm donor may be able to assert parental rights.
Traditional Surrogacy	A woman agrees to be artificially inseminated and carry a child to term. She agrees to waive parental rights.	The birth mother may renege on her promise to waive parental rights. The birth mother may be awarded custody or visitation rights.
Gestational Surrogacy	A woman donates fertilized eggs to a birth mother who will cary the child to term. Birth mother waives parental rights.	Court is likely to enforce such an agreement since the birth mother has no genetic link to the child.
Egg Donations	A woman desiring a child implants a fertilized egg in her uterus. Egg donor waives parental rights.	The egg donor (the genetic mother) may claim parental rights after the birth.

Artificial Insemination

Sometimes a woman is unable to become pregnant through sexual intercourse with her husband. In other cases, a single woman or a woman involved in a same-sex relationship may desire to have a child. These women may choose to become pregnant through **artificial insemination,** whereby sperm is injected into the vagina without the need for intercourse.

When a husband is able to produce sperm, the wife may be injected with his semen. When he is unable to do so (or when the woman has no husband), a suitable donor may be found. No matter who the donor is, when the woman is married, her husband is the legal father and the donor will have no paternal rights. If the mother is unmarried, the donor may be able to assert paternal rights unless he has signed an agreement waiving them. A number of states have enacted laws holding that the donor of semen or ova for use in artificial insemination by a licensed physician has no parental rights or responsibilities toward the child.

Many women obtain semen from a *sperm bank* that requires donors to remain anonymous. However, this approach is not without some degree of risk. For instance, in the 1980s, numerous women visited Dr. Cecil B. Jacobson, a medical doctor specializing in the diagnosis and treatment of infertility. He told his patients they would be inseminated with sperm from their husbands or from anonymous donors participating in the donor insemination program. Instead, the doctor allegedly inseminated the women with his own sperm, thereby becoming the biological father of their children. Dr. Jacobson has been indicted on at least 53 criminal counts of fraud and is the defendant in several civil suits. Imagine the psychological effects this fraud has inflicted on the doctor's patients and their children.

Surrogacy

Some women are medically unable to carry a child to term. As a result, artificial insemination is not a viable alternative for them. However, they may elect to have a child through the services of a **surrogate mother.** This woman contracts to give birth to a child, which she then will give to the prospective parents. There are two basic types of surrogacy arrangements: traditional and gestational. The legal rights and responsibilities of the parties vary depending upon which type is employed.

Traditional Surrogacy

When a woman desiring a child is both infertile and unable to produce a healthy egg, she may arrange to have a child through a surrogate. The surrogate mother is artificially inseminated with sperm from the man selected to father the child. The surrogate mother agrees that the resulting child is to be legally the child of the father and the infertile woman. As a part of this arrangement, she agrees to formally consent to the child being legally adopted by the infertile woman.

Traditional surrogacy carries some risk for the prospective parents. The surrogate mother, after giving birth to the child, may refuse to waive her parental rights. This may prevent the infertile woman from adopting the child. The surrogate mother is not only the woman who gave birth to the child, but the child's genetic mother as well. Like the father, she is the child's natural parent. Because of this fact, a court may override the surrogacy agreement and award custody or visitation rights to the surrogate mother.

Gestational Surrogacy

This arrangement generally is used when a woman cannot carry a fetus to term but can produce healthy eggs. Through *in vitro* fertilization, eggs are surgically removed from the woman's ovaries and are fertilized with a man's semen outside her body. (This sometimes is called a "test-tube baby.") The embryo then is implanted in the surrogate (or gestational) mother's womb. She carries the child to term and, pursuant to the surrogacy agreement, gives the baby to the genetic parents at birth.

With **gestational surrogacy,** the woman desiring a baby and her male companion are the genetic parents of the child. The surrogate mother has no genetic link to the child and, accordingly, may be less likely to persuade a court to award her custody or visitation rights if she fails to live up to the original agreement.

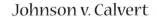

Johnson v. Calvert

851 P.2D 776 (SUP. CT. CAL. 1993)

FACTS   Mark and Crispina Calvert are a married couple who desired to have a child. Despite having a hysterectomy, Crispina's ovaries remained capable of producing eggs. In 1989 Anna Johnson heard about Crispina's plight from a coworker and offered to serve as a surrogate for the Calverts. Mark, Crispina, and Anna signed a contract providing that an embryo created by the sperm of Mark and the egg of Crispina would be implanted in Anna, and the child born would be taken into Mark and Crispina's home "as their child." Anna agreed she would relinquish "all parental rights" to the child in favor of Mark and Crispina. In return, Mark and Crispina would pay Anna $10,000 in a series of installments. Less than a month after the zygote was implanted, an ultrasound test confirmed Anna was pregnant. Unfortunately, relations deteriorated between the two sides. When the child was born, blood tests excluded Anna as the genetic mother. A trial court ruled that Mark and Crispina were the child's "genetic, biological, and natural parents" and that Anna had no parental rights to the child. Anna was denied both custody and visitation rights.

ISSUE   Should Anna be given parental rights over the child?

DECISION   No. We are left with the undisputed evidence that Anna, not Crispina, gave birth to the child and that Crispina, not Anna, is genetically related to him. Both women have thus adduced evidence of a mother and child relationship. Yet, for any child state law recognizes only one natural mother despite advances in reproductive technology rendering a different outcome biologically possible. Because the two women have presented acceptable proof of maternity, we do not believe this case can be decided without inquiring into the parties' intentions as manifested in the surrogacy agreement. Mark and Crispina affirmatively intended the birth of the child, and took the steps necessary to effect in vitro fertilization. But for their acted-on intention, the child would not exist. Anna agreed to facilitate the procreation of Mark and Crispina's child. The parties' aim was to bring Mark's and Crispina's child into the world, not for Mark and Crispina to donate a zygote to Anna. Although the gestative function Anna performed was necessary to bring about the child's birth, it is safe to say that Anna would not have been given the opportunity to gestate or deliver this child had she, prior to implantation, manifested her own intent to be the child's mother. No reason appears why Anna's later change of heart should vitiate the determination that Crispina is the child's natural mother. Any parental rights Anna might successfully assert could come only at Crispina's expense. Thus, Anna has no parental rights to the child.

Enforceability of Surrogacy Contracts

Courts have been reluctant to enforce surrogacy agreements in the traditional surrogacy realm because they look like sophisticated baby-selling contracts. Further, traditional surrogacy appears to be little more than a prearranged adoption. Yet these arrangements often violate the procedural requirements governing adoptions by paying the birth mother and requiring her consent to adoption prior to the birth of the child. Some states have laws making surrogacy contracts unenforceable, while at least one state (Michigan) has made them illegal.

Egg Donations

Sometimes a woman is medically able to carry a fetus to term but is unable to produce healthy eggs. She might have the sperm of her husband mixed with the eggs of a female donor through in vitro fertilization. The fertilized eggs then would be implanted in the wife's uterus. Of course, this process leaves open the risk that the egg donor might claim parental rights.

Egg donations might be a plausible procedure for same-sex, female couples who both wish to "parent" a child. The egg of one female might be fertilized by the sperm of an anonymous male donor through the in vitro procedure. The fertilized egg would then be implanted in the womb of the other woman. In this way, one partner would be the genetic mother of the child, while the other would be the gestational mother. (This approach would be more expensive than an artificial insemination of one of the women.)

An egg donation case differs significantly from a traditional surrogacy arrangement because, with egg donations, the two aspects of the female role in reproduction (the gestational and the genetic) are divided between two women. It also differs from a gestational surrogacy (where the two aspects also are divided) because egg donations involve no intention that the gestational mother give the children to their genetic mother upon birth.

—————————— QUESTIONS AND PROBLEM CASES ——————————

1. Explain the difference between a traditional surrogacy and a gestational surrogacy from a legal standpoint.

2. What legal risk does a marital or cohabiting partner (who is not a biological parent) face when he or she develops an emotional bond with the children of his or her mate? What can the nonbiological parent do to reduce this risk?

3. Under what circumstances is a court likely to extend the parental duty to support children past the age of majority?

4. Mr. Wannamaker and Mrs. Carr were divorced in 1972. As a part of their separation agreement, Mr. Wannamaker contractually promised to pay his children's college expenses. In 1979 Mrs. Carr's new husband adopted the children. Mrs. Carr then filed a contempt action against Mr. Wannamaker when he refused to pay for the college expenses. Should the court order Mr. Wannamaker to pay?

5. Otakar Kirchner (Otto) and Daniella Janikova started dating in September 1989 and began

living together later that year. Seven months later, Daniella became pregnant. She and Otto continued living together and planned to get married. Shortly before the baby's birth, Otto returned to his native Czechoslovakia for two weeks to visit a dying relative. While he was away, a relative from Czechoslovakia telephoned Daniella and told her Otto had resumed a relationship there with a former girlfriend. Distraught, Daniella gathered her belongings and moved into a women's shelter. While living at the shelter, she was persuaded to put the baby up for adoption. Mr. and Mrs. Doe arranged to adopt the baby. At all times the Does were fully aware Daniella planned to tell Otto the child died at birth. They were told Otto would not consent to the adoption and fully acquiesced in Daniella's scheme to tell Otto his child had died at birth. When Otto returned to Chicago prior to Daniella's due date, he and Daniella went through a period of reconciliation. However, she never told him of her plan to place the child for adoption. When the birth took place on March 16, 1991, Otto's efforts to contact Daniella were rebuffed. He was told the baby had died at birth. In the weeks following the birth, Otto, suspicious of the story that the child had died, attempted to discover the truth. Finally, 57 days after the birth, Daniella confessed that the Does had adopted Otto's son. Otto immediately commenced legal action to gain custody of the child. However, through protracted procedural posturing by the Does, the final proceedings were delayed until after the boy's fourth birthday. Is Otto legally entitled to custody of the child?

6. In 1986 Francine Todd and Edward Straub engaged in a romantic relationship and had sexual relations. In December of that year, Todd informed Straub of her desire to have a child. Straub was a divorcee with five children from a previous marriage, and he expressed resistance to fathering another child. Todd threatened to end the relationship, however, unless he agreed to impregnate her. Straub told Todd he would try to impregnate her if she would sign a handwritten agreement promising not to hold him financially or emotionally responsible for any child she might have. Todd signed the agreement, and the couple thereafter began having unprotected sexual intercourse. She became pregnant and gave birth to a child. The birth certificate did not list anyone as the father. Several years later Todd filed a petition asking the court to declare Straub the father of the child and require him to pay child support and certain medical expenses. Straub argued he was merely a "sperm donor" for Todd's artificial insemination and, as a result, the agreement signed by Todd relieved him of parental responsibilities. Is Straub correct?

7. Donald Levin and Barbara Levin Lahnen were married in 1970. Because Donald was sterile, the couple decided Barbara should be inseminated artificially with semen from an anonymous donor. The procedure was successful. Barbara became pregnant and gave birth to a son in 1977. Barbara and Donald were listed as the parents of the child on the birth certificate. Donald supported the child and held him out as his own. The couple

divorced in 1987. The divorce decree included the boy as a child of the marriage and required Donald to pay child support. In 1992 Donald requested the court to vacate the child support order because the child was not his biological son. Should Donald be legally responsible for the child?

8. Olga and Robert McDonald were married on July 9, 1988. Because Olga was unable to conceive naturally, she conceived through an in vitro fertilization. The sperm of her husband was mixed with the eggs of a female donor, and the fertilized eggs were implanted in Olga's uterus. On February 3, 1991, she gave birth to twin girls. Robert later filed for divorce. In his divorce petition, Robert demanded sole custody of the children on the ground that he was the only genetic and natural parent available. He claimed his right to custody was superior to his wife's because she was not the children's natural mother. Is Olga the natural mother of the children for the purpose of resolving the custody dispute?

9. One month before her second birthday, Miranda Gilley nearly drowned in the swimming pool at her apartment complex. She was rescued and temporarily revived, but four months later died from the injuries she had suffered. Her mother, Janet Shoemake, brought suit against the apartment complex owners. The jury attributed 55 percent of the negligence leading to Miranda's death to the apartment complex. However, it also found that Janet negligently failed to properly supervise Miranda. It held Janet 45 percent responsible for her daughter's death. When the apartment complex argued Janet was required to pay 45 percent of the amount owed to the child's estate, Janet claimed she had no liability to Miranda under the parental immunity doctrine. Is Janet correct?

10. Stephanie Kelley met Jeffrey Moyer, a sergeant in the Marine Corps, at a wedding in May 1987. Stephanie and Jeffrey did not date one another, but in July, when Stephanie's roommate moved out, the two agreed to marry. Jeffrey called the marriage a "business relationship" which made it possible for him to receive a married man's privileges through

the military. Stephanie had a replacement roommate to share rent payments, and she qualified for medical insurance available to dependents of military personnel. After they were married, Jeffrey moved into the bedroom vacated by Stephanie's former roommate. They did not have a sexual relationship and each freely dated other people. In April 1988, Stephanie became sexually involved with Paul Comino. He had no knowledge of the marriage, believing Jeffrey merely to be Stephanie's roommate. When Stephanie became pregnant, she told Paul he was the father. A few weeks before the birth and after Jeffrey had moved out, Paul moved in with Stephanie. When the child, Joshua, was born

in December 1988, Paul was identified as the father on the birth certificate. Stephanie and Paul took Joshua to the home they shared and treated him as Paul's natural son. Paul supported Joshua and shared caregiving responsibilities with Stephanie. In April 1991, Stephanie moved out of their family residence and into Jeffrey's home. She told Paul he was not the biological father and threatened to restrict his access to Joshua. Paul filed an action to establish his parental relationship as well as joint custody of Joshua. Stephanie argued Jeffrey is the child's father as a matter of law, since he was her husband at the time of the birth. Is Stephanie correct?

DIVORCE AND FAMILY

John Ward, who served eight years in prison for shooting and killing his first wife, was awarded custody of his 11-year-old daughter. The girl's mother, Mary Ward, is a lesbian and the judge stated he wanted to give the girl a chance to live in "a non-lesbian world." John's lawyer said that his client has been rehabilitated since he shot his first wife in 1974. However, Mary's attorney argued that John had known of Mary's sexual orientation for years and only filed a claim for custody after she sought an increase in child support. She added that he was $1,489 behind in child support payments at the time of the hearing.

Bloomington Herald-Times, February 3, 1996, p. A4.

What factors determine which parent receives custody of the children after a divorce?

Should sexual orientation be a factor when determining a person's fitness to be a parent?

What legal rights does a noncustodial parent have?

Introduction

Well over 3,000 couples are divorced on an average day in the United States. The reasons for this high rate of marital failure are many and varied. In some instances the spouses were too young and immature to fully appreciate the commitment a successful relationship requires. Others were unprepared for the stresses accompanying childrearing or may have allowed financial pressures to distract them from their partner's wants and needs. Many spouses have been physically or emotionally abused by their partners and divorce is literally a means of survival.

Whatever the reasons, 50 percent of today's marriages end in divorce. For everyone involved—husband, wife, children, family, and friends—the demise of the marriage can be extremely painful. Many divorces leave the spouses and their children emotionally and, too frequently, physically scarred. Even amicable divorces tend to be emotionally draining, often infecting both partners with a sense of failure. And, much to the surprise of many divorcing couples, divorce often drastically reduces the participants' economic status.

Chapter Overview

The chapter begins by examining the concept of separation and several procedural aspects of a divorce petition. It then looks at how courts reallocate the property rights of divorcing couples. This includes an introduction to the concept of spousal support. The chapter closes with a discussion of child custody and child support.

Dissolving the Marriage

We should think of "divorce" as a verb rather than a noun. Most couples are stunned to discover that formal dissolution of their marriage does not terminate their relationship. In fact, the process often lasts many years and, for some couples, never ends. This section examines the legal issues that arise during the early stages of the divorce process. It ends with a discussion of pro se divorce (dissolving a marriage without the assistance of a lawyer). This section also contains illustrations that show the various types of legal documents required by most states' judicial systems. (See Figures 20–1 through 20–4 on the following pages.)

http://
www.azleg.state.az.
us/ars/25/title25.htm
provides information
regarding Arizona
laws on dissolution
of marriage.

Separation

The first steps in the divorce process generally occur long before either spouse ever retains an attorney or visits a courtroom. Many couples have separated and reunited numerous times before one or both finally gives up on the relationship. Separations may be either formal or informal.

Legal Separation

Rather than divorce, some people file papers in court requesting a **legal separation.** The court then directs them to live separate and apart without actually terminating the marriage. People may choose this route for religious reasons (they do not believe in divorce). Others select it because they are not certain if they really want to formally end their marriage. They use the separation as a trial divorce.

In its separation order, the court may determine who maintains custody of any children, direct the payment of child support or spousal support, and divide

Figure 20–1: Divorce Petition

STATE OF INDIANA ⎫ SS:
COUNTY OF MONROE ⎭

IN THE MONROE CIRCUIT COURT
CAUSE NO. 53CO

IN RE THE MARRIAGE OF:

_____
                    Petitioner,
and

_____
                    Respondent.

VERIFIED PETITION FOR DISSOLUTION OF MARRIAGE

Comes now the Petitioner and hereby respectfully petitions this Court for a dissolution of marriage pursuant to the provisions of Indiana law. In support of Petition, Petitioner shows the Court as follows:

1. That Petitioner has been a bona fide and continuous resident of the State of Indiana for more than six (6) months and of Monroe County for more than three (3) months immediately preceding the filing of this Peition.

2. That Petitioner and Respondent were duly married on the _____ day of _____, 19_____, and lived together as Husband and Wife until the _____ day of _____, 19 _____, at which time they separated.

3. That the grounds for dissolution of this marriage are irretrievable breakdown without reasonable possibility of reconciliation.

4. Wife is not pregnant.

5. There were born to this marriage on the dates indicated the following named children:

6. The parties have acquired certain properties and debts which should be fairly divided.

WHEREFORE, Petitioner prays that the bonds of matrimony heretofore existing between Petitioner and Respondent be dissolved by a Decree of Marriage Dissolution; the Court order such distribution of the property of the parties as is just and reasonable under the circumstances; the Court make such order pertaining to child custody and control, visitation, health care, reasonable support, and educational expenses as may be necessary; that the court make such further order as is just and reasonable under the circumstances and for all necessary and proper relief in these premises.

Respectfully Submitted,

_____
Petitioner

I affirm under the penalties of perjury that the foregoing representations are true and accurate to the best of my knowledge and belief.

_____
Petitioner

Tammy M. Minger, #14181-53
Minger Law Office
1408 South Walnut St., Suite A
Bloomington, IN 47401
Telephone: (812) 323-2234

their property. However, despite their legal separation, the couple is still married and, accordingly, entitled to spousal benefits under inheritance laws, social security, and many other programs.

Separation Agreements

If one spouse simply leaves the other, that desertion creates a *de facto separation.* One also occurs when both partners mutually agree to live apart without seeking a judicial order. (Some states permit the parties to obtain a divorce solely on the basis of being separated for at least one year.) When couples both agree to separate, they often enter into a **separation agreement** that addresses their child custody, property, financial, and personal arrangements. As with prenuptial agreements (discussed in Chapter 18), courts will not enforce these contracts unless they are entered into knowingly and voluntarily by both spouses.

The Legal Process

Just as the marriage contract is subject to state regulation, the divorce laws also vary from state to state. However, there are many similarities among their rules. The formal legal process usually is triggered when one spouse files a *divorce petition* in a jurisdiction where one or both of the spouses is a resident. After the petition is filed, the court normally issues a *temporary order* providing immediate relief. This often includes temporary awards of child custody, spousal support, child support, and control of marital property. Where there has been marital violence, the court might also issue a restraining order against one or both of the spouses. Temporary relief hearings generally are abbreviated since the court revisits these issues in greater detail during the divorce trial.

Most states require the parties to be separated for a specific time period before granting a divorce. These waiting periods apply even to uncontested divorces because the states hope the marriage still might be preserved. Until the divorce decree is granted, the spouses cannot legally marry anyone else. Even though they have been separated for a considerable time period and the divorce process has dragged on for several years, they still are married to one another. Couples who have a common-law marriage also must terminate their marriage through a formal divorce proceeding; merely separating does not end that legal relationship.

When a divorce is hotly contested, the time between the filing of the divorce petition and the final decree can last several years. In cases where the delay is caused by disagreement over custody, support, or property division issues (rather than the decision to divorce), some courts *bifurcate* the process. In the first stage, the judge quickly ends the marital relationship (giving the ex-spouses freedom to marry other people). The permanent custody, support, and property division issues are resolved in the second stage.

Grounds For Divorce

There has been a nationwide shift to no-fault divorce that has greatly simplified the divorce process. Most states simultaneously have amended their divorce laws to make it more difficult for unwilling spouses to successfully contest the dissolution. As a result, very few divorces involve a full-fledged judicial hearing. In fact, in most cases only the petitioning spouse actually appears before the court.

http:// www.idwr.state.id. us/idstat/TOC/ 32006KTOC.html provides information regarding Idaho law on grounds for divorce.

Fault Divorce

For many years the states only would dissolve a marriage under extreme circumstances. Absent some showing of outrageous conduct or **fault**, a divorce would not be granted. Each state's divorce laws contained a list of grounds for a divorce. These included adultery, cruelty, desertion, alcoholism, and drug abuse. This focus on fault caused a great deal of trauma for unhappily married couples who had not committed any marital misconduct.

Figure 20–2:   Motion for Temporary Order

STATE OF INDIANA   } SS: IN THE MONROE CIRCUIT COURT
COUNTY OF MONROE   }   CAUSE NO. 53CO

IN RE THE MARRIAGE OF:

_____
                    Petitioner,

and   ____

_____
              Respondent.

MOTION FOR PROVISIONAL ORDERS

Petitioner, _____ , states:

1. S/he is the Petitioner in an action for dissolution of marriage, which has been filed in this Court.
2. S/he believes, upon good cause, that the Respondent will dispose of, encumber, hide, transfer or otherwise dissipate the property of the marriage unless s/he is specifically restrained from so doing.
3. Petitioner is without sufficient funds with which to support _____ self and the minor child of the parties or with which to pay h_____ attorney's fees during the pendency of this cause.

WHEREFORE, Petitioner prays for an Order:
a. Restraining and enjoining the Respondent from transferring, dissipating or disposing of property of the marriage;
b. Awarding the Petitioner temporary maintenance and child support; and
c. Setting this cause for preliminary hearing;
d. Awarding Petitioner all other relief in the premises.

_____
Petitioner

I affirm under the penalties of perjury that the foregoing representations are true and accurate to the best of my knowledge and belief.

_____
Petitioner

Respectfully submitted,

_____
Tammy M. Minger
Attorney for Petitioner

Figure 20–3: Summons

STATE OF INDIANA }   SS:
COUNTY OF MONROE }

IN THE MONROE CIRCUIT COURT
CAUSE NO. 53CO

IN RE THE MARRIAGE OF:

_____
           Petitioner,
and

_____
         Respondent.

SUMMONS

THE STATE OF INDIANA TO RESPONDENT:

You have been sued by the Petitioner in the Court stated above. The nature of the proceedings against you appears in the Petition and other documents attached to this Summons.

If you have a claim for relief against the Petitioner arising from the same transaction or occurrence you may be required to assert it in your responsive pleading, if any. Any claim or defense you may have in response to the attached Petition may be raised without written Answer.

The following manner of service of this Summons is hereby designated: _____.

DATED: _____

                                  _____
                                  Pat Haley, Clerk
                                  Monroe Circuit Courts

Tammy M. Minger, #14181-53
Minger Law Office
1408 South Walnut St., Suite A
Bloomington, IN 47401
Telephone: (812) 323-2234

Clerk's Certificate of Mailing

I hereby certify that on the _____ day of _____, 19 _____, I mailed a copy of this Summons and a copy of the Petition to the Respondent, _____, by certified mail, requesting a return receipt, at the address furnished by the Petitioner.

DATED: _____.

                                  _____
                                  Pat Haley, Clerk
                                  Monroe Circuit Courts

Figure 20–4:   Notice of Divorce Hearing

STATE OF INDIANA   } SS: IN THE MONROE CIRCUIT COURT
COUNTY OF MONROE   }   CAUSE NO. 53CO

IN RE THE MARRIAGE OF:

_____
                    Petitioner,
and

_____
           Respondent.

NOTICE OF HEARING

The Court, upon the Motion of the Petitioner, NOW SETS this cause for Preliminary Hearing on _____, 19_____ at _____.

SO ORDERED, this _____ day of _____, 19 _____.

                                             _____
                                             Judge

cc:

Respondent: _____

SHERIFF SERVICE–MONROE COUNTY SHERIFF

No-Fault Divorce

Today there is a widespread renunciation of the need to establish fault before a divorce could be granted. All states now accept some form of **no-fault** divorce and at least 15 have completely eliminated fault grounds. As a result of this trend, couples no longer have to justify their wish to end their marriage. This relieves the divorce petitioner of the need to prove marital misconduct. Instead, one merely needs to assert that the spouses have *irreconcilable differences* or that there has been an *irretrievable breakdown of the marriage.*

Each state has its own rules for determining if its no-fault standards have been met. Some require spouses to first undergo marital counseling or a reconciliation program. Others merely ask for a statement that the spouses tried to work out their differences but failed. Most require the couple to be separated for a prescribed time period before they grant a divorce decree.

Self-Representation

Divorce is greatly simplified (and much cheaper) when a husband and wife agree on how their marital rights and obligations are to be reallocated. When a divorce is amicable, it is not uncommon for the spouses to retain only a single lawyer to guide them through the legal process. And today, couples increasingly are divorcing without the benefit of any legal representation at all.

Many couples who choose the self-representation route do so after purchasing a *divorce kit* from a bookstore. These **pro se divorces** are most common among people of moderate means who have no children and do not own their own home. While attorneys generally are highly critical of "do-it-yourself" divorces, some states have simplified their divorce procedures to assist couples who are in agreement on the terms of their divorce. In fact, some jurisdictions offer pro se litigants self-help form packets and special clinics that provide individualized instructions.

Reallocation of Property Rights

As noted above, the decision to terminate the marriage is only a single step in the divorce process. The court also must reallocate the rights and responsibilities the spouses formerly shared. This generally involves dividing the marital property and determining if one spouse must provide financial support to the other.

http:// www.le.state.ut.us/ ~code/TITLE30/30_02. *htm* provides information regarding Utah property laws in divorce.

Property Division

Even in uncontested divorces, the spouses often are unable to agree on how to divide the property they have accumulated during their time together. When this occurs, the court must make the decision. While the rules governing division of property vary among the states, there are two fundamental methods applied throughout the country. They are the equitable distribution and the community property approaches. (See Figure 20–5.)

Figure 20–5:   Reallocation of Property Rights

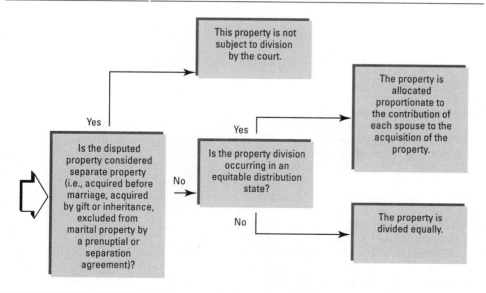

Equitable Distribution

The property distribution laws of most states evolved from common-law rules presuming that each spouse owned the property he or she brought into the marital relationship. The ownership of property acquired after the marriage could be individual or joint, depending on how it was acquired or treated. Thus, an inheritance of the wife was her *separate property*. Similarly, the wages she earned might be her separate property unless she placed them in a joint bank account with her husband; they then became *marital property*.

At least 42 states have modified their common-law rules by enacting **equitable distribution** schemes. These laws treat most property acquired during the marriage as marital property that can be fairly divided by the judge. Gifts or inheritances a spouse receives during the marriage and the property he or she brings into the marriage generally are treated as separate property and are not subject to division by the court. However, some equitable distribution states divide both the marital and the separate property. The equitable distribution laws give judges great discretion in arriving at a fair allocation of property. Courts normally consider the following factors in arriving at an equitable distribution:

1. how long the couple has been married;
2. the age and earning potential of each spouse;
3. the contributions (economic and noneconomic) each partner has made to the relationship; and
4. the living standard enjoyed by the spouses while they were married.

An equitable distribution is not necessarily an equal distribution. Thus, if one spouse made a substantially greater contribution to the marital property, he may receive a greater share of the property division.

A divorcing couple can save a great deal of time and money by jointly resolving the property division issues outside of court in a private separation agreement. Courts rarely disregard these arrangements unless it is clear one party did not knowingly and voluntarily agree to the terms.

Donahue v. Donahue

384 S.E.2D 741 (Sup. Ct. S.C. 1989)

FACTS   Janis and James Donahue were married on February 15, 1979. He is 32 years old and she is 41 years old. They have a 7-year-old child. In the fall of 1979, James entered dental school. His family deposited money for his tuition and books into an account that he maintained separately. Household expenses and money for family support were provided by Janis during the four years James attended dental school and thereafter until the opening of his dental practice. Upon his graduation from dental school in the spring of 1984, the couple moved in with Janis's family for five months before moving into their own home. In January 1984, James opened his own dental practice. Janis cosigned several loans, offering personal property as security, in order to fund the practice. Soon after the practice opened, James began having an extramarital affair. The couple experienced marital discord, and James left the marital home on several occasions, but returned each time shortly after leaving. Finally, Janis filed for divorce on the ground of adultery. The judge found that Janis's direct contributions to the marital estate totaled $251,000 (91 percent) and James's direct contributions totaled $20,112 (9 percent). He distributed 62 percent of the marital property to Janis, including title to the marital home. James argued it was a mistake to award the marital home to Janis because it should only be awarded to one spouse if compelling circumstances exist.

ISSUE   Should the court reconsider the property division?

DECISION   Yes. In order to effect an equitable apportionment, the family court may require the sale of marital property and a division of the proceeds. However, the court should first attempt an "in-kind" distribution of the assets. A family court may grant one spouse title to the marital home as part of the equitable distribution. Here, Janis was awarded the home to compensate her for $23,000 she contributed to the value of the goodwill in James's dental practice. However, goodwill in a solo practice is too speculative to made part of the marital estate subject to equitable distribution. Thus, the award of the marital home to Janis must be reconsidered. At the same time, the judge never explained why he entitled James to 38 percent of the marital property despite his direct contribution of only 9 percent. For this reason, the case must be remanded for reconsideration.

Community Property Distribution

Eight states consider the property and income earned by either spouse during the marriage to be part of a joint economic enterprise and equally owned by each marital partner. Accordingly, they equally divide this **community property** upon dissolution of the marriage. Under a community property distribution, the separate property each spouse brought into the marriage (or received by gift or inheritance) is excluded from this allocation.

A problem arises when the spouses *commingle* their separate property with the community property. For instance, one spouse may receive an inheritance and deposit it in a joint bank account. Funds from this account may be used to pay marital debts over a long time period. The community property states vary widely in how they resolve these situations.

Spousal Support

Historically, upon divorce the husband would be ordered to pay *alimony* to his ex-wife. These weekly or monthly payments (also known as maintenance) often would continue until her death unless she remarried. As a result of the movement toward equitable property distributions, each spouse is expected to become self-supporting after the divorce. Thus, many states either abolished or greatly reduced alimony. Those states that still recognize the concept of alimony no longer presume only the wife should be eligible for it. Thus, if the wife was the major wage-earner, she might be required to make support payments to her ex-husband.

Despite the movement away from alimony, all states still recognize some form of **spousal support.** These are payments to be made to a dependent spouse (usually for no more than seven years) so he or she has an opportunity to become self-supporting. (Many states call this *rehabilitative maintenance.*) In special instances, a court may order spousal support for an indefinite time period. This may occur when there has been a long marriage during which one spouse has become economically dependent on the other at the request of the wage-earner.

Courts consider the resources of the spouse requesting support and the ability of the other spouse to pay when awarding spousal support. In equitable distribution states, the spousal support award and the division of property often are considered together. Thus, the spousal support may come in the form of lump sum payment as part of the property distribution.

As with the division of property, courts often give great deference to private agreements between husbands and wives on spousal support issues. Thus, a growing number of couples (especially those who have already divorced at least once) enter into prenuptial agreements prior to marriage, or separation agreements in anticipation of divorce.

Effect of Marital Misconduct

In some states, marital misconduct affects a court's spousal support or property division award. For instance, in cases of adultery a court may suggest that a husband's extramarital activities led to an unjustified spending of marital assets to the disadvantage of the faithful spouse. This *dissipation of marital assets* might also occur if one spouse is a drug addict or an alcoholic. In any event, the unwarranted spending can reduce the amount of property he will receive.

While 29 states exclude marital misconduct as a factor in awarding spousal support, at least 11 states specifically permit it to be considered. And 8 states deny spousal support to a spouse whose adultery precipitated the divorce. However, courts generally cannot award spousal support solely for the purpose of punishing a spouse who is guilty of some type of marital misconduct (e.g., adultery, desertion, alcoholism). Thus, while fault may be a relevant issue, the court's primary concern in awarding spousal support is to provide for the financial needs of a dependent spouse.

Noah v. Noah

491 So.2d 1124 (Sup. Ct. Fla. 1986)

FACTS   Elizabeth and Richard Noah were married for 10 years. At the time of their divorce, both were employed at the same company (she was a typist and he was a financial analyst). He was in good health, while she had major health problems. They owned five principal assets: a condominium with $35,300 equity; a house having $61,000 equity; furniture valued at $9,000; her car with equity of $600; and his car with equity of $3,300. The equity of this marital property totaled approximately $109,000, all of which was awarded to the wife as lump sum alimony, with the exception of the husband's automobile valued at $3,300. The trial court made this award because Elizabeth was a good wife, in view of her contributions to the marriage, the disparity of their income, Richard's ability to pay alimony, Elizabeth's inability to earn a sum sufficient to support herself, their ages, the length of the marriage, her ill health, and because of Richard's gross marital misconduct. Richard argued the trial court placed undue emphasis on his adulterous affair when making this distribution.

ISSUE   Did the trial court abuse its discretion?

DECISION   Yes. The primary standards to be used in fashioning an equitable alimony award are the needs of one spouse and the ability of the other to pay. However, although Florida has a no-fault divorce system, its divorce laws do retain a vestige of fault by allowing a trial court to consider the adultery of an alimony-seeking spouse. One spouse's adulterous conduct also may be relevant in determining entitlement to alimony when it was longstanding and may have contributed to depletion of the financial resources of the family. However, evidence of Richard's adulterous activity appears to have been presented solely to obtain an increase in the award of alimony. There was no evidence that his misconduct depleted family resources. Thus, we can think of no reason why his adultery should have played a part in fashioning an equitable alimony award. The trial court should reconsider the distribution scheme in light of this decision.

Ethical Issue

Suppose you know that Martin is having an extramarital affair. You also are a good friend of his wife. Should you confront Martin? Should you tell his wife? Would your answer differ if Martin or his wife was one of your close relatives?

Child Custody

During marriage, both parents equally share the legal authority to raise their minor children. There are two fundamental aspects to these custodial rights. First, the couple may jointly make the day-to-day decisions regarding their children's *immediate needs.* These are the things that seem so important to children throughout their early years, like bedtime, television programming, meals, hair length, etc. Second, the parents possess joint authority over the most *fundamental* child-rearing decisions. This gives them equal power to determine religion, education, and medical treatment as well as the other things that strongly influence a person's lifetime development.

Upon dissolution of the marriage, much to the shock and dismay of many parents, the legal system assumes a much more intrusive role in the parenting process. Particularly, in cases where divorced couples are unwilling to cooperate in child-rearing decisions, the courts must forcibly reallocate the parents' custodial rights.

Historical Foundations

Historically, under English common law, a woman possessed few legal rights apart from her father or husband. As a result, upon divorce, a father was presumed to be the natural guardian of his children. This presumption in favor of paternal custody was inherited by early American courts. They granted the father full legal custody unless he abandoned or physically abused his children.

Early in the nineteenth century, U.S. courts recognized that very young children (usually under the age of three) required a mother's nurturing. They established the **tender years doctrine,** which created a judicial preference for maternal

http:// www.cslnet.ctstateu. edu/statutes/title46b/ httoc.htm provides information regarding Connecticut custody laws.

custody when the children were very young. However, as with the paternal preference, this presumption was not absolute. Courts would override it when a parent was guilty of moral impropriety (adultery, cruelty). In fact, by the beginning of the twentieth century, several states erected a statutory presumption that the parent who caused the marital breakup was unfit to act as a custodial parent.

By the mid-1970s, courts overwhelmingly believed all minor children, regardless of their age, were best served by a nurturing maternal environment. Thus, the paternal preference and tender years doctrine gave way to a general preference for maternal custody. Throughout the country it became clear that a mother would gain custody of her children unless the father proved neglect, abuse, or some other type of moral wrongdoing on her part.

Best Interests of the Child

Modern divorce statutes expressly reject any presumption in favor of either parent. They instruct courts to consider the welfare of the children rather than the interests of the parents. This focus on the present and future well-being of the children is known as the **best interests of the child** standard. It reflects the renunciation of stereotypically defined sex roles and the recognition of fuller equality between the sexes. Simultaneously, it arises from a growing recognition that children are persons worthy of legal rights and representation.

Most states have adopted some form of the *Uniform Marriage and Divorce Act*. This model legislation directs courts to consider five criteria when determining what is in the best interests of the child:

1. the wishes of the parents;
2. the wishes of the child;
3. the child's relationships with the parents, siblings, and other people who may significantly affect the child's best interests;
4. the child's adjustment to his home, school, and community; and
5. the mental and physical health of all individuals involved.

While over half of the states require divorce courts to consider each child's custodial preference, judges are not legally obligated to abide by a child's choice. However, in cases where the parents mutually agree on custody, most courts honor their joint decision unless it clearly is not in the best interests of the children.

Parrillo v. Parrillo
554 A.2d 1043 (Sup. Ct. R.I. 1989)

FACTS   Justin and Carla Parrillo were divorced in May 1986. Physical possession of the three children, whose ages ranged from 8 to 13, was awarded to Carla, with Justin having reasonable visitation rights. In early June, Justin filed a motion to have Carla restrained from permitting any "unrelated males" to stay overnight at her residence. Carla acknowledged that her lover, Joseph DiPippo, would remain overnight "once or twice a week behind closed doors." She saw no risk to the children, who were present at those times, because the daughters slept in separate bedrooms about 20 feet away from her bedroom and the son's bedroom was downstairs. When asked if Joseph wore his pajamas in front of the children, Carla explained that when he stayed overnight, he wore a jogging suit. She stated the children liked Joseph but she had no intention of marrying him in the near future. The trial judge concluded the children appeared to be well cared for. However, he did observe that Joseph's overnight visits, in the presence of the children, were not conducive to their general well-being, at least in terms of their psychological welfare. Accordingly, he directed Carla to refrain from allowing any "unrelated males" to stay overnight at her residence when the children were present.

ISSUE   Should the trial court's order be upheld?

DECISION   Yes. The court retains jurisdiction over the custody of the minor children of divorced parents regardless of whether custody was initially established by judicial decree or agreement of the parents. Courts almost universally hold this type of arrangement is a sufficient change in the circumstances and conditions that existed when custody originally was determined to warrant a new consideration of the best interests of the children. In fact, a small number of courts have held the sexual misconduct of the custodial parent is adequate reason to modify the custody decree, even in the absence of any detrimental effect on the children. However, the vast majority of courts considering the issue decline to accept this approach and instead consider the parent's misconduct as a factor in determining the best interests of the children. These courts hold an award of custody will not be modified absent a showing the parent's living arrangement has a detrimental effect upon the children. We cannot fault the trial court's actions. In simple and direct language it ordered the mother to forgo any overnight visitations with Joseph on those occasions when the children are present. He may still visit overnight when the children are not with their mother.

Types of Custody Decrees

Custody decrees decide the two fundamental aspects of child custody. **Physical custody** determines the physical placement of the children, including which of the parents is responsible for their immediate needs (food, clothing, etc.). **Legal custody** decides which of the parents will be both financially and legally responsible for the most fundamental childrearing decisions such as religion, education, and medical treatment. Each of these custodial components must be incorporated in the court's decree. (See Figure 20–6 on page 468.)

Physical Custody

Under *sole physical custody,* the children primarily reside with the custodial parent, although the noncustodial parent may be awarded some visitation rights. With *joint physical custody,* the court divides the children's time between the two parents. However, it need not allocate their physical placement equally. For instance, they might reside with their mother during the week and only stay with their father on weekends. Day-to-day childrearing decisions (bedtime, meals, etc.) are granted to the parent with whom the children are physically placed at any given moment.

Figure 20–6:   Custody Decrees

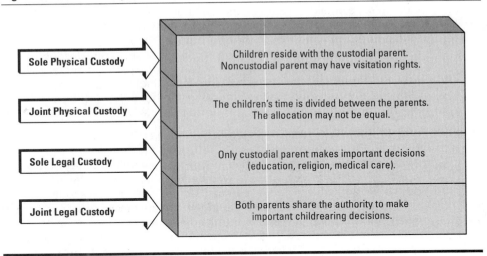

Sole Physical Custody	Children reside with the custodial parent. Noncustodial parent may have visitation rights.
Joint Physical Custody	The children's time is divided between the parents. The allocation may not be equal.
Sole Legal Custody	Only custodial parent makes important decisions (education, religion, medical care).
Joint Legal Custody	Both parents share the authority to make important childrearing decisions.

Legal Custody

When a court awards **sole legal custody,** only one parent possesses the power to make the most important decisions concerning the upbringing of the children (education, religion, medical treatment). Generally, a parent receiving sole legal custody also is awarded sole physical custody, although this is not always true.

Under *joint legal custody,* both parents continue to share most of the childrearing authority they possessed during marriage. The most important decisions affecting the life of the children are retained by both parents regardless of where the children are physically situated. When parents are awarded joint legal custody, they frequently share physical custody as well. This is because many courts believe joint legal/joint physical custody reduces the trauma children experience in the wake of a marital dissolution. However, others contend that the very factors that led to the divorce will similarly destroy such an arrangement. Absent convincing evidence that the divorced parents are sincerely committed to fully cooperate in childrearing decisions, these courts refuse to equally allocate legal and physical custody.

Trapp v. Trapp

526 N.Y.S.2D 95 (A.D. 1 DEPT. 1988)

FACTS   After the divorce of Peter and Regina Trapp, the wife was granted physical custody of their three children, subject to visitation by the husband. The divorce proceeding had been marked by the inability of the spouses, who barely speak to each other, to agree on any issue without resort to the judicial forum. In the four years since commencement of the divorce proceedings, there had been approximately 30 motions and cross-motions between them. Peter consistently refused to cooperate in matters relating to the education and medical care of children. The lower court conceded that the parties had gone through hard problems in their divorce proceedings. Nevertheless, it still believed they had to cooperate on decisions affecting the children. Thus, it awarded both parents joint legal custody.

ISSUE   Should the order of joint legal custody be modified?

DECISION   Yes. Joint legal custody is to be distinguished from joint physical custody, where the children live alternately with both parents. In joint legal custody, although the children actually may live with only one parent, both parents continue to share the same rights and responsibilities they had during the marriage to participate in the decisions affecting their children. In this situation, the day-to-day childrearing decisions are made by the parent with whom the children are living, while decisions with respect to the important issues, such as religious training, education and medical care, and sometimes even less significant matters, such as discipline, diet, and the choice of summer camp, are jointly made. In any event, both arrangements constitute a form of joint custody. The benefits and shortcomings of joint custody have been widely debated. Joint custody has been encouraged primarily as a voluntary alternative for relatively stable, amicable parents behaving in a mature, civilized fashion. It has been rejected where the parties are unable to communicate and make rational, joint decisions on matters relating to the care and welfare of the children. As a court-ordered arrangement imposed upon already embattled and embittered parents, accusing one another of serious vices and wrongs, joint custody can only enhance familial chaos. Where the parties cannot agree on even the simplest of issues, they cannot reasonably be expected eventually to agree on the major areas of concern affecting the children. Joint decision-making cannot be forced on hostile and antagonistic parents. Here, the husband has never shown a capacity for compromise and has litigated virtually every childrearing issue that has arisen. It is obvious these parents cannot jointly decide issues affecting their children and the joint legal custody ordered here would only work a disservice to the children. Thus, Regina Trapp is awarded sole legal custody over matters relating to the choice or change of schools, college or camps and psychological or psychiatric treatment or counseling, and doctors or surgeons. We do, however, believe a distinction should be made between matters involving religion and citizenship, which form a profound part of a child's heritage and generally do not require daily and immediate intervention by the caretaker parent, and those involving education and welfare. Absent a compelling showing to the contrary we leave untouched the provision for joint decision-making over religion and citizenship.

Enforcing Custody Decrees

The custody decrees of one state frequently were not enforced by the courts of other states. This encouraged a divorced parent who was unhappy with a custody order to move the children to another state and seek a rehearing or modification.

Uniform Child Custody Jurisdiction Act

To alleviate this problem, the *Uniform Child Custody Jurisdiction Act* (UCCJA) was promulgated and adopted by each of the 50 states. This model statute encourages cooperation among the states in the enforcement of custody decrees by vesting jurisdiction in the courts of the state where the most significant evidence concerning the children's care, protection, training, and personal relationships is most readily available.

It was hoped that this effort to harmonize the custody rules would deter abductions of children by parents seeking to obtain more favorable custody decrees elsewhere. Thus, the UCCJA cautions courts against exercising jurisdiction or modifying the custody decrees of another state if the children have been improperly taken from the physical custody of the parent entitled to custody.

The UCCJA was not overly successful in creating uniformity around the country. First, the states were slow in adopting its provisions. Second, not all states interpreted its jurisdictional requirements similarly. Thus, child custody determinations still were clouded by conflicting rulings by the courts of different states.

Parental Kidnapping Prevention Act

Congress enacted the *Parental Kidnapping Prevention Act* out of frustration with the UCCJA's failure to ensure uniformity in the resolution of child custody disputes. While this federal statute duplicates the jurisdictional requirements of the UCCJA, it goes a step further by expressly insisting that custody issues be resolved by the courts in the *home state of the children*. It further requires that custody decrees issued by a court with proper jurisdiction be accorded full faith and credit in all other states.

Atkins v. Atkins
823 S.W.2d 816 (Sup. Ct. Ark. 1992)

FACTS   Linda and Sterling Atkins were married in Linda's hometown of Bastrop, Louisiana, and immediately returned to Sterling's hometown of Hamburg, Arkansas, where they resided until they were separated. Bastrop and Hamburg are only 30 miles apart. The couple had only one child, Lindsey, who was born in a Bastrop hospital. On August 15, 1990, while still living in Hamburg, Linda and Sterling separated, and the mother took Lindsey to her parents' home in Bastrop. On August 28, she filed for a separation in Louisiana. On September 7, 1990, Sterling filed a suit for divorce in Arkansas. On October 11, the Louisiana court awarded temporary custody of the child to Linda and ordered Sterling to pay alimony and child support. On February 12, 1991, the Arkansas court refused to accord full faith and credit to the Louisiana decree and granted Sterling a divorce as well as custody of Lindsey. The mother argued that under the *Uniform Child Custody Jurisdiction Act* (UCCJA), once the Louisiana court assumed jurisdiction, the Arkansas court could not hear the matter because the child had a "significant connection" with Louisiana.

ISSUE   Could the Arkansas court lawfully grant custody to the father?

DECISION   Yes. The *Parental Kidnapping Prevention Act* (PKPA) was passed by Congress for cases just like this one because the states' flexible interpretations of the UCCJA provisions (especially those involving "significant connection" and "substantial evidence") can be construed to permit two states to assert jurisdiction concurrently. The existence of concurrent jurisdiction encourages forum shopping among divorcing parents. One of the chief purposes of the PKPA is to avoid jurisdictional competition and conflict between state courts. The principal distinction between the

UCCJA and the PKPA is that the PKPA gives exclusive jurisdiction to the child's home state. "Home state" is defined as the state in which the child lived with his parent or parents for "at least six consecutive months." Accordingly, under the PKPA, the Arkansas court had *exclusive jurisdiction* since it was the *home state*. When the UCCJA and the PKPA conflict, the preemptive federal PKPA controls.

Parenting Plans

As you might imagine, when courts are forced to impose custody arrangements on feuding ex-spouses, there are very few healing and healthful outcomes. The tremendous psychological toll imposed on children by the malicious maneuverings of too many divorced spouses has been well documented by experts in child development. One proposed solution encourages divorcing parents to draft *parenting plans* that formally agree on how their children will be raised. (Washington courts will not issue a divorce decree until the spouses have filed such a plan.)

Many family law experts suggest that this approach conditions both parents to honestly consider the best interests of their children by formally agreeing on the fundamental childrearing issues. Parents also are required to designate a method for resolving future disputes. While parenting plans seem to encourage fathers to take a more active role in postdivorce childrearing, they are not without their critics. Many lawyers argue that vindictive and immature spouses can easily use the planning process to wreak emotional havoc on one another.

Child Support

Most children and their custodial parent (usually the mother) suffer a marked decline in their standard of living in the wake of a divorce. The noncustodial parent (generally the father), on the other hand, often experiences an increase in his standard of living. To offset this outcome, divorce courts generally award the custodial parent some level of child support in the form of weekly or monthly payments from the noncustodial spouse. This money is to be used for the children's support, maintenance, and education, although the custodial parent seldom is required to account for how the money actually is spent.

Numerous factors go into the child support equation. For instance, the parent in the best financial condition generally must pay a greater share of the children's expenses. And, as noted above, a noncustodial parent often is expected to pay money to the custodial spouse. The family's predivorce lifestyle also may determine the amount of support awarded, since most courts do not want the children to suffer a decline in their standard of living. Finally, if the children have unusual medical or educational needs, the child support award is likely to reflect that fact.

http:// *www.law.indiana. edu/codes/in/31/ title-31.html* provides information regarding Indiana law on child support.

Child Support Guidelines

For many years, courts possessed great discretion over the amount of child support they could order. This resulted in tremendous disparities in the financial support children received. To end these inconsistencies, the federal government required states to establish child support guidelines as a condition to receiving federal funding for their public welfare programs. However, because the guidelines were only advisory, they frequently were ignored by the courts. Accordingly, Congress enacted the *Family Support Act of 1988,* which mandates that state support guidelines be followed unless the divorce court stated in writing why the guideline amount was not appropriate.

Types of Guidelines

The *Family Support Act* does not dictate what must be included in the states' child support guidelines. However, there are three basic models in existence. They are: (1) the income shares model, (2) the percentage of income model, and (3) the Melson formula.

Income Shares Model

At least 30 states follow an *income shares model.* This method is premised on the notion that a child should be awarded the proportion of parental income she would have received if the family had stayed together. It establishes the basic level of support to which a child is entitled depending on both parents' combined income. Each individual parent's child support obligation is then based on his or her share of the total parental income.

Percentage of Income Model

At least 12 states follow some version of a *percentage of income model* that bases support payments on a parent's income. (Some states use gross income, while others use net income.) In most states, the parent must provide some fixed percentage of his or her income for child support. For instance, a noncustodial parent may be ordered to pay 17 percent for one child, 25 percent for two, 29 percent for three children, 31 percent for four children, and 34 percent for five or more. A few states reduce the percent of income that must be paid as the parent's income increases.

Melson Formula

The support guidelines of at least four states currently are derived from some version of the *Melson formula.* It is based on three fundamental ideas: (1) parents are entitled to retain income sufficient to meet their most basic needs; (2) parents should not retain more income than absolutely necessary until the basic needs of their children are met; and (3) when the parental income is sufficient to meet the basic needs of the children and parents, the children should share in additional income earned by the parents. This permits the children to benefit from increases in the parents' standards of living.

Other Factors

Courts consider a variety of criteria in deciding whether to deviate from the state guidelines. For instance, extraordinary expenses (medical care, higher education, etc.) may require special consideration by the decision maker. The court's determination of the physical custody of the child often affects the child support obligation of a parent. In many states, the less visitation time a noncustodial parent receives, the more he will be required to pay in the form of child support. Finally, a court may deviate from the established guidelines to accommodate the terms or wishes of the parents when they have freely and fairly negotiated a child support agreement.

College Expenses

Support payments often end when a child reaches the age of 18 or is otherwise emancipated. However, special circumstances may convince a court to extend the support obligation past the age of majority. This might occur if a child were disabled and unable to care for himself.

College expenses provide the most common justification for **postmajority support** obligations. More and more courts view a higher education as a necessity and recognize that children are highly dependent on financial assistance from their parents while they attend college. However, because some courts hesitate to require support past the age of majority, custodial parents often include the obligation to provide college support in a separation agreement or request it in the original divorce petition.

Stack v. Stack

646 So.2d 51 (Civ. App. Ala. 1994)

FACTS   Steven and Rita Stack were divorced in 1988. She was awarded custody of their three minor sons, and Steven was ordered to pay child support of $225 per child per month. In 1992, Rita filed a petition to modify the judgment of divorce, seeking postmajority educational support for the three children. The trial court ordered Steven to pay 35 percent of the college expenses for two of the sons. However, this obligation would be reduced by the amount of any scholarship assistance received by the boys. No postmajority educational support was awarded for the oldest son because he was over the age of majority. Steven appealed, arguing he wants his children to go to college but believes they should pay for their own education.

ISSUE   Should the father be required to pay postmajority educational support for his two younger sons?

DECISION   Yes. A divorced parent has a legal duty to provide, or to aid in providing, a college education if the child demonstrates the ability and willingness to attain a higher education and the parent has sufficient estate, earning capacity, or income to provide financial assistance without undue hardship to himself. One of the boys, Timothy, is a senior in high school and has a 2.8 grade-point average. Timothy currently is taking a college preparatory curriculum and plans to attend college while living at home. John, the youngest son, is in the ninth grade and made the honor role in the first part of his freshman year. He also is taking a college preparatory curriculum and is making A's and B's. Both children desire a college education and have the desire to attain it. The father presented no substantial evidence that providing financial assistance would create an undue hardship for him. Given the fact the father's financial obligation will be reduced as a result of any scholarship assistance Timothy or John may receive and Timothy will continue to live at home, the trial court did not abuse its discretion.

Modifications

As the *Stack* case indicated, courts sometimes modify their support awards. However, they are unlikely to do so unless the party seeking the modification establishes a *material change* of circumstances. (The remarriage of either parent does not automatically qualify as such a change.) Under the *Uniform Marriage and Divorce Act,* courts are instructed to reject modification petitions unless the changed circumstances render the original child support award unconscionable. Substantial changes in the financial status of either spouse have been found to constitute a material change in circumstances, as have the custodial spouse's repeated interference with the noncustodial parent's visitation rights.

Many low- or middle-income families may qualify for special consideration under *Title IV-D* of the *Social Security Act.* Every three years these parents may request a modification review without first having to establish materially changed circumstances.

In Re Marriage of Bethards

526 N.W.2D 871 (CT. APP. IOWA 1994)

FACTS   Connie and Dennis Bethards were divorced in June 1986. The dissolution decree contained custody, visitation, and support provisions for three children. Dennis regularly paid child support and exercised his visitation rights with the children. Dennis learned before the marriage was dissolved that Connie had an affair near the time of the conception of the youngest child, Micah. However, Connie's divorce petition alleged Micah was a child of the marriage, and the issue of paternity was not litigated in the divorce action. Prior to the divorce, Dennis questioned Connie about Micah and she assured him he was the father despite the fact she knew he was not. Dennis asked the court to modify the divorce decree to strike the provision requiring him to pay child support for Micah. Blood testing performed after he filed the petition verified Dennis was not Micah's biological father.

ISSUE   Should the court modify the divorce decree and relieve Dennis from having to pay child support to Micah?

DECISION   Yes. A divorce decree will not be modified as regards child support provisions unless it is proven by a preponderance of the evidence its enforcement will be attended by positive wrong or injustice as a result of material and substantial changes in the circumstances since the date of the original decree. The changed circumstances relied upon must be material and substantial, not trivial, more or less permanent or continuous, not temporary, and must be such as were not within the knowledge or contemplation of the court when the decree was entered. Dennis has met his burden. We have concern about the effect this issue has on Micah and similarly situated children who are deceived in believing a man who is not their biological father is their biological father. There are serious legal and emotional implications in bastardizing Micah. There also are serious legal and emotional implications in failing to do so and in perpetuating a fraud on Micah concerning his biological father. Dennis has been deceived and does not want to be legally determined to be Micah's father. We are without authority to unilaterally make an unrelated man, Dennis, the father of Micah.

Enforcement

Several thousand divorces are granted on an average day in the United States. Yet, of the millions of recipients of child support awards, no more than 50 percent ever collect the entire amount. Under federal law the states are required to provide procedures to aid in the collection of child support. These include intercepting income tax refunds, requiring security deposits with the court, ordering garnishment of wages, and holding nonpaying spouses in contempt of court.

Until recently a spouse easily could avoid his child support obligations by moving to another state. However, all states have now adopted model legislation encouraging interstate cooperation in the collection of child support. These measures include provisions facilitating the maintenance of out-of-state lawsuits as well as establishment of registries of "deadbeat" parents.

Under federal legislation, the *Child Support Recovery Act of 1992,* a parent residing in another state who willfully fails to pay a past-due support obligation may be imprisoned for up to six months for a first offense and for up to two years for repeat offenses. This statute defines a "past-due support obligation" as an amount that has remained unpaid for over one year or that is greater than $5,000.

Some families attempt to collect delinquent child support payments by hiring an attorney—either locally or in the area where the spouse has moved. Others pay a fee (up to 25 percent) to private collection agencies. A third alternative is to seek assistance from the state government. Under this approach, it is possible to pay the local child support enforcement office a fee to pursue the claim through the judicial system. Another variation is to assign the right to collect the child support to the government in return for guaranteed payments under the *Aid to Families with Dependent Children* (AFDC) program.

--- Ethical Issue ---

Suppose you are divorced and have custody of your children. Your ex-spouse is extremely delinquent in making child support payments despite the fact that [s]he easily has the financial means to pay. However, when your children visit with your spouse, they have a wonderful time. Should you tell the children that [s]he is not providing financial support for them?

QUESTIONS AND PROBLEM CASES

1. Under what circumstance is a court likely to consider marital misconduct when making a property division or spousal support award?
2. Explain the difference between physical custody and legal custody.
3. What are the factors the court considers when making an equitable distribution of property upon dissolution of the marriage?
4. What generally must be shown before a court will modify a child support award?

5. Morrison and Ella Narcisse physically separated in August 1986, after approximately 25 years of marriage. During the separation Ella resided in the mortgage-free family home and lived on her income of $23,000 per year. Morrison lived on an annual income of $52,000. On April 27, 1992, the trial court granted Morrison's petition for divorce based on the parties living separate and apart for over one year. It found Ella free from fault

and awarded her permanent alimony of $500 per month. Morrison appealed, arguing that Ella was gainfully employed and fully capable of supporting herself. He supported this argument with the fact she had not requested alimony during the six years they were separated. Ella pointed out that her residence was in dire need of repairs that she could not afford. She explained that she was only able to sustain herself by taking out loans that she now must repay. Should the award of alimony be upheld on appeal?

6. Joseph Pope desired to give his house to his sons, Robert and Tommy. The home was appraised at $32,000. Robert and his wife, Debra, wanted to live in the house, but Tommy preferred to receive cash for the interest given him by his father. Joseph's attorney arranged with a bank for a loan to Robert and Debra in the amount of $16,000 to be secured by a mortgage on the house. The deed conveying the house was in the name of Robert and Debra, and the mortgage was for $16,000. The proceeds of the loan were turned over to Tommy. Ten years later, Robert and Debra borrowed $35,000, secured by a second mortgage on the home, and used the money to improve the home. When the couple were divorced several years later, the court treated the house as marital property and ordered it be sold with the net proceeds to be equally divided between the spouses. Robert appealed from this determination, arguing that half the value of the house constituted nonmarital property and should not have been considered part of the equitable distribution of marital assets. Is Robert correct?

7. Pamela and James Jeffcoat divorced after being married for 15 years. During the marriage, James's father assigned ownership of a life insurance policy to him. When transferred, the policy was subject to a loan. The loan was repaid with marital funds, and the policy premiums were paid with marital funds. James received $41,617 from the insurance company when his father died. This amount was commingled with marital funds in a joint account. In May 1992, when the life insurance proceeds were deposited, the marital account contained $262,113. At the time of the trial, the account contained $67,927. During this period James had exclusive control of the account. In making an equitable distribution, the court credited Pamela with one-half of the $17,000 in premiums paid on the insurance policy. It deemed that the remainder of the $41,617 proceeds ($33,117) belonged to James exclusively as his nonmarital property. Is the trial court correct?

8. Dean and Jane Davidson were married July 14, 1979, in Iowa. They had two children who lived most of their lives in Iowa with their parents. On December 10, 1989, Dean moved to Wisconsin to begin a new job with a local bank. When their residential lease expired on December 31, 1989, Jane and the children joined Dean in Wisconsin. On April 12, 1990, Jane and the children returned to Iowa, ostensibly to visit her family after her father's death. However, in a telephone conversation on April 17, 1990, she informed Dean she did not intend to return to Wisconsin but planned to file an action for divorce in Iowa when she met Iowa's residency requirement. Dean immediately filed a divorce petition in Wisconsin. On April 24, 1990, Jane filed for divorce in Iowa. The Iowa court awarded Jane temporary custody of the children subject to Dean's visitation. The Wisconsin court ruled Wisconsin, rather than Iowa, was the children's home state. It concluded that Jane's petition amounted to a legal fraud upon the Iowa court. The *Uniform Child Custody Jurisdiction Act* (enacted by both states) defines "home state" as *"the state in which the child immediately preceding the time involved lived with the child's parents, a parent, or a person acting as a parent, for at least six months."* Does the Iowa court have jurisdiction because Iowa is the children's home state?

9. When Carla and Alfred Anderson were divorced, their dissolution decree required Alfred to pay child support for their two children. The decree specifically provided: *"Said support shall be payable so long as the children remain dependent."* At the time the decree was entered, Traci, the couple's eldest child, was just beginning her first year of high

school. After she graduated from high school, Carla requested the court to order Alfred to continue paying child support for Traci while she attended Central Washington University. She took the position that the decree allowed postmajority education support because Traci still was factually dependent and, under the language of the decree, support was payable as long as Traci remained dependent. Prior to the parties' separation, Carla and Alfred had generally talked about their hopes and desires for their children to attend college. But they never discussed any specifics. Should the court order Alfred to pay postmajority education support for Traci?

10. Sharon and Bill Davis were married in October 1980. Bill, a dentist, and Sharon, a dental hygienist, had one child born in June 1984. In February 1990, Sharon moved into the guest bedroom, and the couple ceased having sexual relations. On June 8, 1990, Sharon moved out of the house, taking their child with her. She filed for a divorce on the grounds of habitual cruel and inhuman treatment, and irreconcilable differences. Bill counterclaimed for divorce on grounds of desertion, adultery, and habitual drug use. Sharon admitted to one incident of adultery, occurring after separation, at a time when their son was staying with his father. The couple were married for 11 years. During the first 8 or 9 years of marriage, Sharon did all or the majority of the cooking, cleaning, washing, other housework, and childcare. In addition to contributing her own salary to the marital assets, she participated in activities that Bill felt would build his practice. At the outset of the marriage, the couple had no net worth. At the time of the divorce, the marital assets totaled around $400,000. Bill paid the house payments, utilities, telephone, cable, and other basic household expenses from his checking account. Sharon paid for their son's tuition and school expenses, clothes, household needs, and groceries from her account. The trial court dismissed Sharon's claims for divorce and granted Bill a divorce on grounds of adultery and desertion. It awarded custody of the child to Bill and granted Bill use and possession of the marital home. Sharon was given an equity of $12,500 in the house, and would receive that sum if the house were sold. She also was awarded $8,000 in savings. The remaining $380,000 of the jointly acquired marital assets was awarded to Bill. Sharon appealed, claiming the court made an inequitable distribution of the assets in order to punish her for her act of adultery. Should the court recalculate its equitable distribution of the marital assets?

REGULATORY ISSUES

BUYING INSURANCE

When Clifford and Michelle Buckmaster's son was seven years old, he persuaded Mary Ann Diehl's four-year-old daughter to perform oral sex. Soon thereafter, the girl began seeing a therapist because of behavioral changes. He assaulted her again two years later, but this time the girl's mother found out. Diehl sued the boy and his parents for the physical and emotional injuries suffered by her daughter. Fire Insurance Exchange, the company that covered the Buckmasters under a homeowners' insurance policy, claimed that it was under no duty to defend or indemnify the boy or his parents because the policy had an "intentional-acts" exclusion.

Fire Insurance Exchange v. Diehl, 545 N.W.2d 602 (Sup. Ct. Mich. 1996)

What is homeowners' insurance?

What is an exclusion? How do we determine the scope of coverage of an insurance policy?

Is this sexual assault covered by the homeowners' policy?

Introduction

People's lives, health, and property are threatened regularly by forces beyond their control. Each day our newspapers and newscasts report the tragedies suffered by victims of accidents, diseases, crimes, and natural disasters. The staggering costs of these catastrophes would overwhelm most people were it not for the availability of some form of life, property, health, or liability insurance. And yet, despite the vital role that insurance can play in our daily lives, most people know very little about their legal rights and responsibilities under insurance contracts.

The Nature of Insurance

The insurance relationship is contractual in nature. One person pays consideration (a *premium*) to another, who agrees to bear certain risks faced by the first person. Thus, Sarah, knowing she would be financially ruined if her home were destroyed, purchases property insurance from National Insurance. She now is assured that if her house is damaged under circumstances covered by the policy, National must compensate her for her monetary losses. National is the **insurer** and Sarah is the **insured.** Because the insurance proceeds will be paid to Sarah, she also is the **beneficiary** of the policy.

Chapter Overview

This chapter introduces the legal aspects of the insurance relationship. It begins with a survey of the four major types of insurance coverage: life, property, health and accident, and also liability insurance. Special attention is given to automobile insurance because automobile policies often include elements of each of the coverage categories. The chapter closes with a look at the contractual issues underlying the insurance relationship.

Life Insurance

Life insurance generally protects against the financial burdens accompanying the loss of someone's life. Under the terms of a life insurance contract, the insurer promises to pay an agreed-upon sum of money to the beneficiary listed in the policy when the insured dies.

http://
www.state.il.us/INS
is the site of the Illinois Department of Insurance.

Parties to a Life Insurance Policy

The owner of the policy (the person who contracted with the insurer) may be someone other than the insured (the person whose life is insured). For instance, Fred (the owner) may purchase insurance from Equitable Life (the insurer) to cover the life of Fred's wife, Naomi (the insured). As the owner of the policy, Fred can determine who will receive payment upon Naomi's death. This person (the beneficiary) may be Fred, but it also could be someone else designated by Fred.

It is common for the owner and beneficiary of a life insurance policy to be a business partner of the insured. Suppose Adam and Barbara formed a partnership to operate a flower shop. Each of the partners then took out a life insurance policy on the other. When Barbara dies, Adam will receive the proceeds of the policy he took out on her life.

Operation of Life Insurance

The operation of a life insurance contract is relatively simple. At the time of contracting, the owner of the policy selects the beneficiary and the *face value*. When the insured dies, the insurer must pay the face value to the beneficiary. During the course of a life insurance contract, the owner generally may change the identity of the beneficiary.

Hughes v. Scholl

900 S.W.2D 606 (SUP. CT. KY. 1995)

FACTS   Edna Scholl was the wife of Keith Baker for nearly 14 years. During their marriage Keith purchased life insurance policies and named Edna as the beneficiary. At the time of their divorce, Edna and Keith executed a property settlement agreement that did not discuss the insurance policies. In the nine years after the divorce, Keith never changed the beneficiary designations, although he apparently made inquiries of the insurance company about surrendering the policies. After Keith's death, Edna asserted a right to the policies' proceeds. This claim was opposed by Keith's estate, which argued that Edna's status as beneficiary was revoked by the divorce.

ISSUE   Is Edna entitled to the insurance proceeds as the beneficiary?

DECISION   Yes. Keith had nine years during which to designate a new beneficiary. He failed to do so and his inaction might well indicate an intent not to effect a change. A rule that divorce automatically revokes an insured's choice of his former spouse as his life insurance beneficiary unduly interferes with private contract rights and obligations. Moreover, such a rule is unnecessary since a divorced insured who wishes to remove his former spouse as beneficiary may do so with relative ease. On the other hand, insureds who do intend for their former spouses to receive their insurance proceeds would be forced to redesignate them as beneficiaries following divorce. We hasten to add that our holding in no way limits the power of divorcing parties to provide for termination of either spouse's beneficiary expectancy in a property settlement agreement.

Insurable Interest in Life Insurance

A person may not purchase a life insurance policy on the life of another unless the purchaser has a financial interest in the insured's life. This is known as an **insurable interest.** You always may purchase insurance on your own life because you always have an insurable interest in yourself. Similarly, your family members, business partners, and creditors are likely to have an insurable interest in your life.

With life insurance, the insurable interest must exist *at the time the policy was purchased.* It does not have to exist when the insured actually dies. For example, Martin may have purchased a life insurance policy on his business partner, Avery, while they were in business together. Martin can collect on the existing policy even after the partnership is terminated. However, he generally would not be permitted to purchase new insurance on Avery after the partnership ended. A life insurance policy that is purchased by a person who lacks an insurable interest in the life of the insured is void.

Types of Life Insurance

There are two basic types of life insurance: whole life and term insurance. While the insurable interest requirement is the same for both types, there are fundamental differences in their operation.

Whole Life Policies

Under **whole life insurance** the owner must pay a premium for a time period determined by the insurance contract. This may be for the remainder of the insured's life. However, some whole life policies may be paid in full after a set number of years. The greater the risk of the insured's death, the higher the premiums are likely to be.

Whole life policies also have an important savings feature. They often develop a *cash surrender value* that permits the owner to cash in the policy after a set amount of premiums have been paid. Prior to the death of the insured, the owner can terminate the insurance contract and recover a certain percentage of the premiums that have been paid. Whole life policies may also develop a *loan value.* This permits the owner to borrow money from the insurer at favorable rates.

Term Policies

People who want life insurance, but are not interested in the investment features of a whole life policy, may purchase **term life insurance.** Under a term policy, the insurer must pay the face value of the insurance policy if the insured dies within a specified period. Suppose Craig buys a five-year term insurance policy on his own life. If he dies during the five-year period, the insurance company must pay his beneficiary. However, if Craig dies after the term expires, the beneficiary is entitled to nothing.

Craig's policy probably contains a *guaranteed renewability* clause. This allows Craig to renew the policy for additional terms up to a specified age without having to prove he still is in good health. Because Craig's term insurance does not have the investment features of a whole life insurance policy, its premiums are likely to be lower. However, as Craig ages, the level of premiums also will rise. (This would not be the case with a whole life policy.) To offset this disadvantage, Craig's term policy may have a *guaranteed convertibility* feature. This option allows him to convert the policy into whole life insurance.

Annuity Contracts

Many life insurers also offer **annuity contracts.** With an annuity, the insured pays premiums and then receives periodic payments after reaching a certain age. (This differs from an *endowment contract,* which pays a lump sum when the insured reaches a certain age. If the insured dies before reaching the specified age, the lump sum is paid to her beneficiary.) *Variable annuities* have long been available to

http:// *www.allstate.com/ products/life/index. html* is the site of Allstate, a major insurance company. Check this site for information regarding various types of life insurance policies.

people wishing to build up tax-deferred savings to fund their retirement. The actual amount of the annuity payment varies depending on the return the insurer earns on the money it invests.

In recent years, insurers have targeted the growing ranks of older people by offering *immediate fixed annuities.* These contracts require the payment of a designated amount of money, which the insurer can invest. In return the insured is promised periodic, fixed annuity payments for the remainder of his life. While these contracts offer a steady stream of income, they often do nothing to guard against inflation and, if the insured dies prematurely, payments are not made to the heirs. (However, for an additional payment some insurers provide inflation adjustments as well as limited payments to the insured's beneficiaries.)

Viatical Settlements

Prompted by the AIDS crisis, some investors have begun buying life insurance policies from terminally ill people at a discount and collecting the full death benefits when they die. The terminally ill person secures much-needed income in the final years of life when employment is unlikely and medical bills are staggering. The investor pays the premiums on the policy until the insured dies and then collects the full payout. The profit or loss depends on how long the insured person actually lives. These transactions are called **viatical settlements.**

─────────────────────────── Ethical Issue ───────────────────────────

With viatical settlements, the investor's profits are greater if the insured dies quickly. How do you feel about this type of investment?

Property Insurance ▬▬▬▬▬▬▬▬

h t t p : //
www.prudential.com/
insurance/home/inhzz
1000.html is the site
of Prudential, a
major insurance
company. Check this
site for information
regarding various
types of property
insurance policies.

Property insurance policies are *indemnity* contracts that obligate the insurer to pay for actual losses resulting from damage to the insured property. It is necessary to examine the actual insurance policy to determine the extent of the insurer's obligation. The policy stipulates the maximum amount for which the insurer can be held liable as well as the types of losses against which the property is insured.

Types of Property Insurance

There are numerous types of property insurance. Frequently, the term has come to symbolize insurance over *real property* (land and everything firmly attached to the land). Historically, the major peril faced by property owners was losses due to fire. For that reason, fire insurance policies have long been a common type of property insurance. Today, all types of *personal property* are regularly insured. For instance, automobile insurance is a form of personal property insurance coverage.

Landowners commonly purchase **homeowners' insurance,** which provides protection against losses to the insured's dwelling (real property) as well as to any personal property located on or inside the dwelling. In fact, homeowners' policies often insure personal property that has been temporarily removed from the dwelling. Homeowners' insurance also is likely to provide the insured with liability insurance against accidental injuries suffered by guests or other visitors. The case that opened this chapter is concerned with the liability insurance features of a homeowners' policy. Renters may purchase *renters' insurance,* which provides coverage similar to that contained in a homeowners' policy.

Insurable Interest in Property Insurance

A person may not purchase property insurance unless she has an *insurable interest* in the property. This requirement is met by any person who has a financial interest in the insured property. Property owners, renters, and secured creditors (mortgagees or lienholders) all may have an insurable interest in property.

The insurable interest requirement for property insurance differs from its counterpart for life insurance in two important ways. First, the insurable interest for property insurance must exist *at the time the loss occurs* rather than at the time the policy was purchased (the rule for life insurance). For example, First Fidelity extended a $100,000 loan to William and retained a mortgage interest in his house for the full amount of the loan. To protect this interest, First Fidelity also purchased a $100,000 property insurance policy on the house. If the house is destroyed after William has paid off his loan, First Fidelity will not be able to recover under its insurance policy.

Second, a person's insurable interest generally is limited to the amount she will lose if the property is lost or destroyed. Suppose William had paid off most of his mortgage and owed a balance of $20,000. If the house were totally destroyed, First Fidelity would recover only $20,000 from the insurer despite the fact that its insurance policy had a face value of $100,000. However, a purchaser of property has an insurable interest in the full value of the property even if she has paid less than the full purchase price at the time of the loss.

Alberici v. Safeguard Mutual Insurance Company
664 A.2D 110 (SUP. CT. PENN. 1995)

FACTS   Joseph Alberici entered into an agreement to purchase a theatre property for a price of $210,000. The named purchaser on the purchase agreement was "Joseph Alberici or his nominee." A down payment of $21,000 was made by withdrawing funds from a savings account owned jointly by Joseph and his wife, Theresa. After signing the agreement to purchase the theatre, Alberici purchased property insurance on the property in the name of himself and Theresa. Prior to the closing of the sale, the theatre was seriously damaged by fire. Because Joseph was suspected of arson in connection with the fire and ultimately convicted of submitting false fire loss claims, his insurance claims were denied. Theresa's insurance claims also were denied because the insurer argued she did not have an insurable interest in the property.

ISSUE   Did Theresa have an insurable interest in the property?

DECISION   Yes. Before Theresa could recover on the policy in which she had been named as an insured, it must be shown that she possessed an insurable interest in the property. A policy that insures against loss by fire is a contract of indemnity which

continued

protects the insured's interest in the property, not the property itself. One who derives monetary benefit or advantage from the preservation or continued existence of property, or who will suffer monetary loss from its destruction, has an insurable interest in the property. Upon execution of an agreement of sale, a purchaser of real estate has an equitable title to the property and may insure her interest therein. A purchaser's insurable interest is in the entire property, not merely the extent to which she has made payments towards the purchase price. Although the purchase agreement for the theatre property did not specifically identify Theresa has a purchaser, it designated the buyer as "Joseph Alberici or his nominee." Joseph and Theresa had always purchased property together in the past. Further, she accompanied Joseph to inspect the property prior to purchase and the monies to pay for the property had been taken from marital assets. Because Theresa was a purchaser of the property, she had an insurable interest therein. Her interest was in the value of the entire property and not merely her contribution toward the down payment.

Amount of Coverage

When the insured property is damaged or destroyed, the insurance contract must be examined to determine the actual amount the insurer is obligated to pay. There are two basic types of property insurance contracts: open policies and valued policies. (See Figure 21–1.)

Open Policies

Under an **open policy,** the insurer will pay the *fair market value* of the insured property at the time it was destroyed. However, this amount cannot exceed the maximum limits set forth in the contract. For example, Myra purchases an open policy covering her house with a face value of $200,000. While the policy is in effect, the house is totally destroyed by fire. If the house had a fair market value of only $190,000 at the time it was destroyed, $190,000 is the full amount Myra would be paid. If the fair market value was $215,000, Myra's recovery would be limited to $200,000 (the face value of the policy). Most property insurance contracts are open policies.

Valued Policies

Under a **valued policy,** the insurance company must pay the face value of the policy when property is totally destroyed. Thus, even if Myra's home was worth only $190,000 when it was destroyed, she would recover $200,000 under a $200,000 valued policy. If her house was worth $215,000 at the time of destruction, her recovery would be limited to the face value ($200,000) of the valued policy. As a general rule, the face value of the valued policy will be a rough approximation of the insured property's fair market value.

Partial Losses

It is common for a property insurance policy to contain a **coinsurance clause.** This provision, which is triggered when the insured property is partially destroyed, is designed to discourage people from underinsuring their property. Most coinsurance clauses require the insured to purchase insurance equal to at least 80 percent

Figure 21-1:   Recovery for a Total Loss

FACE VALUE OF POLICY	FAIR MARKET VALUE WHEN LOSS OCCURRED	OPEN POLICY RECOVERY	VALUED PROPERTY RECOVERY
$ 200,000	$ 190,000	$ 190,000	$ 200,000
$ 200,000	$ 215,000	$ 200,000	$ 200,000

of the property's fair market value; however, the parties may agree upon any amount. A property owner's failure to meet the coinsurance requirement results in the insurer being liable for less than the full extent of damages when property is partially destroyed.

For example, Arnold purchased a property insurance policy on his house from Independent Insurance Corporation, and the policy has an 80 percent coinsurance clause. The house then suffered $80,000 worth of damages at a time when it had a fair market value of $200,000. Although the coinsurance clause required Arnold to have $160,000 worth of insurance coverage, his policy had a face value of only $120,000. Because he underinsured the house, Arnold will receive only $60,000 (rather than the $80,000 worth of actual damages) from Independent.

The formula for calculating a property insurer's liability for partial losses is:

$$\frac{\text{Amount of Insurance}}{\text{Coinsurance \% } \times \text{ Fair Market Value}} \times \text{Loss} = \text{Insurer's Liability}$$

Using this formula, we can see why Independent Insurance Corporation owed only $60,000 for the $80,000 worth of damage to Arnold's house.

$$\frac{\$120,000}{[(80\%) \times (\$200,000)]} \times \$80,000 = \$60,000$$

There are two important points to be remembered about the coinsurance requirement. First, the fair market value of the insured property is calculated at the time of the loss, rather than at the time the property insurance was originally purchased. As a result, when the property is increasing in value, the insured should be regularly increasing the amount of insurance coverage to reflect that fact. Second, the coinsurance formula only applies to partial losses of property. Thus, if Arnold's house was totally destroyed, Independent would have to pay $120,000 (the face value of the policy). (See Figure 21-2 on page 488.)

Figure 21–2: The Coinsurance Clause

FACE VALUE OF POLICY	AMOUNT OF INSURANCE REQUIRED	FAIR MARKET VALUE AT TIME OF LOSS	ACTUAL LOSS	INSURANCE RECOVERY
$ 120,000	$ 160,000	$ 200,000	$ 80,000	$ 60,000
$ 120,000	$ 160,000	$ 200,000	$ 200,000	$ 120,000

Multiple Insurers

As an indemnity contract, property insurance is intended to compensate the insured for no more than her actual losses. This means that an insured should never receive more than the face value in a valued policy or the fair market value of the property (not to exceed the face value) in an open policy. If greater recoveries were permitted, property owners might overinsure and then intentionally destroy their property. (Of course, an insurer would not be liable if it could proven that any losses were intentionally caused by the insured.)

To prevent people from recovering more than the actual value of their loss, property insurance policies contain a **pro rata clause,** which covers situations where a property owner has purchased insurance coverage from more than one insurer. This provision requires that liability for any loss be apportioned among the insurers.

Suppose Linda purchases insurance to cover her home from two different insurance companies. Her open policy with American Insurance has a face value of $240,000, and a similar policy from Continental Insurance has a face value of $120,000. Her house, which had a fair market value of $240,000, is totally destroyed. Under these circumstances, American owes her $160,000 and Continental is liable for $80,000. (See Figure 21–3.)

The formula for calculating an insurer's liability under a pro rata clause is as follows:

$$\frac{\text{Amount of Insurer's Policy}}{\text{Total Coverage by All Insurers}} \times \text{Loss} = \text{Liability of Insurer}$$

Using this formula, American's insurance liability would be calculated as follows:

$$\frac{\$240,000 \text{ (American's Policy)}}{\$360,000 \text{ (Total by Both Insurers)}} \times \$240,000 = \$160,000$$

Three important points need to be made about pro rata clauses. First, they apply to both partial losses and total losses. Second, an insurer never is liable for

Figure 21–3: Multiple Insurers

POLICY WITH AMERICAN INSURANCE	POLICY WITH CONTINENTAL INSURANCE	TOTAL INSURANCE COVERAGE	TOTAL LOSS	AMERICAN'S LIABILITY	CONTINENTAL'S LIABILITY
$ 240,000	$ 120,000	$ 360,000	$ 240,000	$ 160,000	$ 80,000

more than the face value of its policy. Thus, if Linda's house had fair market value of $380,000 at the time of the loss, American would owe $240,000 and Continental would be liable for $120,000. Linda would be responsible for the rest. Third, pro rata clauses do not apply to life insurance policies. When a person has multiple life insurers, the beneficiary may recover the face value of each policy.

Right of Subrogation

When an insurance company pays a property insurance claim, it obtains the **right of subrogation.** This permits the insurer to pursue whatever legal remedies the insured had against the individual who actually caused the property damage. For instance, Debbie's house was completely destroyed by a fire that was caused when her neighbor, Elwood, negligently burned leaves on a windy day. Nationwide Insurance, Debbie's homeowners' insurer, must pay Debbie for her losses. It then may sue Elwood for the amount of Debbie's claim.

Health and Accident Insurance

The skyrocketing costs of healthcare have focused attention on the need for insurance for hospitalization, medical treatment, and medication. Health and accident insurance was designed to cover these risks.

Basic Coverage

Generally, a single policy can be purchased that provides coverage against the costs of accidents and illnesses. These health and accident policies cover doctors' bills, hospital charges, and the costs of medicine and medical supplies. They may also include lump sum payments for death or disability resulting from accidental causes.

Health and accident insurance contracts frequently designate a list of illnesses and injuries covered by the policy. They may also specifically exclude certain types of illnesses or injuries. Most policies exclude coverage for preexisting health conditions (accidents or illnesses suffered by the insured before the policy's effective date).

Method of Payment

The payment responsibilities of the insurer may vary greatly from policy to policy. Accordingly, the insured should carefully read the health and accident contract in order to fully understand her rights and obligations.

Shared Payment Obligations

Health and accident policies generally require the insurer and the insured to share the payment obligation. One method of doing this is to establish a minimum amount—known as the **deductible**—that the insured must pay before the insurer is obligated to pay anything. The deductible amount varies from policy to policy. However, once it has been paid up for the year, the insurer is responsible for all of the remaining covered expenses.

Some policies obligate the insurer to pay a fixed percentage of the covered medical bills. Modern health and accident policies commonly fix the percentage at 80 percent. However, many policies place a cap on the insured's payment obligation. Thus, in instances of prolonged illness or hospitalization, the insurer may pay a specified percentage up to a fixed amount and then be fully liable for all expenses in excess of that amount.

Time of Payment

The insurance contract also indicates the timing of the insurer's payment obligation. Under many policies the insured must first pay the healthcare provider and then seek reimbursement from the insurer. Other policies instruct the healthcare provider to bill the insurance company directly and then, under a procedure called *balance billing,* later seek payment from the insured for any amounts not covered by insurance.

Cost Control Features

It is more and more common for insurance companies to place a ceiling on the amount they will pay for medical treatments or procedures. These insurers establish *reasonable and customary rates* for various medical services. Many doctors who take Blue Cross & Blue Shield insurance will not charge more than that amount. However, doctors who have no such understanding with an insurer will bill the insured for the balance. Rather than automatically pay such a balance bill, an insured may be wise to check with the doctor to see if it may be waived or reduced.

Group Insurance Coverage

The availability of **group insurance** has helped make health and accident insurance policies available to large numbers of people. These policies, which are provided by employers or other organizations, allow insurers to lower their premiums by spreading the risks over a large number of people. However, the advantages of group insurance may be quickly lost if the insured terminates her employment or other type of group membership.

Suppose Kimberly was insured under her employer's group health and accident policy. When she changes or loses her job, her insurance coverage will end. If Kimberly is fortunate, she will find a new employer who offers a similarly low-priced, group policy. However, this often will not be the case. In many instances, a new insurer will exclude coverage for any accident or extended illness she suffered while with her prior employer. And during any time she is unemployed, it is unlikely she will be able to afford insurance coverage.

In recent years, many states have reformed their laws to create *portable health insurance*. While these measures vary, they usually attempt to guarantee health coverage to people who change or lose jobs by limiting waiting periods for new employees to gain coverage or by requiring insurers to sell individual policies to people who have left their jobs. Current federal law requires private employers who sponsor group health insurance plans to offer self-paid continued group coverage to qualified beneficiaries for at least 18 months after termination of employment.

Liability Insurance

As society becomes more and more litigious, people and businesses are recognizing the growing importance of purchasing liability insurance to cover the costs of defending or settling lawsuits. There are numerous types of liability insurance. For instance, certain types of businesses (taverns, restaurants, and day-care centers) recognize that they might be devastated by personal injury or product liability lawsuits. Accordingly, they purchase business liability coverage. Similarly, employers often purchase workers' compensation insurance to pay off the claims of injured employees. And professionals (doctors, lawyers, accountants) buy malpractice insurance to cover instances where their negligent professional behavior causes injuries to others.

It also is common for people to purchase liability insurance to cover nonbusiness claims. For instance, we generally think of homeowners' and renters' insurance as a form of property insurance. However, these policies also include personal liability protection that is triggered when a visitor is injured by some accidental occurrence in the home of the insured. Automobile policies provide similar liability coverage.

Extent of Coverage

For the most part, liability policies are fairly standard in the types of coverage they offer. They generally exclude protection against claims arising out of the insured's intentional torts and crimes. (It is against public policy to reimburse someone who has committed deliberately wrongful acts.) Therefore, they limit their coverage to protection against claims based on the insured's negligent conduct.

In the case that opened this chapter, the Michigan Supreme Court ruled that the sexual assaults might be covered by the Buckmasters' homeowners' policy. The liability provision covered bodily injury "neither expected nor intended by the insured." The court felt that this language requires the application of a subjective standard of intent. Thus, if a jury finds that the boy intended the acts but not the injuries, his behavior could fall within the insurance coverage. That determination will turn on whether the girl's injuries were reasonably foreseeable to a boy of like age, ability, intelligence, and experience.

Business liability contracts often provide broader protection than personal liability policies. Suppose Ace Company gave a poor job reference for a former employee who, in reality, was an excellent worker. If the ex-employee brought a defamation suit against Ace, the lawsuit might be covered by Ace's business liability coverage despite the fact that defamation is an intentional tort. Some business liability policies cover intentional tort suits, like defamation or invasion of privacy, since they commonly arise in the business environment.

State Farm Fire & Casualty Company v. S.S.

858 S.W.2d 374 (Sup. Ct. Tex. 1993)

FACTS   S.S. contracted genital herpes after engaging in consensual sexual intercourse with G.W. at his home. After S.S. requested that G.W. compensate her for her injuries, G.W. notified State Farm Insurance, the issuer of his homeowners' insurance policy. G.W.'s policy included a provision excluding coverage for intentional injuries. Based on that provision, State Farm questioned whether the policy actually covered S.S.'s claim and rejected her settlement offers for amounts within the policy limits. When S.S. and G.W. settled her claim for $1 million, State Farm refused to pay. It argued that, as a matter of law, the transmission of genital herpes is an intentional injury that is not covered by the homeowners' policy.

ISSUE   Is State Farm correct?

DECISION   No. Generally, the medical community advises herpes infected patients to avoid sexual intercourse when experiencing actual symptoms of the disease in order to prevent transmission of the disease to their sexual partner. However, in recent years, some researchers have espoused the theory that a herpes carrier may be contagious and spread the disease even when the individual is not experiencing any symptoms. G.W.'s policy excludes coverage for *"bodily injury or property damage caused intentionally by or at the direction of the Insured."* While it is undisputed that G.W. intentionally engaged in sexual intercourse without informing S.S. of his condition, the evidence does not indicate that he acted with intent to cause S.S. bodily injury. Instead, it appears that G.W. did not believe it was possible to transmit the disease without an active lesion. The evidence does not demonstrate that G.W. knew that engaging in sexual intercourse with S.S. was substantially certain to result in the transmission of the disease to her. He was operating under the mistaken impression that he could not transmit herpes when he had no active symptoms of the disease.

Insurer's Rights and Obligations

The full extent of the insurer's obligations to the insured can only be determined through a careful reading of the liability insurance contract. However, there are two basic duties one would expect to find in any liability policy: a duty to defend and a duty to pay.

Duty to Defend

When a claim that falls within the coverage of the liability policy is filed against the insured, the insurer has a **duty to defend** the insurer. This generally requires the insurer to hire a competent attorney to represent the insured's interest in the legal dispute. Of course, the duty does not arise unless the insured first notifies the insurance company of the dispute.

When it is not certain if the dispute falls within the policy's coverage, the insurance company faces a quandary. If it neglects to provide legal representation and a court later decides the matter was covered by the policy, the insurer is liable for breaching its duty to defend. In these cases, some insurers seek a declaratory judgment from a court, advising them if a duty to defend has arisen. In other instances, insurers provide temporary representation until they conclusively determine if the duty to defend has arisen.

Duty to Pay

Subject to the coverage limits of the insurance contract, an insurer has a **duty to pay** any damages the court orders the insured to pay. Each policy places a ceiling on the amount for which the insurer is responsible. Thus, if the policy limits the insurance company's liability to $1 million, the insured must pay any claims in excess of that amount.

Many claims never reach the court because the disputing parties attain some type of voluntary settlement. Liability policies generally give the insurer authority to settle claims filed against the insured. In return for the insurance company's payment of a negotiated amount of money, the claimant waives his legal claims against the insured.

Frankenmuth Mutual Insurance Company v. Williams

645 N.E.2D 605 (Sup. Ct. Ind. 1995)

FACTS Tracy Stevens hired Betty White to babysit her two daughters at Betty's home. In early 1989, Michael White, Betty's husband, sexually molested one of the children while she was in Betty's care. He was subsequently convicted of child molesting. On October 18, 1989, Tracy filed suit against Michael for unlawful touching and battery. Three months later, she amended her complaint to add Betty as a defendant, alleging that Betty was negligent in caring for her daughter. Frankenmuth Mutual Insurance Company sold a homeowners' liability insurance policy to Michael and Betty, which was in effect at the time the molestation occurred. The first notice Frankenmuth received that Michael and Betty had been sued came in October 1990 when the company received a subpoena requiring it to produce documents for the trial. The subpoena did not specify the nature of the lawsuit. One month later, Frankenmuth sent a letter to the Whites' attorney stating that Michael's intentional acts were outside the scope of the policy. On April 29, 1991, Betty and Tracy settled the claim against Betty for $75,000. Tracy then attempted to collect the $75,000 from Frankenmuth. The insurance company claimed it had no duty to defend or to pay because it did not receive adequate notice of the lawsuit.

ISSUE Did Frankenmuth receive adequate notice of the lawsuit?

DECISION Yes. Frankenmuth asserts that the subpoena requesting production of the Whites' insurance policy did not constitute notice sufficient for it to be bound by

continued

Betty's settlement. However, the subpoena was accompanied by documents labeled *"Williams v. Michael White and Betty White,"* complete with the cause number of the litigation and the court in which it was pending. The notice looks for all the world as a document from a lawsuit between Tracy and the Whites. Frankenmuth knew of and investigated the incident out of which the lawsuit against Betty arose. Frankenmuth is bound to the terms of the settlement agreement.

http://www.law.indiana.edu/law/incourts/incourts.html

Automobile Insurance

http://
www.state.il.us/ins/
consumerinfo.htm
provides information
from the state of Illi-
nois, or check your
own state or insur-
ance company site.

The high costs of buying or replacing a vehicle, combined with the catastrophic results that often attend automobile accidents, have made it imperative that automobile owners purchase insurance protection. In fact, most states do not permit drivers to register their vehicles without showing proof of insurance.

Types of Automobile Insurance

The standard automobile insurance policy may combine the four basic kinds of insurance: life, property, health and accident, and also liability. However, each policy must be examined to determine its precise terms. There are four types of coverage common to most automobile policies: (1) liability coverage, (2) uninsured motorist coverage, (3) medical coverage, and (4) physical damage coverage.

Liability Coverage

At its most basic level, automobile insurance provides **liability coverage** for automobile accidents. This requires the insurer to cover the costs of bodily injury and property damage the insured inflicts on other people. Suppose Elizabeth, who has an automobile policy with Mutual Insurance, negligently causes her car to collide with a vehicle driven by David. The *bodily injury* feature in Elizabeth's liability coverage will compensate David and the passengers (excluding Elizabeth) in either car for the personal injuries they have suffered. Mutual Insurance also must pay for the damages to David's car because of the *property damage* component of Elizabeth's liability coverage.

The automobile policy probably placed a monetary ceiling on Mutual's liability. In this case, Elizabeth's policy has liability limits of "$100,000/$300,000/$100,000." The first number restricts Mutual's liability to no more than $100,000 for bodily injuries suffered by any one person. The second number ($300,000) is the total liability Mutual has for all bodily injury claims arising out of a single accident. The last number ($100,000) refers to Mutual's maximum liability for property damages resulting from any particular accident. Elizabeth is liable personally for any claims in excess of these limits.

Uninsured Motorist Coverage

If Elizabeth's accident had been caused by David's negligence, she and her passengers could recover their costs from his bodily injury and property insurance. However, if David was not insured or if the accident was caused by an unidentified hit-and-run driver, recovery might be impossible. To protect against these risks, automobile policies provide a type of accident insurance, called **uninsured motorist coverage.** For example, if Elizabeth wins a judgment against David and he is uninsured, her uninsured motorist coverage will pay her costs up to the limits in her liability coverage.

Most policies include *underinsured motorist coverage* as well. This applies if David's policy limits were below the limits of Elizabeth's liability coverage with Mutual Insurance. Suppose David's insurance limited liability for bodily injury to $50,000, while Elizabeth's policy had a $100,000 ceiling. If David's negligence caused Elizabeth $78,000 in injuries, she could recover $50,000 from David's insurer and an additional $28,000 from Mutual Insurance under her underinsured motorist coverage.

Medical Coverage

Automobile policies also provide **medical coverage** that combines the features of accident, liability, and life insurance. For example, because of her policy's medical coverage, Mutual Insurance must reimburse Elizabeth for the injuries she suffered in her traffic accident with David. Similarly, if her passengers cannot recover under her liability coverage because the accident was not Elizabeth's fault, they may be compensated under her medical coverage.

Some medical coverage also has a life insurance feature. Suppose Elizabeth has a $10,000 limit on her medical coverage. If she dies after incurring $6,000 in medical bills, her policy may provide that her heirs will receive *death benefits* of $4,000 (the difference between her policy limit and the $6,000 in medical expenses). Mutual probably has a ceiling on the amount of death benefits it will pay. Thus, if the insurance policy places a $5,000 limit on death benefits, Elizabeth's heirs are entitled to only $5,000 even if her medical expenses were only $2,000.

Physical Damage Coverage

Automobile policies have a property insurance feature that provides **physical damage coverage** for the insured's vehicle. This is commonly called "collision and comprehensive" coverage.

We saw earlier that when Elizabeth's negligence caused the traffic accident, David is paid for damages to his car by Elizabeth's property damage insurance. If her car also is damaged, her *collision* coverage reimburses her for those damages up to the policy limits. However, her policy probably has a deductible clause, which requires Elizabeth to pay part of the costs. If Elizabeth's policy carried a "$500 deductible," she must pay the first $500 of damages to her car.

When Elizabeth purchased her automobile insurance, she probably was given an opportunity to choose the amount of the deductible. If she selected a low deductible, her insurance premiums would be much higher because the insurer's liability would be greater. If she chose a high deductible, her premiums would be lower.

Elizabeth's car could be damaged by causes other than a traffic accident. These causes may include fire, wind, hail, vandalism, and theft. The *comprehensive* feature in her insurance policy covers the costs of these damages. However, coverage probably is limited to the vehicle itself. Thus, Mutual Insurance need not reimburse Elizabeth for any stolen or damaged personal property that was in the car. (The personal property might be covered by her homeowners' or renters' insurance.)

No-Fault Insurance

To relieve the congestion in their courts, many states enacted **no-fault insurance** statutes aimed at converting automobile insurance into a method of compensating accident victims. Under a traditional insurance scheme, if Elizabeth was injured due to David's negligence, she would first recover from Mutual Insurance (her own insurer). Mutual then would sue David. If David was found liable, Mutual would recover from David's automobile insurer.

While there are differences in the no-fault insurance statutes enacted by various states, certain basic similarities do exist. They require that each driver be insured and that when an accident occurs, each person seek recovery from her own insurer. No party (including the insurance companies) has the right to sue another unless their damages exceed certain prescribed limits.

Lindstrom v. Hanover Insurance Company

649 A.2d 1272 (Sup. Ct. N.J. 1994)

FACTS   Kurt Lindstrom, a student at the University of North Carolina—Wilmington, was attending an outdoor party at the university when an occupant of a passing car fired a shot into the crowd. The bullet struck Kurt behind his right ear and pierced his spinal column, rendering him quadriplegic. As a member of his father's household, Kurt was covered by the automobile insurance policy issued by Hanover Insurance Company to the father. At the time of the shooting, a state law required automobile insurers to provide personal-injury-protection benefits, without regard to fault, when the insured and members of his family suffer bodily injury *"as a result of an accident as a pedestrian, caused by an automobile or by an object propelled by or from an automobile."* When Kurt filed for payment under the policy for his medical expenses, Hanover refused to pay.

ISSUE   Should Hanover be required to pay personal-injury-protection benefits to Kurt?

DECISION   Yes. The state's no-fault compulsory automobile-insurance scheme must be liberally construed. The personal-injury-protection coverage it mandates is a social necessity entitled to the broadest application. In short, to accommodate the public interest behind the law, courts must favor the insured and find coverage if possible. This includes giving a broad meaning to the term "accident" as used in the statute. Therefore, an "accident" may, for personal-injury-protection purposes, include the results of intentionally inflicted injury. In this respect, personal-injury-protection coverage differs from both automobile-liability and uninsured-motorist coverage, neither of which applies to injuries caused by an act that is an accident from the victim's perspective but is intended by the actor. These differences are traceable to the significantly different needs each type of coverage satisfies. To be covered under the personal-injury-protection provisions, the act causing the injury may extend to intentional acts when they are a reasonable consequence of the use of an automobile. We are confronted by the depressing reality that in recent years, drive-by shootings have become an increasingly common part of the American experience.

www-camlaw.rutgers.edu/library/search.html

Contractual Issues

Courts often are called upon to determine if a duty to insure exists or to decide if an insurer fully performed its legal obligations. In resolving these disputes, courts generally look to contract law. This is because the insurance relationship basically is contractual in nature. Accordingly, a full understanding of one's rights and obligations under an insurance policy requires a basic knowledge of contract law, coupled with a familiarity with certain statutory rules unique to insurance agreements.

http://
www.touchngo. com:/lglcntr/akstats/ Statutes/Title21.htm contains Alaska's insurance codes.

Mutual Agreement

Disputes often arise over whether an insurance contract was in effect at the time a loss or personal liability arises. Under contract law, there is no enforceable agreement until one party has accepted the other's offer to enter into an insurance relationship. The standard practice in the insurance industry is to treat the potential insured's submission of an application and payment of a premium as merely an offer to enter an agreement. There is no actual insurance contract until the insurer has manifested its intent to accept this offer. What actually constitutes an acceptance may depend on the language in the application, as well as the type of insurance requested. For example, most courts hold that an application for life insurance does not occur until the insurer has signed and mailed the policy to the insured.

------------------------------ Ethical Issue ------------------------------

Do insurance companies have an ethical duty to make certain that applicants understand they are not necessarily insured despite the fact that they have completed an application and paid a premium? Is it ethical for an insurance company to accept the premium and then delay formally accepting the application just in case the applicant suffers a loss during that time period?

Binders

Applications for property insurance often state that coverage begins at the moment the insured signs the application. This provides temporary coverage while the insurer decides whether to accept or reject the offer. These interim policies, known as **binders,** generally are given by an insurance agent when a person is applying for property or automobile insurance. Courts have upheld the enforceability of oral binders.

Insurer Delay

Some courts have ruled that an insurer's retention of a premium for an unreasonable period of time constitutes acceptance of the application for insurance. These courts believe such delays expose people to unfair risks because the applicant is unlikely to seek insurance elsewhere while her application is pending. Several states have enacted laws obligating an insurer to the insurance contract unless it rejects the application in a statutorily prescribed period of time. However, most courts still do not treat unreasonable delay by the insurer as acceptance.

Misrepresentation

Under contract law, when one party misrepresents a material fact to the other, the innocent party may rescind the agreement after discovering the falsity. This rule applies to insurance contracts as well. Applicants who fail to accurately and honestly fill out the application risk having the insurer reject coverage when it discovers the deception.

This can be particularly harsh on applicants who have made unintentional misrepresentations. Accordingly, life insurance policies reduce this harshness in two ways: misstatement of age clauses and incontestability clauses.

Misstatement of Age Clause

Life insurance contracts frequently contain a **misstatement of age clause** that is triggered when the insured understates his age in the application. When the insurance company discovers the misstatement, rather than cancel the entire policy, it merely adjusts the benefits payable upon death to reflect the insured's actual age.

Suppose Nick applied for $100,000 in term life insurance from Equitable Life. When Nick filled out the application he claimed his age was 30. However, he actually was 34. For the premiums Nick was paying, a 34-year-old could have purchased only $75,000 worth of term insurance. Accordingly, upon Nick's death, his beneficiary will receive only $75,000 from Equitable.

Incontestability Clause

Life insurance contracts often contain an **incontestability clause,** which becomes effective after the policy has been in effect for a specified period (often two years). After this time has elapsed, the insurance company loses its right to cancel a policy because of misrepresentations in the application for insurance. However, severe types of fraud are not excused by an incontestability clause. For instance, courts have permitted insurers to cancel policies after it was discovered that an imposter took a required physical examination even though the incontestability period had elapsed. Further, the incontestability clause does not overcome the absence of an insurable interest at the time the policy was purchased.

Contractual Limits on Coverage

Insurers do not provide insurance coverage for every type of loss. The insurance policy, as the legal contract between the insurer and the insured, determines the rights and liabilities of the parties when a loss occurs. Most insurance policies define the extent of insurance coverage for losses that result from various **perils** (causes) in one of three ways: (1) by listing covered perils; (2) by listing excluded perils; or (3) by listing both covered and excluded perils.

Covered Perils

An insurance policy may designate a specific list of **covered perils.** For example, property insurance policies generally protect against fire damage resulting from *hostile fires.* (A hostile fire is one that burns where it was not intended.) Thus, if the insured dropped a painting in the fireplace, it would not be covered. (It was destroyed by a *friendly fire*—one that burned where it was intended.) However, if the fire from the fireplace spread throughout the house or a fire was caused by lightning or an electrical short, the painting would be covered.

There are certain standard perils (losses from hostile fires, hail, wind, vandalism, and flooding from burst pipes) that commonly are listed in most property insurance contracts. If a property owner wishes to obtain additional coverage for other types of risks (earthquake damage), he may request an *add on* from his insurer. Of course, this additional coverage does not come without a price. The insured will be required to pay premiums in excess of those required for a standard policy.

An insured person faces one major obstacle when insured under a policy employing the "covered perils" method. If a loss arises, the insured has the burden of proving it was caused by a covered peril. If this burden is not met, the insurer has no liability on the claim.

Excluded Perils

Some insurance policies provide general protection against loss, but then include a list of **excluded perils.** Damages from floods, earthquakes, and hurricanes are common exclusions in property insurance policies. Life insurance policies commonly exclude coverage if the insured commits suicide within the first two years after purchasing the policy. And all types of insurance contracts regularly exclude liability for damages caused by the intentional acts of the insured.

Under an excluded peril policy, the insured has met her burden of proof when she shows she has suffered a loss. The burden then shifts to the insurer to prove the loss was caused by an excluded peril. If the insurer cannot establish this fact, it must pay on the insurance claim.

In the case that opened the chapter, the insurance company tried to show that the sexual assault fell within the policy's intentional-acts exclusion. However, that provision specifically excluded intentional acts "where the results are reasonably foreseeable." The court argued that a jury might believe that a young boy might not reasonably foresee the injury to the girl. Compare that case with the following one.

Nationwide Insurance v. Board of Trustees
116 F.3d 1154 (7th Cir. 1997)

FACTS   In the early morning hours, Aleck Zavalis, Glenn Schicker, and Conor Gorman, all students at the University of Illinois, stole into the University's Memorial Stadium. They spelled out the letters "F-O-O" with lighter fluid on the playing field. ("Foo" was a word they derived from "Foofur," a lazy hound dog that appeared in a Saturday morning cartoon show during the late 1980s.) Their intent was to light the letters and leave a residue of soot on the Astroturf that would be visible on television or from the bleachers. However, the flames quickly spread and a sizable portion of the playing surface was destroyed. The university, which incurred damages in excess of $600,000, sued the three students. At the time of the mishap, Zavalis's parents maintained a homeowners' insurance policy with Nationwide Insurance. That policy provided public liability coverage for all residents of the Zavalis household including Aleck. However, the policy expressly excluded property damage "which is expected or intended by the insured." Both Zavalis and the university argued that the students' behavior did not fall within the exclusion. Specifically, Zavalis argued that he did not

continued

"expect or intend" the damages because he did not intend to burn any part of the Astroturf. Rather, he and his friends thought that the lighter fluid alone would burn, leaving only a residue of soot on the portions of the Astroturf to which it had been applied.

ISSUE   Does the insurance company have a duty to defend and indemnify Zavalis?

DECISION   No. Sometimes common sense prevails, even in the law. This is one of those occasions. An insured "expects or intends" the injury in question when he acts with an intent or a conscious awareness that damage will result. The mere fact that the actual damage is more severe than the insured anticipated does not, by itself, necessarily establish that he did not "expect or intend" it. The inescapable fact is that Zavalis did intend to damage the Astroturf. Whether he meant to actually scorch it or merely leave a layer of soot on the turf that could be cleaned away later, common sense tells us that his purpose was to damage the field nonetheless. Damage need not be permanent to constitute damage, and defacement certainly qualifies as damage. Here, Zavalis literally played with fire; and although the resulting harm was far beyond what he expected, this was a harm that fell clearly in the policy's exclusion. Therefore, Nationwide is not obligated to defend or indemnify Zavalis.

All Risks Policies

Insurers commonly employ a combination of the covered perils and the excluded perils methods. These insurance contracts, known as **all risks policies,** initially use broad language to set out a general rule of coverage. However, they then lay out specific exclusions that limit the insurer's liability for a wide range of occurrences.

If the insured is not alert, he may be lulled into a false sense of security by the broad coverage language at the beginning of the policy. In many instances, later paragraphs in the contract list numerous exclusions that greatly reduce the breadth of coverage. For this reason, it is extremely important to carefully read the entire insurance contract. (See Figure 21–4.)

Stella Jewelry Mfg. v. Naviga Belgamar
885 F.Supp. 84 (S.D.N.Y. 1995)

FACTS   Judah Rosenberg, the president of Stella Jewelry, traveled to Dallas with two bags of jewelry. After storing the jewelry at the home of Rabbi Jacobson for the night, Rosenberg returned the next morning to retrieve the two bags and parked his car in a circular driveway about 10 feet from the house. After collecting the bags, Rosenberg placed one of them on the ground next to his foot in order to make room for it in the car's trunk. However, when he bent down to pick it up, the bag of jewelry was gone. He stated that "about 10 seconds" elapsed from the moment he placed the bag on the ground until he turned to pick it up, and that during this interval he did not see or hear anything. Stella filed a claim for the jewelry under a property insurance policy it had purchased from Naviga Belgamar, a Belgian insurance corporation. The policy issued to Stella protected against *"All Risks of Physical Loss or Damage."* However, the policy also contained a clause excluding *"Loss resulting from mysterious disappearance."* Naviga denied Stella's insurance claim, arguing that the loss fell within the policy's exclusion for mysterious disappearances.

ISSUE   Did the "mysterious disappearance" clause exclude Stella's loss from insurance coverage?

DECISION   No. Under this type of policy, Stella need only prove the existence of the "all risks" policy and the loss of the covered property. The burden then shifts to Naviga to show that an exclusion to the policy prevents recovery. Defining the term "mysterious disappearance" is difficult. Accordingly, the phrase must be interpreted in light of the business purposes sought to be achieved by the parties and the plain meaning of the words chosen by them to effect those purposes. Carriers which do not wish to insure against all risks customarily incorporate an exclusionary clause in their policies exempting from coverage unexplained loss and mysterious disappearance. This relieves the insurer from liability where the property was misplaced or lost by the insured and not the result of felonious acts of another. In this case, "mysterious disappearance" should be interpreted as a factual circumstance in which a reasonable person could not infer the manner in which the reported loss occurred. However, loss from theft is not excluded from coverage under the policy. And the facts, as related by Rosenberg, indicate only the existence of a theft, albeit a mysterious theft with no evidence of a thief. The mysteriousness exclusion really relates to the credibility of the testimony by Rosenberg. There is no evidence from which one could deduce the bag had blown away or been lost in any other manner than by theft. Under those circumstances no reasonable jury could reach the conclusion that the loss occurred other than by theft.

Figure 21–4:   Recovery Under an All Risks Policy

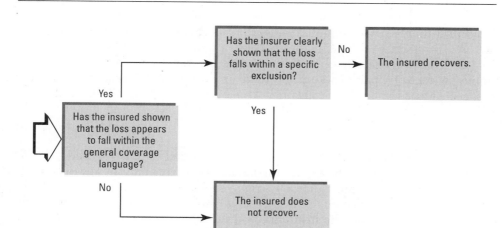

Interpreting Insurance Contracts

While the insurance relationship is contractual in nature, it also is heavily regulated by the states. Thus, one cannot be certain of the rights and obligations of the parties to any insurance contract without some familiarity with the applicable state's insurance laws. However, all states agree that people who buy insurance can be easily confused by the technical language contained in most policies. Accordingly, ambiguities in insurance contracts generally are interpreted in favor of the insured.

Filing an Insurance Claim

The insurance policy specifies the steps that must be taken by a person seeking to recover insurance benefits. First, the insurance company must be given *notification* that a loss or a duty to defend has arisen. (The *Frankenmuth* case, presented earlier in the chapter, rejected an insurer's argument that it was not properly notified of its duty to defend.) Second, the insured must furnish *proof of loss*. Most insurance policies place a *time limit* on the notification and proof of loss requirements. Failure to meet these requirements may cancel the insurer's obligations. However, some policies stipulate that such a delay merely suspends the insurer's obligations until the requirements are met.

Termination

Because of the importance of insurance protection, the states have placed some limitations on the right to terminate a policy. This section explores the two basic ways in which termination occurs: cancellation and lapse.

Cancellation

Cancellation occurs when a party voluntarily extinguishes his or her rights and obligations under the policy. Generally, the insured can do this at any time by notifying the insurer of the desire to cancel. Property and liability insurers possess similar rights to terminate. The insurance policy and state law must be examined to discover the form such notice must take. Property insurance policies often contain lists of activities that automatically cause a cancellation.

Life insurers generally cannot cancel a life insurance contract as long as the premiums are being paid. There are no such restrictions on the right of the insured to cancel. An insured who cancels her whole life policy generally is entitled to recover the accumulated *cash surrender value*.

Lapse

Insurance contracts that are written for a specific period of time (property, liability, and term life) **lapse** at the expiration of that term unless they are renewed. The insured's failure to pay premiums also triggers a lapse. Most states have enacted legislation providing insureds with a *grace period* (often 30 days) after the date when a premium is due. Life insurance policies often have a *reinstatement clause* that allows an insured to reinstate a lapsed policy by paying all past-due premiums and furnishing proof of continued good health.

Nyonteh v. Peoples Security Life Insurance Company
958 F.2D 42 (4TH CIR. 1992)

FACTS Anthony Howell was diagnosed as suffering from chronic granulocytic leukemia and told that, barring a successful bone marrow transplant, he had only a short time to live. Several months later, Howell and his ex-wife, Katherine Nyonteh, applied to Peoples Security Life Insurance for an insurance policy on Howell's life. In answering the health insurance questions on the application, both of them fraudulently concealed Howell's terminal leukemic condition. As a result, the policy was issued in Howell's name. (Ownership was later transferred to Nyonteh.) The policy contained an incontestability clause that became effective after two years. After the policy had been in effect for more than two years, Nyonteh was late in paying her insurance premiums and the policy lapsed. She later applied for reinstatement. In the reinstatement application, both Nyonteh and Howell again concealed Howell's medical condition. The reinstatement contract also contained a two-year incontestability period. Before this incontestability period had elapsed, Howell died.

ISSUE Is Nyonteh entitled to life insurance benefits?

DECISION No. The concealment of a terminal illness leading to imminent death is material to the risk assumed by a life insurance carrier. However, an incontestability clause forecloses untimely challenges based on material misrepresentations in insurance applications. Thus, the principal issue is this case is whether Peoples's right to challenge the insurance policy's validity was barred by the incontestability clause. If the insurance policy had not lapsed, Nyonteh would be entitled to recover the insurance benefits because the two-year period had passed. However, the reinstatement application also included false statements that were material to the risks assumed by Peoples. Because the reinstatement application contained a new period of incontestability that had not run at the time of Howell's death, Peoples was entitled to cancel the policy upon discovering the misrepresentations.

QUESTIONS AND PROBLEM CASES

1. What is a binder? What function does it perform?
2. How does a coinsurance clause reduce the likelihood that a property owner will underinsure property?
3. Describe two ways in which the insurable interest requirement for property insurance differs from its counterpart for life insurance.
4. How does the liability coverage in an automobile policy differ from the physical damage coverage?

5. Western World Insurance Company issued a business liability insurance policy to William Colacurico. The policy insured against liability for bodily injury and property damage at the Unisex Club and other nightclubs or taverns owned by Colacurico. It also contained a provision excluding coverage for *"bodily injury or property damage arising out of assault and battery or out of an act or omission in connection with the prevention or suppression of such acts, whether caused by the insured, his*

employees, patrons, or any other person." Ronald Alvarado filed an action to recover under the liability insurance policy after he was struck by Mark Teaney, a waiter and dancer at the club. According to Alvarado, Teaney hit him in the face and knocked him to the floor for no reason. Under Teaney's version of the altercation, he was showing a customer to a seat in the club when Alvarado blocked his path. Teaney was wearing a costume which he described as "a G-string, some chains, leather and a bull whip." He alleged that when Alvarado grabbed at his crotch area, he struck Alvarado. Do Alvarado's injuries fall within the coverage of the nightclub's business liability policy?

6. Benjamin Born applied for insurance from Medico Life Insurance Company. When filling out the application, Benjamin stated that he had no preexisting medical problems and was in good health. Several months after the policy was issued, Medico discovered that Benjamin had a history of heart disease, degenerative arthritis, and urinary system disorders. May Medico legally cancel the policy?

7. After their separation, Ronald ceased paying premiums on the insurance he held on Karen's life and the policy lapsed. Karen continued paying premiums on the policy she owned on Ronald's life. After Ronald objected to Karen's continued ownership of the policy on his life, the divorce court ordered her to terminate the policy. Should Karen be required to terminate the life insurance policy?

8. Cope purchased a business liability insurance policy for his roofing business from Property Owners Insurance. The policy excluded coverage except in instances of liability "with respect to the conduct of the business" owned by Cope. While the policy was in force, Cope traveled to Montana with a person with whom he did significant business. While on this trip, Cope went snowmobiling with a group of persons; during this activity one of them, Johnson, was accidentally killed. After Johnson's estate filed a wrongful death suit against Cope, Property Owners argued that it

had no obligations under the insurance contract because the accident did not occur with respect to the conduct of Cope's business. Is the insurance company correct?

9. Joseph Ryan was 63 years old and suffering from emphysema. Because of his age and illness, his children decided to seek some form of life insurance for him. Joseph completed an application form for a term insurance policy in the amount of $100,000. His daughter, Deborah, paid the first monthly premium of $107 and the insurer, Metropolitan Life Insurance Company, cashed and deposited the check. Metropolitan's insurance agent told Joseph and his children that coverage would go into effect after the agent signed the application and collected the first month's premium. He then handed Joseph a receipt that explained that if a medical examination was required by the insurer's underwriting rules, coverage would not begin until completion of the examination. The receipt also stated that Metropolitan's insurance agents did not have authority to change or waive the terms of the receipt. One week later, the agent informed Deborah that a medical examination was required by the insurer's underwriting rules and that it would have to be completed before Metropolitan would issue the policy on her father. On the day the medical examination was scheduled, Joseph died of a heart attack before the physical was completed. Four days later, Metropolitan denied Joseph's application for insurance on the grounds the medical examination was not completed. Was Joseph covered by the life insurance policy?

10. Timothy Rick made a series of anonymous telephone calls to the home of Anthony and Susan Rohrer. The calls were of the "hang up" variety, where Rick would not speak after the Rohrers answered the telephone. Rick placed these calls for approximately 40 days in March and April of 1992. After Rick was apprehended, the Rohrers filed a civil suit against him, alleging trespass, nuisance, intentional infliction of emotional distress, and negligence. Rick notified Travelers

Companies, his homeowners' insurance carrier, but Travelers declined to defend him. The homeowners' policy made Travelers liable for damages caused by an "occurrence." It defined "occurrence" as *an accident, including continuous or repeated exposure to substantially the same harmful conditions, which results during the policy period in bodily injury or property damage."* Rick and the Rohrers reached a settlement agreement for $49,000. Under the terms of the agreement, Rick would pay $9,000 and the balance would be subject to collection from Travelers. Rick acknowledged making the telephone calls and stated he did not intend to injure the Rohrers when he made them. Is Travelers correct when it denies coverage for the Rohrers's injuries?

DRIVING A CAR

Officer Mackel was patrolling a high crime area known for its open narcotics trafficking when he saw a late model, black Nissan Pathfinder with heavily tinted windows illegally parked in the middle of the street, effectively blocking traffic. The driver, Billy Howard Stanfield, was talking to a man whom the officer recognized as a known drug dealer. The tinting on the Pathfinder's windows was so dark that Mackel could not see into the vehicle. After approaching the vehicle on the passenger side, Mackel opened the front passenger-side door to determine if Stanfield was armed or had access to a weapon and whether he was alone in the Pathfinder. From his vantage point outside the vehicle, Mackel saw a clear plastic bag of cocaine protruding from a brown paper bag that was overturned on the back seat. Stanfield argued that the cocaine could not be admitted as evidence against him because Mackel had no right to open the passenger door.

United States v. Stanfield, 109 F.3d 976 (4th Cir. 1997).

When may police lawfully stop a motor vehicle?

Do you have the right to refuse when a police officer asks if he may search your car?

Did Officer Mackel have a legal right to open the passenger door of the Pathfinder?

Introduction ▨▨▨▨▨▨▨▨▨▨▨▨▨▨▨▨▨▨▨▨▨

The automobile has had a profound impact on the fabric of American society. Its economic and sociological influences are enormous. Millions of employees manufacture and sell cars, fuel and repair them, and maintain the roads and highways over which they travel. Millions more are dependent upon automobiles for their work and play. Consumers spend a tremendous amount of money purchasing and fueling their cars. With the exception of a house, the family car generally is the most expensive purchase most adults ever make. At the same time, automobiles are major polluters, and traffic accidents take a staggering number of lives. Some sociologists even attribute the breakdown of the family and the growth in teenage pregnancies to the freedom cars brought to our youth.

Despite the tremendous influence motor vehicles have had on society and our individual lives, this country has not promulgated a uniform body of laws governing the purchase and use of automobiles. Instead, courts must draw from contract, tort, property, and criminal law principles when resolving legal disputes involving cars and other motor vehicles. This chapter examines these basic legal issues as they relate to buying, owning, and operating an automobile.

Chapter Overview

The chapter begins with an examination of the contract rules governing the purchase or lease of a car. This is supplemented by a discussion of the options available to an automobile owner when a new or used vehicle has mechanical problems. Attention is then turned to various rules governing the operation of a motor vehicle, including the legal ramifications of driving under the influence of alcohol. This is followed by a review of the responsibilities of automobile drivers and owners when a car is involved in an accident. The chapter closes with a look at the power of law enforcement officials to conduct automobile searches. (Automobile insurance is discussed in Chapter 21.)

Buying a Car ▨▨▨▨▨▨▨▨▨▨▨▨▨▨▨▨▨▨▨▨▨

The purchase of a motor vehicle is governed by contract law. More specifically, it is part of a special branch of contracts known as **sales law.** This is because sales law regulates the formation and performance of contracts for the sale of goods (tangible personal property) and a car is a good. Sales law has been codified in Article 2 of the Uniform Commercial Code. It is fairly uniform throughout the country and, in general, simplifies the contracting process. (Article 2 of the Uniform Commercial Code is introduced in Chapter 8.)

General Sales Duties

Sales law is more concerned with rewarding people's legitimate expectations than it is with enforcing technical rules. Thus, as long as the buyer and seller show an intent to enter into an agreement, they may have an enforceable contract even though they did not agree on all of the terms. This is because the drafters of Article 2 intended to create practical rules reflecting what people actually do when making a purchase. Specifically, they recognized a basic truth in modern life— most contracts are not the product of negotiation between two people with equal

http://
www.law.cornell.edu/
ucc/2/overview.html
provides information
regarding the UCC
on sales.

knowledge and bargaining strength. Instead, consumers frequently are faced with preprinted forms that commercial sellers present on a "take it or leave it" basis. Sales law provides several safeguards to offset the one-sided nature of these **contracts of adhesion.**

Good Faith and Fair Dealing

Article 2 tries to promote fair dealing between contracting partners. Thus, it requires that parties to a sales contract act in **good faith** during the formation and performance of the agreement. Further, it permits courts to refuse to enforce **unconscionable contracts.** Although Article 2 does not define unconscionability, courts have described an unconscionable contract as one that no sensible person not under delusion or duress or in distress would make, and such as no honest and fair person would accept. It generally arises when there is a great disparity in bargaining power that leads the party with lesser power to sign a contract unwillingly or unaware of its terms. This may occur in contracts of adhesion where one party is unlikely to notice or understand unduly harsh terms because they were too technically worded or concealed in fine print. (Unconscionability is discussed in Chapter 9.)

Merchants

http://
www.autosite.com
provides information
on price, sales,
financing, and other
hints on buying and
selling a car.

Sales law frequently imposes higher standards on **merchants** (automobile dealers) than it does on nonmerchants (private sellers). This is because consumers are likely to place more reliance on the expertise of a professional seller. Further, because an automobile dealer merchant generally is more knowledgeable, he often is better able to protect himself.

Written Agreements

Article 2 contains a statute of frauds provision requiring that contracts for the sale of goods for $500 or more be in writing. This **writing requirement** applies whether the seller is a merchant or a private owner. Thus, if Paula orally agrees to sell her car to Mike for $1,200, she may back out of the deal if they had not drafted a written agreement. However, the Uniform Commercial Code provides an exception to its writing requirement when there has been **partial performance.** For instance, if Paula had already delivered the car or if Mike had already paid the purchase price, their oral contract would be enforceable. (See Figure 22–1.)

Parol Evidence

Before signing a written agreement, the parties should make certain that the writing includes all the important terms upon which they have agreed. This is because the **parol evidence rule** generally prohibits a person from varying the terms of a writing by introducing evidence of terms allegedly agreed on prior to, or at the same time as, the writing. Suppose Paula told Mike that if he bought the car and was unhappy with the tape player he could exchange it for a CD player. However, their written agreement stated that Mike took the car "as is." Due to the parol evidence rule, Paula is not required to give Mike the CD player.

Figure 22–1: The Writing Requirement

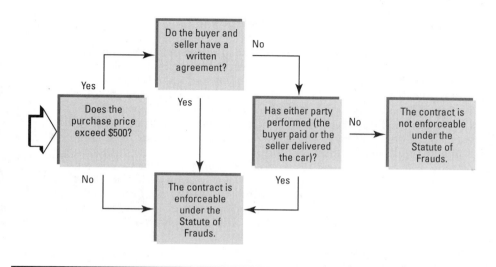

Rules of Construction

When the words used in a written agreement are ambiguous, courts have devised **rules of construction** for resolving subsequent disputes. First, when the parties have used a form contract or the agreement is partly printed and partly written, the written terms override conflicting printed terms. Second, if only one of the parties drafted the contract (as is likely when buying a car from a dealer), all ambiguities are construed against that party. (The writing requirement, parol evidence rule, and the rules of interpretation are discussed in Chapter 9.)

Special Rules

The state and federal governments have drafted numerous other rules governing the sale of automobiles. These regulations recognize the tremendous advantages car dealers have over most consumers when selling motor vehicles. They often are designed to provide consumers with fuller information and to protect them from unfair selling tactics.

Advertising Restrictions

The form and content of advertisements by car dealers often are regulated by state agencies. Because advertisements are commercial speech, they receive no First Amendment protection if they contain false or misleading messages. Further, regulators may require dealers to provide meaningful information to potential buyers so they may rationally determine the advantages and disadvantages of purchasing a particular vehicle.

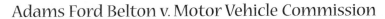

Adams Ford Belton v. Motor Vehicle Commission
946 S.W.2d 199 (Sup. Ct. Mo. 1997)

FACTS   Adams Ford, a car dealership in Missouri, placed an advertisement in the *Kansas City Star* that stated, "$5,000* Guarantees We Will Beat Any Deal, Anywhere, Any Time." The asterisk referred to smaller print at the bottom of the advertisement, which stated, "*All Applicable Rebates to Dealer." The dealership also placed another advertisement in the newspaper that read: "$100 over Ford Factory Invoice on All Models in Stock." Adams Ford was charged with violating two Missouri advertising regulations. The first provides: *"Licensed motor vehicle dealers shall not make any reference to matching or bettering competitors' prices in any advertisement unless all limitations are clearly and conspicuously disclosed. Any policy shall not place an unreasonable burden on the consumer."* The dealer also was charged with violating a second regulation that prohibits licensed dealers from advertising *"a motor vehicle with regard to the invoice price, dealer cost, or any similar term or phrase as consumers equate with cost which is misleading and prohibited."* A hearing officer concluded that Adams Ford had violated both regulations and ordered its dealership license suspended for two days. Adams Ford argued that the advertising regulations violated its First Amendment rights.

ISSUE   Do the regulations violate the dealership's First Amendment rights?

DECISION   No. Though states may not absolutely prohibit commercial advertising that is merely potentially misleading, advertising that is inherently misleading or by experience has proved to be subject to abuse may be regulated. The advertisements prohibited by the first regulation are not protected by the First Amendment because they are inherently misleading and subject to abuse by motor vehicle dealers. The offer was subject to 20 terms and conditions that were not disclosed in the advertisement itself. Among the conditions was a limitation that the "offer expires at the close of business the day the ad runs." The customer was also required to "have made a deposit on the car at the other store." Generally, when customers make a deposit on a vehicle at a dealership, they are usually locked in at that point into purchasing the car or they will lose their deposit. These terms and conditions would likely exclude most customers from availing themselves of the "guarantee." Thus, the "guarantee" is illusory. As for the second regulation, in Missouri, a licensed dealer may not advertise the price of a motor vehicle in relation to "invoice price." There is ample evidence to indicate that as used in the advertisement, "invoice price" is likely to deceive and is, therefore, inherently misleading. In the automobile industry the term "invoice price" has a specialized, unique meaning. An "invoice" generally is understood to mean an itemized statement furnished to a purchaser by a seller and usually specifies the price of goods and services and terms of sale. "Invoice price" ordinarily means the price paid by the dealer for the vehicle. However, within the automotive industry, "invoice price" does not reflect the dealer's price. That price is subject to manipulation by undisclosed dealer rebates, allowances, or incentives. The term "invoice price" is inherently misleading as used in motor vehicle advertisements because of the peculiar meaning given the term by the automotive industry, which is at variance with the commonly understood meaning of the words. A dealer still may advertise the actual sales price or advertise the price in relation to the manufacturer's suggested retail "sticker price" displayed on the vehicle. By contrast, no useful information is conveyed to the consumer by an advertisement of a vehicle with respect to "invoice price."

Odometer Act

The *Vehicle Information and Cost Savings Act,* known as the *Odometer Act,* requires all persons transferring a motor vehicle to give an accurate, written odometer reading to the purchaser or recipient of the transferred vehicle. No person, not even the vehicle's owner, may do anything to cause the odometer to show the wrong mileage unless it is necessary to make repairs. When a seller knows the registered mileage is incorrect, she must disclose that fact on a **mileage disclosure form**. Automobile purchasers should be certain they receive this statement before the title is transferred. Anyone who tampers with an odometer or discloses an inaccurate odometer reading with the intent to defraud may be sued by an injured person in a private civil action. If the suit is successful, the purchaser may recover $1,500 or three times the amount of his damages, whichever is greater.

Diersen v. Chicago Car Exchange
110 F.3D 481 (7TH CIR. 1997)

FACTS In 1994, David Diersen purchased a 1968 Dodge "Charger R/T" from the Chicago Car Exchange (CCE) for $16,790. CCE provided Diersen with a written odometer disclosure statement, as required under the *Odometer Act,* stating that the actual mileage of the vehicle was 22,633. The CCE also provided Diersen with an appraisal document stating that the car had 22,600 original miles, as well as a fact sheet stating that the car had 22,600 miles and just one prior owner. The CCE had purchased the vehicle from Joseph Slaski, who certified to the CCE that the mileage on the car was approximately 22,600 miles and stated that it had but one prior owner. After acquiring the vehicle but before selling it to Diersen, the CCE inspected the vehicle and did not suspect that the odometer reading was inaccurate. After buying the Charger, Diersen conducted an extensive investigation into its title history and discovered that the vehicle had previously been described in title documents as having mileage of 75,000. However, the car's prior owners informed him that the high mileage noted on the title was a discrepancy, arising from a clerical error, and asserted that the vehicle was in fact a low-mileage car. Before Diersen filed this lawsuit, the CCE offered to have him return the car for a complete refund. Diersen refused this offer and sued the CCE for fraud under the *Odometer Act.*

ISSUE Should Diersen recover damages for odometer fraud?

DECISION No. In order to succeed on his claim of odometer fraud, Diersen must demonstrate two essential elements: (1) a violation of the Act's odometer disclosure requirements (i.e., the providing of an inaccurate odometer reading), and (2) an intent to defraud. Diersen claims that the odometer statement provided by the CCE was inaccurate and that the vehicle in question had actually been driven 75,000 miles. But the car's prior owners testified that the Charger was a "low-mileage" vehicle, and that any indication to the contrary on the title had resulted from a clerical error. Diersen introduced evidence from an automobile appraiser that the "worn condition of the driver's seat" and the "damaged condition of the car's oil pan" were consistent with a vehicle that had been driven "greatly in excess of 22,600 miles." However, even if a jury were to agree with Diersen that the odometer statement was inaccurate, that is only *one* of

continued

the elements necessary to prove odometer fraud under the *Odometer Act.* The CCE must have acted with an *intent to defraud* in order to be subject to liability. The record reflects that the CCE relied upon the sworn odometer statement provided by Slaski. One could argue in light of the car's age, the CCE ought to have conducted further inquiry into the car's mileage instead of relying on the figure given by Slaski. However, "mere negligence" is by no means the same as "intent to defraud." Without evidence of fraudulent intent, Diersen cannot prevail on his claim of odometer fraud. Indeed, his allegation of fraudulent or evil intent is belied by the fact that the CCE, in good faith, offered to allow Diersen to return the car for a full refund of his money (an offer he rejected, preferring to pursue this lawsuit).

http://www.law.vill.edu/Fed-Ct/fedcourt.html

Ownership and Registration

http://
www.ink.org/public/
kdor/kdorvehicle.html
is the site of the
Kansas Division of
Motor Vehicles.
Check your state's
home page for simi-
lar information on
auto titles and regis-
trations.

After buying a car, the new owner generally receives two ownership documents: the certificate of title and the certificate of registration. Each performs a different function. (See Figure 22–2.)

Certificate of Title

The **certificate of title** tells the world who owns a motor vehicle. It lists both the purchaser and others who may have a legal interest in the car. This information can be very important (as we will see later) when the buyer has borrowed money to purchase the automobile. It should be kept in a safe place and not in the vehicle because, if the car is stolen, the title can be used to identify the rightful owner.

There often are delays in issuing a certificate of title to the new owner of a car. However, this does not prevent the purchaser from taking title (gaining owner-ship rights) to the vehicle. Under sales law, title generally passes to the buyer of an automobile once the parties' agreement clearly identifies the car that has been bought.

O'Donnell v. American Employers Insurance

622 N.E.2d 570 (Ct. App. Ind. 1993)

FACTS Donald Hummel executed a written purchase order for the purchase of a Chevrolet Corsica from Raisor Pontiac. The purchase order indicated that the total retail price of the car would be $7,681.98 and that Hummel would make a cash down payment of $624.50. It further stated that Purdue Employees Federal Credit Union would be the lienholder for the $7,057.48 balance. Hummel then signed a Retail Installment Contract and Security Agreement with Raisor Pontiac, paid $350.00, and took possession of the vehicle. The following day, he paid the $274.50 balance due on the down payment. Two days later, while driving the Corsica, Hummel collided with another car. At the time of the accident, Raisor Pontiac held the certificate of title and the car bore temporary license plates. Sean O'Donnell, a passenger in the other vehicle, was killed in the collision. Raisor Pontiac did not transfer the certificate of title to Hummel until six days after the accident. At the time of the accident, Raisor Pontiac was insured by American Employers Insurance under a policy that covered its ownership, maintenance, and use of covered vehicles. O'Donnell's parents sued Hummel for the wrongful death of their son. They also claimed that the American Employers' policy covered the accident because Raisor Pontiac was the owner of the car at the time of the accident.

ISSUE   Did Raisor Pontiac own the Corsica when the accident occurred?

DECISION   No. Article 2 provides that title passes to buyer at the time and place at which the seller completes his performance with reference to the physical delivery of the goods, even though a document of title is to be delivered at a different time or place. Thus, title passed to Hummel when he took possession of the car one day before the accident. Raisor Pontiac's continued possession of the certificate of title merely indicated that it was reserving a security interest in the car until it received payment from the Credit Union.

Certificate of Registration

The **certificate of registration** is issued by the state's bureau of motor vehicles. In many states this certificate is not given unless the car meets prescribed safety and environmental standards. The owner may also have to pay certain fees or taxes and show proof of insurance coverage. Certificates of registration often must be renewed on an annual basis, generally when the vehicle's license plates are purchased. The registration usually is kept in the car since police officers are likely to ask to see it when they stop a motor vehicle. Basically, the certificate of registration documents that the automobile may be lawfully operated.

Figure 22–2:   Ownership and Registration

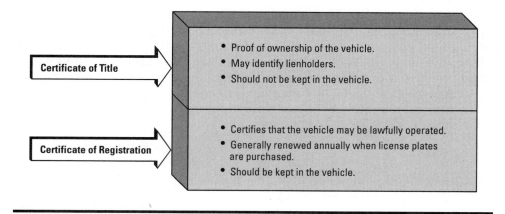

Certificate of Title
- Proof of ownership of the vehicle.
- May identify lienholders.
- Should not be kept in the vehicle.

Certificate of Registration
- Certifies that the vehicle may be lawfully operated.
- Generally renewed annually when license plates are purchased.
- Should be kept in the vehicle.

Risk of Loss

Sometimes a car may be damaged, destroyed, or stolen after the parties have signed an agreement but before the buyer has taken possession of the vehicle. When this occurs, courts first look to the agreement to see if it specifies who bears the **risk of loss.** In the absence of such specific terms, sales law provides the answer. When the seller is a merchant, the risk does not pass to the buyer until she has actually taken possession of the car. However, if the seller is a nonmerchant, the risk passes to the buyer as soon as the seller makes it available.

Suppose Debbie contracts to buy a car from Reliable Auto Sales. If the car is destroyed or stolen while still on the car lot, the automobile dealer must bear the loss. However, the result would be different if Debbie had agreed to buy a car from Harold, a private owner. Once Harold indicated to Debbie that she could pick up the car at her convenience, the risk of loss shifted to her. Of course, Harold might still be liable to Debbie under bailment law if he failed to take reasonable precautions to safeguard the car. (The duties of a bailee are discussed in Chapter 15.) Further, in either the merchant or the nonmerchant case, both the buyer and the seller could insure the vehicle against loss once their agreement was made.

Financing the Purchase

http:// www.edmunds.com/ provides information on financing a car.

The average sticker price for a new car has soared to almost $22,000. Most people cannot write a check for that much money. Accordingly, it should not be surprising that more than 90 percent of all car buyers use some form of financing when buying a car. Suppose Eileen buys a new car from Ace Auto. To finance the purchase, she borrows $15,000 from First Bank and gives the lender a security interest in the car. If Eileen's state requires a certificate of title for motor vehicles, her title should list Eileen as the equitable owner and First Bank as the legal owner. First Bank's name should remain on the certificate of title until the loan has been paid off.

Until First Bank's name is removed from the certificate of title, nobody may take the car free and clear of the bank's security interest. The bank is unlikely to remove its name until the loan balance has been paid in full. As the legal owner, First Bank may repossess the car if it does not receive the loan payments in a timely manner.

Suppose instead that Auto Heaven, an automobile dealership, borrowed money from Bank One. The bank then took a security interest in the dealer's entire inventory. If Chad buys a car from Auto Heaven, he will take title free and clear of the bank's security interest. Thus, his certificate of title will not list Bank One as a legal owner. This exception, known as the *buyer in the ordinary course of business* rule, arises when a car is bought from a dealer. It is not available when a car is purchased from a private owner. (Security interests, buyers in the ordinary course, and repossession are discussed in Chapter 10.)

Leasing

http:// www.spare.autosite. com/new/loanlse/ calc.asp provides leasing tips and other leasing information.

Leasing may be the most publicized way to finance a car today. In 1996, over one-third of all new cars in the country were leased. That number is expected to grow 50 percent by the end of the century. With rising sticker prices, leasing has become an attractive alternative because it generally offers lower monthly payments than conventional financing. However, leasing can be an extremely complex transaction and usually is not as cost-effective as buying.

The Mechanics of Leasing

Automobile leases frequently don't require a down payment other than the first monthly payment and a security deposit equal to the monthly payment. However, payments can be reduced by putting some money down. This is known as *capitalized cost reduction.* Further, the consumer must pay title and registration fees, and many states also assess a *use tax* similar to the sales tax that must be paid when a car is purchased.

Lease agreements require the consumer to pay for *excess wear and damage* to the vehicle when the lease ends. This includes damages such as dents, cracked windshields, torn upholstery, and bald tires. They also impose an *excess mileage fee* (as much as 15 cents a mile) if the car is driven more than an agreed-upon distance (usually 12,000 or 15,000 miles) each year. Finally, many dealers and leasing companies assess a *disposition fee* at the end of the lease to cover the cost of transporting and selling the vehicle. This charge may run several hundred dollars.

At the end of the lease period (typically 24 to 36 months), the consumer does not own the car. *Closed-end* leases give the consumer the option to purchase the vehicle at the end of the lease period for a preset amount, known as the *residual value.* However, not all agreements provide this option. Further, *open-end* leases may require the consumer to pay the difference if the residual value is more than the car's market value when the lease ends.

Regulation of Leasing

Article 2A of the Uniform Commercial Code deals exclusively with leases of goods. In general, its provisions parallel the sales law rules discussed above. However, it does not address many of the complaints levied by consumer groups against automobile leasing companies. In particular, they complain that consumers frequently are not given adequate information to determine if a lease is a good deal or not. In response, several states have enacted auto-lease laws requiring greater disclosure of the financial components of automobile leases. And the Federal Trade Commission has forced the major automakers to fully and clearly disclose important leasing costs such as taxes, title, and registration fees.

Automobile Performance

As we noted above, the purchase of an automobile frequently is an expensive proposition. It often takes a buyer five or more years to pay for a car. Further, while advances in technology have greatly improved the performance of motor vehicles, they also have made it extremely difficult for the average buyer to uncover many latent defects in a new or used vehicle. These modern-day realities are changing the ways in which society views the sale of a car.

Under the traditional contractual model, each party did his best to drive a hard bargain and neither placed much faith in statements of the other. To some extent, this model still governs a transaction when someone purchases a used car from a private owner. However, the expectations of the legal system are changing in instances where the contract is between a consumer and an automobile dealer. In those cases, the law is likely to provide much more protection to the buyer and to make dealers and automakers much more accountable for the quality of the car.

This section explores the rights and responsibilities of buyers and sellers when an automobile does not live up to a buyer's expectations. Specifically, it examines warranties, lemon laws, and automobile recalls. The section closes with a brief look at the legal aspects of automobile repairs.

Express Warranties

When a seller makes promises regarding the quality, condition, or performance of a car, she is making an **express warranty.** An express warranty can arise even when the seller has not used the words "warranty" or "guarantee." In fact, it is not necessary for her to specifically intend to create a warranty. If the seller makes a statement of fact or a promise that relates to the vehicle and becomes part of the basis of the bargain, she has made an express warranty. This might arise from an oral statement or a description of the car in a brochure supplied by the manufacturer or dealer.

Recommendations or mere statements of opinion are not treated as warranties. Accordingly, when a seller describes a particular car as "a great buy," she has not made an express warranty. Sometimes it is difficult to distinguish between a promise regarding the condition or performance of a vehicle and a statement of opinion. Courts are more likely to interpret statements as warranties when they are made by dealers rather than private owners. This is because a buyer is more likely to treat statements made by a dealer as a promise.

Although sellers are not required to give express warranties, federal law regulates the manner in which they may be made. Specifically, sellers must clearly disclose all key elements of the warranty in a single document. Further, they must state whether the warranty is full or limited. A **full warranty** requires the seller to repair the car and replace worn or defective parts free of charge. A **limited warranty,** on the other hand, reduces the seller's duty to repair. For instance, it might limit warranty coverage to only 12 months or 12,000 miles. Or it might cover only replacement parts but not labor charges.

Implied Warranties

A warranty need not be conveyed expressly. Courts seldom hesitate to find an **implied warranty,** particularly when the seller is a merchant, in order to promote higher standards of behavior. Two particular implied warranties frequently are made when a car is sold: the implied warranty of title and the implied warranty of merchantability.

Implied Warranty of Title

The **implied warranty of title** is an implied promise by a seller (a dealer or a private seller) that she has the legal right to sell the car. Included in this warranty is an implied promise that no creditors or mechanics have a security interest or lien on the vehicle. When such an encumbrance does exist, the seller must either pay off the lienholder or disclose the existence of the lien to the buyer before the agreement is finalized.

Implied Warranty of Merchantability

The **implied warranty of merchantability** is a guarantee of the quality and performance standards of the car. Only car dealers (merchants) make this implied warranty. It guarantees that the vehicle is fit for its ordinary purpose and is of customary quality. Of course, a car's customary quality depends on the age and price of the vehicle. Thus, one would expect much better quality and performance from a new car than a high-mileage, used vehicle.

––––––––––––––––– Ethical Issue –––––––––––––––––

Under sales law, private sellers do not make an implied warranty of merchantability when they sell a car. Is it ethical to sell a car to someone when you know it has serious mechanical defects that the buyer cannot readily discover?

Liability Disclaimers

Automobile dealers and manufacturers often attempt to eliminate or limit their liability by inserting a **disclaimer** in the contract. To eliminate the implied warranty of merchantability, the disclaimer must conspicuously use the word "merchantability." Or in the alternative, the seller generally may exclude the warranty of merchantability by using expressions like *"as is"* or *"with all faults."* However, if a full warranty has been given, the seller may not later disclaim or modify any express or implied warranties. Generally, new-car dealers provide limited warranties but then offer to sell buyers an **extended warranty** that expands the time and scope of the original warranty protection.

Lemon Laws

In terms of price and significance, an automobile purchase is an extremely important event in the lives of most consumers. But that purchase can become a nightmare when the seller is unwilling or unable to make certain a new car runs properly. It should be understood that the mere existence of a warranty does not fully protect an automobile purchaser. Consumers have long complained about unscrupulous dealers who don't honor the terms of their warranty or who cannot competently repair a defective vehicle. In fact, under sales law, purchasers of defective cars had no recourse other than to repeatedly bring their cars in for repairs.

In response to an increasing number of lawsuits over automobile warranties and a rising number of complaints from consumer groups, the vast majority of states enacted **lemon laws.** The precise terms of these statutes vary from state to state. However, in general, they require an automobile manufacturer to replace a new vehicle or pay damages to a buyer when its mechanical problems cannot be repaired within an established time period. For instance, California considers a new car to be a "lemon" if it cannot be repaired after four or more attempts or if

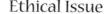
http:// www.autopedia. com/html/HotLinks_ Lemon.html contains information regarding lemon laws for various states.

it has spent more than 30 days in the repair shop during its first year or 12,000 miles. The automaker must buy back the lemon at the original purchase price, including any sales taxes paid by the buyer. If the manufacturer wishes to resell a lemon as a used car, it must mark the car's title to identify it as a lemon.

Hughes v. Chrysler Motors Corporation
542 N.W.2d 148 (Sup. Ct. Wis. 1996)

FACTS   John Hughes purchased a new Dodge Caravan on January 11, 1990. During his first year of ownership, Hughes took the vehicle to the dealer to repair transmission defects on seven separate occasions. Because the repair efforts were unsuccessful, Hughes hired a lawyer. On June 19, 1991, his attorney wrote Chrysler's registered agent in Wisconsin and demanded that Chrysler replace Hughes's car within 30 days with a "comparable new motor vehicle" without any further charge to him. Having received no reply within the 30 days required by statute, his lawyer contacted Chrysler on July 29, 1991 and, at Chrysler's request, mailed a copy of the June 19th demand letter. After receiving a copy of the letter, Chrysler attempted to reach Hughes's attorney by telephone before discovering that Hughes had filed suit on August 22, 1991. On August 23, 1991, Chrysler sent Hughes a letter offering to replace his vehicle without any charge for a model year upgrade or the mileage on his vehicle. Wisconsin's lemon law provides that if a new vehicle does not conform to an applicable express warranty, the nonconformity shall be repaired before the expiration of the warranty or one year after delivery of the vehicle, whichever is sooner. The nonconformity must be repaired within four times and the vehicle cannot be out of service for 30 or more days due to nonconformity. Otherwise, the manufacturer must accept return of the vehicle and, at the direction of the consumer, either replace the vehicle or refund the consumer's full purchase price plus any sales tax, finance charge, and costs, less a reasonable allowance for use. The Wisconsin lemon law is violated if the manufacturer fails to voluntarily replace or repurchase the lemon vehicle within 30 days after the consumer's demand. A manufacturer's failure to comply with this demand entitles the consumer to an action for twice the amount of any pecuniary loss, together with costs and attorney fees. Chrysler argues that a buyer's pecuniary loss is limited to any out-of-pocket expenses that were caused by the manufacturer's violation of the statute. Hughes claims that pecuniary loss includes the purchase price of the car. He contends that allowing the consumer to recover double the purchase price of the automobile effectuates the purposes of the lemon law and strengthens the rights of consumers in dealing with vehicle defects.

ISSUE   Is Hughes entitled to twice the purchase price of the car?

DECISION   Yes. The purpose behind Wisconsin's lemon law was to improve auto manufacturers' quality control and reduce the inconvenience, expense, frustration, fear, and emotional trauma that lemon owners endure. We conclude that the legislature intended to include the purchase price of the car as pecuniary damages. First, if we accept Chrysler's definition of pecuniary loss, then the remedy provided by this statute does not significantly improve upon those remedies available to the consumer before enactment of the lemon law. Second, by including the purchase price of the car as part of the pecuniary loss, the statute provides an incentive to the manufacturer to promptly resolve the matter by making it far more costly to delay. If the only damages available were out of pocket costs, the statute would provide scant incentive to move with dispatch. Third, a potential recovery must be large enough to give vehicle owners the incentive to bring suits against these corporations. We realize that car manufacturers do not deliberately set out to manufacture a lemon. However, an unfortunate fact of life, seemingly as inevitable as night following day, is that occasionally a "lemon" will slip through the line. And when that happens, another unfortunate fact of modern day life is that the cost to the unlucky consumer who purchases that "lemon" is far more than the cost of the car: interrupted, delayed, or even canceled schedules; the time and the trouble, as well as the anxiety and stress that accompany those changes, the apprehension that results every time the consumer gets back into that automobile wondering "what next?" Dependability is a prime objective of every new car buyer. When that is taken away, the loss is far greater than the cost of the car. It is this fact that the legislature recognized when they enacted the lemon law. Its principal motivation is not to punish the manufacturer who, after all, would far prefer that no "lemons" escape their line. Rather, it seeks to provide an incentive to that manufacturer to promptly return those unfortunate consumers back to where they thought they were when they first purchased that new automobile. Chrysler did not respond within the 30 days required by the law. Given that fact, we hold that Hughes can recover double the amount of the purchase price of his automobile. This result is consistent with the underlying purposes and goals of the lemon law.

Automobile Recalls

Federal law requires that automakers notify both the *National Highway Traffic Safety Administration* and vehicle purchasers when manufacturers discover safety defects in their automobiles. At that time, the manufacturers must also indicate how they will address the problem. This might include a **recall.** If this is not done voluntarily, the government may order a recall. The automaker then has three available options for curing the defect: repairing the car, replacing the car, or returning the purchase price.

http:// *www.autosite.com* or *http://www.edmunds. com* provides information on recalls and repairs.

Automobile Repairs

Not all mechanical problems are covered by warranties or the lemon laws. Repairs may be needed after a warranty has expired or, in the case of a purchase from a private seller, the buyer may have received no warranties as to quality or performance. Further, even during a warranty period, damages arising from collisions and buyer abuse or neglect fall outside of the warranty coverage. In these instances, the automobile owner must contract with an automobile mechanic for the necessary repairs.

The Mechanic's Duties

When an automobile mechanic takes possession of a car to make repairs, he is governed by the law of bailments. As such, he owes the car owner a duty of ordinary care and diligence. This means that, as a professional, he must exercise the degree of care that a person in the automobile repair business would be expected to use. Further, he commits a tort if he performs unauthorized or unnecessary repairs. Breach of either bailment or tort duties may result in liability for actual damages. Further, when a mechanic fraudulently performs unnecessary repairs, he may be liable for punitive damages as well.

The Mechanic's Rights

When a mechanic makes necessary repairs to a car, he increases its value. This entitles the mechanic to a **possessory lien,** which gives him the right to maintain possession of the vehicle until he has been paid for the repairs. If the mechanic voluntarily parts with possession before the charges are paid, he loses the lien. However, if the owner recovers the car by fraud or illegal means, the lien still is effective. (See Figure 22–3.)

If the debt is not paid in a reasonable time period, the mechanic frequently has the right to sell the car and pay the charges from the proceeds. Any surplus generally is paid to any other lienholder, such as a bank that financed the owner's purchase of the vehicle. If no other lienholder exists, the surplus money is returned to the owner. Most states have specific procedures a mechanic must follow before he may sell an automobile. They require that he give notice to the owner and advertise the sale. In the absence of such a statute, the mechanic must sue the debtor and obtain a judgment against the automobile owner before the car can be sold.

Figure 22–3:   The Mechanic's Possessory Lien on a Motor Vehicle

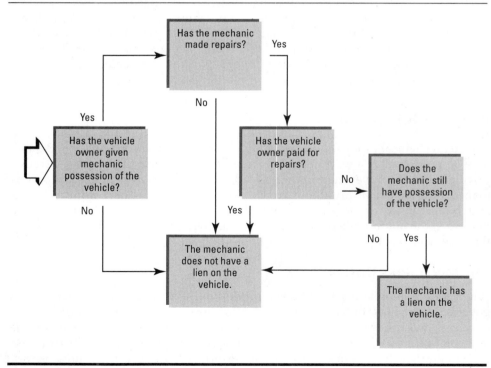

Driving Standards ▬▬▬▬▬▬▬

Despite their many benefits, automobiles impose heavy costs on society. They pollute the air, congest streets and highways, and, when not driven carefully, take lives and destroy property. To minimize these adverse effects, governmental regulators have enacted numerous rules governing the private operation of motor vehicles. This section examines several types of driving standards regulated by the government.

Driver's License

Each state establishes the qualifications that must be met before a person may operate a motor vehicle on public streets and highways. Usually this entails written, driving, and vision tests. States generally allow minors to obtain a **driver's license** after they reach a certain age. Most states have set the age at 16 years, although four states have a minimum license age of 15. Many states award a learner's permit that must be held for a minimum period (usually 10 to 30 days).

A growing number of states issue *graduated licensing,* requiring beginners to drive with adult supervision for up to six months. Teenagers are then eligible for a restricted permit that allows unsupervised driving during daytime hours. Six months later, an unrestricted license is awarded only if the driver's record is free of traffic violations.

As we will see below, a driver's license may be suspended or revoked if a driver fails to comply with motor vehicle laws. Operation of a car without a valid license may be a misdemeanor which could subject the unlicensed driver to a fine and, in some cases, a jail sentence.

Infractions

In a majority of the states, parking and traffic offenses are technically criminal violations even when the maximum punishment is a modest fine. As a result, the violator is entitled to the usual safeguards of the criminal process. A number of states however, have decriminalized parking violations and substituted a civil penalty system. In those jurisdictions, most parking and traffic violations are **infractions** that are not criminal in nature. As civil offenses, they do not subject a driver to any threat of imprisonment. Instead, a judge or hearing officer may require the offender to pay a fine and court costs. In addition, the driver may have her driver's license suspended and be required to attend a driving course. Typical traffic infractions include illegal parking, speeding, disregarding stop signs, no registration or license plates, and failure to wear a seat belt.

Most drivers simply mail a payment with their ticket and the matter is finished. But each state and locality has also established procedures for people to contest tickets. These include the right to an attorney, the right to subpoena witnesses, and the right to a hearing. However, since infractions are not crimes, a police officer is not required to advise a driver of her rights. When a driver fails to either pay the fine or show up for the hearing on the date indicated on the ticket, she may be arrested for *failure to appear.* When this occurs, the state generally suspends the defendant's driving privileges.

http://
www.law.cornell.edu/
states/index.html
provides information
regarding traffic
laws. Choose your
state's home page
to review its traffic
laws.

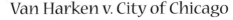

Van Harken v. City of Chicago
103 F.3D 1346 (7TH CIR. 1997)

FACTS   Chicago decriminalized parking violations and substituted a civil penalty system. Under the system, a parking ticket the police officer writes is prima facie evidence of a violation. The owner of the car can either pay the fine written on the ticket (which cannot exceed $100) or challenge the ticket either in writing or in person. These challenges are adjudicated not by regular judges or other governmental employees but by private lawyers whom the city hires as part-time hearing officers. The police officer who wrote the ticket is not expected to participate in the hearing, other than through the ticket itself, which is treated as the equivalent of an affidavit. Ordinarily, the only live participant in the hearing besides the hearing officer is the recipient of the ticket. A manual the city has issued to its hearing officers directs them to conduct a thorough cross-examination of the car owner. The hearing officer can subpoena witnesses (including the police officer) and can consider any documents (photographs, for example) submitted by the car owner. If the hearing officer finds a violation and imposes a fine, the car owner can seek judicial review upon payment of the normal fee for filing a case in court. After Ada Van Harken was found liable for a parking violation, she argued that the city's new system for dealing with parking violations denied her due process for two reasons. First, because such violations were traditionally treated as criminal offenses, she contended that the government could not reclassify them as civil and reduce the procedural safeguards unless it reduced the sanctions as well. Second, she claimed the procedures established by the new ordinance were inadequate even for civil proceedings.

ISSUE   Does the city's system for dealing with parking violations violate due process?

DECISION   No. Van Harken's first argument is without legal merit. Nothing in the due process clause forbids the reclassification of criminal offenses as civil violations. Of course, the state would not be permitted by reclassifying murder as a civil violation to impose the death penalty without the procedural protections that courts have interpreted the Constitution as requiring in capital cases; but the reason would not be the severity of the punishment. A criminal fine of $100 is much less severe than many incontestable civil penalties, so if the government decides to convert it to a civil penalty there is no reason to impose the safeguards of criminal procedure. The traditional system, mindlessly assimilating a parking ticket to an indictment for murder, was archaic and ineffective. Van Harken's second argument also fails. The test for due process when determining if procedural safeguards are inadequate requires a comparison of the costs and benefits of whatever procedure the plaintiff contends is required. If the ticketing police officer was required to attend each hearing, the time and expense to the city would be tremendous. The city would need more police officers. Further, the number of hearings requested would undoubtedly increase because many car owners would think it likely that the officer wouldn't show up—a frequent occurrence at hearings on moving violations. This would require the city to hire more hearing officers. Accordingly, the city's procedures for dealing with parking violations satisfy the requirements of due process.

http://www.vill.edu/Fed-Ct/fedcourt.html

Misdemeanor Offenses

Serious traffic violations are **misdemeanors.** They are criminal offenses. Violations like driving under the influence of alcohol, driving with a suspended license, leaving the scene of an accident, and driving an uninsured vehicle are typical misdemeanor offenses. Penalties for these kinds of traffic violations include fines, court costs, the suspension of driving privileges, and, in some cases, jail time. When charged with a misdemeanor, the driver must appear at the hearing on the scheduled date or he will be charged with failure to appear.

Multiple Violations

Most states provide increased penalties for drivers who commit a certain number of traffic violations within a prescribed time period. These offenders are branded as **habitual traffic offenders.** For instance, the state of Indiana issues a 10-year license suspension for anyone convicted twice in a 10-year period of violations that result in death. Drivers who receive 10 convictions, at least one of which is a serious violation, during a 10-year period may have their licenses suspended for five years.

Many states also assess **points** on the driving record of persons convicted of traffic violations. The number of points allocated to each violation depends on its seriousness. After a driver accumulates a preset number of points, his driver's license is suspended. Satisfactory completion of a driving course may result in the deduction of some points. Further, most states erase points after several years, although they remain on the record for purposes of determining if one is a habitual traffic offender.

Automobiles and Alcohol

Alcohol-related traffic accidents have become a critical social issue in this country. The death and hardship caused by drunk drivers is staggering. For this reason, the laws regulating the operation of an automobile while under the influence of alcohol are becoming stricter and more pervasive.

Driving while intoxicated is a crime and may subject a convicted offender to fines and imprisonment. The conviction of a second drunk driving offense within a prescribed period (often five years) frequently is a felony that triggers much greater fines and longer jail sentences (perhaps three years). In fact, when a drunk driver causes an accident that kills someone, he may even be charged with reckless homicide or murder and imprisoned for as long as 40 years.

All 50 states permit the suspension of the license of drivers who refuse a breath test when they are suspected of drunk driving. Most states require an immediate license suspension or revocation if a driver fails the test. Administering a breath test, and even taking blood samples from a suspected drunken driver over his objection, does not violate his constitutional rights because only physical, rather than testimonial, evidence is involved. To be testimonial, the suspect's communication must make an assertion or disclose information. Thus, the Supreme Court has found unconstitutional the act of requiring an arrested drunk-driving suspect to disclose the date of his sixth birthday because it was testimonial. When eliciting testimonial responses, the police must first advise the accused of his *Miranda* rights.

Fink v. Ryan

673 N.E.2d 281 (Sup. Ct. Ill. 1996)

FACTS   Christopher Fink drove his car into a telephone pole. Afterwards, Fink and a passenger in his car, Jeffrey Almeit, exited the car and found their way to a nearby house. Paramedics and the police were called. When the police arrived, paramedics were immobilizing Fink and Almeit with cervical collars and back boards. The two were transported to a local hospital. Before proceeding to the hospital, police officers investigated the accident scene. The state's Vehicle Code provided that if a traffic accident occurred in which death or serious personal injury resulted and a driver involved in the accident was issued a traffic ticket for a nonequipment offense, the driver would be subject to chemical testing to determine if his driving was impaired by drugs or alcohol. At the hospital, Fink was issued a traffic ticket for failure to reduce speed to avoid an accident. An officer requested that Fink submit to a blood-alcohol content test and Fink was warned of the consequences if he refused—suspension of his driver's license. Fink consented to a blood test and the sample revealed a blood-alcohol concentration above the legal limit. The state sent Fink notice that his driver's license was to be suspended for three months and charged him with driving under the influence of alcohol. Fink challenged the constitutionality of the Vehicle Code, arguing that it allowed an unreasonable search of a driver without probable cause to believe that the driver was chemically impaired.

ISSUE   Does the regulation violate a driver's right to be free from unreasonable searches?

DECISION   No. Under a special needs exception, searches may be reasonable absent individualized suspicion in two types of cases: (1) when the intrusion upon the person to be searched is minor; or (2) when the person to be searched has a diminished expectation of privacy. Illinois has a special need to suspend the licenses of chemically impaired drivers and to deter others from driving while chemically impaired. This specialized need goes beyond the need for normal law enforcement. Thus, a search may be reasonable absent individualized suspicion if a chemical test is nonintrusive or a driver's expectation of privacy has been reduced. Although a driver does not lose all reasonable expectation of privacy simply because the automobile and its use are subject to government regulation, that pervasive regulation reduces a driver's expectation of privacy. While driving on the road, one reasonably expects less privacy than one expects within the confines of a residence. Further, no reasonable driver expects to leave the scene of a serious accident moments after its occurrence. With law enforcement personnel investigating the accident and other personnel attending to the participants' physical conditions, a driver expects less privacy. Finally, the statute premises chemical testing on an arrest as evidenced by the issuance of a ticket for a nonequipment offense. Drivers issued such tickets are released only after posting bail in the form of a current Illinois driver's license, a bond certificate, or cash. Because the movement of an arrested driver is already subject to restrictions, the administering of a chemical test poses a minimal additional intrusion. Thus, we conclude that this statute falls within the special needs exception to the Fourth Amendment.

http://www.findlaw.com/

Traffic Accidents

The number of automobiles on the streets and highways at any one time, coupled with the high speeds at which people travel, makes it highly likely that each of us will be involved in one or more traffic accidents during our life. In light of this fact, it is essential that we have some awareness of our legal duties and potential liabilities when traffic accidents occur.

The Driver's Duties

When a driver is involved in a traffic accident, she is required to stop at the scene. She must then give her name, address, and the registration number of her vehicle to the driver and any occupant of any automobile involved in the accident. She may also be required to actually show her driver's license to those people so they may be more certain of her identity.

While at the scene, the driver must determine if any injured people need medical assistance and, if they do, make arrangements for them to receive such care. The driver also must give immediate notice of the accident to the appropriate law enforcement agency if there has been a death or injury. When there is no death or injury, she may not be required to contact the police unless there is property damage over a prescribed amount. (For example, in Indiana if the damage appears to be at least $750, the police must be notified within 10 days.)

If a driver causes damage to an unattended vehicle, she must locate and inform the driver or operator. If this is not reasonable, she may leave a note on the car giving her name, address, and a brief description of what happened. Likewise, when a driver damages someone's property along a roadway, she should attempt to locate the owner. If she cannot find this person, the driver must contact the appropriate law enforcement officials.

The Driver's Liability for Accidents

Whether or not a driver is liable for death, personal injury, or property damage generally is determined by negligence analysis. Thus, in most cases, the driver is legally responsible if the injuries or damages resulted from his lack of reasonable care. (However, several states have *guest statutes* that preclude passengers from recovering damages from the driver of their vehicle.) In cases where the driver causing the accident committed a traffic violation, the court would use negligence per se if the rule that was violated was designed to protect against accidents like the one that occurred. (Negligence and negligence per se are discussed in Chapter 7.)

The Owner's Liability for Accidents

A car owner may be liable for accidents involving her vehicle even though someone else was driving the car. This might occur under *respondeat superior* if the car was negligently driven by an employee of the owner in the scope of her employment. Further, the owner could be liable under *direct liability* if she negligently permitted an unsafe driver to use the vehicle. (Respondeat superior and direct liability are discussed in Chapter 12.) Further, a number of states hold the owner liable when one of her family members negligently drives the car and injures someone. Finally, the owner of a car may be liable if an accident results from her failure to maintain her vehicle in good repair. (See Figure 22–4.)

Automobile Stops and Searches

People have less privacy rights in their automobiles than they do in their homes. This stems, in part, from the fact that drivers have a reduced expectation of privacy since the ownership and operation of licensed vehicles is so heavily regulated. Further, courts recognize that law enforcement officers literally risk their lives each time they stop a vehicle. Accordingly, they give the police wide latitude to protect their safety from hidden dangers in a car. Finally, because a vehicle can be quickly and easily moved and it takes time to obtain a search warrant, the police are permitted to conduct warrantless searches when they have probable cause to believe there is evidence of a crime in a motor vehicle. (See Figure 22–5.)

Investigative Stops

As a general rule, police must observe specific facts that give them a reasonable basis to suspect a law has been violated before they may stop a vehicle. This could be a moving violation (speeding, drunk driving, etc.) or an equipment offense (no brake light, loud muffler, etc.). However, it is unlikely that a parking violation is a sufficiently serious offense to justify an **investigative stop.** In the case that opened this chapter, Officer Mackel had a legal right to detain and question Stanfield because Stanfield was committing a traffic offense by blocking traffic in the middle of the street.

Figure 22–4:   The Vehicle Owner's Liability for Accidents

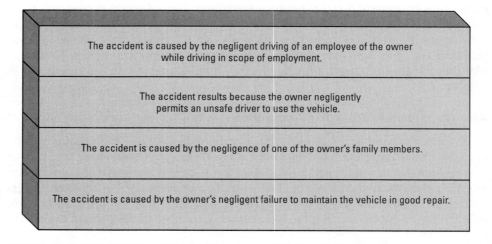

The accident is caused by the negligent driving of an employee of the owner while driving in scope of employment.

The accident results because the owner negligently permits an unsafe driver to use the vehicle.

The accident is caused by the negligence of one of the owner's family members.

The accident is caused by the owner's negligent failure to maintain the vehicle in good repair.

Figure 22–5: Vehicle Stops and Searches

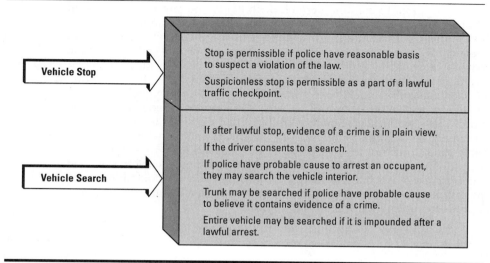

Sometimes police stop a vehicle that appears to be in violation of the law. However, after a brief check they discover that no laws were broken. At that point, further detention and interrogation should cease. The following case considers this issue.

People v. Redinger

906 P.2D 81 (SUP. CT. COLO. 1995)

FACTS Russell Wise, a state patrol officer, observed Thomas Redinger's vehicle traveling along the highway. Because Wise did not see a license plate or temporary sticker on the rear of Redinger's car, he determined that Redinger had violated provisions of Colorado's motor vehicle laws. Wise activated the overhead lights on his police car and Redinger drove to the side of the road. Wise then pulled over behind Redinger, got out of the patrol car, and walked toward Redinger's vehicle. As he neared Redinger's vehicle, Wise observed a valid temporary registration plate properly displayed in the rear window on the driver's side of the car. After Wise reached the driver's side of the vehicle, he explained why he had stopped the car and requested Redinger to produce a driver's license, registration, and proof of insurance. While Redinger was removing his wallet from a jacket pocket, a small clear bag containing a white powdery substance fell onto his leg. Having observed the bag, Wise asked Redinger to step out of the car. He retrieved the bag and asked Redinger to identify its contents. Redinger said the bag contained crystal methamphetamine. When Redinger was later charged with possession of a controlled substance, he argued that the bag should be excluded from evidence because the search was illegal.

ISSUE Did Wise have the right to detain and question Redinger after he learned that no violation of the motor vehicle law had occurred?

continued

DECISION   No. Police officers may require drivers of motor vehicles to stop and to respond to investigative questions if they have a reasonable suspicion that the driver has committed or is about to commit a crime. Such limited governmental intrusion without probable cause is justified as a consequence of the mobile nature of motor vehicles and the desire to encourage conscientious police investigations. The stop, which is investigatory rather than accusatory in nature, allows police to determine whether the initial reasonable suspicion was justified. When, as here, the purpose for which the investigative stop was instituted has been accomplished and no other reasonable suspicion exists to support further investigation, there is no justification for continued detention and interrogation of citizens. Wise stopped Redinger's vehicle because he had a reasonable suspicion that Redinger had violated the motor vehicle law. At the moment he stopped Redinger's car, Wise was authorized to investigate that reasonable suspicion. Prior to questioning Redinger, Wise learned that his initial suspicion was unfounded and that no violation of the motor vehicle law had occurred. The purpose of the initial investigation having been satisfied, and absent any other basis for detaining or questioning Redinger, Wise's conduct in requiring Redinger to produce information was unwarranted.

Vehicle Searches

After lawfully stopping a car, police may order its occupants out of the vehicle. When the stop was triggered by a nonarrestable offense (illegal turn, missing mirror) and there is no probable cause to believe the car contains evidence of a specific crime, police may not search the vehicle without the driver's consent. However, if they see evidence of a crime in plain view, the police may arrest the occupants and search the inside of the car.

In the case that opened this chapter, the court was concerned about the tremendous risks police officers face when they approach a vehicle with heavily tinted windows. In fact, for just that reason, 28 states have enacted laws either regulating or prohibiting tinted windows. The court ruled that the officer acted reasonably in opening the passenger door. Because the cocaine was then in plain view, it was admissible as evidence.

When the police have probable cause to arrest an occupant of a car, they may search the vehicle's interior including the contents of any containers within the passenger compartment. They may not search the trunk, absent the driver's consent, unless they have probable cause to believe it contains evidence of a crime. However, if subsequent to an arrest the car is towed and impounded, police may search the entire vehicle so they may take an inventory of its contents.

Ethical Issue

Our traffic laws are so numerous and the possibility of minor equipment failure on most cars is so great that police generally could lawfully stop most vehicles. Yet the police seldom stop cars for such minor violations. Is it right for police to stop cars on the pretext of correcting a minor violation when, in reality, they are hoping to discover evidence of a greater crime?

Traffic Checkpoints

There is an exception to the rule that police must have a reasonable basis for believing that a law has been broken before they may stop a motor vehicle. The Supreme Court has permitted law enforcement officials to make suspicionless stops of vehicles at certain types of **traffic checkpoints.** Police regularly erect these roadblocks to screen cars for unlicensed drivers, safety violations, drunken drivers, illegal drugs, and illegal aliens.

In the past, many states required that the time and location of traffic checkpoints be publicized in advance so drivers could avoid them. However, absent such a regulation, an announcement is not necessary. Courts demand that a checkpoint be planned and operated in a manner that minimizes the discretion of the officers staffing the roadblock. Further, they insist that the checkpoints be no more intrusive than necessary. The next case examines these concerns.

State v. Damask
936 S.W.2d 565 (Sup. Ct. Mo. 1996)

FACTS The Franklin County Sheriff's Department set up a drug enforcement checkpoint at the eastbound I-44 exit where Highway AH crosses I-44 by an overpass. Franklin County had been operating such checkpoints for several months in an attempt to thwart drug trafficking along I-44, a known drug corridor. The sheriff's department placed two signs that read "DRUG ENFORCEMENT CHECKPOINT ONE MILE AHEAD" approximately one-quarter mile west of exit 242 on both sides of the eastbound lanes of I-44. Exit 242 is in a remote area and offers no services to travelers. Eastbound travelers arrive at exit 242 after recently passing exits offering gas, food, and lodging services. A motorist would have little reason to leave I-44 at exit 242 unless he was a local resident. Contrary to the signs along the highway, the sheriff's deputies set up the checkpoint at the top of the eastbound exit 242 ramp. Eastbound cars exiting I-44 found fully marked law enforcement vehicles at the stop sign at the top of the exit ramp. The officers' written procedures instructed them to approach a vehicle and check for a valid driver's license and registration. They also were to ask the motorist why he stopped at that exit. If the response did not arouse suspicion, the motorist was permitted to leave. If the circumstances aroused suspicion, the officers were to ask for permission to search the vehicle. If the driver refused, the police would use a drug-sniffing dog to examine the exterior of the car. When Richard Damask stopped at the checkpoint, he was asked why he exited there. He stated that he was turning around to get food. However, the police saw a cup of warm coffee and fast food bags in the car. He also appeared nervous. After Damask denied the police permission to search his car, an officer approached with the police dog. The dog alerted to the trunk. The police then searched the trunk and found a duffle bag filled with packages of marijuana. The entire stop and search took approximately five minutes.

ISSUE Was the stop and search lawful?

continued

DECISION   Yes. Generally, seizures that are not based upon a particularized suspicion of criminal activity are unreasonable. However, stopping motorists on public highways may be reasonable even in the absence of such suspicion as long as they strike a reasonable balance between the public interest in preventing criminal activity and the individual's right to be free from arbitrary interference by law officers. In addressing this balance, courts must weigh three elements: (1) the gravity of the state's interest served by the checkpoint; (2) the checkpoint's effectiveness in advancing the public interest; and (3) the degree to which the checkpoint interferes with or intrudes upon motorists. As to the first prong, it is clear that the state's interest in interdicting drug trafficking is beyond serious dispute. The second prong also is met. The Franklin County checkpoint was set up along a popular route for the transport of narcotics. Further, the remoteness of exit 242 made it unlikely that travelers, other than local residents, would exit at that point unless they were trying to avoid the checkpoint they believed was one mile further down the interstate. Finally, a constitutionally permissible checkpoint is designed so as to minimize both interference with legitimate traffic and the amount of discretion the field officers may wield in operating the roadblock. On average, vehicles were stopped for no more than two minutes and the initial investigation was limited to a check of license and registration and questions as to why the driver exited there. The officers had little discretion. They were required to follow specific written procedures. And, perhaps most important, the plans eliminated all discretion as to which cars would be stopped by requiring that all exiting vehicles be stopped. Because this checkpoint was operated in a nondiscriminatory fashion as to the initial stops and because it effectively advanced an important state interest, with minimal intrusion to motorists, it is constitutional.

QUESTIONS AND PROBLEM CASES

1. What is an implied warranty of merchantability? Does it accompany every sale of an automobile?

2. When may the police lawfully stop a motor vehicle?

3. What guarantees does an automobile mechanic have that he will be paid for repairs he makes on a motor vehicle?

4. What is the difference between a vehicle's certificate of title and its certificate of registration?

5. A rule promulgated by the Louisiana Motor Vehicle Commission prohibits the use of the term "invoice" in any advertisement for the sale of a motor vehicle. The regulation permits an automobile dealer to advertise the actual proposed selling price of a car or an amount above or below the "Manufacturer's Suggested Retail Price," the standardized price set by the industry for any model car with the same equipment. The purpose of the regulation is to eliminate misleading advertisements. Joe Conte Toyota, an automobile dealership, wishes to run the following advertisement in a local newspaper offering automobiles for sale: "*$49.00 over Factory Invoice.**" The advertisement copy would include a disclaimer: *Dealer invoice may not reflect actual dealer cost. Or in the alternative the disclaimer might read: *Invoice price indicates amount dealer paid distributor for car. Due to various factory rebates, holdbacks and incentives, actual dealer cost is lower than invoice price. The dealership has asked you if its ad, with either of the disclaimers, would violate state law. Is the ad permissible?

6. Sharon Wright signed a form contract to purchase a used Subaru from T & B Auto

Sales. The contract stated, in capital letters: "UNLESS DEALER FURNISHES BUYER WITH A SEPARATE WRITTEN WARRANTY OR SERVICE CONTRACT . . . DEALER HEREBY DISCLAIMS ALL WARRANTIES, EXPRESS OR IMPLIED, INCLUDING ANY IMPLIED WARRANTIES OF MER-CHANTABILITY . . . ON ALL USED VEHI-CLES WHICH ARE HEREBY SOLD—AS IS—NOT EXPRESSLY WARRANTED OR GUARANTEED." When Wright took posses-sion of the car, she received a T & B Auto Sales Used Vehicle Guarantee that stated, in part: "The automobile is warranted for a period of 30 days from the date of delivery, or 1,000 miles, whichever comes first. This 50-50 guarantee means that the dealer will make any necessary mechanical repairs in his shop at a cost to the buyer of only 50 percent of the dealer's current list on both parts and labor, except where such repairs have become nec-essary by abuse, negligence, or collision." The fifth clause stated: "No other guarantees, representations, or agreements expressed or implied have been made to the buyer." Wright returned the car for repairs during the first month when it was overheating and the oil light stayed on continuously. Wright had repeated mechanical problems with the car for the next six months until, finally, it would not start at all. Wright then had the car towed to another garage where it was discovered that the heads on the engine were reversed and on the wrong side. This caused the engine to overheat and allowed oil and water to mix. As a result, the engine was near melt-down. After being forced to replace the engine, Wright sued T & B for her towing charges, repair costs, and loss of the use of the car. At the time of the engine replacement she had driven the car nearly 10,000 miles. Is T & B liable to Wright?

7. When Thompson discovered that his trans-mission was leaking, he took the car to Mr. Transmission, a transmission repair business. Thompson told the mechanic he wanted the transmission seals replaced and signed a work order. He expected to pay their adver-tised fee of $69.95. When Thompson returned for his car, he found that the transmission, which did not have to be taken apart to replace the seals, had been removed from the car and was disassembled. He was told that the transmission would have to be rebuilt or replaced and that installing a rebuilt transmis-sion for $377 would be the quickest solution. Thompson had Mr. Transmission install a rebuilt transmission, and paid for it under protest since he had not authorized his trans-mission to be disassembled. When the rebuilt transmission began to leak, Thompson sued Mr. Transmission for unauthorized disassem-bly and destruction of his operating transmis-sion. He requested both actual and punitive damages. Is Thompson entitled to such dam-ages? Explain.

8. John Allred was stopped for a driving infrac-tion. He was not advised of his *Miranda* rights before being asked to recite the alphabet from "c" to "w" at the roadside, in the presence of three police officers. Allred instead recited from "e" to "w." Should the results of Allred's counting test be suppressed because his con-stitutional rights were violated?

9. Dennis Tyler got a parking ticket issued by a deputy sheriff of Alameda County. The ticket indicated he had parked in a bus zone and that the penalty for the violation was $250. Tyler submitted a timely request to the county for initial administrative review, asserting that his car was next to, but not in, the bus zone. The county issued a decision, finding no grounds to warrant cancellation of the park-ing ticket. The printed notice informed Tyler that if he was not satisfied with the findings of the initial review, he could contest the decision to a hearing officer by sending a written explanation of the reasons for contest-ing the decision plus the full amount of the parking fine. If he prevailed at the hearing, the parking penalty would be refunded. Tyler argued that requiring him to prepay the park-ing penalty as a precondition to filing an appeal denied him due process of law. Courts use a balancing test to determine if the gov-ernment may require payment of a penalty in

advance of an administrative hearing. The test requires the court to weigh three factors: the extent of the interest affected, the risk of erroneous deprivation, and the burdens on the government. May the county require Tyler to prepay the ticket before considering his appeal?

10. The Michigan State Police established a sobriety checkpoint program, following an advisory committee's guidelines. In the first hour- and-fifteen-minute check, 126 cars passed through the checkpoint. The average delay per car was 25 seconds as police officers briefly examined drivers for signs of intoxication. Two drivers were detained for field sobriety tests, one of whom was arrested for driving under the influence. A third driver who did not stop was arrested for driving under the influence. May the police lawfully conduct the sobriety checkpoints? Explain.

CHAPTER 23

LAW AND THE INTERNET

Jake Baker, a University of Michigan student, posted several stories on a "sex stories" newsgroup on the Internet. One story graphically described the torture, rape, and murder of a woman. Further, in this story he named the victim—a female student with whom he had taken a class. The newsgroup to which Baker's story was posted is an electronic bulletin board, the contents of which are publicly available via the Internet. A Canadian read the stories and he and Baker exchanged e-mail discussing how they could kidnap a woman. When a Michigan graduate read the postings and complained to school officials, the FBI began an investigation. Baker was arrested and charged with five counts of a federal crime—the interstate transmission by electronic mail of a threat to kidnap or injure. Each count was punishable by up to five years in prison. After being charged, Baker was suspended from the university. He argued that his postings were entitled to First Amendment protection.

United States v. Baker, 890 F.Supp. 1375 (E.D.Mich. 1995).

Should the charges against Baker be dismissed?
What rights are available to Internet users?
Are the traditional legal rules regulating conduct
   applicable to Internet users?

Introduction

The Internet, a worldwide network of computers, was created almost 30 years ago as a research medium for scientists and academics. By the early 1990s, with the advent of the World Wide Web, businesses and consumers discovered the wonders of electronic communication. Like any new frontier, one of the Internet's initial attractions may have been its lawlessness. It allowed anybody to publish anything, with the potential to reach millions of households around the world.

Today, this renegade spirit is colliding head-on with growing demands that governmental regulators tame the Internet's Wild West mentality. As with all new frontiers, the permanent settlers are arriving. More and more businesses have set up shop on the Internet. Schools are incorporating it into their curricula and encouraging children to tap into the Web. Even the traditional media companies are expanding to the multimedia World Wide Web. Finally, numerous governmental agencies at the state and federal level are rushing to establish their own Web sites. With each new arrival there are increasing calls for legal controls to provide order to what had once been a virtual free-for-all.

The extent to which many traditional legal and constitutional doctrines are transferable to the Internet is not always clear. For instance, today with an investment of less than one thousand dollars any person can "publish" a message that simultaneously reaches millions of people across the country. Is this what the Founding Fathers envisioned when they crafted the First Amendment's protection for freedom of the press? And our legal definition of pornography is based on "community standards." If sexually explicit materials originating in California are downloaded in Tennessee, which "community" decides if the photos are pornographic? These are just two of the legal controversies that have confronted courts and regulators. Web users should develop a general understanding of the areas of the law most frequently implicated by Internet use. These include free speech, privacy, intellectual property, criminal law, contracting, and jurisdiction. Armed with this knowledge, they can better identify the current rules governing the Internet and more accurately predict future regulatory efforts.

Chapter Overview

The chapter opens with a look at the First Amendment issues implicated by regulation of the Internet. These include obscenity, child pornography, indecent materials, and online advertising. Attention is then turned to three important types of online misconduct: defamation, computer crime, and online torts. Personal jurisdiction and privacy rights also are discussed in this section. This is followed by a look at two forms of intellectual property that are threatened by electronic communications: copyrights and trademarks. The intellectual property section also examines the legal issues implicated by online domain names. The chapter closes with a brief overview of the legal aspects of contracting in cyberspace.

http://
www.law.cornell.
edu/constitution/
constitution.
billofrights.html#
amendmenti
contains the text of
the First
Amendment.

Freedom of Expression

Attempts to regulate online activity often implicate First Amendment concerns. After all, electronic mail (e-mail), mailing list services (listservs), newsgroups, and chat rooms provide increasingly popular means of communication. And the World Wide Web may be compared to a vast library containing millions of indexed publications that are readily available to readers. Likewise, it is a vast shopping mall offering access to a wide variety of goods and services. Finally, the Web allows people and organizations to quickly and easily communicate on any number of topics with a worldwide audience. Accordingly, the First Amendment's protection for free expression may be the most important source of legal rights on the Internet.

Regulation of Speech

The constitutional safeguards for free speech are not absolute. (Freedom of expression is discussed in Chapter 5.) For instance, the First Amendment protects against only governmental interference with speech. Thus, private online companies may place any number of restrictions on the exchange of information by their members. Further, governmental restrictions on online expression may pass constitutional scrutiny if they meet certain standards. For instance, the government may not regulate the content of noncommercial messages unless the restriction (1) is furthering a compelling governmental interest and (2) interferes with the expression no more than is necessary to advance the government's interest. Consider the following case.

http:// *wings.buffalo.edu/ Complaw* provides information and links about computer law.

American Civil Liberties Union v. Zell

977 F. Supp. 1228 (N.D. Ga. 1997)

FACTS   Georgia passed a law making it a crime for any person to knowingly "transmit any data through a computer network for the purpose of setting up, maintaining, operating, or exchanging data with an electronic mailbox . . . [or] homepage . . . if such data uses any individual name . . . to falsely identify the person." A variety of Internet users challenged the constitutionality of the statute. They argued that it has tremendous implications for Internet users, many of whom "falsely identify" themselves on a regular basis for the purpose of communicating about sensitive topics without subjecting themselves to ostracism or embarrassment.

ISSUE   Is the regulation constitutional?

DECISION   No. Enforcement of the statute should be enjoined because it imposes content-based restrictions which are not narrowly tailored to achieve the state's purported compelling interest. Because the identity of the speaker is no different from other components of a document's contents that the author is free to include or exclude, the statute's prohibition of Internet transmissions which "falsely identify" the sender constitutes a presumptively invalid content-based restriction. The state may impose content-based restrictions only to promote a "compelling state interest" and only through the use of "the least restrictive means" to further the articulated interest. The statute's asserted purpose, fraud prevention, is a compelling interest. However, the statute is not narrowly tailored to achieve that end and instead sweeps innocent, protected speech within its scope. Specifically, by its plain language the criminal prohibition applies regardless of whether a speaker has any intent to deceive or whether deception actually occurs. Therefore, it could apply to a wide range of transmissions which "falsely identify" the sender, but are not "fraudulent" within the specific meaning of the criminal code.

Online Obscenity

Computer bulletin board systems have been heavily criticized as major distributors of obscene material. In response to consumer complaints, private online companies and public libraries with Internet access sites have experimented with blocking access to objectionable materials. Further, law enforcement officials regularly conduct sting operations to uncover and prosecute those who disseminate obscene materials.

Obscene expression is not entitled to First Amendment protection. Thus, once a particular message is found to be obscene, its author or publisher is automatically subject to criminal liability since such expression may be banned completely. Courts have fashioned a three-part test for deciding if expression is obscene: (1) whether the average person applying contemporary community standards would find the work, taken as a whole, appeals to the prurient interest; (2) whether the work depicts or describes, in a patently offensive way, sexual conduct specifically prohibited by local law; and (3) whether the work, taken as a whole, lacks serious literary, artistic, political, or scientific value. (See Figure 23–1.)

State and federal laws prohibiting the distribution of obscene materials pose special problems for Internet users. This is because sexually explicit materials may be simultaneously downloaded in numerous communities throughout the country. Yet each community is free to determine whether the particular material is obscene. Thus, material that is legally permitted in one community may be found obscene, and illegal, in another. Despite the confusion this can create for online distributors, courts permit prosecution to be brought either in the district of dispatch or the district of receipt, and obscenity is determined by the standards of the community where the trial takes place.

Figure 23–1:   Online Obscenity Test

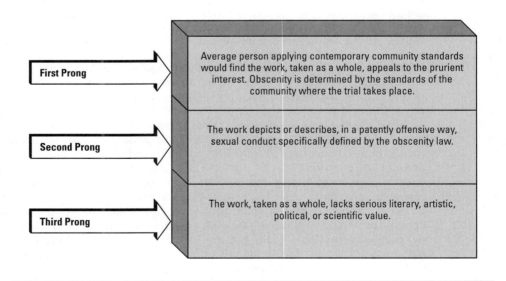

Child Pornography

Like obscenity, child pornography does not receive any First Amendment protection. In fact, material that is not otherwise obscene may be completely prohibited if it depicts children engaging in sexual conduct. Courts have liberally construed the ban against child pornography for several reasons. First, visual depictions of minors participating in sexual activities threaten the welfare of children by creating a permanent record of such activity. Second, the advertising and selling of such materials increases the demand for further sexual exploitation of minors.

The *Child Pornography Prevention Act of 1996* (CPPA) was enacted to prevent the use of computer technology to convey the impression that children were used in sexually explicit photographs or images. The CPPA recognizes that computer technology makes possible the altering of otherwise innocent pictures of children to create visual depictions of those same children engaging in sexual activities. Congress believed that computer-generated images depicting children participating in sexual activities are just as dangerous to the welfare of minors as material using actual children. In passing the legislation, Congress concluded that the dangers of child pornography are not limited to its effect on the children actually used in the photographs. It recognized a third rationale for prohibiting child pornography: it stimulates the sexual appetites and encourages the activities of child molesters and pedophiles. The following case upholds the constitutionality of the CPPA.

Free Speech Coalition v. Reno

1997 U.S. DIST. LEXIS 12212 (N.D. CAL. 1997)

FACTS Congress passed the *Child Pornography Prevention Act of 1996* to combat the use of computer technology to produce pornography that conveys the impression that children were used in the photographs or images. In passing this legislation, Congress recognized that the dangers of child pornography are not limited to its effect on the children actually used in the pornography. Additionally, child pornography stimulates the sexual appetites and encourages the activities of child molesters and pedophiles, who use it to feed their sexual fantasies. Child pornography also is used by child molesters and pedophiles as a device to break down the resistance and inhibitions of their victims or targets of molestation, especially when these are children. Congress recognized that computer technology is capable of altering perfectly innocent pictures of children to create visual depictions of those children engaging in any imaginable form of sexual conduct. These computer generated pictures are often indistinguishable from photographic images of actual children. Computer generated images which appear to depict minors engaging in sexually explicit conduct are just as dangerous to the well-being of children as material using actual children. The statute defines child pornography as *"any visual depiction, including any photograph, film, video picture, or computer or computer-generated image or picture, whether made or produced by electronic, mechanical, or other means, of sexually explicit conduct, where (A) the production of such visual depiction involves the use of a minor engaging in sexually explicit conduct; (B) such visual depiction is, or appears to be, of a minor engaging in sexually explicit conduct."* The statute provides an affirmative defense for violations if *"(1) the alleged child pornography was produced using an*

continued

actual person or persons engaging in sexually explicit conduct; (2) each such person was an adult at the time the material was produced; and (3) the defendant did not advertise, promote, present, describe, or distribute the material in such a manner as to convey the impression that it is or contains a visual depiction of a minor engaging in sexually explicit conduct."

ISSUE   Does this child pornography statute violate the First Amendment?

DECISION   No. The government may impose reasonable restrictions on the time, place, or manner of protected speech, provided the restrictions are justified without reference to the content of the regulated speech, that they are narrowly tailored to serve a significant governmental interest, and that they leave open ample alternative channels for communication of the information. The statute is content-neutral. It clearly was passed in order to prevent the secondary effects of the child pornography industry. The statute clearly advances important and compelling government interests. These are the protection of children from the harms brought on by child pornography and the industry that such pornography has created. Furthermore, it burdens no more speech than necessary in order to protect children from the harms of child pornography. Although there may be a degree of ambiguity in the phrase "appears to be a minor," any ambiguity can be resolved by examining whether the work was marketed and advertised as child pornography. Given that the goal of the statute is to prevent the digital manipulation of images to create child pornography even when no children were actually used in the production of the material, the statute meets that goal by regulating the narrowest range of materials that might fall within the targeted category. Congress clearly intended to exclude from its reach materials that do not involve the actual or apparent depiction of children.

Indecent Materials

http://
*FloridaLawFirm.com/
infolaw.html* contains
cases, documents,
articles, and links on
topics in this section.

Much of the sexually explicit material on the Internet is neither obscene nor child pornography. It is merely indecent. Such expression is entitled to First Amendment protection and, therefore, cannot be entirely prohibited by the government. However, it can be regulated if the government is furthering a compelling interest in the least intrusive manner.

For many years, the courts have permitted broad regulation of indecent materials that are aired on radio or television. In part, this has been because of the pervasive influence that the broadcast media have on our daily lives. Courts also have recognized the unique accessibility of radio and television to children. Congress cited these same concerns when it enacted the *Communications Decency Act of 1996.* That statute sought to criminalize the transmission of indecent or patently offensive displays over the Internet.

It is not clear that indecency on the Internet creates the same threats as its counterpart on radio and television. Internet users seldom encounter indecent materials accidentally. Most sexually explicit images are preceded by warnings as to their content. This is not the same as radio or television where a listener or viewer may accidentally discover an indecent broadcast. Further, systems have been developed that assist parents in controlling the materials that may be accessed on a home computer. The U.S. Supreme Court took these differences into consideration when it struck down part of the *Communications Decency Act* in the following case.

Reno v. American Civil Liberties Union

117 S.Ct. 2329 (U.S. Sup. Ct. 1997)

FACT   The *Communications Decency Act of 1996* contains two provisions that have direct application to the Internet. First, the "indecent transmission" provision prohibits the knowing transmission of obscene or indecent messages to any recipient under 18 years of age. Second, the "patently offensive display" provision prohibits the knowing sending or displaying of patently offensive messages in a manner that is available to a person under 18 years of age. The breadth of these two prohibitions is qualified by two affirmative defenses. One covers those who take "good faith, reasonable, effective, and appropriate actions" to restrict access by minors to the prohibited communications. The other encompasses those who restrict access to covered material by requiring certain designated forms of age proof, such as a verified credit card or an adult identification number or code.

ISSUE   Do the "indecent transmission" and "patently offensive display" provisions violate the First Amendment?

DECISION   Yes. There are ambiguities concerning the scope of the statute's coverage. For instance, each of the two provisions uses a different linguistic form. The first uses the word "indecent," while the second speaks of material that depicts or describes in terms "patently offensive." This will provoke uncertainty among speakers about how the two standards relate to each other, and just what they mean. This vagueness is a matter of special concern for two reasons. First, the statute is content-based regulation of speech that has an obvious chilling effect on free speech. Second, this is a criminal statute which threatens violators with penalties including up to two years in prison for each violation. The severity of criminal sanctions may well cause speakers to remain silent rather than communicate even arguably unlawful words, ideas, and images. Given the vague contours of the coverage of the statute, it unquestionably silences some speakers whose messages would be entitled to constitutional protection. Further, it lacks the precision that the First Amendment requires when a statute regulates the content of speech. In order to deny minors access to potentially harmful speech, the statute effectively suppresses a large amount of speech that adults have a constitutional right to receive and to address to one another. That burden on adult speech is unacceptable if less restrictive alternatives would be at least as effective in achieving the legitimate purpose that the statute was enacted to serve. In evaluating the free speech rights of adults, we have made it perfectly clear that sexual expression which is indecent but not obscene is protected by the First Amendment. It is true that we have repeatedly recognized the governmental interest in protecting children from harmful materials. But that interest does not justify an unnecessarily broad suppression of speech addressed to adults. It is at least clear that the strength of the government's interest in protecting minors is not equally strong throughout the coverage of this broad statute. For instance, a parent who sent his 17-year-old college freshman information on birth control via e-mail could be incarcerated even though neither he, his child, nor anyone in their home community, found the material "indecent" or "patently offensive" if the college town's community thought otherwise. The first provision may continue to block obscene speech since it enjoys no First Amendment protection. But the statute cannot stand as it relates to indecent and patently offensive material.

http://www.law.vill.edu/Fed-Ct/fedcourt.html

——————————————————— Ethical Issue ———————————————————

A Virginia public library recently implemented an Internet policy requiring that all library computers with Internet access use filtering software to block child pornography, obscene material, and material deemed harmful to juveniles. However, several library patrons have filed suit, arguing that the library is using filtering software that blocks legitimate, non-pornographic information. Should public libraries limit the access of adults to offensive but nonpornographic materials?

Online Advertising

The World Wide Web promises to drastically alter the way in which businesses advertise their goods and services. Web sites and electronic bulletin boards now permit interactive contact with potential customers around the world. This allows businesses to tailor their advertising to the wants and needs of individual customers rather than broadcast a single message to a wide audience.

Regulating Commercial Speech

As a form of commercial speech, an online advertisement is entitled to less First Amendment protection than is noncommercial speech. For instance, false, misleading, or deceptive ads may be prohibited entirely. Further, the government needs only to establish that it has a substantial interest (something less than a compelling interest) to justify regulating commercial speech. (The commercial speech test is explained in Chapter 5.)

Computer Junk Mail

The increasing use of computers for commercial purposes has led to growing complaints over the online version of junk mail. Modern mass advertisers use automated programs to compile the e-mail addresses of Internet users. They then hawk their wares at minimal cost by sending millions of unsolicited ads to e-mail users. Private online companies complain that these mass e-mailings, known as **spam,** overload their e-mail servers and threaten to clog the Internet.

There are several remedies available to private online companies whose members are being bombarded by spam. First, they may take private actions to block the mass mailings from reaching their system. This is not illegal since, as private companies, they are not required to grant access to advertisers. Second, they may sue the advertisers for trespass. This remedy is discussed later in the chapter in *CompuServe v. Cyber Promotions.*

Online Misconduct ▰▰▰▰▰▰▰▰▰▰

http://
www.netlaw.com or
http://FloridaLawFirm.
com/iplaw/index.html
contains cases, information, and links on various computer law issues.

The steady movement of people and businesses to cyberspace is carrying human interaction to new levels. And, as with any new frontier, friction among the inhabitants is inevitable. Yet many Internet users strenuously resist the extension of traditional legal rules and regulations to cyberspace, calling instead for self-regulation. Despite this resistance, law enforcement officials are actively policing the Internet to discourage serious misconduct and protect the rights of the innocent.

Jurisdiction

Law enforcement officials and private individuals generally cannot enforce rules against online misconduct without the assistance of the courts. However, a court cannot adjudicate a misconduct case unless it has personal jurisdiction over the defendant. For a court to have jurisdiction, the defendant either must be a resident of the forum state or, if he is a nonresident, must have knowingly or purposefully availed himself of the privilege of doing business in the state. For crimes and intentional torts, personal jurisdiction is even easier to find. They generally subject an online offender to the jurisdiction of the state where the victim resides.

Cybersell v. Cybersell

130 F.3D 414 (9TH CIR. 1997)

FACTS   Cybersell (Cybersell AZ) is an Arizona corporation that provides Internet and Web advertising and marketing services, including consulting. It filed to register the name "Cybersell" as a service mark in August 1994. The application was approved and the grant was published in October 1995. Cybersell operated a Web site using the mark from August 1994 through February 1995. The site was then taken down for reconstruction. In the summer of 1995, a Florida corporation operating under the name Cybersell (Cybersell FL) was formed to provide business consulting services for strategic management and marketing on the Web. At the time Cybersell FL chose its name, Cybersell AZ had no home page on the Web and had not yet received its service mark. Cybersell FL created a Web page. The home page had a logo with the name "CyberSell" at the top. It proclaimed in large letters "Welcome to CyberSell." When Cybersell AZ discovered the Cybersell FL Web page, it sent an e-mail asserting that it held the "Cybersell" service mark. Cybersell immediately changed the name of Cybersell FL to WebHorizons and replaced the CyberSell logo at the top of its Web page with WebHorizons. However, the WebHorizons page still said "Welcome to CyberSell." Cybersell AZ filed a complaint in a federal district court in Arizona alleging trademark infringement. Cybersell FL moved to dismiss for lack of personal jurisdiction.

ISSUE   Does Arizona have personal jurisdiction over the Florida corporation?

DECISION   No. We use a three-part test to determine whether a district court may exercise specific jurisdiction over a nonresident defendant: (1) The nonresident defendant must do some act or consummate some transaction with the forum or perform some act by which he purposefully avails himself of the privilege of conducting activities in the forum, thereby invoking the benefits or protections; (2) the claim must be one which arises out of or results from the defendant's forum-related activities; and (3) exercise of jurisdiction must be reasonable. The "purposeful availment" requirement is satisfied if the defendant has taken deliberate action within the forum state or if he has created continuing obligations to forum residents. So far as we are aware, no court has ever held that an Internet advertisement alone is sufficient to subject the advertiser to jurisdiction in the plaintiff's home state. Here, Cybersell FL has conducted no commercial activity over the Internet in Arizona. All that it did was post an

continued

essentially passive home page on the Web, using the name "CyberSell." While there is no question that anyone, anywhere could access that home page and thereby learn of the services offered, we cannot see how from that fact alone it can be inferred that Cybersell FL deliberately directed its merchandising efforts toward Arizona residents. Cybersell FL did nothing to encourage people in Arizona to access its site, and there is no evidence that any part of its business (let alone a continuous part of its business) was sought or achieved in Arizona. In short, Cybersell FL has done no act and has consummated no transaction, nor has it performed any act by which it purposefully availed itself of the privilege of conducting activities, in Arizona, thereby invoking the benefits and protections of Arizona law. We conclude that the essentially passive nature of Cybersell FL's activity in posting a home page on the World Wide Web does not qualify as purposeful activity invoking the benefits and protection of Arizona. As it engaged in no commercial activity and had no other contacts via the Internet or otherwise in Arizona, Cybersell FL lacks sufficient minimum contacts with Arizona for personal jurisdiction to be asserted over it.

http://www.law.vill.edu/Fed-Ct/fedcourt.html

Defamatory Speech

Online discussions often are characterized by a rough and tumble attitude. This may stem, in part, from the fact that users often converse anonymously. In many respects, this spontaneity is a refreshing departure from the social niceties that moderate most face-to-face encounters. However, because bulletin board messages may reach millions of Internet users within a matter of seconds, disparaging remarks have a tremendous capacity to injure people, products, or businesses.

Defamation Law

Under traditional law, people who publish false statements that injure another's reputation may be liable for the intentional tort of **defamation.** Oral defamation is called *slander,* and written defamation is *libel.* (Defamation is discussed in Chapter 7.) False statements about a business's products or service create a cause of action for *disparagement.*

Defamatory or disparaging statements are not actionable unless they are published, false, and injurious. Publication occurs when the defendant communicates the false statement to someone other than the plaintiff. In many defamation cases, the plaintiff has difficulty proving injury. However, when the false statement was written, the courts presume that such injury occurred. Further, injury is presumed when the false statement accuses the plaintiff of having committed a serious crime or of having a "loathsome" disease.

Defamation Liability

Under traditional tort law, anyone who falsely publishes a defamatory or disparaging statement is liable to the injured plaintiff. This often is difficult in the online context since many Internet users operate under an alias. However, some online service companies, when confronted by a court subpoena, have revealed an author's true identity.

Some injured plaintiffs have sued the online service company that operated the bulletin board where the defamatory statement appeared. Originally, courts made the determination of liability turn on whether the bulletin board operator was acting as a distributor or publisher. If the company was a distributor, it was considered to be a passive conduit that could not be held liable absent some showing of fault. Publishers, on the other hand, were companies who exercised editorial control over the content of the bulletin board. Because of their active role, they could be liable as if they had originally written the false statement.

The distinction between publishers and distributors seems to have been abolished by passage of the *Communications Decency Act*. That statute immunizes computer service providers from liability for information that originates with third parties. The following case, *Zeran v. America Online,* confronts this issue head-on.

Zeran v. America Online

129 F.3D 327 (4TH CIR. 1997)

FACTS   On April 25, 1995, an unidentified person posted a message on an America Online (AOL) bulletin board advertising "Naughty Oklahoma T-Shirts." The posting described the sale of shirts featuring offensive and tasteless slogans related to the April 19th bombing of the federal building in Oklahoma City. Those interested in purchasing the shirts were instructed to call "Ken" at Ken Zeran's telephone number in Seattle, Washington. As a result of this anonymously perpetrated prank, Zeran received a high volume of calls, comprised primarily of angry derogatory messages, but also including death threats. Zeran could not change his phone number because he relied on its availability to the public in running a business out of his home. Later that day, Zeran called AOL and informed a company representative of his predicament. The employee assured Zeran that the posting would be removed from AOL's bulletin board, but explained that as a matter of policy AOL would not post a retraction. The next day, an unknown person posted another message advertising additional shirts with new tasteless slogans related to the Oklahoma City bombing. Again, interested buyers were told to call Zeran's phone number, to ask for "Ken," and to "please call back if busy" due to high demand. The angry, threatening calls intensified. Over the next four days, an unidentified party continued to post messages on AOL's bulletin board, advertising additional items with still more offensive slogans. During this time period, Zeran called AOL repeatedly and was told by company representatives that the individual account from which the messages were posted would soon be closed. By April 30th, Zeran was receiving an abusive phone call approximately every two minutes. Zeran sued AOL, claiming it was liable for the defamatory speech initiated by the third party. He argued that once he notified AOL of the unidentified third party's hoax, AOL had a duty to remove the defamatory posting promptly, to notify its subscribers of the messages's false nature, and to effectively screen future defamatory material. AOL contended that the *Communications Decency Act of 1996* immunizes computer service providers like AOL from liability for information that originates with third parties.

continued

ISSUE   Is AOL immune from liability?

DECISION   Yes. One of the many means by which individuals access the Internet is through an interactive computer service. AOL is just such an interactive computer service. Much of the information transmitted over its network originates with the company's millions of subscribers. They may transmit information privately via electronic mail, or they may communicate publicly by posting messages on AOL bulletin boards, where the messages may be read by any AOL subscriber. The pertinent language of the *Communications Decency Act* states: "No provider or user of an interactive computer service shall be treated as the publisher or speaker of any information provided by another information content provider." By its plain language, it creates a federal immunity to any cause of action that would make service providers liable for information originating with a third-party user of the service. Specifically, the statute precludes courts from entertaining claims that would place a computer service provider in a publisher's role. The purpose of this immunity is not difficult to discern. It was enacted to maintain the robust nature of Internet communications and, accordingly, to keep governmental interference in the medium to a minimum. None of this means, of course, that the original culpable party who posts defamatory messages would escape accountability. However, Congress made a policy choice not to deter harmful online speech through the separate route of imposing tort liability on companies that serve as intermediaries for other parties' potentially injurious messages. The purpose of the immunity is evident. Interactive computer services have millions of users. The amount of information communicated via interactive computer services is therefore staggering. The specter of tort liability in an area of such prolific speech would have an obvious chilling effect. Faced with potential liability for each message republished by their services, interactive computer service providers might choose to severely restrict the number and type of messages posted. Another important purpose of the statute was to encourage service providers to self-regulate the dissemination of offensive material over their services. Congress was concerned that courts would treat service providers who actively screened and edited messages posted on bulletin boards as publishers of any defamatory statements. This could trigger a strict liability standard. Fearing that the specter of strict liability would deter service providers from blocking and screening offensive material, Congress enacted the statute's broad immunity. Even distributors, rather than publishers, are immune from liability under the act. If computer service providers were subject to distributor liability, they would face potential liability each time they received notice of a potentially defamatory statement. Because they would be subject to liability only for the publication of information, and not for its removal, they would have a natural incentive simply to remove messages upon notification whether the contents were defamatory or not.

http://www.law.vill.edu/Fed-Ct/fedcourt.html

Computer Crime

http://
www.fraud.com is
the site of the FTC's
National Fraud Information Center, with
a link to Internet
fraud information.

Both the federal government and the states have enacted legislation designed to curb computer crime. For instance, most states have laws prohibiting unauthorized access to, or use of, a computer. And the federal government expressly outlaws unauthorized access to government computers, computers containing restricted government information, and the computers of credit card issuers.

Some individuals have discovered ways to access the services of commercial service providers without paying their fees. This theft of services is illegal. It also is illegal for hackers to alter or destroy data stored in another's computer. In fact, any activity that is illegal offline probably is criminal online as well. Much of the criminal activity that occurs online violates one or more traditional criminal statutes. This includes theft, distributing obscene materials, destruction of property, and trespass.

In the case that opened the chapter, Jake Baker was charged with transmitting in interstate commerce threats to injure or kidnap another. However, the court dismissed the charges. First, most of the statements were sent by e-mail and therefore were not communicated to the general public. Second, the court did not believe that Baker's messages constituted a true threat. Instead, it viewed the communications as only a rather savage and tasteless piece of fiction.

Online Torts

Even when the government does not proceed with a criminal action, the injured party may have a remedy. As the court acknowledged in the previous case (*Zeran v. America Online*), a defamed person has a tort remedy against the author of the defamatory statement. Likewise, most of the crimes noted above are intentional torts as well. As such, they provide the injured party with a civil cause of action for damages. Consider the following case, where an online service company convinced the court that a spam distributer has committed the intentional tort of trespass.

CompuServe v. Cyber Promotions
962 F.Supp. 1015 (S.D. Ohio 1997)

FACTS CompuServe operates a computer communication service through a proprietary nationwide computer network. In addition to allowing access to the extensive content available within its own proprietary network, CompuServe also provides its subscribers with a link to the much larger resources of the Internet. This allows its subscribers to send and receive electronic messages, known as "e-mail," by the Internet. Cyber Promotions is in the business of sending unsolicited e-mail advertisements on behalf of itself and its clients to hundreds of thousands of Internet users, many of whom are CompuServe subscribers. CompuServe ordered Cyber to stop using CompuServe's computer equipment to process and store the unsolicited e-mail. Instead, Cyber sent an increasing volume of e-mail solicitations to CompuServe subscribers. CompuServe then attempted to block the flow of Cyber's e-mail transmissions to its computer equipment, but to no avail. CompuServe argued that Cyber's actions amount to trespass to personal property, which entitles CompuServe to injunctive relief to protect its property.

ISSUE Does CompuServe have a viable claim for trespass against Cyber?

continued

DECISION Yes. Internet users often pay a fee for Internet access. However, there is no per-message charge to send electronic messages over the Internet and such messages usually reach their destination within minutes. Thus, electronic mail provides an opportunity to reach a wide audience quickly and at almost no cost to the sender. It is not surprising that some companies, like Cyber, have begun using the Internet to distribute advertisements by sending the same unsolicited commercial message to hundreds of thousands of Internet users at once. Cyber refers to this as "bulk mail," while CompuServe calls it "junk mail." In the vernacular of the Internet, unsolicited e-mail advertising is sometimes referred to as "spam." E-mail sent to CompuServe subscribers is processed and stored on CompuServe's proprietary computer equipment. Thereafter, it becomes accessible to CompuServe's subscribers, who can access CompuServe's equipment and electronically retrieve those messages. CompuServe has received many complaints from subscribers threatening to discontinue their subscription unless CompuServe prohibits mass mailers from using its equipment to send unsolicited advertisements. CompuServe asserts that the volume of messages generated by such mass mailings places a significant burden on its equipment which has finite processing and storage capacity. CompuServe receives no payment from the mass mailers for processing their unsolicited advertising. However, CompuServe's subscribers pay for their access to CompuServe's services in increments of time and thus the process of accessing, reviewing, and discarding unsolicited e-mail costs them money, which is one of the reasons for their complaints. A trespass to property may be committed by intentionally using or intermeddling with property possessed by another. Electronic signals generated and sent by computer have been held to be sufficiently physically tangible to support a trespass cause of action. It is undisputed that CompuServe has a possessory interest in its computer systems. Further, Cyber's contact with CompuServe's computers is clearly intentional. Any value CompuServe realizes from its computer equipment is wholly derived from the extent to which that equipment can serve its subscriber base. However, Cyber's tactics have placed a tremendous burden on that equipment. CompuServe clearly has a viable claim for trespass to personal property and is entitled to injunctive relief to protect its property.

Online Privacy

Most Internet users do not realize how little privacy they have while online. For instance, most universities and employers claim property interests in the e-mail correspondence on their systems. In a growing number of cases, employees are being fired after their employers discover inappropriate messages in their e-mail. Further, computer hackers sometimes infiltrate e-mail systems and gain access to confidential materials.

Even the simple act of visiting a Web site may reveal private information about the computer user to marketers and managers. For example, Netscape's browser contained a feature, known as "cookies," that allowed Internet merchants to track precisely what users were looking at in their Web sites. (Netscape now allows its customers to deactivate the cookies feature.) And it is not at all uncommon for Web sites to give out users' names, addresses, and social security numbers to any interested parties.

At present, government and corporate leaders agree that electronic commerce on the Internet will not be successful without some privacy guarantees. However, there still exists a strong debate over whether these protections should come from government regulation or private cooperation. In late 1997, the Federal Trade Commission (FTC) criticized companies that falsely hold themselves out as following information privacy policies on their Web sites. The FTC warned that it might treat failure to abide by the stated policy as a deceptive trade practice. And, in early 1998, a group of look-up services providers agreed on a set of guidelines restricting the manner in which personal information (like someone's social security number) would be disseminated. The FTC gave its stamp of approval to this self-regulation.

--------------------------- Ethical Issue ---------------------------

Under current laws, a private employer may intercept an employee's e-mail if the employer is the provider of the e-mail system in the workplace. The employer need not give notice to the employee and may continue monitoring the communications as long as they relate to business matters. Should employers engage in unannounced monitoring of e-mail?

Intellectual Property Rights ▬▬▬▬

Online communication is made possible by the transmission of digital information. Computer technology allows us to transform text, photographs, sound recordings, and movies into a series of ones and zeros. Thus, tangible property is transformed into a digital form that can be read by a computer. These files can then be downloaded into their original form.

Ownership of the original materials (text, photographs, etc.) is governed by intellectual property law. With the development of computer technology, courts have been forced to extend the traditional concepts of property ownership to cyberspace. This section examines three areas where intellectual property laws and cyberspace often meet: copyrights, trademarks, and domain names.

Copyrights

Federal copyright law gives certain exclusive rights to those who create original works such as books, songs, photographs, paintings, movies, and computer software. Copyright protection has been extended to traditional works even after they have been converted to digital form. As soon as an original work comes into existence, it is protected by copyright law. However, before making the work available to the public, it generally is wise to give *notice* of the copyright. This might include the word "copyright" followed by the name of the copyright owner. Further, the owner should *register* the copyright with the Copyright Office of the Library of Congress. This is because registration generally is necessary before the owner may sue for copyright infringement.

http://
www.law.cornell.edu/
topics/copyright.html
contains links to sites
on copyrights.

Ownership Rights

A copyright owner has the exclusive right to:

1. reproduce the copyrighted work;
2. prepare derivative works (adaptations) based on the original material;
3. distribute copies of the copyrighted work to the public by sale or other transfer; and
4. display the copyrighted works publicly.

Copyright law generally blocks anyone else from exercising these rights without the consent of the copyright owner.

Copyright Infringement

To bring a case of **copyright infringement,** the plaintiff must prove: (1) ownership of a valid copyright, and (2) copying by defendant of constituent elements of the work that are original. Once the plaintiff has established the ownership and copying elements, she can establish a direct infringement by proving that the defendant exercised any of the ownership rights described in the previous paragraph. (See Figure 23–2).

Playboy Enterprises v. Hardenburgh

1997 U.S. Dist. LEXIS 19310 (N.D. Ohio 1997)

FACTS   Russ Hardenburgh operated a computer bulletin board service (BBS) named "Rusty-N-Edie's BBS." For a fee, subscribers received access to certain files that were otherwise off-limits to the general public, and had the right to download a set number of megabytes of electronic information from these files every week. The central BBS grew to 124 computers, with nearly 6,000 subscribers. Approximately 110,000 files were available for downloading, nearly half of which were graphic image files (GIFs). A GIF is created by scanning a photograph to create digital data that can be run through a computer. To increase its stockpile of available information, and thereby its attractiveness to customers, Hardenburgh provided an incentive to encourage subscribers to upload information onto the BBS. They were given a "credit" for each megabyte of electronic data that they uploaded onto the system. For each credit, the subscriber was entitled to download 1.5 extra megabytes of electronic information, in addition to the megabytes available under the normal terms of subscription. Information uploaded onto the BBS went directly to an "upload file" where a BBS employee checked the new files to ascertain whether they were pornographic or blatantly protected by copyright. In the course of scanning online systems to make certain that its copyrighted materials were not being made available to computer users, Playboy Enterprises discovered that Hardenburgh was making Playboy photographs available to his BBS subscribers. Playboy sued Hardenburgh for direct and/or contributory copyright infringement. Hardenburgh replied that any Playboy photographs that appeared on the BBS were placed there by his subscribers, not BBS employees.

ISSUE   Is Hardenburgh liable to Playboy for copyright infringement?

DECISION   Yes. Playboy has clearly established that many of the photographs available on the BBS were copies of photographs to which Playboy was the copyright owner. Thus, to prove direct infringement, Playboy merely needs to prove that Hardenburgh violated any of Playboy's exclusive rights to the copyrighted material. These include Playboy's right to (a) reproduce the photographs, (b) distribute copies of the photographs to the public by sale or other transfer of ownership, and (c) display the photographs publicly. Direct copyright infringement requires some element of direct action or participation and setting up a computer bulletin board is not one of those activities. That being said, the facts in this case are sufficient to establish that Hardenburgh engaged in two activities reserved to copyright owners. He distributed and displayed copies of Playboy photographs in violation of Playboy's copyrights. This finding hinges on two crucial facts: (1) his policy of encouraging subscribers to upload files, including adult photographs, onto the system, and (2) his policy of using a screening procedure in which a BBS employee viewed all files in the upload file and moved them into the generally available files for subscribers. These two facts transform Hardenburgh from a passive provider of a space in which infringing activities happened to occur to an active participant in the process of copyright infringement. Similarly, Hardenburgh violated Playboy's right of public display. He displayed copies of Playboy's photographs to the public by adopting a policy which allowed his employees to place those photographs in files available to subscribers. Finally, a party is liable for contributory copyright infringement where it, with knowledge of the infringing activity, induces, causes or materially contributes to the infringing conduct of another. Hardenburgh clearly induced, caused, and materially contributed to any infringing activity which took place on his BBS. He encouraged subscribers to upload information including adult files. Also, he had at least constructive knowledge that infringing activity was likely to be occurring on his BBS.

Figure 23–2:   Bringing a Copyright Infringement Action

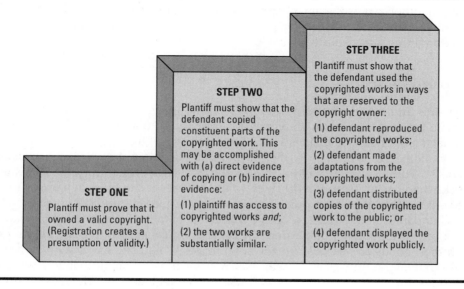

STEP ONE
Plantiff must prove that it owned a valid copyright. (Registration creates a presumption of validity.)

STEP TWO
Plantiff must show that the defendant copied constituent parts of the copyrighted work. This may be accomplished with (a) direct evidence of copying or (b) indirect evidence:
(1) plaintiff has access to copyrighted works *and*;
(2) the two works are substantially similar.

STEP THREE
Plantiff must show that the defendant used the copyrighted works in ways that are reserved to the copyright owner:
(1) defendant reproduced the copyrighted works;
(2) defendant made adaptations from the copyrighted works;
(3) defendant distributed copies of the copyrighted work to the public; or
(4) defendant displayed the copyrighted work publicly.

Fair Use

Portions of copyrighted materials may be copied, adapted, or distributed without the owner's permission if they fall within the **fair use** doctrine. This defense may be extended to protect certain online uses of copyrighted material. The copyright act sets out four factors for evaluating whether a use is a fair use:

1. purpose and character of the use (Commercial uses are presumptively unfair.);
2. nature of the copyrighted work (The scope of fair use is greater for informational work than for creative work.);
3. amount and substantiality of portions used (Fair use may apply if there are substantial differences between the copyrighted work and the derivative work); and
4. effect on the market (Fair use does not apply if the use diminishes the value or marketability of the original work.).

Trademarks

http://
www.law.cornell.
edu/topics/trademark.
html contains infor-
mation and links on
trademarks.

A **trademark** is any word, name, symbol, or device used by a manufacturer or seller to identify her products and to distinguish them from the products of competitors. A **service mark** is similar to a trademark except it is used to identify and distinguish services. The *Lanham Act* prohibits a person from using another's mark without permission "in connection with the sale, offering for sale, distribution or advertising of any goods or services on or in connection with which such use is likely to cause confusion, or to cause mistake, or to deceive."

Trademark law was designed to help buyers identify favored goods and services. Thus, it traditionally permitted multiple parties to use the same mark for different classes of goods or services since such use was not likely to confuse consumers. However, **trademark dilution** laws have changed the traditional trademark analysis. Trademark dilution laws protect "distinctive" or "famous" marks from unauthorized uses even when confusion is not likely to occur. This is because trademark dilution laws focus on protecting the investment of trademark owners, while traditional trademark laws were intended to protect consumers.

Domain Names

Web sites and other information sources on the Internet are addressed using a domain name system. Domain names are arranged so that, reading from right to left, each part of the name gives a more localized area of the Internet. One purpose of domain names is to identify the person or organization that owns a particular Web site. The domain name system also allows Internet users to locate Web sites quickly and easily. Thus, if a user knows or can deduce the domain name associated with a Web site, he can quickly access that site. (See Figure 23–3 on page 552.)

Companies doing business on the Internet generally prefer to use their trademark or service mark as their domain name since consumers readily identify it with their goods or services. However, while more than one entity may own the same trademark, only one of them may register it as a domain name. Network Solutions, Inc. (NSI), manages most domain name registrations. However, it does not make an independent determination of an applicant's right to use a domain name. It merely checks to make certain that an applicant's domain name is not the same as one that already is registered. Thus, NSI is insulated from trademark infringement or dilution lawsuits since it does not make commercial use of domain names as trademarks. However, companies that register another's trademark as their domain name may be liable for infringement or dilution.

Panavision International v. Toeppen

945 F.Supp. 1296 (C.D. Cal. 1996)

FACTS Panavision International owns several federally registered trademarks, including "Panavision" and "Panaflex," which it uses in connection with its theatrical motion picture and television camera and photographic equipment business. After registering the *panavision.com* domain name, Dennis Toeppen established a Web site displaying aerial views of Pana, Illinois. At no time did he use the name in connection with the sale of any goods or services. When Panavision attempted to establish a Web site under its own name, it discovered that Toeppen already had registered that domain name. Therefore, Panavision was unable to register and use its trademark as an Internet domain name. When Panavision notified Toeppen of its desire to use the *panavision.com* domain name, he demanded $13,000 to discontinue his "use" of the domain name. Toeppen then registered Panavision's "Panaflex" trademark as the domain name *panaflex.com*. The *panaflex.com* Web site contains only the word "hello." Toeppen also is the registered owner of several other domain names that are based on trademarks and trade names. Panavision asserts that Toeppen is in the business of registering well-known marks and exacting payment from the marks' owners before he will relinquish control of the domain names.

ISSUE: Has Toeppen violated the federal trademark dilution laws?

DECISION: Yes. Traditionally, trademark law has permitted multiple parties to use the same mark for different classes of goods or services. Trademark law only prohibited use of the same mark on competing goods or services where there was a likelihood of consumer confusion as to the origin of the goods or services with which the user associated the mark. Trademark dilution laws, however, changed the traditional trademark analysis. Trademark dilution laws protect "distinctive" or "famous" trademarks from certain unauthorized uses of the marks regardless of a showing of competition or likelihood of confusion. Indeed, the very purpose of dilution statutes is to protect trademarks from damage caused by the use of the marks in non-competing endeavors. Whereas traditional trademark law sought primarily to protect consumers, dilution laws place more emphasis on protecting the investment of the trademark owners. Still, dilution laws do promote consumer welfare: if trademarks are valuable to consumers, then protecting businesses' investments in trademarks will benefit consumers by increasing the willingness of businesses to invest in the creation of recognized marks. An area in which trademark law will have an impact on the Internet involves disputes over the right to use particular domain names. While trademark law permits multiple parties to use the same mark for different classes of goods and services, the current organization of the Internet permits only one use of a domain name, regardless of the goods or services offered. That is, although two or more businesses can own the trademark "Acme," only one business can operate on the Internet with

continued

the domain name *acme.com*. Still, some Internet trademark disputes can be resolved under trademark dilution law. The federal trademark dilution statute provides that "the owner of a famous mark shall be entitled . . . to an injunction against another person's commercial use in commerce of a mark or trade name, if such use begins after the mark has become famous and causes dilution of the distinctive quality of the mark." The distinctiveness and fame of the "Panavision" marks are well established and undisputed. Registration of a trademark as a domain name, without more, is not a commercial use of the trademark and therefore is not within the prohibitions of the statute. However, in this case Toeppen has made a commercial use of the Panavision marks. His "business" is to register trademarks as domain names and then to sell the domain names to the trademark's owners. Toeppen traded on the value of the marks as marks by attempting to sell the domain names to Panavision. This conduct injured Panavision by preventing the company from exploiting its marks and injured consumers because it would have been difficult to locate Panavision's Web site if Panavision had established one under a name other than its own. Dilution is defined as the lessening of the capacity of a famous mark to identify and distinguish goods and services. Toeppen was able not merely to lessen the capacity of the Panavision marks to identify Panavision's goods and services, but to eliminate their capacity to identify and distinguish Panavision's goods and services on the Internet. This case does not grant trademark owners preemptive rights in domain names. This decision merely holds that registering a famous mark as a domain name for the purpose of trading on the value of the mark by selling the domain name to the trademark owner violates the federal dilution statute.

Figure 23–3:   Domain Names

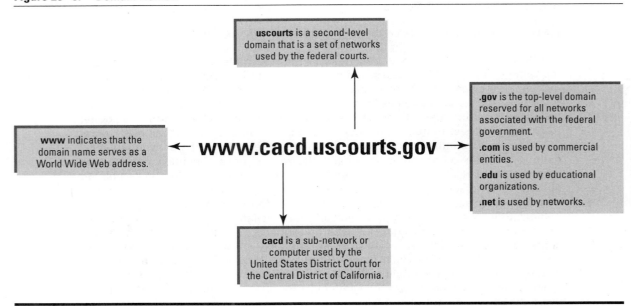

Contracting in Cyberspace ▬▬▬▬

As more and more businesses establish a presence on the Internet, electronic contracting is becoming quite common. Contracts may be formed through the exchange of e-mail messages, or users may order goods or services they find advertised on a Web site. For the most part, traditional contract rules can be easily adapted to the Internet. (Contract law is discussed in Chapters 8 and 9.)

Article 2 of the Uniform Commercial Code provides a uniform legal framework for the formation and enforcement of contracts for the sale of goods. Currently an Article 2B is being drafted that adapts the Uniform Commercial Code rules to cyberspace. Article 2B aims to provide a framework for contractual relationships among entities heavily involved in cyberspace. For the most part, however, its provisions will parallel the rules laid out in Article 2.

Contract Formation

The fact that a particular transaction was negotiated electronically should not pose a serious obstacle to contract formation. After all, many oral contracts are enforceable. In instances where a user orders goods or services from a Web site, the traditional contract rules could easily govern. The Web site display may be viewed as an advertisement, which constitutes little more than an invitation to make an offer. When a user orders goods or services displayed on the Web site, he is making an offer that can be accepted or rejected by the seller.

However, there may be some differences. For instance, under traditional contract law, an acceptance generally is effective as soon as it is dispatched. It is unlikely that Article 2B will follow this rule. Instead an electronic acceptance is not likely to be effective until it actually is received by the offeror.

Writing

Under the Uniform Commercial Code, a contract for the sale of goods in excess of $500 must be in writing. Similarly, the common-law statute of frauds requires a writing for contracts that cannot be performed within one year. However, the need for a writing is not a serious obstacle to an electronic contract. As long as the electronic messages can be reduced to a tangible form (printed out), they should qualify as a writing.

Shrinkwrap Contracts

Oftentimes, computer software is sold in packages containing a disk or CD-ROM. The software arrives in a package with some contractual terms printed on the outside. One such term states that the buyer accepts the **shrinkwrap** terms by opening the package. Current drafts of Article 2B of the Uniform Commercial Code would make shrinkwrap terms enforceable if they meet three conditions: (1) the user must have had an opportunity to review the terms; (2) the user is clearly informed of what actions she must do to accept the terms; and (3) the user must have voluntarily accepted the terms. Consider the following "shrinkwrap" case. (This case appeared as the opening vignette to Chapter 2.)

Hill v. Gateway 2000

105 F.3D 1147 (7TH CIR. 1997)

FACTS   Rich and Enza Hill ordered a Gateway 2000 computer system by telephone. They paid by giving their credit card number during the telephone conversation. The computer arrived in a box that also contained a list of terms, said to govern the contract unless the Hills returned the computer within 30 days. One of the terms in the box containing the computer was an arbitration clause. Rich and Enza Hill kept the computer for more than 30 days before complaining about its components and performance. When they ultimately filed suit, Gateway asked the court to enforce the arbitration clause. In response, the Hills claimed that the arbitration clause did not stand out. They conceded that they noticed the statement of terms but denied reading it closely enough to discover the agreement to arbitrate. Accordingly, they argued that they should be permitted to go to court.

ISSUE   Should the court enforce the arbitration clause?

DECISION   Yes. A contract need not be read to be effective; people who accept contractual offers take the risk that the unread terms may in retrospect prove unwelcome. Practical considerations support allowing vendors to enclose the full legal terms with their products. If the staff at the other end of the telephone for direct-sales operations such as Gateway's had to read the four-page statement before taking the buyer's credit card number, the droning voice would anesthetize rather than enlighten many potential buyers. Others would hang up in rage over the waste of their time. Customers as a group are better off when vendors skip costly and ineffectual steps such as telephonic recitation, and use instead a simple approve-or-return device. Competent adults are bound by such documents, read or unread. Perhaps the Hills would have had a better argument if they had been first alerted to the bundling of hardware and legal-ware after opening the box and wanted to return the computer in order to avoid disagreeable terms, but were dissauded by the expense of shipping. This raises an interesting question, but one that need not detain us because the Hills knew before they ordered the computer that the carton would include *some* important terms, and they did not seek to discover these in advance. Shoppers have three principal ways to discover these things. First, they can ask the vendor to send a copy before deciding whether to buy. Second, shoppers can consult public sources (computer magazines, the Web sites of vendors) that may contain this information. Third, they may inspect the documents after the product's delivery. The Hills took the third option. By keeping the computer beyond 30 days, the Hills accepted Gateway's offer, including the arbitration clause.

http://www.law.vill.edu/Fed-Ct/fedcourt.html

QUESTIONS AND PROBLEM CASES

1. What is meant by the term "spam"? What problems does it create?

2. What does it take for a court to have jurisdiction over a person who engages in online misconduct?

3. Why does the domain name system frequently cause problems for trademark owners?

4. America Online (AOL) is a private online company. Its subscribers pay fees for the use of AOL resources, access to AOL, and access to and use of AOL's e-mail system and its connection to the Internet. Cyber Promotions, an advertising agency, provides advertising services for companies and individuals wishing to advertise their products and services via e-mail. Cyber sends its e-mail via the Internet to members of AOL, members of other commercial online services, and other individuals with an Internet e-mail address. On January 26, 1996, AOL advised Cyber that it was upset with Cyber's dissemination of unsolicited e-mail to AOL members over the Internet. AOL subsequently sent a number of "e-mail bombs" to Cyber's Internet service providers. These "e-mail bombs" occurred when AOL gathered all unsolicited e-mail sent by Cyber to undeliverable AOL addresses, altered the return path of such e-mail, and then sent the altered e-mail in a bulk transmission to Cyber's service providers in order to disable the service providers. Cyber claims that as a result of AOL's "e-mail bombing," two of its service providers terminated their relationship with Cyber and a third refused to enter into a contract with it. AOL, on the other hand, counters that Cyber has no right to send literally millions of e-mail messages each day to AOL's Internet servers free of charge and resulting in the overload of the e-mail servers. Does the First Amendment prohibit AOL from blocking the unsolicited e-mail sent by Cyber to AOL members?

5. CompuServe develops and provides computer-related products and services, including CompuServe Information Service (CIS), an online general information service or "electronic library" that subscribers may access from a personal computer or terminal. Subscribers to CIS pay a membership fee and online time usage fees, in return for which they have access to the thousands of information sources available on CIS. Subscribers may also obtain access to over 150 special interest "forums," which are comprised of electronic bulletin boards, interactive online conferences, and topical databases. One forum available is the Journalism Forum, which focuses on the journalism industry. One publication available as part of the Journalism Forum is Rumorville USA, a daily newsletter that provides reports about broadcast journalism and journalists. Rumorville is published by Don Fitzpatrick Associates. CompuServe has no employment, contractual, or other direct relationship with Fitzpatrick. It also has no opportunity to review Rumorville's contents before they are uploaded into CompuServe's computer banks, from which they are immediately available to approved CIS subscribers. Cubby, Inc., developed Skuttlebut, a computer database designed to publish and distribute electronically news and gossip in the television and radio industries. Skuttlebut was created to compete with Rumorville. Cubby alleges that on several occasions, Rumorville published false and defamatory statements relating to Skuttlebut, and that CompuServe carried these statements as part of the Journalism Forum. Cubby sued CompuServe for defamation. CompuServe claims it cannot be held liable for them because it did not know and had no reason to know of the statements. Should CompuServe be held liable for the defamatory statements? Explain.

6. SportsNet is a national computer network service whereby sports memorabilia dealers may communicate to purchase and sell merchandise. There are two features on SportsNet, a mailbox and a bulletin board. The

mailbox feature is personal in nature and allows a person to send messages exclusively to another SportsNet user, similar to e-mail. The bulletin board feature allows a person to send messages to all members accessing SportsNet. Rosario Fuschetto and Jeff Meneau communicated with each other over both the bulletin board and mailbox features of SportsNet. After the two started arguing over several matters, Fuschetto posted a note on the bulletin board feature, accessible to all subscribers of SportsNet, explaining his arguments with Meneau. As a result, Meneau brought suit against Fuschetto for defamation of character. Fuschetto argued that the bulletin board communications were a "periodical" under the Wisconsin statute. The statute provides that before a libel lawsuit may be brought against any *"newspaper, magazine, or periodical, the libeled person shall first give those alleged to be responsible or liable for the publication a reasonable opportunity to correct the libelous matter."* Accordingly, he contended that the lawsuit must be dismissed because Meneau was required to demand a retraction before he could bring suit. Were the bulletin board communications a periodical under the terms of the Wisconsin statute?

7. Lockheed owns the federally registered "SKUNK WORKS" service mark for "engineering, technical consulting, and advisory services with respect to designing, building, equipping, and testing commercial and military aircraft and related equipment. Despite this fact, several companies registered domain names such as *skunkwrks.com, skunkworks.com, skunkwerks.com, the-skunkwerks.com,* and *theskunkworks.com.* Lockheed claims that Network Solutions, Inc. (NSI) directly infringed its "SKUNK WORKS" service mark by accepting the domain name registrations. Is NSI liable to Lockheed for direct infringement and dilution of the Lockheed service mark?

8. Juno Online is an online provider with approximately 1.5 million subscribers. Juno Lighting is a manufacturer and retailer of recessed and track lighting. Juno Lighting has used the Juno name in its logo since 1976 and holds two federal trademarks for the name "Juno." In December 1994, Juno Online registered the domain name *juno.com* with Network Solutions (NSI), and began providing free e-mail service to customers. Because Juno Online registered the domain name *juno.com* with NSI, no other business or person could obtain that address. Juno Lighting sent a letter to NSI requesting that NSI cancel Juno Online's domain name *juno.com*. Subsequently, Juno Lighting obtained, by registering with NSI, the domain name *Juno-online.com*. According to Juno Lighting, this was done in order to prevent others from obtaining the name, thus allowing Juno Lighting to transfer the domain name to Juno Online to help resolve this dispute. Juno Online alleges that Juno Lighting's registration of the domain name *juno-online.com* is unlawful. The *Lanham Act* states that *"any person who, on or in connection with any goods or services, . . . uses in commerce any word, term, name, symbol, or device [that] is likely to cause confusion . . . or to deceive as to affiliation, connection or association . . . shall be liable in a civil action."* Juno Lighting claims that, because it has merely acquired the domain name and has not used it, it has not violated the *Lanham Act*. Does Juno Lighting's registration of the domain name *juno-online.com* violate the law?

9. Richard King owns a small cabaret featuring live entertainment in Columbia, Missouri. He operates the club under the name "The Blue Note." Bensusan Restaurant runs an enormously successful jazz club in New York City called "The Blue Note," which name was registered as a federal trademark for cabaret services. In 1993, a Bensusan representative wrote to King demanding that he cease and desist from calling his club The Blue Note. Nothing further was heard from Bensusan until 1996 when King, through a local Website design company, permitted that company to create a Web site on the Internet for King's cabaret. The Web site describes King's establishment as "Mid-Missouri's finest live entertainment venue, . . . located in beautiful Columbia, Missouri." It also contains a disclaimer stating that it "should not be confused in any way, shape, or form with the . . . Blue

Note, located in New York. The Cyperspot is created to provide information for Columbia, Missouri area individuals only." Bensusan filed a lawsuit against King in a federal district court in New York. King moved for a dismissal on the ground that New York lacked personal jurisdiction over the dispute. The appropriate New York statute provides that a New York court may exercise personal jurisdiction over a nonresident who commits a tortious act within the state. Does King's use of the Web site subject him to the personal jurisdiction of a New York court?

10. Robert and Carleen Thomas operated the Amateur Action Computer Bulletin Board System (AABBS) from their home in Milpitas, California. Its features included e-mail, chat lines, public messages, and files that members could access, transfer, and download to their own computers and printers. The AABBS contained approximately 14,000 files depicting images of bestiality, oral sex, incest, sado-masochistic abuse, and sex scenes involving urination. Actual access to the files, however, was limited to members who were given a password after they paid a membership fee and submitted a signed application form that Robert reviewed. A U.S. Postal Inspector purchased a membership under an assumed name. He then dialed the AABBS's telephone number, logged on, and, using his computer/modem in Memphis, Tennessee, downloaded several files. Afterwards, Robert and Carleen were charged in Tennessee with violating federal obscenity laws and knowingly using and causing to be used a combined computer/telephone system for the purpose of transporting obscene, computer-generated materials in interstate commerce. Ultimately, Robert and Carleen were sentenced to 37 and 30 months of incarceration, respectively. In determining their guilt, the court used the community standards of obscenity in Tennessee rather than in California. Should the community standards of Tennessee govern this case?

A

Abandonment- An act that occurs when a tenant wrongfully vacates the premises prior to the expiration of a lease.

Actual authority- The authority of an agent within the confines of the agency agreement. Such authority can be **express** (oral or written) or **implied.**

Actual causation- A requirement of causation in which it can be shown that a plaintiff's injuries would not have occurred if the duties of the defendant had not been breached.

Adoption disclosure statutes- State laws that allow disclosure of adoption records to adopted persons over 21 years of age.

Adversary system- The legal network of laws, rules, and procedures characterized by opposing parties who contend against each other for a result favorable to themselves.

Affirm a decision- An appellate court's decision in agreement with a lower court's verdict.

Agency- The relationship between an agent and a principal. An **agent** is a person who acts for the benefit of and under the direction of another person, called the **principal.**

Agency at will- The power to terminate an agency agreement at any time.

Agency shop- Where workers are free to decide whether or not they wish to become union members, but must pay union dues even if they decide against union membership.

Alternative dispute resolution (ADR)- A means of resolving civil disputes without litigation.

Annuity contract- Life insurance contracts for which the insured pays premiums and then receives periodic payments after reaching a certain age.

Annulment- Official state denial of the existence of a marital contract despite the couple's securing a license and having the marriage ceremony.

Answer- A document from a defendant that responds to a complaint paragraph by paragraph, and which is filed in court and forwarded to the plaintiff.

Apparent authority- When in the absence of actual authority, a principal, through words, action, or inaction, permits an agent to hold herself out as possessing actual authority.

Arbitral award- The decision or determination for a party in an arbitration case.

Arbitration- The settlement of a dispute by a nonjudicial third party who makes a decision after hearing the case.

Arraignment- The initial appearance of the accused before the judge or magistrate, during which the accused is informed of constitutional rights, advised of charges, and given an opportunity to plead guilty or not guilty.

Assault- An intentional tort that occurs when one person intentionally places another in the apprehension of immediate harm; it is not necessary for any physical contact to occur.

Assignment- The act of transferring to another all or part of one's property, interest, or rights.

Attachment- The act by which a borrower gives a lender a security interest in property (collateral).

Attorney-client privilege- A privilege that prevents a lawyer or a client from disclosing confidential communications made by a client for the purpose of furnishing or obtaining professional legal advice or services.

B

Bailment- The delivery of goods or personal property by one person **(bailor)** to another **(bailee)** in trust until it is to be returned to the bailor or to some other person designated by the bailor.

Bargaining unit- A group of employees who choose to unionize and who share similar job classifications and similar concerns about terms of employment.

Battery- The intentional tort that occurs when one person touches another in a harmful or offensive way without consent.

Bearer paper- An instrument that does not specifically identify the person to whom it is payable.

Bench trial- A trial in which a judge decides a matter without the assistance of a jury.

Beneficiary- One who benefits from an act of another.

559

Bilateral contract- A contract in which both parties promise something to each other; a promise for a promise.

Bill of Rights- The first 10 amendments of the Constitution, which restrain the power of the government to arbitrarily interfere with people's rights.

Binder- A special agreement in which the seller accepts the buyer's offer to purchase. It commonly arises in insurance and real estate transactions.

Bona fide occupational qualification (BFOQ)- The special requirements of a job that make it lawful for an employer to discriminate on the basis of sex, religion, or national origin, but not on race or color.

Breach- The breaking or violating of a law, right, obligation, engagement, or duty by omission or by commission.

C

Capacity - The ability of a person to legally perform an act.

Causa mortis gift- A gift made in contemplation of the donor's death, which may be conditional.

Child pornography- Material that may not be otherwise obscene, but depicts children engaging in sexual conduct.

Choice of law clause- A clause in a business contract that specifies the state whose law will govern in any disputes that arise from the contract.

Civil law- Laws and rules (generally contract and tort laws) that result in monetary, and sometimes punitive, damages.

Cohabitation- Living together as if married, but without the license and ceremony.

Commercial speech- Speech, such as advertising, that proposes a commercial transaction.

Common law- Law created by the courts.

Common-law crime- Behavior that is so outrageous as to be treated as criminal in the absence of a criminal statute.

Common-law marriage- Living together as man and wife without license and ceremony as long as there is cohabitation and an intent to be married, and the couple is held as husband and wife before others. Only 12 states still permit common-law marriages.

Community property- Property or income earned by either spouse during a marriage that is considered by laws in eight states to belong to both spouses, and must be divided equally upon dissolution of the marriage.

Complaint- A document that sets out the basis of a claim against a defendant, and that details the plaintiff's interpretation of the relevant facts, legal issues, and remedy being sought.

Computer crime- Criminal activity performed via computer that includes most traditional criminal statutes, such as theft, distributing obscene materials, destruction of property, and trespass.

Condominium- A multifamily structure with separate units individually owned, but common areas owned by all of the co-owners as tenants in common.

Conflict of interest- A situation in which an agent's interests are not consistent with the best interests of the principal.

Conflict of laws- The power of courts to determine, when inconsistencies between laws of different states or countries occur, which body of law will govern.

Consanguinity- Blood relationship or common ancestry.

Consent restraints - Devices used to control the number of shareholders in a close corporation.

Consideration- In contracts, what the parties give to each other as their part of the contract performance. A price that a promisee must pay before a promisor's promise will be enforceable.

Constructive eviction- The substantial interference by the landlord with a tenant's quiet enjoyment of the rented property, through means such as lack of heat or hot water.

Contact veto- A provision of adoption disclosure statutes that allows relatives of an adopted person to prevent contact by the adopted person.

Contingency fee- An agreement between attorney and client where the attorney agrees to represent the client with compensation to be a percentage of the amount recovered.

Contracts of adhesion- Preprinted contracts provided by commercial sellers.

Conversion- Similar to trespass, but more serious in that it deprives another of personal property for an unreasonable period of time.

Cooperative- Ownership of a building by a group of people who pay rent to reside within the premises.

Copyright- Laws that give certain exclusive rights to those who create original works and do not allow anyone else to exercise those rights without the permission of the copyright owner.

Corporation- An artificial person or legal entity created by or under the authority of the laws of a state, which is distinct from its shareholders, who are not personally liable for the corporation's debts. Legally, a corporation is treated like a person, and can sue and be sued.

Courts of appeals- Federal courts that review the decisions of the district courts that fall within their geographic region to determine whether the lower courts have properly interpreted and applied the law.

Crime- A wrong against society that results in fine, imprisonment, or a death penalty.

Criminal law- Laws and rules that govern duties to society at large that can result in fines, imprisonment, or a death penalty.

Criminal procedure- The body of law governing the procedures by which crimes are investigated, prosecuted, judged, and punished. It includes constitutional protections to persons accused of committing crimes.

Custodial interrogation- Questioning initiated by law enforcement officers after a person is taken into custody or otherwise deprived of freedom of action in any significant way.

Cyberspace- The lines of communications between computers.

D

Deed- The document in real estate that transfers ownership interests.

Defamation- The intentional publishing or speaking of false statements about another that causes injury to that person's reputation, and includes libel and slander.

Default judgment- A court judgment for which a plaintiff files a petition when a defendant does not respond to the summons and complaint. When this occurs, the plaintiff wins everything requested in the complaint.

Defendant- A party who must defend himself or herself in a legal action; the person against whom a legal action is brought.

Deficiency judgment- A judgment against a borrower that allows a lender to sue the borrower for the remaining balance of a loan if foreclosure does not provide enough money to settle the lender's claims.

Deposition- A witness's oral testimony under oath prior to trial.

Directed verdict- A verdict in favor of the defendant, frequently requested by the defendant's attorney, and granted only when the plaintiff fails to present evidence sufficient to support his or her claim.

Disclaimer- A notice intended to limit liability.

Discovery- The process by which the parties of a legal proceeding gather the information necessary to resolve the dispute.

District courts- Federal courts that hear both criminal and civil matters; the *trial courts* in the federal system.

Diversity cases- Cases that arise when the parties to a legal dispute are citizens of different states or countries and that may be heard by federal courts if the dispute is for more than $50,000.

Divorce- Legal dissolution of a marriage.

Doctrine of necessaries- A doctrine of common-law marriage that authorizes a spouse to purchase the necessities of life and charge them to his/her spouse when [s]he fails to provide them.

Domain name system- An address system on the Internet that identifies the owner of the Internet site.

Domestic torts Suits brought by one spouse against another, generally for negligence such as physical injury or emotional distress, but usually not intentional torts.

Double jeopardy- Prosecution more than once for the same crime; prohibited by the Fifth Amendment.

Draft- A negotiable instrument through which one person orders another person to pay money to a third person.

Due Process clause- In the Fifth Amendment, the statement prohibiting the federal government from depriving any person of life, liberty, or property, without due process of law, or legal recourse; the Fourteenth Amendment applies the same standard to the states.

Duty to disclose- A seller's duty to disclose material facts about the product being purchased that the buyer could not have discovered through a reasonable investigation.

E

Earnest money- Money from a real estate buyer that is held by the broker and shows the buyer's good-faith intention to purchase the property; it is retained by the seller if the buyer wrongfully fails to complete the transaction.

Easement- The right of access to another's real property. **Affirmative easement** is the right to make use of another's real property. **Negative easement** is the right of a person to prevent a neighbor from making certain uses of the neighbor's land.

Eminent domain- The power to take private property for public use.

Employee- One who is hired to work for another and qualifies as a statutory employee under the day-to-day control of the employer to be protected by employment laws.

Employment-at-will- The predominant employment doctrine in the U.S. that generally gives an employer the right to fire an employee at any time for any reason, or for no reason.

Endowment contract- Life insurance policy that is paid in a lump sum when the insured reaches a certain age.

Enumerated powers- Doctrine by which Congress can only exercise the delegated powers granted to it by the Constitution.

Equity- Justice administered by fairness, rather than by the strictly formulated rules of common law.

Establishment clause- A First Amendment clause that limits the ability of the government to engage in or support religion.

Eviction- The act of depriving a person of the possession of land or rental property that the person has held or leased.

Exclusionary rule- A judicially created rule that states that evidence obtained as a result of unreasonable search and seizure may not be used in a criminal trial against the accused.

Exculpatory clause- Waiver of claims provisions intended to create an assumption of risk defense; such clauses do not relieve a defendant from liability for intentional or reckless behavior.

Executive agencies- Administrative agencies exclusively within the executive branch of the government.

Executive orders- Rule-making authority given by Congress in the federal government to the president, and by state congresses in the states to governors, and that have the force of law.

ex post facto **laws ("After the fact")-** Laws that punish people for crimes committed before the law was passed; these are prohibited by the Constitution.

Express agreement- A contract that is agreed to orally or in writing.

Express warranty- A warranty in which a seller explicitly makes promises regarding the quality, condition, or performance of the goods being sold.

F

Federalism- Division of governing power between the federal government and the states.

Federal question- A dispute in law that may be brought before a federal court, and that arises when there has been a violation of federal law or of rights protected by the U.S. Constitution.

Felony- Serious criminal offense, such as murder, rape, or kidnapping.

Fiduciary- A person who is legally required to act in the best interests of another, rather than pursue his or her own personal interests.

Fiduciary relationship- A relationship between an agent and a principal that requires the agent to act in the best interests of the principal rather than pursue his or her own interests.

Fixture- Personal property that is firmly attached to the earth's crust and thereby becomes real property.

Foreclosure- The option of a lender to repossess collateral, sell it, and apply the proceeds of the sale to a borrower's loan.

Forfeiture- An option for a seller in an installment real estate contract where the buyer defaults to cancel the contract and retake possession of the property.

Forum non conveniens- The power of a court to determine if a trial would be more convenient and just to the parties if it were conducted in another forum.

Forum selection clause- A clause in a contract that specifies the place where any litigation must be brought.

Franchise- A business that, for a fee, has the right to sell an established product and use a proven method to sell successfully.

Fraudulent- Based on fraud, the intentional perversion of truth for the purpose of inducing another to part with some valuable belonging or legal right.

Free Exercise clause- A First Amendment clause preventing the government from opposing any religion; freedom of religion.

Full warranty- A warranty in which the seller is responsible for the buyer's damages resulting from worn or defective parts of the goods sold.

G

Garnishment- A creditor's legal recourse to obtain repayment, by which the court seizes a portion of the debtor's wages to pay the creditor.

General partnership- An association of two or more people who carry on as co-owners a business for profit.

Grand jury- A body of citizens with the duty to determine in criminal cases if a crime has been committed and if there is sufficient evidence and reason to go to trial.

Guarantor- One who makes a secondary promise to pay the debts of another.

Guest statutes - State laws that preclude automobile passengers from recovering damages from the driver of their vehicle in an accident.

H

Heartbalm statutes- State laws that abolish or strictly limit the cause of action for breach of promise to marry.

Heirs- Persons who receive a decedent's assets and liabilities when there is no will.

Holder in due course- A person who holds a negotiable instrument, and took it for value in good faith, without notice of any claim against it.

Hostile environment- A type of harassment that occurs when supervisors or coworkers subject an employee to intimidation, ridicule, or insult based on the employee's gender.

I

Implied agreement- A contract that arises from circumstances and is not expressed by the parties.

Implied powers- Powers granted to Congress that are not specifically stated in the Constitution, but are implied.

Implied warranty- A warranty that is not explicit but is assumed, such as an **implied warranty of merchantability,** which is a guarantee of quality and performance made by car dealers, or an **implied warranty of title,** in which it is implied that a seller has the legal right to sell a good.

Implied warranty of habitability- An implied guarantee that a new home is free of hidden defects that would make it unsafe or unsuitable for human habitation.

Income shares model- State methods in child support issues of a divorce that states that the child should be awarded the proportion of parental income that would have been received if the family had stayed together.

Incontestability clause- The clause in a life insurance policy that becomes effective after a specific period of the policy's life through which the insurer loses its right to cancel the policy if there are misrepresentations in the original application for the policy.

Indemnity contract- Property insurance contracts that obligate the insurer to pay for actual losses resulting from damage to the insured property.

Independent agencies- Administrative agencies that are not part of the executive branch of government, but are headed by a board or commission.

Independent contractor- One who is hired to work for another but does not qualify as a statutory employee under the day-to-day control of the employer, and is not protected by most employment laws.

Indictment- In a criminal case, acts in the same manner as a complaint in a civil case, and is brought about by a grand jury.

Infraction- Minor civil offenses that have been decriminalized, such as traffic and parking violations.

Injunction- A court order preventing someone from doing something in cases where the nonbreaching party would otherwise suffer irreparable harm.

Injurious falsehood- Defamation of a business product or service; also, disparagement.

Insurable interest- Financial interest vested in property or in another person's life.

Interrogatory- A detailed list of questions submitted by an attorney during discovery.

Interspousal immunity- Historically, a court ruling that prevents one spouse from bringing a negligence or intentional tort suit against the other.

Inter vivos gift- An unconditional gift; once it is delivered, the donor cannot revoke it.

Intestate- Without a will.

Inverse condemnation- An action to obtain compensation when governmental action effectively denies property owners the reasonable use of their land.

Investigative stop- The right of the police to detain and question the driver of an automobile if specific observable facts give them a reasonable basis to suspect that a law has been violated.

J

Joint and several liability clause- The clause in most leases that makes each tenant responsible for the other tenants' share of the rent.

Joint tenancy- A situation in which two or more persons are given equal rights and responsibilities to property transferred to them with the specific intent to create joint tenancy.

Judgment creditor- The winning party in a trial.

Judgment debtor- The losing party in a trial, who must pay damages or otherwise abide by the court's decision.

Judgment non obstante veredicto- ("Not withstanding the verdict") A judgment entered by order of the court for either the plaintiff or the defendant even though there has been a verdict for one or the other.

Judicial review- Power of courts to review and interpret decisions of other levels of government.

Jurisprudence- The science of law or legal thought.

L

Latent defects- Defects to property that are hidden dangers.

Laws- A set of principles developed by a legitimate authority that have general application to society and threaten sanctions against those who fail to comply with the principles.

Legal interpretation- The power of the courts to determine the meaning of laws through the plain meaning of the language, the legislative history of the law, the purpose of the law, and the accommodation of public policy.

Legal positivism- The rule of law that states all laws must be enforced to the letter.

Legal realism- A theory of law that focuses on the day-to-day application of law rather than on theoretical rules.

Legal reasoning- A type of critical thinking that combines basic analytical thinking with a recognition of the special features of the U.S. legal system, and is a useful tool in both legal and nonlegal situations.

Liability- A broad legal term meaning responsibility.

Libel- Written defamation.

Lien- A claim or charge on property for payment of some debt or obligation.

Limited liability company- A company that combines the taxation characteristics of a partnership with the limited liability features of a corporation.

Limited partnership- A partnership in which some partners (**general partners**) have unlimited liability, while others (**limited partners**) have only their investments at risk and do not participate in the firm's management.

Limited warranty- A warranty in which the seller's liability for worn or defective parts is somehow limited.

Litigation- A lawsuit. A legal action that occurs when the disputants petition the courts to settle their differences.

Living will- A document that specifies that life-sustaining treatment be withheld or discontinued when there is no hope of the recovery of the person who drafted and signed the document.

M

Mailbox rule- An agreement is made the instant the offeree dispatches the acceptance via an authorized means of acceptance.

Malpractice- A term that is applied to professional misconduct or unreasonable lack of skill.

Marital confidence privilege- The requirement of spouses to keep confidential the statements or admissions made by one another during marriage.

Marriage evasion statutes- State laws that prohibit recognition of marriages performed out-of-state by persons seeking to avoid the requirements of their state of residence.

Marriage validation statutes- State laws that recognize a marriage that is validly performed in another state.

Mechanic's lien- A claim on property by persons who furnish labor or provide materials for the improvement of real estate when the repairs or materials are unpaid.

Mediation- A method of dispute resolution that calls in a neutral third party to help the disputants reach a compromise.

Mens rea- Criminal intent when violating a law.

Merchantable title- During a seller's transference of property, this means the property does not have any claims against it that would interfere with the buyer's possession.

Mini-trial- A private, voluntary, informal method of alternative dispute resolution in which attorneys for both sides briefly present the facts of their case before officials for each side with authority to settle, usually with a neutral third party present.

Miranda warning- The warning to criminal defendants before interrogation by police regarding the right to an attorney and the right to remain silent.

Misdemeanor- Criminal offense less serious than a felony, such as disorderly conduct, possession of small amounts of marijuana, or check deception.

Mistake- In contracts, an error as to the material terms in a contract that is not the result of misstatements by one of the parties. In **mutual mistakes,** both parties to the contract are in error. In **unilateral mistakes,** only one party is in error.

Mortgage- A three-party transaction involving the buyer (**mortgagor**), the lender (**mortgagee**), and the seller in securing a loan for the purchase of real estate.

Motion to dismiss- A motion filed by a defendant asking the court to dismiss a case.

N

Natural law- A higher set of rules than enacted laws that is based on ethics and morality to promote justice.

Necessary and proper clause- In Article I, §8 of the Constitution, the clause that gives Congress the power ". . . to make all Laws which shall be necessary and proper for carrying into execution . . ."

Negligence- Unintentional wrong against another.

Negligence per se- Violation of a public safety statute.

Negotiable instruments- Substitutes for money that can pass through the financial system.

Negotiation- A method of dispute resolution that requires both sides to make a good-faith effort to resolve a dispute; once agreement is reached, a binding contract spells out the new obligations of both parties. In commercial law, the processes by which rights to checks and other negotiable instruments pass from one person to another.

Noncommercial speech- Pure or political speech, protected by the Constitution.

Nuisance The interference of another's rights to use and quietly enjoy property.

O

Obscenity- Oral, written, or otherwise visual expression or material that the average person applying community standards would find as appealing to the prurient interest, that depicts sexual conduct specifically prohibited by local law, and that taken as a whole lacks serious literary, artistic, political, or scientific value. This is not the same as **indecent material**, which displays or depicts sexually explicit content, but does not meet the three criteria for obscenity, and is protected by the First Amendment.

Open-end lease- An automobile lease that may require the consumer to pay the difference if the residual value is more than the car's market value at the end of the lease.

Open policy- A property insurance policy through which the insurer is to pay the fair market value of the insured property at the time it was destroyed.

Open shop- Where a union represents the bargaining unit, but individual workers are not required to become members or pay dues.

Order paper- An instrument that is payable to a specifically identified person.

Ordinances - Laws passed by city and county governments within a state that may not conflict with state or federal laws.

P

Paralegal- A person with legal skills who is not an attorney but works under the supervision of an attorney to perform tasks relating to the practice of law.

Parental liability statutes- State laws that impose financial responsibility on parents when their children commit intentional torts that injure people or property.

Parol Evidence rule- The contract rule that holds that a person cannot use evidence of statements made before or at the same time as a writing to contradict any of the written terms of a contract.

Patent defects- Defects to property that are readily observable.

Periodic tenancy- Tenancy of a leased property when no specific duration is stated in the rental agreement.

Plaintiff- A party who brings about a legal action.

Pleadings- Formal claims and defenses by parties to a suit, with the intended purpose of providing notice of what is to be expected at the trial.

Point system- State system of allocating points for traffic violations of licensed drivers, the number of points based on the seriousness of the violations. When reaching a preset number of points, the driver's license is suspended.

Police powers - Powers given to the states to pass laws protecting the health, safety, and general welfare of their citizens.

Portable health insurance- Insurance that guarantees health coverage to persons who change or lose jobs, by limiting waiting periods for new employees to gain coverage or by requiring insurers to sell individual policies to people who have left jobs.

Possessory lien- An artisan or mechanic's right to maintain possession of personal property until paid for any repairs or improvements done to it.

Precedent- A case or court decision that serves as an example or authority for identical or similar cases or questions of law that arise later.

Preemption- A doctrine whereby the supremacy clause dictates that state laws conflicting with valid federal laws are unconstitutional.

Prenuptial agreement (or **antenuptial agreement**)- An agreement between a couple before marriage that generally concerns property and support rights, personal rights and responsibilities, and custody and support obligations to children born during marriage.

Pretrial conference- A private meeting with the lawyers on both sides of a dispute and the judge on the case, to honestly assess the nature of the claims.

Private law- Legally binding obligations created by private persons through their power to contract, but that are subordinate to other sources of law.

Pro bono ("For the good")- A Latin term used to describe work or legal services performed free of charge.

Procedural law- Rules designed to control the manner in which rights and duties are determined.

Procedural unconscionability- In contracts, focuses on the manner in which the contract was negotiated and whether each party had reasonable opportunity to understand the terms and conditions of the contract.

Promissory estoppel- A promise that causes another to act in reliance on it.

Promissory note- A negotiable instrument through which one person promises to pay money to another person on demand or at a particular time in the future.

Pro rata **clause-** A clause in a property insurance policy that apportions financial resonsibility among multiple insurers and prevents the insured from recovering more than the actual value of the loss.

Pro se **divorce-** "Do-it-yourself" divorce, without legal representation and usually used when there are no property or child-custody issues between a couple.

Proximate causation- A requirement of causation in which the defendant is liable only for the outcomes that should reasonably have been foreseen at the time the duty was breached.

Q

Quasi contract- A contract imposed by the court in a situation where no contract exists but the court wants to avoid unjust enrichment.

Quitclaim deed- A deed that conveys to the buyer whatever title the seller has in the property, but that does not guarantee that there are no competing claims to the property.

R

Residual value- In a closed-end automobile lease, the preset amount remaining at the end of the lease period that the consumer may pay to purchase the car.

Res ipsa loquitur **("The thing speaks for itself")-** A rule of evidence whereby the negligence of a person may be inferred from the mere fact that the injury in question occurred.

Respondeat superior **("Let the master answer" or vicarious liability)** The theory of liability that applies to situations where an agent commits a tort in the scope of her agency, thereby subjecting her principal to liability.

Restrictive covenants- Restrictions limiting the future use of property.

Retainer- An initial fee paid to an attorney by the client upon agreement to perform the requested legal services.

Retaliatory eviction- A landlord's eviction of, or refusal to renew leases with, tenants who complain about housing code violations.

Reverse a decision- An appellate court's decision against a lower court's verdict. If a case must be reheard because of improper interpretation of law, it is **reversed and remanded** for the lower court to retry.

Revocation- An offeror's withdrawal of an offer.

Right of redemption- The right of a borrower to recover collateral by paying off a loan prior to foreclosure.

Rules of construction- Court rules regarding the resolution of disputes when words of a written agreement are ambiguous.

S

Sanctions- Penalties.

Savings clause- A clause providing that termination of the landlord/tenant relationship does not affect the former tenant's liability for rent.

Service mark- Any word, name, symbol, or device used by a services provider as identification to distinguish it from its competitors.

Settlement- The process of resolving a dispute outside of court.

Sexual harassment- Illegal discrimination based on sex. **Quid pro quo** harassment occurs when employment is conditioned upon the employee submitting to unwelcome sexual advances.

Slander- Spoken defamation.

Small claims court- State courts that provide an inexpensive forum for the resolution of small civil suits.

Sociological jurisprudence- Interpretation of laws that looks past the plain meaning of words to promote social agendas in keeping with social evolution.

Sole proprietorship- A business organization with only one owner.

Solicitation- Asking, enticing, or encouraging someone to engage in illegal conduct. Also, advertising services or drumming up business through advertising.

Spam- Mass e-mailings for advertising that are said to overload e-mail servers.

Spendthrift clause- A clause in a trust agreement that prevents creditors or other assignees from gaining access to the beneficiaries' interests.

Spousal testimony privilege- The requirement of spouses not to testify against one another in criminal proceedings.

Standing- The "standing to sue" doctrine, which means a party has sufficient stake in a dispute to obtain judicial resolution. Standing requires that the plaintiff must have suffered an injury in fact, that there be causal connection between the plaintiff's injury and defendant's conduct, and that the injury will be redressed by a favorable decision by the court.

Stare decisis - A term meaning "let the decision stand," which states that a court, in making a decision, should follow the rulings of prior cases that have similar facts or precedents.

Statute- A formal, written law, either federal, state, city, or county.

Statute of frauds- State requirements that certain contracts generally must be in writing to be enforceable.

Strict liability- Liability without fault.

Subagent- The agent of an agent.

Sublease- The transfer of some of one's interest, property, or rights as a tenant to another.

subpoena- A command by the court for a witness to appear at the trial at a certain time and place to give testimony.

Substantive law- Laws that establish the rights and duties that members of a society possess.

Summary judgment- A decision by a judge on a case based on the information in the pleadings and facts uncovered during the discovery process.

Summary process statutes- Statutes that provide landlords with quick judicial procedures for regaining possession of rented property when tenants violate terms of the lease.

Summons- In a civil suit, an official notification to a defendant of the claims against him or her, ordering him or her to appear in court at a specified time. The actual presentation of the summons to the defendant is known as **service of process,** and the person who presents it is a **process server.** Also, in a criminal case, an order to appear in court.

Supremacy clause- The statement in Article VI, section 2, of the Constitution that states that the Constitution and federal laws are the supreme laws of the land, and conflicting state laws are unconstitutional.

Supreme Court- The highest appellate court in the United States and the final authority on the interpretation of federal statutes and the U. S. Constitution.

Surety- One who makes an original promise to pay the debts of another.

Surrender- An agreement between a landlord and tenant that relieves the tenant of further liability, including the duty to pay rent, under the lease.

Symbolic speech- Expression that is not written or oral, such as cross-burning or displaying a swastika, some of which is protected by the Constitution.

T

Tenancy at sufferance- Tenancy that continues after a lease has expired until the landlord either demands possession of the property or elects to treat the relationship as a new tenancy.

Tenancy by the entirety- A form of co-ownership similar to a joint tenancy, except neither of the parties may unilaterally transfer their property interest.

Tenancy-in-common- A situation in which two or more persons are given equal rights and responsibilities to property transferred to them.

Tender years doctrine- Historically, a doctrine that created judicial preference for maternal custody in a divorce when the children were very young.

Term life insurance- Life insurance that is only for a specific term, or time period, after which it is no longer in effect.

Testator- A person who leaves a will.

Tort- Intentional or negligent wrong against an individual.

Trademark- Any word, name, symbol, or device used by a manufacturer or seller to identify its products and to distinguish them from those of competitors.

Trademark dilution laws- Laws that protect distinctive or famous marks from unauthorized uses even when confusion with another trademark is not likely to occur.

Treasure trove- Property that has been hidden or concealed for such a length of time that its true owner is undiscoverable or deceased.

Trespass- Intentional and unlawful entry onto property possessed by another, or causing some harmful substance to enter such property.

trial de novo **("A new trial")-** In a small claims case, the parties appeal and must completely retry the case as if they never had the original proceeding.

Trust- The holding of property for the benefit of another, by a person with legal rights to the property.

Trustee- A fiduciary who owes a duty of loyalty to administer a trust for the benefit of the beneficiary.

U

Unconscionability- In contracts, when terms are grossly unfair to one party, usually when the party lacks knowingness and voluntariness.

Unconscionable contract- A contract that no sensible person not under delusion or duress or in distress would make, or no honest and fair person would accept.

Unilateral contract- A contract in which one party promises something in exchange for another party's act; a promise for an act.

Union shop- Where workers are required to join the union at the end of a grace period after becoming an employee.

V

Valid contract- A contract for which all of the legal requirements imposed by contract law are met.

Valued policy- A property insurance policy through which the insurer is to pay the face value of the policy when property is totally destroyed.

Venue - The concept of determining which court is the proper place for a lawsuit to be brought.

Verdict- The formal decision made by a jury (or by a judge in a bench trial), reported to and accepted by the court, on the matters on trial.

Viatical settlement- The purchase of a life insurance policy from a terminally ill person by an investor who pays the premiums until the insured person dies, and then collects the full payout.

Voidable contract- A contract that could be canceled by one of the parties, and is enforceable unless the party with the right to cancel exercises that right.

Void contract- A contract in which the parties fail to comply with the basic contract requirements.

W

Warranty deed- A deed that conveys to the buyer the title to property, with the promise that the property is free and clear of any competing claims.

Whole life insurance- Life insurance for which the owner of the policy must pay a premium for a time period determined by the insurance contract, and that is effective until the owner dies.

Will- A document written by a testator that is signed and witnessed in the presence and sight of the testator and the witnesses, and is valid if the testator was of sound mind and legal age at the time the will was made.

Writing requirement- A statute-of-frauds provision requiring that contracts for the sale of goods worth $500 or more be in writing, the exception being **partial performance,** when part of an oral contract has been fulfilled.

Writ of certiorari- A writ to a lower court from a higher court indicating that the higher court is willing to review the lower court decision.

Writ of execution- A legal document obtained by the judgment creditor from the court directing the sheriff to seize assets of the judgment debtor to satisfy the judgment.

Z

Zoning ordinances- Ordinances that regulate the use of real estate.

QUICKEN BUSINESS LAW PARTNER®3 EXERCISES

This portion of the text is intended to help you in your personal legal and business issues. Through the *Quicken Business Law Partner*®3 documents, you can learn to read and understand legal and business forms, letters, and other documents. These exercises will help you understand your rights as a debtor, and what to do when you can't get the other side to a contract to make good on a promise. For example, do you have the right to request a credit report? How would you do it? What if you wanted to file a suit to collect damages? What language would you use and what would the form for a complaint look like?

With the help of *Quicken Business Law Partner*®3 software, you can now work through the following exercises to understand how law and rights look when you put them into action. You will gain firsthand experience in drafting a letter of complaint to a breaching contract party. You can learn how to make requests for information from the federal government. You will even learn how to exercise your right under federal law to obtain a copy of your own credit report.

In the following scenarios you might be able to find help in solving a dispute with your landlord. You could discover a way to have your business handled for you if you must be out of town. You can learn about various employment contracts. With these exercises you bring together your own questions, your knowledge of the law, and your skills for critical thinking in solving individual problems.

An answer section after the exercises (pp. 577–581) provides answers to most of the exercises so that you can check your application skills. Challenge exercises are more comprehensive and may be assigned by your instructor. Just remember to read the assignment carefully, review the *Quicken Business Law Partner*®3 forms and documents, and apply your knowledge gained from this text to the circumstances to find a solution. You will gain valuable knowledge and skills in resolving the inevitable legal issues that cross everyone's path.

Exercise 1

Government Power and Individual Rights (Chapters 4 and 5)

Government Records

Review the "Request for FBI and CIA Records in the Government" section of the *Quicken Business Law Partner*®*3* and answer the following questions:

1. If you used this letter request, what would you obtain?

2. If the agency indicates it will withhold the records you have requested, what information must it give?

Challenge Exercise
Write and request your own records.

Exercise 2

Government Power and Individual Rights (Chapters 4 and 5)

Freedom of Information Request

Review the "FOI Request" in the *Quicken Business Law Partner*®*3* and answer the following questions:

1. What information does the requestor need to provide to the agency?

2. What does the letter request if your request is not addressed to the proper agency?

Exercise 3

Bill of Sale (Chapter 8)

Refer to the "Bill of Sale" in the *Quicken Business Law Partner*®*3* and answer the following questions:

1. What does property sold "AS IS" mean?

2. What does a bill of sale do?

3. Is a bill of sale different from a document of title?

Note: Exercises 4 through 10 are based on the following facts:

David and Maria Lopez contracted with Tolleson Carpet for the purchase and installation of carpet in their home for a total price of $4,281. While the installers were moving the furniture in the Lopezes' family room in order to remove the old carpet and install the new, one worker swung a roll of carpet around in such a way that it hit the screen of the Lopezes' wide-screen television. Maria Lopez witnessed this event but could not get close enough to inspect the television screen when it happened.

After the carpet installation was complete, both David and Maria noticed the scratch. Maria told David, "That's just where that worker scraped the roll of carpet when they were moving the furniture." The Lopezes' television was two months old at the time of the carpet installation, so they had a repair service examine the screen. Replacement cost for the screen, including labor, was estimated at $671.

Maria called Tolleson's manager, Frank Fairbanks, and explained the problem with the television screen. "Look," Fairbanks responded, "you can't prove we did that. That's not our problem. Besides, read your contract. It says right in there that we have no liability for any damages to your house or furniture that occurs while we're installing your carpet." Maria hung up and told David, "I guess I could put it all in writing and maybe the company could respond."

Exercise 4

Breach of Contract and Withholding Payment (Chapters 8 and 9)

They Scratched my Wide-Screen TV, Now What?

Refer to the "BBB/Attorney General Letter of Complaint" provided in the *Quicken Business Law Partner*®*3* Documents.

1. What details will Maria and David need to fill in to draft the complaint?

2. What documents do you think they should attach to their complaint?

3. Can you think of means of alternative dispute resolution that might help Maria and David and Tolleson's to resolve their differences?

Challenge Exercise
Help Maria draft a letter of complaint using the form provided in the *Quicken Business Law Partner*®*3* Documents. Do you have all the information you need?

Exercise 5

Stop Payment Orders (Chapter 11)

We Need to Get that Check Back!

David has just given Tolleson a check for $2,281, the balance due on the carpet contract. "I wonder if there is anything I can do to get my money back until this issue with the television screen is resolved," David wondered.

Review Chapter 11 in the text and determine whether David can take any action with the check to Tolleson. Refer to the *Quicken Business Law Partner®3* Credit Documents, the "Stop Payment on a Check" form, and answer the following questions:

1. Can Lopez rightfully stop payment on the check to Tolleson?

2. Must the drawer give a reason for the stop payment?

3. According to the stop payment form, who will pay the costs and fees for stopping payment?

4. Will the bank be held liable if the stop payment order should not have been requested by the drawer?

5. Who will be held liable if the stop payment order was wrongfully issued?

Challenge Exercise

Review Chapter 11 and discuss the validity of Tolleson's disclaimer for damages that occur while they are installing carpet. What information would Lopez need to stop payment on the check? Draft a stop payment order for Lopez and be sure to customize it for their fact circumstances.

Exercise 6

Notice of Dishonor (Chapter 11)

The Saga of the Wide-Screen TV Continues

After Tolleson deposited the Lopezes' check, it is notified that the check has been dishonored by the Lopezes' bank. Review Chapter 11 and determine Tolleson's rights. Answer the following question:

1. Is Tolleson required to notify Lopez of the bank's dishonor of the check?

Turn to the "Quicken Bad Check Notice" under the Credit Document section, and answer the following questions:

2. According to the notice, what will happen if payment is not made immediately?

3. Is interest accruing?

Challenge Exercise

Help Tolleson by also drafting a follow-up letter to David and Maria Lopez with a demand for payment.

Exercise 7

Collection Activities (Chapter 10)

Collection Efforts for the Carpet Begin

With no response from the Lopezes, Tolleson has referred the matter to a collection agency. The collection agency has contacted the Lopezes and demanded payment. The letter from the collection agency includes the following paragraphs:

> *Tolleson Carpet has made repeated demands for payment on your carpet contract.*
>
> *Please pay the amount due ($2,281.00) today so that your credit rating is not affected by your nonpayment of this binding obligation.*
>
> *If payment is not received within 10 days, we shall proceed with all rights and remedies afforded Tolleson by law.*

Review the *Quicken Business Law Partner®3* Credit Documents and answer the following questions:

1. Has the collection agency violated any laws with its demand letter?

2. What rights could the Lopezes assert?

Challenge Exercise

Help the Lopezes draft a letter responding to the collection agency's demand for payment.

Exercise 8

Credit Reports (Chapter 10)

Now the Screen Scratch Might Affect my Credit Rating

Maria and David Lopez are concerned that their problems with Tolleson may have resulted in a blemish on their previously flawless credit report. Review the *Quicken Business Law Partner*®3 Credit Documents. Refer to the request for a credit report and answer the following questions:

1. What must be included with a request for a credit report in order to obtain the report?

2. Why would the inclusion of a social security number be important?

Challenge Exercise

Help the Lopezes make the appropriate request. Be sure to list any additional information you would need in order to make the request.

Exercise 9

Small Claims Court (Chapter 2)

The Lawsuit for the Carpet Payment

Suppose that the Lopezes still have not paid the remaining balance for the carpet and Tolleson wishes to proceed with a suit to recover the amount due from them. Refer to the *Quicken Business Law Partner*®3 Credit Documents and the "Small Claims Worksheet" and answer the following questions:

1. Go to the list of state small claims limits in the document. Does the claim against the Lopezes qualify for small claims court in your state? Suppose the Lopezes have paid all but the $671 for the television screen; would the Tolleson suit then qualify for small claims court in your state?

2. What additional information do you need to complete the checklist?

3. Who is the plaintiff in this suit? Who is the defendant?

4. Which state has the highest small claims court maximum?

Challenge Exercise

Complete the small claims checklist for Tolleson.

Exercise 10

Filing a Lawsuit (Chapter 2)

The Suit for the Television Screen Scratch

Suppose the Lopezes make the $2,281 payment to Tolleson and then file suit against the company to collect the $671 for the repair of their television screen. Refer to the *Quicken Business Law Partner*®3 Credit Documents and the portion on "Defending A Lawsuit—Business" and answer the following questions:

1. In this situation, who is the plaintiff? Who is the defendant?

2. What additional information do you need to complete the form?

Challenge Exercise

Complete the checklist as thoroughly as you can for Tolleson with the information you have been given.

Exercise 11

Contracts (Chapters 8 and 9)

General Contract: Products

Review the "General Contract—Products" form in the General Business Documents of *Quicken Business Law Partner*®3 and answer the following questions:

1. What happens if the buyer fails to make a payment?

2. What is the time given for delivery?

3. Who pays the costs if improper packaging produces damages to the goods?

4. Who pays the taxes in this transaction?

5. What are the inspection rights under the contract?

6. Are these inspection rights different from those given under the UCC?

7. What is *force majeure*?

8. Give examples listed as *force majeure*.

9. What do the parties agree to do in the event there is a dispute between them?

10. What is the pledge of confidentiality?

11. Is an assignment of this contract permitted?

Exercise 12

Borrowing Money (Chapter 10)

The Role of Guarantors

Refer to Chapter 10 and the "Guaranty" in the *Quicken Business Law Partner®3* and answer the following questions:

1. What type of guaranty is this?

2. How long does the guaranty last?

3. Does the creditor have to notify the guarantor if the debtor defaults?

4. Does the creditor have to notify the guarantor if he loans more money to the debtor?

5. Does the creditor have to show diligence in collection before turning to the guarantor?

6. What can the creditor change without notice to the guarantor?

7. Is the guarantor released if the creditor does change terms?

Exercise 13

Borrowing Money (Chapter 10)

Promissory Notes

Refer to the "Promissory Note" in the *Quicken Business Law Partner®3* Documents and answer the following questions:

1. How are payments applied?

2. In what currency is the note payable?

3. Review Chapter 10. Is it possible to have a negotiable promissory note in the United States when the note is not payable in U.S. currency?

Exercise 14

Credit Applications and Denial (Chapter 10)

Assume you have been denied a loan for the purchase of a car. Refer to Chapter 10 and the "Challenge to a Denial of Credit" in the *Quicken Business Law Partner®3* program.

1. What requests for information are made in the letter?

Exercise 15

Powers of Attorney: Agency Relationships (Chapter 12)

How Do I Close on a House When I'm Out of the Country?

Nancy Travis, a photographer for *National Geographic*, lives in Scarsdale, New York. The National Geographic Society has just given Nancy an assignment in the Andes that will run from June 1, 1999, until July 14, 2000. Nancy will depart on May 29, 1999, for South America.

Nancy is single and has just purchased a house. The closing on her house is scheduled for June 15, 1999, and because of title searches and mortgage paperwork, she has learned that this date is the earliest she can expect for the closing. In addition, Nancy will be receiving an inheritance of 22,000 shares of IBM stock from her late uncle's estate that is scheduled for a final distribution hearing on June 20, 2000.

Nancy is concerned because she can't handle all of these personal transactions when she is out of the country working. "They'll need my signature on documents for the closing and the stock transfer. And the papers aren't even completed yet, so I can't sign them in advance. There won't even be any papers for the stock until the judge signs them after the hearing. How can I sign for the shares then?"

Jake Truitt, a lifelong friend of Nancy's, has offered to help in whatever way he can to handle the transactions while Nancy is gone but notes, "I just can't see that they will accept my signature."

Review the material on agency in Chapter 12. Then turn to the *Quicken Business Law Partner®3* program and refer to the "Power of Attorney" Documents.

1. What authority does a general power of attorney give?

2. According to the agreement, is Jake entitled to compensation?

3. Can Jake serve under the power of attorney without compensation?

4. Can Nancy revoke the power of attorney?

Refer to the "Special Power of Attorney" in the *Quicken Business Law Partner®3* Documents.

5. What is the distinction between this document and the general power of attorney?

6. Is the agent entitled to compensation?

Challenge Exercise

Can you help Nancy with her dilemma? Explain the pros and cons of a power of attorney to Nancy. Using the information you have been given, draft a power of attorney for Nancy.

Exercise 16

Getting a Job (Chapter 13)

Confidentiality Agreement

Review the "Confidentiality Agreement" in the *Quicken Business Law Partner*®*3* and answer the following questions:

1. What is the definition of confidential information?

2. What kinds of information would you list as being confidential? Refer to Chapter 13.

Exercise 17

Getting a Job (Chapter 13)

Consulting Agreement

Review the "Consulting Agreement" in the *Quicken Business Law Partner*®*3* and answer the following questions:

1. Will the consultant be an independent contractor or an employee?

2. Why is this distinction important? What differences exist between hiring an independent contractor and hiring an employee? Refer to Chapter 13.

Exercise 18

Getting a Job (Chapter 13)

Employment Agreement

Review the "Employment Agreement" in the *Quicken Business Law Partner*®*3* and answer the following questions:

1. How long will the employment last?

2. Is an employment of this length legal?

3. How are the parties to the agreement to give notice?

Exercise 19

Getting a Job (Chapter 13)

Regulation of Employment

Review the "Social Security Earnings Benefit Request" in the *Quicken Business Law Partner*®*3* and answer the following questions:

1. What information is this request designed to obtain for you?

2. What are the penalties for making a request to obtain this information on someone other than yourself without their permission?

Challenge Exercise

Write and obtain your own SS-Earnings benefit statement.

Exercise 20

Getting a Job (Chapter 13)

Letter of Acceptance

Review the *Quicken Business Law Partner*®*3* "Letter of Acceptance" under Employment and answer the following questions:

1. Prior to the time of the use of this document, what interaction had the parties had regarding employment?

2. How would a letter like this help the employee? Be sure to review Chapter 13.

Exercise 21

Getting a Job (Chapter 13)

Non-Compete Agreement: Antitrust and Employment

Review the "Non-Compete Agreement" in the *Quicken Business Law Partner*®*3* and answer the following questions:

1. What types of activities does the agreement prohibit?

2. What remedies are given for violation of the agreement?

3. Refer to Chapter 13 and discuss why and when this type of agreement would be necessary.

Exercise 22

Starting a Business (Chapter 14)

Corporate Bylaws

Review the "Corporate Bylaws" in the *Quicken Business Law Partner®3* and answer the following questions:

1. How often will meetings of shareholders be held?

2. Who can call a special meeting?

3. When must notice of a meeting be given?

4. What constitutes a quorum for meetings?

5. Can a quorum be met with proxy representation?

6. Can a director be removed without cause?

7. List the offices provided by the bylaws.

8. Who elects the officers?

9. How are the bylaws amended?

10. Can you own shares in the corporation without actually having stock certificates?

Exercise 23

Starting a Business (Chapter 14)

Articles of Incorporation

Review the Articles of Incorporation in the *Quicken Business Law Partner®3* and answer the following questions:

1. List the information needed for incorporation using this document.

2. Is this same information required under the MBCA? Refer to Chapter 14.

3. Will the corporation provide indemnity for its officers and directors?

4. Refer to Chapter 14. What does indemnity for officers and directors mean?

Challenge Exercise

Draft your own articles of incorporation.

Exercise 24

Property (Chapter 15)

Copyright Application: Intellectual Property

Review the "Copyright Application" in the *Quicken Business Law Partner®3* and answer the following questions:

1. List the types of works that can be copyrighted.

2. If a book is written by an employee during the course of employment, who has the right to the copyright?

Exercise 25

Renting an Apartment (Chapter 17)

Real Estate Leases

Refer to Chapter 17 and the "Real Estate Lease—Commercial" in the *Quicken Business Law Partner®3* and answer the following questions:

1. When is the rent due under the lease?

2. Who is responsible for insurance on the property?

3. How does either party give notice to the other according to the lease?

4. What happens if a portion of the lease agreement is unenforceable?

Exercise 26

Renting an Apartment (Chapter 17)

The Defective Apartment

The heating in your apartment does not work, and it is February in North Conway, New Hampshire. Refer to Chapter 17 and the "Complaint to the Landlord" in *Quicken Business Law Partner®3*.

1. What two things does the note to the landlord accomplish?

2. What rights do tenants generally have regarding the conditions of their leased premises?

Challenge Exercise

Draft a letter of complaint for a problem in your own apartment.

Exercise 27

Renting an Apartment (Chapter 17)

Residential Leases

Refer to the "Residential Lease" in the *Quicken Business Law Partner*®*3* and Chapter 17 and answer the following questions:

1. What provisions do you see in the residential lease that are not found in the commercial lease?

2. What is the habitability clause, and what does it do for the tenant?

Exercise 28

Renting an Apartment (Chapter 17)

Rental Application

Refer to the "Rental Application" in the *Quicken Business Law Partner*®*3* and answer the following questions:

1. What happens if a tenant submits an application and is approved by the landlord and then fails to rent the premises?

2. Will the landlord be permitted to do a credit check?

3. List the grounds on which the landlord can't discriminate.

4. What rights does the tenant have if rejected by the landlord?

Challenge Exercise

What problematic questions do you see in the application?

Exercise 29

Renting an Apartment (Chapter 17)

The Rental Property Inspection

Refer to the "Renter's Inspection Worksheet" in the *Quicken Business Law Partner*®*3* and answer the following questions:

1. What are the general standards for the condition of the premises that the parties confirm through sign-off on this inspection sheet?

2. What effect does this checklist have on termination rights of the tenant?

3. For what defects does the tenant assume the risk?

4. What does the tenant agree to do with respect to the smoke detector?

Exercise 30

Bill of Sale for Motor Vehicles (Chapter 22)

Refer to the "Bill of Sale—Motor Vehicles" in the *Quicken Business Law Partner*®*3* and answer the following questions:

1. What differences are there between the bill of sale and the bill of sale for motor vehicles?

2. What happens if the seller makes a false statement regarding the vehicle's mileage?

3. What promise does the seller make in the bill of sale about the vehicle's odometer?

Answers

Exercise 1

1. All information about you held by the FBI and CIA with certain exceptions such as information related to any ongoing investigations.
2. The agency must disclose why the information is being withheld.

Exercise 2

1. The requestor must provide what documents he/she is looking for and for what period.
2. That the request be forwarded to the proper agency.

Exercise 3

1. When the phrase "AS IS" appears in a contract, it means that both the implied warranty of merchantability and the implied warranty of fitness for a particular purpose are disclaimed. The goods are sold with all their defects, and the buyer assumes the risk of those defects. Subsequently discovered defects cannot be a basis for suit or liability against the seller.
2. A bill of sale is evidence of a transfer of title.
3. A bill of sale is evidence of a transfer of title but is not itself a document of title.

Exercise 4

1. Maria and David will need to tell their story in their letter as it is reflected in the facts. They will need to spell out their issues about the carpet layers and the television screen.
2. Copies of the documents Maria and David should attach are: the carpet contract; the purchase contract for the television (to show it was a relatively new purchase at the time of the carpet problem); and the estimate for the repair. Maria and David could attach affidavits from people who had seen the screen before the installation (including themselves) that attest to the fact the screen was not scratched prior to the installers' conduct.
3. Maria and David and the Tollesons could sit with a mediator and try to work out a fair solution such as at least splitting the cost of the screen repair. They could also try arbitration in which the arbitrator could propose a solution.

Exercise 5

1. Yes. Lopez can stop payment on the check, but this action is not a final determination for the contract rights that might exist between the parties. Stopping payment on the check is simply a means for the Lopezes to gain leverage in terms of resolution of the dispute. By stopping payment, they are not in the position of having to seek money from Tolleson. Tolleson will be forced to deal with the issues the Lopezes have raised in order to obtain payment.
2. Yes, the drawer must give a reason for the stop payment order. In this case, the Lopezes would simply explain that they are stopping payment because of a contract dispute.
3. The drawer bears the cost of stopping payment on a check.
4. No. The bank is not liable because it has no way of knowing whether the contract complaint is legitimate. The bank puts a clause in its stop payment forms to protect it—stopping the payment at the customer's direction without agreeing to assume the liability if it is wrong.
5. The drawer has full liability to the payee for a wrongful stop payment order. This liability rests where it should because the stop payment order is the result of a dispute between the drawer and the payee. To the extent the drawer is wrong, the parties' contractual liability will take over and determine damages.

Exercise 6

1. Yes. Tolleson is required to notify the Lopezes because the primary party, or at least the first party for presentment of the instrument, the bank, has refused to pay. In order to attach liability of the secondary party (the drawer), the payee must give notification of dishonor.
2. If payment of the amount of the check is not made immediately, Tolleson will make an additional charge and there will be no further credit extended to the Lopezes.
3. Yes. Interest does accrue during the entire time that Tolleson attempts to collect the amount due from the Lopezes.

Exercise 7

1. The collection agency has not violated any of the provisions of the *Fair Debt Collections Practices Act* assuming that the notice is given privately. The notice contains a classic collector's hedge in that it does not threaten a suit directly in case the creditor or the agency decides not to proceed with such action. The notice is broad enough that any additional action could be taken, but not so specific that the agency would be making a threat it would not carry out, which is a violation of the FDCPA.

2. The Lopezes could respond that they wish to have no further contact from the collection agency and the contact would have to stop. If the Lopezes do assert their rights to no further contact, the issue about the scratched screen will come to a head because it is intertwined with the issue of payment, and any legal action by Tolleson to collect the amount due will enable the Lopezes to respond with their claim for damages to their TV.

Exercise 8

1. Personal ID (copy), the appropriate fee, social security number, and addresses for the last five years.
2. The social security number is included because mix-ups between individuals with the same names can be avoided when the SS# is used. Also, phony requests are at least reduced because the SS# is more difficult to come by than a name and address. The additional information on addresses is also requested to match persons with reports correctly. Because of numerous lawsuits over the past few years of mix-ups in identification, credit reporting agencies take additional precautions with respect to data and the release of credit reports.

Exercise 9

1. Simply review the chart provided in the *Quicken* "Small Claims Worksheet" and match it to your state. In most states the $671 qualifies for small claims court.
2. To complete the small claims checklist, you will need an address for Tolleson as well as its business status—i.e., a corporation, sole proprietorship, etc.
3. Tolleson is the plaintiff, and the Lopezes would be the defendants.
4. With a maximum of $15,000, Florida and Delaware have the highest small claims court jurisdiction.

Exercise 10

1. In this factual situation, the Lopezes will be the plaintiffs and Tolleson will be the defendant.
2. Tolleson will need to check with its employees or contractors who installed the carpeting to see what happened. Tolleson must find and provide any documentation it has regarding the incident.

Exercise 11

1. The failure of the buyer to make a payment is considered a material breach.

2. "Time is of the essence" is the time given for delivery—ASAP would be the standard.
3. The seller absorbs the loss if the goods are damaged due to improper packaging.
4. The buyer is to pay the taxes.
5. The inspection rights include the right to open, test, and view.
6. The inspection rights afforded under the contract are about the same as those given under Article 2, with the exception that the buyer must give written notice of rejection and the reasons for such rejection.
7. A *force majeure* is an event that interferes with the performance of the contract that is beyond the parties' control and was not anticipated by them.
8. Examples of *force majeure* in the contract include acts of God, fire, explosion, vandalism, storms, riots, military action, wars, and insurrections.
9. If the matter has not been resolved in five days, they agree to go to binding arbitration.
10. A pledge of confidentiality is an agreement not to disclose the terms of the agreement or any proprietary information regarding the product.
11. No. Assignment of the contract is not permitted.

Exercise 12

1. This is an absolute and unconditional guaranty.
2. There can be no revocation of this guaranty, and it lasts until all obligations under the original credit contract are satisfied.
3. No. As is typical in most guaranty contracts, the creditor need not notify the guarantor of the debtor's default.
4. No. The creditor need not notify the guarantor if additional loans are made by the creditor to the debtor.
5. No. The creditor need not show due diligence in collection because this guaranty is an unconditional guaranty of payment. Only in a guarantor of collection situation must a creditor establish due diligence before demanding payment from the guarantor.
6. The creditor can change the payment terms of the credit agreement and release the collateral without giving notice to the guarantor.
7. No. The guarantor is not released if the creditor changes the terms.

Exercise 13

1. Payments under the note are applied first to accrued interest and then to principal.
2. The note is payable in U.S. currency.
3. Yes. A note can still be negotiable even though it is

payable in a currency that is foreign to the country in which the note is made or either party is located. So long as the note is payable in a medium of exchange recognized by some country, it is negotiable and valid.

Exercise 14

1. The information requested in the *Quicken* form is whether a consumer reporting agency was used, and, if so, which one. The letter also requests a description of the nature of the investigation conducted.

   An important tip in checking a credit denial is to be certain that the creditor had the information on you—did they have the right credit report and the right person?

Exercise 15

1. A general power of attorney gives Jake full authority to run Nancy's business affairs. He can open, maintain, and close bank accounts and securities accounts. He is given full access to safe-deposit boxes. He can sell, exchange, buy, invest, and reinvest assets. He can purchase insurance and collect debts. He can enter into binding contracts on Nancy's behalf. He can exercise her stock options; employ help; and sell, mortgage, and lease property. If Nancy had any kind of business operations, he could run them with full authority. He can prepare, sign, and file government documents on Nancy's behalf.

   This general power of attorney is an enormously broad one that gives Jake full and complete authority over any of Nancy's property and legal issues. In this case, a general power of attorney may be more than Nancy wishes to give to Jake.

2. Yes. Jake is entitled to reasonable compensation plus reimbursement for expenses.

3. Yes. Jake could serve as a gratuitous agent, but this form entitles him to compensation. Because Jake is helping Nancy as a friend, they will need to change this portion of the form. Remember, forms are not customized for individual needs and there are legal issues and implications for each clause.

4. Yes. Nancy can revoke the power of attorney at any time. Nancy may want to put a time limitation on the power of attorney. Nancy could also put a transaction limitation on it in that she could direct the transactions for which Jake has authority.

5. The special power of attorney in the *Quicken Business Law Partner*®*3* requires that the specific matters for which there is authority be spelled out; the

power of attorney is limited in scope in that transactional limitations are placed on the delegated authority.

6. Yes. Jake is again entitled to compensation. He could serve as a gratuitous agent, but the clause on compensation would have to be deleted from the document.

Exercise 16

1. The definition of confidential information given in the document is proprietary information not generally known to the public.

2. Information about customers including customer lists, new products, strategies, supply chain management techniques, planned ad campaigns, etc.

Exercise 17

1. The consultant will be an independent contractor.

2. This distinction is important because of wage tax and liability issues, and workers' compensation coverage issues. For an employee, an employer must pay wage taxes, if the employer is fully liable for acts within the scope of employment and subjects the employee to workers' compensation system rules. An independent contractor pays his or her own wage taxes and is not covered by workers' compensation. The employer would also not be liable for the torts of an independent contractor.

Exercise 18

1. It is an "at will" agreement—it can be terminated at any time.

2. Yes. It is legal. There are some exceptions such as terminating a whistleblower that would prevent termination because such a termination would be retaliatory in nature.

3. Notices must be given in writing.

Exercise 19

1. Your history of wages and applicable social security withholding as well as what benefits you could expect under SS programs.

2. Making a request for another without their permission is a violation of federal law that carries fines and/or imprisonment.

Exercise 20

1. From the document, we can conclude that the parties had a conversation about a contract for employment.

2. A letter such as this would help the employee prove that some type of a contract exists. It would

be contemporaneous evidence of discussions of employment. It also serves as a formal acceptance of an oral offer. Further, the failure of the employer to correct any misunderstandings about the conversation and offer of employment would allow the employee to rely on the oral promise and begin the process of terminating another job or moving.

Exercise 21

1. The types of activities prohibited under the agreement are: competing directly or indirectly, soliciting customers for business, inducing employees to leave, and revealing confidential business information.
2. Monetary remedies as well as injunctive relief are afforded under the agreement.
3. This type of agreement is necessary to prevent employees from obtaining proprietary information and then using it to start their own businesses or taking it to other employers who are competitors.

Exercise 22

1. The shareholders will hold meetings at least once each calendar year.
2. A special meeting of shareholders can be called by the president, the board, or a majority of the outstanding shareholders of voting shares.
3. Notice of a meeting must be given no later than 10 days prior to the meeting. The time can be measured from the time the notice is mailed and not when it actually is received by the shareholders.
4. A quorum is the majority of the outstanding voting shares.
5. Yes. Proxies can be used to make up a quorum.
6. Yes. A director can be removed with or without cause.
7. The offices provided in these bylaws include the president, vice president, secretary, and treasurer. More than one office can be held by a single person.
8. The officers are elected by the directors.
9. The bylaws can be amended by the directors or the shareholders by a majority of a quorum of voting shares.
10. Yes. You can own shares in the corporation without having to have certificates as evidence.

Exercise 23

1. Under these sample incorporation documents, the information needed is the total number of shares, the registered agent for the corporation, the purpose of the corporation, and the names of the directors.

2. No. The MBCA does not require all the information noted in these articles of incorporation. These articles require more information that is permitted and possibly desirable from the standpoint of the parties' rights.
3. Yes. The corporation's officers and directors will enjoy the protection of indemnity from the corporation.
4. Indemnity means that the officers and directors can be reimbursed for the expenses they incur in defending their conduct with respect to the corporation. There can be some exceptions such as when the directors and officers engage in fraud.

Exercise 24

1. The types of works that can be copyrighted are music, books, movies, television shows, magazines, newspapers, periodicals, and software.
2. The employer has the right to the copyright because the employer provided the resources for its development.

Exercise 25

1. The rent is due on the first day of each month.
2. Both the landlord and the tenant are responsible for carrying insurance on their respective properties. Tenants would have to carry their own insurance, for example, on their furniture. Landlords would carry an owner's policy on the property.
3. Notice must be given in writing.
4. If one portion of the lease is uneforceable, it is to be struck from the lease so that the remainder can be enforced.

Exercise 26

1. The letter serves two very important purposes: the landlord is put on notice of a heating problem in the apartment, and the landlord is given a time within which to solve the problem.
2. Most states give residential tenants a warranty of habitability, which means that the premises are fit and habitable at the time of the lease. The *Uniform Residential Landlord Tenant Act* (URLTA) also provides tenants with rights in the event the basic essentials of habitation (such as heat, water, and, in some circumstances, air conditioning) cease to work. Those rights include the right to make a demand for repair (which is what this *Quicken* letter is designed to do), and then the right to self-help or make the repairs themselves and then bill the landlord or deduct that amount from the rent. However, all these rights begin with the notice to the landlord of the problem.

Exercise 27

1. Some of the provisions in the residential lease not found in the commercial lease include the condition of the dwelling unit, extended absences of the tenant from the property, and the rights and obligations with respect to the keys.
2. The habitability clause simply puts into the official language of the lease the rights most tenants have in most states: that the premises are in habitable condition at the commencement of the lease.

Exercise 28

1. The tenant whose application is approved by the landlord and who fails to enter into a lease agreement will lose his or her application fee. The reason for such damages is that the landlord expends time and effort (and in some cases fees for the credit report) in processing an application.
2. Yes. The application form authorizes the landlord to do a credit check.
3. The grounds on which a landlord can't discriminate are race, religion, national origin, age, and disability.
4. If the applicant makes a written request for the reason for rejection of the application, the landlord has 60 days within which to respond to the applicant.

Exercise 29

1. The general standards that the checklist is intended to confirm are that the premises are in good, clean, sanitary order and in good condition and repair.
2. By signing off on the inspection sheet, the tenant agrees to return the premises to the landlord in the same condition as when the inspection occurs.
3. The tenant assumes the risk for any defects in the rental property that he knew of or should have known of through inspection of the property.
4. The tenant agrees to test the smoke detector at least every other week and to be certain that it has an alkaline battery that is in working order.

Exercise 30

1. A bill of sale for motor vehicles has more details including a description of the car (make, model, etc.) as well as the mileage.
2. A false statement about the mileage on the car is a federal offense and can result in fines and/or imprisonment.
3. The seller promises that the odometer is in good working order and that it has not been tampered with so as to affect the recorded mileage on the car.

B APPENDIX

The Constitution of the United States

Preamble

We the people of the United States, in order to form a more perfect union, establish justice, insure domestic tranquility, provide for the common defense, promote the general welfare, and secure the blessings of liberty to ourselves and our posterity, do ordain and establish this Constitution for the United States of America.

Article I

SECTION 1. All legislative powers herein granted shall be vested in a Congress of the United States, which shall consist of a Senate and House of Representatives.

SECTION 2.1. The House of Representatives shall be composed of members chosen every second year by the people of the several States, and the electors in each State shall have the qualifications requisite for electors of the most numerous branch of the State legislature.

2. No person shall be a representative who shall not have attained to the age of twenty-five years, and been seven years a citizen of the United States, and who shall not, when elected, be an inhabitant of that State in which he shall be chosen.

3. Representatives and direct taxes shall be apportioned among the several States which may be included within this Union, according to their respective numbers, which shall be determined by adding to the whole number of free persons, including those bound to service for a term of years, and excluding Indians not taxed, three fifths of all other persons.[1] The actual enumeration shall be made within three years after the first meeting of the Congress of the United States, and within every subsequent term of ten years, in such manner as they shall by law direct. The number of representatives shall not exceed one for every thirty thousand, but each State shall have at least one representative; and until such enumeration shall be made, the State of New Hampshire shall be entitled to choose three, Massachusetts eight, Rhode Island and Providence Plantations one, Connecticut five, New York six, New Jersey four, Pennsylvania eight, Delaware one, Maryland six, Virginia ten, North Carolina five, South Carolina five, and Georgia three.

4. When vacancies happen in the representation from any State, the executive authority thereof shall issue writs of election to fill such vacancies.

5. The House of Representatives shall choose their speaker and other officers; and shall have the sole power of impeachment.

SECTION 3.1. The Senate of the United States shall be composed of two senators from each State, chosen by the legislature thereof, for six years; and each senator shall have one vote.

2. Immediately after they shall be assembled in consequence of the first election, they shall be divided as equally as may be into three classes. The seats of the senators of the first class shall be vacated at the expiration of the second year, of the second class at the

---

[1] See the Fourteenth Amendment.

expiration of the fourth year, and of the third class at the expiration of the fourth year, and of the third class at the expiration of the sixth year, so that one third may be chosen every second year; and if vacancies happen by resignation, or otherwise, during the recess of the legislature of any State, the executive thereof may make temporary appointments until the next meeting of the legislature, which shall then fill such vacancies.[2]

3. No person shall be a senator who shall not have attained to the age of thirty years, and been nine years a citizen of the United States, and who shall not, when elected, be an inhabitant of that State for which he shall be chosen.

4. The Vice President of the United States shall be President of the Senate, but shall have no vote, unless they be equally divided.

5. The Senate shall choose their other officers, and also a president pro tempore, in the absence of the Vice President, or when he shall exercise the office of the President of the United States.

6. The Senate shall have the sole power to try all impeachments. When sitting for that purpose, they shall be on oath or affirmation. When the President of the United States is tried, the chief justice shall preside: and no person shall be convicted without the concurrence of two thirds of the members present.

7. Judgment in cases of impeachment shall not extend further than to removal from office, and disqualification to hold and enjoy any office of honor, trust or profit under the United States: but the party convicted shall nevertheless be liable and subject to indictment, trial, judgment and punishment, according to law.

SECTION 4.1. The times, places, and manner of holding elections for senators and representatives, shall be prescribed in each State by the legislature thereof; but the Congress may at any time by law make or alter such regulations, except as to the places of choosing senators.

2. The Congress shall assemble at least once in every year, and such meeting shall be on the first Monday in December, unless they shall by law appoint a different day.

SECTION 5.1. Each House shall be the judge of the elections, returns and qualifications of its own members, and a majority of each shall constitute a quorum to do business; but a smaller number may adjourn from day to day, and may be authorized to compel the attendance of absent members, in such manner, and under such penalties as each House may provide.

[2] See the Seventeenth Amendment.

2. Each House may determine the rules of its proceedings, punish its members for disorderly behavior, and, with the concurrence of two thirds, expel a member.

3. Each House shall keep a journal of its proceedings, and from time to time publish the same, excepting such parts as may in their judgment require secrecy; and the yeas and nays of the members of either House on any question shall, at the desire of one fifth of those present, be entered on the journal.

4. Neither House, during the session of Congress, shall, without the consent of the other, adjourn for more than three days, nor to any other place than that in which the two Houses shall be sitting.

SECTION 6.1. The senators and representatives shall receive a compensation for their services, to be ascertained by law, and paid out of the Treasury of the United States. They shall in all cases, except treason, felony, and breach of the peace, be privileged from arrest during their attendance at the session of their respective Houses, and in going to and returning from the same; and for any speech or debate in either House, they shall not be questioned in any other place.

2. No senator or representative shall, during the time for which he was elected, be appointed to any civil office under the authority of the United States, which shall have been created, or the emoluments whereof shall have been increased during such time; and no person holding any office under the United States shall be a member of either House during his continuance in office.

SECTION 7.1. All bills for raising revenue shall originate in the House of Representatives; but the Senate may propose or concur with amendments as on other bills.

2. Every bill which shall have passed the House of Representatives and the Senate, shall, before it becomes a law, be presented to the President of the United States; if he approves he shall sign it, but if not he shall return it, with his objections to that House in which it shall have originated, who shall enter the objections at large on their journal, and proceed to reconsider it. If after such reconsideration two thirds of that House shall agree to pass the bill, it shall be sent, together with the objections, to the other House, by which it shall likewise be reconsidered, and if approved by two thirds of that House, it shall become a law. But in all such cases the votes of both Houses shall be determined by yeas and nays, and the names of the persons voting for and against the bill shall be entered on the journal of each House respectively. If any bill shall not be returned by the President within ten days (Sundays excepted) after it shall have been presented to him, the same shall be a law, in like manner as if he had signed it, unless the Congress by their adjournment prevent its return, in which case it shall not be a law.

3. Every order, resolution, or vote to which the concurrence of the Senate and the House of Representatives may be necessary (except on a question of adjournment) shall be presented to the President of the United States; and before the same shall take effect, shall be approved by him, or being disapproved by him, shall be repassed by two thirds of the Senate and House of Representatives, according to the rules and limitations prescribed in the case of a bill.

SECTION 8. The Congress shall have the power

1. To lay and collect taxes, duties, imposts, and excises, to pay the debts and provide for the common defense and general welfare of the United States; but all duties, imposts, and excises shall be uniform throughout the United States;

2. To borrow money on the credit of the United States;

3. To regulate commerce with foreign nations, and among the several States, and with the Indian tribes;

4. To establish a uniform rule of naturalization, and uniform laws on the subject of bankruptcies throughout the United States;

5. To coin money, regulate the value thereof, and of foreign coin, and fix the standard of weights and measures;

6. To provide for the punishment of counterfeiting the securities and current coin of the United States;

7. To establish post offices and post roads;

8. To promote the progress of science and useful arts, by securing for limited times to authors and inventors the exclusive rights to their respective writings and discoveries;

9. To constitute tribunals inferior to the Supreme Court;

10. To define and punish piracies and felonies committed on the high seas, and offenses against the law of nations;

11. To declare war, grant letters of marque and reprisal, and make rules concerning captures on land and water;

12. To raise and support armies, but no appropriation of money to that use shall be for a longer term than two years;

13. To provide and maintain a navy;

14. To make rules for the government and regulation of the land and naval forces;

15. To provide for calling forth the militia to execute the laws of the Union, suppress insurrections and repel invasions;

16. To provide for organizing, arming, and disciplining the militia, and for governing such part of them as may be employed in the service of the United States, reserving to the States respectively, the appointment of the officers, and the authority of training the militia according to the discipline prescribed by Congress.

17. To exercise exclusive legislation in all cases whatsoever, over such district (not exceeding ten miles square) as may, by cession of particular States, and the acceptance of Congress, become the seat of the government of the United States, and to exercise like authority over all places purchased by the consent of the legislature of the State in which the same shall be, for the erection of forts, magazines, arsenals, dockyards, and other needful buildings; and

18. To make all laws which shall be necessary and proper for carrying into execution the foregoing powers, and all other powers vested by this Constitution in the government of the United States, or in any department or officer thereof.

SECTION 9.1. The migration or importation of such persons as any of the States now existing shall think proper to admit, shall not be prohibited by the Congress prior to the year one thousand eight hundred and eight, but a tax or duty may be imposed on such importation, not exceeding ten dollars for each person.

2. The privilege of the writ of habeas corpus shall not be suspended, unless when in cases of rebellion or invasion the public safety may require it.

3. No bill of attainder or ex post facto law shall be passed.

4. No capitation, or other direct, tax shall be laid, unless in proportion to the census or enumeration herein before directed to be taken.[3]

5. No tax or duty shall be laid on articles exported from any State.

6. No preference shall be given by any regulation of commerce or revenue to the ports of one State over those of another: nor shall vessels bound to, or from, one State be obliged to enter, clear, or pay duties in another.

7. No money shall be drawn from the treasury, but in consequence of appropriations made by law; and a regular statement and account of the receipts and expenditures of all public money shall be published from time to time.

8. No title of nobility shall be granted by the United States: and no person holding any office of profit or trust under them, shall, without the consent of the Congress, accept of any present, emolument, office, or title, of any kind whatever, from any king, prince, or foreign State.

[3] See the Sixteenth Amendment.

SECTION 10.1. No State shall enter into any treaty, alliance, or confederation; grant letters of marque and reprisal; coin money; emit bills of credit; make anything but gold and silver coin a tender in payment of debts; pass any bill of attainder, ex post facto law, or law impairing the obligation of contracts, or grant any title of nobility.

2. No State shall, without the consent of the Congress, lay any imposts or duties on imports or exports, except what may be absolutely necessary for executing its inspection laws: and the net produce of all duties and imposts laid by any State on imports or exports, shall be for the use of the treasury of the United States; and all such laws shall be subject to the revision and control of the Congress.

3. No State shall, without the consent of the Congress, lay any duty of tonnage, keep troops, or ships of war in time of peace, enter into any agreement or compact with another State, or with a foreign power, or engage in war, unless actually invaded, or in such imminent danger as will not admit of delay.

Article II

SECTION 1.1. The executive power shall be vested in a President of the United States of America. He shall hold his office during the term of four years, and, together with the Vice President, chosen for the same term, be elected as follows:

2. Each State shall appoint, in such manner as the legislature thereof may direct, a number of electors, equal to the whole number of senators and representatives to which the State may be entitled in the Congress: but no senator or representative, or person holding an office of trust or profit under the United States, shall be appointed an elector.

The electors shall meet in their respective States, and vote by ballot for two persons, of whom one at least shall not be an inhabitant of the same State with themselves. And they shall make a list of all the persons voted for, and of the number of votes for each; which list they shall sign and certify, and transmit sealed to the seat of the government of the United States, directed to the president of the Senate. The president of the Senate shall, in the presence of the Senate and House of Representatives, open all the certificates, and the votes shall then be counted. The person having the greatest number of votes shall be the President, if such number be a majority of the whole number of electors appointed; and if there be more than one who have such majority, and have an equal number of votes, then the House of Representatives shall immediately choose by ballot one

of them for President; and if no person have a majority, then from the five highest on the list the said House shall in like manner choose the President. But in choosing the President, the votes shall be taken by States, the representation from each State having one vote; a quorum for this purpose shall consist of a member or members from two thirds of the States, and a majority of all the States shall be necessary to a choice. In every case, after the choice of the President, the person having the greatest number of votes of the electors shall be the Vice President. But if there should remain two or more who have equal votes, the Senate shall choose from them by ballot the Vice President.[4]

3. The Congress may determine the time of choosing the electors, and the day on which they shall give their votes; which day shall be the same throughout the United States.

4. No person except a natural born citizen, or a citizen of the United States, at the time of the adoption of this Constitution, shall be eligible to the office of President; neither shall any person be eligible to that office who shall not have attained to the age of thirty-five years, and been fourteen years a resident within the United States.

5. In the case of removal of the President from office, or of his death, resignation, or inability to discharge the powers and duties of the said office, the same shall devolve on the Vice President, and the Congress may by law provide for the case of removal, death, resignation, or inability, both of the President and Vice President, declaring what officer shall then act as President, and such officer shall act accordingly, until the disability be removed, or a President shall be elected.

6. The President shall, at stated times, receive for his services a compensation, which shall neither be increased nor diminished during the period for which he shall have been elected, and he shall not receive within that period any other emolument from the United States, or any of them.

7. Before he enter on the execution of his office, he shall take the following oath or affirmation:—"I do solemnly swear (or affirm) that I will faithfully execute the office of President of the United States, and will to the best of my ability, preserve, protect and defend the Constitution of the United States."

SECTION 2.1. The President shall be commander in chief of the army and navy of the United States, and of the militia of the several States, when called into the actual service of the United States; he may require the opinion, in writing, of the principal officer in each of the

---

[4] Superseded by the Twelfth Amendment.

executive departments, upon any subject relating to the duties of their respective office, and he shall have power to grant reprieves and pardons for offenses against the United States, except in cases of impeachment.

2. He shall have power, by and with the advice and consent of the Senate, to make treaties, provided two thirds of the senators present concur; and he shall nominate, and by and with the advice and consent of the Senate, shall appoint ambassadors, other public ministers and consuls, judges of the Supreme Court, and all other officers of the United States, whose appointments are not herein otherwise provided for, and which shall be established by law: but the Congress may by law vest the appointment of such inferior officers, as they think proper, in the President alone, in the courts of law, or in the heads of departments.

3. The President shall have power to fill up all vacancies that may happen during the recess of the Senate, by granting commissions which shall expire at the end of their next session.

SECTION 3. He shall from time to time give to the Congress information of the state of the Union, and recommend to their consideration such measures as he shall judge necessary and expedient; he may, on extraordinary occasions, convene both Houses, or either of them, and in case of disagreement between them with respect to the time of adjournment, he may adjourn them to such time as he shall think proper; he shall receive ambassadors and other public ministers; he shall take care that the laws be faithfully executed, and shall commission all the officers of the United States.

SECTION 4. The President, Vice President, and all civil officers of the United States, shall be removed from office on impeachment for, and conviction of, treason, bribery, or other high crimes and misdemeanors.

Article III

SECTION 1. The judicial power of the United States shall be vested in one Supreme Court, and in such inferior courts as the Congress may from time to time ordain and establish. The judges, both of the Supreme and inferior courts, shall hold their offices during good behavior, and shall, at stated times, receive for their services, a compensation, which shall not be diminished during their continuance in office.

SECTION 2.1. The judicial power shall extend to all cases, in law and equity, arising under this Constitution, the laws of the United States, and treaties made, or which shall be made, under their authority;—to all cases

affecting ambassadors, other public ministers and consuls;—to all cases of admiralty and maritime jurisdiction;—to controversies to which the United States shall be a party;—to controversies between two or more States; between a State and citizens of another State;[5]—between citizens of different States;—between citizens of the same State claiming lands under grants of different States, and between a State, or the citizens thereof, and foreign States, citizens or subjects.

2. In all cases affecting ambassadors, other public ministers and consuls, and those in which a State shall be party, the Supreme Court shall have original jurisdiction. In all the other cases before mentioned, the Supreme Court shall have appellate jurisdiction, both as to law and to fact, with such exceptions, and under such regulations as the Congress shall make.

3. The trial of all crimes, except in cases of impeachment, shall be by jury; and such trial shall be held in the State where the said crimes shall have been committed; but when not committed within any State, the trial shall be at such place or places as the Congress may by law have directed.

SECTION 3.1. Treason against the United States shall consist only in levying war against them, or in adhering to their enemies, giving them aid and comfort. No person shall be convicted of treason unless on the testimony of two witnesses to the same overt act, or on confession in open court.

2. The Congress shall have power to declare the punishment of treason, but no attainder of treason shall work corruption of blood, or forfeiture except during the life of the person attainted.

Article IV

SECTION 1. Full faith and credit shall be given in each State to the public acts, records, and judicial proceedings of every other State. And the Congress may by general laws prescribe the manner in which such acts, records and proceedings shall be proved, and the effect thereof.

SECTION 2.1. The citizens of each State shall be entitled to all privileges and immunities of citizens in the several States.[6]

2. A person charged in any State with treason, felony, or other crime, who shall flee from justice, and be found in another State, shall on demand of the executive

[5] See the Eleventh Amendment.
[6] See the Fourteenth Amendment, Section 1.

authority of the State from which he fled, be delivered up to be removed to the State having jurisdiction of the crime.

3. No person held to service or labor in one State under the laws thereof, escaping into another, shall in consequence of any law or regulation therein, be discharged from such service or labor, but shall be delivered up on claim of the party to whom such service or labor may be due.[7]

SECTION 3.1. New States may be admitted by the Congress into this Union; but no new State shall be formed or erected within the jurisdiction of any other State, nor any State be formed by the junction of two or more States, or parts of States, without the consent of the legislatures of the States concerned as well as of the Congress.

2. The Congress shall have power to dispose of and make all needful rules and regulations respecting the territory or other property belonging to the United States; and nothing in this Constitution shall be so construed as to prejudice any claims of the United States, or of any particular State.

SECTION 4. The United States shall guarantee to every State in this Union a republican form of government, and shall protect each of them against invasion; and on application of the legislature, or of the executive (when the legislature cannot be convened) against domestic violence.

Article V

The Congress, whenever two thirds of both Houses shall deem it necessary, shall propose amendments to this Constitution, or, on the application of the legislature of two thirds of the several States, shall call a convention for proposing amendments, which in either case, shall be valid to all intents and purposes, as part of this Constitution when ratified by the legislatures of three fourths of the several States, or by conventions in three fourths thereof, as the one or the other mode of ratification may be proposed by the Congress; provided that no amendment which may be made prior to the year one thousand eight hundred and eight shall in any manner affect the first and fourth clauses in the ninth section of the first article; and that no State, without its consent, shall be deprived of its equal suffrage in the Senate.

Article VI

1. All debts contracted and engagements entered into, before the adoption of this Constitution, shall be as valid against the United States under this Constitution, as under the Confederation.[8]

2. This Constitution, and the laws of the United States which shall be made in pursuance thereof; and all treaties made, or which shall be made, under the authority of the United States, shall be the supreme law of the land; and the judges in every State shall be bound thereby, anything in the Constitution or laws of any State to the contrary notwithstanding.

3. The senators and representatives before mentioned, and the members of the several State legislatures, and all executive and judicial officers, both of the United States and of the several States, shall be bound by oath or affirmation to support this Constitution; but no religious test shall ever be required as a qualification to any office or public trust under the United States.

Article VII

The ratification of the conventions of nine States shall be sufficient for the establishment of this Constitution between the States so ratifying the same.

Done in Convention by the unanimous consent of the States present the seventeenth day of September in the year of our Lord one thousand seven hundred and eighty-seven, and of the independence of the United States of America the twelfth. In witness whereof we have hereunto subscribed our names.

Amendments

First Ten Amendments passed by Congress September 25, 1789. Ratified by three-fourths of the States December 15, 1791.

Amendment I

Congress shall make no law respecting an establishment of religion, or prohibiting the free exercise thereof; or abridging the freedom of speech, or of the press; or the right of the people peaceably to assemble, and to petition the government for a redress of grievances.

Amendment II

A well regulated militia, being necessary to the security of a free State, the right of the people to keep and bear arms, shall not be infringed.

---

[7] See the Thirteenth Amendment.

[8] See the Fourteenth Amendment, Section 4.

Amendment III

No soldier shall, in time of peace be quartered in any house, without the consent of the owner, nor in time of war, but in a manner to be prescribed by law.

Amendment IV

The right of the people to be secure in their persons, houses, papers, and effects, against unreasonable searches and seizures, shall not be violated, and no warrants shall issue, but upon probable cause, supported by oath or affirmation, and particularly describing the place to be searched, and the person or things to be seized.

Amendment V

No person shall be held to answer for a capital, or otherwise infamous crime, unless on a presentment or indictment of a grand jury, except in cases arising in the land or naval forces, or in the militia, when in actual service in time of war or public danger; nor shall any person be subject for the same offense to be twice put in jeopardy of life or limb; nor shall be compelled in any criminal case to be a witness against himself, nor be deprived of life, liberty, or property, without due process of law; nor shall private property be taken for public use without just compensation.

Amendment VI

In all criminal prosecutions, the accused shall enjoy the right to a speedy and public trial, by an impartial jury of the State and district wherein the crime shall have been committed, which district shall have been previously ascertained by law, and to be informed of the nature and cause of the accusation; to be confronted with the witnesses against him; to have compulsory process for obtaining witnesses in his favor, and to have the assistance of counsel for his defense.

Amendment VII

In suits at common law, where the value in controversy shall exceed twenty dollars, the right of trial by jury shall be preserved, and no fact tried by a jury shall be otherwise reexamined in any court of the United States, then according to the rules of the common law.

Amendment VIII

Excessive bail shall not be required, nor excessive fines imposed, nor cruel and unusual punishments inflicted.

Amendment IX

The enumeration in the Constitution of certain rights shall not be construed to deny or disparage others retained by the people.

Amendment X

The powers not delegated to the United States by the Constitution, nor prohibited by it to the States, are reserved to the States respectively, or to the people.

Amendment XI

Passed by Congress March 5, 1794. Ratified January 8, 1798.

The judicial power of the United States shall not be construed to extend to any suit in law or equity, commenced or prosecuted against one of the United States by citizens of another State, or by citizens or subjects of any foreign State.

Amendment XII

Passed by Congress December 12, 1803. Ratified September 25, 1804.

The electors shall meet in their respective States, and vote by ballot for President and Vice President, one of whom, at least, shall not be an inhabitant of the same State with themselves; they shall name in their ballots the person voted for as President, and in distinct ballots, the person voted for as Vice President, and they shall make distinct lists of all persons voted for as President and of all persons voted for as Vice President, and of the number of votes for each, which lists they shall sign and certify, and transmit sealed to the seat of the government of the United States, directed to the President of the Senate;—The President of the Senate shall, in the presence of the Senate and House of Representatives, open all the certificates and the votes shall then be counted;—The person having the greatest number of votes for President, shall be the President, if such number be a majority of the whole number of electors appointed; and if no person have such majority, then from the persons having the highest numbers not exceeding three on the list of those voted for as President, the House of Representatives shall choose immediately, by ballot, the President. But in choosing the President, the votes shall be taken by States, the representation from each State having one vote; a quorum for this purpose shall consist of a member or members from two thirds of the States, and a majority of all the States shall be necessary to a choice. And if the House of Representatives shall not choose a President whenever the right of choice shall devolve upon them, before the fourth day of March next following, then the Vice President shall act as President, as in the case of the death or other constitutional disability of the President. The person having the greatest number of votes as Vice President shall be the Vice President, if such number be a majority of the whole number of electors appointed, and if no person have a majority, then from the two highest numbers on the list, the Senate shall choose the Vice President; a quorum for the purpose shall consist of two thirds of the whole number of Senators, and a majority of the whole number shall be necessary to a choice. But no person constitutionally ineligible to the office of President shall be eligible to that of Vice President of the United States.

Amendment XIII

Passed by Congress February 1, 1865. Ratified December 18, 1865.

SECTION 1. Neither slavery nor involuntary servitude, except as punishment for crime whereof the party shall have been duly convicted, shall exist within the United States, or any place subject to their jurisdiction.

SECTION 2. Congress shall have power to enforce this article by appropriate legislation.

Amendment XIV

Passed by Congress June 16, 1866. Ratified July 23, 1868.

SECTION 1. All persons born or naturalized in the United States, and subject to the jurisdiction thereof, are citizens of the United States and of the State wherein they reside. No State shall make or enforce any law which shall abridge the privileges or immunities of citizens of the United States; nor shall any State deprive any person of life, liberty, or property, without due process of law; nor deny to any person within its jurisdiction the equal protection of the laws.

SECTION 2. Representatives shall be apportioned among the several States according to their respective numbers, counting the whole number of persons in each State, excluding Indians not taxed. But when the right to vote at any election for the choice of electors for President and Vice President of the United States, representatives in Congress, the executive and judicial officers of a State, or the members of the legislature thereof, is denied to any of the male inhabitants of such State, being twenty-one years of age, and citizens of the United States, or in any way abridged, except for participation in rebellion, or other crime, the basis of representation therein shall be reduced in the proportion which the number of such male citizens shall bear to the whole number of male citizens twenty-one years of age in such State.

SECTION 3. No person shall be a senator or representative in Congress, or elector of President and Vice President, or hold any office, civil or military, under the United States, or under any State, who having previously taken an oath, as a member of Congress, or as an officer of the United States, or as a member of any State legislature, or as an executive or judicial officer of any State, to support the Constitution of the United States, shall have engaged in insurrection or rebellion against the same, or given aid or comfort to the enemies thereof. But Congress may by a vote of two thirds of each House, remove such disability.

SECTION 4. The validity of the public debt of the United States, authorized by law, including debts incurred for payment of pensions and bounties for services in suppressing insurrection or rebellion, shall not be questioned. But neither the United States nor any State shall assume or pay any debt or obligation incurred in aid of insurrection or rebellion against the United States, or any claim for the loss or emancipation of any slave; but all such debts, obligations, and claims shall be held illegal and void.

SECTION 5. The Congress shall have power to enforce, by appropriate legislation, the provisions of this article.

Amendment XV

Passed by Congress February 27, 1869. Ratified March 30, 1870.

SECTION 1. The right of citizens of the United States to vote shall not be denied or abridged by the United States or by any State on account of race, color, or previous condition of servitude.

SECTION 2. The Congress shall have power to enforce this article by appropriate legislation.

Amendment XVI

Passed by Congress July 12, 1909. Ratified February 25, 1913.

The Congress shall have power to lay and collect taxes on incomes, from whatever source derived, without apportionment among the several States, and without regard to any census or enumeration.

Amendment XVII

Passed by Congress May 16, 1912. Ratified May 31, 1913.

The Senate of the United States shall be composed of two senators from each State, elected by the people thereof, for six years; and each senator shall have one vote. The electors in each State shall have the qualifications requisite for electors of the most numerous branch of the State legislature.

When vacancies happen in the representation of any State in the Senate, the executive authority of such State shall issue writs of election to fill such vacancies: Provided, That the legislature of any State may empower the executive thereof to make temporary appointments until the people fill the vacancies by election as the legislature may direct.

This amendment shall not be so construed as to affect the election or term of any senator chosen before it becomes valid as part of the Constitution.

Amendment XVIII

Passed by Congress December 17, 1917. Ratified January 29, 1919.

After one year from the ratification of this article, the manufacture, sale, or transportation of intoxicating liquors within, the importation thereof into, or the exportation thereof from the United States and all territory subject to the jurisdiction thereof for beverage purposes is hereby prohibited.

The Congress and the several States shall have concurrent power to enforce this article by appropriate legislation.

This article shall be inoperative unless it shall have been ratified as an amendment to the Constitution by the legislatures of the several States, as provided in the Constitution, within seven years from the date of the submission hereof to the States by Congress.

Amendment XIX

Passed by Congress June 5, 1919. Ratified August 26, 1920.

The right of citizens of the United States to vote shall not be denied or abridged by the United States or by any State on account of sex.

The Congress shall have power by appropriate legislation to enforce the provisions of this article.

Amendment XX

Passed by Congress March 3, 1932. Ratified January 23, 1933.

SECTION 1. The terms of the President and Vice President shall end at noon on the 20th day of January, and the terms of Senators and Representatives at noon on the 3d day of January, of the years in which such terms would have ended if this article had not been ratified; and the terms of their successors shall then begin.

SECTION 2. The Congress shall assemble at least once in every year, and such meeting shall begin at noon on the 3d day of January, unless they shall by law appoint a different day.

SECTION 3.

If, at the time fixed for the beginning of the term of the President, the President-elect shall have died, the Vice President-elect shall become President. If a President shall not have been chosen before the time fixed for the beginning of his term, or if the President-elect shall have failed to qualify, then the Vice President-elect shall act as President until a President shall have qualified; and the Congress may by law provide for the case wherein neither a President-elect nor a Vice President-elect shall have qualified, declaring who shall then act as President, or the manner in which one who is to act shall be selected, and such person shall act accordingly until a President or Vice President shall have qualified.

SECTION 4. The Congress may by law provide for the case of the death of any of the persons from whom the House of Representatives may choose a President whenever the right of choice shall have devolved upon them, and for the case of the death of any of the persons from whom the Senate may choose a Vice President whenever the right of choice shall have devolved upon them.

SECTION 5. Sections 1 and 2 shall take effect on the 15th day of October following the ratification of this article.

SECTION 6. This article shall be inoperative unless it shall have been ratified as an amendment to the Constitution by the legislatures of three-fourths of the several States within seven years from the date of its submission.

Amendment XXI

Passed by Congress February 20, 1933. Ratified December 5, 1933.

SECTION 1. The eighteenth article of amendment to the Constitution of the United States is hereby repealed.

SECTION 2. The transportation or importation into any State, Territory, or possession of the United States for delivery or use therein of intoxicating liquors in violation of the laws thereof, is hereby prohibited.

SECTION 3. This article shall be inoperative unless it shall have been ratified as an amendment to the Constitution by conventions in the several States, as provided in the Constitution, within seven years from the date of the submission thereof to the States by the Congress.

Amendment XXII

Passed by Congress March 24, 1947. Ratified February 26, 1951.

SECTION 1.   No person shall be elected to the office of the President more than twice, and no person who has held the office of President, or acted as President, for more than two years of a term to which some other person was elected President shall be elected to the office of the President more than once. But this article shall not apply to any person holding the office of President when this article was proposed by the Congress, and shall not prevent any person who may be holding the office of President, or acting as President, during the term within which this article becomes operative from holding the office of President or acting as President during the remainder of such term.

SECTION 2.   This article shall be inoperative unless it shall have been ratified as an amendment to the Constitution by the legislatures of three-fourths of the several States within seven years from the date of its submission to the States by the Congress.

Amendment XXIII

Passed by Congress June 16, 1960. Ratified April 3, 1961.

SECTION 1.   The District constituting the seat of Government of the United States shall appoint in such manner as the Congress may direct:

A number of electors of President and Vice President equal to the whole number of Senators and Representatives in Congress to which the District would be entitled if it were a State, but in no event more than the least populous State; they shall be in addition to those appointed by the States, but they shall be considered, for the purposes of the election of President and Vice President, to be electors appointed by a State; and they shall meet in the District and perform such duties as provided by the twelfth article of amendment.

SECTION 2.   The Congress shall have power to enforce this article by appropriate legislation.

Amendment XXIV

Passed by Congress August 27, 1962. Ratified February 4, 1964.

SECTION 1.   The right of citizens of the United States to vote in any primary or other election for President or Vice President, for electors for President or Vice President, or for Senator or Representative in Congress, shall not be denied or abridged by the United States or any State by reason of failure to pay any poll tax or other tax.

SECTION 2.   The Congress shall have power to enforce this article by appropriate legislation.

Amendment XXV

Passed by Congress July 6, 1965. Ratified February 23, 1967.

SECTION 1.   In case of the removal of the President from office or of his death or resignation, the Vice President shall become President.

SECTION 2.   Whenever there is a vacancy in the office of the Vice President, the President shall nominate a Vice President who shall take office upon confirmation by a majority vote of both Houses of Congress.

SECTION 3.   Whenever the President transmits to the President pro tempore of the Senate and the Speaker of the House of Representatives his written declaration that he is unable to discharge the powers and duties of his office, and until he transmits to them a written declaration to the contrary, such powers and duties shall be discharged by the Vice President as Acting President.

SECTION 4.   Whenever the Vice President and a majority of either the principal officers of the executive departments or of such other body as Congress may by law provide, transmit to the President pro tempore of the Senate and the Speaker of the House of Representatives their written declaration that the President is unable to discharge the powers and duties of his office, the Vice President shall immediately assume the powers and duties of the office as Acting President.

Thereafter, when the President transmits to the President pro tempore of the Senate and the Speaker of the House of Representatives his written declaration that no inability exists, he shall resume the powers and duties of his office unless the Vice President and a majority of either the principal officers of the executive department or of such other body as Congress may by law provide, transmit within four days to the President pro tempore of the Senate and the Speaker of the House of Representatives their written declaration that the President is unable to discharge the powers and duties of his office. Thereupon Congress shall decide the issue, assembling within forty-eight hours for that purpose if not in session. If the Congress, within twenty-one days after receipt of the latter written declaration, or, if Congress is not in session, within twenty-one days after Congress is required to assemble, determines by two-thirds vote of both Houses that the President is unable to discharge the powers and duties of his office, the Vice

President shall continue to discharge the same as Acting President; otherwise, the President shall resume the powers and duties of his office.

Amendment XXVI
Passed by Congress March 23, 1971. Ratified July 5, 1971.

SECTION 1.   The right of citizens of the United States, who are eighteen years of age or older, to vote shall not be denied or abridged by the United States or by any State on account of age.

Amendment XXVII
Passed by Congress September 25, 1789. Ratified May 18, 1992.

No law, varying the compensation for the services of the Senators and Representatives, shall take effect, until an election of Representatives shall have intervened.

SUBJECT INDEX